Contents

Preface

The fundamental aim underlying the writing of *Biological Science* was the desire to emphasise the unifying scientific nature of biological systems despite the amazing diversity in structure and function seen at all levels of biological organisation.

Books 1 and 2 comprise a complete text for the A-level student, following all syllabuses in Biological Sciences and incorporating all the topic areas recommended by the GCE Interboard Working Party on the A-level common core in Biology (published 1983). The text will also be relevant to all first-year University and Further Education College students studying the Biological Sciences.

Each chapter is designed to provide comprehensive, up-to-date information on all topics in Biological Sciences, and the accuracy and relevance of this information has been checked by leading authorities in the appropriate fields and by practising teachers and examiners. The text includes:
- clearly written factual material,
- a carefully selected series of thoroughly pretested practical investigations relevant to the A-level course,
- a variety of types of question designed to stimulate an enquiring approach and answers to them.

Whilst it is recognised that the study of Biological Science follows no set pattern, the content of books 1 and 2 has been arranged so that each book contains material approximating to each year of a two-year course.

The appendices, which provide information and techniques vital to the study of Biological Science at this level, recognise that many students do not study Chemistry and Physics to the same level. Mathematical, physical and chemical concepts related to Biological Sciences are emphasised throughout the text, as appropriate.

Acknowledgements

The authors and publisher wish to acknowledge the many friends, colleagues, students and advisers who have helped in the production of *Biological Science*.

In particular, we wish to thank:
Dr R. Batt, Dr Claudia Berek, Professor R.J. Berry, Dr A.C. Blake, Dr John C. Bowman, Mr R. Brown, Dr Fred Burke, Mr Richard Carter, Dr Norman R. Cohen, Dr K.J.R. Edwards, Mr Malcolm Emery, Mr Nick Fagents, Dr James T. Fitzsimons, Dr John Gay, Dr Brij L. Gupta, Dr David E. Hanke, the late Dr R.N. Hardy, Reverend J.R. Hargreaves, Dr S.A. Henderson, Mr Michael J. Hook, Mr Colin S. Hutchinson, Illustra Design Ltd, Dr Alick Jones, Mrs Susan Kearsey, Dr Simon P. Maddrell FRS, Professor Aubrey Manning, Dr Chris L. Mason, Mrs Ruth Miller, Dr David C. Moore, A. G. Morgan, Dr Rodney Mulvey, Dr R.E. Riley, Dr David Secher, Dr John M. Squire, the late Professor James F. Sutcliffe, Miss Anne C. Tallantire, Dr R.M. Taylor, Dr Eric R. Turner, Dr Paul Wheater, Dr Brian E.J. Wheeler, Dr Michael Wheeler.

The authors are particularly indebted to Mrs Adrienne Oxley, who patiently and skilfully organised the pretesting of all the practical exercises. Her perseverance has produced exercises that teachers, pupils and laboratory technicians can depend upon.

However, the authors accept full responsibility for the final content of these books.

Finally, the authors wish to express their thanks to their wives and families for the constant support and encouragement shown throughout the preparation and publication of these books.

We also wish to thank the following for permission to use their illustrations, tables and questions.
Figures: 14.10, 14.13, 14.15*c*, 14.15*d*, 20.1, 20.26, 21.17, Centre for Cell and Tissue Research, York; 14.11*a*, 20.2, 24.8*b*, Heather Angel; 14.11*b*, A–Z Collection; 14.12, data from L.J. Briggs & H.L. Shantz (1916)*J. Agr. Res*, **5**, 583–649; 14.16*c*, 14.16*d*, 14.42, 18.11, 19.4, 20.39, 20.41*a*, 21.26*a*, 21.26*b*, 22.18, 23.15, 23.31, Biophoto Associates; 14.19, data from R.N. Robertson & J.S. Turner (1945) *Austral. J. Exp. Biol. Med. Sci.*, **23**, 63; 14.21*a*, 14.21*b*, 14.21*c*, Dr Chris Marshall; 14.22, Anderson & Cronshaw (1970) *Planta*, **91**, 173–80, Springer-Verlag; 14.25*a*, 14.25*b*, Dr Martin Zimmerman, Harvard University; 14.28, Professor B.E.S. Gunning (1977) *Science Progress*, **64**, 539–68, Blackwell Scientific Publications Ltd.; 14.29, 14.47, E.G. Springthorpe (1973) *An introduction to functional systems in animals*, Longman by permission of the Longman Group Limited; 14.30, A.E. Vines & N. Rees (1972) *Plant and animal biology*

(4th ed.) vol. 1, by permission of Pitman Publishing Ltd., London; 14.31, 19.7, J.A. Ramsay (1968) *A physiological approach to lower animals* (2nd ed.) Cambridge University Press; 14.38a, 14.38b, 14.39a, 14.39b, 14.18, 14.49, 16.8, 19.21a, 19.21b, 20.32, Dr Paul Wheater; 14.40, 14.59, A.G. Clegg & P.C. Clegg (1963) *Biology of the mammal* (2nd ed.) Heinemann Medical Books; 14.46, 14.56, 16.27, 17.45, K. Schmidt-Nielsen (1979) *Animal physiology* (2nd ed.) Cambridge University Press; 14.54, 14.55, J.H. Green (1968) *An introduction to human physiology*, Oxford University Press; 14.63, E. Florey (1967) *An introduction to general and comparative animal physiology*, W.B. Saunders & Co.; 14.64, G. Chapman (1967) *The body fluids and their functions*, Studies in Biology no. 8, Edward Arnold; 14.70, Emil Bernstein & Eila Kairinen, Gillette Research Institute *Science*, **173**, cover 27 August 1971, copyright © 1971 by the American Association for the Advancement of Science; 14.72, from *The development of the immune system*, Max Cooper & Alex Lawton, copyright © 1974 by Scientific American Inc., all rights reserved; 14.78, Macfarlane Burnet (1971) *Genes, dreams and realities*, MTP Press Ltd.; 15.2a, 15.2b, 17.48a, 17.48b, 17.48c, Roy Edwards; 15.3, W.O. James (1963) *An introduction to plant physiology* (6th ed.) Oxford University Press; 15.16, Dr B.E. Juniper; 15.17, P.E. Pilet (1975) *Planta*, **122**, 299–302; 15.18, T Swarbrick *Harnessing the hormone*, Grower Publications Ltd.; 15.20, 20.28, Long Ashton Research Station; 15.24, Centre Nationale de la Recherche Scientifique *Regulateurs naturels de la croissance vegetale* (1964); 15.27, Dr Peter Evans, Southampton University; 15.33, Professor Anton Lang (1957) *Proc. Natl. Acad. Sci. USA*, **43**, 709–17; 16.25a, E.D. Adrian & Y. Zotterman (1926) *J. Physiol.*, **61**, 151–71; 16.25b, B. Katz (1950) *J. Physiol.*, **111**, 261–82; 16.31, R. Schmidt (ed.) (1978) *Fundamentals of sensory physiology*, Springer-Verlag; 16.43a, 16.43b, Dr I. Hunter-Duvar, The Hospital for Sick Children, Toronto; 16.46, P.J. Bentley (1976) *Comparative vertebrate endocrinology*, Cambridge University Press; 16.65, 16.66, Caroline E.G. Tutin; 16.57a, N. Tinbergen (1953) *The herring gull's world*, Collins; 16.57b, N. Tinbergen & A. Purdeck (1950) *Behaviour*, **3**, 1–38; 16.58, J. Brady (1979) *Biological clocks*, Studies in Biology no. 104, Edward Arnold; 16.59, Niall Rankin/Eric and David Hosking; 16.60, A. Watson (1970) *J. Reprod. Fert.*, Suppl. **11**, 3–14; 16.61, J.S. Huxley (1914) *Proc. Zool. Soc. Lond.*, **1914(2)**, 491–562; 16.63, R.A. Hinde (1970) *Animal behaviour* (2nd ed.) McGraw-Hill Book Company, reproduced with permission; 16.64, 16.65, N. Tinbergen (1951) *A study of instinct*, Oxford University Press; 16.68, J.B. Messenger (1977) *Symp. Zool. Soc. Lond.*, **38**, 347–76 by permission of the Zoological Society of London; 17.15, Lee D. Peachey (1965) *Journal of Cell Biology*, **25**, 209–31; 17.17, P.M.G. Munro, Biopolymer Group, Imperial College; 17.18, A. Freundlich, Biopolymer Group, Imperial College; 17.19, Dr J. Squire, Biopolymer Group, Imperial College; 17.25b, David Harrison (1971) *Advanced biology notes*, by permission of Macmillan, London and Basingstoke; 17.31, 17.35, from *Cells and organelles*, 2nd edition by Alex B. Novikoff & Eric Holtzman, copyright © 1970, 1976 by Holt, Rinehart and Winston, reprinted by permission of Holt, Rinehart and Winston, CBS College Publishing; 17.32, M.A. Sleigh (1974) Cilia and flagella, Academic Press Inc.; 17.49, E.J. Sains, *The Racing Pigeon*, London; 17.57, Topham; 18.9, C.J. Martin (1930) *Lancet*, (2) **108**, 561; 18.14, R.N. Hardy (1979) *Temperature and animal life*, Studies in Biology no. 35 (2nd ed.) Edward Arnold; 18.21, Royal Veterinary College, Histology Department; 19.2, J. Zanefeld (1937) *J. Ecology*, **25**, 431–68; 19.3, E.H. Mercer (1959) *Proc. Roy. Soc. Lond.* B, **150**, 216–36, plate 16; 19.8, J.W.L. Beament (1958) J. Exp. Biol., **35**, 494–519;

19.11, G. Parry (1960) in *The physiology of crustacea* vol. 1, ed. T.H. Waterman, 341–66, Academic Press Inc.; 19.14, A.P.M. Lockwood (1963) *Animal body fluids and their regulation*, Heinemann Educational; 19.19, Professor A. Clifford Barger, Harvard Medical School; 20.11a, 20.11b, Gurdon (1977) *Proc. Roy. Soc. Lond.* B, **198**, 211–47; 20.23; Hermann Eisenbeiss; 20.25, Howard Jones; 20.31, *Research in reproduction* (1976) **8**, no.4, by permission of the International Planned Parenthood Federation; 20.41b, Dr Everett Anderson/Science Photo Library; 20.48, *Research in reproduction* (1972) **4**, no. 5, by permission of the International Planned Parenthood Federation; 20.49a, 20.49b, 20.49c, 20.49d, Marion J. Boorman; 21.3, data from L.R. Wallace (1948) *J. Agric. Sci.*, **38**, 93, and H. Palsson & B. Vergés (1952) *J. Agric. Sci.*, **42**, 93; 21.7, A.L. Batt (1980) *Influences on animal growth and development*, Studies in Biology no. 116, Edward Arnold; 21.8, J. Hammond (ed.) (1955) *Progress in the physiology of farm animals*, **2**, 341, Butterworths; 21.12, R. Soper & S.T. Smith (1979) *Modern biology*, by permission of Macmillan, London and Basingstoke; 21.13, J.L. Durrer & J.P. Hannon (1962) *Am. J. Physiol.*, **202**, 375; 21.15, data from R. Desveaux & M. Kogane-Charles (1952) *Annls. Inst. Nat. Rech. Agron. Paris*, **3**, 385–416, © INRA-PARIS 1952; 21.29, Gene Cox; 21.34, The Natural History Photographic Agency; 22.2, 22.7a, 22.7b, 22.8,, 22.9, Dr S.A. Henderson, Department of Genetics, University of Cambridge; 22.3a, 23.26, ARC Poultry Research Centre; 22.11b, 22.11c, H. G. Callan (1963) *Int. Rev. Cytol.*, **15**, 1; 22.11 Professor H.G. Callan, University of St Andrews; 22.14, 22.24 E.J. Ambrose & D.M. Easty (1977) *Cell biology* (2nd ed.), Nelson, by permission of Van Nostrand Reinhold (UK); 22.20, from *The genetic code I*, F.H.C. Crick, copyright © 1962 by Scientific American Inc., all rights reserved; 22.25a, O.L. Miller Jr & B.A. Hamkalo, Visualization of bacterial genes in action, *Science*, **169**, 392–5, 24 July 1970, copyright © 1970 by the American Association for the Advancement of Science; 24.3, RIDA Photo Library; 24.6, G. Matthews (1939) *Climate of evolution* (2nd ed.) vol. 1, New York Academy of Sciences; 24.7, Eric Hosking; 24.8, D. Lack (1947) *Darwin's finches*, Cambridge University Press; 24.9a, Bruce Coleman Ltd.; 24.9b, *Pig farming* magazine, Ipswich; 24.14, T.H. Hamilton (1967) *Process and pattern in evolution*, Macmillan, London and Basingstoke; 24.18, The Zoological Society of London; 24.19, V.M. Ingram (1963) *Haemoglobins in genetics and evolution*, © 1963, Columbia University Press, reprinted by permission; 25.3; M.N. Karn & L.S. Penrose (1951) *Ann. Eugenics, London*, **16**, 147–64; 25.4, D.S. Falconer (1953) *J. Genetics*, 51, 470–501; 25.5a, 25.5b, Photo A.G.P.M.; 25.6, Semences Nickerson, France; 25.8, D.F. Jones, Connecticut Agricultural Experiment Station 25.9, John Haywood; 25.10a, 25.10b, Dr H.B.D. Kettlewell; 25.11, H.B.D. Kettlewell (1958) *Heredity*, **12**, 51–72, by permission of Longman 25.12, M.A. Tribe, I. Tallan and M.R. Eraut (1978) *Case Studies in Genetics*, Cambridge University Press; 25.13, John Haywood.

Tables: 14.7, T.E. Weier, C.R. Stocking & M.G. Barbour (1970) *Botany: an introduction to plant biology* (4th ed.), John Wiley & Sons Inc.; 16.1, A.L. Hodgkin (1958) *Proc. Roy. Soc. Lond.*, **148**, 1–37; 16.18, W.H. Thorpe (1963) *Learning and instinct in animals*, Methuen; 19.2, K. Schmidt-Nielsen (1979) *Animal physiology* (2nd ed.), Cambridge University Press; 24.6, M.O. Dayhoff & R.V. Eck (1967–8) *Atlas of protein sequence and structure*, National Biomedical Research Foundation, Silver Spring, Md.

Cover: Cockchafer in flight. Stephen Dalton/NHPA.

Chapter Fourteen

Transport

The exchange of substances between individual cells and their environments takes place by the physical process of diffusion (which includes osmosis) and the active processes of active transport and endocytosis or exocytosis. Within cells, substances generally move by diffusion, but active processes, such as cytoplasmic streaming, can also occur. Over short distances these means of transport are rapid and efficient and in unicellular organisms, and multicellular organisms which possess a large surface area to volume ratio, they operate efficiently enough for specific transport systems to be unnecessary. For example, respiratory gases are exchanged by diffusion between the body surface and the environment in small organisms such as the earthworm.

In larger and more complex organisms, cells may be too widely separated from each other and from their external environments for these processes to be adequate. Specialised long-distance transport systems which can move substances more rapidly become necessary. Materials are generally moved by a mass flow system, **mass flow** being the bulk transport of materials from one point to another as a result of a pressure difference between the two points. It is a characteristic of mass flow that all the materials, whether they be in solution or suspension, are swept along at similar speeds as in a river, unlike diffusion, where molecules move independently of each other according to their diffusion gradients. Some of the mass flow systems of plants and animals are summarised in table 14.1.

Transport in plants

Table 14.2 page 474 summarises the major groups of substances that move through plants and gives details of the major routes and mechanisms for uptake, transport and elimination.

The movement of substances through the conducting, or vascular, tissues of plants is termed **translocation**. In vascular plants (Pteridophytes and Spermatophytes) the vascular tissues are highly specialised and are called **xylem** and **phloem**. Xylem translocates mainly water, mineral salts, some organic nitrogen and hormones from the roots to the aerial parts of the plant. Phloem translocates a variety of organic and inorganic solutes, mainly from the expanded leaves to other parts of the plant.

The study of translocation has important economic applications. For example, it is useful to know how herbicides, fungicides, growth regulators and nutrients enter plants, and the routes that they take through plants, in order to know how best to apply them, and to judge possible effects that they might have. Also, plant pathogens such as fungi, bacteria and viruses are sometimes translocated and such knowledge could influence treatment or preventive measures. One relatively recent innovation has been the introduction of fungicides described as **systemic** which are translocated through the plants and provide longer-term, and more thorough, protection from such important diseases as mildews.

Table 14.1 Some mass flow systems of animals and plants.

Mass flow system	Material(s) moved	Driving force	Location
Plants			
vascular system:			
xylem (chapter 14)	mainly water and mineral salts	transparation and root pressure	vascular plants: Pteridophyta and Spermatophyta
phloem (chapter 14)	mainly organic food, e.g. sucrose	mechanism not fully understood	
Animals			
alimentary system (chapter 10)	food and water	muscles of alimentary canal	Annelida, Mollusca, Arthropoda, Chordata
respiratory system (chapter 11)	air or water	respiratory muscles	Mollusca, Chordata
blood vascular system (chapter 14)	blood	heart or contractile blood vessels	Annelida, Mollusca, Arthropoda, Chordata
lymphatic system (chapter 14)	lymph	general muscular activity in the body	Mammalia

Table 14.2 Movement of substances through plants.

	Uptake	Transport	Elimination
Water			
route	root hairs	xylem	stomata (cuticle and lenticels)
mechanism	osmosis	mass flow (root pressure)	diffusion of water vapour
Solutes			
route	root hairs	xylem (mainly inorganic solutes) phloem (mainly organic solutes)	shedding of leaves, bark, fruits and seeds; otherwise retained until death or passed to next generation in embryo of seed
mechanism	diffusion or active transport	mass flow	controlled by plant growth substances
Gases*			
route	stomata, lenticels, root epidermis	intercellular spaces and through cells	stomata, lenticels, root epidermis
mechanism	diffusion	diffusion	diffusion

* Movement of gases is considered in further detail in chapter 11.

14.1 Plant water relations

14.1.1 Osmosis

An understanding of plant water relations depends upon an understanding of the physical processes of osmosis and diffusion, which are explained in section A1.5. There it is pointed out that osmosis can be regarded as a special kind of diffusion in which water molecules are the only molecules diffusing owing to the presence of a differentially permeable membrane which does not allow the passage of solute particles. Water molecules move from a region of their high concentration (a dilute solution) to a region of their low concentration (a more concentrated solution) through a differentially permeable membrane. It is known that this process occurs more rapidly than can be accounted for by straightforward diffusion, and that mass flow is involved. It can, however, be explained in terms of diffusion.

14.1.2 Osmotic pressure (OP) and osmotic potential (π)

Osmotic pressure is the pressure* a solution would generate if enclosed within an osmometer and allowed to come to equilibrium with pure water. The more concentrated a solution, the greater is its OP.

The term **osmotic potential** is now more commonly used, since under normal circumstances the 'pressure' referred to is only a potential (theoretical) pressure, and only becomes a real pressure under the special circumstances of the osmometer experiment (see section A1.5.2). By convention, osmotic potential is given a negative sign, and osmotic pressure a positive sign. Throughout this chapter the abbreviation OP is used to mean osmotic pressure, with a positive sign, because negative signs can be confusing.

* Pressure was formerly measured in atmospheres (atm), but now pascals are used (Pa) (see section A4.3).
  $1 \text{ Pa} = 1 \text{ Nm}^{-2}$ (N = newton)
  $1 \text{ bar} = 0.987 \text{ atm} = 10^5 \text{ Pa} = 100 \text{ kPa}$
  $1 \text{ atm} = 1.0132 \text{ bar} = 1.0132 \times 10^5 \text{ Pa} = 101.32 \text{ kPa}$

14.1.3 Water potential (symbol ψ, the Greek letter psi)

Plant physiologists now use the term water potential,* ψ, when describing the tendency of water molecules to move from one place to another. More traditional terms that may be encountered are described in the addendum, section 14.1.10.

Water moves from a region of higher water potential to one of lower water potential.

By convention, water potential for pure water at atmospheric pressure is zero. All solutions at atmospheric pressure have lower water potentials and therefore negative values of ψ. Osmosis can be redefined as the movement of water molecules from a region of higher water potential to a region of lower water potential through a differentially permeable membrane.

If a pressure greater than atmospheric pressure is applied to pure water or a solution, its water potential increases. Thus, water potential can be raised to a positive value, as for plasma in the glomerulus of the kidney. At atmospheric pressure, the water potential of a solution is determined by its osmotic pressure, and is usually expressed in pressure units:

$$\psi^{\text{solution}} = -\text{OP}^{\text{solution}}$$

Advantage of using water potential

Water potential can be regarded as the tendency of water to leave a system. A higher (that is less negative) water

* The origin of the term water potential may be of interest. It is a fundamental term derived from thermodynamics and describes the free energy of water in a given system, such as in soil or in a cell. Water molecules, like other molecules, always move down gradients of free energy, from higher to lower free energy, according to the laws of entropy. The process is called **diffusion**. The **water potential** of a system is the difference between the free energy of water in that system and of pure water at atmospheric pressure. It is usually expressed in pressure units by biologists, though it can also be expressed in energy units.

For a more detailed account, written with biology teachers and A-level students in mind, see Bradbeer, Thomason & Bradbeer (Dec. 1980) *School Science Review*, **62**, 272–3, no. 219 and Hutchinson. C.S. & Sutcliffe, J.F. (Summer 1983) *J. Biol.Ed.*, **17**, 123–30.

potential implies a greater tendency to leave. If two systems are in contact, water will move from the system with the higher water potential to the one with the lower potential.

Using the term water potential, the tendency for water to move between any two systems can therefore be measured, not just from cell to cell in a plant, but also for example from soil to root, from leaf to air or from soil to air. Water can be said to move through a plant down a continuous gradient of water potential from soil to air. The steeper the potential gradient, the faster the flow of water along it.

14.1.4 Movement of water between solutions by osmosis

The terms mentioned above can only be used with confidence if they are properly understood. The following question, together with questions 14.5–14.8, can be a useful test of this understanding.

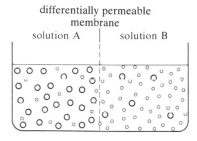

Fig. 14.1 *Two solutions separated by a differentially permeable membrane*

14.1 Study fig 14.1 in which two solutions are separated by a differentially permeable membrane.

(a) Which solution has the higher concentration of water molecules?

(b) Which solution is more concentrated, that is has the higher concentration of solute?

(c) In which direction will osmosis occur?

(d) Which solution has the higher osmotic pressure?

(e) Which of the following two values of ψ is higher:

   (i) −2 000 kPa, (ii) −1 000 kPa?

(f) Which solution has the higher water potential (ψ)?

(g) What is the relationship between OP and ψ of a solution at atmospheric pressure?

14.1.5 Osmosis and plant cells

The differentially permeable membranes of particular relevance in the water relations of plant cells are shown in fig 14.2. The cell wall is usually freely permeable to substances in solution, so is not an osmotic barrier. The cell contains a large central vacuole whose contents, the cell sap or vacuolar sap, contribute to the osmotic pressure of the cell. The two important membranes are the plasma membrane and the tonoplast. In plant water relations, the plasma membrane, cytoplasm and tonoplast can be regarded as acting together as one differentially permeable membrane.

Experiment 14.1: To investigate osmosis in living plant cells

Materials

onion bulb or young rhubarb
  epidermis
microscope
2 slides and cover-slips
scalpel and forceps

distilled water
1 M sucrose solution
2 teat pipettes
filter paper

Method

Remove a strip of epidermis from the inner surface of one of the fleshy storage leaves of the onion bulb, or from the young rhubarb petiole. Rhubarb has the advantage of having coloured cell sap, but onion epidermis is easier to peel off. The epidermis can be removed by first slitting it with a scalpel, then lifting and tearing back the single layer of cells with fingers or forceps. Quickly transfer the epidermal strip to a slide and add two or three drops of distilled water. Carefully add a cover-slip and examine the cells with a microscope. Identify and draw a few epidermal cells. Repeat using another strip of epidermis and 1 M sucrose solution instead of distilled water. Observe the strip over a period of 15 min and draw any changes observed in one or more representative cells at high power. The possibility of reversing the process observed can be investigated by irrigating with distilled water under the cover-slip to wash away the sucrose solution. Use filter paper to absorb any excess liquid.

Results

Fig 14.3 shows the appearance of onion epidermal cells left in 1 M sucrose solution for varying lengths of time.

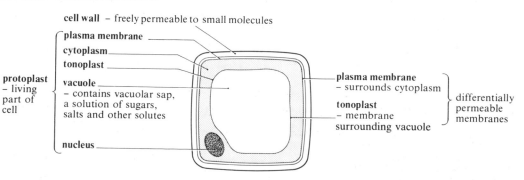

Fig 14.2 *Differentially permeable membranes of a typical vacuolated plant cell. Note that the plasma membrane would normally be pressed tightly up against the cell wall*

cell wall – freely permeable to small molecules

plasma membrane
cytoplasm
tonoplast

protoplast – living part of cell

vacuole – contains vacuolar sap, a solution of sugars, salts and other solutes

nucleus

plasma membrane – surrounds cytoplasm

tonoplast – membrane surrounding vacuole

} differentially permeable membranes

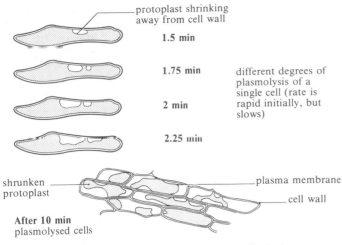

protoplast shrinking away from cell wall

1.5 min

1.75 min — different degrees of plasmolysis of a single cell (rate is rapid initially, but slows)

2 min

2.25 min

shrunken protoplast — plasma membrane — cell wall

After 10 min plasmolysed cells

Fig 14.3 *Appearance of onion epidermal cells during plasmolysis. Strips of epidermal cells were left in 1 M sucrose solution for varying lengths of time*

14.1.6 Plasmolysis and turgor pressure (TP)

If a cell is in contact with a hypertonic solution, that is a solution of lower water potential than its own contents, then water leaves the cell by osmosis through the plasma membrane. Water is lost first from the cytoplasm and then from the vacuole through the tonoplast. The protoplast, that is the living contents of the cell within the cell wall, shrinks and eventually pulls away from the cell wall. This process is called **plasmolysis**, and the cell is said to be **plasmolysed**. The point at which plasmolysis is just about to happen is called **incipient plasmolysis**. At incipient plasmolysis the protoplast has just ceased to exert any pressure against the cell wall, so the cell is **flaccid**. Water will continue to leave the protoplast until its contents are of the same water potential as the external solution. No further shrinkage then occurs.

> **14.2 What occupies the space between the cell wall and the shrunken protoplast in plasmolysed cells?**

The process of plasmolysis is usually reversible without permanent damage to the cell. If a plasmolysed cell is placed in pure water or a hypotonic solution, that is a solution of higher water potential than the contents of the cell, water enters the cell by osmosis. As the volume of the protoplast increases it begins to exert pressure against the cell wall and stretches it. The wall is relatively rigid, so the pressure inside the cell rises rapidly. The pressure exerted by the protoplast against the cell wall is called **turgor pressure (TP)**. Sometimes the term **wall pressure (WP)** is used instead, referring to the pressure of the wall against the protoplast. The two pressures are equal and opposite in direction. As the turgor pressure of the cell gradually increases, due to water entering by osmosis, the cell becomes turgid. Full turgidity, that is maximum TP, is achieved when a cell is placed in pure water. When the

tendency for water to enter a cell is exactly balanced by turgor pressure, the amount of water leaving the cell equals that entering the cell. There is no further net uptake of water and the cell is now in equilibrium with the surrounding solution. The contents of the cell are still likely to be of higher osmotic pressure than the external solution because only a small amount of water is needed to raise the turgor pressure to the equilibrium point, and this is not sufficient to dilute the cell contents significantly. Turgor pressure therefore accounts for the fact that at equilibrium the osmotic pressure of a plant cell can be greater than that of the external solution.

Turgor pressure is a real pressure rather than a potential one, and can only develop to any extent if a cell wall is present. Animal cells have no cell wall and the plasma membrane is too delicate to prevent the cell expanding and bursting in a hypotonic solution. Animal cells must therefore be protected by osmoregulation (chapter 19).

> **14.3 What is the TP of a flaccid cell?**
>
> **14.4 Which organisms, apart from plants, possess cell walls?**

14.1.7 Movement of water between solutions and cells by osmosis

When considering the tendency for water to move by osmosis between a plant cell and an external solution, the water potential of the cell must be compared with the water potential of the solution, since water always moves from higher to lower water potential. The water potential of the cell must equal the water potential of the external solution at equilibrium.

As previously stated, at atmospheric pressure the water potential of a solution is determined by its osmotic pressure:

$$\psi^{solution} = -\,OP^{solution}$$

The water potential of a cell is determined by two factors, its osmotic pressure and its turgor pressure. As with the external solution, the higher the osmotic pressure of the solution inside the cell, the lower its water potential. However, an increase in turgor pressure inside a cell increases the tendency for water to leave the cell (or resists water entry), that is an increase in turgor pressure increases the water potential of the cell. This can be summarised in the equation below:

$$\psi^{cell} = TP^{cell} - OP^{cell}*$$

At equilibrium, $\psi^{cell} = \psi^{solution}$ or $\psi^{int} = \psi^{ext}$

where 'int' means internal solution, and 'ext' means external solution.

* ψ^{cell} is better expressed as $\psi_w = \psi_p + \psi_s$ (see Addendum, section 14.1.10).

The problems below are useful in testing understanding of the terms used so far. It will be necessary to remember the following points:

(1) water always moves from higher water potential to lower water potential;

(2) for two systems to be in equilibrium, they must have equal water potential;

(3) in most cases the quantities of water entering and leaving plant cells are not sufficient to significantly change their osmotic pressures (osmotic pressure is therefore assumed to remain constant in the following calculations) though turgor pressures do change significantly.

> **14.5** Describe what happens if a cell at incipient plasmolysis, with an OP of 2 000 kPa, is placed in a solution of OP 1 200 kPa. What are the ψ and TP of the cell at equilibrium?
>
> **14.6** If the OP of the vacuolar sap of a cell in equilibrium with pure water at atmospheric pressure is 1 100 kPa, what is its TP?
>
> **14.7** If a cell is equilibrated with pure water and then transferred to a sucrose solution with a water potential of −800 kPa,
>
> (a) what is the difference in ψ between the cell contents and the external solution at the time of transfer?
>
> (b) would water enter or leave the cell?
>
> (c) would the TP of the cell increase or decrease?

14.1.8 Movement of water between cells by osmosis

Consider the situation in fig 14.4, in which two vacuolated cells possessing different water potentials are in contact.

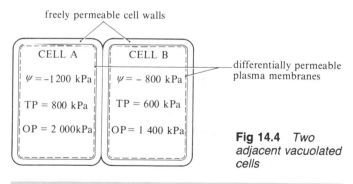

Fig 14.4 *Two adjacent vacuolated cells*

> **14.8** (a) Which cell has the higher water potential?
>
> (b) In which direction will water move by osmosis?
>
> (c) What will be the water potential of the cells at equilibrium?
>
> (d) What will be the osmotic pressures and turgor pressures of the cells at equilibrium?

Experiment 14.2: To determine the mean osmotic pressure of the cell sap in a sample of plant cells using the method of incipient plasmolysis

There are several methods available for determining osmotic pressure of plant cells, but the most convenient is that of incipient plasmolysis. It makes use of the following relationships:

(1) ψ of a cell = TP − OP; ψ of a solution = −OP.

(2) $\psi^{cell} = \psi^{solution}$ when the two are in equilibrium.

Samples of the tissue being investigated are allowed to come to equilibrium in a range of solutions of different concentrations (water potentials) and the aim is to find which solution causes incipient plasmolysis, that is shrinkage of the protoplasts to the point where they just begin to pull away from the cell walls. At this point turgor pressure is zero since no pressure is exerted by the protoplasts against the cell walls, so $\psi^{cell} = -OP^{cell} = \psi^{solution} = -OP^{solution}$ (from (1) and (2) above). In other words, the solution causing incipient plasmolysis has the same osmotic pressure as the cell sap.

In practice, osmotic pressure varies between cells in the same tissue and so some plasmolyse in more dilute solutions than others. Incipient plasmolysis is said to have been reached when 50% of the cells have plasmolysed. At this point 50% of the cells are unplasmolysed and the average cell can be said to be at incipient plasmolysis. The osmotic pressure obtained is a mean value for the tissue.

Materials

onion bulb or rhubarb petiole
6 petri dishes
6 test-tubes
test-tube rack
labels or wax pencil
2 × 10 cm³ or 25 cm³ graduated pipettes
2 × 100 cm³ beakers
brush (fine paintbrush)
distilled water
1 M sucrose solution
fine forceps
Pasteur pipettes
slides and cover-slips
microscope
graph paper
razor blade or sharp scalpel

Method

(An alternative method using beetroot is described after this first method.)

(1) Label six petri dishes and six test-tubes appropriately for each of the following sucrose solutions: 0.3 M, 0.35 M, 0.4 M, 0.45 M, 0.5 M and 0.6 M.

Table 14.3 Sucrose dilution table for experiment 14.2.

Concentration of sucrose solution	Volume of distilled water/cm³	Volume of 1M sucrose solution/cm³
0.30 M	14	6
0.35 M	13	7
0.40 M	12	8
0.45 M	11	9
0.50 M	10	10
0.60 M	8	12

(2) Using a 10 cm³ or 25 cm³ graduated pipette, a beaker of distilled water and a beaker of 1M sucrose solution, make up 20 cm³ of sucrose solution of the required concentration in each test-tube. Table 14.3 shows the amounts used.

(3) Make sure that the solutions are mixed thoroughly by shaking. This is very important. Add the solutions to the appropriate petri dishes.

(4) **Onion.** Remove one of the fleshy storage leaves of an onion. While it is still attached to the leaf, cut the inner epidermis into six squares of approximately 5 mm side using a razor blade or scalpel. Remove each of the six squares using fine forceps and immediately place one square of tissue into each petri dish. Agitate each dish gently to ensure that the tissue is completely immersed and washed with the sucrose solution. Leave for about 20 min.

   Rhubarb. Score the outer epidermis into six squares of approximately 5 mm side and remove the epidermis as described for the onion.

(5) Remove the tissue from the 0.60 M solution and, using a brush, mount it on a slide in sucrose solution of the same concentration. Add a cover-slip and examine with a microscope.

(6) Select a suitable area of cells using low power. Switch to a medium or high power objective and move the slide through the selected area, recording the state (plasmolysed or unplasmolysed) of the first 100 cells viewed. Cells in which there is any sign of the protoplast pulling away from the cell wall should be counted as plasmolysed.

(7) Repeat for all other squares of tissue, mounting them in their respective solutions.

(8) From the total number of cells counted and number plasmolysed determine the percentage of plasmolysed cells for each solution. Plot a graph of percentage of plasmolysed cells (vertical axis) against molarity of sucrose solution (horizontal axis).

(9) Read off from the graph the molarity of the sucrose solution which causes 50% of the cells to plasmolyse.

(10) Plot a graph of osmotic pressure (vertical axis) against molarity of sucrose solution (horizontal axis) using the data provided in table 14.4.

(11) From this graph determine the osmotic pressure of the solution which caused 50% plasmolysis. This is equal to the mean osmotic pressure of the cell sap.

Table 14.4 Osmotic pressures of given sucrose solutions at 20 °C.

Concentration of sucrose solution (molarity)	Osmotic pressure/kPa	Osmotic pressure/atm
0.05	130	1.3
0.10	260	2.6
0.15	410	4.0
0.20	540	5.3
0.25	680	6.7
0.30	820	8.1
0.35	970	9.6
0.40	1 120	11.1
0.45	1 280	12.6
0.50	1 450	14.3
0.55	1 620	16.0
0.60	1 800	17.8
0.65	1 980	19.5
0.70	2 180	21.5
0.75	2 370	23.3
0.80	2 580	25.5
0.85	2 790	27.5
0.90	3 010	29.7
0.95	3 250	32.1
1.00	3 510	34.6
1.50	6 670	65.8
2.00	11 810	116.6

Results

A typical graph for onion epidermis is shown in fig 14.5. Similar results are obtained using rhubarb epidermis.

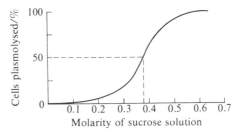

Fig 14.5 *Percentage of onion epidermal cells plasmolysed in different concentrations of sucrose solution*

14.9 What is the osmotic pressure of onion epidermal cells if 50% of the cells plasmolysed in 0.38 M sucrose solution?

Use of beetroot tissue

Beetroot is a less convenient material to use, but a combination of this experiment with experiment 14.3 would enable an estimation of the turgor pressure of beetroot cells to be made, although it should be pointed out that different beetroots may have different water potentials and osmotic pressures. Beetroots normally have a higher osmotic pressure than onion or rhubarb because they have more sugar and inorganic salts in their vacuoles.

Modifications to the method are as follows.

(1)–(3) As for onion and rhubarb experiment above, except use solutions of the following concentrations: 0.4 M, 0.45 M, 0.5 M, 0.55 M, 0.6 M and 0.7 M.

(4) Cut a rectangular 'chip' of beetroot with square ends of approximately 5×5 mm. Thin sections (maximum 0.5 mm thick) should be cut from the end of this chip using a razor blade. The thinner the sections, the easier it is to count plasmolysed cells. The coloured sap enables easy detection of plasmolysis. The sections could be cut immediately before the practical class and kept in distilled water. Add several sections of beetroot tissue to each sucrose solution, and leave for about 30 min. Meanwhile examine similar sections, mounted in distilled water, with a microscope to become familiar with the appearance of the unplasmolysed cells. The margins of the sections are likely to be thinner and easier to examine. Some damaged cells may be colourless, and some small cells near vascular tissue may be seen. These can be ignored in subsequent counts.

(5)–(11) As before, starting with tissue from 0.7 M solution.

Results

A set of results obtained for beetroot is given in table 14.5.

Table 14.5 Percentage of beetroot cells plasmolysed in different concentrations of sucrose solution.

Molarity of sucrose solution	Percentage of plasmolysed cells*
0.30	2.5
0.40	3.5
0.45	13.5
0.50	74.0
0.55	100.0
0.60	100.0

* Sample size 200 cells.

> **14.10** What is the mean osmotic pressure of the beetroot cells used in this experiment? (You will need to draw a graph to determine this.)

Experiment 14.3: To determine the water potential of a plant tissue

Water potential is a measure of the tendency of water molecules to pass from one place to another. The principle in this experiment is to discover a solution, of known water potential, in which the tissue being examined neither gains nor loses water. Samples of the tissue are allowed to come to equilibrium in a range of solutions of different concentrations and the solution which induces neither an increase nor a decrease in mass or volume of the tissue has the same water potential as the tissue. The method described below relies on volume rather than mass changes.

Materials

fresh potato tuber or fresh beetroot
6 petri dishes
5 test-tubes
test-tube rack
labels or wax pencil
2×10 cm³ or 25 cm³ graduated pipettes
tile
distilled water
1 M sucrose solution
scalpel or knife
2×100 cm³ beakers
graph paper

Method

(1) Label six petri dishes appropriately, one for each of the following: distilled water, 0.1 M, 0.25 M, 0.5 M, 0.75 M and 1.0 M sucrose solutions. Label five test-tubes appropriately, one for each of the sucrose solutions.

(2) Using a graduated pipette, a beaker of distilled water and a beaker of 1 M sucrose solution, make up 20 cm³ of sucrose solution of the required concentration in each test-tube. A dilution table is useful as described in experiment 14.2 (table 14.3).

(3) Shake the tubes to mix the solutions thoroughly.

(4) Pour the solutions into the appropriate petri dishes. Add 20 cm³ of distilled water to the sixth petri dish.

(5) Place the petri dishes on graph paper, making sure their lower surfaces are dry.

(6) Using the knife or scalpel, cut 12 rectangular strips of tissue approximately 2 mm thick, 5 mm wide and as long as possible (about 5 cm) from a slice of tissue (2 mm thick) taken from the middle of a large beetroot or potato. It is important to work quickly to avoid loss of water through evaporation as this would lower the water potential of the tissue.

(7) Completely immerse two strips in each petri dish and immediately measure their lengths against the graph paper seen through the bottoms of the dishes. Agitate the contents of each dish to wash the strips.

(8) Leave in covered petri dishes for at least 1 h, preferably 24 h.

(9) Measure the lengths again, and calculate the mean percentage change in length. Plot a graph of the mean percentage change in length (vertical axis) against the molarity of the sucrose solution (horizontal axis). Changes in length are proportional to changes in volume.

(10) Read off from the graph the molarity of the sucrose solution which causes no change in length.

(11) Plot a graph of osmotic pressure (vertical axis) against molarity of sucrose solution (horizontal axis) using the data provided in table 14.4.

(12) From this graph, determine the osmotic pressure of the solution which caused no change in length. The water potential of the tissue is determined according to the following:

$$\psi^{\,cell} = \psi^{\,external\ solution} = -OP^{external\ solution}$$

(13) If beetroot has been used and its osmotic pressure determined from experiment 14.2, calculate the turgor pressure from:

$$\psi = TP - OP$$

Results

More accurate results are likely to be obtained by pooling class results. See table 14.6 for specimen results.

Table 14.6 Lengths of beetroot strips left in distilled water or different concentrations of sucrose solution for 24 h.

Molarity of sucrose solution	Length of beetroot strip at start/cm			Length of beetroot strip after 24 h/cm		
	1	2	3	1	2	3
0.00 (distilled water)	4.8	5.0	5.3	5.0	5.3	5.6
0.10	5.1	4.8	4.9	5.3	4.9	5.1
0.20	5.1	4.9	4.9	5.2	4.9	5.0
0.25	5.2	4.8	5.0	5.2	4.9	5.0
0.30	4.9	4.9	5.0	4.9	5.0	5.1
0.40	4.9	5.0	4.8	4.9	5.0	4.8
0.50	5.0	4.8	5.1	4.8	4.7	5.0
0.60	4.8	5.0	5.0	4.6	4.9	4.9
0.75	4.9	4.9	5.0	4.6	4.7	4.8
0.90	4.9	5.0	4.9	4.5	4.7	4.7
1.00	4.8	4.9	4.9	4.7	4.6	4.4
1.50	4.9	4.9	4.9	4.5	4.1	4.5

14.11 What is the mean water potential of beetroot cells from the data in table 14.6? (You will need to determine mean percentage changes in length and draw graphs.)

14.12 Why are at least two strips of tissue added to each dish?

14.13 Why are the petri dishes covered when left?

14.14 If the osmotic pressure of beetroot cells is 1 400 kPa and their water potential is −950 kPa, what is their mean turgor pressure?

14.15 Consider the experiment illustrated in fig 14.6 in which the hollow inflorescence stalk (scape) of a dandelion (*Taraxacum officinale*) is first cut longitudinally into four strips 3 cm long, and the pieces then immersed in distilled water or sucrose solutions of different concentrations.

(a) Why did cutting the scape longitudinally result in immediate curling back of the cut strips?

(b) Why did scape B bend further outwards in distilled water?

(c) Why did scape C bend inwards in concentrated sucrose solution?

(d) Why did scape A retain the same curvature in dilute sucrose solution?

(e) Which of the following could be determined for scape cells using this method: osmotic pressure, water potential or turgor pressure? Design an experiment to determine the relevant value, giving full experimental details.

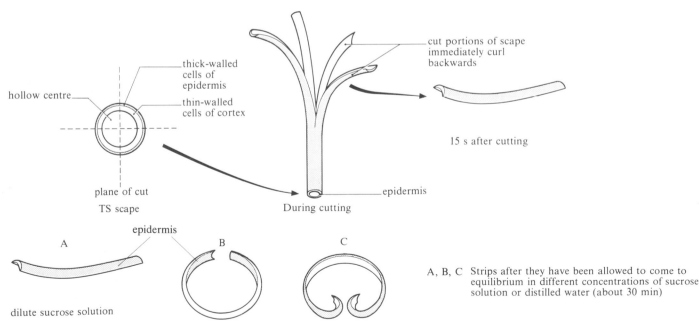

thick-walled cells of epidermis

thin-walled cells of cortex

hollow centre

plane of cut

TS scape

During cutting

epidermis

cut portions of scape immediately curl backwards

15 s after cutting

epidermis

A — dilute sucrose solution

B — distilled water

C — concentrated sucrose solution (1 M) or drying in air

A, B, C Strips after they have been allowed to come to equilibrium in different concentrations of sucrose solution or distilled water (about 30 min)

Fig 14.6 *Experiment on dandelion scapes. Investigation of the effects of distilled water and sucrose solutions on the curvature of strips of dandelion scape*

14.1.9 Effect of heat and alcohols on membranes

The differential permeability of cell membranes can be destroyed by certain chemicals and treatments, such as ethanol and high temperatures. The membranes are still present but behave as if holes had been punched through them and they no longer provide a barrier to the passage of large molecules such as sucrose. High temperature and alcohols denature membrane proteins and increase fluidity of membrane lipids; alcohols at high concentrations can also dissolve lipids.

> **14.16** The red colour of beetroot is contained in the cell vacuoles. Using this information, design experiments to investigate the effects of heat and ethanol on the differential permeability of beetroot cell membranes.

14.1.10 Addendum

(1) Use of the term water potential has replaced use of the older terms of diffusion pressure deficit and suction pressure. The origins and meanings of the older terms are explained below.

Diffusion pressure deficit (DPD), and **suction pressure (SP)**. It has been stated that osmosis can be regarded as a special kind of diffusion in which only water molecules move. The tendency for water molecules to move used to be expressed by the term diffusion pressure (DP). The greater the concentration of water molecules in a solution, the greater is the DP of the solution. At atmospheric pressure (that is in the absence of hydrostatic pressure), pure water therefore has the maximum DP, and when substances dissolve in water they lower the DP of the solution. Solutions always have a lower DP than pure water at atmospheric pressure; the more concentrated a solution, the less concentrated the water and the lower its DP.

A solution was therefore said to have a **diffusion pressure deficit** (DPD) with respect to pure water, whose DPD is set arbitrarily at zero. The more concentrated the solution, the greater is its DPD. For a given solution DPD = OP at atmospheric pressure. The term DPD replaced the term **suction pressure** (SP). The origin of the latter came from the idea that in osmosis a hypertonic solution sucked water from a hypotonic solution. The hypertonic solution was therefore said to have a higher suction pressure. It is now realised that the driving force for water movement comes from the hypotonic solution with its higher water potential (or diffusion pressure).

The relationship between the terms discussed is summarised thus:

$$-\psi = DPD = SP$$

For a solution at atmospheric pressure:

$$-\psi = DPD = OP = SP$$

(2) Instead of the equation

$$\psi^{cell} = TP^{cell} - OP^{cell}$$

plant physiologists prefer to use the equation

$$\psi_w = \psi_s + \psi_p$$

where ψ_w is the water potential of the cell, ψ_s is the contribution made by the solute concentration to the water potential (ψ_s is negative and equals osmotic pressure) and ψ_p is the contribution made by the turgor pressure to the water potential (this is zero or positive).

14.2 Movement of water through the flowering plant

Water in the plant is in direct contact with water in the soil and with water vapour in the air around the plant. It has already been stated that water moves from higher to lower water potentials. Plant physiologists therefore think of water as moving through plants from a region of higher water potential in the soil to a region of lower water potential in the atmosphere, down a gradient of water potentials. The water potential of moderately dry air is several tens of thousands of kilopascals below that of the plant; hence there is a great tendency for water to leave the plant.

Most of the water entering the plant does so via the root hairs. It travels across the root cortex to the xylem, ascends in the xylem to the leaves and is lost by evaporation from the surface of the mesophyll cells before diffusing out through the stomata. This latter process is called **transpiration**, and the flow of water from the roots to the transpiring surfaces forms the **transpiration stream**. It is estimated that less than 1% of the water absorbed is used by the average plant. Uses of water are given in section 5.1.2.

14.3 Transpiration and movement of water through the leaf

Water normally leaves the plant as a vapour. The change from a liquid state to a vapour state requires the addition of energy, called the **latent heat of evaporation**. This energy is provided by the Sun (solar energy) and according to the most widely accepted theory of transpiration, the **cohesion–tension theory**, it is this energy that maintains the flow of water through the entire plant. Transpiration is the loss of water vapour from the surface of a plant, and may occur from the following three sites (relative losses when stomata are open are indicated in brackets).

(1) **Stomata:** by evaporation of water from cells and diffusion of the water vapour through stomata, the pores found in the epidermis of leaves and green stems (about 90%).

(2) **Cuticle:** by evaporation of water from the outer walls of epidermal cells through the waxy cuticle covering the epidermis of leaves and stems (about 10%, varying with thickness of cuticle).

(3) **Lenticels:** by evaporation of water through lenticels (minute proportions, although this is the main source of water loss from deciduous trees after leaf fall).

The quantities of water lost by transpiration can be very large. A herbaceous plant, such as cotton or sunflower, can lose between 1–2 dm³ of water per day, and a large oak tree more than 600 dm³ per day.

14.17 Why does transpiration occur mainly through leaves?

Water is brought to the leaf in the xylem of vascular bundles which spread to form a fine branching network throughout the leaf. The branches end in one or a few xylem vessels or tracheids possessing little lignification. Water can therefore escape easily through their cellulose walls to the mesophyll cells they supply. Fig 14.7 shows the three pathways which water can subsequently follow, namely the apoplast pathway (cell walls), the symplast pathway (cytoplasm and plasmodesmata) and the vacuolar pathway (from vacuole to vacuole).

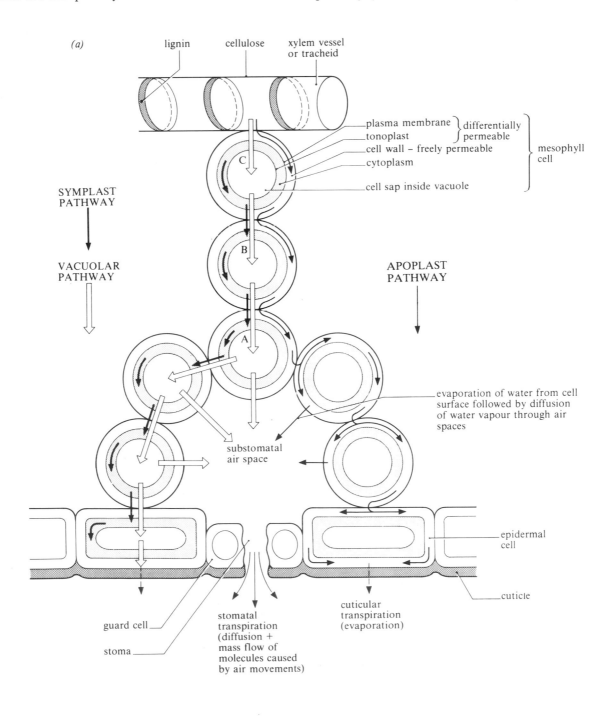

482

Fig 14.7 *(a) (facing page) Diagrammatic representation of water movement through a leaf. There are three possible pathways: the symplast and vacuolar pathways are shown to the left, the apoplast pathway to the right. Cells A, B and C are referred to in the text. Thickness of cell walls has been exaggerated. (b) (right) Diagrammatic representation of a group of cells summarising possible pathways of water (and solute) movement. More than one pathway may be used simultaneously. Such pathways may be used across the leaf and across the root cortex. Movement of ions by the vacuolar pathway would involve active transport. The apoplast pathway is the most important, and the vacuolar pathway the least important (negligible)*

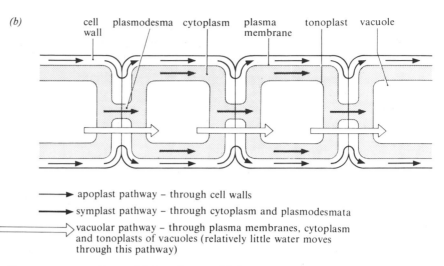

(b)

——→ apoplast pathway – through cell walls

——→ symplast pathway – through cytoplasm and plasmodesmata

====⟹ vacuolar pathway – through plasma membranes, cytoplasm and tonoplasts of vacuoles (relatively little water moves through this pathway)

14.3.1   The apoplast (apoplasm) pathway

The **apoplasm** is the system of adjacent cell walls which is continuous throughout the plant (except for the Casparian strip in roots, section 14.5.2). Up to 50% of a cellulose cell wall may be 'free space' which can be occupied by water. As water evaporates from the mesophyll cell walls into the intercellular air spaces, tension develops in the continuous stream of water in the apoplasm, and water is drawn through the walls in a mass flow by the cohesion of water molecules (section 14.4). Water in the apoplasm is supplied from the xylem.

14.3.2   The symplast (symplasm) pathway

The **symplasm** is the system of interconnected protoplasts in the plant. The cytoplasm of neighbouring protoplasts is linked by the plasmodesmata, the cytoplasmic strands which extend through pores in adjacent cell walls (fig 14.7b). The exact structure of plasmodesmata is not yet fully explained, so to what extent they form channels for the movement of materials is not known. However, it seems likely that once water, and any solutes it contains, is taken into the cytoplasm of one cell it can move through the symplasm without having to cross further membranes. Water would move down a water potential gradient, as in the vacuolar pathway (section 14.3.3). Movement might be aided by cytoplasmic streaming. The symplasm is a more important pathway of water movement than the vacuolar pathway.

14.3.3   The vacuolar pathway

In the vacuolar pathway water moves from vacuole to vacuole through neighbouring cells, crossing the symplasm and apoplasm in the process and moving through plasma membranes and tonoplasts by osmosis (fig 14.7b). It moves down a water potential gradient, set up as follows.

Water evaporates from the wet walls of the mesophyll cells into the intercellular air spaces, particularly into the larger substomatal air spaces. Taking cell A in fig 14.7a as an example, loss of water from the cell would result in a decrease in its turgor pressure and its water potential. Cell B would then have a higher water potential than cell A (at equilibrium they would be equal). Water will therefore move from cell B to cell A, thus lowering the water potential of cell B relative to cell C. In this way a gradient of water potential is set up across the leaf from a higher potential in the xylem to a lower potential in the mesophyll cells. Water enters the mesophyll cells from the xylem by osmosis. Although it is convenient to describe the movement of water in a step-by-step fashion, it should be stressed that the water potential gradient that develops across the leaf is a continuous one, and water moves smoothly down the gradient as a liquid would in moving along a wick.

It is sometimes imagined that water moves across the leaf in response to a gradient of osmotic pressures. However, although a water potential gradient exists, there is no evidence to suggest that osmotic pressures of the relevant cells differ significantly from one another. Differences in water potential are due mainly to differences in turgor pressure (remember that loss of a small amount of water from a cell has a much greater effect on turgor pressure than on osmotic pressure). The same applies to the root (section 14.5) where gradients of turgor pressure and water potential, but not necessarily of osmotic pressure, exist.

14.3.4   Exit of water through stomata

The three pathways described above end with water evaporating into air spaces. From here water vapour diffuses through the stomata, following the path of least resistance in moving from a high water potential inside the leaf to a much lower one outside the leaf. In dicotyledons, stomata are usually confined to, or are more numerous in, the lower epidermis. Control of stomatal opening is discussed in section 14.3.9. Immediately next to the leaf is a layer of stationary air whose thickness depends on the dimensions and surface features of the leaf, such as hairiness, and also on wind speed. Water vapour must diffuse through this layer before being swept away by moving air (mass flow). The thinner the stationary layer, the faster is the rate of transpiration. There is a diffusion gradient from the stationary layer back to the mesophyll

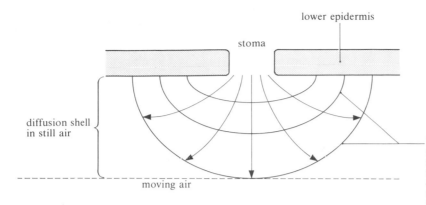

lower epidermis

stoma

diffusion shell in still air

moving air

Arrows represent curved paths of diffusion of water molecules

Fig 14.8 *Diffusion of water molecules from a stoma. Note that the diffusion gradient is steeper at the edges of the pore*

Lines represent contours of equal concentration of water molecules (equal water potential); the steeper the water potential gradient, the closer together the contours and the faster the rate of diffusion. The fastest rates are therefore from the edges of the pores. This 'edge effect' means that water loss and gaseous exchange are more rapid through a large number of small holes than through a smaller number of large holes with the same total area

cells. Theoretically each stoma has a diffusion gradient, or 'diffusion shell' around it, as shown in fig 14.8. In practice the diffusion shells of neighbouring stomata overlap in still air to form one overall diffusion shell.

14.3.5 Measuring the rate of transpiration

Transpiration can easily be demonstrated by placing a bell jar over a potted plant with the pot enclosed in a plastic bag to prevent water loss from the soil. As transpiration occurs, a fluid collects on the inside of the bell jar which is shown to contain water when tested with cobalt(II) chloride paper (blue to pink in water) or anhydrous copper(II) sulphate crystals (white to blue in water).

Measuring absolute rates of transpiration can be difficult, but satisfactory results, at least for the purposes of comparison, can be obtained by means of the two simple experiments described below.

Experiment 14.4: To investigate and measure factors affecting rate of transpiration using a potometer

A **potometer** is a piece of apparatus designed to measure the rate of water uptake by a cut shoot or young seedling. It does not measure transpiration directly, but since most of the water taken up is lost by transpiration, the two processes are closely related. Potometers are available commercially, but a simple version may be set up as shown in fig 14.9.

Materials

potometer (fig 14.9: conical filter flask, short rubber tubing, rubber bung with a single hole, hypodermic syringe and needle, graduated capillary tube)
large black polythene bag   stop clock
large transparent   thermometer
   polythene bag   vaseline (petroleum jelly)
small electric fan   leafy shoot, such as lilac
retort stand and clamp   bucket

Method

(1) Select a suitable leafy plant, cut off the shoot and immerse the cut end immediately in a bucket of water to minimise the risk of air being drawn into the xylem. Immediately cut the shoot again under water, with a slanting cut, a few centimetres above the original cut. The stem must be thick enough to fit tightly into the bung of the potometer.

(2) Submerge a conical filter flask in a sink of water to fill it with water. Transfer the leafy shoot from bucket to sink and again immediately make a slanting cut a few centimetres above the last cut. Fit the shoot into the bung of the flask under water and push the bung in to make a tight fit.

(3) Submerge the graduated capillary tube, with rubber tubing attached, in the sink, fill it with water and attach it to the side arm of the filter flask.

(4) Remove the apparatus from the sink and set up the syringe with the needle pushed into the rubber tubing as shown in fig 14.9. The syringe can be clamped in a vertical position. The joint between shoot and bung should be smeared with vaseline to make certain it is airtight.

(5) As the shoot takes up water the end of the water column in the capillary tube can be seen to move. It may be returned to the open end of the tube by pushing in water from the syringe. Allow the shoot to equilibrate for 5 min whilst regularly replacing the water taken up.

(6) Measure the time taken for the water column to move a given distance along the capillary tube and express the rate of water uptake in convenient units, such as cm min^{-1}. A number of readings should be taken to ensure that the rate is fairly constant, and the mean result calculated. The temperature of the air around the plant should be noted.

(7) Each time the air bubble reaches the end of the graduated section of the tube return it to its original position with the syringe.

(8) The effects of some of the following factors on rate of uptake of water could be investigated:

Fig 14.9 *A simple potometer*

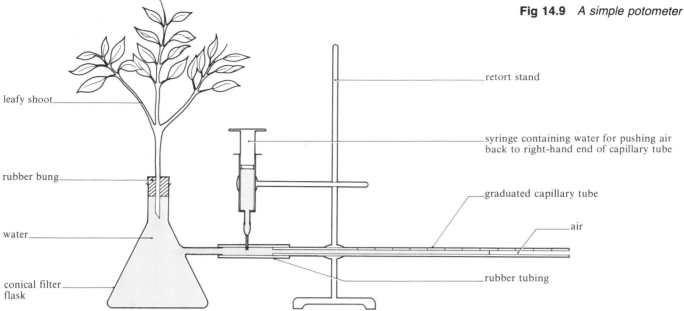

leafy shoot

rubber bung

water

conical filter flask

retort stand

syringe containing water for pushing air back to right-hand end of capillary tube

graduated capillary tube

air

rubber tubing

(a) wind – use a small electric fan (do not strongly buffet the leaves or the stomata will close);

(b) humidity – enclose the shoot in a transparent plastic bag;

(c) darkness – enclose the shoot in a black polythene bag;

(d) removal of half the leaves – is the transpiration rate halved?

(e) vaselining upper and/or lower epidermises of the leaves to prevent water loss.

In each case sufficient time should be allowed to ensure that the new rate has been attained. It is not always possible to change only one condition at a time; for example, enclosing the plant in a transparent bag will also lead to some reduction in light intensity.

Absolute rate of water uptake

Results can be converted to actual volume of water taken up per unit time, such as $cm^3\ h^{-1}$, if the volume of the graduated scale corresponding to each division is determined.

Most of the water taken up is lost through the leaves. An estimate of rate of water loss per unit leaf area can be obtained by measuring the volume of water lost as described above and then removing all the leaves and determining their surface area. The latter can be obtained by drawing the outlines of the leaves on graph paper and counting the enclosed squares. Using these data results can be expressed as $cm^3\ h^{-1}\ m^{-2}$ leaf area.

Results

The effects of wind, temperature, humidity and darkness are discussed in section 14.3.6.

14.3.6 Effects of environmental factors on transpiration

Plants exhibit many morphological and anatomical features which enable them to reduce transpiration losses if dry conditions are encountered. Such features are described as **xeromorphic** and are considered below. Plants growing in dry habitats and thus subjected to drought are called **xerophytes** and possess many xeromorphic features which are described in more detail in section 19.3.2. Plants growing under conditions in which there is normally an adequate water supply are called **mesophytes**, but nevertheless can show xeromorphic features.

Light

Light affects transpiration because stomata usually open in the light and close in darkness. At night, therefore, only small amounts of water are lost by cuticular, and possibly lenticular transpiration. As stomata open in the morning, transpiration rates increase.

One group of succulent plants, the Crassulaceae, open their stomata at night and close them during the day as a means of reducing water losses. Carbon dioxide enters the stomata at night, is fixed into an organic acid, and then released again inside the leaf for photosynthesis during the day.

Temperature

Given the presence of light, the external factor which has the greatest effect on transpiration is temperature. The higher the temperature, the greater the rate of evaporation of water from mesophyll cells and the greater the saturation of the leaf atmosphere with water vapour. At the same time, a rise in temperature lowers the relative humidity of the air outside the leaf. Both events result in a steeper concentration gradient of water molecules from leaf atmosphere to external atmosphere. The steeper this gradient, the faster is the rate of diffusion. Alternatively, it can be said that water potential increases inside the leaf while decreasing outside the leaf.

The temperature of the leaf is raised by solar radiation. Pale-coloured leaves reflect more of this radiation than normal leaves and therefore do not heat up as rapidly. The pale colour is usually due to a thick coat of epidermal hairs, waxy deposits or scales, and is a xeromorphic feature.

Humidity and vapour pressure

Low humidity (low water vapour pressure) outside the leaf favours transpiration because it makes the diffusion gradient of water vapour (or water potential gradient) from the moist leaf atmosphere to the external atmosphere steeper. As the concentration of water vapour in the external atmosphere, that is the humidity, rises, the diffusion gradient becomes less steep. Water vapour pressure of the atmosphere also decreases with altitude as atmospheric pressure decreases. High altitude plants therefore often show xeromorphic adaptations to reduce transpiration rates.

A xeromorphic feature of some leaves is the presence of sunken stomata, that is stomata in grooves or infoldings of the epidermis, around which a high humidity can build up and reduce transpiration losses. In some cases the whole leaf may roll up enclosing a humid atmosphere, such as in *Ammophila* (marram grass) (fig 14.10). A coat of

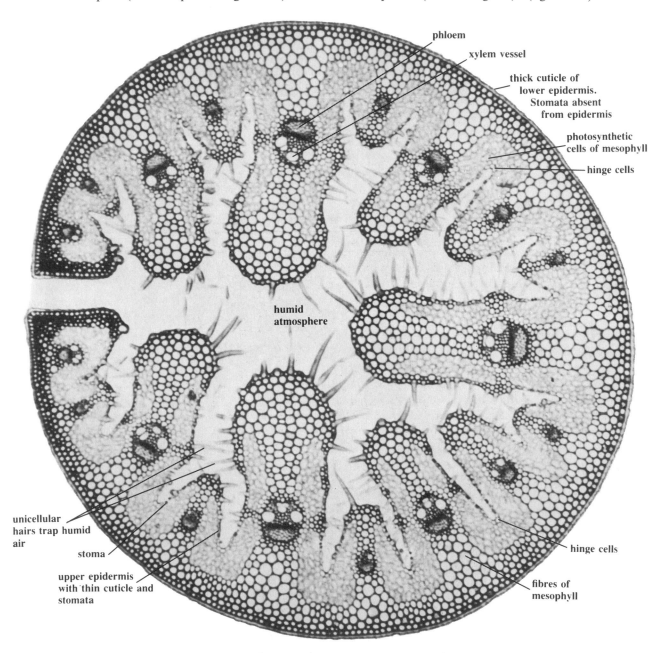

Fig 14.10 *A transverse section of the xeromorphic leaf of* Ammophila *(marram grass) to show distribution of tissues. The leaf is shown in the rolled condition*

epidermal hairs or scales will tend to trap a layer of still moist air next to the leaf, thus reducing transpiration.

Wind

In still air a shell of highly saturated air builds up around the leaf, thus reducing the steepness of the diffusion gradient between leaf atmosphere and external atmosphere. Any disturbance, that is mass flow of the air, will generally sweep away this shell. Thus windy conditions result in increased transpiration rates, the increase being most pronounced at low wind speeds. High winds may result in stomatal closure and cessation of stomatal transpiration.

Hairs and scales trap still air as described above, tending to reduce transpiration rates.

Availability of soil water

As soil dries out, water usually binds more tightly to soil particles. Also, though of less importance, the soil solution becomes more concentrated, that is its water potential decreases. There is therefore less tendency for water to enter by osmosis. Reduced water uptake is followed shortly by a reduction in transpiration rate as there is greater resistance to movement of water through the plant, and a less steep water potential gradient from the soil through the plant to the atmosphere.

14.3.7 Effect of plant or internal factors on the rate of transpiration

The effects of some xeromorphic adaptations on transpiration rates have been considered above. Further examples of the ways in which such 'internal' as opposed to 'external' (environmental) factors can operate are given below.

Leaf surface area and surface area to volume ratio

Transpiration of a plant increases with its total leaf surface area, and with leaf surface area to volume ratio. Reduction of leaf surface is achieved when leaves are reduced to needles, such as in *Pinus* and other conifers, or to spines, as in cacti. There may also simply be a reduction in size in dry conditions. The shedding of leaves in dry or cold seasons by deciduous plants is a xeromorphic adaptation. In cold seasons water may be unavailable through being frozen and the rate of water movement through the plant is also lower at low temperatures.

Surface area to volume ratio can be reduced by using the stem as the main photosynthetic organ, as in cacti. Fig 14.11 shows the characteristic reduction in leaf surface area of succulents like cacti.

Cuticle

In general, the thinner the cuticle the greater the rate of cuticular transpiration, although the composition of the cuticle is also important. Where it is thin, as in ferns, 30–45% of the transpiration losses can be through the cuticle. It may assume particular importance if stomatal

transpiration is minimal and water is scarce.

The upper surfaces of dicotyledonous leaves, which are exposed to direct solar radiation and are less protected from air currents than the lower surfaces, often possess thicker cuticles than their lower surfaces. Increased wax deposits on leaves can virtually eliminate cuticular transpiration. Also, waxy leaves are usually shiny and so reflect more solar radiation.

Stomata

In general, the greater the number of stomata per unit area, the greater is the rate of stomatal transpiration; however, their distribution is also important. For example, the lower surfaces of dicotyledonous leaves usually have more stomata than their upper surfaces (table 14.7), whereas monocotyledonous leaves, which are generally held vertically rather than horizontally, have similar upper and lower surfaces with similar stomatal distributions (see maize and oat, table 14.7). On average, fewer stomata occur in plants adapted to dry conditions. The number may vary within the same species as a result.

Table 14.7 Stomatal densities in the leaves of some common plants

| Plant | Number of stomata/cm^{-2} | |
	upper epidermis	lower epidermis
Monocotyledons		
maize (*Zea mais*)	5 200	6 800
oat (*Avena sativa*)	2 500	2 300
Dicotyledons		
apple (*Malus* spp.)	0	29 400
bean (*Phaseolus vulgaris*)	4 000	28 100
cabbage (*Brassica* spp.)	14 100	22 600
lucerne (*Medicago sativa*)	16 900	13 800
Nasturtium	0	13 000
oak (*Quercus* spp.)	0	45 000
potato (*Solanum tuberosum*)	5 100	16 100
tomato (*Lycopersicon esculentum*)	1 200	13 000

Based on Weier, T. E., Stocking, C. R. and Barbour, M. G. (1970) *Botany, an Introduction to Plant Biology*, 4th ed., John Wiley & Sons, p. 192.

Experiment 14.5: To investigate stomatal distribution

Materials

    clear nail varnish
    slides and cover-slips
    fine forceps
    fresh fully expanded leaves
    microscope

Method

A convenient means of examining stomatal distribution is to make a replica of the leaf surface using clear nail varnish. Spread a thin layer of the nail varnish over the leaf

Fig 14.11 *Succulent plants. (left) Silver Cholla (Opuntia echinocarpa) (right) Kalarchoe verticilitta*

using the brush in the bottle. Allow it to dry, then peel off the thin replica with fine forceps, lay it on a slide and add a cover-slip. It may be mounted in water for convenience. Examine with a microscope. Count the number of stomata in a given field of view and repeat several times in different areas. Obtain a mean value. Determine the area of the field of view of the microscope by measuring the diameter with a calibrated slide or transparent ruler and using the formula πr^2 for the area, where r is the radius and $\pi = 3.142$. The number of stomata per square centimetre can then be calculated.

Compare the densities of stomata in upper and lower epidermises of the same leaf, and in different species. Is there any correlation between stomatal densities and the habitats of plants?

14.18 Examine fig 14.12. Describe and explain the relationships between the three variables shown.

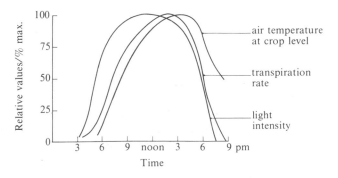

Fig 14.12 *Relationship between light intensity, air temperature and transpiration rate from lucerne leaves. (From data by L. J. Briggs & H. L. Shantz (1916) J. Agr. Res., 5, 583–649; cited by A. C. Leopold (1964) Plant growth and development, p. 396. McGraw-Hill)*

14.3.8   Functions of transpiration

Transpiration has been described as a 'necessary evil' because it is an inevitable, but potentially harmful, consequence of the existence of wet cell walls from which evaporation occurs. Water vapour escapes along the route used for gaseous exchange between the plant and its environment, which is essential for the processes of photosynthesis and respiration. The route is mainly through stomata, as already discussed. If there was no cuticle, stomata would be unnecessary and gaseous exchange would be even more efficient. However, loss of water could not then be controlled. The cuticle reduces water loss and further control is exercised by the stomata, which in most plants are highly sensitive to water stress and close, for example, under conditions of drought. They also usually close during the night when photosynthesis ceases. Loss of water can lead to wilting, serious desiccation, and often death of a plant if conditions of drought are experienced. There is good evidence that even mild water stress results in reduced growth rate and, in crops, to economic losses through reductions in yield.

Despite its apparent inevitability, it is worth questioning whether there might be some advantages associated with transpiration. Two possibilities are as follows.

(1) It has been suggested that the transpiration stream is necessary to distribute mineral salts throughout the plant, since these move with the water. Whilst this may be true, it seems probable that very low transpiration rates would suffice. For example, mineral salt supply to leaves is just as great at night, when transpiration is low, as during the day because the xylem sap is more concentrated at night. Uptake of mineral salts is largely independent of the transpiration stream, but high rates of water uptake may serve to draw water and dissolved substances from more remote regions of the soil.

(2) The evaporation of water from mesophyll cells that accompanies transpiration requires energy and therefore results in cooling of the leaves in the same way that sweating cools the skin of mammals. This is sometimes important under conditions of direct sunlight when leaves absorb large amounts of radiant energy and experience rises in temperature which, under extreme conditions, can inhibit photosynthesis. However, it is unlikely that the cooling effect is of significance under normal conditions. Plants that live in hot climates usually have other means of counteracting heat stress.

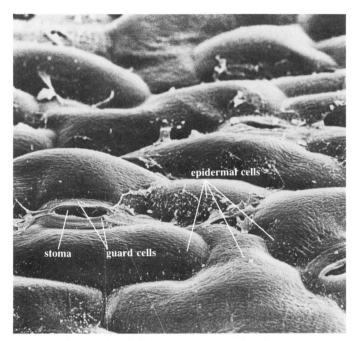

Fig 14.13 *Scanning electron micrograph of stomata on the lower surface of a leaf*

14.3.9 Stomata – structure and mechanism of opening and closing

Stomata are pores in the epidermis through which gaseous exchange occurs. They are found mainly in leaves, but also in stems. Each stoma is bounded by two guard cells which, unlike the other epidermal cells, possess chloroplasts. The guard cells control the size of the stoma by changes in their turgidity. The appearance of guard cells and stomata is well revealed by the scanning electron microscope, as shown in fig 14.13.

The appearance of epidermal cells, guard cells and stomata in surface view, as seen with the light microscope, is dealt with in section 8.1. Fig 14.14 is a diagram of a section through a typical stoma, and shows that the guard cell walls are unevenly thickened, the wall furthest from the pore (termed the dorsal wall) being thinner than that next to the pore (the ventral wall). Also, the cellulose microfibrils that make up the walls are arranged so that the ventral wall is less elastic than the dorsal wall, and some

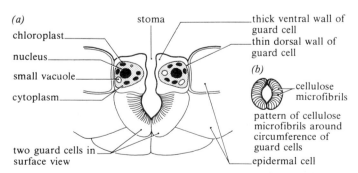

Fig 14.14 (a) *Vertical section through a stoma, showing also part of the lower surface of the leaf.* (b) *Pattern of cellulose microfibrils in guard cell walls*

form hoops around the sausage-shaped guard cells as shown in fig 14.14*b*. As the cells inflate with water, that is become turgid, the hoops tend to restrict the cells to an increase in length only. Because the ends of the guard cells are joined, and also because the thin dorsal walls stretch more easily than the thick ventral walls, each cell assumes a semicircular shape (fig 14.14). Thus a hole, the stoma, appears between the guard cells. The same effect can be obtained by inflating a sausage-shaped balloon which has had a piece of adhesive tape stuck along one side to mimic the non-elastic ventral wall of the guard cell.

Conversely, when the guard cells lose water and turgidity, the pore closes. The question remains as to how the turgidity changes are brought about.

A traditional hypothesis, the 'starch–sugar hypothesis', suggested that an increase in sugar concentration in guard cells during the day led to an increase in their osmotic pressure and entry of water by osmosis. However, sugar has never been shown to accumulate in guard cells to the extent necessary to cause the observed changes in osmotic pressure. It has now been shown that an accumulation of potassium ions and associated anions occurs in guard cells during the day in response to light and is sufficient to account for the observed changes. In darkness, potassium ions (K^+) move out of the guard cells into surrounding epidermal cells. There is still doubt about which anion balances the potassium. In some, but not all, species studied large quantities of organic acid anions, such as malate, accumulate. At the same time the starch grains that appear in guard cell chloroplasts in darkness decrease in size, suggesting that starch is converted to malate in light. A possible route is:

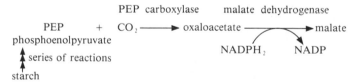

(Compare C_4 photosynthesis, section 9.8.2.)

Some species, such as *Allium cepa* (onion), have no starch in their guard cells. Here malate does not accumulate during stomatal opening and inorganic anions, such as chloride (Cl^-), may be taken up with the cations.

Certain questions remain to be answered. For example, why is light necessary for stomatal opening, and what function is served by the chloroplasts apart from starch storage? Is malate converted back to starch in darkness? In 1979 it was shown that the enzymes of the Calvin cycle are absent from the chloroplasts of guard cells of *Vicia faba* (broad bean), and the thylakoid system is poorly developed, although chlorophyll is present. Normal C_3 photosynthesis therefore cannot occur and starch cannot be made by this route. This might help to explain why starch is made at night rather than during the day as in normal photosynthetic cells. Another interesting fact is that guard cells lack plasmodesmata and are therefore relatively isolated from other epidermal cells.

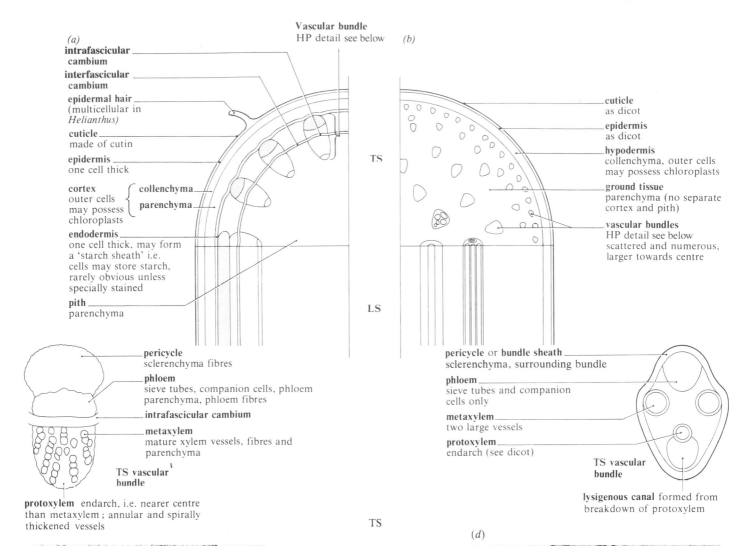

(a)

intrafascicular cambium

interfascicular cambium

epidermal hair (multicellular in *Helianthus*)

cuticle made of cutin

epidermis one cell thick

cortex outer cells may possess chloroplasts — **collenchyma** / **parenchyma**

endodermis one cell thick, may form a 'starch sheath' i.e. cells may store starch, rarely obvious unless specially stained

pith parenchyma

Vascular bundle HP detail see below

(b)

TS

LS

cuticle as dicot

epidermis as dicot

hypodermis collenchyma, outer cells may possess chloroplasts

ground tissue parenchyma (no separate cortex and pith)

vascular bundles HP detail see below scattered and numerous, larger towards centre

pericycle sclerenchyma fibres

phloem sieve tubes, companion cells, phloem parenchyma, phloem fibres

intrafascicular cambium

metaxylem mature xylem vessels, fibres and parenchyma

TS vascular bundle

protoxylem endarch, i.e. nearer centre than metaxylem; annular and spirally thickened vessels

pericycle or **bundle sheath** sclerenchyma, surrounding bundle

phloem sieve tubes and companion cells only

metaxylem two large vessels

protoxylem endarch (see dicot)

TS vascular bundle

lysigenous canal formed from breakdown of protoxylem

TS

(c)

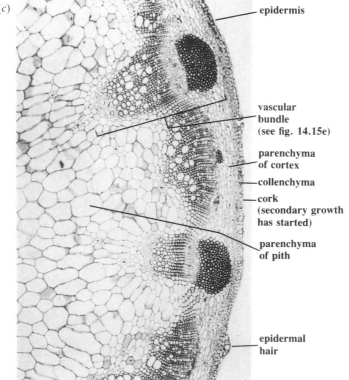

epidermis

vascular bundle (see fig. 14.15e)

parenchyma of cortex

collenchyma

cork (secondary growth has started)

parenchyma of pith

epidermal hair

(d)

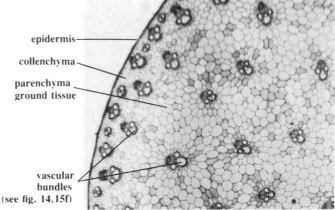

epidermis

collenchyma

parenchyma ground tissue

vascular bundles (see fig. 14.15f)

Fig 14.15 (a) (top left) *Primary anatomy of the stem of a typical dicotyledon,* Helianthus annuus *(sunflower).* (b) (top right) *Anatomy of the stem of a typical monocotyledon,* Zea mais *(maize).* (c) (above left) *Low power micrograph of part of a TS of the stem of* Helianthus. (d) (above right) *Low power micrograph of part of a TS of the stem of* Zea. (e) (facing page, top left) *High power micrograph of a TS of a vascular bundle from a stem of* Helianthus. (f) (facing page, top right) *High power micrograph of a TS of a vascular bundle from a stem of* Zea (g) (facing page, centre) *Micrograph of an LS of the stem of* Helianthus (h) (facing page, bottom) *Micrograph of an LS of the stem of* Zea

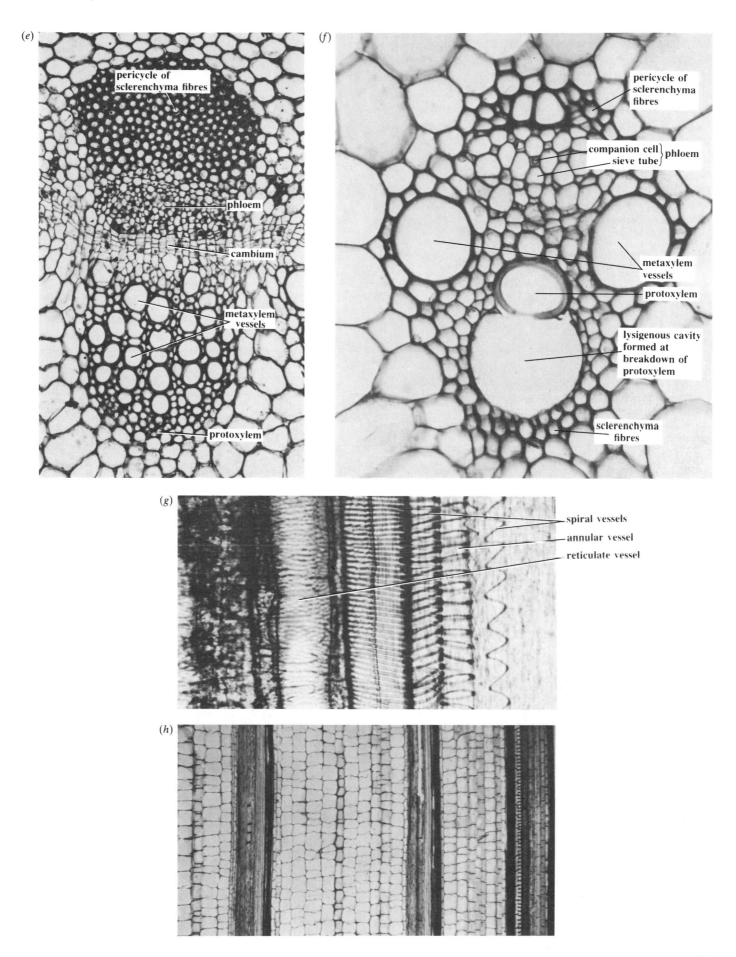

(e)

pericycle of sclerenchyma fibres

phloem

cambium

metaxylem vessels

protoxylem

(f)

pericycle of sclerenchyma fibres

companion cell } phloem
sieve tube }

metaxylem vessels

protoxylem

lysigenous cavity formed at breakdown of protoxylem

sclerenchyma fibres

(g)

spiral vessels

annular vessel

reticulate vessel

(h)

14.4   Ascent of water in the xylem

Xylem in flowering plants contains two types of water-transporting cell, the tracheid and the vessel, whose structures as seen in the light microscope are discussed in section 8.2.1, together with the appearance of vessels as seen with the scanning electron microscope (fig 8.11). The structure of the secondary xylem (wood) is dealt with in section 21.6.6.

Xylem, together with phloem, forms the vascular or conducting tissue of higher plants. Vascular tissue consists of bundles of tubes called **vascular bundles** whose structure and arrangement in the primary stems of dicotyledonous plants (dicots) and monocotyledonous plants (monocots) are shown in fig 14.15.

14.19   Summarise in table form the major differences in primary structure between dicot and monocot stems.

14.20   What is the overall shape of the following tissues in three dimensions: (*a*) epidermis, (*b*) xylem, (*c*) pericycle of dicots and (*d*) pith?

The fact that water can move up the xylem may be demonstrated by immersing the cut end of a shoot in a dilute solution of a dye, such as eosin. The dye rises in the xylem and spreads through the network of veins in the leaves. Sectioning and examination with a light microscope reveals the stain to be in the xylem.

Better evidence that xylem conducts water is given by 'ringing' experiments. These were among earlier experiments done before radioactive isotopes made the tracing of substances through living organisms much easier. In one type of ringing experiment an outer ring of bark, including phloem, is removed and, in the short term, this does not affect the upward movement of water. However, lifting a flap of bark, removing a section of xylem, and replacing the flap of bark leads to rapid wilting.

Any theory for water movement up the xylem has to account for the following observations.
(1) Xylem vessels are dead tubes with narrow lumens ranging in diameter from 0.01 mm in 'summer wood' to about 0.2 mm in 'spring wood'.
(2) Large quantities of water are carried at relatively high speeds, up to 8 m h^{-1} being recorded in tall trees and commonly in other plants at 1 m h^{-1}.
(3) To move water through such tubes to the height of a tall tree requires pressures of around 4 000 kPa. The tallest trees, the giant sequoias or redwoods of California (conifers and therefore possessing only tracheids, not vessels) and *Eucalyptus* trees or blue gums of Australia, can reach heights greater than 100 m. Water will rise in fine capillary tubes due to its high surface tension, a phenomenon called **capillarity**, but could rise only about 3 m in even the finest xylem vessels by this method.

The **cohesion–tension theory** (or cohesion theory) of water movement adequately accounts for these observations. According to this theory, evaporation of water from the cells of a leaf is responsible for raising water from the roots. Evaporation results in a reduced water potential in the cells next to the xylem as described in section 14.3. Water therefore enters these cells from the xylem sap which has a higher water potential, passing through the moist cellulose cell walls of the xylem vessels at the ends of the veins, as shown in fig 14.7.

The xylem vessels are full of water and as water leaves them a tension is set up in the columns of water. This is transmitted back down the stem all the way to the root by **cohesion** of water molecules. Water molecules have high cohesion, that is tend to 'stick' to each other, because, being polar, they are electrically attracted to each other and are held together by hydrogen bonding (section 5.1.2). They also tend to stick to the vessel walls, a force called **adhesion**. The high cohesion of water molecules means that a relatively large tension is required to break a column of water, that is a water column has a high tensile strength. The tension in the xylem vessels builds up to a force capable of pulling the whole column of water upwards by means of mass flow, and water enters the base of the columns in the roots from neighbouring root cells. It is essential that the xylem walls should also have high tensile strength if they are not to buckle inwards, as happens when sucking up a soggy straw. Lignin and cellulose both provide this strength. Evidence that the contents of xylem vessels are under high tension comes from measuring diurnal changes in the diameters of tree trunks using an instrument called a dendrogram. The minimum diameters are recorded during daylight hours when transpiration rates are highest. The minute shrinkage of each xylem vessel under tension combines to give a measurable shrinkage in diameter of the whole trunk.

Estimates of the tensile strength of a column of xylem sap vary from about 3 000–30 000 kPa, the lower estimates being the more recent. Water potentials of the order required to generate enough tension to raise water, about −4 000 kPa, have been recorded in leaves, and it seems likely that xylem sap has the required tensile strength to withstand this tension, though there may be a tendency for the columns to break, particularly in vessels of relatively large diameter.

Critics of the theory point to the fact that any break in a column of sap should stop its flow, the vessel tending to fill with air and water vapour, a process known as **cavitation**. Shaking, bending and shortage of water can all induce cavitation. It is well known that the water content of tree trunks gradually decreases during summer as the wood becomes filled with air. This is made use of in the lumber industry because such wood floats more easily. However, breaks in water columns do not greatly affect water flow rates. The explanation may be that water flows from one vessel to another, or by-passes air-locks by moving through neighbouring parenchyma cells and their walls. Also, it is calculated that only a small proportion of the vessels need be functional at any one time to account for the observed flow rates. In some trees and shrubs water moves only through the younger outer wood, which is therefore called **sapwood**. In oak and ash, for example, water moves mainly through the vessels of the current year, the rest of the sapwood acting as a water reserve. New vessels are added throughout the growing season, mostly early in the season when flow rates are higher.

A second force involved in water movement up the xylem is **root pressure**. This can be observed and measured when a freshly cut root stump continues to exude sap from its xylem vessels. The process is inhibited by respiratory inhibitors such as cyanide, lack of oxygen and low temperatures. The mechanism probably depends on active secretion of salts or other solutes into the xylem sap, thus lowering its water potential. Water then moves into the xylem by osmosis from neighbouring root cells.

The positive hydrostatic pressure of around 100–200 kPa (exceptionally 800 kPa) that is generated by root pressure is usually not sufficient alone to account for water movement up the xylem but it is no doubt a contributing factor in many plants. It can be sufficient, however, in slowly transpiring herbaceous plants, when it can cause guttation. **Guttation** is the loss of water as drops of liquid from the surface of a plant (as opposed to vapour in transpiration). It is favoured by the same conditions that favour low transpiration rates, including dim light and high humidity. It is common in many rain forest species and is frequently seen at the tips of the leaves of young grass seedlings.

14.21 Summarise the properties of xylem which make it suitable for the long-distance transport of water and solutes.

14.5 Uptake of water by roots

The primary structures of typical dicot and monocot roots are shown in fig 14.16.

14.22 Summarise in table form the major differences in primary structure between typical dicot and monocot roots.

Water is absorbed mainly, but not exclusively, by the younger parts of roots in the regions of the root hairs. As a root grows through the soil, new root hairs develop a short distance behind the zone of elongation and older hairs die. These hairs are tubular extensions of epidermal cells (fig 14.16) and greatly increase the available surface area for uptake of water and mineral salts. They form a very intimate relationship with soil particles.

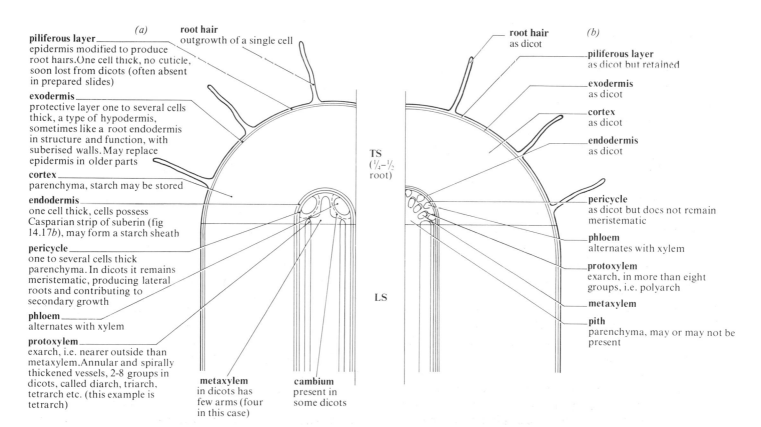

Fig 14.16 (a) *Primary anatomy of the root of a typical dicotyledon*, Ranunculus *(buttercup). (b) Primary anatomy of the root of a typical monocotyledon*, Zea mais *(maize). (c) and (d) overleaf*

493

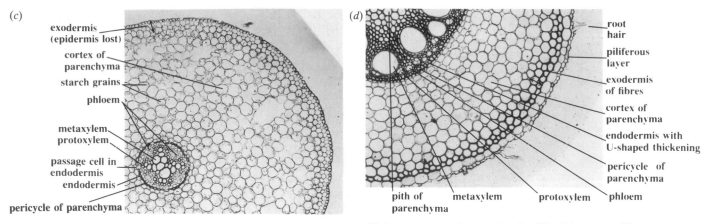

(c) exodermis
(epidermis lost)

cortex of
parenchyma

starch grains

phloem

metaxylem
protoxylem

passage cell in
endodermis

endodermis

pericycle of parenchyma

(d) root
hair

piliferous
layer

exodermis
of fibres

cortex of
parenchyma

endodermis with
U-shaped thickening

pericycle of
parenchyma

phloem

pith of parenchyma   metaxylem   protoxylem

(c) Low power micrograph of a TS of the root of Ranunculus

(d) Low power micrograph of a TS of the root of Zea

Fig 14.17*a* is a diagrammatic representation of the pathway taken by water across a root. A water potential gradient exists across the root from higher potential in the piliferous layer to lower potential in the cells adjacent to the xylem. This gradient is maintained in two ways:

(1) by water moving up the xylem, as described, setting up tension in the xylem and thus lowering the water potential of its sap;

(2) the xylem sap has a higher osmotic pressure than the dilute soil solution.

Water moves across the root by pathways similar to those in the leaf, namely apoplast, symplast and vacuolar pathways.

14.5.1   Symplast and vacuolar pathways

As water moves up the xylem in the root, it is replaced by water from neighbouring parenchyma cells,

such as cell A in fig 14.17*a*. As water leaves cell A, the water potential of cell A decreases and water enters it from cell B by osmosis or through the symplasm in exactly the same way as described for cells A and B in the leaf (section 14.3.2). Similarly the water potential of cell B then decreases and water enters it from cell C and so on across the root to the piliferous layer.

The soil solution is normally fairly dilute, so it has a higher water potential than cells of the piliferous layer, which include the root hairs. Water therefore enters the root from the soil by osmosis.

> **14.23**   Arrange the following in order of ψ: soil solution, xylem sap, cell A, cell B, cell C, root hair cell. (Use the symbol > (greater than).)

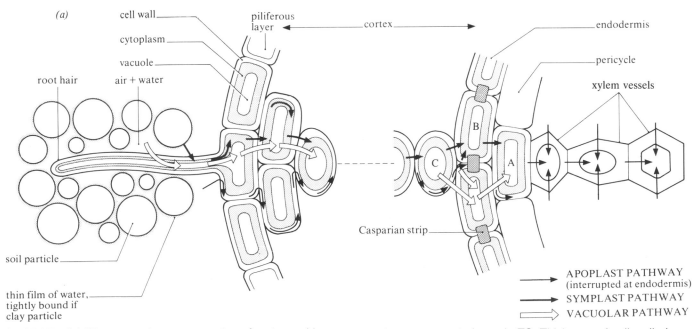

(a) cell wall

piliferous layer

cortex

endodermis

cytoplasm

vacuole

air + water

root hair

pericycle

xylem vessels

B

C

A

Casparian strip

soil particle

thin film of water,
tightly bound if
clay particle

→ APOPLAST PATHWAY
(interrupted at endodermis)

→ SYMPLAST PATHWAY

⇨ VACUOLAR PATHWAY

Fig 14.17 *(a) Diagrammatic representation of water and ion movement across a root shown in TS. Thickness of cell walls is exaggerated for clarity. Cells A, B, C are referred to in the text. The apoplast pathway is of greatest importance for both water and solutes. The symplast pathway is less important, except for salts in the region of the endodermis. Movement along the vacuolar pathway is negligible. (b)* and *(c)* facing page

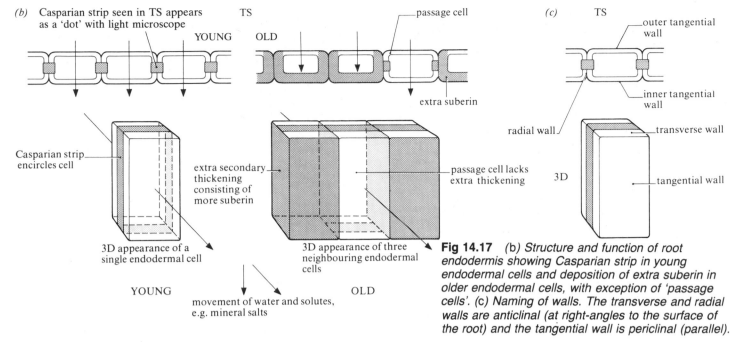

(b) Casparian strip seen in TS appears as a 'dot' with light microscope

TS

YOUNG   OLD

passage cell

extra suberin

Casparian strip encircles cell

extra secondary thickening consisting of more suberin

3D appearance of a single endodermal cell

3D appearance of three neighbouring endodermal cells

passage cell lacks extra thickening

YOUNG   OLD

movement of water and solutes, e.g. mineral salts

(c)   TS

outer tangential wall

inner tangential wall

radial wall

transverse wall

3D

tangential wall

Fig 14.17 *(b) Structure and function of root endodermis showing Casparian strip in young endodermal cells and deposition of extra suberin in older endodermal cells, with exception of 'passage cells'. (c) Naming of walls. The transverse and radial walls are anticlinal (at right-angles to the surface of the root) and the tangential wall is periclinal (parallel).*

14.5.2   Apoplast pathway

The apoplast pathway operates in much the same way as in the leaf (section 14.3.1). However, there is one important difference. When water moving through spaces in the cell walls reaches the endodermis its progress is barred by the waterproof substance called **suberin** which is deposited in the cell walls in the form of bands called **Casparian strips**. These strips prevent apoplastic movement of water (fig 14.17b) and therefore water and salts must pass through the plasma membrane under the cytoplasmic control of the endodermal cell. In this way, it is believed, control by living cells is exercised over the movement of water and mineral salts from soil to xylem. Such control is necessary to regulate salt movement and may be a protective measure against entry of toxic substances, fungal pathogens, and so on. It is interesting to note that when endodermal cells are plasmolysed, their cytoplasm remains attached to the Casparian strip even when shrinking away from the rest of the cell wall. As roots get older suberisation in the endodermis often gets more extensive as shown in fig 14.17b. This blocks the normal exit of water and mineral salts through the inner tangential walls. However, plasmodesmata may stay as pores in these walls, and 'passage cells' in which no extra thickening occurs also remain to allow water and solute movement.

The relative importance of apoplast, symplast and vacuolar pathways is not known.

14.6   Uptake of mineral salts and their transport across roots

As part of their nutrition, plants require certain mineral elements in addition to the carbohydrates made in photosynthesis. The uses of these elements are described in table 9.10. In higher plants minerals are taken up from the soil or surrounding water by roots. Uptake is greatest in the region of the root hairs.

Mineral elements exist in the form of ions in salts, and in solution the ions dissociate and move about freely. In attempting to explain the uptake and movement of mineral ions, the following facts must be taken into account.

(1) Cell membranes, including the plasma membrane and tonoplast, are not truly semi-permeable but differentially permeable, allowing to varying extents the passage of substances other than water, such as ions.

(2) Active transport can occur across cell membranes. This requires energy in the form of ATP, made during respiration, and can lead to an accumulation of ions against a concentration gradient (section 7.2.2).

(3) There is a continuous system of cell walls, the apoplasm, extending inwards from the piliferous layer of the root. Water, and any solutes it contains, enters the system from the soil by mass flow and to a lesser extent by diffusion.

(4) Water moves through the apoplasm as part of the transpiration stream.

Fig 14.18 shows the uptake of potassium ions by young cereal roots which had previously been thoroughly washed in pure water. After 90 min the respiratory inhibitor potassium cyanide was added to the solutions.

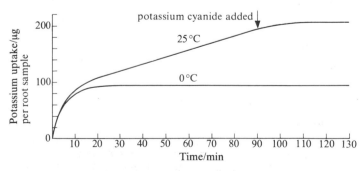

Fig 14.18 *Absorption of potassium ions by young cereal plants in aerated solution*

14.24 (a) Describe the uptake of potassium ions at 0 °C and 25 °C.
(b) Explain the differences described, and the effect of potassium cyanide (KCN).

Similar results to those in fig 14.18 can be obtained with isolated tissues, those of storage organs, such as carrot, being commonly used. The data shown in fig 14.19 confirm the inhibition of respiration by potassium cyanide.

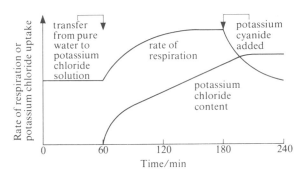

Fig 14.19 *Rate of respiration and uptake of potassium chloride by carrot discs. (Based on data by Robertson & Turner (1945))*

14.25 Fig 14.19 shows that the rate of respiration of carrot discs increases when they are transferred from pure water to potassium chloride solution. From the results shown, account for this increase.

14.26 Why does the rise in potassium chloride content stop when KCN is added?

14.27 In an experiment similar to that described in fig 14.18, but involving phosphate uptake, 16% of the phosphate taken up by barley roots over a short period could be washed out after transferring to pure water again. Explain.

14.28 Could ions reach the xylem entirely by means of the apoplast pathway?

To summarise so far, the uptake of ions by roots is a combination of **passive uptake**, whereby ions move by mass flow and diffusion through the apoplasm, and **active uptake**, or **active transport**, whereby ions can be taken up into cells against a concentration gradient using energy from respiration.

Active transport is selective and dependent on respiration, whereas diffusion is non-selective and not dependent on respiration. Each cell of the root cortex is bathed in a solution similar in composition to that of the soil solution as a result of passive uptake. Thus there is a large surface area for ion uptake.

Ions moving in the apoplasm can only reach the endodermis, where the Casparian strip prevents further progress as described in section 14.5.2. To cross the endodermis, ions must pass by diffusion or active transport through the plasma membranes of endodermal cells, entering their cytoplasm and possibly their vacuoles. Thus the plant monitors and controls which types of ions eventually reach the xylem.

14.29 How could you demonstrate, using a radioactive ion and autoradiography, that the endodermis is a barrier to the movement of ions through cell walls?

Ions can also move through the symplast pathway. Once they are taken into the cytoplasm of one cell, they can move through the symplasm without having to cross further membranes. The symplasm extends from the piliferous layer right through to the xylem. Fig 14.17a summarises the possible ways in which ions can cross the root.

The final stage in the movement of mineral salts across the root is the release of ions into the xylem. To achieve this, ions must leave living cells at some stage, crossing back through a plasma membrane. This could be by diffusion or active transport.

14.7 Translocation of mineral salts through plants

The pathway of mineral salts across the root to the xylem, described above, is the first stage in their translocation. Once in the xylem, they are distributed throughout the plant by the transpiration stream, in which they move by mass flow. Movement of the mineral elements in the xylem can be demonstrated by ringing experiments like those already described, in which removal of tissues external to the xylem, such as phloem, has no effect on upward movement of ions. Analysis of the xylem sap also reveals that although some of the nitrogen travels as inorganic nitrate or ammonium ions, much of it is carried in the organic form of amino acids and related compounds. Some conversion of these ions to amino acids must therefore take place in the roots. Similarly small amounts of phosphorus and sulphur are carried as organic compounds.

Thus, although xylem and phloem are traditionally regarded as conducting inorganic and organic materials respectively, the distinction is not clear-cut. In addition, a small amount of exchange between xylem and phloem is common and phloem carries significant quantities of mineral elements away from organs other than the root, as discussed below.

The chief **sinks**, that is sites of utilisation, for mineral elements are the growing regions of the plant, such as the apical and lateral meristems, young leaves, developing fruits and flowers, and storage organs. Unloading of solutes from xylem occurs at the fine vein endings and entry of solutes into cells can take place by diffusion and active uptake. Transfer cells (section 14.8.6) may sometimes be involved.

14.7.1 Recirculation and remobilisation

Very often the path from roots to sinks via xylem or phloem is not the end of translocation of mineral elements. Generally speaking, xylem makes the initial delivery of a given element to an organ, and then phloem carries away the element for continued translocation up or down the plant if it is not required by that organ. This **recirculation** can be investigated with radioactive isotopes and is shown to be a common phenomenon. In one experiment, the roots of a maize plant were separated into two beakers of nutrient solution, one containing radioactive phosphorus. Within 6 h the phosphorus had travelled up the stem in the xylem, back down in the phloem and had been detected in the second beaker. This is part of the evidence which suggests that phosphorus circulates continuously and rapidly within the xylem and phloem of plants. Other elements are less mobile. Sulphur, for example, is mainly removed during its first circulation, and calcium is notoriously immobile, being virtually trapped in any organ where it is deposited because it has poor mobility within the phloem.

Often an element will stay in an organ for some time and then be **remobilised**, that is leave the organ for some other part of the plant after having served some useful function. This occurs during sequential senescence (ageing) of leaves, when older dying leaves export much of their mineral content to younger leaves. Similarly, prior to abscission of leaves by deciduous trees and shrubs useful minerals can be conserved by remobilising them for storage elsewhere. Development of flowers, fruits and seeds, and storage organs also involves remobilisation. Directional control of the movement of nutrients is under the influence of plant growth substances, particularly cytokinins (section 15.2.7). The elements most readily mobilised are phosphorus, sulphur, nitrogen and potassium.

14.8 Translocation of organic solutes in phloem

In those multicellular plants where certain parts of the plant, such as roots, are some distance from the sites of photosynthesis, there is a need for a transport system to circulate the products of photosynthesis. In vascular plants phloem is the tissue which carries these organic products away from the leaves, the main organs of photosynthesis, to other parts. Phloem consists of sieve elements, companion cells, parenchyma, fibres and sclereids. Its structure, as revealed by the light microscope, is described in section 8.2.2. The sieve elements are arranged end to end to form sieve tubes, each element being separated from the next by a sieve plate. Fig 14.20 summarises the relationship between autotrophic cells producing organic food and those receiving the food. Note from fig 14.20 that movement of organic solutes must be up and down in the same plant, that is bidirectional. This contrasts with movement in the xylem, which is only upwards. Note also that storage organs act either as sources

Fig 14.20 *Movement of organic solutes in a green plant*

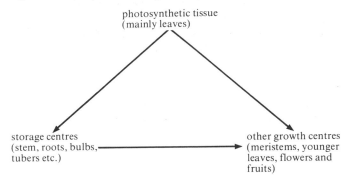

(losing food) or as sinks (gaining food) at different times.

Typically, about 90% of the total solute carried in the phloem is the carbohydrate sucrose, a disaccharide. This is a relatively inert and highly soluble sugar, playing little direct role in metabolism and so making an ideal transport sugar, being unlikely to be used in transit. Once at its destination it can be converted back to the more active monosaccharides. It can be present in very high concentrations, up to 25% mass to volume in the phloem of plants such as sugarcane.

It should be noted that phloem also carries certain mineral elements in various forms, particularly nitrogen and sulphur in the form of amino acids, phosphorus in the form of inorganic phosphate ions and sugar phosphates, and potassium ions. Small amounts of vitamins, growth substances such as auxins and gibberellins, artificially applied chemicals, viruses and other components may also be present. The importance of phloem in recirculation and remobilisation of mineral elements is in section 14.7.1.

Evidence for the circulation of carbon within the plant can be obtained by supplying leaves with carbon dioxide containing the radioactive isotope ^{14}C. Radioactive carbon dioxide is fixed in photosynthesis and ^{14}C passes into an organic solute such as sucrose. Its movement around the plant can then be traced by various techniques used to locate radioactive isotopes, such as autoradiography, application of a Geiger counter to the plant surface, or extraction of the isotope from different parts. Ultimately, both phloem and xylem will be intimately associated in the circulation of carbon. For example, carbon in the form of sucrose may reach the roots and there be used in the conversion of nitrates to amino acids. The latter, containing the carbon, can then travel up the shoots in the xylem.

Experiment 14.6: To investigate the pattern of distribution of the products of photosynthesis in a pea plant

The experiment and data below are based on the Independent Television schools' programme *An investigation of photosynthesis and assimilate transport*. Providing the terms of licence granted by the Independent Television Companies to local authorities are complied with, this programme could be usefully recorded on a videocassette recorder.

In the experiment below, carbon dioxide containing the radioactive isotope of carbon, ^{14}C, is supplied to photosynthesising pea plants (*Pisum sativum*). ^{14}C is a useful isotope because it has a long half-life (5 570 years) and therefore retains its radioactivity throughout the experiment. (Compare ^{11}C which has a half-life of 20.5 min.) It is also relatively safe to handle because it emits only weak radiation (low energy β particles).

$^{14}CO_2$ is used by the plant in photosynthesis in exactly the same way as the usual carbon dioxide ($^{12}CO_2$) and is incorporated into the products of photosynthesis (assimilates). The movement of these assimilates can be followed in the experiment because they contain ^{14}C; they are said to be ^{14}C-labelled.

Method

Fig 14.21 outlines the stages of an experiment in which $^{14}CO_2$ is fed either to a lower leaf or an upper leaf of separate pea plants with one pod. After feeding and allowing 24 h for transport of ^{14}C-labelled assimilates from the leaves to other parts of the plant, the pattern of distribution of activity is revealed either by autoradiography (fig 14.21) or by measuring the amount of ^{14}C in each plant part. If autoradiography is done first, the plants can subsequently be cut up and used for the second determination which involves combustion.

(b)

(a)

(c)

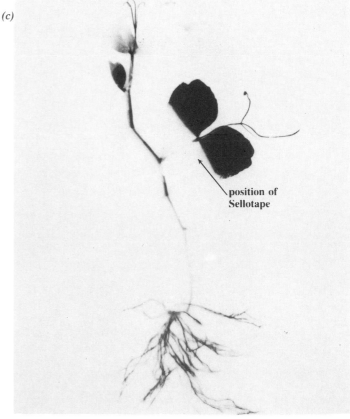

position of Sellotape

498

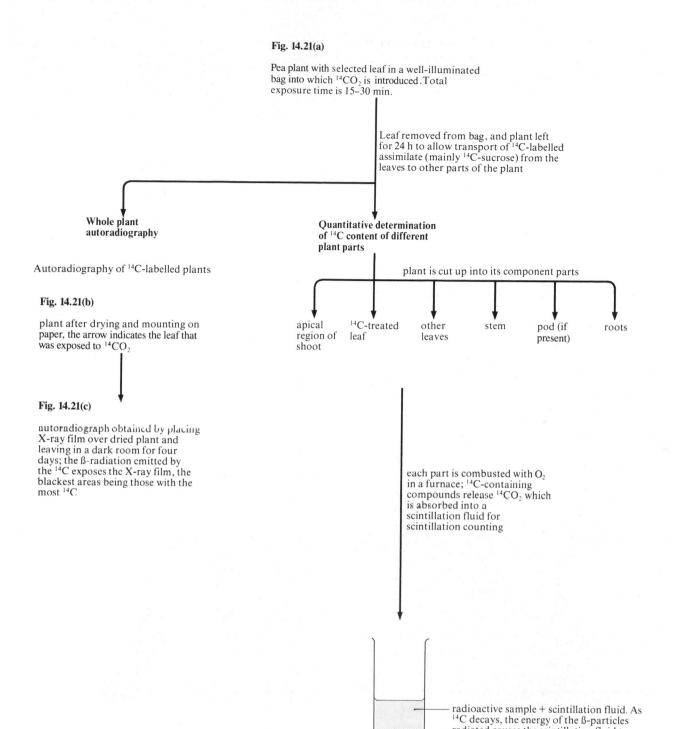

Fig. 14.21(a)

Pea plant with selected leaf in a well-illuminated bag into which $^{14}CO_2$ is introduced. Total exposure time is 15–30 min.

Leaf removed from bag, and plant left for 24 h to allow transport of ^{14}C-labelled assimilate (mainly ^{14}C-sucrose) from the leaves to other parts of the plant

Whole plant autoradiography

Autoradiography of ^{14}C-labelled plants

Fig. 14.21(b)

plant after drying and mounting on paper, the arrow indicates the leaf that was exposed to $^{14}CO_2$

Fig. 14.21(c)

autoradiograph obtained by placing X-ray film over dried plant and leaving in a dark room for four days; the ß-radiation emitted by the ^{14}C exposes the X-ray film, the blackest areas being those with the most ^{14}C

Quantitative determination of ^{14}C content of different plant parts

plant is cut up into its component parts

apical region of shoot

^{14}C-treated leaf

other leaves

stem

pod (if present)

roots

each part is combusted with O_2 in a furnace; ^{14}C-containing compounds release $^{14}CO_2$ which is absorbed into a scintillation fluid for scintillation counting

radioactive sample + scintillation fluid. As ^{14}C decays, the energy of the ß-particles radiated causes the scintillation fluid to fluoresce; the sample is placed in an instrument called a scintillation counter where the tiny flashes of light emitted are amplified to generate an electrical signal and a count rate is obtained which is proportional to the amount of ^{14}C present

Fig 14.21 (opposite and above) *Stages in an experiment to investigate the pattern of distribution of ^{14}C-labelled assimilates in a pea plant*

Results

Fig 14.21 shows the results of autoradiography. Table 14.8 shows the results of counting the ^{14}C in each plant part.

Table 14.8 Radioactivity of different parts of a pea plant 24 h after feeding with $^{14}CO_2$.

Plant part	Upper leaf treated/counts min^{-1}*	Lower leaf treated/counts min^{-1}*
apical region of shoot	1 123	759
^{14}C-treated leaf	11 325	11 372
other leaves	234	168
stem	819	1 160
pod	9 055	4 937
roots	842	2 700

* Corrected for background radiation which is always present as a result of cosmic radiation.

14.30 (a) From table 14.8 calculate the percentage distribution of radioactivity in each plant and thereby compare directly the patterns of ^{14}C-assimilate distribution in the two plants. What are the main similarities and differences in the pattern of ^{14}C export from the upper and lower leaves?
(b) Consider the significance of these similarities and differences in relation to the growth of the plant and its parts. (It may help you if you draw a simple diagram of a pea plant with about eight leaves, with a pod positioned by the third leaf from the top, then indicate the direction and degree of assimilate movement from both an upper and lower leaf to the pod and to the root system.)

14.8.1 Features of phloem translocation

Although an adequate hypothesis for xylem translocation has been established, there is still controversy about the mechanism of phloem translocation. Before considering possible mechanisms for phloem translocation it is useful to list some outstanding facts which any hypothesis has to account for, and which make the problem such a difficult one to solve.

(1) **The quantity of material moved can be very large.** It is estimated, for example, that as much as 250 kg of sugar can be conducted down the trunk of a large tree during a growing season.
(2) **The rate of flow is high, commonly 20–100 cm h^{-1}.** Maximum rates in excess of 600 cm h^{-1} have been recorded.

14.31 If sucrose were moving at 100 cm h^{-1} through sieve tubes where sieve elements were 200 μm long, how long would it take a given molecule of sucrose to pass through one sieve element?

Translocation values of 10–25 g dry mass h^{-1} cm^{-2} of sieve tube cross-sectional area are commonly obtained for dicotyledonous stems.

(3) **The distances travelled can be very large.** The tallest trees, such as *Eucalyptus*, may be over 100 m tall. The leaves of *Eucalyptus* trees are located mainly near the top of the trunk, so assimilates must travel the length of the stem and often a considerable distance through the roots.
(4) **The amount of phloem is not great.** In a tree trunk, the functional phloem tissue is a layer only about the thickness of a postcard around the circumference. It forms the innermost layer of the bark of woody stems and roots, the older phloem becoming stretched and dying as the plant grows and its circumference increases.
(5) **The sieve tubes are very fine, not more than 30 μm in diameter.** This is comparable with a very fine human hair. At regular intervals the tubes are spanned by sieve plates with pores of even smaller diameter. The smaller the diameter of the tubes and pores, the greater is their resistance to the passage of fluid, and the greater the force required to move it.

14.32 How many sieve plates per metre would be encountered by a sucrose molecule moving through a sieve tube whose sieve elements were 400 μm long?

(6) Apart from sieve plates, sieve tubes have other structural features which must be taken into account.

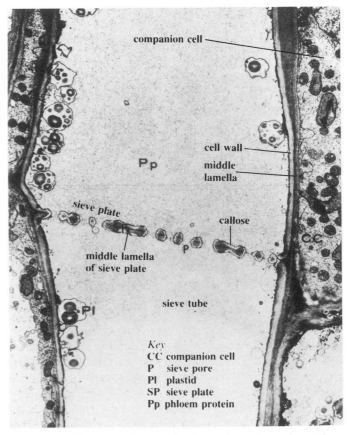

Fig 14.22 *Electron micrograph of a mature sieve element*

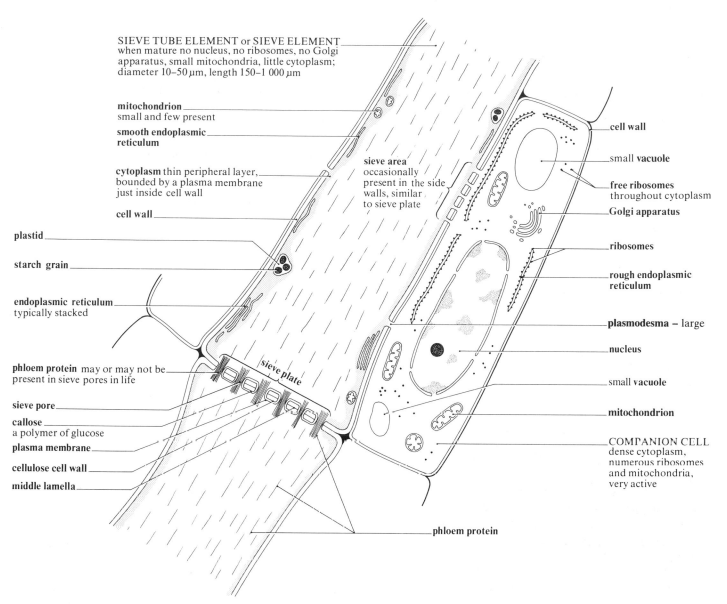

SIEVE TUBE ELEMENT or SIEVE ELEMENT
when mature no nucleus, no ribosomes, no Golgi
apparatus, small mitochondria, little cytoplasm;
diameter 10–50 µm, length 150–1 000 µm

mitochondrion
small and few present

smooth endoplasmic
reticulum

cytoplasm thin peripheral layer,
bounded by a plasma membrane
just inside cell wall

cell wall

plastid

starch grain

endoplasmic reticulum
typically stacked

phloem protein may or may not be
present in sieve pores in life

sieve pore

callose
a polymer of glucose

plasma membrane

cellulose cell wall

middle lamella

sieve plate

sieve area
occasionally
present in the side
walls, similar
to sieve plate

cell wall

small vacuole

free ribosomes
throughout cytoplasm

Golgi apparatus

ribosomes

rough endoplasmic
reticulum

plasmodesma – large

nucleus

small vacuole

mitochondrion

COMPANION CELL
dense cytoplasm,
numerous ribosomes
and mitochondria,
very active

phloem protein

Fig 14.23 *Diagrammatic LS of sieve tube elements and a companion cell as seen with the electron microscope. If the sieve tube is damaged, for example by a grazing animal, more callose is rapidly deposited, blocking the sieve plate and preventing loss of valuable solutes from the sieve tube*

14.8.2   Ultrastructure of sieve tubes

In contrast with xylem vessels, which are dead empty tubes with few, if any, internal obstructions, phloem sieve tubes are living and do apparently contain obstructions to the flow of solution, namely the sieve plates and, to a lesser extent, the cytoplasm. Since the mechanism of movement is still unclear, it is important in the search for evidence to study the structure of sieve tubes in more detail than can be revealed by the light microscope. Fig 14.22 is an electron micrograph of a mature sieve element, and fig 14.23 is a diagram showing the main features of sieve elements and their neighbouring companion cells.

During development of a sieve element from a meristematic cell its nucleus degenerates, making it an unusual example of a living cell with no nucleus; in this respect it is like mammalian red blood cells. At the same time many other profound changes take place, the results of which are shown in fig 14.23. The cell walls at each end of the element develop into sieve plates. These are formed when the plasmodesmata of the end walls enlarge greatly to form sieve pores. A surface view of a sieve plate is shown in fig 8.12. The effect of all the changes is to leave a tube-like structure with a wide lumen and a very narrow, indistinct, peripheral layer of living cytoplasm bounded by a plasma membrane.

Closely associated with each sieve element are one or more companion cells, parenchyma cells which are derived from the same parent cell as the neighbouring sieve element. Companion cells have dense cytoplasm with small vacuoles, and the usual cell organelles. They are metabolically very active, as indicated by their numerous mitochondria and ribosomes (fig 14.23). They show a very close structural and physiological relationship with sieve elements, being essential for their survival because when companion cells die, so do sieve elements.

In dicotyledonous and some monocotyledonous plants

sieve elements develop large quantities of a fibrous protein called **phloem protein** (P-protein). This sometimes forms deposits large enough to be seen with the light microscope. Such deposits were once called 'slime bodies' or 'slime plugs', but the material is not carbohydrate in nature and therefore not a true mucilaginous slime. There is much debate as to whether or not the fibres of protein are normally present in the sieve pores, where they are sometimes, but not always, seen in the electron microscope. One of the great problems of preparing phloem tissue for electron microscopy is that the contents of sieve tubes are thought to be under high hydrostatic pressure, possibly as great as 3 000 kPa. Cutting a specimen for fixation might therefore release this pressure and the sudden surge of sieve tube contents might result in phloem protein and the other contents being swept into and plugging the sieve plates. Any phloem protein seen in the sieve pores might therefore be due to a surge artefact. A number of attempts have been made to get round this problem. For example, wilting a plant before cutting it should eliminate or reduce hydrostatic pressure. Electron microscopy of wilted plants reveals the sieve pores are sometimes plugged, sometimes unplugged and sometimes partially plugged. This and other techniques have so far failed to resolve the problem.

14.8.3 Evidence for movement in phloem

It is important, especially in view of the discussion so far, to be certain that organic solutes really are carried in the phloem sieve tubes. The earliest evidence for movement of sugars and other compounds in phloem came from ringing experiments, in which a ring of tissue containing phloem was removed from the outer region of the stem, leaving the xylem intact. Malpighi obtained evidence in 1675 for ascent of water in wood and descent of food in 'bark'. He removed rings of bark from trees (bark contains the phloem) and found that the leaves did not wilt, but that growth below the ring was greatly reduced.

Mason and Maskell, working with cotton plants in Trinidad during the 1920s and 1930s, did many ringing experiments, one of which is described in fig 14.24. From the results of the experiments shown in fig 14.24, Mason and Maskell concluded that some lateral exchange of sugars can take place between xylem and phloem when they are in contact and the phloem is interrupted (fig 12.24a) but that downward movement occurs in phloem (b and c).

Two simple types of experiment have been done to show the movement of sucrose in phloem. In 1945 a non-radioactive isotope of carbon, ^{13}C, was introduced into a plant as $^{13}CO_2$ and detected by mass spectrometry. A ring of phloem was killed with a fine jet of steam and translocation of ^{13}C-labelled sucrose through this section was shown to be prevented. Movement of mineral elements in the xylem is not affected by such treatment. In the second experiment, microautoradiography of stem sections from plants fed with $^{14}CO_2$ revealed radioactivity in the phloem. The introduction of radioactive tracers in the 1930s and 1940s provided a tremendous boost to work on translocation.

Confirmation that movement is through the sieve tubes comes from a neat type of experiment in which the ability of aphids to feed on translocating sugars is made use of. The aphid penetrates the plant tissues with its specially modified mouthparts; these include extremely fine, tube-like 'stylets' which are pushed slowly through the plant's tissues to the phloem. They can be shown to penetrate individual sieve tubes, as revealed by fig 14.25.

If the aphid is anaesthetised with carbon dioxide and the body removed, leaving the stylets in the plant, the contents of the sieve tube will continue to be forced up the tube of the mouthparts by the hydrostatic pressure in the sieve tube, and the oozing fluid can be collected by microcapillary tubes. This technique has found a number of useful applications, for example in estimating rate of flow through sieve tubes (rate of exudation from tube) and in analysing their contents.

Finally, improvements in the sensitivity of film used in microautoradiography have enabled precise location of the weakly emitting isotope of hydrogen, tritium (^{3}H), in sieve tubes rather than other phloem cells. The isotope is supplied as part of an amino acid or sucrose.

Experiments have also established that different materials are carried up and down the phloem at the same time, although it is probable that this bidirectional movement is in neighbouring sieve tubes rather than in the same sieve tube.

14.8.4 Mechanism of translocation in phloem

The facts which any hypothesis must account for are summarised in section 14.8.1. A picture of active phloem has been presented in the previous sections in which large quantities of material move at relatively rapid speeds through very fine sieve tubes. Within the tubes are apparent obstructions, the sieve plates, and other structural features such as phloem protein for which no certain roles have been found. Combine these facts with the further fact that the system is delicate and easily damaged by interference, and it is not surprising that research workers have found it difficult to establish the mechanism of translocation through sieve tubes.

Most workers now believe that a mass flow of solution occurs through sieve tubes, involving the bulk movement of water and solutes in the same direction, unlike diffusion in which molecules and ions move independently of each other. Diffusion itself is too slow to account for the rates observed. The evidence for mass flow through sieve tubes is summarised below.

(1) When phloem is cut, sap can be induced to exude, apparently by mass flow. This is sometimes utilised commercially as a source of sugar. For example the sugar palm exudes 10 dm^3 of sugar-rich sap per day.

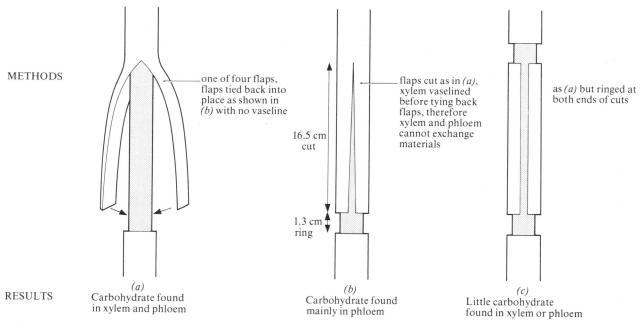

METHODS

one of four flaps, flaps tied back into place as shown in (b) with no vaseline

16.5 cm cut

1.3 cm ring

flaps cut as in (a), xylem vaselined before tying back flaps, therefore xylem and phloem cannot exchange materials

as (a) but ringed at both ends of cuts

RESULTS

(a)
Carbohydrate found in xylem and phloem

(b)
Carbohydrate found mainly in phloem

(c)
Little carbohydrate found in xylem or phloem

Fig 14.24 *Ringing experiments on cotton plants carried out by Mason and Maskell*

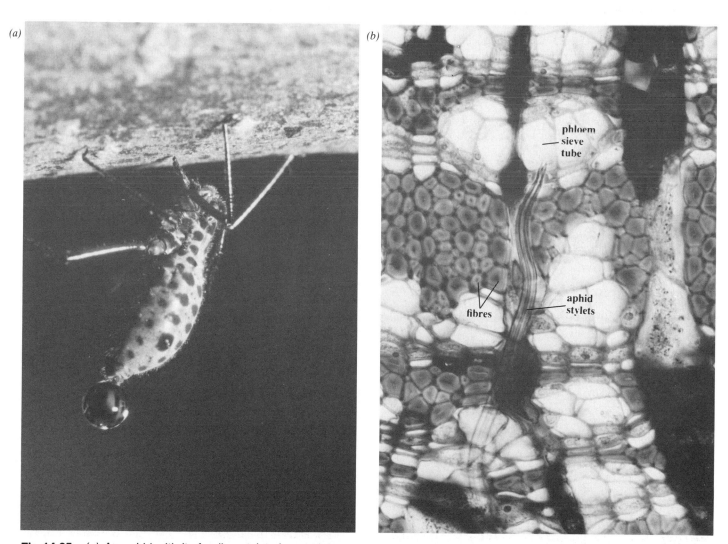

(a)

(b)

phloem sieve tube

fibres

aphid stylets

Fig 14.25 *(a) An aphid with its feeding stylets inserted through a leaf epidermis. (b) Feeding stylets of an aphid inserted into a sieve tube*

(2) The prolonged exudation of sucrose solutions from aphid stylets, as described in section 14.8.8, is evidence of hydrostatic pressure in the sieve tubes.

(3) Certain viruses are moved in the phloem translocation stream, indicating mass flow rather than diffusion since the virus is passive and not in solution.

The main debate concerns the mechanism by which mass flow is brought about, and the major hypotheses will be discussed.

Münch's hypothesis or pressure flow hypothesis

In 1930, Münch put forward a purely physical hypothesis to explain how mass flow might be brought about in sieve tubes. It can be illustrated by the model shown in fig 14.26.

In the model there is an initial tendency for water to pass by osmosis into A and C, but the tendency is greater for A because the solution in A is more concentrated than that in C. As water enters A, a turgor pressure (hydrostatic pressure) builds up in the closed system A–B–C, forcing water out of C. Mass flow of solution occurs through B along the hydrostatic pressure gradient so generated. There is also an osmotic gradient from A to C. Eventually the system comes into equilibrium as water dilutes the contents of A and solutes accumulate at C. The model can be applied to living plants. The leaves which make sugar during photosynthesis, thus raising the OP of the leaf cells, are represented by A. Water, brought to the leaf in xylem (D), enters the leaf cells by osmosis, raising their turgor pressure. At the same time, sugars are used in the sinks, such as roots (C), for various purposes including respiration and synthesis of cellulose. This lowers the OP of these cells. A hydrostatic pressure gradient exists from leaves to roots, or, in more general terms, from sources to sinks, resulting in mass flow. Equilibrium is not reached because

solutes are constantly being used at the sinks (C) and made at the sources (A).

The Münch hypothesis is a purely physical explanation and so does not explain why sieve tubes must be living and metabolically active. It also does not explain the observation that leaf cells are capable of loading sieve tubes against a concentration gradient, that is the fact that the OP of sieve tubes is greater than that of the leaf cells. The hypothesis has therefore been modified to include an active loading mechanism of solutes into the sieve tubes. The osmotic and hydrostatic pressure gradient therefore starts in the tubes rather than in the photosynthetic cells. It is also believed that unloading at the sinks is an active process.

Evidence for Münch's hypothesis

(1) The hypothesis predicts that mass flow will occur through sieve tubes and this seems to occur (the evidence is given above).

(2) The hypothesis requires the existence of an osmotic gradient and high turgor (hydrostatic) pressure in the phloem. These have been demonstrated in a number of plants.

Evidence against Münch's hypothesis

(1) The hydrostatic pressure gradients required to move solutes at the observed rates are relatively high. Assuming the sieve pores are completely open, a gradient of 100 kPa m^{-1} might be adequate, but it is still doubtful if such large gradients exist. If the sieve tube pores are obstructed, such as with cytoplasm or phloem protein, the required pressures become unrealistic.

(2) The Münch hypothesis does not explain the occurrence of sieve plates or phloem protein, both of which would seem to be barriers to mass flow.

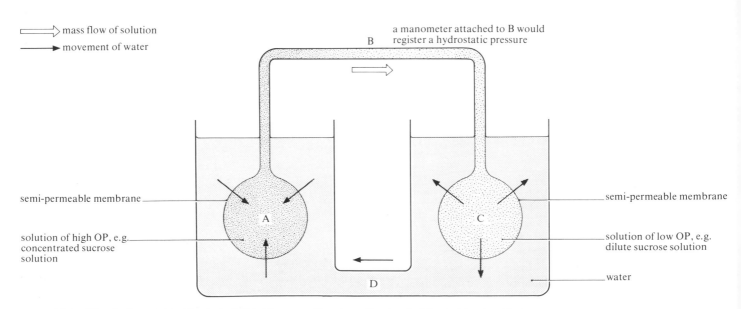

Fig 14.26 *Physical model to illustrate Münch's mass flow hypothesis of phloem translocation*
Equivalents in living plant
A: source, such as leaf; B: phloem; C: sink, such as roots, meristems, fruits; D: xylem, cell walls and intercellular spaces

Electroosmosis

A mechanism involving electroosmosis was proposed independently by Fensom in 1957 and Spanner in 1958. The phenomenon of electroosmosis is illustrated in fig 14.27.

It depends upon the presence of an ionic solution in which a fixed charged surface occurs. The surface becomes charged when the molecules of which it is composed lose ions. For example, if hydrogen ions leave an insoluble molecule, such as a fibrous protein, when it is placed in water, the positively charged hydrogen ions can move freely in solution leaving behind a negatively charged, immobile molecule. The solution then carries a mobile positive charge which balances the fixed negative charge. If a potential difference is applied across the charged surface, the positive ions move towards the negative electrode (cathode). Each ion is surrounded by a shell of water molecules (fig 5.5) which moves with the ions, together with other ions and uncharged molecules, such as sucrose, in a mass flow of the whole solution past the fixed charge (fig 14.27).

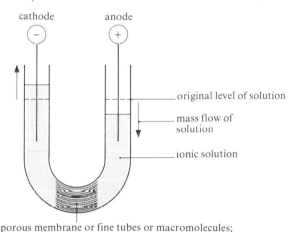

cathode   anode

original level of solution

mass flow of solution

ionic solution

porous membrane or fine tubes or macromolecules; they are fixed in position and have charged surfaces

Fig 14.27 *Electroosmosis. In the case illustrated, the fixed surface is negatively charged and the solution carries a corresponding net positive charge*

In sieve tubes, fixed charged surfaces could be provided by the cell walls, including the sieve plates, and the phloem protein (P-protein), all of which would be negatively charged under the alkaline conditions usually found in phloem. Spanner's hypothesis has been modified several times, but his 'final restatement', published in 1979,* can be outlined as follows.
(1) Mass flow is initiated by the loading of sieve tubes and operates as described by Münch.
(2) P-protein is loosely packed in the sieve pores, possibly as a result of mass flow.
(3) There is a high concentration of potassium ions (K^+) in the sieve tube solution. These and other cations can pass through the sieve plate, but anions are repelled by the negative charge of the phloem protein (and cell walls).

* D. C. Spanner (1979) *Plant, Cell and Environment*, **2**, 107–21.

(4) A potential difference (PD) builds up across the sieve plate because anions begin to accumulate above it. The net charge is negative above the plate and positive below it.
(5) Once a critical PD is reached, a local surge of H^+ ions (protons) occurs from the wall of the sieve tube, through its plasma membrane and into the tube, reducing pH (increasing H^+ concentration).
(6) This more than balances the negative charge and reverses the PD across the plate, temporarily making the local environment above the plate positively charged.
(7) This positive charge causes electroosmosis of K^+ ions through the sieve plate, past the fixed negative charge of the P-protein. Movement of potassium and other cations induces a mass flow of solution.
(8) A proton pump in the sieve tube membrane quickly restores the high pH of the sieve tube by actively pumping out protons from the sieve tube. Energy for this is supplied by ATP from the companion cells and sieve tubes.
(9) The original PD begins to build up again.

The overall result is that translocation through sieve tubes is by mass flow, as proposed by Münch, but is boosted by electroosmosis at the sieve plates. The boosting is in the form of brief pulses. It does not necessarily take place simultaneously at all sieve plates and there may or may not be a particular sequence of 'firing' at different sieve plates. A pulsed, rather than smooth, flow may therefore occur through sieve tubes.

Evidence for the electroosmosis hypothesis

(1) A role for companion cells, in supplying ATP, is established.
(2) High levels of potassium ions are found in sieve tubes.
(3) The hydrostatic pressures required are lower than those for Münch's hypothesis.
(4) A role is given for sieve plates: they provide a charged porous structure allowing the flow of solutes by electroosmosis. There is also a possible role for phloem protein, if this is found in the sieve pores.

Evidence against the electroosmosis hypothesis. The hypothesis is largely circumstantial, that is there is no direct evidence for it. For example, the postulated changes in potential difference have not been measured. Also, it has not been demonstrated that the sieve tube walls act as a reservoir for hydrogen ions.

The relay hypothesis

A major criticism of Spanner's hypothesis is that massive expenditures of metabolic energy would be needed to maintain the observed flow rates, since pumping takes place over the relatively small area of the sieve plates. In 1979, Alexander Lang suggested that pumping could occur over a much larger surface area if it took place across the membranes of adjacent, overlapping sieve tubes in the region of the overlap. The pumping process could be similar to that which is involved in loading and unloading sieve tubes at source and sink. Movement of solutes would still occur along a pressure gradient between source and sink, as postulated by Münch, but a much smaller overall gradient would be required. This 'relay mechansim' is therefore a mass flow mechanism which reconciles some of the conflicting evidence for and against Münch's hypothesis. It is supported by the observation that solutes move readily in and out of sieve tubes along their lengths, such as between phloem and xylem.

Other hypotheses

It should be noted that other hypotheses for phloem transport have been put forward, including some form of cytoplasmic streaming, and the existence of cytoplasmic strands ('transcellular strands') supported by the sieve plates and extending long distances through the sieve tubes suggests that solutions could in some way be pumped along the strands. Like electroosmosis, these ideas are interesting but as yet are supported by little, if any, experimental evidence.

14.8.5 First-aid mechanisms – a possible role for sieve plates, phloem protein and plastids

One danger faced by all plants is damage from being eaten by animals. If sieve tubes are ruptured, leakage of high energy substances such as sucrose would be costly to the plant. Usually damaged sieve tubes are sealed within minutes by deposition of callose across the sieve plates, blocking the sieve pores. This represents a possible role for sieve plates. It has been suggested that in dicotyledons, the phloem protein serves an even more rapid first-aid function by blocking the sieve pores as soon as the tube is broken. This is due to the pressure surge mentioned in section 14.8.2. In monocotyledons, where phloem protein is usually scarce, the same role may be performed by plastids found in sieve tubes.

14.8.6 Loading sieve tubes

It has been shown that the sucrose concentration in sieve tubes in leaves is commonly between 10–30%, whereas it forms only about a 0.5% solution in the photosynthetic cells where it is produced. Loading of sieve tubes therefore occurs against a concentration gradient. Both symplast and apoplast routes are possible in the short journey, 3 mm at most, from chloroplasts to sieve tubes.

In 1968 a modified type of companion cell was reported by Gunning and fellow workers. It has numerous internal protuberances of the cell wall, a result of extra thickening. This in turn results in an approximately tenfold increase in surface area of the plasma membrane lining the wall. It is thought that such cells are thus modified for active uptake of solutes from neighbouring photosynthetic cells and that they actively load their adjacent sieve elements through

complex, extensive plasmodesmata. The numerous mitochondria in their cytoplasm provide energy for this. These modified cells are called **transfer cells**, and similar examples of plant cells with wall ingrowths have since been found in many situations where short-distance transport occurs, including xylem parenchyma. Similar cells can easily be seen in a toluidine blue-stained, hand-cut section of a *Tradescantia* node. They are not found in all plants, but are common in the pea family and some other families. Fig 14.28 shows their appearance when viewed with an electron microscope.

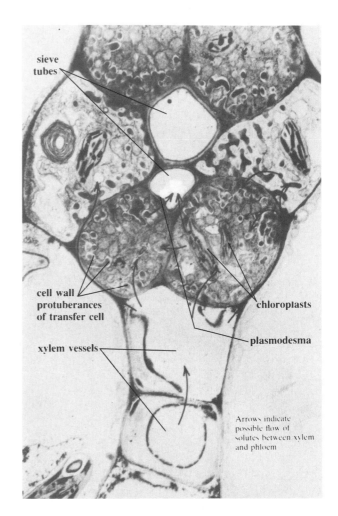

Fig 14.28 *Transverse section of a minor vein in a leaf of Senecio vulgaris. The phloem region, in the top half of the picture, shows six parenchyma cells centred around two sieve elements. Pairs of companion cells modified as A-type transfer cells lie both above and below the sieve elements. There is a B-type transfer cell to each side. The A- and the B-types differ strikingly in the relative density of their cytoplasm, in the polarity of their zones of wall ingrowths, and in their connections with the sieve elements: plasmodesmata between sieve elements and A-types are common, but are very rare between sieve elements and B-types. In the lower half of the picture two xylem elements occupy the centre, while to each side there are parts of two large bundle sheath cells. Arrows indicate some of the possible routes for intraveinal retrieval of solutes delivered to the apoplast in the xylem (see text). Magnification × 6 560*

Transport in animals

In the animal kingdom, the protozoa, coelenterates and platyhelminths lack a specific system for the transport and distribution of materials. The organisms in these phyla possess a large surface area to volume ratio, and diffusion of gases over the whole body surface is sufficient for their needs. Internally, the distance that materials have to travel is again small enough for them to move by diffusion or cytoplasmic streaming (section 7.2.4).

As organisms increase in size and complexity so the quantity of materials moving in and out of the body increases. The distance that materials have to travel within the body also increases, so that diffusion becomes inadequate as a means for their distribution. Some other method of conveying materials from one part of the organism to another is therefore necessary. This generally takes the form of a mass flow system.

14.9 General characteristics of a circulatory system

The purpose of a circulatory system is to provide rapid mass flow of materials from one part of the body to another over distances where diffusion would be too slow. On reaching their destination the materials must be able to pass through the walls of the circulatory system into the organs or tissues. Likewise, materials produced by these structures must also be able to enter the circulatory system.

Every circulatory system possesses three distinct characteristics:
(1) a circulatory fluid, generally called blood;
(2) a contractile, pumping device to propel the fluid around the body, this may either be a modified blood vessel or a heart;
(3) tubes through which the fluid can circulate, called blood vessels.

Two distinct types of circulatory system are found in the higher invertebrates and vertebrates. They are the open and closed vascular systems.

The open vascular system (most arthropods, some cephalopod molluscs, tunicates). Blood is pumped by the heart into an aorta which branches into a number of arteries. These open into a series of blood spaces collectively called the **haemocoel**. Blood under low pressure moves slowly between the tissues, gradually percolating back into the heart via open-ended veins. Distribution of blood to the tissues is poorly controlled.

The closed vascular system (echinoderms, cephalopod molluscs, annelids, vertebrates). Blood is pumped by the heart rapidly around the body under sustained high pressure and back to the heart. It is confined to a series of specific vessels and not permitted to come into contact with the body tissues. Distribution of blood to the tissues is able to be adjusted. The only entry and exit to this system is through the walls of the blood vessels.

Blood vessels are named according to their structure and function. Vessels conveying blood away from the heart are called **arteries**. These branch into smaller arteries called **arterioles**. The arterioles divide many times into microscopic **capillaries** which are located between the cells of nearly all the body tissues. It is here that exchange of materials between blood and tissues takes place.

Within the organ or tissue the capillaries reunite forming **venules** which begin the process of returning blood to the heart. The venules join to form **veins**. It is these blood vessels that actually pass the blood back into the heart. The anatomy of each type of blood vessel is discussed in detail later in section 14.12.

14.10 The development of transport systems in animals

In the protozoa circulation of materials is primarily achieved by protoplasmic streaming. Coelenterates rely on movements of their body wall to create water currents in the enteron which circulate food, water and dissolved gases. The musculo-epithelial and flagellate cells of the endoderm assist in this activity. Platyhelminths have a very thin, flattened shape, enabling materials to be exchanged within the organism and with its environment by diffusion.

14.10.1 Annelids

Annelids are coelomate animals. The presence of a coelom separates the body wall from the internal organs and confers the advantage of independence of movement of internal structures such as the gut. However, this is countered by the need for some form of connecting system between the two regions which enable food, gases and waste substances to be transported between the environment and the gut or vice versa. It is at the coelomate level that a blood system evolved in order to connect gut and body wall.

The earthworm – a closed blood vascular system

There is a well-developed blood system in which blood circulates around the body through a system of closed blood vessels. The largest blood vessel is the longitudinal, **dorsal vessel** which has muscular walls. It is situated above the alimentary canal. Peristaltic contractions originate at the rear end of the vessel and drive blood forwards towards the anterior end of the animal, backflow being prevented by a series of valves. Each valve is formed from a fold of endothelium within the blood vessel. The dorsal vessel is the main collecting vessel and receives blood from the body wall, gut, nerve cord and nephridia. The names of the main segmental vessels are given in figs 14.29 and 14.30.

Fig 14.29 (right) *Segmental distribution of blood in* Lumbricus *in regions behind the clitellum. (From A. E. Vines & N. Rees (4th edition, 1972) Plant and animal biology, Vol. I, Pitman)*

Fig 14.30 (below) *Main blood vessels in the earthworm (Lumbricus terrestris). (From E. G. Springthorpe (1973) An introduction to functional systems in animals, Longman)*

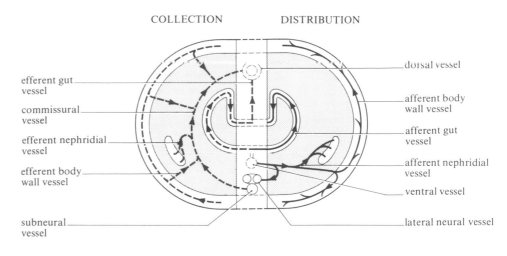

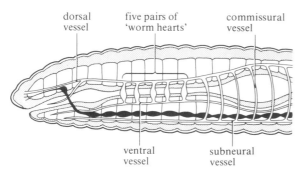

The dorsal vessel connects with the smaller, more contractile, ventral vessel via five pairs of contractile 'pseudohearts' located in segments 7–11. Each 'pseudoheart' possesses four valves which permit the blood to flow only towards the ventral vessel.

The blood flows posteriorly in the ventral vessel. It is distributed to the nephridia, nerve cord, gut and body wall by a series of segmental blood vessels. In addition the nerve cord is supplied with blood by the longitudinal, subneural vessel which runs below it.

Within the various organs of the worm, capillary networks enable materials to be exchanged between blood and tissues. Eventually the blood passes back to the dorsal vessel, when it can once again begin its journey through the closed blood vascular system of the worm.

The blood itself is red in colour, containing haemoglobin (section 14.13.1) dissolved in the plasma. It transports oxygen, carbon dioxide, soluble excretory materials and foodstuffs around the body. Colourless amoeboid cells which have a defensive function also circulate in the blood.

14.10.2 Arthropoda

The coelom is drastically reduced in the arthropods and its place taken by the haemocoel. This is a network of blood-filled spaces called **sinuses** in which the internal organs are suspended. Gaseous exchange in most arthropods is effected by the tracheal system (section 4.10), and the blood vascular system is not used for transporting respiratory gases. Arthropod blood is colourless, containing no haemoglobin, and serves to transport dissolved foodstuffs and excretory materials and to circulate colourless amoeboid leucocytes.

The cockroach – an open blood vascular system

There is only one blood vessel in the cockroach, the dorsal blood vessel, and the posterior part of it is modified into a distinct heart, whilst the anterior end is called the **aorta**. The heart lies in a large sinus which is a modified part of the haemocoel called the **pericardium** (fig 14.31). There are 13 dilations or chambers in the heart, three are located in the thoracic segments and ten in the abdomen. Every chamber except the most posterior possesses a pair of lateral openings called **ostia**. Each ostium is fitted with a valve which permits blood to enter but not leave the chamber. Between adjacent chambers are more valves which prevent backward flow of the blood. Intersegmental alary muscles are attached to the ventral wall of the heart, and when these muscles contract they increase the volume of the heart and create a negative pressure. This draws in blood from the pericardium through the ostia. When the alary muscles relax and the heart contracts, blood is propelled forwards into the aorta. This divides into several arteries which are open-ended. Consequently blood pours out of them into blood sinuses where it bathes the organs of the insect directly. Eventually the blood percolates back into the pericardium and ultimately into the heart.

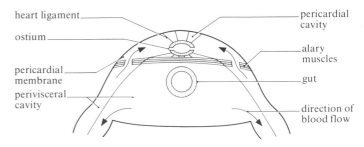

Fig 14.31 *Schematic transverse section to show open blood vascular system of an insect. (After Ramsay (1968) A physiological approach to lower animals, Cambridge University Press)*

14.10.3 Vertebrate circulatory systems

All vertebrate circulatory systems possess a well-defined muscular heart, lying in a ventral position in the region of the pectoral girdle. The heart is responsible for conveying blood rapidly to all parts of the animal's body. Arteries convey blood away from the heart, whilst veins pass blood from the body to the heart. Another system, the lymphatic system, is also present and supplements the activities of the circulatory system.

Comparative embryological studies indicate that, in all vertebrate embryos, six lateral arterial arches emanate from the ventral aorta and unite to form a pair of lateral dorsal aortae which eventually merge into a single median dorsal aorta (fig 14.32). Fish are the only vertebrates to exhibit this arrangement in anything like its original form in the adult condition. In all other vertebrates the embryonic pattern has been extensively modified.

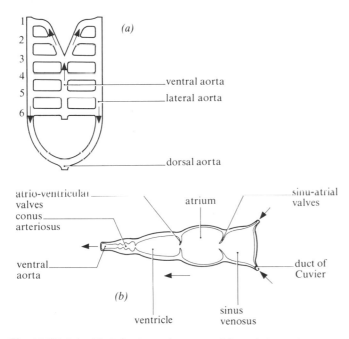

Fig 14.32 (a) *Vertebrate embryo condition of the blood vascular system. Six arterial arches branch from the ventral aorta, eventually rejoining to form lateral aortae. (b) Embryonic heart*

The dogfish

The dogfish heart (fig 14.33*b*), which is confined within a pericardial cavity, is S-shaped and consists of two main chambers, an **atrium** and a **ventricle**. Blood from the general body circulation enters a thin-walled chamber, the **sinus venosus**, which precedes the heart. From here it passes into the weakly muscular atrium by a negative

pressure developed in the surrounding pericardium. It is passed on to the thicker, more muscular ventricle. When this contracts, blood is pumped via the **conus arteriosus** into a ventral aorta. Valves between the atrium and ventricle and the ventricle and conus arteriosus prevent backflow of blood. The conus arteriosus is highly elastic and easily stretched by the pressure of the blood leaving the ventricle. In turn, its elastic walls act on the blood and force it forwards at a more uniform speed, thus enhancing a continuous flow of blood in the ventral aorta.

In the dogfish five pairs of afferent branchial arteries branch from the ventral aorta and carry deoxygenated blood to the gills (fig 14.33*a*). Within the gills the arteries divide many times into numerous fine capillaries. Eventually they rejoin to form efferent branchial arteries. These carry oxygenated blood and form a series of four loops which encircle the perimeter of each of the first four internal branchial clefts. A single blood vessel from the anterior part of the fifth branchial cleft opens into the fourth loop. Four epibranchial vessels from either side of the body convey the blood from the loops backwards and towards the midline where they join to form the dorsal aorta. Anteriorly the dorsal aorta divides and joins the internal carotid arteries, and supplies oxygenated blood to the head. Posteriorly the dorsal aorta branches many times into arteries which supply the rest of the body with oxygenated blood.

As blood flows through the heart only once during each circuit of the body, the dogfish is said to possess a single circulation (fig 14.33*c*). The blood pressure falls as it passes through the gill capillaries and is low in the dorsal aorta. The blood pressure falls even further after it has passed through the capillaries of the body organs. This is because of the resistance to its flow exerted by the various capillary networks of the body. Consequently, return of blood to the heart is very slow. To offset this apparent disadvantage, large blood spaces called **sinuses**, which provide little resistance to blood flow, are present. Raised anterior and posterior cardinal sinuses, together with laterally placed veins, return blood to the region of the heart where it passes to the sinus via a pair of Cuvierian veins. Backflow of blood in the veins is prevented by valves, and forward flow enhanced by the body muscles squeezing these vessels.

In the posterior region of the fish there are blood vessels called **portal veins**. These are blood vessels with capillary beds at both ends. Blood from the small intestine passes to the liver via the hepatic portal vein, and blood from the tail to the kidney via renal portal veins. Thus the blood of the dogfish having already passed through the capillaries of the gills passes through two sets of capillaries of the portal systems – three sets of capillaries in all.

Dogfish blood contains oval-shaped, nucleated red blood cells and amoeboid leucocytes suspended in plasma. The lymphatic system is comprised of lymphatic vessels emptying into two dorsal longitudinal collecting ducts which finally return their contents (that is lymph) to the blood via the cardinal sinuses.

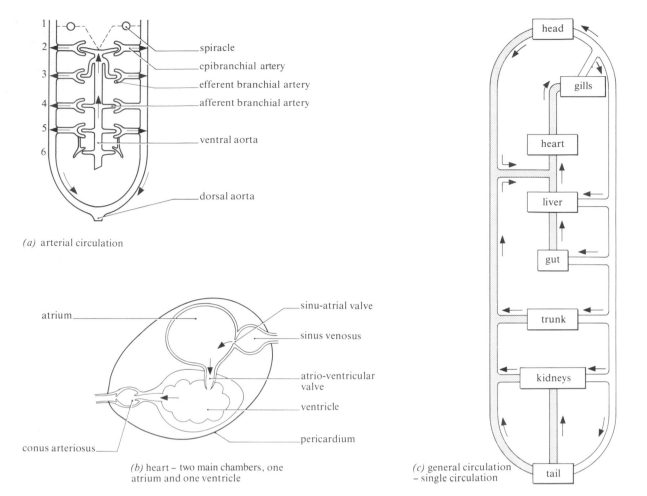

(a) arterial circulation

(b) heart – two main chambers, one atrium and one ventricle

(c) general circulation – single circulation

Fig 14.33 *Dogfish arterial blood supply. Six arterial arches are reduced to five, the first gill slit is modified as a spiracle. Direct branchial vessels have split up to form afferent, efferent and epibranchial arteries. This gives a greater surface area of the blood system in the gill region for gaseous exchange*

Amphibia – the frog

In the adult frog the heart and aortic circulation show modifications which can be correlated with its semi-terrestrial mode of life. Lungs have developed and replaced gills as respiratory organs, and a new circulation, the pulmonary circulation between the lungs and heart, has been established. There is no longer a need to retain all the aortic arches to supply branchial arches, and some have been put to new uses whilst others have been lost. The third arch has become the carotid artery and transports blood anteriorly to the head (fig 14.34*a*). The fourth is the systemic, conveying oxygenated blood to the rest of the body via the dorsal aorta, whilst the sixth arch transports deoxygenated blood from the heart to the lungs via the pulmonary artery. The first, second and fifth arches have disappeared.

The heart consists of three main chambers, two atria and one ventricle (fig 14.34*b*). Blood which has been oxygenated at the lungs is returned to the left atrium via the pulmonary vein, whilst deoxygenated blood from the body is passed to the right atrium via the sinus venosus by the anterior and posterior venae cavae. At no time does the

blood in the atria mix. However, both atria contract at the same time and deliver their blood to the single ventricle. The inner surface of the dorsal and ventral walls of the ventricle is built up into ridges which prevent mixing of the blood to some extent. When the blood passes from the ventricle to the conus arteriosus, mixing is further prevented by a spiral valve which incompletely divides the conus into two distinct corridors. The dorsal passage, called the **cavum pulmocutaneous**, leads to the pulmonary arch which, besides running to the lungs, also sends branches to the skin, whilst the ventral **cavum aorticum** takes blood to the carotid and systemic arches.

It is clear that there are two distinct circuits which the blood can take, one to the lungs and one to the body. This may be regarded as a partial double circulation, where blood, after passing from the heart to the lungs, is returned again to the heart before passing to the body (fig 14.34*c*). The separation of oxygenated and deoxygenated blood in this system is not entirely complete.

The blood vascular system of a frog is a very special system suitable for an amphibious animal. When the frog is relatively inactive, oxygen diffuses into the capillaries

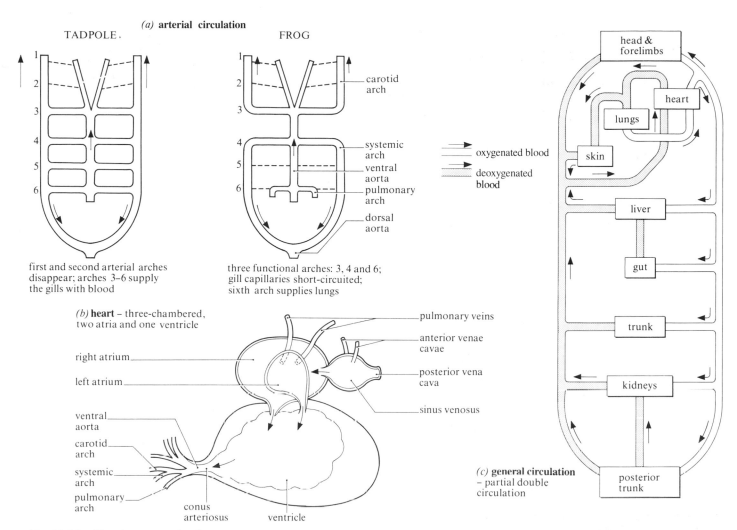

(a) **arterial circulation**

TADPOLE.　　　　　　　FROG

first and second arterial arches
disappear; arches 3–6 supply
the gills with blood

three functional arches: 3, 4 and 6;
gill capillaries short-circuited;
sixth arch supplies lungs

(b) **heart** – three-chambered,
two atria and one ventricle

right atrium

left atrium

ventral
aorta

carotid
arch

systemic
arch

pulmonary
arch

conus
arteriosus　　　ventricle

pulmonary veins

anterior venae
cavae

posterior vena
cava

sinus venosus

oxygenated blood

deoxygenated
blood

head &
forelimbs

heart

lungs

skin

liver

gut

trunk

kidneys

posterior
trunk

(c) **general circulation**
– partial double
circulation

Fig 14.34　*Blood system of a frog*

under the skin and is transported to the right atrium of the heart via the subclavian vein. The lungs are not used except under conditions of strenuous action. Thus normally the left atrium receives little oxygenated blood.

Veins replace sinuses in the venous system of the frog. Blood is returned to the sinus venosus by anterior and posterior venae cavae which receive blood from veins leaving the major organs of the body. Renal and hepatic portal veins are also present.

Intercellular channels containing lymph (section 14.12.1) drain into lymphatic vessels. Eventually the lymph is pumped into the venous system at two points, one anterior and one posterior. A pair of small contractile lymph hearts in each region drive the lymph into the veins.

Frog's blood consists of nucleated erythrocytes containing haemoglobin, and a variety of white cells suspended in the plasma. They include macrophages, lymphocytes, granulocytes and monocytes (section 14.11.2).

Reptilia – the crocodile

Here the heart consists of four chambers, two atria and two ventricles, the right side being more or less completely separated from the left side (fig 14.35). Therefore the crocodile possesses a double circulatory system with almost complete separation of oxygenated blood in the left side from deoxygenated blood on the right side. The conus arteriosus has been replaced by three distinct arteries which form arches directly from the ventricle. They are the right systemic arch, which gives rise to the carotid arteries, the left systemic arch, and the pulmonary arch.

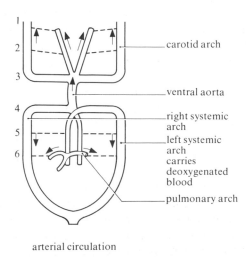

carotid arch

ventral aorta

right systemic
arch

left systemic
arch
carries
deoxygenated
blood

pulmonary arch

arterial circulation

Fig 14.35　*Reptile arterial blood supply – the crocodile*

511

Aves and Mammalia – general

The heart is four-chambered in birds and mammals. The right atrium and ventricle are completely separated from the left atrium and ventricle (fig 14.36b). This means that oxygenated and deoxygenated blood are also kept completely separate. In order for blood in the right side of the heart to get to the left side, it must first pass through the lungs (fig 14.36c). For blood from the left side to get to the right side it has first to pass round the body. This double circulation ensures that oxygenated blood flowing to the tissues is under high pressure and not, as is the case of fish, under low pressure. As the blood passes through the lungs before it passes to the body, this ensures that it is well oxygenated before it reaches the actively respiring organs.

> **14.33** Why is it an advantage in birds and mammals for oxygenated blood to flow to the tissues under high pressure?

The arterial system is further reduced in birds and mammals. Birds retain only the right half of the systemic arch, whilst mammals retain the left half (fig 14.36a). The third arch persists as the carotid arch and the sixth as the pulmonary arch. Within the venous system the posterior vena cava replaces the renal portal system. Therefore blood from the posterior parts of the body is returned directly to the heart, thus increasing the speed at which blood can be supplied back to the tissues.

14.11 Composition of mammalian blood

Blood is composed of cells bathed in a fluid matrix called **plasma**. The cells constitute about 45% by volume of the blood, whilst the other 55% is represented by the plasma.

14.11.1 Plasma

Plasma is a pale yellow liquid. It consists of 90% water and 10% of a variety of substances in solution and suspension, some of which are normally maintained at constant concentrations, whilst the concentrations of others may fluctuate within narrow limits according to their rates of removal or supply from particular organs. The major components of blood plasma together with their functions are shown in table 14.9.

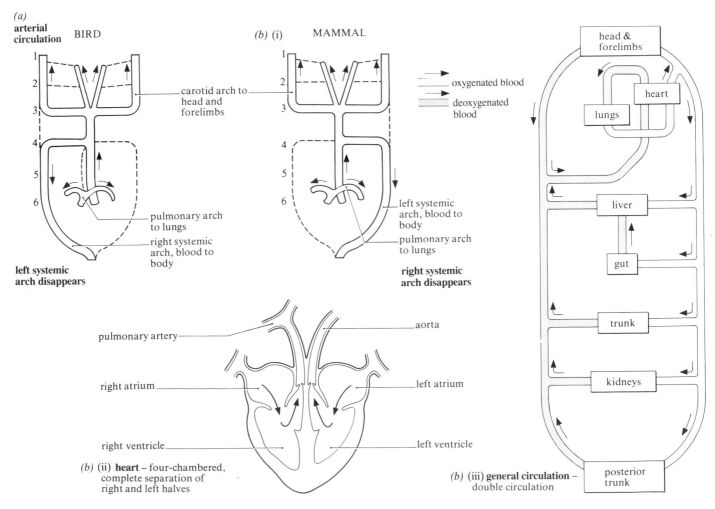

Fig 14.36 (a) Bird and (b) mammal arterial blood systems

512

Table 14.9 Components of blood plasma and their functions.

Constituent	Function
Constituents maintained at a constant concentration	
Water	Major constituent of lymph. Provides tissue cells with water. Conveys many dissolved materials round the body. Aids maintenance of blood pressure and blood volume
Plasma proteins	
Serum albumin	Very abundant. Binds plasma calcium
Serum globulins:	
α-globulin	Binds thyroxine and bilirubin
β-globulin	Binds iron, cholesterol and the vitamins A, D and K
γ-globulin	Binds antigens and is important in the body's immunological reactions. Generally called antibody. Also binds histamine
Prothrombin	A catalytic agent which takes part in the blood-clotting process
Fibrinogen	Takes part in blood-clotting process
Enzymes	Participate in metabolic activities
Mineral ions	
These include: Na^+, K^+, Ca^{2+}, Mg^{2+}, $H_2PO_4^-$, HPO_4^{2-}, PO_4^{3-}, Cl^-, HCO_3^-, SO_4^{2-}	All help collectively to regulate osmotic pressure and pH levels of the blood. They also exert a variety of other effects on the cells of the body; e.g. Ca^{2+} may act as a clotting factor, regulate muscle and nerve cell sensitivity, influence the sol–gel condition within cells
Constituents that occur in varying concentrations	
Dissolved products of digestion	
Dissolved excretory products	All are being constantly transported to and from cells within the body
Vitamins	
Hormones	

14.11.2 Blood cells

Erythrocytes

These are the red blood cells. Characteristically in Man they are small, enucleated and appear as circular biconcave discs. Their average diameter is 7–8 µm, which is approximately the same as the internal diameter of blood capillaries. Their particular shape permits a larger surface area to volume ratio than that of a sphere, and therefore increases the area which can be used for gaseous exchange. Each cell is very thin, thus permitting efficient diffusion of gases from its surface inwards. Its membrane is pliable and this property allows the erythrocyte to squeeze through capillaries whose internal diameters are smaller than its own.

The mechanism of production of erythrocytes is known as **haemopoiesis** and the tissue which gives rise to them is called **haemopoietic tissue**. In an infant, all bones contain haemopoietic tissue, whilst in adults the principal regions of erythrocyte production are the bones of the pelvis, ribs, sternum, vertebrae, clavicles, scapulae and skull. There are approximately five million erythrocytes per cubic millimetre of blood. However this figure varies according to the age, sex and state of health of each individual.

An important characteristic of erythrocytes is the presence of haemoglobin which combines reversibly with oxygen to form oxyhaemoglobin in areas of high oxygen concentration, and releases the oxygen in regions of low oxygen concentration. They also contain the enzyme carbonic anhydrase which plays a role in carbon dioxide transport (section 14.13.4).

In the adult, each erythrocyte has a life span of about three months after which time it is destroyed in the spleen or liver. The protein portion of the erythrocyte is broken down into its constituent amino acids; the iron of the haem portion is extracted and stored in the liver as ferritin (an iron-containing protein). It may be re-used later in the production of further erythrocytes or as a component of cytochrome. The remainder of the haem molecule is broken down into two bile pigments, bilirubin and biliverdin. Both are ultimately excreted by way of the bile into the gut.

Between 2–10 million erythrocytes are destroyed and replaced each second in the human body. The rate of destruction and replacement is determined by the amount of oxygen in the atmosphere which is available for carriage by the blood. If the quantity carried is low, then the marrow is stimulated to produce more erythrocytes than the liver destroys. This is one of the ways in which mammals acclimatise to the reduced oxygen content at high altitudes. When the oxygen content is high, the situation is reversed.

White blood cells – leucocytes

These cells are larger than erythrocytes, and present in much smaller numbers, there being about 7 000 per cubic millimetre of blood. All are nucleated. They play an important role in the body's defence mechanisms against disease. Although they are nucleated their life span in the bloodstream is normally only a few days. There are two main groups of white blood cell, the granulocytes and the agranulocytes.

Table 14.10 Cellular components of blood (diagrams not drawn to scale).

Component	Origin	Number of cells/mm^{-3}	Function	Structure
Erythrocytes	bone marrow	5 000 000	transport of oxygen and some carbon dioxide	
Leucocytes	bone marrow			
(a) Granulocytes (72% of total white blood cell count)				
neutrophils (70%)		4 900	engulf bacteria	
eosinophils (1.5%)	bone marrow	105	anti-histamine properties	
basophils (0.5%)		35	produce histamine and heparin	
(b) Agranulocytes (28%)				
monocytes (4%)	bone marrow	280	engulf bacteria	
lymphocytes (24%)	bone marrow lymphoid tissue spleen	1 680	production of antibodies	
Platelets	bone marrow	250 000	initiate blood-clotting mechanism	

Granulocytes (polymorphonuclear leucocytes). These originate in the bone marrow but are produced by cells different from those that make erythrocytes. Each cell contains a lobed nucleus and granular cytoplasm (table 14.10). All are capable of amoeboid movement. Granulocytes can be further subdivided into neutrophils, eosinophils and basophils.

Neutrophils (phagocytes). These constitute 70% of the total number of white cells. They are able to squeeze between the cells of the capillary walls and enter the intercellular spaces. This process is called **diapedesis**. From here they move to infected areas of the body. They are actively phagocytic and engulf and digest disease-causing bacteria (section 14.13.5).

Eosinophils. They possess cytoplasmic granules which stain red when the dye eosin is applied to them. Generally they represent only 1.5% of the total number of white cells, but their population increases in people with allergic conditions such as asthma or hayfever. It is thought that eosinophils possess anti-histamine properties. The number of eosinophils present in the bloodstream is under the control of hormones produced by the adrenal cortex.

Basophils. They represent 0.5% of the white blood cell population and produce heparin and histamine. The granules in these cells stain blue with basic dyes such as methylene blue.

Agranulocytes (mononuclear leucocytes). These cells possess non-granular cytoplasm and either an oval or bean-shaped nucleus. Two main types exist.

Monocytes (4%). These are formed in the bone marrow and have a bean-shaped nucleus. They are actively phagocytic and ingest bacteria and other large particles. They are able to migrate from the bloodstream to inflamed areas of the body and act in the same manner as neutrophils.

Lymphocytes (24%). These are produced in the thymus gland and lymphoid tissues from precursor cells which originate from the bone marrow. The cells are rounded and possess only a small quantity of cytoplasm. Amoeboid movement is limited. Their major function is to cause or mediate immune reactions (such as antibody production, graft rejection and tumour cell killing). The life span of these particular cells can vary from a matter of days in rodents up to ten years or more in humans.

14.11.3 Platelets

Platelets are irregularly shaped membrane-bound cell fragments, frequently enucleated and formed from large bone marrow cells called **megakaryocytes**. They function to initiate the mechanism of blood clotting. There are about 250 000 platelets per cubic millimetre of blood.

Experiment 14.7: Preparation of a blood smear

Materials

disposable towels
cotton wool swabs
70% alcohol
sterile disposable lancet
two slides
sealable container
Leishman's stain
distilled water
glycerine
cover-slip
freshly prepared aqueous sodium chlorate solution

Method

(1) Thoroughly wash both hands using soap and water. Those giving blood samples must pay particular attention to washing the site chosen for sampling. Dry the hands using only disposable towels.
(2) Shake the wrist of one hand downwards several times to force blood into the hand.
(3) Sterilise an area 5–10 mm from the lower corner of the nail of the little finger (fig 14.37a) using a cotton wool swab that has been soaked in 70% alcohol and allow it to dry.
(4) Remove a new sterile disposable lancet from its packet just prior to its use. DO NOT permit the sharp end to touch anything.
(5) Puncture the skin in the chosen area using the lancet and then place the lancet in a sealable container. Lancets must be used once only.
(6) Transfer the drop of blood which appears onto one end of a sterile slide. Avoid any contact between the punctured skin and the slide.
(7) Using a fresh cotton wool swab, wipe the site of the puncture again with 70% alcohol and apply slight pressure if necessary to stop blood flow. Put all used swabs in the container with the lancets.

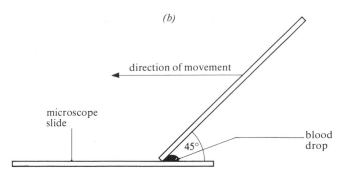

(b)

direction of movement

microscope slide

45°

blood drop

Fig 14.37 *(b) Preparation of a blood smear*

(8) Take another microscope slide, hold it at an angle of 45° and touch the drop of blood with it. Then push the second slide along the first slide (fig 14.37b) in a direction away from the drop of blood to make a blood smear.
(9) Allow the smear to dry for several minutes so permitting the cells to stick to the slide. This may be done by holding the slide above a bench lamp or waving it in the air.
(10) Add six drops of Leishman's stain and leave for 60 s.
(11) Add six drops of distilled water and mix with the stain by rocking the slide.
(12) Leave for 15 min and then rinse off the stain with water.
(13) Add a drop of glycerine to the preparation, followed by a cover-slip, and view the smear under a microscope.
(14) Erythrocytes will be stained pink, platelets and the nuclei of white blood cells will be stained blue.
(15) Any blood spilt on the bench or elsewhere during the experiment must be wiped up immediately using a freshly prepared aqueous solution of sodium chlorate.
(16) Great care should be taken to avoid contamination of the skin with blood from another person. If this should occur, however, the contaminated area must be cleaned immediately with sodium chlorate diluted with water to ten times its volume, and then washed thoroughly with soap and water.
(17) At the end of the practical both hands must be washed with soap and water and dried using disposable towels.
NB Because of the risk of contamination through broken skin, participation in this practical by people with any kind of open wound should be avoided.

(a)

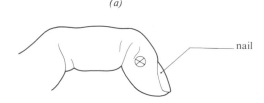

nail

Fig 14.37 *(a) Point where blood may be taken from the finger. It is easier to insert the lancet if the finger is crooked at the top joint*

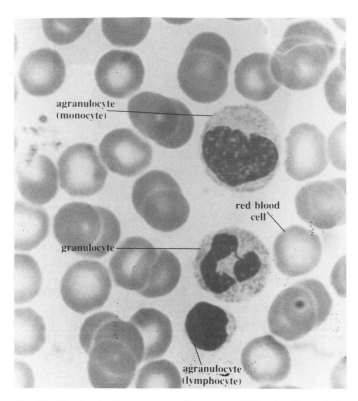
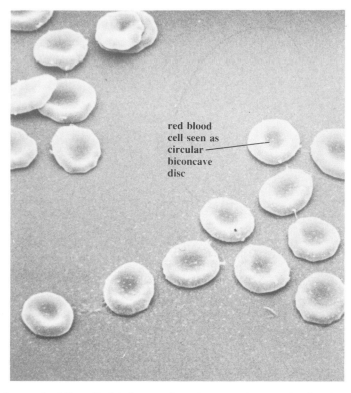

Fig 14.38 (a) A blood smear showing red blood cells and three types of white cell. (b) A scanning electron micrograph of red blood cells of a mammal

Table 14.11 Comparison in structure and function of an artery, capillary and vein (diagrams are not drawn to scale).

Artery	Capillary	Vein
Transport blood away from the heart	Link arteries to veins. Site of exchange of materials between blood and tissues	Transport blood towards the heart
Tunica media thick and composed of elastic, muscular tissue	No tunica media. Only tissue present is squamous endothelium. No elastic fibres	Tunica media relatively thin and only slightly muscular. Few elastic fibres
No semi-lunar valves	No semi-lunar valves	Semi-lunar valves at intervals along the length to prevent backflow of blood
Pressure of blood is high and pulsatile	Pressure of blood falling and non-pulsatile	Pressure of blood low and non-pulsatile
Blood flow rapid	Blood flow slowing	Blood flow slow
Low blood volume	High blood volume	Increased blood volume
Blood oxygenated except in pulmonary artery	Mixed oxygenated and deoxygenated blood	Blood deoxygenated except in pulmonary vein

Artery diagram: lumen, tunica externa of collagen fibres, tunica intima of endothelium, tunica media of smooth muscle and elastic fibres

Capillary diagram: endothelial cell

Vein diagram: lumen, tunica externa of collagen fibres, tunica intima, tunica media of smooth muscle fibres and a few elastic fibres

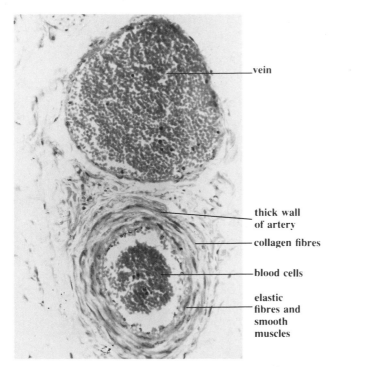

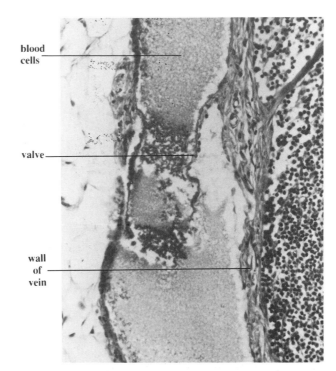

Fig 14.39 *(a) TS of an artery and a vein. (b) LS of a vein showing a valve*

14.12   The mammalian circulatory system

As blood circulates continuously round the body it passes through a series of arteries, capillaries and veins. Basically each artery and vein consists of three layers, an inner lining of squamous endothelium, the **tunica intima**, a middle layer of smooth muscle and elastic fibres, the **tunica media**, and an external layer of fibrous connective tissue possessing collagen-fibres, the **tunica externa** (table 14.11 and fig 14.39(a)).

The large arteries in close proximity to the heart (that is the aorta, subclavians and carotids) must be able to contend with the high pressure of blood leaving the ventricles of the heart. The walls of these vessels are thick and the middle layer is mainly composed of elastic fibres. This enables them to dilate but not rupture during ventricular systole (section 14.12.3). When systole ceases, the arteries contract and promote an even flow of blood along their length (fig 14.40).

The arteries further away from the heart have a similar structure but possess more smooth muscle fibres in the middle layer. They are supplied with neurones from the sympathetic nervous system. Stimulation from this system regulates the diameter of these arteries and this is important in controlling the flow of blood to different parts of the body.

Blood passes from the arteries into smaller vessels called arterioles. In all of these except the pulmonary arterioles, the tunica media consists entirely of smooth muscle fibres supplied with neurones from the sympathetic nervous system (section 16.2). Many arterioles possess precapillary 'sphincters' (figs 14.41 and 14.42) at their capillary ends.

When these structures contract, blood is prevented from flowing through the capillary network. Also present in certain regions of the body are arterio-venous cross-connections, which act as short-circuit routes between arterioles and venules and serve to regulate the quantity of blood which flows through the capillary beds according to the needs of the body.

Blood passes from the arterioles into capillaries, the smallest of all blood vessels in the body. They form a vast network of vessels pervading all parts of the body, and are

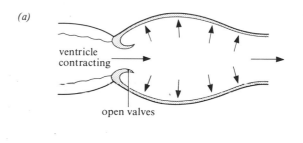

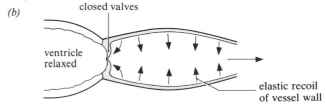

Fig 14.40 *Diagram demonstrating how the arteries near the heart assist in maintaining a continuous flow of blood in spite of a discontinuous flow received from the ventricles. (From Clegg & Clegg (2nd edition, 1963) Biology of the mammal, Heinemann Medical Books)*

517

so numerous that no capillary is more than 0.5 mm from any cell. They are 7–10 μm in diameter and their walls, consisting solely of endothelium, are permeable to water and dissolved substances. It is here that exchange of materials between the blood and body cells takes place.

Blood from the capillary beds drains into venules, whose walls consist of a thin layer of collagen fibres. They pass the blood into veins which eventually convey it back to the heart.

A vein possesses less muscle and elastic fibres in its

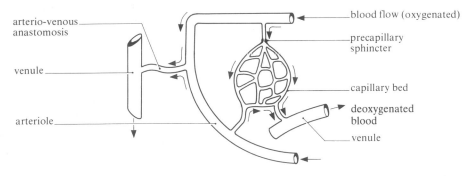

Fig 14.41 *The possible routes that blood may take between arteriole, capillary bed and venule*

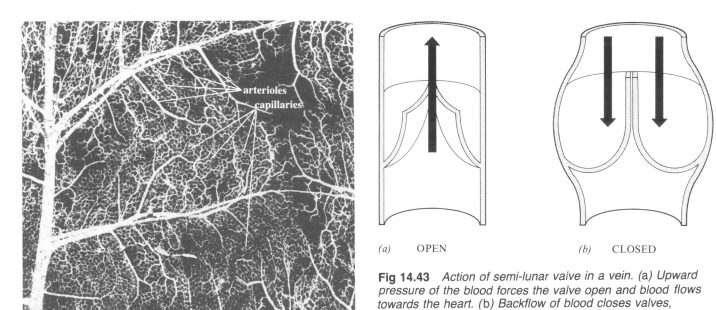

Fig 14.42 *Capillary bed showing arterioles and capillaries*

(a)　OPEN　　　(b)　CLOSED

Fig 14.43 *Action of semi-lunar valve in a vein. (a) Upward pressure of the blood forces the valve open and blood flows towards the heart. (b) Backflow of blood closes valves, blood therefore cannot flow away from the heart*

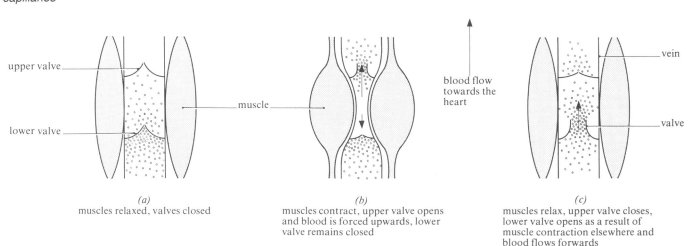

(a)
muscles relaxed, valves closed

(b)
muscles contract, upper valve opens and blood is forced upwards, lower valve remains closed

(c)
muscles relax, upper valve closes, lower valve opens as a result of muscle contraction elsewhere and blood flows forwards

Fig 14.44 *Diagram illustrating how muscle contraction around a vein aids one-way flow of blood towards the heart*

middle layer than an artery and the diameter of its lumen is greater. Semi-lunar valves (fig 14.43) are present, being formed from folds of the inner walls of the vein which are permeated by elastic fibres. They function to prevent backflow of blood thereby maintaining a unidirectional blood flow. A number of veins are located between the large muscles of the body (as in the arms and legs). When these muscles contract they exert pressure on the veins and squeeze them flat (fig 14.44). This assists the venous flow to the heart. A general plan of the mammalian double circulation is shown in fig 14.45.

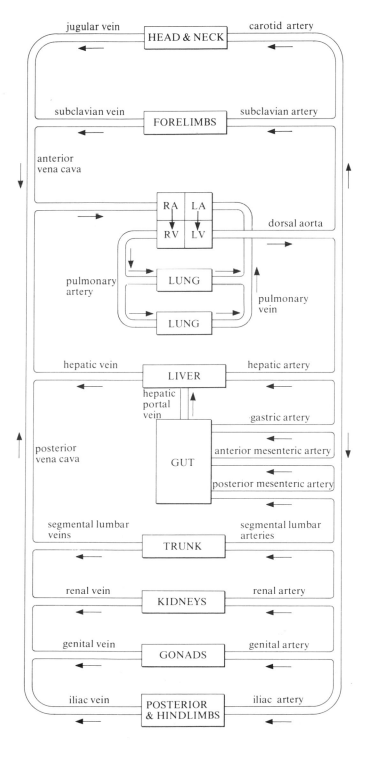

Fig 14.45 *Mammalian double circulatory system. Principal blood vessels are shown but not capillary beds*

14.12.1 Formation of intercellular fluid

Intercellular, or tissue, fluid is formed when blood passes through the capillaries. The capillary walls are permeable to all components of the blood except the erythrocytes and plasma proteins.

The osmotic pressure exerted by the plasma proteins is about 25 mm Hg* and this far exceeds the OP in the tissue fluid. Under these conditions one would normally expect tissue fluid to flow into the blood plasma. However, the blood pressure at the arterial end of a capillary is about 32 mm Hg. Therefore fluid passes from the capillary into the minute spaces between the cells to form the inter-cellular fluid. It is through the tissue fluid that exchange of materials between blood and tissues occurs.

The blood cannot afford to constantly lose so much fluid and therefore much of it is returned. This occurs in two ways.

(1) At the venous end of the capillary blood pressure has fallen to 12 mm Hg and therefore below the OP exerted by the plasma proteins. Thus there is a net flow of tissue fluid back into the capillary (fig 14.46).

(2) The rest of the intercellular fluid drains into blindly ending lymphatic capillaries, and once inside these the fluid is termed **lymph**. The lymphatic capillaries join to form larger lymphatic vessels. The lymph is moved through the vessels by contraction of the muscles surrounding them, and backflow is prevented by valves present in the major vessels which act in a similar fashion to those found in veins (fig 14.48).

The lymphatic vessels of the legs join to those from the alimentary canal to form the thoracic duct. This empties the lymph into the blood system in the neck region via the left subclavian vein. The right lymphatic duct drains lymph back into the bloodstream via the right subclavian vein (fig 14.47).

Situated at intervals along the lymphatic system are lymph glands or nodes. Lymphocytes, in the course of circulation through the blood and lymph, 'rest' and accumulate in the lymph nodes. They produce antibodies and are an important part of the body's immune system. The nodes (fig 14.49) also filter out bacteria and foreign particles from the lymph, which are ultimately ingested by phagocytes.

* In medicine, the unit of pressure commonly used is still millimetres of mercury (mm Hg). For comparison with SI units, see section A4.3.3.

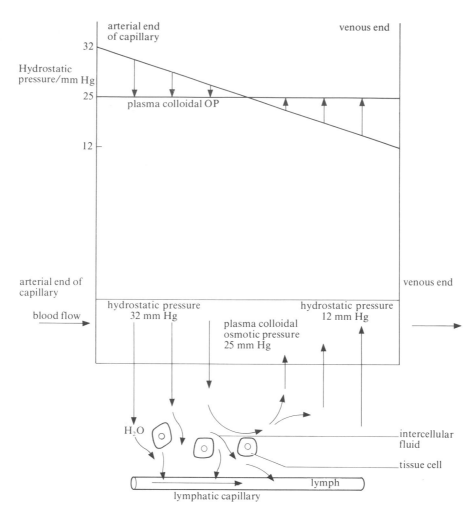

Fig 14.46 *Formation of tissue fluid and lymph. Some tissue fluid is reabsorbed at the venous end of the capillary whereas the remainder is collected in lymphatic capillaries. (After K. Schmidt-Nielsen (1980)* Animal physiology, *2nd ed., Cambridge University Press)*

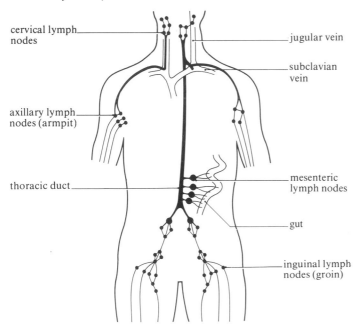

Fig 14.47 *Human lymphatic system. (From E. G. Springthorpe 1973)* An introduction to functional systems in animals, *Longman)*

14.12.2 The mammalian heart

The heart is situated between the two lungs and behind the sternum in the thorax. It is surrounded by a conical-shaped sac, the pericardium, the outer part of which consists of non-distensible white fibrous tissue, whilst the inner part is made up of two membranes. The inner of the two membranes is attached to the heart whilst the outer one is attached to the fibrous tissue. Pericardial fluid is secreted between them which reduces the friction between the heart walls and surrounding tissues when the heart is beating. The general inelastic nature of the pericardium as a whole prevents the heart from being overstretched or overfilled with blood.

There are four chambers in the heart, two upper thin-walled atria and two lower thick-walled ventricles (fig 14.50). The right side of the heart is completely separated from the left. The atria function to collect and retain blood temporarily until it can pass to the ventricles. The distance from atrium to ventricle is very small, hence the power of contraction of the atria does not have to be very great. The right atrium receives deoxygenated blood from the general circulation of the body whilst the left

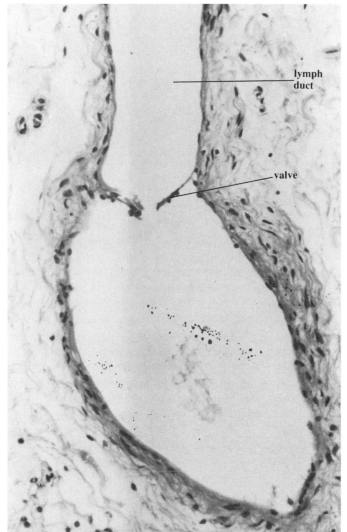

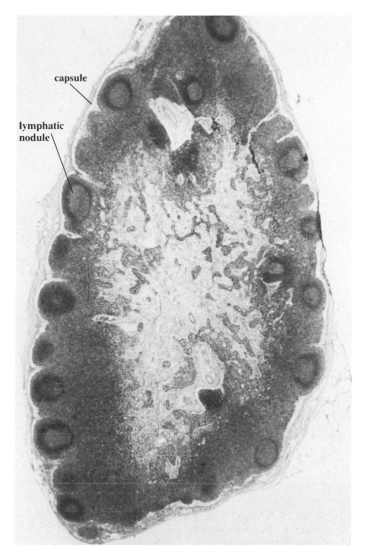

Fig 14.48 *LS through lymph vessel showing an internal valve*

Fig 14.49 *Section through a lymph gland*

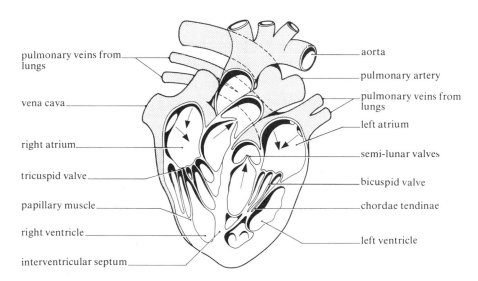

Fig 14.50 *Section through mammalian heart*

521

atrium receives oxygenated blood from the lungs. The muscular wall of the left ventricle is at least three times as thick as that of the right ventricle. This difference can be correlated with the fact that the right ventricle has only to supply the pulmonary circulation whilst the left ventricle pumps blood through the much larger systemic circulation of the body. Correspondingly the blood entering the aorta from the left ventricle is at a much higher blood pressure (approximately 105 mm Hg) than the blood entering the pulmonary artery (16 mm Hg).

> **14.34** What other advantages are there in supplying the pulmonary circulation with blood at a lower pressure than that of the systemic circulation?

As the atria contract they force blood into the ventricles, and rings of muscle which surround the venae cavae and pulmonary veins at their point of entry into the atria contract and close off the veins. This prevents reflux of blood into the veins. The left atrium is separated from the left ventricle by a bicuspid (two-flapped) valve, whilst a tricuspid valve separates the right atrium from the right ventricle. Attached to the ventricular side of the flaps are fibrous cords which in turn attach to conical-shaped papillary muscles which are extensions of the inner wall of the ventricles. These valves are pushed open when the atria contract, but when the ventricles contract the flaps of each valve press tightly closed so preventing reflux of blood to the atria. At the same time the papillary muscles contract so tightening the fibrous cords. This prevents the valves from being turned inside out. Pulmonary and aortic pocket

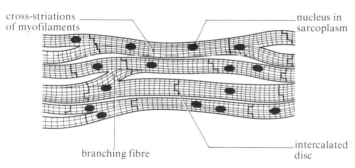

Fig 14.51 *Structure of cardiac muscle*

Fig 14.52 *Photograph of cardiac muscle*

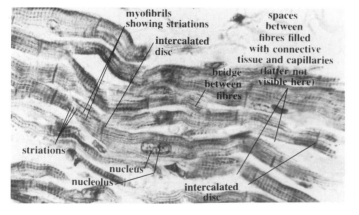

valves guard the point of entry of blood into these vessels and prevent regurgitation of blood back into the ventricles.

The walls of the heart are composed of cardiac muscle fibres, connective tissue and tiny blood vessels. Each muscle fibre possesses one or two nuclei, myofilaments and many large mitochondria. The fibres branch and cross-connect with each other to form a complex net-like arrangement. This permits contraction waves to spread quickly amongst the fibres and enhance the contraction of the chambers as a whole. No neurones are present in the wall of the heart (figs 14.51 and 14.52).

14.12.3 The cardiac cycle

The cardiac cycle refers to the sequence of events which take place during the completion of one heartbeat. It is as follows.

(1) Deoxygenated blood, under low pressure, enters the right atrium and oxygenated blood enters the left atrium. These chambers gradually become distended. Initially the bicuspid and tricuspid valves are closed, but as pressure in the atria rises, as they fill with blood, it eventually exceeds that of the ventricles and the valves are pushed open. Some of the blood flows into the relaxed ventricles. This resting period of the heart chambers is called **diastole** (fig 14.53*a*).

(2) When diastole ends, the two atria contract simultaneously. This is termed **atrial systole** and results in more blood being conveyed into the ventricles (fig 14.53*b*). Almost immediately the ventricles contract. This is called **ventricular systole** (fig 14.53*c*). When this occurs the bicuspid and tricuspid valves are closed. The ventricular pressure rises and soon exceeds the blood pressure in the aorta and pulmonary artery, forcing the aortic and pulmonary valves open. Thus blood is expelled from the heart into these elastic-walled vessels. During ventricular systole blood is forced against the closed atrio-ventricular valve and this produces the first heart sound ('lub').

(3) Ventricular systole ends and is followed by **ventricular diastole** (fig 14.53*d*). The high pressure developed in the aorta and pulmonary artery tends to force some blood back towards the ventricles and this closes the aortic and pulmonary artery pocket valves. Hence backflow is prevented. The impact of this backflow against the valves causes the second heart sound ('dub'):

ventricular systole = 'lub'
ventricular diastole = 'dub'

The repeated recoil of the elastic arterial vessels as a result of ventricular systole forces the blood into the pulmonary and systemic circulations as a series of pulses. As blood is propelled further and further away from the heart, the pulses become less and less pronounced until, in the capillaries and veins, blood flows evenly (figs 14.55 and 14.56).

One complete heartbeat consists of one systole and one diastole and lasts for about 0.8 s (fig 14.54).

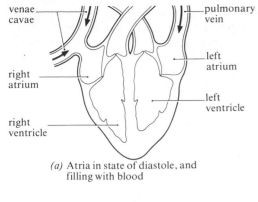

venae cavae — pulmonary vein

right atrium — left atrium

right ventricle — left ventricle

(a) Atria in state of diastole, and filling with blood

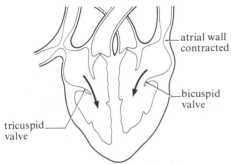

atrial wall contracted

bicuspid valve

tricuspid valve

(b) Atrial systole forces blood into ventricles. Bicuspid and tricuspid valves open. Sphincters of venae cavae and pulmonary veins closed

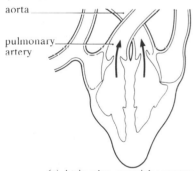

aorta

pulmonary artery

(c) Atria relax, ventricles contract. Blood propelled into aorta and pulmonary artery

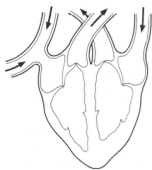

(d) Pocket valves of aorta and pulmonary artery close. Atria begin to refill. Ventricles in state of diastole

Fig 14.53 *Sequence of heart actions involved in one complete heartbeat – the cardiac cycle*

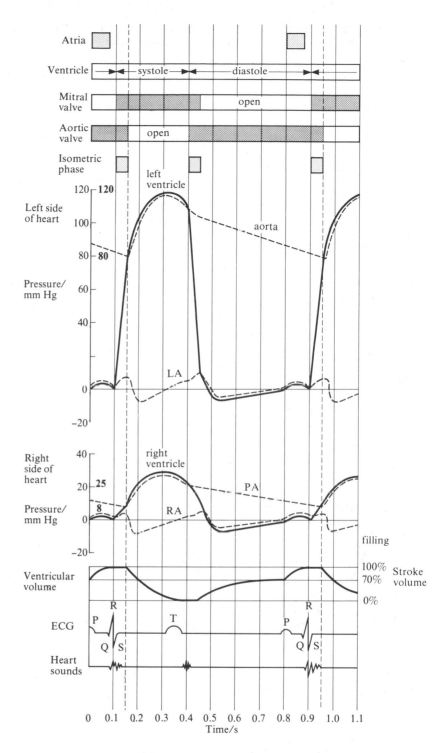

Fig 14.54 *The sequence of events in the cardiac cycle starting with the onset of atrial systole. Part of the subsequent cycle is shown. PA, blood pressure in the pulmonary artery; RA, right atrial pressure; LA, left atrial pressure. (From J. H. Green (1968)* An introduction to human physiology, Oxford University Press)

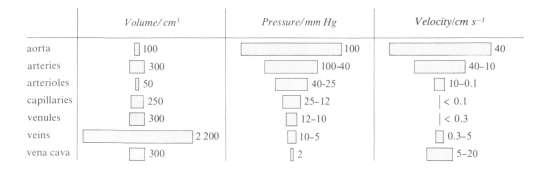

	Volume/cm³	Pressure/mm Hg	Velocity/cm s⁻¹
aorta	100	100	40
arteries	300	100–40	40–10
arterioles	50	40–25	10–0.1
capillaries	250	25–12	< 0.1
venules	300	12–10	< 0.3
veins	2 200	10–5	0.3–5
vena cava	300	2	5–20

Fig 14.55 *Distribution of blood volume, pressure and velocity in the human vascular system. (From K. Schmidt-Nielsen (1980)* Animal physiology, *2nd ed., Cambridge University Press)*

Fig 14.56 *Blood pressure throughout the human circulatory system. (From J. H. Green (1968)* An introduction to human physiology, *Oxford University Press)*

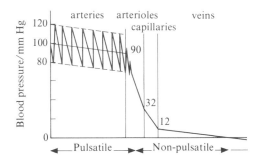

14.12.4 Mechanism of heart excitation and contraction

When a heart is removed from a mammal and placed in well-oxygenated Ringer solution at 37 °C it will continue to beat rhythmically for a considerable time, without stimuli from the nervous or endocrine systems. This demonstrates the myogenic nature of the heart, that is it possesses its own inherent or 'built-in' mechanism for initiating contraction of the cardiac muscle fibres.

Myogenic control of heartbeat rate

The stimulus for contraction of the heart originates in a specific region of the right atrium called the **sino-atrial node** (or S-A node for short) close to the point of entry of the venae cavae. The S-A node is a vestige of the sinus venosus seen in the heart of lower vertebrates. It consists of a small number of diffusely orientated cardiac fibres, possessing few myofibrils, and a few nerve endings from the autonomic nervous system. The S-A node initiates the heartbeat, but the rate at which it beats can be varied by stimulation from the autonomic nervous system.

The cells of the S-A node maintain a differential ionic concentration across their membranes of −90 mV. These cells have a permanently high sodium conductance, that is to say that sodium ions continually diffuse into the cells. This produces a depolarisation which leads to a propagated action potential (section 16.1.1) being set up in the cells adjacent to the S-A node. As this wave of excitation passes across the muscle fibres of the heart it causes them to contract. The S-A node is known as the pacemaker of the heart because each wave of excitation begins here and acts as the stimulus for the next wave of excitation.

Once contraction has begun it spreads through the walls of the atria via the network of cardiac fibres at the rate of 1 m s⁻¹. Both atria contract more or less simultaneously. The atrial muscle fibres are completely separated from those of the ventricles by the atrio-ventricular septum of connective tissue, except for a region in the right atrium called the **atrio-ventricular node** (A-V node).

The tissues of the A-V node are similar to those of the S-A node and supply a bundle of specialised fibres, the A-V bundle, which provide the only route for the transmission of the wave of excitation from the atria to the ventricles. There is a delay of approximately 0.15 s in conduction from the S-A node to the A-V node, thus permitting atrial systole to be completed before ventricular systole begins.

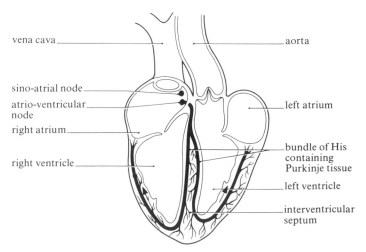

Fig 14.57 *Position of the sino-atrial and atrio-ventricular nodes, and the bundle of His*

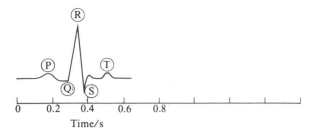

Fig 14.58 *An electrocardiogram (ECG) trace demonstrating the change in electrical potential across the heart during one cardiac cycle. P, atrial depolarisation over the atrial muscle and spread of excitation from the sino-atrial node equivalent to atrial systole; Q, R and S, ventricular systole; T, ventricular diastole begins*

The A-V bundle is connected to the **bundle of His**, a strand of modified cardiac fibres which gives rise to finer branches known as **Purkinje tissue**. Impulses are conducted rapidly along the bundle at 5 m s^{-1}, ultimately proceeding to all parts of the ventricles. Both ventricles are stimulated to contract simultaneously, and the wave of ventricular contraction begins at the apex of the heart and spreads upwards squeezing blood out of the ventricles towards the arteries which pass vertically upwards out of the heart (figs 14.57 and 14.58).

Certain characteristics of cardiac muscle make it suited to its role of pumping blood round the body throughout the life of the mammal. Once cardiac muscle has begun to contract it cannot respond to any other stimulus until it begins to relax. This is known as the **refractory period**. The length of time that the cardiac muscle is in this condition is called its absolute refractive period (fig 14.59). This period is longer than that of other types of muscle, and enables the muscle to contract vigorously and rapidly without becoming fatigued. It is thus impossible for the heart to develop a state of sustained contraction called **tetanus**, or to develop an oxygen debt.

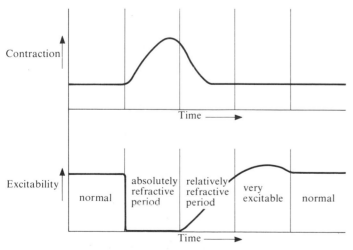

Fig 14.59 *The refractory period of cardiac muscle. The upper figure shows a record of the contraction of the muscle, the lower figure shows the varying excitability of the muscle to stimuli. (From Clegg & Clegg (2nd edition, 1963) Biology of the mammal, Heinemann Medical Books)*

14.12.5 Regulation of heartbeat rate

The intrinsic rate of the heartbeat is controlled by the activity of the S-A nodes as described earlier. Even when removed from the body and placed into an artificial medium the heart will continue to beat rhythmically, albeit more slowly. In situ, however, the body's demands on its circulatory system are constantly changing and the heart rate has to be continuously adjusted accordingly. This is achieved by the dynamic and integrated activity of two types of control system, one nervous and the other chemical. This is a homeostatic response whose overall function is to maintain constant conditions within the bloodstream even though conditions around it are constantly changing.

The amount of blood flowing from the heart over a given period of time is known as the **cardiac output** and depends upon the volume of blood expelled at each beat (the stroke volume) and the heart rate. These three variables are related by the expression

$$\text{cardiac output} = \text{stroke volume} \times \text{heart rate}$$

and it is the cardiac output which is the important variable. One way of controlling cardiac output is by varying the heart rate.

Nervous control of heart rate

Within the medulla oblongata of the hindbrain are several regions concerned with cardiovascular control. In all regions, part of their function is to control the heart rate. Two vagus nerves carrying parasympathetic fibres leave the cardio-inhibitory centre of the medulla oblongata and run, one on either side of the trachea, to the heart. Here nerve fibres lead to the S-A node, A-V node and the bundle of His. Impulses passing along the vagus nerve reduce the heart rate. Other nerves, of the sympathetic system, have their origin in the pressor region of the vasomotor centre of the medulla, run parallel to the spinal cord and emerge from the thoracic region to the S-A node. Stimulation by these nerves results in an increase in the heart rate. It is the integrated activity of the inhibiting and accelerating effects, occurring within the medulla oblongata, that controls the heart rate.

Sensory fibres from stretch receptors within the walls of the aortic arch, the carotid sinuses and the vena cava run to the cardio-inhibitory centre in the medulla. Impulses received from the aorta and carotids decrease the heart rate, whilst those from the vena cava stimulate the pressor centre which increases the heart rate. As the volume of blood passing to any of these vessels increases so does the distension of the vessels, and this increases the number of impulses transmitted to the cardiovascular centres in the medulla.

For example, under conditions of intense activity body muscles contract strongly and this increases the rate at which venous blood returns to the heart. Consequently the vena cava is distended by large quantities of blood and the heart rate is increased. At the same time the increased

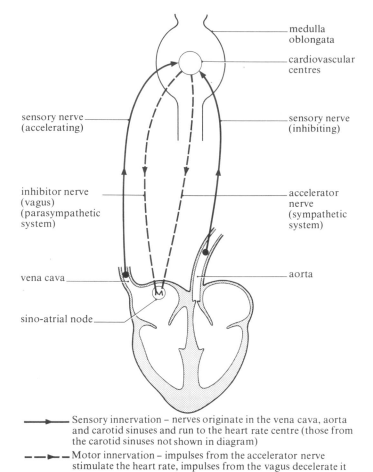

| Sensory innervation – nerves originate in the vena cava, aorta and carotid sinuses and run to the heart rate centre (those from the carotid sinuses not shown in diagram) |
| Motor innervation – impulses from the accelerator nerve stimulate the heart rate, impulses from the vagus decelerate it |

Fig 14.60 *Neurones connecting the heart to the cardiovascular system*

blood flow to the heart places the cardiac muscle of the heart under tension. Cardiac muscle responds to this tension by contracting more strongly during systole and pumping out an increased volume of blood (the stroke volume). This relationship between the volume of blood returned to the heart and cardiac output was named after the English physiologist Starling and is known as **Starling's law**.

The increased stroke volume stretches the aorta and carotids which in turn, via stretch reflexes, signal the cardio-inhibitory centre to slow the heart rate. Therefore there is an automatic fail-safe mechanism which serves to prevent the heart from working too fast, and to enable it to adjust its activity in order to cope effectively with the volume of blood passing through it at any given time (fig 14.60).

Non-nervous control of heart rate

There are a number of non-nervous stimuli which act directly on cardiac muscle or on the S-A node. They are briefly summarised in table 14.12.

Many activities affect the cardiovascular centre in some way or other, for example emotions, such as blushing or turning white with anger, sights and sounds. In such instances sensory impulses are transmitted to the brain

Table 14.12 Non-nervous agencies affecting heart rate.

Non-nervous stimulus	Effect on heart rate
High pH	Decelerates
Low pH (e.g. high CO_2 levels, as is the case during active exercise)	Accelerates
Low temperature	Decelerates
High temperature	Accelerates
Mineral ions Endocrine factors (e.g. thyroxine, insulin, sex hormones, adrenaline, pituitary hormones)	The rate is influenced directly or indirectly

where they pass to the cardiovascular centre via interconnecting pathways. Under such stimulation the cardiovascular centre responds accordingly (table 14.12).

It should be noted that this centre is influenced at any given moment by a combination of nervous and non-nervous agencies, and never by a single one. The activity of the cardiovascular centre also fluctuates according to the health and age of the individual.

14.12.6 Regulation of blood pressure

Blood pressure depends on several factors: heart rate, strength of heartbeat, blood output (stroke volume) and resistance to blood flow by the blood vessels (peripheral resistance). Heart rate and stroke volume have been discussed in the last section. Resistance to blood flow is altered by contraction (**vasoconstriction**) or relaxation (**vasodilation**) of the smooth muscle in the blood vessel walls, especially those of the arterioles. This peripheral resistance is increased by vasoconstriction but decreased by vasodilation. Increased resistance leads to a rise in blood pressure, whereas a decrease produces a fall in blood pressure. All such activity is controlled by a vasomotor centre in the medulla oblongata.

Nerve fibres run from the vasomotor centre to all arterioles in the body. Changes in the diameter of these blood vessels are produced principally by variation in the activity of constrictor muscles. The dilator muscles play a somewhat less important role.

Vasomotor centre activity is regulated by impulses coming from pressure receptors (**baroreceptors**) located in the walls of the aorta and carotid sinuses in the carotid arteries (fig 14.61). Stimulation of parasympathetic fibres in these areas, caused by increased cardiac output, produces vasodilation throughout the body and consequent reduction in blood pressure, as well as a slowing of the heart rate. The converse occurs when blood pressure is low. In this case, a fall in blood pressure increases impulse transmission along sympathetic fibres. This causes body-wide vasoconstriction and a compensatory rise in blood pressure.

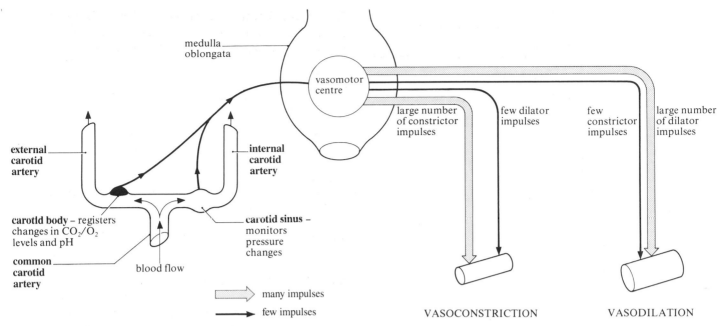

Fig 14.61 *Interrelationships between the carotid body, carotid sinus, vasomotor centre and general circulatory system*

Chemical control of the vasomotor centre

Blood arriving at the carotid bodies carrying a high concentration of carbon dioxide stimulates chemoreceptors in these regions to transmit impulses to the vasomotor centre (fig 14.61). Nerve fibres leaving the chemoreceptors synapse with fibres from the carotid sinus prior to passing to the vasomotor centre. When the vasomotor centre is stimulated in this way it sends impulses to the blood vessels to vasoconstrict and therefore raises blood pressure. As increased carbon dioxide concentration in the body is usually brought about by increased activity by body tissues, the blood containing the carbon dioxide will be transported more rapidly to the lungs where expulsion of carbon dioxide in exchange for oxygen can take place more quickly.

Carbon dioxide can also directly affect the behaviour of the smooth muscle of the blood vessel itself. When a tissue suddenly becomes very active, producing a large quantity of carbon dioxide, the carbon dioxide acts directly on the blood vessels in the vicinity and stimulates them to dilate. This increases their own blood supply thus allowing more oxygen and glucose to reach the active cells. It must be remembered, however, that when the carbon dioxide leaves this localised area it will have the effect of promoting vasoconstriction elsewhere via vasomotor activity. This is a good illustration of how dynamic and adjustable the control of blood pressure and therefore circulation and distribution of blood can be.

Other agencies, such as types of emotional stress (for example excitement, pain and annoyance), increase sympathetic activity and therefore blood pressure. Also when the adrenal medulla is stimulated to produce adrenaline by impulses from higher nervous centres this again increases the rate of heartbeat, promotes bodywide vasoconstriction

and therefore raises blood pressure. The significance of the control of heart rate and blood pressure is described further in section 18.1.5.

> **14.35** When an animal is wounded, its overall blood pressure rises, but the area in the vicinity of the wound swells as a result of local vasodilation. Why?
>
> **14.36** Outline the main adjustments that occur to the heart rate and circulatory system just before, during and after a 100 m race.

14.13 Functions of mammalian blood

Mammalian blood performs many major functions. In the following list, the first five functions are carried out solely by the plasma.

(1) Transport of soluble organic compounds from the small intestine to various parts of the body where they are stored or assimilated, and transport from storage areas to places where they are used.
(2) Transport of soluble excretory materials from tissues where they are produced to the organs of excretion.
(3) Transport of metabolic by-products from areas of production to other parts of the body.
(4) Transport of hormones from the glands where they are produced to all parts of the body or certain target organs. This facilitates communication within the body.
(5) Distribution of heat from the deeply seated organs. This serves to dissipate excess heat and to aid the maintenance of a uniform body temperature.

(6) Transport of oxygen from the lungs to all parts of the body, and carriage of carbon dioxide produced by the tissues in the reverse direction.

(7) Defence against disease. This is achieved in three ways:
  (a) clotting of the blood which prevents excessive blood loss and entry of pathogens;
  (b) phagocytosis, performed by the granulocytes which engulf and digest bacteria which find their way into the bloodstream;
  (c) immunity mediated by antibodies and/or lymphocytes.

(8) Maintenance of a constant blood osmotic pressure and pH as a result of plasma protein activity. As the plasma proteins and haemoglobin possess both acidic and basic amino acids they can combine with or release hydrogen ions and serve to minimise pH changes over a wide range of pH values.

14.3.1 Oxygen carriage

It is the haemoglobin molecule, found in the erythrocytes, which is responsible for the transport of oxygen round the body. Haemoglobin is a tetrameric protein with a relative molecular mass of 68 000. It possesses four haem prosthetic groups, responsible for the characteristic red colour of the blood, linked to four globin polypeptide chains. A ferrous iron atom is located within each haem group, and each of these can combine loosely with one molecule of oxygen (fig 14.62).

$$Hb + 4O_2 \rightleftharpoons HbO_8$$

Combination of oxygen with haemoglobin, to form oxyhaemoglobin, occurs under conditions when the partial pressure of oxygen is high, such as in the lung alveolar capillaries. When the partial pressure of oxygen is low, as in the capillaries which supply metabolically active tissues, the bonds holding oxygen to haemoglobin become unstable and oxygen is released. This diffuses in solution into the surrounding cells.

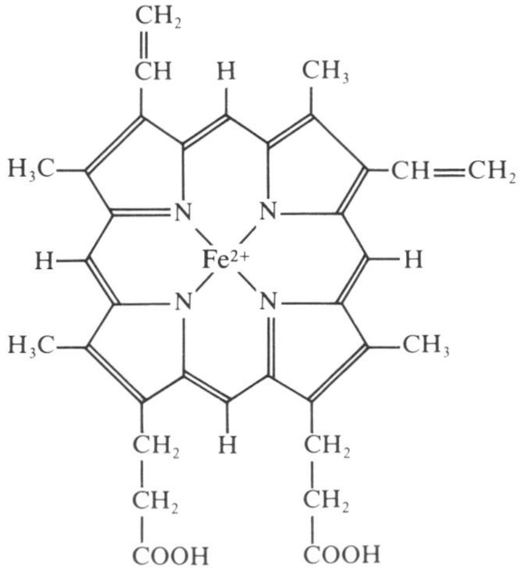

The amount of oxygen that can combine with haemoglobin is determined by the oxygen tension. This is expressed as a partial pressure and is the fraction of oxygen found in the air. It is still measured in millimetres of mercury. For example, atmospheric pressure at sea level is 760 mm Hg. Approximately one-fifth of the atmosphere is oxygen, therefore the partial pressure of oxygen in the atmosphere at sea level is $\frac{1}{5} \times 760 = 152$ mm Hg. When the percentage oxygen saturation of blood is plotted against the partial pressure of oxygen an S-shaped curve, called the **oxygen dissociation curve**, is obtained (fig 14.63).

Analysis of the curve indicates that for physiological reasons haemoglobin is completely saturated with oxygen at a point known as the **loading tension**. This is taken as the tension when 95% of the pigment is saturated and coincides with a partial pressure of about 73 mm Hg in the example given in fig 14.63. At higher partial pressures of oxygen further uptake of oxygen can occur, but 100% saturation of haemoglobin is rarely achieved. At an oxygen partial pressure of approximately 30 mm Hg only 50% of the haemoglobin is present as oxyhaemoglobin, and at a partial pressure of zero no oxygen is attached to the haemoglobin molecule. Over the steep part of the curve, a small decrease in the oxygen partial pressure of the environment will bring about a sizeable fall in the percentage saturation of haemoglobin. The oxygen given up by the pigment is available to the tissues.

But why is the curve S-shaped? The explanation lies in the way that haemoglobin binds to oxygen. It involves the phenomenon of allostery (section 6.6). When an oxygen molecule combines with the ferrous iron atom of a single haem unit it distorts its shape slightly. This distortion is registered by the whole molecule which changes its shape accordingly. Further structural alterations occur when

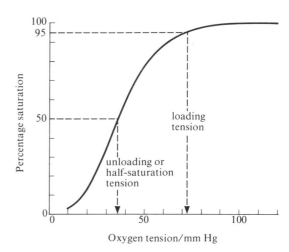

Fig 14.63 *Diagram to explain the terminology applied to oxygen dissociation curves of oxygen-carrying pigments. Loading tension is the tension at which 95% of the pigment is saturated with oxygen; unloading tension is the tension at which 50% of the pigment is saturated with oxygen. (From Florey (1966) An introduction to general and comparative physiology, W.B. Saunders & Co.)*

Fig 14.62 *A single haem molecule*

oxygen molecules attach to the second and third haem groups, each one facilitating much faster uptake of oxygen than the preceding one. When the last haem monomer is ready to pick up oxygen it does so several hundred times faster than the first.

The converse reaction occurs when oxyhaemoglobin is exposed to regions where the partial pressure of oxygen is low, as in actively respiring tissues. The first oxygen molecule is released to the tissues very rapidly, but the second, third and fourth molecules are given up much less readily and only at a very reduced partial pressure of oxygen.

In regions with an increased partial pressure of carbon dioxide the oxygen dissociation curve is shifted to the right. This is known as the **Bohr effect** or **shift** (fig 14.64).

14.37 What is the physiological significance of the Bohr effect?

14.38 Consider fig 14.65. The oxygen dissociation curve of the foetus is to the left of that of its mother. Why is this so?

14.39 The oxygen dissociation curve of the South American llama, which lives in the High Andes at an altitude of about 5 000 m above sea level, is located to the left of most other mammals (fig 14.66). Why is this so?

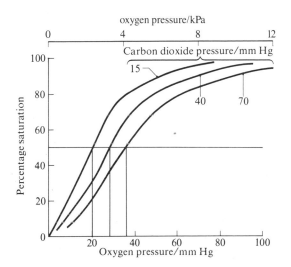

Fig 14.64 (above) *Oxygen dissociation curves of haemoglobin illustrating the Bohr effect at different pressures of carbon dioxide. (From Garth Chapman (1967) The body fluids and their functions,* Studies in Biology No. 8, Arnold)

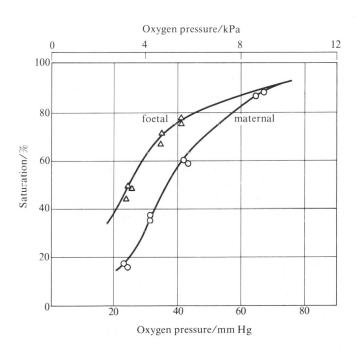

Fig 14.65 (above) *Oxygen dissociation curves of foetal and maternal blood of a goat*

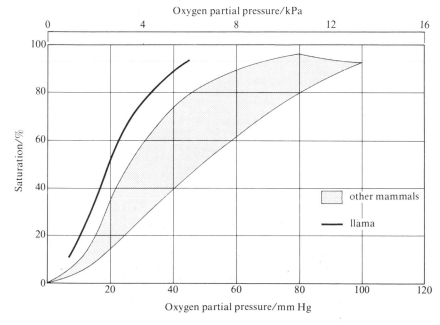

Fig 14.66 (left) *Oxygen dissociation curves of the llama and other mammals*

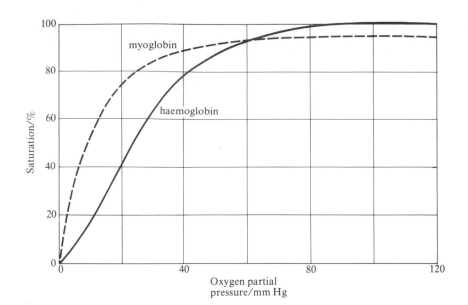

Fig 14.67 *Comparison of haemoglobin and myoglobin oxygen dissociation curves. Myoglobin remains 80% saturated with oxygen until the partial pressure of oxygen falls below 20 mm Hg. This means that myoglobin retains its oxygen in the resting cell but gives it up when vigorous muscle activity uses up the available oxygen supplied by haemoglobin*

14.13.2 Myoglobin

The myoglobin molecule is widely distributed in animals and is particularly common in skeletal muscle tissues of mammals. It displays a great affinity for oxygen and its oxygen dissociation curve is displaced well to the left of haemoglobin (fig 14.67). In fact it only begins to release oxygen when the partial pressure of oxygen is below 20 mm Hg. In this way it acts as a store of oxygen in resting muscle, only releasing it when supplies of oxyhaemoglobin have been exhausted. Myoglobin is very similar to the haemoglobin subunits with respect to both amino acid sequence and three-dimensional structure, but the myoglobin molecules do not associate to form tetramers and so cannot show cooperative oxygen binding. The two proteins have presumably evolved from a common ancestral molecule.

14.13.3 Carbon monoxide and haemoglobin

The affinity of the ferrous ions in haemoglobin for carbon monoxide is several hundred times as great as it is for oxygen. Therefore haemoglobin will combine with any carbon monoxide available in preference to oxygen to form a relatively stable compound called **carboxyhaemoglobin**. If this occurs oxygen is prevented from combining with haemoglobin, and therefore the transport of oxygen round the body by the blood is no longer possible. In Man, collapse follows quickly after exposure to carbon monoxide and, unless the victim is removed from the gas, asphyxiation is inevitable. Removal from the gas must be followed by administering a pure oxygen–carbon dioxide mix since the oxygen tension in air is insufficient to replace the carbon monoxide attached to the haemoglobin.

14.13.4 Carriage of carbon dioxide

Carbon dioxide is carried by the blood in three different ways.

In solution (5%). Most of the carbon dioxide carried in this way is transported in physical solution. A very small amount is carried as carbonic acid (H_2CO_3).

Combined with protein (10–20%). Carbon dioxide combines with the amine (NH_2) group of haemoglobin to form a neutral carbamino-haemoglobin compound. The amount of carbon dioxide that is able to combine with haemoglobin depends on the amount of oxygen already being carried by the haemoglobin. The less the amount of oxygen being carried by the haemoglobin molecule, the more carbon dioxide that can be carried in this way:

$$HHbNH_2 + CO_2 \longrightarrow HHbN-C\overset{\overset{\displaystyle H}{|}}{}{\overset{\displaystyle O}{\underset{\displaystyle OH}{}}}$$

haemoglobin

carbamino-haemoglobin

As hydrogencarbonate (85%). Carbon dioxide produced by the tissues diffuses passively into the bloodstream and passes into the erythrocytes where it combines with water to form carbonic acid. This process is catalysed by the enzyme carbonic anhydrase found in the erythrocytes and takes less than one second to occur. Carbonic acid then proceeds to dissociate into hydrogen and hydrogencarbonate ions:

$$CO_2 + H_2O \rightleftharpoons H_2CO_3 \rightleftharpoons H^+ + HCO_3^-$$

When the erythrocytes leave the lungs their oxyhaemoglobin (represented as HbO_2) is weakly acidic and associated with potassium ions. This may be represented as

$KHbO_2$. In areas of high carbon dioxide concentrations (as at the tissues), oxygen is easily given up by oxyhaemoglobin. When this happens the haemoglobin becomes strongly basic. In this state it dissociates from the potassium ions and readily accepts hydrogen ions from carbonic acid forming haemoglobinic acid (H.Hb). The potassium ions associate with hydrogencarbonate ions to form potassium hydrogencarbonate.

$$KHbO_2 \rightleftharpoons KHb + O_2$$
$$H^+ + HCO_3^- + KHb \rightleftharpoons H.Hb + KHCO_3$$
$$\text{(haemoglobinic acid)}$$

By accepting hydrogen ions, haemoglobin acts as a buffer molecule and so enables large quantities of carbonic acid to be carried to the lungs without any major alteration in blood pH.

The plasma membrane of an erythrocyte is relatively impermeable to the passage of sodium and potassium ions, however a cation pump operates and expels large numbers of sodium ions into the plasma. The majority of hydrogencarbonate ions formed within the erythrocyte diffuse out into the plasma along a concentration gradient and combine with sodium to form sodium hydrogencarbonate. The loss of hydrogencarbonate ions from the erythrocyte is balanced by chloride ions diffusing into the erythrocyte from the plasma. Thus electrochemical neutrality is maintained. This phenomenon is called the 'chloride shift'. Potassium hydrogencarbonate, formed in the erythrocyte, is also capable of dissociating, and some of the chloride ions which enter the erythrocyte combine with potassium ions to form potassium chloride, whilst the hydrogencarbonate ions diffuse out. When hydrogencarbonate leaves the erythrocyte, the excess H^+ ions which remain decrease the pH within the erythrocyte causing the dissociation of potassium oxyhaemoglobin ($KHbO_2$) into oxygen and potassium haemoglobin (fig 14.68).

When the erythrocytes reach the lungs the reverse process occurs.

14.40 Summarise how carbon dioxide in the blood is expelled as gaseous carbon dioxide by the lungs.

14.13.5 Defensive functions of the blood

Every mammal is equipped with a complex system of defensive mechanisms which are designed to enable it to withstand attacks by pathogens, and to remove foreign materials from its system. Three defensive mechanisms are discussed here:
(1) clotting of blood } both contributing to
(2) phagocytosis } wound healing
(3) immune response to infection.

Clotting

When a tissue is wounded blood flows from it, and coagulates to form a blood clot. This prevents further blood loss and entry of pathogenic micro-organisms and is of clear survival value to the animal concerned. It is just as important that blood in undamaged vessels does not clot. The highly complex series of reactions that take place in order for coagulation to be achieved serves at the same time to prevent it from occurring unnecessarily. The whole clotting process depends on at least 12 clotting factors working in harmony with each other. Only the main factors are described in this account.

Blood escaping from a superficial wound is exposed to the air, and mixes with substances oozing from the damaged cells and ruptured platelets. Thromboplastin, a lipoprotein released from injured tissues, together with clotting factors VII and X (plasma enzymes) and calcium ions, catalyses the conversion of inactive plasma protein prothrombin to thrombin. Thrombin is a proteolytic enzyme that hydrolyses the large soluble globular plasma protein molecule, fibrinogen, into smaller units which then associate to form a meshwork of long tangled needle-like fibres of insoluble fibrillar fibrin (fig 14.69). When

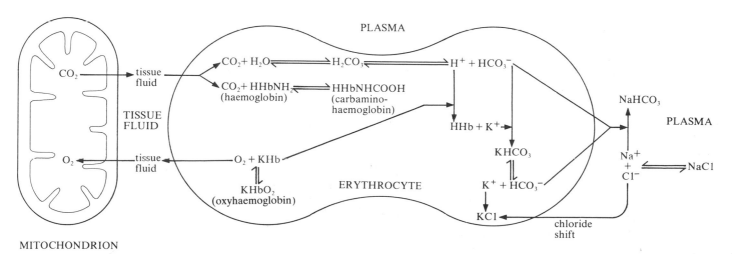

Fig 14.68 *Carbon dioxide carriage by the plasma and erythrocyte and its role in the release of oxygen at the tissues*

531

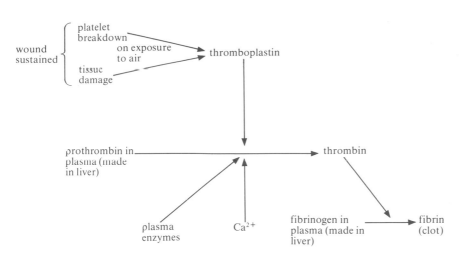

wound sustained {
platelet breakdown
tissue damage
} on exposure to air → thromboplastin

prothrombin in plasma (made in liver) ──────────→ thrombin

plasma enzymes   Ca²⁺

fibrinogen in plasma (made in liver) → fibrin (clot)

Fig 14.69 *Major features involved in the clotting process*

Fig 14.70 (below) *A red blood cell enmeshed in fibrin in a blood clot*

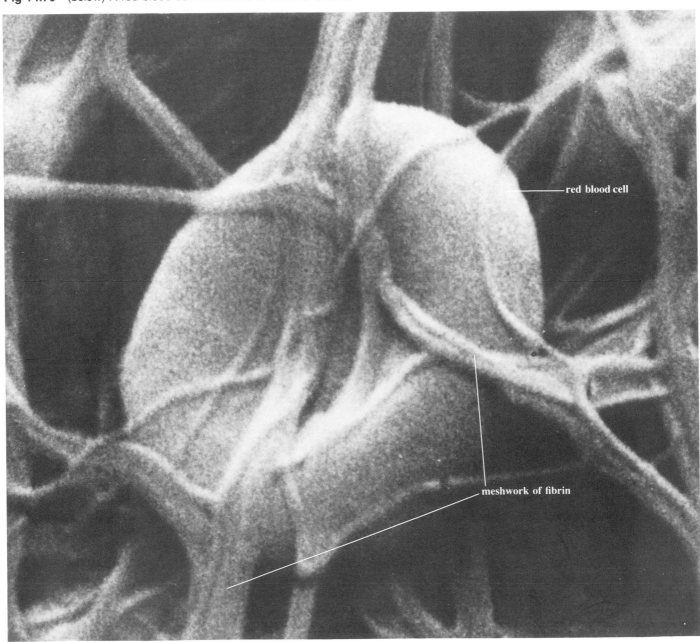

red blood cell

meshwork of fibrin

fibrinogen has been removed from the plasma, the fluid which remains is called **serum**. Blood cells become trapped in the meshwork (fig 14.70) and a blood clot is formed. It dries to form a scab which acts to prevent further blood loss, and as a mechanical barrier to the entry of pathogens.

Because the clotting process is so elaborate, it means that the absence or low concentration of any of the essential clotting factors could produce excessive bleeding. Such a condition is known as **haemophilia**. For example, if an essential factor necessary for the action of thromboplastin is absent or only present in minute amounts, the individual will bleed profusely from any minor cut. Haemophilia is due to an inheritable gene mutation and is transmitted on an X chromosome. The condition is usually seen only in males, with females being carriers, since the abnormal allele is carried on the X chromosome and is recessive to the normal allele on the other X chromosome (section 23.6.1).

Clotting does not occur in undamaged blood vessels because the lining of the vessels is very smooth and does not promote platelet or cell rupture. Also present are substances which actively prevent clotting. One of these is heparin, present in low concentrations in the plasma and produced by most cells found in the connective tissues and the liver. It serves to prevent the conversion of prothrombin into thrombin, and fibrinogen to fibrin and is widely used clinically as an anticoagulant.

If a clot does form within the blood circulation it is called a **thrombus** and leads to a medical condition known as **thrombosis**. This may happen if the endothelium of a blood vessel is damaged and the roughness of the damaged area promotes platelet breakdown and sets in motion the clotting process. Coronary thrombosis, a thrombus developing in the coronary artery of the heart, is particularly dangerous and can lead to a swift death.

Phagocytosis

This function is generally carried out by neutrophils. These are amoeboid cells which are attracted to areas where cell and tissue damage has occurred. The stimulus for this migration appears to be some of the chemicals liberated by the ruptured blood cells and tissues. The neutrophils are able to recognise any invading bacteria. This capability is enhanced by plasma proteins called **opsonins**, which become attached to the surfaces of the bacteria and in some way make them more recognisable. Then the bacteria are engulfed in an amoeboid fashion and a phagosome is formed (fig 14.71). Small lysosomes fuse with the phagosome, forming a phagolysosome. Lysozyme and other hydrolytic enzymes, together with acid, are poured into the phagolysosome from the lysosomes and the bacteria are digested. Ultimately the soluble products of bacterial digestion are absorbed into the surrounding cytoplasm of the neutrophil.

Neutrophils are able to squeeze through the walls of blood capillaries, a process called **diapedesis**, and move about in the tissue spaces. In organs such as the liver,

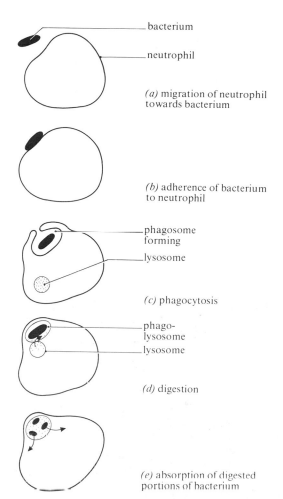

(a) migration of neutrophil towards bacterium

(b) adherence of bacterium to neutrophil

(c) phagocytosis

(d) digestion

(e) absorption of digested portions of bacterium

Fig 14.71 *Phagocytosis of a bacterium by a neutrophil*

spleen and lymph nodes, large resident phagocytes, usually termed **macrophages**, are present. Their role is to engulf toxic foreign particles as well as microbes, and to retain them for long periods of time, often permanently. In this way infection can often be localised. The macrophages together with the neutrophils form the body's reticuloendothelial system.

Inflammation

When an area of the body is wounded, the localised reaction of the tissue surrounding the wound is to become swollen and painful. This is called inflammation and is due to the escape of chemicals, including histamine and 5-hydroxytryptamine, from the damaged tissues. Collectively they cause local vasodilation of capillaries. This increases the amount of blood in the area and raises the temperature locally. Permeability of the capillaries is also increased, permitting escape of plasma into the surrounding tissues and a consequent swelling of the area, a condition known as **oedema**. This plasma contains bacteriocidal factors, antibodies and neutrophils, all of which help to combat spread of infection. Fibrinogen is also present to assist blood clotting if necessary, and the excess tissue fluid tends to dilute and negate any potential toxic irritants.

Wound healing

Towards the end of the inflammatory phase, cells called fibroblasts appear and secrete collagen. This is a fibrous protein and becomes linked to polysaccharide to form a meshwork of randomly arranged fibrous scar tissue. Vitamin C is important for collagen formation; without it hydroxyl groups cannot be attached to the collagen molecule and so it remains incomplete. After about 14 days the disorganised mass of fibres is reorganised into bundles arranged along the lines of stress of the wound. Numerous small blood vessels begin to ramify through the wound. They function to provide oxygen and nutrients for the cells involved in repairing and healing the wound.

Whilst these processes are going on within the wound, the epidermis around it is also engaged in repair and replacement activity. Some epidermal cells migrate into the wound and ingest much of the debris and fibrin of the blood clot which has formed over the wound. When the epidermal cells meet, they unite to form a continuous layer under the scar. When this is complete the scab sloughs off thus exposing the epidermis to the surrounding atmosphere.

Summary of events

(1) Wound occurs, blood flows.
(2) Clotting process occurs.
(3) Inflammation occurs.
(4) White cells migrate into wound. They absorb foreign matter and bacteria, and remove cell debris.
(5) Fibroblasts enter the wound and synthesise collagen which is built up into scar tissue.
(6) Epidermal cells remove any final debris in the wound, and also begin to dismantle the scar.
(7) Epidermis creates a new skin surface in the area of the wound.
(8) Scab sloughs off.

If the wound is small, phagocytosis is usually sufficient to cope with any pathogenic invasion. However, if there is considerable damage, the immune response of the body is put into action.

14.14 The immune system

Immunity has been defined by Sir Macfarlane Burnet as

'the capacity to recognise the intrusion of material foreign to the body and to mobilise cells and cell products to help remove that particular sort of foreign material with greater speed and effectiveness'.

Basic definitions

An **antibody** is a molecule synthesised by an animal in response to the presence of foreign substances for which it has a high affinity. Each antibody is a protein molecule called an **immunoglobulin** (formerly globulin). Its structure consists of two heavy H-chains of 50 000–60 000 relative molecular mass, and two light L-chains of 23 000 relative molecular mass. Functionally the antibody has a constant and variable part, the variable part acting something like a key which specifically fits into a lock (fig 14.72). Each organism can produce thousands of antibodies with different specificities, recognising all kinds of foreign substances.

The name **antigen** or **immunogen** is given to the foreign material that elicits antibody formation. Antigen usually takes the form of a protein or polysaccharide structure on the surface of microbial organisms or as a free molecule. Two systems of immunity have been developed by mammals, a cell-mediated immune response and a humoral response.

The division of labour in the immune system is caused by the development of two types of lymphocytes, the T and B cells. Both types arise from precursor cells in the bone marrow. The influence of the thymus gland is essential in making the T cells immunologically competent, and it is thought that the placenta, foetal liver and bone marrow exert a similar influence over the development of the B cells. Within each type there is an enormous capacity for recognising each of the millions of antigens that exist. When an antibody–antigen reaction occurs it serves to fix

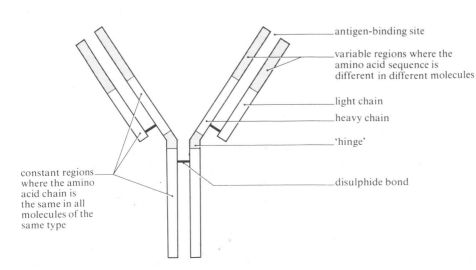

constant regions where the amino acid chain is the same in all molecules of the same type

antigen-binding site

variable regions where the amino acid sequence is different in different molecules

light chain

heavy chain

'hinge'

disulphide bond

Fig 14.72 *Immunoglobulin antibody molecule. Antigens are bound between the light and heavy chains of the variable regions. (From M. Cooper & A. Lawton (1972) The development of the immune system, Scientific American)*

and nullify the action of the antigen, thereby preventing it from acting upon the body in a harmful way.

Cell-mediated response. T cells possessing membrane receptors which recognise antigen are stimulated to proliferate and produce a clone of T cells. These cells then either combat micro-organisms and/or effect the rejection of foreign tissues.

Humoral immune response. B cells recognise antigen in a similar way to T cells. However their response is different. They are stimulated to proliferate and form a plasma cell clone. The plasma cells synthesise and liberate antibodies into the blood plasma and tissue fluid. Here the antibodies adhere to the surfaces of bacteria and speed up their phagocytosis, or combine with and neutralise toxins produced by micro-organisms.

14.14.1　The thymus gland and the development of T cells

The thymus gland is situated in the thorax under the sternum and close to the ventral side of the heart. It begins to function during the embryonic period of the individual and is at its most active at the time of, and just after, birth. After the period of weaning it decreases in size and soon ceases to function.

Evidence that the thymus gland is important in the development of the immune response can be demonstrated by the following experiments.

(1) Removal of the gland from a newborn mouse results in death from a chronic deficiency of lymphocytes in its tissue fluid and blood.

(2) Tissue from another mouse grafted onto an experimental newborn mouse with the gland removed is unable to recognise and react with antigens.

(3) If the thymus gland is removed from a much older mouse, this mouse suffers no adverse effects.

The stem cells of the bone marrow, which give rise to T lymphocytes, must pass through the tissue of the thymus gland before they can become fully functional. The mechanism employed for the maturation of T lymphocytes has yet to be clearly understood, but it is known that the thymus secretes a hormone called **thymosin** which may promote T lymphocyte maturation. However, the role of the thymus as an endocrine organ has yet to be clearly established. The spleen and other lymph glands possess small numbers of lymphocytes at birth.

The cortex of the thymus gland is packed with lymphocytes, and those resident in the gland are called **thymocytes**, in order to distinguish them from the T lymphocytes circulating in the blood and body fluids (fig 14.73). Most thymocytes are immature, but a few are capable of reacting with antigen. When they do, they proliferate and manufacture complex molecules called **lymphokines** which aid in the attack and elimination of foreign particles. Mature, antigen-specific T lymphocytes are also required to help B lymphocytes mature and produce their antibody.

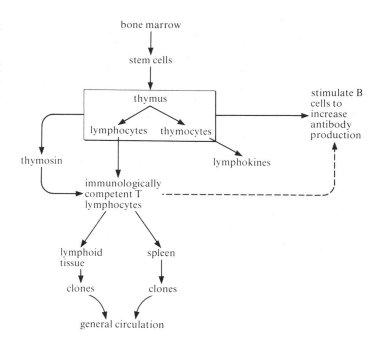

Fig 14.73　*T-cell differentiation and activity*

T cells constantly leave the thymus and pass to the lymph nodes and spleen. Here, if an antigen is recognised by a T cell, the T cell divides to form a clone of cells, all of which can identify and react with the antigen (fig 14.74). An individual T lymphocyte combats foreign cells by producing a receptor for antigen which is built into its plasma membrane. When this sensitised lymphocyte recognises a complementary antigen, it attaches itself to it, rather like a key fitting into a lock, and destroys it. T cells regularly leave the lymphoid tissues to circulate in the blood and tissue fluid. Their constant circulation increases their chances of meeting and combating antigens.

14.14.2　B cell production

Stem cells that will eventually become B lymphocytes must undergo further differentiation outside the bone marrow. This may be in the liver, spleen or lymph nodes.

When surface receptors (immunoglobulins) on the B lymphocytes detect complementary antigens, the B lymphocytes are stimulated to divide repeatedly and differentiate into plasma cell clones and memory cells (fig 14.74). The plasma cells, being genetically identical with each other, proceed to synthesise large quantities of antibody of the same kind.

These antibody-producing cells live for only a few days, but during that time they are able to synthesise and secrete nearly 2 000 identical antibody molecules per second.

The lymphatic memory cells are important in activating the body's response to a second infection of the antigen. Very little is known about memory cells, only that they exist and that in some way they enable an individual who has been exposed to an antigen once to respond more

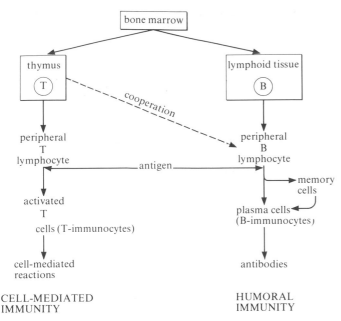

Fig 14.74 *Comparison of cell-mediated and humoral immunity*

promptly and vigorously in a second encounter. This is called the **secondary response** and it results in a massive outpouring of antibody which quickly neutralises the harmful effect of the antigen (fig 14.76). Thus immunity is achieved. However, it must be remembered that immunity to one antigen does not protect the individual against any other antigens. Each time a new antigen gains entry into the body, the appropriate complementary antibody must be produced if disease is to be prevented.

14.14.3 Classes of immunoglobulins and their biological activities

There are five classes of immunoglobulin antibodies. Each class is determined by the type of heavy chain in its molecule, and demonstrates different activities. The light chains in the immunoglobulins are specified as either **kappa** or **lambda**. Their structural details need not be discussed here. Table 14.13 indicates some of the activities of the immunoglobulins.

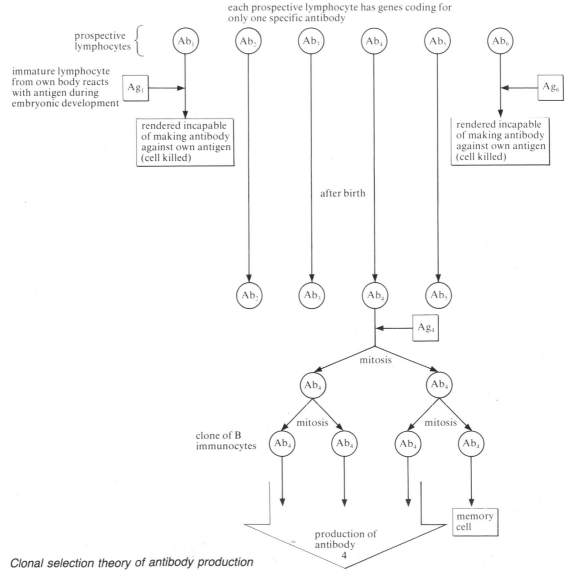

Fig 14.75 *Clonal selection theory of antibody production*

Table 14.13 Classes of immunoglobulins and their biological activities.

Immuno-globulin	Heavy chain	Activity
IgM	mu	First class of antibody to appear in the serum after injection of antigen. It initiates the body's primary response
IgG	gamma 1 ,, 2 ,, 3 ,, 4	Principal antibody in serum. Initiates the body's secondary response
IgA	alpha 1 ,, 2	Major class of antibody in external secretions such as saliva, tears, bronchial and intestinal mucus. Operates as body's first line of defence against bacterial and viral antigens
IgD	delta	Little secreted. It is membrane-bound, but its function is as yet unknown
IgE	epsilon	Possibly involved in reactions to allergens. Functions otherwise unknown

14.14.4 The clonal selection theory of antibody formation

This theory was developed by Jerne, Burnet, Talmage and Lederberg in the 1950s and is generally accepted as a working model for antibody production (fig 14.75). Its essential points are as follows.

(1) There exists in every individual a very wide range of lymphocytes, each of which is capable of recognising only one specific antigen.

(2) The specificity of an antibody (which is a protein) is determined by its amino acid sequence, which in turn is determined by the lymphocyte's own unique DNA base sequence. Therefore the ability to synthesise a specific antibody is predetermined before the cell ever meets the antigen.

(3) Small amounts of antibody are produced by each cell as it matures and some of it becomes interlocked into its plasma membrane where it acts as a receptor site for its complementary antigen.

(4) It is thought that if an immature lymphocyte meets with an antigen corresponding to its antibody during embryonic life, then the lymphocyte is killed. Therefore an animal will not synthesise antibody against its own macromolecules and becomes self-tolerant.

(5) When antigen locks into the receptor site of a mature lymphocyte, somehow the genetic apparatus of the lymphocyte is stimulated to produce antibody. Contact with the antigen is necessary for the lymphocyte to differentiate and divide into a clone of plasma cells synthesising antibody, and into memory cells.

(6) As all plasma cells are genetically identical, they all make the same antibody.

(7) The memory cells persist after the disappearance of the antigen, and in some way retain the capacity to be stimulated by antigen if it reappears. This is called **immunological memory** (fig 14.76), and is responsible for the body's secondary response which generally confers immunity on an animal against the specific antigen.

14.14.5 Types of immunity

Natural passive immunity

Preformed antibodies from one individual are passed into another individual of the same species. This only affords temporary protection against infection, for as the antibodies do their job, or are broken down by the body's natural processes, their number diminishes and protection is slowly lost. For example, antibodies from a mother can cross the placenta and enter her foetus. In this way they provide protection for the baby until its own immune system is fully functional. Passive immunity may also be conferred by colostrum, the initial secretion of the mammary glands, from which antibodies are absorbed from the intestines of the baby.

Acquired passive immunity

Here antibodies which have been preformed in one individual are extracted and then injected into the blood of another individual which may or may not be of the same species. For example, specific antibodies used for combating tetanus and diphtheria are cultured in horses and later injected into Man. They act prophylactically to prevent tetanus and diphtheria respectively. This type of immunity is again short lived.

Natural active immunity

The body manufactures its own antibodies when exposed to an infectious agent. Because memory cells, produced on exposure to the first infection, are able to stimulate the production of massive quantities of antibody when exposed to the same antigen again, this type of immunity is most effective and generally persists for a long time, sometimes even for life (fig 14.76).

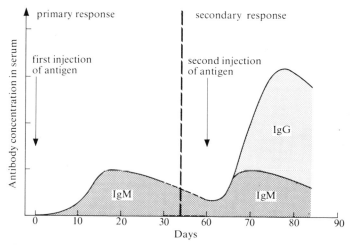

Fig 14.76 *Primary and secondary response to an initial and later dose of antigen. The secondary response is more rapid and intense than the first*

This is achieved by injecting small amounts of antigen, called the **vaccine**, into the body of an individual. The whole process is called **vaccination** or **immunisation**. The small dose of antigen is usually safe because the antigen is either killed or attenuated. This ensures that the individual does not contract the disease itself, but is stimulated to manufacture antibodies against the antigen. Often a second, booster injection is given and this stimulates a much quicker production of antibody which is long lasting and which protects the individual from the disease for a considerable time. Several types of vaccine are currently in use.

(1) **Toxoids.** Exotoxins produced by tetanus and diphtheria bacilli are detoxified with formaldehyde, yet their antigen properties remain unimpaired. Therefore vaccination with the toxoid will stimulate antibody production without producing symptoms of the disease.

(2) **Killed organisms.** Some dead viruses and bacteria are able to provoke a normal antigen–antibody response and are used for immunisation purposes.

(3) **Attenuated organisms.** Modified but living organisms are injected into the body. They are able to multiply without producing disease. Attenuation may be achieved by culturing the organisms at higher temperatures than normal or by adding specific chemicals to the culture medium for long periods of time. Attenuated vaccines for tuberculosis, measles, rubella and poliomyelitis are now in general use.

14.14.6 Blood groups

When a patient receives a blood transfusion it is imperative that he receives blood that is compatible with his own. If it is incompatible, a type of immune response occurs. This is because the donor's red cell membranes possess mucopolysaccharides known as **agglutinogens** which act as antigens and react with antibodies (agglutinins) in the recipient's plasma. The result is that the donor's cells are agglutinated (the cells link or attach to each other when the antigens on the surface of their cells interact with the antibodies). Two agglutinogens exist and they are named A and B respectively. The complementary plasma agglutinins are named a and b, and are present in the plasma all of the time. They are not produced in response to the donor's agglutinogen as is the case in the immune reactions already studied. A person with a specific agglutinogen in the red cells does not possess the corresponding agglutinin in the plasma. For example, anyone with agglutinogen A in the red cell membranes has no agglutinin a in the plasma and is classified under blood group A. If only B agglutinogens are present the blood group is B. Should both agglutinogens be present the blood group will be AB, whilst if no agglutinogens are present the blood group is designated O (table 14.14).

When transfusion occurs it is important to know what

Table 14.14 Blood groups.

Blood group	O	A	B	AB
Percentage of population	46%	42%	9%	3%
Agglutinogen	–	A	B	A + B
Agglutinin	a + b	b	a	–

Fig 14.77 *Interactions between human blood groups. Cell agglutinogens are denoted by capital letters, agglutinins by small letters*

will happen to the cells of the donor. If there is a likelihood of them being agglutinated by the recipient's plasma antibodies then transfusion should not take place.

Fig 14.77 indicates the consequences of mixing different blood groups together. Individuals with blood group O are termed **universal donors** because their blood can be given to anyone. It possesses cells which will not be agglutinated by the recipient's plasma agglutinins. Although group O possesses a and b agglutinins there will be very little agglutination of the recipient's cells because the donated plasma is diluted so much by the recipient's blood that it is ineffective in its agglutination activity. Individuals with group AB can receive blood from anyone and are called **universal recipients**. However, they can only donate to blood group AB.

14.14.7 The rhesus factor

Of the total population, 85% possess red cells containing an agglutinogen called the rhesus factor and are termed **rhesus positive**. The remainder of the population lack the rhesus agglutinogen and are therefore regarded as **rhesus negative**. Rhesus negative blood does not usually contain rhesus agglutinins in its plasma. However, if rhesus positive blood enters a rhesus negative individual the recipient responds by manufacturing rhesus agglutinins.

The practical importance of this observation is made obvious when a rhesus negative mother bears a rhesus positive child. During the later stages of the pregnancy, fragments of the rhesus positive cells of the foetus may enter the mother's circulation and cause the mother to produce rhesus agglutinins. These can infiltrate the foetus and destroy foetal red cells. Normally the agglutinins are not formed in large enough quantities to unduly affect the first-born child. However, subsequent rhesus positive children can suffer chronic destruction of their red cells. A rhesus baby is usually premature, anaemic and jaundiced, and its blood needs to be completely replaced by a transfusion of healthy blood. This treatment may now be undertaken whilst the baby is still in the womb.

Protection against the rhesus positive–negative reaction

(1) Consider a rhesus negative mother of blood group O, carrying a rhesus positive child of any blood group other than O. Should foetal cells enter the maternal circulation, the mother's a and b agglutinins will destroy them before the mother has time to manufacture anti-rhesus agglutinins.

(2) If an intravenous injection of anti-rhesus agglutinins, called **anti-D**, is given to a rhesus negative mother within 72 h of her giving birth, sensitisation of the rhesus negative mother by rhesus positive foetal cells is prevented. Apparently the anti-D attaches itself to the foetal cells which are in the mother's circulation and affects them in such a way that they are not recognised by the mother's antibody forming cells and hence the antibody process in the mother is not set in motion (fig 14.78).

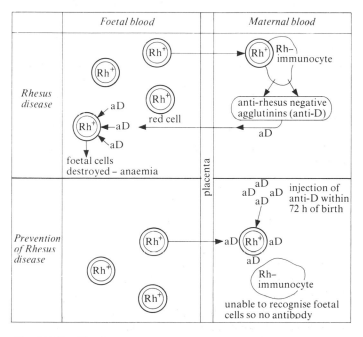

Fig 14.78 *The basis of Rhesus disease and its prevention. (From Burnet (1978)* Genes, dreams and realities, *Pelican)*

14.14.8 Transplantation

Replacement of diseased tissues or organs by healthy ones is called transplantation and is a technique used increasingly in surgery today. However, when foreign tissue is inserted into or onto another individual it is rejected by the recipient because it acts as an antigen, so stimulating the immune response in the recipient. The following terms are used for the different kinds of transplantation.

Autograft – tissue grafted from one area to another on the same individual.

Isograft – a graft between two genetically identical individuals such as identical twins.

Allograft – a tissue grafted from one individual to another individual of the same species but of different genetic constitution.

Xenograft – a graft between individuals of different species such as from pig to Man.

Only allografting will be discussed here.

As blood is a fluid tissue, then simple blood transfusion can be regarded as an allograft. Here rejection results in agglutination of the donor's red cells as discussed earlier. When rejection of tissue, such as skin, occurs the following sequence of events takes place.

(1) The skin allograft initially develops blood vessels in the first 2–3 days and generally looks healthy.

(2) During the next six days its vascularisation decreases, and a great number of T lymphocytes and monocytes (sections 14.14.1 and 14.11.2) gather in the vicinity of the graft.

(3) Two days later the graft cells begin to die and the graft is eventually cast off.

Prevention of graft rejection

There are several means of preventing graft rejection currently in use, listed as follows.

(1) Tissue matching – this is an obvious and necessary precaution to take prior to any surgery.

(2) Exposure of bone marrow and lymph tissues to X-irradiation tends to inhibit blood cell production and therefore slows down rejection.

(3) Immunosuppression – here the principle is to use agents which inhibit the entire activity of the immune system. When this occurs graft rejection is delayed, but the main problem with this technique is that the patient becomes susceptible to all other kinds of infections. It has also been shown that immunosuppression may make the patients more prone to develop cancer.

If the disadvantages of non-specific immunosuppression are to be overcome then ways must be found of suppressing only the T cells response to the antigens of the graft. In this way the rest of the patient's immune system would remain unimpaired and continue to function normally. The most promising approach is to treat the patient (or his bone marrow) with antibody that recognises and destroys the T lymphocytes responsible for the graft rejection.

14.14.9 The interferon system

Interferon is a generic term which it is now realised applies to a number of proteins with similar properties. Human interferons have been divided into three groups α, β and γ depending on which type of cell they are produced by. The interferon α group consists of several species. They are all of similar molecular mass (about 20 000).

The most widely studied property of interferon is its ability to 'interfere' with the replication of viruses. It is produced in mammalian and avian cells in response to viral attack and appears to be an effective anti-viral agent on most types of cell against all viruses to a greater or lesser extent.

When a cell is attacked by a virus, a number of things happen. The virus will multiply, but at the same time the host cell is stimulated to produce interferon (fig 14.79). This is released from the cell and when it comes into contact with adjacent cells it renders them resistant to virus attack. To do this interferon triggers a series of events which lead to an inhibition of viral protein synthesis, viral RNA transcription and in some cases assembly and release of virus particles. Thus interferon, itself, is not anti-viral but brings about an 'anti-viral state' which involves cellular changes that then inhibit virus replication. The production of interferon can be stimulated by a whole variety of factors apart from virus attack, such as some inactivated viruses, double-stranded RNA, man-made double-stranded oligonucleotides and bacterial endotoxins. It would seem that interferon is produced as a result of an 'abuse' of the cell.

Interferon is biologically extremely active. Mouse interferon has an activity of 2×10^9 units per milligram of protein, where one unit will bring about a 50% reduction in virus production. This means that as little as one molecule per cell may be necessary to render a cell resistant to virus infection.

The interferons have a wide range of other effects including inhibiting cell growth. Recent results show that this effect may mean that they will be useful as anti-cancer agents under certain circumstances. There are also effects on the immune system and marked changes in the properties of cell membranes.

Thus it would seem that the interferon system may play an important role in the protection of the body against viruses.

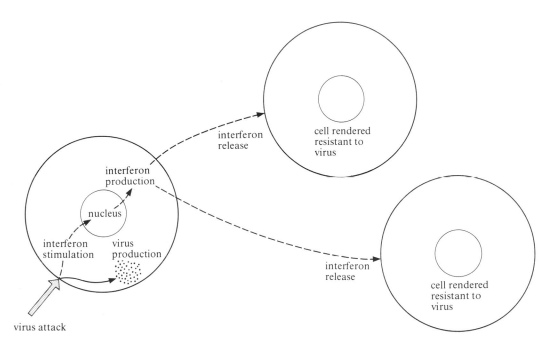

Fig 14.79 *Interferon production and activity*

Chapter Fifteen

Coordination and control in plants

Plants, like animals, need some form of internal coordination if their growth and development is to proceed in an orderly fashion, with suitable responses to their environment. Unlike animals, plants do not possess nervous systems and rely entirely on chemical coordination. Their responses are therefore slower and they often involve growth. Growth, in turn, can result in movement of an organ. In this chapter plant movements will be examined before studying the various ways in which plants coordinate their activities.

15.1 Plant movements

It is a characteristic of all but a few unicellular plants that they do not show locomotion (movement of the entire organism). However, movements of individual plant organs are possible and are modified by the sensitivity of the plant to external stimuli. Movements induced by external stimuli fall into three categories: tropisms (tropic movements), nasties (nastic movements) and taxes (tactic movements).

> **15.1** What is the basic reason for the fact that animals show locomotion whereas plants do not?

15.1.1 Tropisms

A **tropism** is a movement of part of a plant in response to, and directed by, an external stimulus. The movement is almost always a growth movement. Tropic responses are described as positive or negative depending on whether growth is towards or away from the stimulus respectively. Some examples of tropisms are shown in table 15.1.

> **15.2** Complete a fourth column to table 15.1 to show for each response how it is advantageous to the plant involved.
>
> **15.3** How could growth be modified to cause a tendril to coil round a solid object?

Phototropism and geotropism will be discussed in more detail later in this chapter (sections 15.2.1 and 15.2.2).

Table 15.1 Examples of tropisms.

Stimulus	Type of tropism	Examples
Light	Phototropism	Shoots and coleoptiles positively phototropic. Some roots negatively phototropic, e.g. adventitious roots of climbers like ivy
Gravity	Geotropism	Shoots and coleoptiles negatively geotropic. Roots positively geotropic. Rhizomes, runners, dicotyledonous leaves **diageotropic***. Lateral roots, stem branches **plagiogeotropic***
Chemical	Chemotropism	Hyphae of some fungi positively chemotropic, e.g. *Mucor*. Pollen tubes positively chemotropic in response to chemical produced at micropyle of ovule
Water	Hydrotropism (special kind of chemotropism)	Roots and pollen tubes positively hydrotropic
Solid surface or touch	Haptotropism (thigmotropism)	Tendrils positively haptotropic, e.g. leaves of pea. Central tentacles of sundew, an insectivorous plant positively haptotropic (section 9.12.2)
Air (oxygen)	Aerotropism (special kind of chemotropism)	Pollen tubes negatively aerotropic

*diageotropism: growth at 90° to gravity, that is horizontal growth.
plagiogeotropism: growth at some other angle to gravity, that is not horizontal or directly towards or away from gravity.

15.1.2 Taxes

A **taxis** is a movement of an entire cell or organism (that is locomotion) in response to, and directed by, an external stimulus. As with tropisms they can be described as positive or negative, and can be further classified according to the nature of the stimulus. Note that this kind of movement is not confined to plants. Examples are given in table 15.2.

> **15.4** Design an experiment to demonstrate the preferred light intensity of *Euglena* or *Chlamydomonas* in phototaxis.

Table 15.2 Examples of taxes.

Stimulus	Taxis	Examples
Light	Phototaxis	Positive: *Euglena* swims towards light, chloroplasts move towards light Negative: Earthworms, blowfly larvae, woodlice and cockroaches move away from light
Chemical	Chemotaxis	Positive: Sperms of liverworts, mosses and ferns swim towards substances released by the ovum, motile bacteria move towards various food substances Negative: Mosquitoes avoid insect repellent
Air (oxygen)	Aerotaxis (special kind of chemotaxis)	Positive: motile aerobic bacteria move towards oxygen
Gravity	Geotaxis	Positive: Planula larvae of some coelenterates swim towards sea bed Negative: Ephyra larvae of some coelenterates swim away from sea bed
Magnetic field	Magnetotaxis	Certain motile bacteria
Resistance	Rheotaxis	Positive: *Planaria* move against water current, moths and butterflies fly into the wind

15.5 Fig 15.1 illustrates the distribution of motile bacteria 10 min after being placed under a cover-slip with a filament of a green alga. (*a*) Name a genus of a suitable alga for the experiment. (*b*) Put forward a hypothesis to account for the final distribution of the bacteria. (*c*) How could you check your hypothesis?

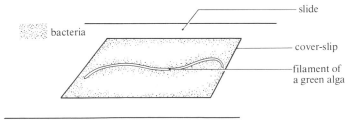

Fig 15.1 *Distribution of motile bacteria on a slide*

15.1.3 Nasties

A **nasty** is a non-directional movement of part of a plant in response to an external stimulus. The direction of movement is determined by the structure of the responding organ. Movement is the result of growth or a turgor change and small movements are typically amplified by the particular positioning of the responding cells.

The 'sleep movements' (**nyctinasty**) of certain flowers and leaves, whereby they open and close in response to light intensity (**photonasty**) or temperature (**thermonasty**), are nastic because they are merely triggered by external stimuli and are directed internally. Some flowers, such as crocus and tulip, close at night by the lower sides of petals growing more rapidly (**hyponasty**). Opening is caused by more rapid growth of the upper sides (**epinasty**). Many leaves or leaflets, particularly of leguminous plants, such as clover and *Mimosa*, have structures called pulvini. A **pulvinus** is a swelling at the base of a petiole or leaflet which possesses large parenchyma cells. Rapid turgor pressure changes in these cells result in the pulvinus acting as a hinge and bringing about movement.

Haptonastic movements, where the stimulus is touch, are among the most fascinating of plant movements, since they include rapid and elaborate responses. The well-known 'sensitive plant' *Mimosa pudica* is sensitive to touch as well as a variety of other stimuli. It exhibits normal sleep movements but responds very rapidly to shock (**seismonasty**) such as a sharp blow, injury, or sudden change in temperature or light intensity. If leaflets at the tip are shocked, they fold upwards in seconds. If the stimulus is strong or sustained, successive pairs of leaflets fold up and the stimulus eventually passes through the whole leaf, resulting in the petiole drooping (fig 15.2). The stimulus will pass in the reverse direction if the stem is stimulated. Fig 15.2 shows the three sites at which pulvini are found. The stimulus is thought to be transmitted by a hormone moving through the xylem; electrical changes are associated with its passage but there is no nervous system.

Insectivorous plants show some of the most elaborate movements in the plant kingdom, some of which are haptonastic.

15.1.4 Kinesis

A type of locomotory response not so far mentioned is **kinesis**. Since this is virtually confined to the animal kingdom it is discussed in chapter 16 with animal behaviour.

15.2 Plant growth substances

Chemical coordination in animals is controlled by **hormones**, chemicals working in minute concentrations at sites some distance from their sites of synthesis. Plants are coordinated by chemicals which do not necessarily move from their sites of synthesis and hence, by definition, should not always be termed hormones. In view of this and because their effects are usually on some aspect of growth, they are called **growth substances**. It is also important to stress that the precise mechanisms of action of the plant growth substances so far discovered are far from clear and that analogies with the better understood animal hormones may be misleading. Plant growth substances are certainly essential for plant development, but to what extent they act

Fig 15.2 *Response of the 'sensitive plant'* (Mimosa pudica) *to shock.* (left) *before* (right) *after*

as 'triggers' for changes in growth or as 'integrating chemicals', modifying processes triggered by other unknown events, is not certain. It should be borne in mind that growth can be divided into the three stages of cell division, cell enlargement and cell differentiation (specialisation) and that these have particular locations in plants (section 21.6). It can be expected, therefore, that the action and distribution of different plant growth substances will reflect this. Five major types of growth substance are recognised: auxins, gibberellins, cytokinins, abscisic acid and ethene (ethylene). Generally speaking, cytokinins are associated with cell division, auxins and gibberellins with cell enlargement and differentiation, abscisic acid with resting states (such as lateral buds) and ethene with senescence (ageing).

In this chapter, each type of growth substance will first be discussed separately, and then key stages in the life cycle of a plant will be discussed to emphasise the fact that growth substances often work in association with each other to achieve their effects.

15.2.1 Auxins and phototropism

Discovery of auxins

The discovery of auxins was the result of investigations into phototropism that began with the experiments of Charles Darwin and his son Frances. Using oat coleoptiles as convenient material (fig 15.3), they showed that the growth of shoots towards light was the result of some 'influence' being transmitted from the shoot tip to the region of growth behind it. Some of their experiments are summarised in

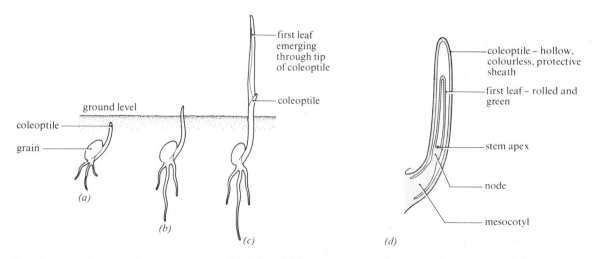

Fig 15.3 *Germination of a typical grass seedling: (a) (b) and (c) stages in germination, (d) section of coleoptile at stage* (b)

543

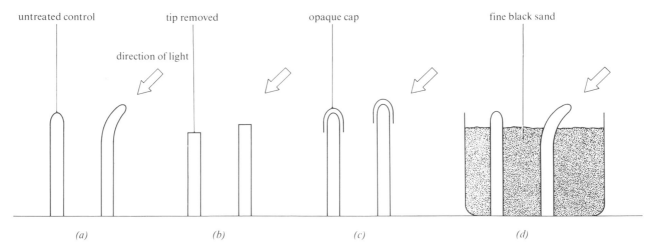

untreated control | tip removed | opaque cap | fine black sand

direction of light

(a)   *(b)*   *(c)*   *(d)*

Fig 15.4 *Darwin's experiments on phototropism using oat coleoptiles. (a), (b), (c) and (d) separate experiments showing treatment* (left) *and result* (right)

fig 15.4, the diagrams representing results obtained from many seedlings.

> **15.6** (*a*) List carefully the conclusions you could draw from experiments (*a*)–(*d*) in fig 15.4, given that the curvature was due to growth in the region behind the tip. (*b*) Why was experiment (*c*) necessary, bearing in mind the result from experiment (*b*)?

If the tropic response is analysed in terms of the following: stimulus → receptor → transmission → effector → response, then the largest gap in our knowledge remains the nature of the transmission. In 1913 the Danish plant physiologist Boysen-Jensen added to our knowledge. Fig 15.5 summarises some of his experiments.

> **15.7** What extra information is provided by Boysen-Jensen's experiments?
>
> **15.8** If these experiments were repeated in uniform light, draw diagrams to show what results you would expect. Give reasons for your answers.

In 1928 the Dutch plant physiologist Went finally proved the existence of a chemical transmitter. His aim had been to intercept and collect the chemical as it passed back from the tip and to demonstrate its effectiveness in a variety of tests. He reasoned that a small diffusing molecule should pass freely into a small block of agar jelly, whose structure is such that relatively large spaces exist between its molecules. Fig 15.6 illustrates some of his experiments.

> **15.9** What would you conclude from the results shown in fig 15.6?
>
> **15.10** What result would you expect if the treated block had been placed on the right side of the decapitated coleoptile in experiment (*b*)?

A further experiment of note carried out by Went is illustrated in fig 15.7. In control experiments the tip was exposed to uniform light or darkness before transfer of agar blocks, and the degree of curvature induced by blocks A and B was the same. Unilateral illumination of the tip, however, resulted in unequal distribution of the chemical in blocks A and B (fig 15.7). Not only does this support the

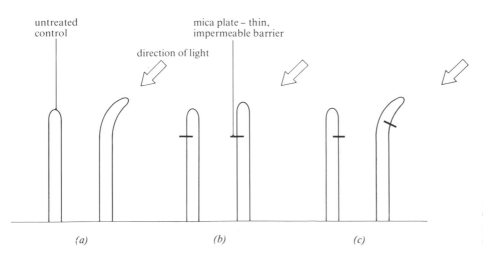

untreated control | mica plate – thin, impermeable barrier

direction of light

(a)   *(b)*   *(c)*

Fig 15.5 *Boysen-Jensen's experiments on phototropism using oat coleoptiles, (a), (b) and (c), separate experiments showing treatment* (left) *and result* (right)

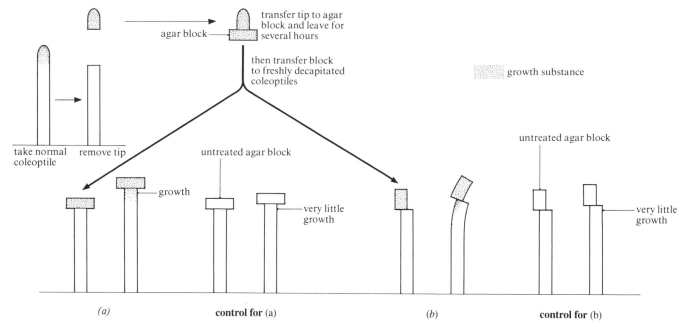

Fig 15.6 *Went's experiments, (a) and (b), separate experiments showing treatment (left) and result (right). Control experiments are shown alongside. All treatments were carried out in darkness or uniform light*

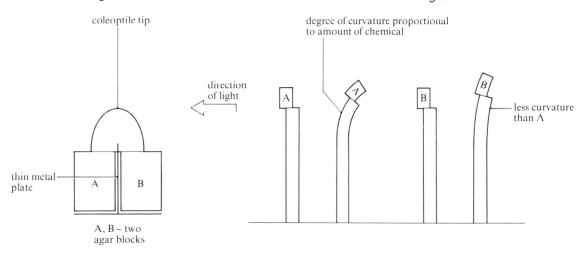

Fig 15.7 *Went's experiment showing effect of unilateral light on distribution of the chemical (auxin)*

conclusions from Boysen-Jensen's experiments about the effect of light on the distribution of the chemical, but it shows how a test for measuring the amount of the chemical present, that is a bioassay, can be set up. A **bioassay** is an experiment in which the amount of a substance is found by measuring its effects in a biological system. Went showed that the degree of curvature of oat coleoptiles was directly proportional to the concentration of the chemical (at normal physiological levels).

The chemical was subsequently named 'auxin' (from the Greek *auxein*, to increase). In 1934 it was identified as indoleacetic acid (IAA). IAA was soon found to be widely distributed in plants and to be intimately concerned with cell enlargement. Fig 15.8 summarises present beliefs concerning the movement of IAA during unilateral illumination of coleoptiles. It should be pointed out, however, that the coleoptile is the simplest system so far

studied and that others appear to be more complex. Also, there is little evidence for the development of auxin gradients in the critical period before the response is measured.

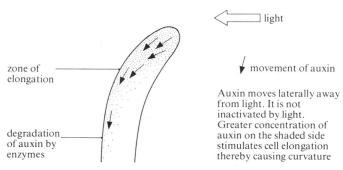

Fig 15.8 *Hypothesis for effect of unilateral illumination on distribution of auxin in a coleoptile*

Structure of IAA

The structure of IAA is shown in fig 15.9.

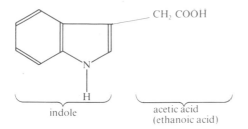

Fig 15.9 *Structure of IAA (indoleacetic acid)*

Other chemicals with similar structures and activity were soon isolated, and some such substances have been synthesised, making a whole class of plant growth substances called auxins. Some of these are discussed below in section 15.2.5.

Synthesis and distribution of auxins

Auxins are made continuously in the shoot apex and young leaves. Movement away from the tip is described as basipetal (from apex to base of the organ) and polar (in one direction only). It moves, apparently by diffusion, from cell to cell and is eventually inactivated and degraded by enzymes. Long-distance transport can also occur via the vascular system (mainly phloem) from shoots to roots. A little auxin is probably made in roots. The effects of different auxin concentrations on shoot growth can be investigated by means of an experiment such as experiment 15.1.

Experiment 15.1: To investigate the effects of indoleacetic acid (IAA) on the growth of oat coleoptiles

The aim of the experiment is to investigate the effect of various concentrations of IAA on growth of oat coleoptiles. Growth is affected by white light and therefore cutting and transferring of coleoptiles during the experiment should be carried out under red light or in the minimum amount of light possible. Sucrose solution is used in the experiment as energy will be required for growth, and sucrose is an energy source. The apical tip (3 mm) of each coleoptile is removed in order to prevent natural auxins produced by the coleoptile from having an effect on growth.

Materials

germinating oat seedlings with coleoptiles at least 1.5 cm long (Soak 100 oat grains in water overnight, place the soaked seeds on damp paper towelling in a dish, cover the dish with aluminium foil and place in the dark to germinate (five days in an incubator at 20 °C). In order to obtain the 60 coleoptiles required for each experiment, at least 100 grains should be soaked to allow for germination failure.)
6 test-tubes in a test-tube rack
6 petri dishes + lids
5 × 5 cm³ graduated pipettes
25 cm³ measuring cylinder or 10 cm³ graduated pipette
coleoptile cutter (fig 15.10)
paint brush
stock IAA solution (1 g dm⁻³) (IAA is not readily soluble in water and is therefore first dissolved in ethanol: dissolve 1 g of IAA in 2 cm³ ethanol and dilute to 900 cm³ with distilled water. Warm the solution to 80 °C and keep at this temperature for 5 min. Make up to 1 dm³ with distilled water. Adjust quantities according to final volume required.)
2% sucrose solution
distilled water

Method

(1) Take six test-tubes and six petri dishes and label them A–F.
(2) Add 18 cm³ of 2% sucrose solution to each test-tube.
(3) Using a clean 5 cm³ pipette, add 2 cm³ of IAA solution to tube A and mix the two solutions thoroughly.
(4) Using a fresh pipette transfer 2 cm³ of solution from tube A to tube B and mix the contents of tube B thoroughly.
(5) Using a fresh pipette each time, transfer 2 cm³ from tube B to tube C, mix, then 2 cm³ from tube C to tube D, mix, then 2 cm³ from tube D to tube E.
(6) Add 2 cm³ distilled water to tube F.
(7) Transfer the solutions from tubes A–F to petri dishes A–F.
(8) Take 60 germinated oat seedlings and cut 10 mm lengths of coleoptile, starting about 2 mm back from the tips. Use a double-bladed cutter with the blades held exactly 10 mm apart by a series of washers, two nuts and two bolts (see fig 15.10). If the tips of the coleoptiles are placed in a line, several lengths can be cut simultaneously.
(9) Using a paint brush, transfer 10 lengths of coleoptile to each dish avoiding cross contamination of the solutions (the greater the number of coleoptiles used, the more statistically valid the results).
(10) Place a lid on each and incubate the dishes at 25 °C for three days in the dark.
(11) Remeasure the lengths of coleoptiles as accurately as possible.

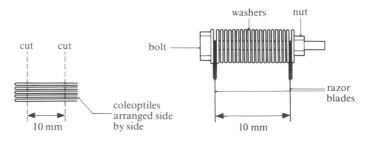

Fig 15.10 *Cutting 10 mm lengths of coleoptiles*

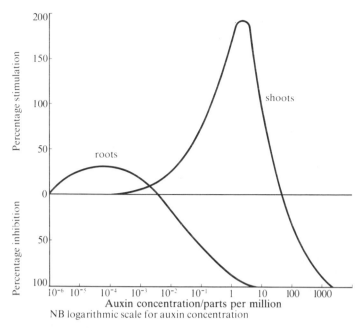

Fig 15.11 *Effect of auxin concentration on growth responses of roots and shoots. Note that concentrations of auxin which stimulate shoot growth inhibit root growth*

(12) Ignoring the largest and smallest figures for each dish, calculate the mean (average) length.

(13) Plot a graph of mean length (vertical axis) against IAA concentration in parts per million (horizontal axis).

> **15.11** What is the concentration in parts per million (ppm) of IAA in each petri dish (1 g dm^{-3} = 1 000 ppm)?

(14) Comment on the results and compare them with fig 15.11. More accurate results can be obtained by combining class results.

15.2.2 Auxins and geotropism

It is a common observation that roots are positively geotropic, that is grow downwards, and shoots are negatively geotropic, that is grow upwards. That gravity is the stimulus responsible can be demonstrated by using a piece of equipment called a **klinostat** (fig 15.12). As the chamber rotates, all parts of the seedling receive, in turn, equal stimulation from gravity. A speed of four revolutions per hour is sufficient to eliminate the one-sided effect of gravity and to cause straight shoot and root growth. A non-rotating control shows the normal response to gravity, with shoot growing up and root growing down. It is important to ensure even illumination during the experiment (or to carry it out in darkness) so that there can be no directional response to light.

The involvement of auxins in geotropism is demonstrated by the experiment shown in fig 15.13, which uses the techniques introduced by Went. Auxin moves out of the horizontally placed coleoptile tip but moves downwards as it does so. The greater auxin concentration on the lower

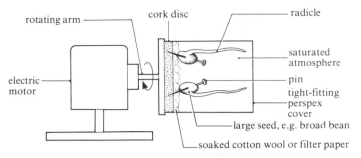

Fig 15.12 *(above) Klinostat showing broad beans after several days growth with rotation*

Fig 15.13 *(below) Effect of gravity on distribution of auxin from a horizontal coleoptile tip*

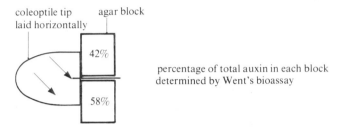

surface of an intact coleoptile would stimulate greater cell elongation here, and hence upward growth.

Decapitation of a root tip removes its sensitivity to gravity, but it is not so easy to demonstrate movement of auxins in roots because very low concentrations are present, and these do not give convincing results in the bioassay described. An interesting result though is obtained from the experiment shown in fig 15.14.

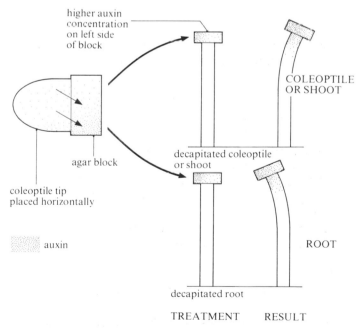

Fig 15.14 *Effect of uneven auxin distribution on growth of decapitated coleoptile and root*

> **15.12** What can you conclude from the experiment shown in fig 15.14?

547

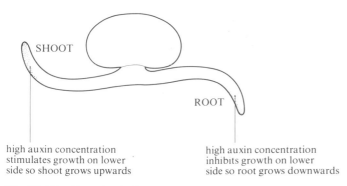

SHOOT

ROOT

high auxin concentration
stimulates growth on lower
side so shoot grows upwards

high auxin concentration
inhibits growth on lower
side so root grows downwards

Fig 15.15 *Hypothesis for redistribution of auxin in a horizontally placed seedling*

Observations of this type led to the hypothesis summarised in fig 15.15, which suggests that the opposite responses of roots and shoots are due to different sensitivities to auxin. Modifications of the hypothesis in the light of recent findings are discussed later in this section.

The different sensitivity of roots to auxin (fig 15.11) could also explain the negative phototropism shown by some; the higher accumulation of auxin on the shaded side would cause inhibition of growth with the result that cells on the light side would elongate faster and the root would grow away from light.

An important aspect of plant growth regulation has thus been revealed. It is not only the nature of the growth substance which is relevant (qualitative control) but the amount of that substance (quantitative control).

The gravity-sensing mechanism

The question now arises as to how the gravity stimulus is detected. Darwin showed that removal of the root cap, the group of large parenchyma cells that protect the root tip as it grows through the soil, abolishes the geotropic response. A section of the root cap reveals the presence of large starch grains contained in amyloplasts within the cells (fig 15.16).

It was suggested as long ago as 1900 that these cells act as **statocytes**, that is gravity receptors, and that the starch grains are **statoliths**, structures which move in response to gravity. The so-called '**starch–statolith hypothesis**' proposes that sedimentation of the starch grains through the cells occurs so that they come to rest on the lower sides of the cells with respect to gravity (fig 15.16). In some unknown way this affects the distribution of growth substances which are known to be produced sometimes in the root apex, sometimes in the root cap and sometimes in both. There is much evidence to support this hypothesis. All plant organs which are sensitive to gravity contain statocytes. They are found, for example, in the vascular bundle sheaths of shoots. Plants from which the starch grains have been removed by certain treatments lose their sensitivity to gravity, but regain it if allowed to make more starch.

15.13 How is this mechanism of gravity detection similar to that in animals?

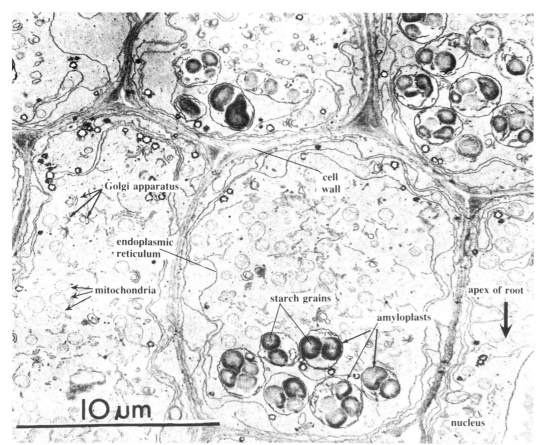

Golgi apparatus

cell wall

endoplasmic reticulum

mitochondria

starch grains

amyloplasts

apex of root

nucleus

10 μm

Fig 15.16 *Electron micrograph of section of root cap showing amyloplasts with starch grains located at the bottoms of the cells*

Modern hypotheses on geotropism

In coleoptiles the gravity response seems to be mediated by auxins as described above, but with most shoots a geotropic response is still obtained if the tip is removed, and there is still doubt as to whether movement of auxin is involved. In roots, auxin redistribution does occur, but probably not dramatically enough to account for the observed changes in growth rates. Transmission of a growth inhibitor from the root cap to the zone of elongation has been shown, but this is not necessarily auxin. Several groups of workers have been unable to find auxin in the root caps of maize seedlings, a common experimental plant. Instead, abscisic acid, a well-known growth inhibitor, has been found. Ethene, another growth inhibitor, could also be involved. Finally, gibberellins (growth promoters) have been found in higher concentrations than normal in the rapidly growing sides of both shoots and roots when they are geotropically stimulated.

> **15.14** What can you conclude from the experiments shown in fig 15.17? Controls, using untreated agar, showed no curvature. When IAA was used instead of abscisic acid no significant curvature was obtained.

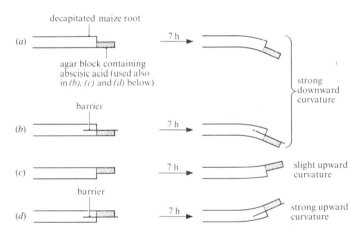

Fig 15.17 *Effect of abscisic acid on geotropic response to decapitated roots. (Based on experiments by Pilet, 1975.)*

15.2.3 Mode of action of auxins

The effect of auxins on cell enlargement is now reasonably well understood. During cell extension the rigid cellulose framework of the cell wall must be loosened. Extension then occurs by a combination of osmotic swelling as water enters the cell and by the laying down of new cell wall material. The orientation of the existing cellulose microfibrils probably helps to determine the direction of extension. 'Wall loosening' is induced by acid conditions, and by auxins. In 1973 four different groups of workers all demonstrated that auxins stimulate hydrogen ion (proton) secretion. This causes a lowering of pH outside the cell (increase in acidity) and hence wall loosening, possibly by an enzyme with a low pH optimum. The ability to maintain a high osmotic potential inside the cell, and availability of water to enter the cell and generate turgor pressure, are also necessary.

15.2.4 Other effects of auxins

Apart from stimulating cell elongation and hence shoot growth, auxins have a number of other important roles in the plant, summarised in table 15.4. Further details of their roles in differentiation, apical dominance, abscission and fruit growth are given later under the appropriate headings.

15.2.5 Commercial applications of auxins

Discovery of IAA led to the synthesis by chemists of a wide range of active compounds with similar structure. Synthetic auxins have proved commercially useful in a variety of ways. They are cheaper than IAA to produce, and often more physiologically active because plants generally do not have the necessary enzymes to break them down. Table 15.3 gives some examples with their structures and summaries of their uses. Chlorine substitutions in the structures often increase activity. Fig 15.18 shows the effect of treating tomatoes with a fruit-setting auxin.

Fig 15.18 *The three large trusses were set by spraying with beta naphthoxy acetic acid. The small one in the bottom left-hand corner was not sprayed – and produced only one normal size tomato*

549

Table 15.3 Commercial applications of auxins.

Type of Auxin	Examples with structures	Uses
Indoles and naphthyls	NAA (naphthalene acetic acid) [structure] —CH₂—COOH (compare with IAA fig 15.9) Indole propionic acid [structure] —COOH	**Fruiting** – help natural fruit set; sometimes cause fruit setting in absence of pollination (parthenocarpy) **Rooting hormone** – promote rooting of cuttings
Phenoxyacetic acids*	2,4-D (2,4-dichlorophenoxyacetic acid) [structure] O—COOH, Cl, Cl 2,4,5-T (2,4,5-trichlorophenoxyacetic acid) as above but extra chlorine atom in 5 position of ring MCPA (2-methyl-4-chlorophenoxyacetic acid) as 2,4-D but methyl group (CH₃) in 2 position of ring instead of chlorine	**Selective weedkillers** – kill broad-leaved species (dicotyledons). Used in cereal crops and on lawns. Also in conifer plantations for scrub clearance (conifers unaffected). 2,4-D/2,4,5-T mix used in Vietnam war by US as the defoliant 'Agent Orange' **Potato storage** – inhibit sprouting of potatoes **Fruiting** – prevent premature fruit drop (retard abscission)
Benzoic acids	2,3,6-trichlorobenzoic acid [structure] Cl, COOH, Cl, Cl 2,4,6-trichlorobenzoic acid as above except chlorine atom in 4 position instead of 3 position of ring	Powerful **weedkillers**

*Cause plants to outgrow themselves. Growth distorted. Respiration excessive. 2,4,5-T is being phased out owing to concern about its contaminant, dioxin, which is the most toxic substance known to Man. Dioxin causes, for example, cancer, foetal abnormalities and a particularly severe form of acne called chloracne.

15.2.6 Gibberellins

Discovery of gibberellins

During the 1920s a team of Japanese scientists at the University of Tokyo was investigating a particularly damaging worldwide disease of rice seedlings, caused by the fungus *Gibberella* (now called *Fusarium*). Infected seedlings became tall, spindly and pale and eventually died or gave poor yields. By 1926 a fungal extract had been isolated which induced these symptoms in rice plants. An active compound was crystallised by 1935 and a further two by 1938. These compounds were called **gibberellins**, after the fungus. Language barriers and then the Second World War delayed the initiation of work in the West, but immediately after the war there was competition between British and American groups to isolate these chemicals. In 1954 a British group isolated an active substance which they called **gibberellic acid**. This was the third, and most active, gibberellin (**GA₃**) isolated by the Japanese. Gibberellins were isolated from higher plants during the 1950s, but the chemical structure of GA₃ was not completely worked out until 1959 (fig 15.19). Now more than 50 naturally occurring gibberellins are known, all differing only slightly from GA₃.

Structure of gibberellins

All are **terpenes**, a complex group of plant chemicals related to lipids; all are weak acids and all contain the 'gibbane' skeleton (fig 15.19).

gibbane skeleton

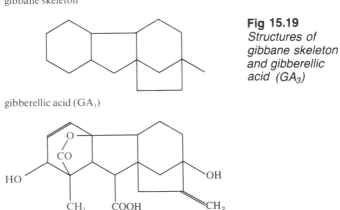

gibberellic acid (GA₃)

Fig 15.19 *Structures of gibbane skeleton and gibberellic acid (GA₃)*

Synthesis and distribution of gibberellins

Gibberellins are most abundant in young, expanding organs, being synthesised particularly in young apical leaves (possibly in chloroplasts), buds, seeds and root tips.

550

They migrate after synthesis in a non-polar manner, that is up or down the plant from the leaves. They move in phloem and xylem.

Effects of gibberellins

Like the auxins, the principal effect of gibberellins is on stem elongation, mainly by affecting cell elongation. Thus genetically dwarf varieties of peas and maize are restored to normal growth and dwarf beans can be converted into runner beans (fig 15.20). Stem growth of normal plants is promoted. Further information, relating to interaction with auxins, is given in section 15.3.

One of the classic effects of gibberellins, which has been much studied in an attempt to understand their mechanism of action, is the breaking of dormancy of certain seeds, notably of cereals. Germination is triggered by soaking the seed in water. After imbibing water the embryo secretes gibberellin which diffuses to the aleurone layer, stimulating synthesis of several enzymes, including α-amylase (fig 15.21). These catalyse the breakdown of food reserves in the endosperm and the products of digestion diffuse to the embryo, where they are used in growth.

15.15 (*a*) What is the substrate of α-amylase? (*b*) What is the product of the reaction it catalyses? (*c*) What other enzyme is required to complete digestion of its substrate? (*d*) Why is α-amylase so important in cereal seeds?

15.16 Explain the role of storage proteins in the aleurone layer by reference to fig 15.21.

Experiment 15.2: To test the following two hypotheses, (*a*) that gibberellin can stimulate breakdown of starch in germinating barley grains and (*b*) that gibberellin is produced in the embryo

The presence of amylase in barley seeds can be detected by placing a cut seed on the surface of agar containing starch. If the surface is moist, amylase will diffuse from the seed and catalyse digestion of the starch. Addition of iodine to the agar would stain remaining starch blue-black, revealing a clear 'halo' of digestion around the seed. The size of this circular zone gives a rough indication of how much amylase was present. In practice, sterile handling techniques are an important precaution because contaminating bacteria and fungi may also produce amylase.

With careful experimental design, further hypotheses may be tested (see, for example, Coppage, J. & Hill, T. A. (1973) *J. Biol. Ed.* **7**, 11–18).

Fig 15.20 *The influence of gibberellic acid (GA) on the growth of variety* Meteor *dwarf pea. The plant on the left received no GA and shows the typical dwarf habit. The remaining plants were treated with GA; the dose per plant in micrograms is shown. With doses up to 5 micrograms there is increased growth of the stems with increase in GA dosage. This is the principle of the dwarf pea assay of gibberellins*

Fig 15.21 *Role of gibberellin in mobilising food reserves of barley grain during breaking of dormancy*

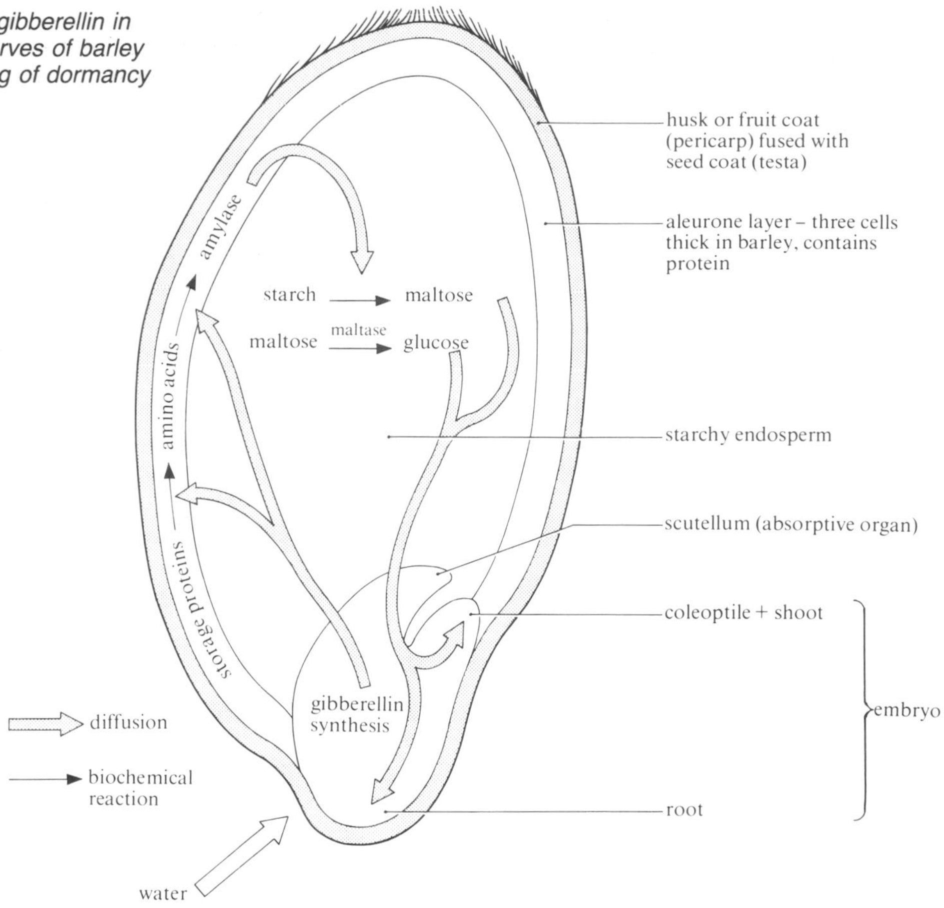

husk or fruit coat (pericarp) fused with seed coat (testa)

aleurone layer – three cells thick in barley, contains protein

amylase

starch → maltose

maltose $\xrightarrow{\text{maltase}}$ glucose

amino acids

starchy endosperm

scutellum (absorptive organ)

coleoptile + shoot

storage proteins

gibberellin synthesis

embryo

⇨ diffusion

→ biochemical reaction

root

water

Materials (per student)

white tile
scalpel
forceps
50 cm³ beaker
labels or chinagraph pencil
iodine/potassium iodide solution
sterile distilled water in sterile flasks (×3)
5% sodium hypochlorite solution or commercial sterilising fluid, e.g. Milton's or 70% alcohol
two starch agar plates (sterile): 1% agar containing 0.5% starch poured to a depth of about 0.25 cm in sterile Petri dishes
two starch–gibberellin agar plates: as above but add gibberellin (GA₃) to the agar before autoclaving at the concentration of 1 cm³ of 0.1% GA₃ solution per 100 cm³ agar (final concentration 10 ppm GA₃) (Gibberellin does not dissolve readily in water and is best dissolved in ethanol; some of the GA₃ is destroyed during autoclaving but the seeds are sensitive to concentrations as low as 10^{-5} ppm GA₃.)
dehusked barley grains: to dehusk barley grains, soak them in 50% (v/v) aqueous sulphuric acid for 3–4 h and then wash thoroughly (about ten times) in distilled water; violent shaking of the grains in a conical flask removes most of the husks; grains should be used immediately, since soaking starts germination. Alternatively, 'embryo'

and 'non-embryo' halves can be separated (see below) and stored under dry conditions in a fridge for a maximum of 2–3 days. Wheat grains are naked and do not need dehusking, and may be used as a substitute for barley.

Method

(1) Take two starch agar, and two starch–gibberellin agar plates appropriately labelled +GA or −GA. These have been sterilised. Label one of each type 'embryo' and the other 'non-embryo'.

(2) Cut at least two dry barley grains transversely in half (fig 15.22) on a tile, thus separating into 'embryo' and 'non-embryo' halves.

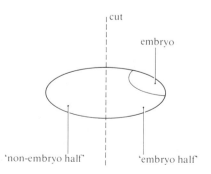

cut

embryo

'non-embryo half'   'embryo half'

Fig 15.22 *Cutting a barley grain for experiment 15.2*

(3) Sterilise the halves in 5% sodium hypochlorite solution for 5 min. Then wash in three changes of sterile distilled water in sterile flasks.

(4) Using forceps sterilised by rinsing in 70% alcohol, place the halves immediately in the relevant dishes, cut face downwards, with minimal lifting of lids as follows:

−GA	+GA	−GA	+GA
embryo $\frac{1}{2}$	embryo $\frac{1}{2}$	non-embryo $\frac{1}{2}$	non-embryo $\frac{1}{2}$

(5) Incubate for 24–48 h at 20–30 °C.

(6) Test for presence of starch in each dish by flooding surfaces of agar with I_2/KI solution. Draw the final appearance of each dish. Discuss the results.

> **15.17** Using starch agar it is often possible to demonstrate an association of amylase activity with fingerprints. Suggest reasons for this association.
>
> **15.18** What further experiment could you do, given the facilities, to prove that gibberellin causes synthesis of *new* amylase rather than activating pre-existing amylase?
>
> **15.19** How could you prove that amylase synthesis takes place in the aleurone layer?
>
> **15.20** How might the effect of gibberellin on barley seeds be used as a bioassay for gibberellin activity?

Other effects of gibberellins

Further effects of gibberellins on flowering, fruit growth and dormancy and their involvement in photoperiodism and vernalisation are discussed later under the appropriate headings. Their effects are summarised in table 15.4.

Mode of action of gibberellins

The mechanism of action of gibberellins remains unclear. In cereal grains GA_3 has been shown to stimulate synthesis of new protein, particularly α-amylase, and is effective in such low concentrations (as little as 10^{-5} μg cm^{-3}) that it must be operating at a profound level in cell metabolism, such as the 'switching' on or off of genes which takes place during cell differentiation (section 22.7). No conclusive evidence that this is so has yet been obtained, and higher concentrations are required for its other effects. In cell elongation it is dependent on the presence of auxins.

Commercial applications of gibberellins

Gibberellins are produced commercially from fungal cultures. They promote fruit setting and are used for growing seedless grapes (parthenocarpy). GA_3 is used in the brewing industry to stimulate α-amylase production in barley, and hence promote 'malting'. A number of synthetic growth retardants act as 'anti-gibberellins', that is they inhibit the action of gibberellins. Application of these often results in short (dwarf), sturdy plants with deep green leaves and sometimes greater pest and disease resistance. They take up less space and may in the future lead to higher yields per acre; also they are less inclined to blow over.

15.2.7 Cytokinins

Discovery of cytokinins

During the 1940s and 1950s efforts were made to perfect techniques of plant tissue culture. Such techniques provide an opportunity to study development free from the influence of other parts of the organism, and to study effects of added chemicals. While it proved possible to keep cells alive, it was difficult to stimulate growth. During the period 1954–6 Skoog, working in the USA, found that coconut milk contained an ingredient that promoted cell division in tobacco pith cultures. Coconut milk is a liquid endosperm (food reserve) and evidence that it contained growth substances had already been obtained in the 1940s when it had been studied as a likely source of substances to promote embryo growth. In a search for other active substances a stale sample of DNA happened to show similar activity, although a fresh sample did not. However, autoclaving fresh DNA produced the same effect and the active ingredient was shown to be chemically similar to the base adenine, a constituent of DNA (section 5.6). It was called **kinetin**. The term 'kinin' was used by Skoog for substances concerned with the control of cell division. Later the term **cytokinin** was adopted, partly from cytokinesis, meaning cell division, and partly because kinin has an entirely different meaning in zoology (it is a blood polypeptide). The first naturally occurring cytokinin to be chemically identified was from young maize (*Zea mais*) grains in 1963 and hence called **zeatin**. Note again the chemical similarity to adenine (fig 15.23).

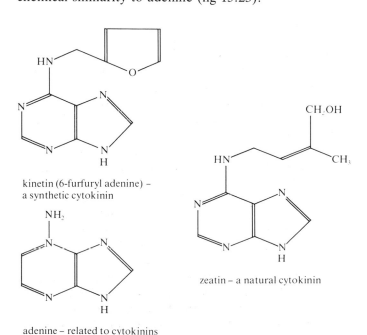

kinetin (6-furfuryl adenine) – a synthetic cytokinin

zeatin – a natural cytokinin

adenine – related to cytokinins

Fig 15.23 *Structures of kinetin, zeatin and adenine*

553

Table 15.4 Roles of plant growth substances in plant growth and development.

Process affected	Auxins	Gibberellins
Stem growth	**Promote cell enlargement in region behind apex.** Promote cell division in cambium.	**Promote cell enlargement in presence of auxin.** Also promote cell division in apical meristem and cambium. **Promote 'bolting' of some rosette plants**
Root growth	**Promote at very low concentrations. Inhibitory at higher concentrations**, e.g. geotropism?	Usually inactive
Root initiation	**Promote growth of roots from cuttings and calluses**	Inhibitory
Bud (shoot) initiation	Promote in some calluses but sometimes antagonistic to cytokinins and inhibitory. Sometimes promote in intact plant if apical dominance broken (see below).	Promote in chrysanthemum callus. Sometimes promote in intact plant if apical dominance broken
Leaf growth*	Inactive	Promote
Fruit growth	**Promote.** Can sometimes induce parthenocarpy.	**Promote.** Can sometimes induce parthenocarpy.
Apical dominance	**Promote, i.e. inhibit lateral bud growth**	Enhance action of auxins
Bud dormancy*	Inactive	**Break**
Seed dormancy*	Inactive	**Break**, e.g. cereals, ash
Flowering*	Usually inactive (promote in pineapple)	**Sometimes substitute for red light.** Therefore promote in long-day plants, inhibit in short-day plants
Leaf senescence	Delay in a few species	Delay in a few species
Fruit ripening	—	—
Abscission	**Inhibit.** Sometimes promote once abscission starts or if applied to plant side of abscission layer	Inactive
Stomatal mechanism	Inactive	Inactive

Process Affected	Cytokinins	Abscisic acid	Ethene
Stem growth	**Promote cell division in apical meristem and cambium** Sometimes inhibit cell expansion	**Inhibitory, notably during physiological stress, e.g. drought, waterlogging**	**Inhibitory, notably during physiological stress**
Root growth	Inactive or inhibit primary root growth	Inhibitory, e.g. geotropism?	Inhibitory, e.g. geotropism?
Root initiation	Inactive or promote lateral root growth	—	—
Bud (shoot) initiation	Promote, e.g. in protonemata of mosses	—	—
Leaf growth*	Promote	—	—
Fruit growth	**Promote.** Can rarely induce parthenocarpy	—	—
Apical dominance	**Antagonistic to auxins, i.e. promote lateral bud growth**	—	—
Bud dormancy*	**Break**	**Promotes**, e.g. sycamore, birch	**Breaks**
Seed dormancy*	**Break**	**Promotes**	—
Flowering*	Usually inactive	Sometimes promote in short-day plants and inhibit in long-day plants (antagonistic to gibberellins)	Promotes in pineapple
Leaf senescence	**Delay**	Sometimes promotes	—
Fruit ripening	—	—	**Promotes**
Abscission	Inactive	**Promotes**	—
Stomatal mechanism	Promotes stomatal opening	**Promotes closing of stomata under conditions of water stress (wilting)**	Inactive?

*Light and temperature are also involved – see photoperiodism and vernalisation.
NB The information presented in this table is generalised. The growth substances do not necessarily always have the effects attributed to them and variation in response between different plants is common. It is best to pay closest attention to the positive effects. Those stressed in bold type are the most important for the A-level student.

Synthesis and distribution of cytokinins

Cytokinins are most abundant where rapid cell division is occurring, particularly in fruits and seeds where they are associated with embryo growth. Evidence suggests that in mature plants they are frequently made in the roots and move to the shoots in the transpiration stream (in xylem). Cytokinins may be re-exported from leaves via the phloem.

Effects of cytokinins

Cytokinins, by definition, promote cell division. They do so, however, only in the presence of auxins. Gibberellins may also play a role, as in the cambium. Their interaction with other growth substances is discussed later in section 15.3.2.

One of the intriguing properties of cytokinins is their ability to delay the normal process of ageing in leaves. If a leaf is detached from a plant it will normally senesce very rapidly, as indicated by its yellowing and loss of protein, RNA and DNA. However, addition of a spot of kinetin will result in a green island of active tissue in the midst of yellowing tissue. Nutrients are then observed to move to this green island from surrounding cells (fig 15.24).

> **15.21** Study fig 15.24 and then answer the following.
> (a) What difference is there in the fate of applied amino acid between an old leaf and a young leaf?
> (b) Why should there be this difference?
> (c) What is the effect of kinetin on distribution of radioactive amino acid in old leaves?

Even when kinetin is applied to dying leaves on an intact plant a similar, though less dramatic, effect occurs. It has been shown that levels of natural cytokinins decrease in senescing leaves. A natural programme of senescence may therefore involve movement of cytokinins from older leaves to younger leaves via the phloem.

Cytokinins are also implicated in many stages of plant growth and development (table 15.4 and section 15.3).

Mode of action of cytokinins

The similarity of cytokinins to the base adenine, a component of the nucleic acids RNA and DNA, suggests that they may have a fundamental role in nucleic acid metabolism. Some unusual bases, derived from transfer RNA molecules, have been shown to have cytokinin activity, raising the possibility that cytokinins are involved in transfer RNA synthesis. Whether this is true or not, it does not necessarily account for their role as growth substances, and further evidence is still being sought.

Commercial applications of cytokinins

Cytokinins prolong the life of fresh leaf crops such as cabbage and lettuce (delay of senescence) as well as keeping flowers fresh. They can also be used to break dormancy of some seeds.

15.2.8 Abscisic acid

Discovery of abscisic acid

Plant physiologists have more recently obtained evidence that growth inhibitors, as well as growth promoters like auxins, gibberellins and cytokinins, are important in the normal regulation of growth. It had long been suspected that dormancy was caused by inhibitors when a group at the University of Aberystwyth, led by Wareing, set about trying to find them in the late 1950s. In 1963, an extract from birch leaves was shown to induce dormancy of birch

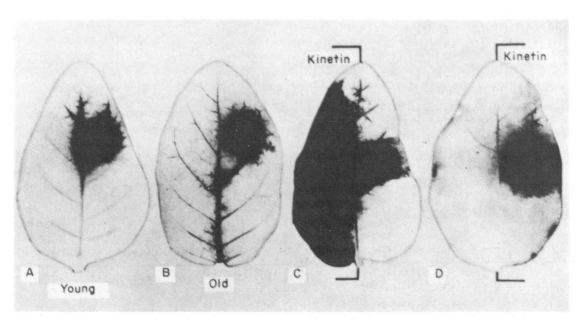

Fig 15.24 *Effect of kinetin upon translocation of an amino acid in tobacco leaves. Radioactive amino acid was supplied as indicated and after a period of translocation the leaves were exposed to photographic film. In the resulting autoradiographs, the areas containing the amino acid appear black*

buds. The leaves had been treated with short days to mimic approaching winter. Pure crystals of an active substance were isolated from sycamore leaves in 1964. The substance was called **dormin**. It turned out to be identical to a compound isolated by another group in 1963 from young cotton fruit. This accelerated abscission and was called **abscisin II** (abscisin I is a similarly acting, but chemically unrelated and less active compound). In 1967 it was agreed to call the substance **abscisic acid (ABA)**. It has been found in all groups of plants from mosses upwards and a substance that plays a similar role, lunularic acid, has been found in algae and liverworts.

Structure of abscisic acid

Like the gibberellins, ABA is a terpenoid and has a complex structure (fig 15.25). It is the only growth substance in its class.

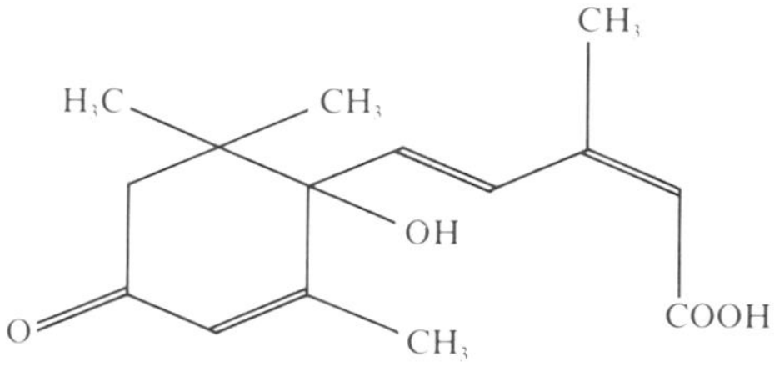

Fig 15.25 *Structure of abscisic acid*

Synthesis and distribution of ABA

ABA is made in leaves, stems, fruits and seeds. The fact that isolated chloroplasts can synthesise it again suggests a link with the carotenoid pigments, which are also made in chloroplasts. Like the other growth substances, ABA moves in the vascular system, mainly in the phloem. It also moves from the root cap by diffusion (see geotropism).

Effects of ABA

Table 15.4 summarises the effects of ABA on growth and development. It is a major inhibitor of growth in plants and is antagonistic to all three classes of growth promoters. Its classical effects are on bud dormancy (including apical dominance), seed dormancy and abscission (see section 15.3.4) but it also has roles in wilting, flowering, leaf senescence and possibly geotropism. It is associated with stress, particularly drought. In wilting tomato leaves, for example, the ABA concentration is 50 times higher than normal and ABA is thought to bring about closure of stomata. High concentrations stop the plant growing altogether.

Mode of action of ABA

This is unknown.

Commercial applications of ABA

ABA can be sprayed on tree crops to regulate fruit drop at the end of the season. This removes the need for picking over a long time-span.

15.2.9 Ethene (Ethylene)

Discovery of ethene as a growth substance

It was known in the early 1930s that ethene gas speeded up ripening of citrus fruits and affected plant growth in various ways. Later it was shown that certain ripe fruits, such as bananas, gave off a gas with similar effects. In 1934 yellowing apples were shown to emit ethene and it was subsequently shown to emanate from a wide variety of ripening fruits and other plant organs, particularly from wounded regions. Trace amounts are normal for any organ.

Structure of ethene

See fig 15.26.

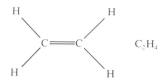

Fig 15.26 *Structure of ethene (ethylene)*

Synthesis and distribution of ethene

As mentioned above, ethene is made by most or all plant organs. Despite being a gas it does not generally move freely through the system of air spaces in the plant because it tends to escape more easily from the plant surface. However, movement of the water-soluble precursor of ethene from waterlogged roots to shoots in the xylem has been demonstrated.

Effects of ethene

Ethene is known chiefly for its effects on fruit ripening and the accompanying rise in rate of respiration (the climacteric) which occurs in some plants (section 15.3.5). Like ABA it acts as a growth inhibitor in some circumstances and can promote abscission of fruits and leaves. Its effects are summarised in table 15.4.

Commercial applications of ethene

Ethene induces flowering in pineapple and stimulates ripening of tomatoes and citrus fruits. Fruits can often be prevented from ripening by storage in an atmosphere lacking oxygen; ripening can subsequently be regulated by application of ethene with oxygen. The commercial compound 'ethephon' breaks down to release ethene in plants and is applied to rubber plants to stimulate the flow of latex.

15.3 Synergism and antagonism

Having studied individual growth substances it has become clear that they generally work by interacting with one another, rather than each controlling its own

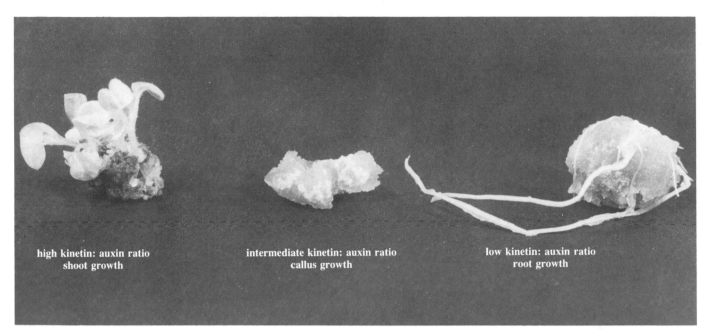

Fig 15.27 *Cultures of tobacco callus. The culture medium in each case contains IAA (2 mg dm⁻³). The culture 0.2 mg dm⁻³ kinetin (centre) continues growth as a callus; with a lower kinetin addition (0.02 mg dm⁻³) it initiates roots and with a higher kinetin addition (0.5 mg dm⁻³) it initiates shoots*

specific aspect of growth. Two kinds of control emerge. In the first, two or more substances supplement each other's activities. It is often found that their combined effect is much greater than the sum of their separate effects. This is called **synergism** and the substances are said to be **synergistic**. The second kind of control occurs when two substances have opposite effects on the same process, one promoting and the other inhibiting. This is called **antagonism** and the substances are said to be **antagonistic**. Here the balance between the substances determines response.

Some of the better understood phases of plant growth and development can now be studied and the importance of synergism and antagonism demonstrated.

15.3.1 Shoot growth

The effect of gibberellins on elongation of stems, petioles, leaves and hypocotyls is dependent on the presence of auxins.

> **15.22** How could you demonstrate this experimentally?

15.3.2 Cell division and differentiation

Cytokinins promote cell division only in the presence of auxins. Gibberellins sometimes also play a role, as in the cambium when auxins and gibberellins come from nearby buds and leaves. The interaction of cytokinins with other growth substances was demonstrated in the classic experiments of Skoog in the 1950s, already mentioned. His team showed the effect of various concentrations of kinetin and auxin on growth of tobacco pith callus. A high auxin to cytokinin ratio promoted root

formation whereas a high kinetin to auxin ratio promoted lateral buds which grew into leafy shoots. Undifferentiated growth would occur if the growth substances were in balance (fig 15.27).

15.3.3 Apical dominance

Apical dominance is the phenomenon whereby the presence of a growing apical bud inhibits growth of lateral buds. It also includes the suppression of lateral root growth by growth of the main root. Removal of a shoot apex results in lateral bud growth, that is branching. This is made use of in pruning when bushy rather than tall plants are required.

> **15.23** (a) What plant growth substance is made in the shoot apex? (b) Design an experiment to show whether it is responsible for apical dominance.

It is interesting to note that auxin levels at the lateral buds are often *not* high enough to cause inhibition of growth. Auxins exert their influence in an unknown way, possibly by somehow 'attracting' nutrients to the apex. In cocklebur it appears that the fall in auxin level in the stem after decapitation permits the lateral buds to inactivate the high levels of ABA that they contain. Gibberellins often enhance the response to IAA. Kinetin application to lateral buds, however, often breaks their dormancy, at least temporarily. Kinetin plus IAA causes complete breaking of dormancy. Cytokinins are usually made in the roots and move in the xylem to the shoots. Perhaps, therefore, they are normally transported to wherever auxin is being made, and they combine to promote bud growth.

Apical dominance is a classic example of one part of a

557

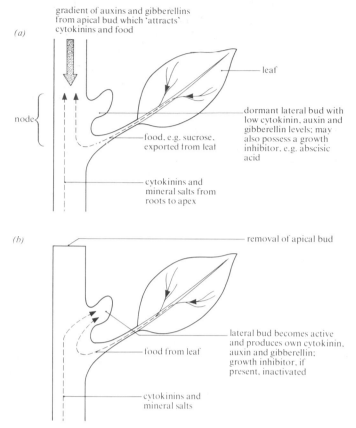

(a)

gradient of auxins and gibberellins from apical bud which 'attracts' cytokinins and food

leaf

node

dormant lateral bud with low cytokinin, auxin and gibberellin levels; may also possess a growth inhibitor, e.g. abscisic acid

food, e.g. sucrose, exported from leaf

cytokinins and mineral salts from roots to apex

(b)

removal of apical bud

lateral bud becomes active and produces own cytokinin, auxin and gibberellin; growth inhibitor, if present, inactivated

food from leaf

cytokinins and mineral salts

Fig 15.28 *Possible involvement of plant growth substances in apical dominance, (a) in presence of apical bud, (b) after removal of apical bud*

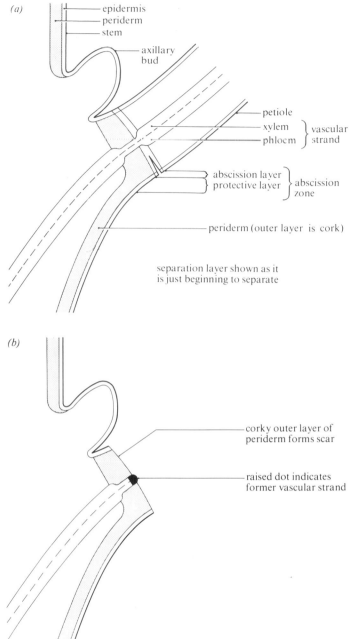

(a)

epidermis
periderm
stem

axillary bud

petiole

xylem

phloem

} vascular strand

abscission layer
protective layer

} abscission zone

periderm (outer layer is cork)

separation layer shown as it is just beginning to separate

(b)

corky outer layer of periderm forms scar

raised dot indicates former vascular strand

Fig 15.29 *Abscission zone of a leaf, (a) during abscission, (b) after abscission*

plant controlling another via the influence of a growth substance. This is called **correlation** (fig 15.28).

15.3.4 Abscission

Abscission is the organised shedding of part of the plant, usually a leaf, unfertilised flower or fruit. At the base of the organ, in a region called the **abscission zone**, a layer of living cells separates by breakdown of their middle lamellae, and sometimes breakdown of their cell walls. This forms the **abscission layer** (fig 15.29). Final shedding of the organ occurs when the vascular strands are broken mechanically, such as by the action of wind. A protective layer is formed beneath the abscission layer to prevent infection or desiccation of the scar, and the vascular strand is sealed. In woody species the protective layer is corky, being part of the tissue produced by the cork cambium, namely the periderm (section 21.6).

Abscission of leaves from deciduous trees and shrubs is usually associated with the onset of winter, but in the tropics it often occurs with the onset of a dry season. In both cases it affords protection against possible water shortage, leaves being the main organs through which water is lost by transpiration. In winter, for example, soil water may be unavailable through being frozen. In

evergreen species, abscission is spread over the whole year and the leaves are usually modified to prevent water loss.

It has been shown that as a leaf approaches abscission, its output of auxin declines. Fig 15.30 summarises the effect of auxin on abscission. It is worth noting that once abscission has been triggered, auxins seem to accelerate the process.

Abscisic acid (ABA) acts antagonistically to auxin by promoting abscission in some fruits. Unripe seeds produce auxins, but during ripening auxin production declines and ABA production may rise. In developing cotton fruits, for example, two peaks of ABA occur. The first corresponds to

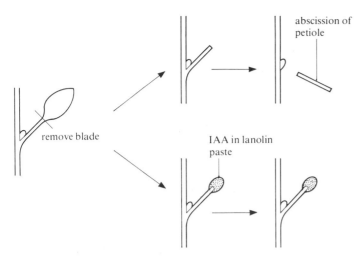

Fig 15.30 *Effect of auxin (IAA) on abscission of a leaf petiole. Removal of leaf blade leads to abscission of the petiole. IAA substitutes for the presence of the leaf blade*

the 'June drop' when self-thinning of the plants occurs: only the aborted immature fruitlets have high ABA levels at this stage. The second corresponds with seed ripening.

There is some doubt as to whether ABA also affects leaf abscission. Applications of high concentrations are effective, but this could be a result of stimulating ethene production. Ethene is produced by senescing leaves and ripening fruits and always stimulates abscission when applied to mature organs. Some deciduous shrubs and trees produce ABA in their leaves just before winter (section 15.5.1) but this may be purely to induce bud dormancy.

Abscission is of immense horticultural significance because of its involvement in fruit drop. Commercial applications of auxins and ABA reflect this and have been discussed earlier in this chapter.

If flowers are not fertilised they are generally abscised (see 'fruit set' below).

15.3.5 Pollen tube growth, fruit set and fruit development

Germinating pollen grains are a rich source of auxins as well as commonly stimulating the tissues of the style and ovary to produce more auxin. This auxin is necessary for 'fruit set', that is retention of the ovary, which becomes the fruit after fertilisation. Without it abscission of the flower normally occurs. After fertilisation, the ovary and the ripe seeds continue to produce auxins which stimulate fruit development.

A few natural examples are known where fruit development proceeds without fertilisation, and therefore without seed development, for example banana, pineapple and some seedless varieties of oranges and grapes. Such development is called **parthenocarpy**. Unusually high auxin levels occur in these ovaries. Parthenocarpy can sometimes be artificially induced by adding auxins, as in tomato, squash and peppers. Seedless pea pods can just as

easily be induced! Gibberellins have the same effect in some plants, such as the tomato, including some that are not affected by auxins, for example cherry, apricot and peach. Developing seeds are not only a rich source of auxins and gibberellins, but also of cytokinins (section 15.2.7). These growth substances are mainly associated with development of the embryo and accumulation of food reserves in the seed, and sometimes in the pericarp (fruit wall) from other parts of the plant.

Fruit ripening is really a process of senescence and is often accompanied by a burst of respiratory activity called the **climacteric**. This is associated with ethene production. The subsequent roles of ethene and ABA in fruit abscission were discussed in section 15.3.4.

15.4 Phytochrome and effects of light on plant development

The importance of environmental stimuli to the growth and orientation of plant organs has already been discussed with plant movements. The stimulus which has the widest influence on plant growth is light. Not only does it provide the energy for photosynthesis and influence plant movements, but it directly affects development. The effect of light upon development is called **photomorphogenesis**.

15.4.1 Etiolation

Perhaps the best way to demonstrate the importance of light is to grow a plant in the dark! Such a plant lacks chlorophyll (is chlorotic) and therefore appears white or pale yellow rather than green. The shoot internodes become elongated and thin and it is described as **etiolated**. In dicotyledonous plants, the epicotyl or hypocotyl (section 21.6.2) elongates in hypogeal or epigeal germination respectively and the plumule tip is hooked. Dicotyledonous leaves remain small and unexpanded. In monocotyledonous plants, the mesocotyl elongates during germination and the leaves may remain rolled up. In all leaves, chloroplasts fail to develop normal membrane systems and are called **etioplasts**. Plants make less supporting tissue and are fragile and collapse easily. Eventually they use up their food reserves and die unless light is reached for photosynthesis. Yet as soon as the plant is exposed to light, normal growth ensues. The significance of etiolation is that it allows maximum growth in length with minimum use of carbon reserves which, in the absence of light, the plant cannot obtain by photosynthesis.

15.24 How does the morphology of an etiolated plant suit it for growing through soil?

15.4.2 Discovery of phytochrome

The first stage in any process affected by light must be the absorption of light by a pigment, the so-called **photoreceptor**. The characteristic set of wavelengths of

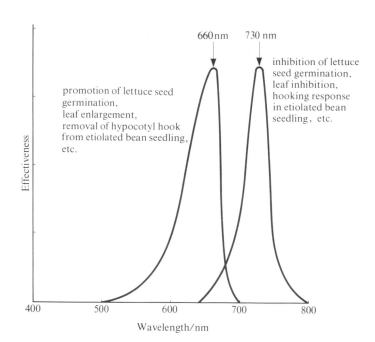

Fig 15.31 *Typical action spectra of a phytochrome-controlled response*

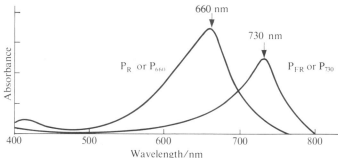

Fig 15.32 *Absorption spectra of the two forms of phytochrome*

light it absorbs form its absorption spectrum (section 9.3.2); remaining wavelengths are reflected and give the substance a characteristic colour (chlorophyll, for example, absorbs red and blue light and reflects green light).

The seeds of many plants germinate only if exposed to light. In 1937 it was shown that, for lettuce seeds, red light promoted germination but far-red light (longer wavelength) inhibited germination. Borthwick and Hendrick, working at the US Department of Agriculture in the 1950s, plotted an **action spectrum** for the germination response (a spectrum of wavelengths showing their relative effectiveness at stimulating the process). Fig 15.31 shows that the wavelength most effective for germination was about 660 nm (red light) and for inhibition of germination about 730 nm (far red light).

They also showed that only brief exposures of light were necessary and that the effects of red light were reversed by far-red light and vice versa. Thus the last treatment in an alternating sequence of red/far-red exposures would always be the effective one. The US team eventually isolated the pigment responsible in 1960 and called it **phytochrome**. Phytochrome, as they predicted, is a blue-green pigment existing in two interconvertible forms. One form, P_{FR} or P_{730} absorbs far-red light and the other, P_R or P_{660}, absorbs red light. Absorption of light by one form converts it rapidly and reversibly to the other form (within seconds or minutes depending on light intensity):

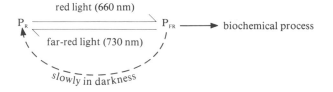

Normal sunlight contains more red than far-red light, so the P_{FR} form predominates during the day. This is the physiologically active form, but reverts slowly to the more stable, but inactive, P_R form at night. Phytochrome was shown to consist of a pigment portion attached to a protein. It is present in minute amounts throughout plants (hence it is not visible, despite its colour (but is particularly concentrated in the growing tips. Its absorption spectrum is shown in fig 15.32.

15.25 What is the difference between an absorption spectrum and an action spectrum?

A number of developmental processes are mediated by low intensities of red light and reversed by far-red light or darkness, showing the involvement of phytochrome (fig 15.31 and table 15.5). The most significant of these is flowering, which is discussed later. The involvement of phytochrome in a process is shown by matching the action spectrum of the response with the absorption spectrum of phytochrome.

15.4.3 Photoperiodism and flowering

One of the important ways in which light exerts its influence on living organisms is through variations in daylength (**photoperiod**). The further from the equator, where days are almost a constant 12 hours, the greater the seasonal variation in daylength. Thus daylength is an important environmental signal in temperate latitudes where it varies between about 9 and 15 hours during the year. The effects of photoperiod on animals are discussed in section 16.8.5. In plants it is a matter of common observation that phenomena such as flowering, fruit and seed production, bud and seed dormancy, leaf fall and germination are closely attuned to seasonal influences like daylength and temperature, and that survival of the plant depends on this.

The process involving the most profound change is flowering, when shoot meristems switch from producing leaves and lateral buds to producing flowers. The impor-

Table 15.5 Some phytochrome-controlled responses in plants.

General process affected	Red light promotes
Germination*	Germination of some seeds, e.g. some lettuce varieties
	Germination of fern spores
Photomorphogenesis (light-controlled development of form and structure)	Leaf expansion in dicotyledons. Leaf unrolling in grasses (monocotyledons). Chloroplast development (etioplasts converted to chloroplasts: see etiolation). Greening (protochlorophyll converted to chlorophyll). Inhibition of internode growth (including epicotyl, hypocotyl, mesocotyl), i.e. preventing of etiolation. Unhooking of plumule in dicotyledons
Photoperiodism	Stimulates flowering in long-day plants. Inhibits flowering in short-day plants. See flowering

*Experiments designed to investigate the effects of light on seed germination are described by J. W. Hannay in *J. Biol. Ed.* (1967) **1**, 65–73. The variety of lettuce suggested, 'Grand Rapids', is no longer available but some modern varieties could be screened for suitability. Such varieties currently available are 'Dandie', 'Kloek' and 'Kweik'. 'Dandie' is probably the most reliable but is fairly expensive because it is a winter-forcing variety. It is available from Suttons in small packets or from F. W. King & Co., Coggeshall, Essex in 10 g packets (enough for about 250 dishes of 50 seeds each). *Phacelia* seeds make an interesting contrast to lettuce.
NB In this experiment a green leaf can be used as a far-red filter.

Table 15.6 Classification of plants according to photoperiodic requirements for flowering.

Short-day plants (SDPs)	Long-day plants (LDPs)
e.g. cocklebur (*Xanthium pennsylvanicum*), chrysanthemum, soybean, tobacco, strawberry	e.g. henbane (*Hyoscyamus niger*), snapdragon, cabbage, spring wheat, spring barley
Flowering induced by dark periods longer than a critical length, e.g. cocklebur 8.5 h; tobacco 10–11 h (Under natural conditions equivalent to days shorter than a critical length, e.g. cocklebur 15.5 h; tobacco 13–14 h)	Flowering induced by dark periods shorter than a critical length, e.g. henbane 13 h (Under natural conditions equivalent to days longer than a critical length, e.g. henbane 11 h)

Day-neutral plants

e.g. cucumber, tomato, garden pea, maize, cotton
Flowering independent of photoperiod

NB Tobacco (SDP) and henbane (LDP) both flower in 12–13 h daylength.

tance of photoperiod in flowering was discovered as early as 1910 but was first clearly described by Garner and Allard in 1920. They showed that tobacco plants would flower only after exposure to a series of short days. This occurred naturally in autumn, but could be induced by artificially short days of seven hours in a greenhouse in summer. As they examined other plants it became obvious that some required long days for flowering (**long-day plants**) and some would flower whatever the photoperiod once mature (**day-neutral plants**).

Additional complications have since been found. For example, some plants are day-neutral at one temperature, but not at another; some require one daylength followed by another; in some, the appropriate daylength only accelerates flowering and is not an absolute requirement.

An important advance in our understanding came when it was shown that it is really the length of the dark period which is critical. Thus short-day plants are really long-night plants. If they are grown in short days, but the long night is interrupted by a short light period, flowering is prevented. Long-day plants will flower in short days if the long night period is interrupted. Short dark interruptions, however,

do not cancel the effect of long days. Table 15.6 summarises the three main categories of plant.

15.4.4 Quality and quantity of light

The next step is to find the quality (colour) and quantity of light required. Remembering that the cocklebur (SDP) will not flower if its long night is interrupted, experiments revealed that red light was effective in preventing flowering, but that far-red light reversed the effect of red light. Therefore phytochrome is the photoreceptor. These experiments were, in fact, part of the programme which led to the discovery of phytochrome. As would be expected, a LDP held in short days is stimulated to flower by a short exposure to red light during the long night. Again this is reversed by far-red light. The last light treatment always determines response.

In some, though not all, cases low light intensities for a few minutes are effective, again typical of a phytochrome-controlled response. The higher the intensity used, the shorter the exposure time required.

Table 15.7 Effect of red/far-red light interruptions of long nights on flowering of cocklebur (after Downs, R. J. (1956) *Plant Physiol.* **31**, 279–84).

Red light		Two minutes red light followed by FR light	
Floral stage	Duration of red light/s	Floral stage	Duration of FR light/s
6.0	0	0.0	0
5.0	5	4.0	12
4.0	10	4.5	15
2.6	20	5.5	25
0.0	30	6.0	50

15.4.5 Perception and transmission of the stimulus

It was shown in the mid-1930s that the light stimulus is perceived by the leaves and not the apex where the flowers are produced.

In addition to this, a cocklebur plant with just one induced leaf will flower even if the rest of the plant is under non-inductive conditions. This implies that some agent, that is a hormone, must pass from the leaf to the apex to bring about flowering. This concept is supported by the observation that the flowering stimulus can be passed from an induced plant to a non-induced plant by grafting, and that the stimulus is apparently the same for SDP, LDP and day-neutral plants because grafting between these is successful. The hypothetical flowering hormone has been called '**florigen**' but has never been isolated. Indeed, its existence is doubted by some plant physiologists.

15.4.6 Mode of action of phytochrome

How, then, does phytochrome exert its control? At the end of a light period it exists in the active P_{FR} form. At the end of a short night its slow transition back to the inactive P_R form, which takes place in darkness, may not be complete. It can be postulated, therefore, that in LDPs P_{FR} promotes flowering and in SDPs it inhibits flowering. Only long nights remove sufficient P_{FR} from the latter to allow flowering to occur. Unfortunately, short exposures to far-red light, which would have the same effect as a long night, cannot completely substitute for long nights, so the full explanation is more complex. Some time factor is also important.

We do know that gibberellins can mimic the effect of red light in some cases. Gibberellic acid (GA_3) promotes flowering in some LDPs, mainly rosette plants like henbane which bolt before flowering. (Bolting is a rapid increase in stem length.) GA_3 also inhibits flowering in some SDPs. Antigibberellins (growth retardants) nullify these effects.

So, does P_{FR} stimulate gibberellin production, and is this the flowering hormone? There are too many exceptions for this to be the case. Abscisic acid inhibits flowering in some LDPs, such as *Lolium*, but induces it in some SDPs, such as strawberry. In short, our understanding of the flowering process is still incomplete.

15.5 Vernalisation and flowering

Some plants, especially biennials and perennials, are stimulated to flower by exposure to low temperatures. This is called **vernalisation**. Here the stimulus is perceived by the mature stem apex, or by the embryo of the seed, but not by the leaves as in photoperiodism. As with photoperiod, vernalisation may be an absolute requirement (such as in henbane) or may simply hasten flowering (as in winter cereals).

Long-day plants (for example cabbage), short-day plants (such as chrysanthemum) and day-neutral plants (such as ragwort) can all require vernalisation. The length of chilling required varies from four days to three months, temperatures around 4 °C generally being most effective. Like the photoperiodic stimulus, the vernalisation stimulus can be transmitted between plants by grafting. In this case the hypothetical hormone involved was called **vernalin**. It has subsequently been discovered that during vernalisation gibberellin levels increase, and application of gibberellins to unvernalised plants can substitute for vernalisation (fig 15.33). It is now believed that 'vernalin' is a gibberellin. It is clear now that photoperiodism and vernalisation serve to synchronise the reproductive behaviour of plants with their environments, ensuring reproduction at favourable times of the year. They also help to ensure that members of the same species flower at the same time and thus encourage cross-pollination and cross-fertilisation, with the attendant advantages of genetic variability.

Fig 15.33 *Carrot plants (var.* Early french forcing*). left: control; centre: maintained at 17°C but supplied 10 mg of gibberellin daily for 4 weeks; right: plant given vernalizing cold treatment (6 weeks). All photographed 8 weeks after completion of cold treatment*

15.5.1 Photoperiodism and dormancy

The formation of winter buds in temperate trees and shrubs is usually a photoperiodic response to shortening days in the autumn, for example in birch, beech and sycamore. The stimulus is perceived by the leaves and, as mentioned before, abscisic acid (ABA) levels build up. ABA moves to the meristems and inhibits growth. Short days also induce leaf fall from deciduous trees (abscission). Often buds must be chilled before dormancy can be broken ('**bud-break**'). Similarly some seeds require a cold stimulus ('**stratification**') after imbibing water before they will germinate, thus preventing them from germinating prematurely once ripe. This is discussed further in section 21.10. Gibberellins can substitute for the cold stimulus, and natural bud-break is accompanied by a rise in gibberellins as well as, in many cases, a fall in ABA. Breaking of bud dormancy in birch and poplar has been shown to coincide with a rise in cytokinins.

Apart from buds and seeds, storage organs are involved in dormancy and again photoperiod is important. For example, short days induce tuber formation in potatoes, whereas long days induce onion bulb formation.

> **15.28** Some buds remain dormant throughout the summer. What causes dormancy here?

Chapter Sixteen

Coordination and control in animals

Irritability or **sensitivity** is a characteristic feature of all living organisms and involves their ability to respond to a stimulus. In all organisms some degree of internal coordination and control is necessary in order to ensure that the events of the stimulus and response bear some mutual relationship associated with the maintenance of the steady-state (chapter 18) and survival of the organism.

Animals, unlike plants, have two different but related systems of coordination: the **nervous system** and the **endocrine system**. The former is fast acting, its effects are localised and it involves electrical and chemical transmission, whereas the latter is slower acting, its effects are diffuse and it relies on chemical transmission through the circulatory system. It is thought that the two systems have developed in parallel in the majority of multicellular animals.

16.1   The nervous system

The nervous system is composed of highly differentiated cells whose function is to detect sensory information, code this in the form of electrical impulses and transmit them, often over considerable distances, to other differentiated cells capable of producing a response.

All sensory information (**stimuli**) is detected in multi-cellular animals by modified nerve cells called **sensory receptors** and the structure and function of these is described in section 16.5. This sensory information is passed on to **effector cells** which produce a response which is associated in some way with the stimulus. The structure and function of effectors is described briefly in section 16.6 and chapter 17.

Interposed between the receptors and effectors are the conductile cells of the nervous system, the **neurones**. These are the basic structural and functional units of the nervous system and ramify throughout the organism forming an elaborate communication network. Types of neurone, and their structures, are shown and described in section 8.6. The structural complexity and organisation of the neurones within the network is related to the phylogenetic position of the organism and ranges from the primitive nerve net of the coelenterates (section 16.3) to the complex central nervous system of mammals (section 16.2). Whereas the former is purely a communication system, the latter provides, in addition, facilities for the storage, retrieval and integration of information.

16.1.1   The nature of the nerve impulse

The transmission of information along neurones as electrical impulses and its effects on muscle contraction and glandular secretion have been known for over 200 years. Details of the mechanisms, however, were established only in the last 40 years following the discovery of certain axons in squid which have a diameter of approximately 1 mm (1000 μm). These **giant axons** (supplying the muscles of the mantle involved in escape responses) had large enough diameters to permit the earliest electrophysiological investigations to be carried out on them.

The apparatus currently used to investigate electrical activity in neurones is shown in fig 16.1. The **microelectrode**, composed of a small glass tube drawn out to a fine point of 0.5 μm diameter, is filled with a solution capable of conducting an electric current, such as 3M potassium chloride. This is inserted into an axon and a second electrode, in the form of a small metal plate, is passed into the saline solution bathing the neurone being investigated. Both electrodes are connected by leads to a **preamplifier** to complete the circuit. The preamplifier increases the signal strength in the circuit approximately 1 000 times and provides the input to a **dual-beam cathode ray oscilloscope**. All movements of the microelectrode are controlled by a **micromanipulator**, a device with adjusting knobs similar to those of the microscope, which enables delicate control over the position of the tip of the microelectrode.

When the tip of the microelectrode penetrates the axon plasma membrane, the beams of the oscilloscope separate. The distance between the beams indicates the potential difference between the two electrodes of the circuit and can be measured. This value is called the **resting potential (RP)** of the axon and is approximately −65 mV in all species investigated. The negative sign for the resting potential indicates that the membrane of the axon is **polarised**, that is the inside of the axon is negative with respect to the outside of the axon. In sensory cells, neurones and muscle cells this value changes with the activity of the cells and hence they are known as **excitable cells**. All other living cells show a similar potential difference across the membrane, known as the **membrane potential**, but in these cells this is constant and so they are known as **non-excitable cells**.

Resting potential

The resting potential of most mammalian neurones is constant as long as the cell remains inactive due to lack of

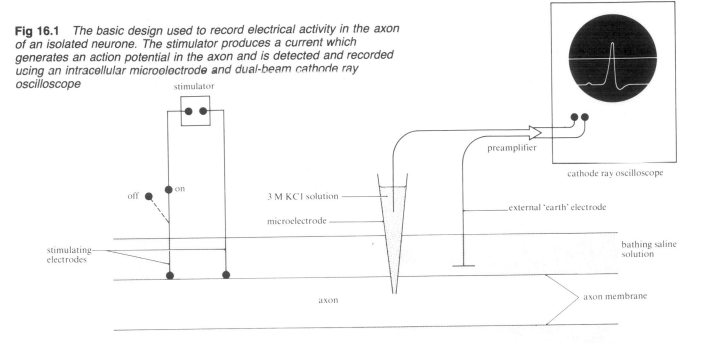

Fig 16.1 *The basic design used to record electrical activity in the axon of an isolated neurone. The stimulator produces a current which generates an action potential in the axon and is detected and recorded using an intracellular microelectrode and dual-beam cathode ray oscilloscope*

stimulation. Curtis and Cole in the USA, and Hodgkin and Huxley in England, in the late 1930s revealed the resting potential to be a physico-chemical phenomenon set up and maintained by the differential concentration of ions across the axon membrane and the selective permeability of the membrane to the ions. Analyses of the intracellular fluid of the axon and the extracellular sea water bathing the axon showed that ionic electrochemical gradients exist as shown in table 16.1.

Table 16.1. Ionic concentrations of extracellular and intracellular fluids in squid axon. (Values given are approximations in mmol kg^{-1} H$_2$O, data from Hodgkin, 1958)

Ion	Extracellular concentration	Intracellular concentration
K$^+$	20	400
Na$^+$	460	50
Cl$^-$	560	100
A$^-$	0	370
(Organic anions)		

The axoplasm inside the axon has a high concentration of potassium (K$^+$) ions and a low concentration of sodium (Na$^+$) ions, in contrast to the fluid outside the axon which has a low concentration of K$^+$ ions and a high concentration of Na$^+$ ions. (The distribution of chloride (Cl$^-$) ions is ignored in the following descriptions since it does not play a vital role in the activities under consideration.)

These electrochemical gradients are maintained by the active transport of ions against their electro-chemical gradients by specific regions of the membrane known as **cation** or **sodium pumps**. These constantly active carrier mechanisms are driven by energy supplied by ATP and

couple the removal of Na$^+$ ions from the axon with the uptake of K$^+$ ions as shown in fig 16.2a.

The active movement of these ions is opposed by the **passive** diffusion of the ions which constantly pass down their electrochemical gradients as shown in fig 16.2b at a rate determined by the permeability of the axon membrane to the ion. K$^+$ ions have an ionic mobility and membrane permeability which is 20 times greater than that of Na$^+$ ions, therefore K$^+$ loss from the axon is greater than Na$^+$ gain. This leads to a net loss of K$^+$ ions from the axon, and the production of a **negative** charge within the axon. The value of the resting potential is largely determined by the K$^+$ electrochemical gradient.

Changes in the permeability of the membrane of excitable cells to K$^+$ and Na$^+$ ions lead to changes in the potential difference across the membrane and the formation of action potentials in, and the propagation of nerve impulses along, the axon.

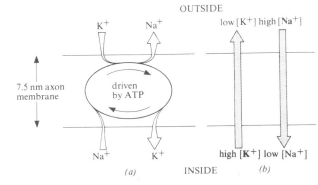

Fig 16.2 *Active and passive ionic movements associated with the production of a negative (−) potential within the axon. (a) The Na$^+$/K$^+$ coupled cation pump actively exchanges ions which pass across the membrane by passive diffusion down their electrochemical gradients as shown in (b)*

Action potential

The experimental stimulation of an axon by an electrical impulse, as shown in fig 16.3, results in a change in the potential across the axon membrane from a negative inside value of about -70 mV to a positive inside value of about $+40$ mV. This polarity change is called an **action potential** or **spike** and appears on the cathode ray oscilloscope as shown in fig 16.3.

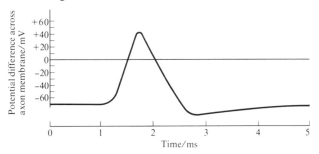

Fig 16.3 *A typical action potential in squid axon*

An action potential is generated by a sudden momentary increase in the permeability of the axon membrane to Na^+ ions which enter the axon. This increase in sodium **conductance** (the electrical equivalent of permeability)

increases the number of positive ions inside the axon and reduces the membrane potential from its resting value of -70 mV. The change in membrane potential is called **depolarisation**. Sodium conductance and depolarisation influence each other by **positive feedback**, that is an increase in one factor reinforces an increase in the other, and this produces the steep rising phase of the action potential. Calculations have revealed that relatively few Na^+ ions (about 10^{-6}% of the internal Na^+ present, depending upon axon diameter) enter the axon and produce the depolarisation of about 110 mV associated with the action potential. At the peak of the action potential, sodium conductance declines (**Na inactivation**) and about 0.5 ms after the initial depolarisation, potassium conductance increases and K^+ ions diffuse out of the axon. As K^+ ions diffuse outwards the internal positive charge is replaced by a negative charge. This **repolarisation** of the membrane is shown by the falling phase of the action potential 'spike' and results in the membrane potential assuming its original level.

From the above account it can be seen that whilst the resting potential is determined largely by K^+ ions, the action potential is determined largely by Na^+ ions (fig 16.4).

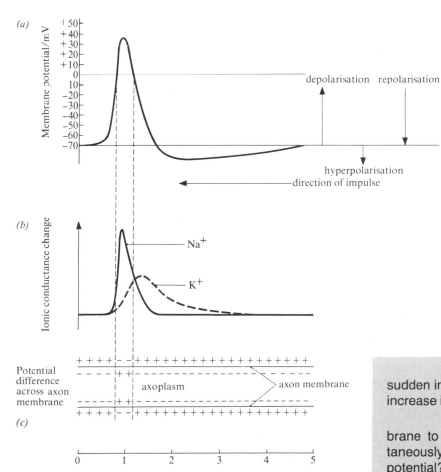

Fig 16.4 *Diagrams to show the relationships between (a) the membrane potential, (b) ionic conductance and (c) the potential distribution across the axon membrane during production of an action potential*

16.1 Give two reasons why there is a sudden influx of Na^+ ions into the axon following an increase in Na^+ permeability of the axon membrane.

16.2 If the permeability of the axon membrane to Na^+ ions and K^+ ions increased simultaneously what effect would this have on the action potential?

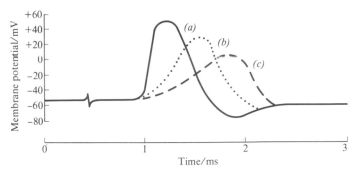

Fig 16.5 *Membrane potentials recorded from squid axons bathed in isotonic sea water containing different relative concentrations of ions*

16.3 Hodgkin and Katz, in 1949, investigated the effect of Na⁺ ions on the production of action potentials in squid axons. Intracellular microelectrodes recorded action potentials from axons bathed in different concentrations of isotonic sea water. The results are shown in fig 16.5. Which action potentials correspond with axons placed in normal sea water, one-half sea water and one-third sea water? Explain the effect of these solutions on the action potentials.

Features of action potentials

Initiation of an action potential. Stimulation of sensory cells leads to depolarisation of their membranes and if this reaches a certain threshold value in the sensory neurone, the **threshold stimulus intensity**, it will set up an action potential. For any given neurone the **amplitude** (fig 16.3) of the action potential is always constant, and increasing the strength or number of stimuli have no effect on this. For this reason action potentials are described as **all-or-nothing** events.

Transmission of nerve impulses. Information is transmitted through the nervous system as a series of nerve impulses, which travel as action potentials. A nerve impulse passes along an axon as a wave of depolarisation accompanied by a wave of negativity along the surface of the axon marking the position, at any instant, of the action potential. Action potentials are **propagated**, that is self-generated, along the axon by the effects of Na⁺ ions entering the axon. This creates an area of positive charge and a flow of current is set up in a **local circuit** between this active area and the negatively charged resting region immediately ahead. The current flow in the local circuit reduces the membrane potential in the resting region and this depolarisation produces an increase in sodium permeability and the development of an all-or-nothing action potential in this region. Repeated depolarisations of immediately adjacent regions of the membrane result in the action potential being moved or propagated along the axon. Action potentials are propagated along the axon without change in amplitude and are capable of being transmitted over an infinite distance, that is, they are **non-decremental**. The reason for this is that the production of an action potential at each point along the axon is a self-generating event resulting from a change in the local concentration of ions. So long as the extra- and intracellular environments of the axon have the necessary differential ionic concentrations an action potential at one point will generate another action potential in its adjacent region.

Refractory period. Nerve impulses only pass along the axon in one direction from active region to resting region. This is because the previously active region undergoes a recovery phase during which the axon membrane cannot respond to a depolarisation by a change in sodium conductance, even if the stimulus intensity is increased. The phase is called the **absolute refractory period** and lasts for about 1 ms. Following this is a period lasting for 5–10 ms called the **relative refractory period** during which a high-intensity stimulus may produce a depolarisation. The refractory period is also a limiting factor in the speed of conduction of the nerve impulse.

16.4 Describe the ionic changes occurring across the axon membrane during the refractory period.

Speed of conduction. In non-myelinated axons (section 16.2), typical of those found in invertebrates, the velocity of the propagated action potential depends on the longitudinal resistance of the axoplasm. The resistance, in turn, is related to the diameter of the axon such that the smaller the diameter the greater the resistance. In the case of fine axons (<0.1 mm) the high resistance of the axoplasm has an effect on the spread of current and reduces the length of the local circuits so that only the region of the membrane immediately in front of the action potential is involved in the local circuit. These axons conduct impulses at about 0.5 m s⁻¹. Giant axons, typical of many annelids, arthropods and molluscs, have a diameter of approximately 1 mm and conduct impulses at velocities up to 100 m s⁻¹, which are ideal for conducting information vital for survival.

16.5 Explain, in terms of the resistance of the axoplasm and local circuits, why giant axons conduct impulses at greater velocities than fine axons.

In vertebrates, the majority of neurones, particularly those of the spinal and cranial nerves, have an outer covering of myelin derived from the spirally wound Schwann cell (section 8.6.3). Myelin is a fatty material with a high electrical resistance and acts as an electrical insulator in the same way as the rubber and plastic covering of electrical wiring. The combined resistance of the axon membrane and myelin sheath is very high but where breaks in the myelin sheath occur, as at the **nodes of Ranvier**, the resistance to current flow between the axoplasm and the extra-cellular fluid is lower. It is only at these points that local circuits are set up and current flows across the axon membrane generating the next action potential. This means, in effect, that the action potential 'jumps' from node to node and passes along the myelinated axon faster than the series of smaller local currents in a non-myelinated axon. This type of conduction is called **saltatory** (*saltare*, to jump) and can lead to conduction velocities of up to 120 m s^{-1} (fig 16.6).

Temperature has an effect on the rate of conduction of nerve impulses and as temperature rises to about 40 °C the rate of conduction increases.

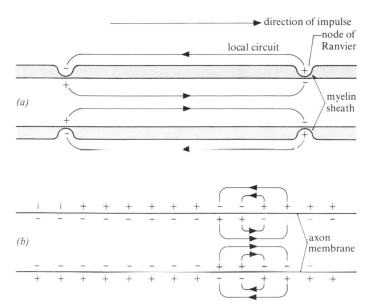

Fig 16.6 *Diagrams showing the difference in lengths of the local circuits produced (a) in a myelinated axon and (b) a non-myelinated axon. In (a) conduction is described as saltatory since the action potential effectively 'jumps' from node to node*

16.6 Why do myelinated axons of frog having a diameter of 3.5 μm conduct impulses at 30 m s^{-1} whereas axons of the same diameter in cat conduct impulses at 90 m s^{-1}?

Coding of nervous information. Nerve impulses pass through the nervous system as propagated, all-or-nothing action potentials with a fixed amplitude for a given species, for example 110 mV in squid axon. Information cannot therefore be passed as an amplitude code and is passed instead as a **frequency code**. This code was first described by Adrian and Zotterman in 1926. They demonstrated that the frequency of nerve impulses is directly related to the intensity of the stimulus giving rise to the impulses.

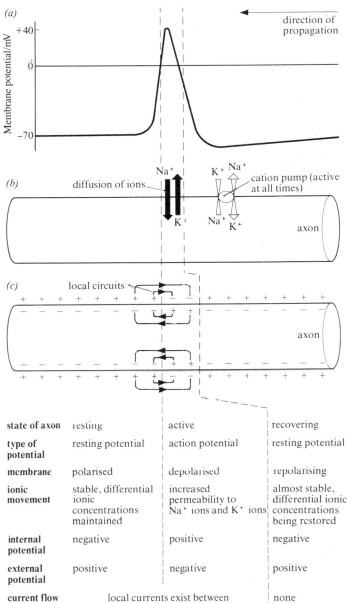

state of axon	resting	active	recovering
type of potential	resting potential	action potential	resting potential
membrane	polarised	depolarised	repolarising
ionic movement	stable, differential ionic concentrations maintained	increased permeability to Na⁺ ions and K⁺ ions	almost stable, differential ionic concentrations being restored
internal potential	negative	positive	negative
external potential	positive	negative	positive
current flow	local currents exist between resting and active regions		none

Fig 16.7 *Summary diagrams showing the events accompanying the production of local circuits within the axon and the propagation of an action potential in a non-myelinated axon, (a) action potential and direction of propagation, (b) ionic movements across the axon membrane, (c) current flow in local circuits*

16.1.2   The synapse

A synapse is an area of functional, but not physical, contact between one neurone and another for the purpose of transferring information. Synapses are usually found between the fine terminal branches of the axon of one neurone and the **dendrites** (**axodendritic synapses**) or **cell body** (**axosomatic synapses**) of another neurone. The number of synapses is usually very large, providing a large surface area for the transfer of information. For example, over 1 000 synapses may be found on the dendrites and cell body of a motor neurone in the spinal cord. Some cells in the brain may receive up to 10 000 synapses (fig 16.8).

569

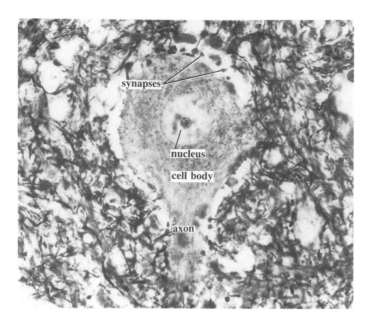

Fig 16.8 *Scanning electron micrograph of a motor neurone transmission at a neuronal synapse.*

There are two types of synapses, **electrical** and **chemical**, depending upon the nature of transfer of information across the synapse. A structurally dissimilar, but functionally similar, form of synapse exists between the terminals of a motor neurone and the surface of a muscle fibre and this is called a **neuromuscular junction**. Details of the structure and physiological differences between the synapse and the neuromuscular junction are described later in this section.

Structure of the chemical synapse

Chemical synapses are the commonest type of synapse found in vertebrates and they consist of a bulbous expansion of a nerve terminal called a **synaptic knob** or **bouton terminale** lying in close proximity to the membrane of a dendrite. The cytoplasm of the synaptic knob contains mitochondria, smooth endoplasmic reticulum, microfilaments and numerous **synaptic vesicles**. Each vesicle has a diameter of approximately 50 nm and contains a chemical **neurotransmitter substance** responsible for the transmission of the nerve impulse across the synapse. The membrane of the synaptic knob nearest the synapse is thickened as a result of cytoplasmic condensation and forms the **presynaptic membrane**. The membrane of the dendrite is also thickened and termed the **postsynaptic membrane**. These membranes are separated by a gap, the **synaptic cleft**, of 20 nm. The presynaptic membrane is modified for the attachment of synaptic vesicles and the release of transmitter substance into the synaptic cleft. The postsynaptic membrane contains large protein molecules which act as **receptor sites** for the transmitter substances and numerous **channels** and **pores**, normally closed, for the movement of ions into the postsynaptic neurone (fig 16.10*a*).

Synaptic vesicles contain a transmitter substance which is produced either in the cell body of the neurone and passes down the axon to the synaptic knob by axoplasmic streaming through microtubules, or directly in the synaptic knob. In both cases synthesis of transmitter substances requires enzymes produced by ribosomes in the cell body. In the synaptic knob the transmitter substance is 'packaged' into vesicles and stored pending release. The two main transmitter substances in vertebrate nervous systems are **acetylcholine (ACh)** and **noradrenaline**, although other substances exist and are described at the end of this section. Acetylcholine is an ammonium compound with the formula as shown in fig 16.9. It was the first transmitter substance to be isolated and was obtained by Otto Loewi, in 1920, from the endings of parasympathetic neurones of the vagus nerve (section 16.2) in frog heart. The detailed structure of noradrenaline is described in section 16.6.6. Neurones releasing acetylcholine are described as **cholinergic neurones** and those releasing noradrenaline are described as **adrenergic neurones**.

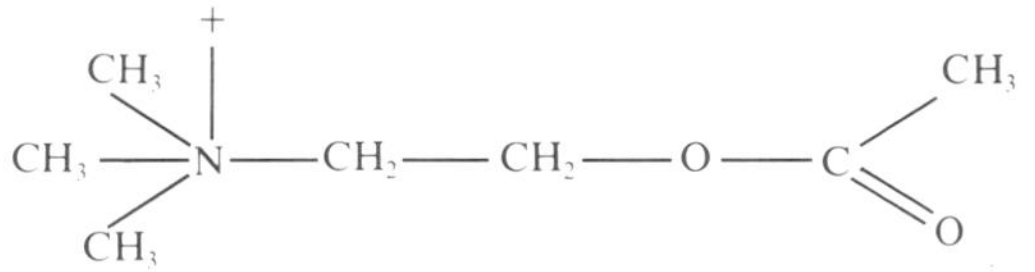

Fig 16.9 *Structural formula of acetylcholine*

Mechanisms of synaptic transmission

The arrival of nerve impulses at the synaptic knob is thought to depolarise the presynaptic membrane and increase the permeability of the membrane to Ca^{2+} ions. As the Ca^{2+} ions enter the synaptic knob they cause the synaptic vesicles to fuse with the presynaptic membrane and rupture (**exocytosis**), discharging their contents into the synaptic cleft. This is known as **excitation–secretion coupling**. The vesicles then return to the cytoplasm where they are refilled with transmitter substance. Each vesicle contains about 3 000 molecules of acetylcholine.

The transmitter substance diffuses across the synaptic cleft, imposing a delay of about 0.5 ms, and attaches to a specific receptor site on the postsynaptic membrane which recognises the molecular structure of the acetylcholine molecule. The arrival of the transmitter substance causes a change in the configuration of the receptor site leading to channels opening up in the postsynaptic membrane and the entry of ions which either **depolarise** or **hyperpolarise** (fig 16.4*a*) the membrane according to the nature of the transmitter substance released and the molecular properties of the postsynaptic receptor sites. Having produced a change in the permeability of the postsynaptic membrane the transmitter substance is immediately lost from the synaptic area by reabsorption by the presynaptic membrane, or diffusion out of the cleft or by hydrolysis by enzymes. In the case of **cholinergic** synapses acetylcholine is hydrolysed to choline by the enzyme **acetylcholinesterase (AChE)**, situated on the postsynaptic membrane, and reabsorbed into the synaptic knob to be recycled into acetylcholine by synthetic pathways in the vesicles (fig 16.10).

At **excitatory** synapses ion-specific channels open up allowing Na^+ ions to enter and K^+ ions to leave down their respective concentration gradients. This leads to a depolarisation in the postsynaptic membrane. The depolarising response is known as an **excitatory postsynaptic potential (e.p.s.p.)** and the amplitude of this potential is usually small but longer lasting than that of an action potential. The amplitude of e.p.s.p.s fluctuates in steps, suggesting that transmitter substance is released in 'packets' rather than individual molecules. Each 'step' is thought to correspond to the release of transmitter substance from one synaptic vesicle. A single e.p.s.p. is normally unable to produce sufficient depolarisation to reach the threshold required to propagate an action potential in the post-synaptic neurone. The depolarising effect of the e.p.s.p.s is additive, a phenomenon known as **summation**. Two or more e.p.s.p.s arising simultaneously at different regions on the same neurone may produce collectively sufficient depolarisation to initiate an action potential in the postsynaptic neurone. This is **spatial** (related in space) **summation**. The rapid repeated release of transmitter substance from several synaptic vesicles by the same synaptic knob as a result of an intense stimulus produces individual e.p.s.p.s which are so close together that they summate and give rise to an action potential in the postsynaptic neurone. This is **temporal** (related in time) **summation**. Therefore impulses can be set up in a single postsynaptic neurone as a result of either weak stimulation by several of its presynaptic neurones or repeated stimulation by one of its presynaptic neurones.

At **inhibitory** synapses the release of transmitter substance increases the permeability of the postsynaptic membrane by opening up ion-specific channels to Cl^- and K^+ ions. As the ions move down their concentration gradients they produce a hyperpolarisation of the membrane known as an **inhibitory postsynaptic potential (i.p.s.p.)**.

Transmitter substances are neither inherently excitatory nor inhibitory. For example, acetylcholine has an excitatory effect at most neuromuscular junctions and synapses, but has an inhibitory effect on neuromuscular junctions in cardiac muscle and visceral muscle. These opposing effects are determined by events occurring at the postsynaptic membrane. The molecular properties of the receptor sites determine which ions enter the postsynaptic cell, which in turn determines the nature of the change in postsynaptic potentials as described above.

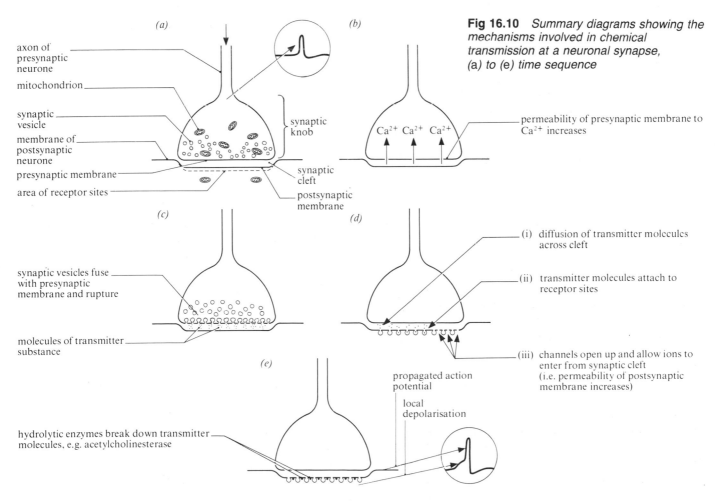

Fig 16.10 *Summary diagrams showing the mechanisms involved in chemical transmission at a neuronal synapse, (a) to (e) time sequence*

(a)

axon of presynaptic neurone

mitochondrion

synaptic vesicle

membrane of postsynaptic neurone

presynaptic membrane

area of receptor sites

synaptic knob

synaptic cleft

postsynaptic membrane

(b)

Ca^{2+} Ca^{2+} Ca^{2+}

permeability of presynaptic membrane to Ca^{2+} increases

(c)

synaptic vesicles fuse with presynaptic membrane and rupture

molecules of transmitter substance

(d)

(i) diffusion of transmitter molecules across cleft

(ii) transmitter molecules attach to receptor sites

(iii) channels open up and allow ions to enter from synaptic cleft (i.e. permeability of postsynaptic membrane increases)

(e)

hydrolytic enzymes break down transmitter molecules, e.g. acetylcholinesterase

propagated action potential

local depolarisation

571

Electrical synaptic transmission

Transmission across some synapses in many animals, including those of the coelenterate nerve net and vertebrate nervous systems, occurs by the flow of an electrical current between the pre- and postsynaptic membranes. The gap between these membranes is only 2 nm and the combined resistance to the flow of current by membranes and fluid in the cleft is very low. There is no delay in transmission time across the synapses and they are not susceptible to the action of drugs or other chemicals.

Neuromuscular junction

The neuromuscular junction is a specialised form of synapse found between the nerve terminals of a motor neurone and the **endomysium** of muscle fibres (section 17.4.2). Each muscle fibre has a specialised region, the **motor end-plate**, where the axon of the motor neurone divides and forms non-myelinated branches 100 nm wide running in shallow troughs on the membrane cell surface. The muscle cell membrane, the **sarcolemma**, has many deep folds called **junctional folds** as shown in fig 16.11. The cytoplasm of the motor neurone axon terminal has the same contents as the synaptic knob, and on stimulation releases acetylcholine by the same mechanisms as previously described. Changes in the structure of receptor sites on the sarcolemma increase the permeability of the sarcolemma to Na^+ and K^+ ions and a local depolarisation known as **end-plate potential** (**EPP**) is produced which is sufficient to lead to a propagated action potential passing along the sarcolemma and down into the fibre via the **transverse tubule system** (**T-system**) (section 17.4.7). This action potential results in the initiation of muscular contraction.

Functions of synapses and neuromuscular junctions

The primary function of neuronal synapses and neuromuscular junctions within the vertebrate nervous system is the transmission of information between receptor and effector. Several other significant functional features arise out of the structure and organisation of these sites of chemical secretion. They are summarised as follows.

(1) **Unidirectionality**. The release of transmitter substance at the presynaptic membrane, and the location of receptor sites on the postsynaptic membrane, ensure that nerve impulses pass in one direction along a given pathway. This gives **precision** to the nervous system.

(2) **Amplification**. Sufficient acetylcholine is released at the neuromuscular junction by each nerve impulse to excite the postsynaptic membrane to produce a propagated response in the muscle fibre. Thus nerve impulses arriving at the neuromuscular junction, however weak, are adequate to produce a response from the effector, thereby increasing the **sensitivity** of the system.

(3) **Adaptation or accommodation**. The amount of transmitter substance released by a synapse steadily falls off in response to constant stimulation until the supply of

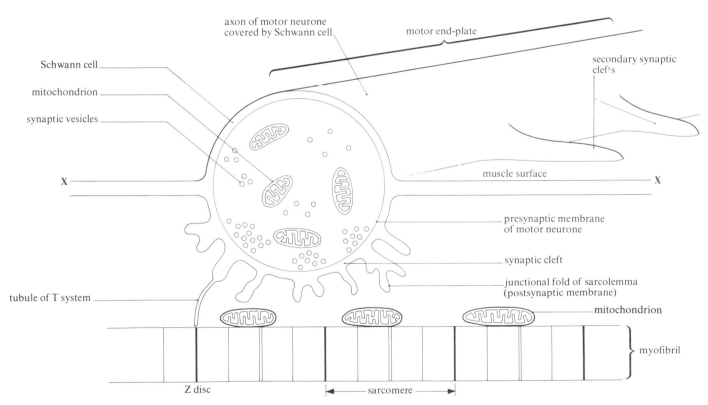

Fig 16.11 *Diagram showing the structure of a motor end plate and neuromuscular junction. The upper part of the diagram above* **X — X** *shows the course of the axon of a motor neurone on the surface of the muscle – the motor end plate. The part of the diagram below* **X — X** *shows the ultrastructure of the neuromuscular junction*

transmitter substance is exhausted and the synapse is described as **fatigued**. Further information passing along this pathway is inhibited and the adaptive significance of fatigue is the prevention of damage to an effector due to overstimulation. Adaptation also occurs at the level of the receptor and this is described in section 16.4.2.

(4) **Integration**. A postsynaptic neurone may receive impulses from a large number of excitatory and inhibitory presynaptic neurones. This is known as **synaptic convergence** and the postsynaptic neurone is able to summate the stimuli from all the presynaptic neurones. This spatial summation enables the synapse to act as one region for the integration of stimuli from a variety of sources and the production of a coordinated response. **Facilitation** occurs at some synapses and this involves each stimulus leaving the synapse more responsive to the next stimulus. In this way subsequent reduced stimuli may evoke a response and this is used to increase the sensitivity of certain synapses. Facilitation is not temporal summation in that it is a chemically mediated response of the postsynaptic membrane and not an electrical summation of postsynaptic membrane potentials.

(5) **Discrimination**. Temporal summation at synapses enables weak background stimuli to be filtered out before it reaches the brain. For example, information from exteroceptors in the skin, the eyes and ears receive constant stimuli from the environment which has little immediate importance for the nervous system. Only *changes* in intensity of stimuli are significant to the nervous system and these increase the frequency of stimuli and pass across the synapse and evoke a response.

(6) **Inhibition**. The transmission of information across synapses and neuromuscular junctions may be prevented postsynaptically by the activity of certain chemical blocking agents, described in the next section, or presynaptically. Presynaptic inhibition occurs at synaptic knobs that are in close contact with synaptic knobs from inhibitory synapses. Stimulation of these inhibitory synapses reduces the number of synaptic vesicles released by the inhibited synaptic knob. This arrangement enables a given nerve terminal to produce a variable response depending upon the activity of its excitatory and inhibitory synapses.

Chemical influences on the synapse and neuromuscular junction

Chemical substances carry out a variety of different functions in the nervous system. The effects of some chemical substances are widespread and well known, such as the excitatory effects of acetylcholine and adrenaline, whereas the effects of other substances are localised and, as yet, require further clarification. Some of these substances and their functions are described in table 16.2.

Several drugs used in the alleviation of psychiatric

Table 16.2. Summary table of chemical substances affecting the synapse and neuromuscular junction in mammals

Substance	Site of action	Function
acetylcholine	vertebrate nervous system	excitation or inhibition
gamma aminobutyric acid(GABA)	mammalian brain	inhibition
dopamine serotonin (5-hydroxytryptamine) noradrenaline	mammalian brain	excitation
lysergic acid diethylamide(LSD) mescaline	mammalian brain	produce hallucinations by mimicking the actions, or acting as antagonists, of other transmitter substances
tetanus toxin	presynaptic membrane	prevents release of inhibiting transmitter substance
botulinum toxin	presynaptic membrane	prevents release of acetylcholine
nicotine	postsynaptic membrane	mimics action of acetylcholine
eserine strychnine organophosphorus weedkillers and insecticides	postsynaptic membrane	inactivates acetylcholinesterase and prevents breakdown of acetylcholine
curare	postsynaptic membrane of neuromuscular junction	blocks action of acetylcholine
atropine	parasympathetic postganglionic endings	blocks action of acetylcholine
muscarine	parasympathetic postganglionic endings	mimics action of acetylcholine

disorders such as anxiety and depression are believed to be effective due to their ability to interact with chemical transmission at synapses. Many tranquillisers and sedatives, such as the tricyclic anti-depressant **imipramine** and **reserpine** and **monoamine oxidase inhibitors**, exert their effects by interacting with transmitter substances or their receptor sites. For example, monoamine oxidase inhibitors prevent the activity of an enzyme involved in the breakdown of adrenaline and noradrenaline and, presumably, are effective in treating depression by prolonging the effects of these transmitter substances. Hallucinogenic drugs, such as **lysergic acid diethylamide** (**LSD**) and **mescaline**, are believed to produce their effects by either mimicking the actions of naturally occurring brain transmitter substances or having antagonistic effects on other transmitter substances.

Recent research into the activity of the pain-suppressing opiate drugs, **heroin** and **morphine** in the mammalian brain have revealed the presence of naturally occurring (**endogenous**) substances having similar effects. These substances which react with the opiate receptors are collectively called

573

endorphins. Many so far have been identified and the best known are a group of low relative molecular mass peptides known as **enkephalins**, for example **metenkephalin** and β-**endorphin**. They are thought to reduce pain, influence emotion and are involved with certain types of mental illness.

This research has opened up new ideas on brain functioning and offers a biochemical basis for the control of pain and healing by such diverse activities as hypnosis, acupuncture and faith healing. Many more chemical substances of this type have yet to be isolated, identified and have their function determined. As techniques of extracting and analysing substances found in such minute quantities continue to improve, it is only a matter of time before they will help to provide a more complete understanding of brain activity.

16.2   The vertebrate nervous system

The nervous system of vertebrates is characterised by the structural and functional diversity of its neurones and their complex organisation within the body.

There are several systems of classification of the vertebrate nervous system and all have advantages and limitations. The system given in fig 16.12 divides the peripheral nervous system according to the position of innervation in the body. Internuncial neurones, modified nerve cells of the brain and sense organs are not included in this classification.

16.2.1   The peripheral nervous system

Spinal nerves arise from the spinal cord and emerge between adjacent vertebrae along most of the length of the spinal cord. They all carry both sensory and motor neurones and are described as **mixed** nerves. Further details of spinal nerves and the spinal cord are given below. **Cranial nerves** arise from the ventral surface of the brain and, with one exception, supply receptors and effectors of the head. There are 10 pairs of cranial nerves in lower vertebrates and 12 in mammals, numbered I–XII in Roman numerals. Not all cranial nerves are mixed (table 16.3).

The tenth cranial nerve, the **vagus**, includes an important motor nerve of the autonomic nervous system supplying the heart, bronchi and alimentary canal.

16.2.2   Reflex action and reflex arcs

The simplest form of irritability associated with the nervous system is **reflex action**. This is a rapid, automatic stereotyped response to a stimulus and because it is not under the conscious control of the brain it is described as an **involuntary action**. The neurones forming the pathway taken by the nerve impulses in reflex action make up a **reflex arc**. The simplest reflex arc found in animals involves a single neurone and the following pathway:

This level of organisation characterises the nervous system of coelenterates. Reflex arcs in all animal groups showing a greater level of structural and functional complexity than coelenterates include at least two neurones, an **afferent** or **sensory neurone** (*a*, towards) carrying impulses from a receptor towards an aggregation of nervous tissue which may be a **ganglion, nerve cord** or the **central nervous system**, and an **efferent** or **motor neurone** (*e*, away from) carrying impulses away from this aggregation to an effector (fig 16.13). There is a wide range of reflexes showing varying structural and functional complexity broadly involving four courses of action.

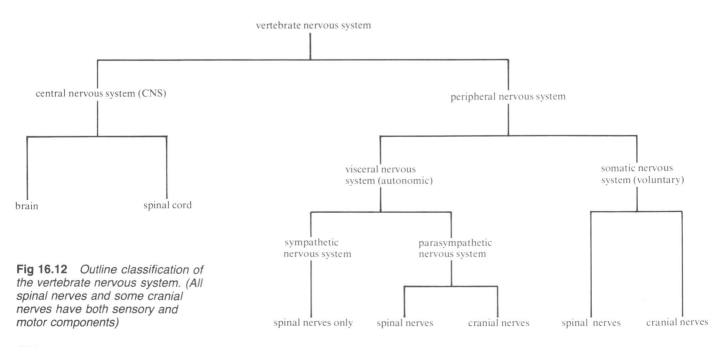

Fig 16.12 *Outline classification of the vertebrate nervous system. (All spinal nerves and some cranial nerves have both sensory and motor components)*

Table 16.3. Summary of mammalian cranial nerves, their innervations and functions

Cranial nerve	Name	Type	Innervation	Function
I	olfactory	sensory	olfactory organ	smell
II	optic	sensory	retina	sight
III	oculomotor	motor	four eye muscles	eye movements
IV	trochlear	motor	one eye muscle	eye movements
V	trigeminal	mixed	jaw muscles, teeth, skin of face	jaw movements, touch and pain receptors
VI	abducens	motor	one eye muscle	eye movements
VII	facial	mixed	cheek, face muscles, tongue	salivation, facial expression, sweet, sour, salt taste
VIII	auditory	sensory	cochlea, semicircular canals	hearing, balance
IX	glossopharyngeal	mixed	tongue, pharyngeal muscle	bitter taste, swallowing
X	vagus	mixed	larynx, pharynx, heart, gut	speech, swallowing, decrease heart rate, stimulus for peristalsis
XI	accessory	motor	head and neck	head movement
XII	hypoglossal	motor	tongue	tongue movement

(1) **Monosynaptic reflex**. This is the simplest reflex arc seen in vertebrates. The sensory neurone synapses directly on to the motor neurone cell body. Only one synapse in the central nervous system is involved in this arc. These reflexes are common in vertebrates and are involved in the control of muscle tone and posture, such as the knee jerk or patellar reflex. In these reflex arcs no neurones pass to the brain and reflex actions are carried out without the involvement of the brain because they are routine and no conscious thought or decision is required for their operation. They are economical on the number of neurones in the central nervous system and do not make trivial demands on the brain which can 'concentrate' on more important matters.

(2) **Polysynaptic spinal reflex**. This has at least two synapses situated within the central nervous system as a result of the inclusion of a third type of neurone in the arc: an **internuncial (intermediate or relay)** neurone. The synapses are found between the sensory neurone and internuncial neurone and between the internuncial neurone and the motor neurone as shown in fig 16.13*b*. This type of reflex arc provides a simple illustration of localised reflex action within the spinal cord. Fig 16.14 shows a much simplified example of the **spinal reflex** associated with the reflex action following pricking a finger on a pin.

Simple reflex arcs such as (1) and (2) allow the body to make automatic involuntary homeostatic adjustments to changes in the external environment, such as the iris–pupil reflex and balance during locomotion, and also in the internal environment, such as breathing rate and blood pressure, and to prevent damage to the body as in cuts and burns.

(3) **Polysynaptic spinal/brain reflexes**. Here the sensory neurone synapses in the spinal cord with a second

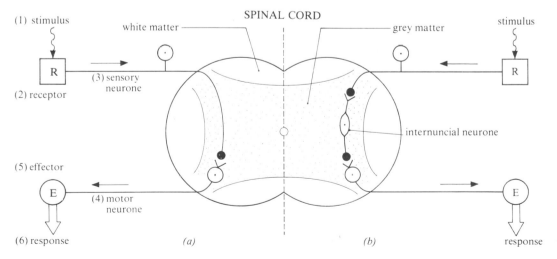

Fig 16.13 *Diagrammatic representation of two simple forms of reflex arc, (a) monosynaptic reflex arc, including the main features of a reflex arc (numbered 1 to 6) (b) simple polysynaptic reflex arc. (**R** represents receptor, **E** represents effector)*

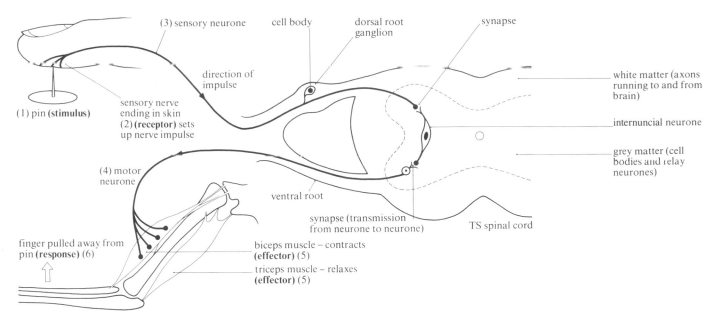

Fig 16.14 *A simplified example of reflex action and a reflex arc. (The numbers in brackets refer to the basic structures in any reflex arc shown in Fig 16.13)*

sensory neurone which passes to the brain. The latter sensory neurones are part of the **ascending nerve fibre tract** and have their origin in the pre-internuncial neurone synapse (fig 16.15*a*). The brain identifies this sensory information and stores it for further use.

Alternatively motor activity may be initiated at any time by the brain and impulses transmitted down motor neurones in **descending nerve fibre tracts** to synapse directly with spinal motor neurones in the post-internuncial synaptic region (fig 16.15*b*).

(4) **Conditioned reflexes**. These are forms of reflex actions where the type of response is modified by past experience. These reflexes are coordinated by the brain. **Learning** forms the basis of all conditioned reflexes, such as in toilet training, salivation on the sight and smell of food and awareness of danger (section 16.9).

Many simple reflex situations arise where there are two immediate responses involving the activity of a given set of muscles which can either contract or relax and produce opposite responses. The normal spinal reflex response in such situations would pass through the reflex arc shown in fig 16.14, but 'conditions' associated with the stimulus may modify the response. In these situations more complex reflex pathways exist involving excitatory and inhibitory neurones.

For example, if any empty metal baking tin is picked up and found to be extremely hot, burning the fingers, it will probably be dropped immediately whereas a boiling hot, cooked casserole in an expensive dish, equally hot and painful, will probably be put down, quickly but gently. The reason for the difference in the response reveals the involvement of conditioning and memory, followed by a conscious decision by the brain.

Fig 16.15 *Simplified diagram of sections through the brain and spinal cord showing (a) the pathway of sensory impulses from receptor, via the spinal cord, to the cerebral cortex, and (b) the pathway of motor impulses, initiated within the cortex to effector, via the spinal cord*

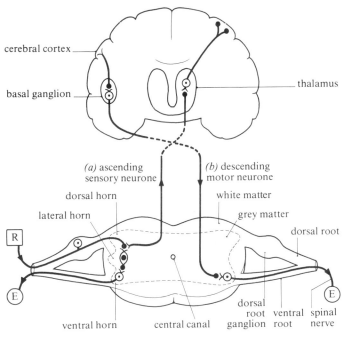

In this situation reflex pathways exist as shown in fig 16.16.

The stimulus in both cases produces impulses passing to the brain in an ascending sensory neurone. When the information reaches the brain it is interpreted and associated with related sensory information coming from other sense organs, for example the eyes, concerning the *cause* of the stimulus. The incoming

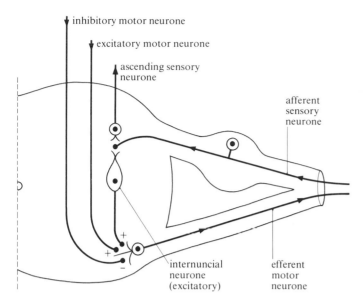

inhibitory motor neurone

excitatory motor neurone

ascending sensory neurone

afferent sensory neurone

internuncial neurone (excitatory)

efferent motor neurone

Fig 16.16 *Simplified diagram showing the relationships within the spinal cord between an internuncial neurone and the modifying effects of excitatory and inhibitory motor neurones from the brain*

information is compared with stored information concerning the nature and cause of the present stimulus and the likely outcome of allowing the spinal reflex to proceed. In the case of the metal tin, the brain computes that no further damage to either the body or the tin will occur if it is dropped and so initiates impulses in an **excitatory** motor neurone. This passes down the spinal cord to the level where the stimulus entered and synapses with the cell body of the motor neurone of the spinal reflex. Such is the speed of conduction through the pathway described above that the impulses from the excitatory motor neurone reach the spinal motor neurone at the same time as impulses from the internuncial neurone. The combined effect of these sends excitatory impulses to the muscle effector along the spinal motor neurone and the tin is dropped.

In the case of the casserole dish, the brain computes that dropping the casserole would probably scald the legs and feet, ruin the meal and break an expensive dish, whereas holding it until it could be put down safely would not cause much more damage to the fingers. If this decision is reached, impulses are initiated which pass down the spinal cord in an **inhibitory** motor neurone. These impulses arrive at the synapse with the spinal motor neurone at the same time as stimulatory impulses from the internuncial neurone and the latter are cancelled out. No impulses pass along the motor neurone to the muscle effector and the dish is held. Simultaneous brain activity would initiate an alternative muscle response which would result in the dish being put down quickly and safely.

The accounts of reflex arcs and reflex activity given above are, of necessity, simplified generalisations. The whole process of the coordination, integration and control

of body functions is much more complex. For example, neurones connect different levels of the spinal cord together, controlling say the arms and legs, so that activity in one can be related to the other whilst at the same time other neurones from the brain achieve overall control.

Whilst combined activity of the brain and endocrine system is important in the coordination of many nervous activities described later in the chapter, another reflex system, based solely on neuronal activity, exists for the control of visceral activities. This is the autonomic nervous system.

16.2.3 The autonomic nervous system

The autonomic nervous system (*autos*, self; *nomos*, governing) is that part of the peripheral nervous system controlling activities of the internal environment that are normally involuntary, such as heart rate, peristalsis and sweating. It consists of motor neurones passing to the smooth muscles of internal organs. Most of the activity of the autonomic nervous system is integrated locally within the spinal cord or brain by **visceral reflexes** and does not involve the conscious control of higher centres of the brain. However, some activities, such as the control of anal and bladder sphincter muscles, are also under the conscious control of the brain and control of these has to be learned. It is thought that many other autonomic activities may be able to be controlled by conscious effort and learning: many forms of meditation and relaxation have their physiological roots in the control of autonomic activities, and considerable success has already been achieved in regulating heart rate and reducing blood pressure by conscious control or 'will power'. The overall control of the autonomic nervous system is maintained, however, by centres in the medulla and hypothalamus (see section 16.2.4). These receive and integrate sensory information and coordinate this with information from other parts of the nervous system to produce the appropriate response.

The autonomic nervous system is composed of two types of neurones, an unmyelinated **preganglionic** neurone, which leaves the central nervous system in the ventral root of the segmental nerve before synapsing with several unmyelinated **postganglionic** neurones leading to effectors.

There are two divisions of the autonomic nervous system: the **sympathetic** and the **parasympathetic nervous systems**. The two systems differ primarily in the structural organisation of their neurones and these differences are shown in fig 16.17.

In the sympathetic nervous system the synapses and cell bodies of the postganglionic neurones in the trunk region are situated in ganglia close to the spinal cord. Each **sympathetic ganglion** is connected to the spinal cord by a **white ramus communicans** and to the spinal nerve by a **grey ramus communicans** as shown in fig 16.18. Adjacent segmental sympathetic ganglia on each side of the spinal cord are linked together by the sympathetic nerve tract to form a chain of sympathetic ganglia running alongside the

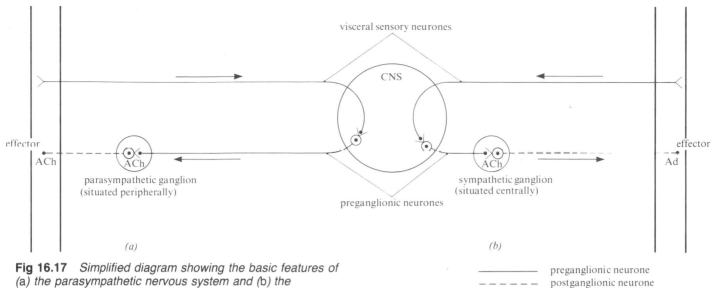

(a)

(b)

Fig 16.17 *Simplified diagram showing the basic features of (a) the parasympathetic nervous system and (b) the sympathetic nervous system (visceral sensory neurones are not part of the autonomic nervous system)*

——————	preganglionic neurone
— — — — —	postganglionic neurone
ACh	acetylcholine
Ad	noradrenaline

Fig 16.18 *Simplified diagram showing the position of a sympathetic ganglion and its relationship to the spinal cord and spinal nerve*

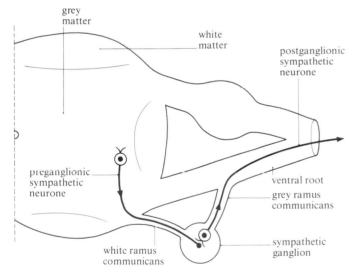

spinal cord. The ganglia of the parasympathetic nervous system are situated close to, or within, the effector organ.

Other differences between the two systems include the nature of the chemical transmitter substance released at the postganglionic effector synapse, their general effects on the body and the conditions under which they are active. These differences are summarised in table 16.4.

The sympathetic and parasympathetic nervous systems generally have opposing effects on organs they supply and this enables the body to make rapid and precise adjustments of visceral activities in order to maintain a steady state. For example, an increase in heart rate due to the release of noradrenaline by sympathetic neurones is compensated for by the release of acetylcholine by parasympathetic neurones. This action prevents heart rate becoming excessive and will eventually restore it to its normal level when secretion from both systems balances out. A summary of the antagonistic effects of these systems is shown in table 16.5.

16.2.4 The central nervous system

The **central nervous system** (**CNS**) develops from an infolding of the ectoderm immediately above the embryonic notochord and forms a dorsal, hollow neural tube running the length of the animal. The neural tube differentiates during development to form an expanded anterior region, the **brain**, and a long cylindrical **spinal cord**.

The central nervous system is covered by three membranes called **meninges** and is completely encased within the protective bones of the skull and vertebral column. The outer membrane forms the tough **dura mater** attached to the periosteum of the skull and vertebrae, and the inner **pia mater** which directly overlies the nervous tissues. Between the two is the **arachnoid** 'membrane', composed of pillars of connective tissue supporting a space beneath it, the **subarachnoid space**, which contains the **cerebrospinal fluid** (**CSF**). Most of this fluid is contained in the central canal of the spinal cord and continues forward to occupy four expanded regions, the **ventricles**, of the brain. The fluid bathes the outside and inside of the brain and blood vessels lie within it for the supply of nutrients and oxygen to the nervous tissues and the removal of wastes (see fig 16.19). The cells of the vascular **anterior** and **posterior choroid plexuses** in the roof of the brain secrete CSF and provide a link between the fluid outside and inside the brain. About 100 cm³ of fluid is present in the CNS and, apart from its nutritive and excretory functions, it supports the nervous tissues and protects them against mechanical shock. A continual circulation of fluid is maintained by ciliated cells lining the ventricles and central canal.

Table 16.4. Summary of the differences between the sympathetic and parasympathetic nervous systems

Feature	Sympathetic	Parasympathetic
Origin of neurones	Emerges from cranial, thoracic and lumbar regions of CNS	Emerges from cranial and sacral regions of CNS
Position of ganglion	Close to spinal cord	Close to effector
Length of fibres	Short preganglionic fibres Long postganglionic fibres	Long preganglionic fibres Short postganglionic fibres
Number of fibres	Numerous postganglionic fibres	Few postganglionic fibres
Distribution of fibres	Preganglionic fibres innervate a wide area	Preganglionic fibres innervate a restricted region
Area of influence	Effect diffuse	Effect localised
Transmitter substance	Noradrenaline released at effector	Acetylcholine released at effector
General effects	Increases metabolite levels Increases metabolic rate Increases rhythmic activities Lowers sensory threshold	Decreases metabolite levels None Decreases rhythmic activities Restores sensory threshold to normal levels
Overall effect	Excitatory homeostatic effect	Inhibitory homeostatic effect
Conditions when active	Dominant during danger, stress and activity; controls reactions to stress	Dominant during rest Controls routine body activities

Table 16.5 Summary of the effects of the sympathetic and parasympathetic nervous systems on the body

Region	Sympathetic	Parasympathetic
Head	Dilates pupils None Inhibits secretion of saliva	Constricts pupils Stimulates secretion of tears Stimulates secretion of saliva
Heart	Increases amplitude and rate of heart beat	Decreases amplitude and rate of heart beat
Lungs	Dilates bronchi and bronchioles Increases ventilation rate	Constricts bronchi and bronchioles Decreases ventilation rate
Gut	Inhibits peristalsis Inhibits secretion of alimentary juices Contracts anal sphincter muscle	Stimulates peristalsis Stimulates secretion of alimentary juices Inhibits contraction of anal sphincter muscle
Blood	Constricts arterioles to gut and smooth muscle Dilates arterioles to brain and skeletal muscle Increases blood pressure Increases blood volume by contraction of spleen	Maintains steady muscle tone in arterioles to gut, smooth muscle, brain and skeletal muscle Reduces blood pressure None
Skin	Contracts erector pili muscles of hair Constricts arterioles in skin of limbs Increases secretion of sweat	None Dilates arterioles in skin of face None
Kidney	Decreases output of urine	None
Bladder	Contracts bladder sphincter muscle	Inhibits contraction of bladder sphincter muscles
Penis	Induces ejaculation	Stimulates erection
Glands	Releases adrenaline from adrenal medulla	None

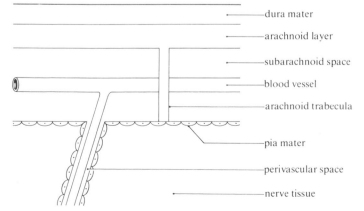

— dura mater
— arachnoid layer
— subarachnoid space
— blood vessel
— arachnoid trabecula
— pia mater
— perivascular space
— nerve tissue

Fig 16.19 *Diagram showing the structure of the meninges and associated blood vessels. Notice that the channels through the nerve tissue are lined by the pia mater*

The functions of the central nervous system involve the coordination, integration and control of most nervous activities and it works in conjunction with the peripheral nervous system. In higher organisms, advanced forms of nervous activity, such as memory and intelligence, are possible due to the increased size of certain regions of the brain.

The spinal cord

The spinal cord is a dorso-ventrally flattened cylinder of nervous tissue running from the base of the brain to the lumbar region and protected by vertebrae. It consists of an H-shaped central core of **grey matter**, composed of nerve cell bodies, dendrites and synapses surrounding a central canal, and an outer layer, the **white matter**, containing nerve fibres whose fatty myelin sheaths give it its characteristic colour. There are 31 pairs of segmental **spinal nerves** present and these divide close to the spinal cord to form two branches called the **dorsal root** and **ventral root**. Sensory neurones enter the dorsal root and have their cell bodies in a swelling, the **dorsal root ganglion**, close to the spinal cord. The sensory neurones then enter the dorsal horn of the grey matter where they synapse with **internuncial** (intermediate or relay) neurones. These, in turn, synapse with motor neurones in the **ventral horn** and leave the spinal cord via the ventral root (fig 16.15). Since there are many more internuncial neurones than motor neurones, some integration must occur within the grey matter. Some sensory neurones synapse directly with motor neurones in the ventral horn, as in the familiar knee-jerk reflex (fig 16.13a). In the thoracic, upper lumbar and sacral regions a **lateral horn** is present (fig 16.15) containing the cell bodies of the preganglionic autonomic neurones. The white matter is composed of groups of nerve fibres, forming tracts, running between the grey matter and the brain and providing a means of communication between spinal nerves and the brain. **Ascending tracts** carry sensory information to the brain and **descending tracts** relay motor information to the spinal cord.

The functions of the spinal cord include acting as a coordinating centre for simple spinal reflexes, such as the knee-jerk response, and autonomic reflexes, such as contraction of the bladder, and providing a means of communication between spinal nerves and the brain.

The brain

The brain is the swollen anterior end of the vertebrate neural tube and it coordinates and controls the activities of the whole nervous system. The brain is composed entirely of groups of cell bodies, nerve tracts and blood vessels. The **nerve fibre tracts** form the **white matter** of the brain and carry bundles of neurones to and from various regions called '**nuclei**' or **centres** composed of groups of cell bodies and synapses collectively forming the **grey matter** of the brain. The tracts connect the various 'nuclei' together and link the brain and spinal cord. During the phylogenetic development of the vertebrate brain the number of tracts and the complexity of their interconnections have increased. The 'nuclei' vary in size from isolated groups of several hundred cells to large regions such as the cerebral cortex and the cerebellar cortex in Man consisting of several hundred million cells.

The structure of the vertebrate brain. The vertebrate brain differentiates initially into three regions during its embryological development and these are the **forebrain, midbrain** and **hindbrain**. Primitively, these three regions are associated with the coordination of the senses of smell, sight and balance respectively. Subsequent development of the brain varies between and within each vertebrate class, and the original tripartite structure becomes obscured as the forebrain and hindbrain each subdivide. The adult vertebrate brain has five regions, and they assume a particular significance within each class associated with the mode of life and level of structural and functional complexity attained by the class. Some regions of the brain have increased in size reflecting their importance whereas others have diminished. The overall structure of the generalised vertebrate brain is shown in fig 16.20 and a summary showing the development of the regions of the brain in non-mammalian and mammalian vertebrates is given in table 16.6.

Fish are very dependent upon smell in order to find food and have large olfactory lobes to accommodate the sensory input. A large cerebellum coordinates movements, and the large optic lobes act partly in visual responses but mainly as the main coordination centre of the brain. The optic lobes form the dominant feature of the amphibian brain where they have the same functions as in fish. Reptiles show a reduction in the size of the midbrain and an increase in the size of the forebrain. This trend continues in birds with an increase in the sizes of the thalamus and corpora striata where most of the complex, instinctive behavioural activities of birds are coordinated. Finally, mammals are characterised by a large pair of cerebral hemispheres covering a well-developed thalamus. These two structures, containing nuclei and tracts respectively, reflect the dependence placed on the storage of sensory information and the integration of all voluntary activities. The medulla shows little change in relative size throughout the vertebrates and this stresses the importance placed on the reflex control of all essential functions such as heart rate.

Methods of studying brain function

Little knowledge of the functions of the various regions of the brain can be obtained by simply studying their anatomy and histology. Whilst this provides valuable information about structural interrelationships, it does not explain the physiological activities occurring in the brain. Brain activity has been studied using electrophysiological techniques, including the use of **electroencephalograms**. Good electrical contact is made between electrodes and the scalp using electrode jelly and electrical changes produced by the activity of many cells of the cerebral cortex are detected,

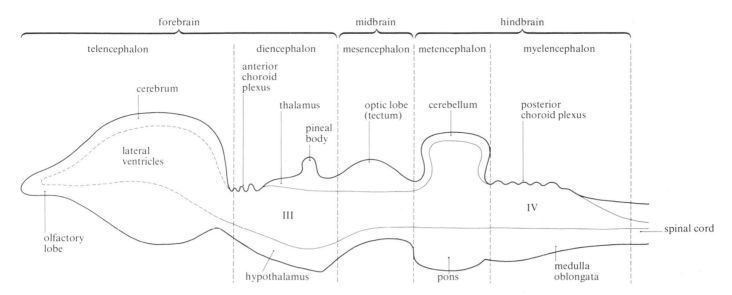

Fig 16.20 *Diagram showing a median section of a generalised vertebrate brain. The numbers refer to the positions of the IIIrd and IVth ventricles*

Table 16.6. The origins and regions of the vertebrate brain

Embryonic division	Adult region	Structural/functional regions	
		Non-mammal	Mammal
forebrain	telencephalon	olfactory lobes (fish) neopallium (reptiles) corpora striata (birds)	cerebral hemispheres basal ganglia
	diencephalon	thalamus hypothalamus	thalamus hypothalamus
midbrain	mesencephalon	optic lobes (amphibia) tectum	corpora quadrigemina
hindbrain	metencephalon	cerebellum pons	cerebellum pons
	myelencephalon	medulla oblongata	medulla oblongata

amplified and recorded on a pen trace. Three major wave frequencies have been detected. α-**waves** are recorded from relaxed subjects with their eyes closed and they usually mask the higher frequency β-**waves** which are present at all times and best seen in patients under anaesthesia. The absence of β-waves or any electrical activity from the brain of a patient indicates 'brain-stem-death' and, along with cessation of heart beat and ventilation is taken as a clinical definition of death. δ-**waves** have the lowest frequency and greatest amplitude and are recorded during sleep. Whilst electroencephalograms yield little immediate information regarding brain function, they are valuable in diagnosing the position of localised brain abnormalities, and, for example, the various forms of epilepsy. Epilepsy is a result of excessive activity of the

CNS and occurs in two forms. The first, *grand mal* produces powerful convulsions lasting from several seconds to minutes whereas the second, *petit mal* produces mild convulsions lasting for much shorter periods of time.

Investigations of brain function are carried out on the brains of patients under local anaesthesia. In one type of investigation patients describe sensations produced whilst various regions of the brain are electrically stimulated. This technique enables motor activities of regions of the cerebral cortex to be mapped (fig 16.23). Likewise recordings of electrical activity obtained using microelectrodes inserted into cell bodies or axons in specific regions during stimulation of sensory cells and organs have enabled maps to be drawn showing regions of brain sensory function.

The structure and functions of the human brain

The following account of the brain is brief and represents a summary of current knowledge of the structures and functions of the human brain. Elaboration of function and evidence for this is omitted except where it is considered necessary for clarification. In this chapter the brain is considered from a structural standpoint and the activities of each region shown in table 16.6 are described in turn. By necessity this approach and account is a gross oversimplification since many brain activities span several regions, and it is useful to bear in mind that functionally there are three main interrelated regions, the cerebrum (cerebral hemispheres), the cerebellum and the brain stem, the latter being composed of the medulla, pons, mesencephalon and thalamus. The brain stem is an extension of the spinal cord and contains complex neuronal pathways controlling cardiovascular function, ventilation, gastrointestinal function, eye movement, equilibrium and most of the stereotyped activities of the body.

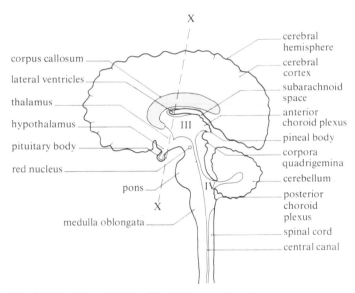

Fig 16.21 (above) *Simplified diagram showing a vertical section through the human brain (the numbers indicate the ventricles of the brain)*

Fig 16.22 (below) *Simplified diagram showing a cross-section of the human brain through **X — X** on Fig. 16.21*

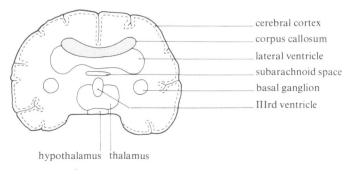

Telencephalon

This is the anterior region of the forebrain and consists of the **cerebrum** and **basal ganglia**. The cerebrum forms the roof and walls of the telencephalon and is greatly enlarged to form the left and right cerebral hemispheres covering most of the brain. The basal ganglia occupy the floor of the telencephalon.

Cerebrum. The cerebral hemispheres are composed of a thin outer layer (3 mm) of densely packed nerve cells (10^9) forming a region of grey matter called the **cerebral cortex**. Beneath this is a central mass of white matter composed of nerve fibre tracts. Left and right cerebral hemispheres are linked by a broad nerve fibre tract called the **corpus callosum** and the surface area of the cortex is increased by numerous infoldings called **convolutions**. Each cerebral hemisphere is divided, for convenience, into four lobes as shown in fig 16.23, and electrophysiological techniques have enabled three discrete areas to be recognised according to the functions their cells perform. These areas are:

(1) **sensory** – receiving impulses indirectly from receptors (input),

(2) **association** – interpreting the input, storing the input and initiating a response in the light of similar past experience, and

(3) **motor** – transmitting impulses to effectors (output).

The interrelationships between the above areas enable the cerebral cortex to dominate and coordinate all voluntary and some involuntary activities of the body, including highly developed functions such as memory, learning, reasoning, conscience and personality. If the cerebral cortex is entirely destroyed it would not cause death but the patient would show no spontaneous activity. The patient would be able to respond to certain stimuli but would be unable to learn or reason and all visible signs of intelligence and personality would disappear. Only those reflexes controlled predominantly by the medulla and cerebellum, such as feeding and sleeping, would remain.

Sensory areas are the input areas of the cortex and receive sensory impulses via ascending tracts from receptors originating from most parts of the body. The sensory areas form localised regions of the cortex associated with certain senses as shown in fig 16.23. The size of the region is related to the number of receptors in the sensory structure.

Association areas are so named for several reasons. First, they associate incoming sensory information with previously perceived information stored in memory units, so that the information is 'recognised'. Secondly, the information is associated with incoming sensory information from other receptors. Thirdly, the information is 'interpreted' and given meaning within its present context and, if necessary, the interpreted information is associated with the 'computed' most appropriate response which the association area initiates and passes to its associated motor area. Association areas, therefore, are involved in memory,

16.23 *Diagram showing the positions of the four main lobes of the brain: frontal, parietal, occipital and temporal. Superimposed on these are the major: sensory, association and motor areas and centres. The positions of certain regions of the brain associated with specific activities and regions of the body are also shown*

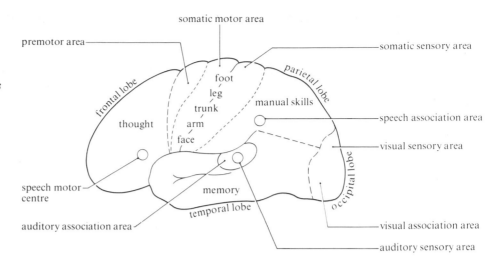

learning and reasoning, and the degree of success of the outcome may be loosely termed **intelligence**.

Several major association areas are adjacent to their related sensory area; for example, the **visual association area** is situated immediately anterior to the visual cortex in the **occipital lobe** where, in a visual context, it carries out the association functions described above. Some association areas may have a restricted specialised function and these are linked to other association centres that can further develop the activity. For example, the **auditory association area** only interprets sounds into broad categories which are relayed to more specialised association areas such as the **speech association area** where 'sense' is made of the words. Speech is initiated in the **speech motor centre** which is an example of the third type of functional area found in the cerebrum.

Motor areas are the output areas of the cortex where motor impulses are initiated to pass to voluntary muscles via descending tracts originating in the white matter of the cerebrum.

Many motor impulses pass directly to the spinal cord through two large **pyramidal tracts (corticospinal tracts)** via the brain stem. All other motor impulses pass through **extrapyramidal tracts** which contain motor impulses from other regions of the brain such as the basal ganglia and cerebellum. In the medulla all tracts cross over so that impulses from the left cerebral cortex innervate the right side of the body and vice versa.

Neurones passing through the pyramidal tracts have their cell bodies in the motor cortex and their axons pass directly to synapse with the motor neurones that they activate in the spinal segment at the point where the latter emerge. There are no intervening synapses in the brain, therefore impulses and subsequent responses are neither delayed nor modified en route. Localised regions of the motor cortex have been mapped, and examples of these are shown in fig 16.23. The size of each specific motor area is related to the complexity of the motor activity.

The main extrapyramidal tract is the **reticulospinal tract** which relays motor neurones from the **reticular formation** situated in the brain stem between the thalamus and medulla. Motor impulses from various regions of the brain controlling muscular activity pass to specific areas of the reticular formation where this activity is modified by impulses from the cortex and becomes either **inhibitory** or **excitatory**. For example, impulses from the cerebellum and **premotor area** of the cortex, a region involved in the control of coordinated movements, pass to an area of the reticular formation in the medulla where the combined effect stimulates **inhibitory motor neurones**. These have a suppressive regulatory effect on muscle activity enabling complex coordinated movements of the body to occur, such as the varied control involved in angling, directing and powering a tennis racquet, cricket ball or violin bow, according to circumstances. Other combinations of motor impulses stimulate **excitatory motor neurones**; in fact, the overall motor output of the reticular formation is excitatory.

Most sensory neurones run to the reticular formation before passing to the cortex via the thalamus. Some of these sensory neurones form the **reticular activating system** and are responsible for activating the cortex and arousing the body from its natural state of sleep. Underactivity or destruction of the reticular activating system induces deep sleep or coma respectively. Many general anaesthetics are thought to act by temporarily blocking synaptic transmission in this system. The reticular activating system is also believed to be responsible for producing and sustaining motivation and concentration hence the inverse relationship between tiredness and concentration.

Finally, the functions of certain regions of the cortex, particularly the large anterior regions, the **prefrontal lobes**, are still uncertain. These regions, along with others in the brain, are called **silent areas** because they fail to produce either sensation or response when stimulated electrically. They are believed to be responsible for our individual characteristics or **personality**. The removal of the lobes or cutting the tracts leading from them to the rest of the brain (**prefrontal lobotomy**) was used to relieve acute anxiety states in patients but it has been discontinued. The side-effects included a reduction in mental awareness, intelligence, judgement and creativity and gave an indication of the functions of the prefrontal lobes.

Basal ganglia. These are regions of the forebrain containing cell bodies receiving motor neurones from parts of the cortex and passing on impulses to the reticular formation. The functions of the basal ganglia are varied, but one ganglion, for example, provides inhibitory stimuli for the antagonistic control of muscle tone during slow movements. Damage to this basal ganglion produces the tremor of the hands associated with Parkinson's disease, a form of muscle paralysis.

Diencephalon

This is the posterior region of the forebrain and its dorsal and lateral regions form the **thalamus** and the ventral region forms the **hypothalamus**. The **pineal body** arises in this region and its function is described in section 16.6.3.

Thalamus. The majority of sensory neurones carrying impulses to the cortex terminate in the thalamus. Here the origin and nature of the impulses are 'analysed' and relayed to the appropriate sensory areas of the cortex by neurones originating in the thalamus. It therefore acts as a processing, integrating and relay centre for all sensory information. In this function it shows similarities to a switchboard in a telephone exchange. Information from certain regions of the cortex is modified by the thalamus, which is also thought to be involved in the perception of pain and pleasure. Part of the reticular formation, whose function was described above for the cerebral motor areas, originates in the thalamus. The dorsal region immediately anterior to the thalamus, the **anterior choroid plexus**, facilitates transfer of substances between the CSF in the third ventricle and the subarachnoid space (fig 16.21).

Hypothalamus. This is the main coordinating and control centre for the autonomic nervous system. It receives sensory neurones from all the visceral receptors and taste and smell receptors. Information is relayed from here to effectors via the medulla and spinal cord, and is used in the regulation and control of heart rate, blood pressure, ventilation rate and peristalsis. Other regions of the hypothalamus contain specific centres for the initiation of feeding, drinking and sleeping, and behavioural activities associated with aggression and reproduction. The hypothalamus is the most vascular region of the brain and monitors the metabolite and hormone levels of the blood as well as blood temperature. Using this information the hypothalamus, in association with the pituitary gland situated immediately beneath it, directs and controls the release of most of the hormones from the body, and maintains the steady-state composition of the blood and tissues. The detailed neuroendocrine role of the hypothalamus is described in section 16.6.2.

Mesencephalon

This connects the anterior two regions of the brain to the posterior two regions and, therefore, all nerve fibre tracts within the brain pass through this region which is part of the brain stem. The roof of the mesencephalon is composed of the **tectum** consisting of the four **corpora quadrigemina** and these function as visual and auditory reflex centres. The superior pair of corpora quadrigemina receive sensory neurones from the eyes and muscles of the head and control visual reflexes. For example, they control the movement of the head and eyes to fix and focus on an object. The inferior pair of corpora quadrigemina receive sensory neurones from the ears and muscles of the head and control auditory reflexes such as the movement of the head to locate and detect the source of a sound.

Situated in the floor of the mesencephalon are many centres or nuclei controlling specific subconscious stereotyped muscular movements, such as bending forwards and backwards and rotation of the head and trunk. For example, stimulation of part of one of these nuclei, the **red nucleus**, causes the head and upper trunk to extend backwards.

Metencephalon

The dorsal region of the metencephalon forms the **cerebellum** and the ventral region forms the **pons**.

Cerebellum. This is made up of the two **cerebellar hemispheres** and, like the cerebrum, has its grey matter on the outside. The grey matter contains characteristically large flask-shaped **Purkinje** cells bearing many dendrites. These cells receive impulses concerning muscular movement from a number of different sources, including sensory receptors in the balance organs (the vestibular apparatus) of the ear concerned with balance, proprioceptors in joints, tendons and muscles and motor centres of the cortex. The cerebellum is thought to integrate this information and produce coordinated muscular activity in all the muscles involved in a given movement including the reflex control of body posture. Damage to the cerebellum results in jerky, poorly controlled movements. The cerebellum is vital to the control of rapid muscular activities such as running, typing and even talking. All the activities of the cerebellum are involuntary but may involve learning in their early stages. During these training periods the cortex directs the control of the cerebellum and concentration is required, such as when learning to walk, swim or ride a bicycle. Once the skill is acquired reflex control by the cerebellum takes over.

Pons. This forms the part of the brain stem in the floor of the metencephalon and, apart from acting as a bridge (*pons*, bridge) carrying ascending and descending tracts, it contains several 'nuclei' relaying impulses to the cerebellum.

Myelencephalon

This is the posterior region of the brain and is continuous

with the spinal cord. It is composed of the dorsally situated **posterior choroid plexus** and the ventro-lateral **medulla oblongata**.

In the medulla the ascending and descending nerve fibre tracts cross over from left to right and vice versa. The eighth to twelfth cranial nerves originate from the medulla and it contains important reflex centres for the regulation of autonomic activities including the control of heart rate (chapters 14 and 18), blood pressure (chapters 14 and 18), ventilation rate (chapters 11 and 18), swallowing, salivation, sneezing, vomiting and coughing.

16.3 The phylogenetic development of the nervous system

A study of animal phylogeny shows a progressive increase in structural and functional complexity from protozoa to mammals. Several trends and patterns in the organisation of organ systems have become established and this is clearly reflected in the development of the nervous system as shown by a study of irritability in protozoa, coelenterates, annelids, arthropods and mammals.

In protozoa the ability to respond to a stimulus resides within a single cell of the organism. There is no spatial separation between the stimulus and response and the cell functions as both receptor and effector. Investigations carried out on irritability in *Amoeba* suggested that the mechanism of transducing a stimulus, for example prodding it with a blunt needle, involves the plasma membrane and the granular endoplasm. The mechanism probably involves the release of energy by an ATP/ATPase system which provides energy for amoeboid movement (section 17.6.1) thus enabling *Amoeba* to make an avoidance response to the stimulus.

The development of multicellular organisation in the coelenterates has led to an increase in spatial separation of stimulus and response, receptor and effector. Fortunately, the attainment of the multicellular state was accompanied by tissue differentiation and the appearance of nerve cells linking receptor to effector, thus overcoming difficulties of spatial separation. The nervous system of primitive coelenterates, for example *Hydra*, is a **nerve net** or **plexus** composed of a single layer of short multipolar neurones in synaptic contact throughout the organism. Impulses spread out in all directions from the point of stimulation and at each synapse an impulse is lost. This impulse is used, effectively, to 'charge' the synapse so that subsequent impulses can cross the synapse. This process is called **facilitation** and, since an impulse is lost at each synapse in facilitating (making easier) the passage of the next impulse, the mechanism of conduction is called **decremental conduction**. Nervous conduction in these organisms is therefore slow, due to the number of synapses to cross, and spatially restricted because impulses die out as they progress outwards from the stimulus. This system is useful in producing localised responses, say within a tentacle, but of little value to the whole organism unless the stimulus is **intense** or **prolonged**. In most advanced coelenterates, such as jellyfish and sea anemones, in addition to the nerve net there is a system of elongate bipolar neurones arranged in tracts, called **through conduction tracts**, and able to transmit impulses rapidly over considerable distance and without apparent loss. This system enables the organism to make fairly rapid responses of the whole body to harmful stimuli, such as the withdrawal of tentacles, and this foreshadows the aggregation of neurones into nerves seen in higher organisms.

In the annelids the association of neurones into nerves has resulted in a nervous system consisting of a single longitudinal tract, the **ventral nerve cord**, running the entire length of the organism. This consists of paired segmentally arranged ganglia joined by connecting neurones and supplying segmental nerves to the tissues of each segment as shown in fig 17.37.

As a result of the unidirectional method of locomotion, annelids possess a head. This structure is specialised to assist with feeding and, since it is the first part of the body to come into contact with new environmental situations, it contains all the sensory structures necessary to detect stimuli associated with these situations. The increased input of sensory information from these receptors to the nervous system is dealt with by the enlarged anterior end of the nerve cord. This concentration of feeding apparatus, sense organs and nervous tissue into one region is called **cephalisation**. It should be emphasised though that the term applies to the development of *all* the features associated with the head and not just the nervous tissue. The degree of cephalisation shown by an organism varies according to the level of structural complexity attained by the organism and its mode of life.

The annelid nervous system shows all the basic features found in all other invertebrate groups. The enlarged anterior region of the nerve cord forms a pair of **cerebral ganglia** situated above the pharynx and linked to the ventral nerve cord by a pair of **circumpharyngeal connectives**.

In arthropods the basic organisation of the nervous system is almost identical to that of annelids except that the cerebral ganglia overlie the oesophagus and consequently are linked to the ventral nerve cord by **circumoesophageal connectives**. Cerebral ganglia are analogous to the vertebrate brain but do not possess the same degree of autonomy over the entire nervous system as seen in vertebrates. For example, removal of the head of an invertebrate has very little effect on movement, whereas in vertebrates the brain initiates and controls all movement of the body. Invertebrate cerebral ganglia, in fact, appear to act simply as relay centres between receptors and effectors and their role in integration and coordination is limited to a few neuroendocrine responses such as the timing of reproductive activities in annelids and the control of ecdysis and moulting in arthropods (section 21.7.3).

16.4   Sensory receptors

The coordinated activity of an organism relies upon a continuous input of information from the internal and external environments. If this information leads to a change in activity or behaviour of the animals, it is a **stimulus**. The specialised region of the body detecting the stimulus is known as a **sensory receptor**.

The simplest and most primitive type of receptor consists of a single unspecialised primary sense cell composed of a single sensory neurone whose terminal end is capable of detecting the stimulus and giving rise to a nerve impulse passing to the central nervous system, for example, skin mechanoreceptors such as the **Pacinian corpuscle** (section 16.5.1). More complex receptors are known as **secondary sense cells**, and they consist of modified epithelial cells able to detect stimuli. These form synaptic connections with their sensory neurones which transmit impulses to the CNS, for example mammalian taste buds (fig 16.31). The most complex receptors are **sensory organs** composed of a large number of sense cells, sensory neurones and associated accessory structures. The mammalian eye and ear show the level of complexity which is attained by sense organs. In the eye there are two types of secondary sense cells, rods and cones, many connecting neurones and many accessory structures such as the lens and iris.

The accessory structures often serve the double function of eliminating the effects of unwanted stimuli and amplifying the effects of desired stimuli.

On the basis of the position of the receptor and the stimulus three types of receptor are identified:

(1) **exteroceptors** – these respond to stimuli originating outside the body, as with the ear and sound;
(2) **interoceptors** – these respond to stimuli originating inside the body, such as blood pressure and carbon dioxide receptors in the carotid arteries;
(3) **proprioceptors** – these respond to stimuli concerned with the relative positions and movements of muscles and the skeleton.

An alternative, and somewhat preferable, system of classification is based on the type of stimulus detected by the receptor, and this is shown in table 16.7.

Table 16.7. Types of receptors and the stimuli detected by them

Type of receptor	Type of stimulus energy	Nature of stimulus
photoreceptor	electromagnetic	light
electroreceptor	electromagnetic	electricity
mechanoreceptor	mechanical	sound, touch, pressure, gravity
thermoreceptor	thermal	temperature change
chemoreceptor	chemical	humidity, smell, taste

Animals only detect stimuli existing in one of the forms of energy shown in table 16.7. Structures transforming stimulus energy into electrical responses in axons are known as **transducers** and, in this respect, receptors act as **biological transducers**.

All receptors transform the energy of the stimulus into a localised non-propagated electrical response which initiates nerve impulses in the neurone leaving the receptor. Thus receptors **encode** a variety of stimuli into nerve impulses which pass into the central nervous system where they are decoded and utilised to produce the required responses as shown in fig 16.13b. The type of response and its extent and duration are all directly related to the nature of the stimulus.

16.4.1   The mechanism of transduction

All sensory cells are excitable cells, and they share with nerve cells and muscle cells the ability to respond to an appropriate stimulus by producing a rapid change in their electrical properties. When not stimulated, sensory cells are able to maintain a resting potential as described in section 16.1.1, but respond to a stimulus by producing a change in membrane potential. Bernard Katz, in 1950, using a specialised stretch receptor known as a muscle spindle was able to demonstrate the presence of a depolarisation in the immediate region of the sensory nerve ending in the muscle spindle. This localised depolarisation is found only in the sensory cell and is known as the **generator** or **receptor potential**. Subsequent investigations involving intracellular recordings, made by penetrating the membranes of receptor cells in muscle spindles and the mechanoreceptors of the skin, the Pacinian corpuscles, have revealed the following information about transduction:

(1) the generator potential results from the stimulus producing a non-selective increase in the permeability of the sensory cell membrane to sodium and potassium ions which flow down their electro-chemical gradients;
(2) the magnitude of the generator potential varies with the intensity of the stimulus;
(3) when the generator potential reaches a predetermined threshold it gives rise to a propagated action potential in the sensory axon leading from the sensory cell (fig 16.24);
(4) the frequency of the nerve impulses in the sensory axon is directly related to the intensity of the stimulus.

This latter point was, in fact, established in Cambridge in 1926 by Lord Adrian, who demonstrated that sensory information is carried by all-or-nothing action potentials as a frequency code. We now know that only the generator potential exhibits an amplitude code but, following the attainment of a certain threshold value in the sensory neurone, this gives rise to a propagated all-or-nothing response in the sensory neurone.

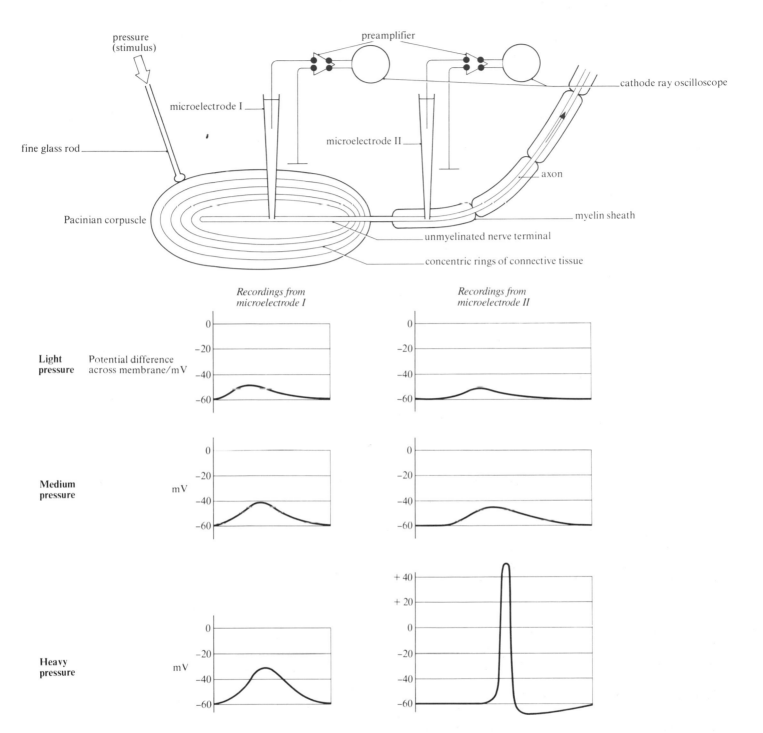

Fig 16.24 *The electrical activity recorded by two microelectrodes (I) and (II) inserted into (I) the axon terminal within a Pacinian corpuscle and (II) the axon of the sensory neurone leaving the corpuscle. As the pressure on the fine glass rod, acting as the stimulus is increased, the amplitude of the localised, non-propagated generator potential increases and at a certain threshold produces a propagated action potential in the sensory neurone*

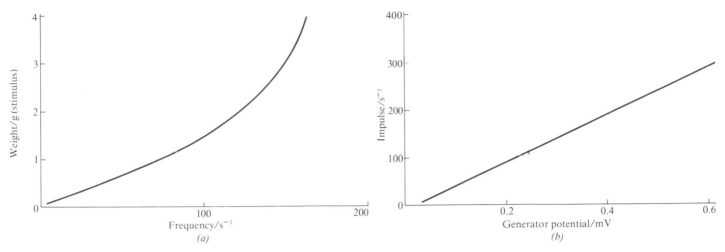

16.25 *Graphs obtained during investigations on frog muscle spindles (a) after Adrian and Zotterman, 1926 and (b) after Katz, 1950*

16.7 Study the graphs shown in fig 16.25, obtained from investigations on frog muscle spindle, and describe the relationship between stimulus, generator potential, and frequency of nerve impulses.

16.4.2 Properties of receptors

The input to the central nervous system from receptors provides the organism with all the essential information to enable it to survive. As a rule a single receptor cell cannot monitor the whole range of a given type of stimulus, however the organism needs to have information concerning the strength or intensity of each stimulus in order to produce the correct response. Receptors have two major properties which increase their effectiveness and efficiency. These are **sensitivity** and **discrimination** and they are obtained by the following structural and functional adaptations.

Parallel sensory cells with various thresholds

Some sense organs, such as stretch receptors in muscle, are composed of many sense cells having a range of thresholds. Those having a low threshold are stimulated by weak stimuli, and as the strength of the stimuli increases they respond by producing an increasing number of impulses in the sensory neurone leaving the sense cell. At a given point saturation occurs and the frequency of impulses in the neurone cannot be increased. A further increase in intensity of stimulus will excite sense cells with higher thresholds, and these too will produce a frequency of responses which is proportional to the intensity of the applied stimulus. In this way the range of receptors is extended (fig 16.26).

Adaptation

Most receptors initially respond to a strong constant stimulus by producing a high frequency of impulses in the sensory neurone. The frequency of these impulses gradually declines and this reduction in response, with time, is called **adaptation**. For example, on entering a room you may immediately notice a clock ticking but after a while become unaware of its presence. The rate and extent of adaptation in a receptor cell is related to its function and there are two types, rapidly and slowly adapting receptors.

Rapidly adapting receptors (phasic receptors) respond to changes in stimulus level by producing a high frequency of impulses at the moments when the stimulus is switched 'on' or 'off'. For example, the Pacinian corpuscle and other receptors concerned with touch and the detection of sudden changes act in this way and register the *dynamic* aspects of a stimulus.

Slowly adapting receptors (tonic receptors) register a constant stimulus with a slowly decreasing frequency of impulses. For example, crayfish stretch receptors register *static* aspects of a stimulus associated with more or less steady conditions.

Adaptation is thought to be related to a decrease in the permeability of the receptor membrane to ions due to sustained stimulation. This progressively reduces the amplitude and duration of the generator potential and when this falls below the threshold level the sensory neurone ceases to fire.

The advantage of adaptation of sense cells is that it provides the animal with precise information about changes in the environment. At other times the cells remain quiescent, thus preventing overloading of the central nervous system with irrelevant and unmanageable information. This contributes to the overall efficiency and economy of the nervous system and enables it to ignore static background information and to concentrate on monitoring aspects of the environment having most survival value.

Convergence and summation

A high degree of sensitivity is achieved in many sense organs by an anatomical arrangement of sense cells and

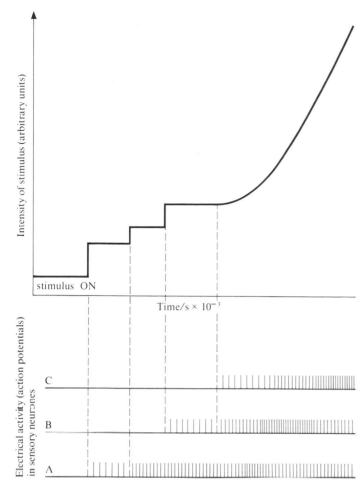

16.26 *The frequency of action potentials produced in sensory neurones leaving three sense cells, **A**, **B** and **C**, each having different threshold levels. In the case of **B** and **C** the point at which the receptors become active coincides with the saturation point of the sense cell with the lower threshold*

sensory neurones known as **convergence**. In such cases, several sense cells are connected to, or converge on, a single sensory neurone. These cells are characteristically small, are found in large numbers and are extremely sensitive to stimuli. Whilst the effect of a stimulus on a single one of these cells would not produce a response in the sensory neurone, the combined effect of the simultaneous stimulation of several cells is cumulative. This cumulative stimulatory effect produced in the sensory neurone is known as **summation** and is similar in function to the summative effect described for synapses in section 16.1.2 and effectors in sections 16.6 and 17.4.5. A good example of convergence and summation is provided by rod cells of the mammalian retina. Some of these cells are capable of detecting a single quantum of light, but the generator potential produced is inadequate to produce a propagated action potential in a neurone of the optic nerve. However, several rods (ranging from two or three to several hundred) are connected to a single optic nerve fibre by a bipolar neurone. Stimulation of at least six rods is required to produce an impulse in an optic nerve fibre. The

increased **visual sensitivity** produced by this arrangement of rods is highly adapted to dim-light vision and is well developed in nocturnal species such as owls, badgers and foxes. This high degree of sensitivity, however, is linked with a decrease in visual precision, as may be observed when attempting to read in poor light. In the human eye and that of many other diurnal species (active during daylight) this problem is counteracted by the presence of cones which, with few exceptions, do not show convergence or summation. What cones lose in sensitivity they gain in **discrimination** as described in section 16.5.4.

Spontaneous activity

Some receptors produce nerve impulses in sensory neurones in the absence of stimulation. This system is not as meaningless as it might appear as it has two important advantages. Firstly it increases the sensitivity of the receptor by enabling it to make an immediate response to a stimulus that would normally be too small to produce a response in the sensory neurone. Any slight change in the intensity of the stimulus will now produce a change in the frequency of impulses along the sensory neurone. Secondly the direction of the change in stimulus can be registered by this system as an increase or decrease in the frequency of the response in the sensory neurone. For example, infra-red receptors in pits in the face of the rattlesnake which act as direction finders in locating prey and predators show spontaneous activity and are sensitive and able to discriminate increases or decreases in temperature of 0.1 °C.

Feedback control of receptors

The threshold of some sense organs can be raised or lowered by efferent impulses from the central nervous system. This 'resets' the sensitivity of the receptor to respond to different ranges of stimulus intensities with equal sensitivity. In many cases the mechanism of control involves feedback from the receptors, which produces changes in accessory structures enabling the receptor cells to function over a new range. This occurs, for example, in the muscle spindle and the iris of the eye.

Lateral inhibition

This phenomenon is important in increasing both sensitivity and discrimination in a receptor. The basic principle involves the mutual inhibition of response from adjacent sense cells when stimulated. Investigations carried out on the individual sense organs (**ommatidia**) of the compound eye of the horseshoe crab, *Limulus*, revealed that adjacent ommatidia produce a lower response if stimulated simultaneously than they do if stimulated independently. This is significant in accentuating the differences between two adjacent areas stimulated by different intensities. Fig 16.27 shows a model system based on visual perception and demonstrates how light falling on two adjacent receptors is enhanced at the bright/dim boundary thereby 'highlighting' the edge. This effect forms the basis of the optical illusion shown in fig 16.28.

Lateral inhibition in the human eye increases the resolving power or **visual acuity** of the eye. The resolving power of a system is its ability to distinguish two or more stimuli of equal intensity as separate stimuli. For example, the distance at which two black lines of equal density can be seen as separate lines and not as a single line is a measure of the eyes' resolving power. The visual acuity of the human eye is very high and in part is due to lateral inhibition but mainly to the anatomical arrangement of cones in the retina. Light from two sources falling on the same or immediately adjacent cones is not resolved as coming from two sources. However, light from two sources falling on cones separated by only one cone can be perceived as separate sources. Approximately 95% of the seven million

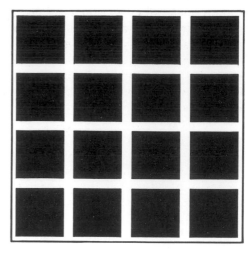

Fig 16.28 *The above diagram illustrates an optical illusion which may be caused by lateral inhibition. The grey spots at the intersections of the white lines are thought to be produced by the image of the white lines inhibiting adjacent receptors which fail to be stimulated. The lack of stimulation from the dark areas and the stimulation from the white lines combine to produce the sensation of grey at the intersections of the white lines*

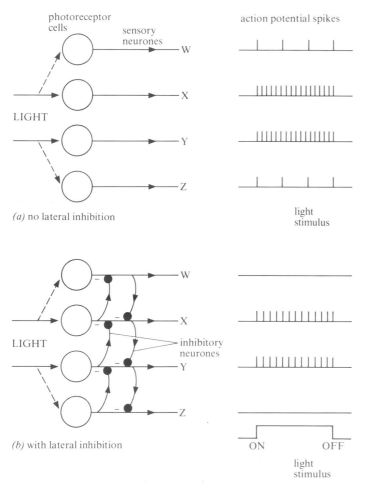

(a) no lateral inhibition

(b) with lateral inhibition

Fig 16.27 *The diagram shows action potentials recorded from four adjacent ommatidia **W**, **X**, **Y** and **Z**. **X** and **Y** are stimulated directly by a narrow beam of light whilst **W** and **Z** are stimulated weakly by light scattered from the beam stimulating **X** and **Y**. In (a) with no lateral inhibition **W** and **Z** are excited and action potentials are recorded in their sensory neurones. In (b) with lateral inhibition direct stimulation excites **X** and **Y** and inhibitory neurones linking these with **W** and **Z** prevent any propagated action potentials being set up in the latter. This mechanism sharpens the contrast, as perceived by the cerebral ganglia, as a result of the differential illumination of adjacent photoreceptors. The same principle applies to the rods and cones of the vertebrate eye (after Lamb, Ingram, Johnson and Pitman, 1980)*

cones in the eye are situated within a 1 mm diameter **fovea** in the centre of the retina. Here they each have a bipolar neurone connecting them to their *own* sensory neurone of the optic nerve. It is the absence of convergence and the close packing of cones in the fovea that is responsible for the high visual acuity.

16.5 Structure and function of receptors

There is enormous variation in the structure and function of receptors in the animal kingdom. In this section the structure and function of some mammalian receptors is considered briefly and detailed consideration is given only to the mammalian eye and ear, and the arthropod eye.

16.5.1 Mechanoreceptors

Mechanoreceptors are considered the most primitive type of receptors and may respond to a range of mechanical stimuli such as pressure, gravity, displacement and vibration.

Touch and pressure

The distinction between touch and pressure is one of degree, and the detection of these stimuli depends on the position of the receptors within the skin. Touch receptors sensitive to small pressures are found close to the surface of the skin and are composed of many fine, free endings of sensory neurones (primary sense cells). These may be situated in the epidermis or attached to hairs in the hair follicle and respond to deformation of the skin and hairs.

Touch receptors are localised in certain regions of the body and account for the increased sensitivity in these regions. For example, two stimuli may be resolved by the tip of the tongue when 1 mm apart whereas this is only possible at a distance of 60 mm in the middle of the back.

Specialised sense organs known as **Meissner's corpuscles** are situated immediately beneath the epidermis and respond to touch (fig 16.29). They consist of the single convoluted ending of a neurone enclosed within a fluid-filled capsule. **Pacinian corpuscles** are situated in the dermis, joints, tendons, muscles and mesenteries of the gut, and consist of the ending of a single neurone surrounded by connective tissue lamellae. They respond to pressure (fig 16.24).

All touch and pressure receptors are thought to produce a generator potential as a result of deformation of the receptor membrane leading to an increase in the permeability of the receptor cell to ions.

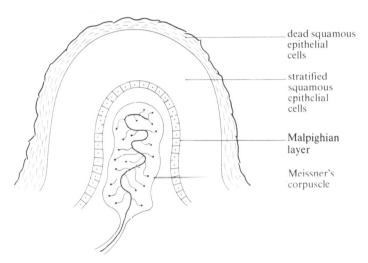

Fig 16.29 *Simplified diagram of a touch receptor, Meissner's corpuscle, showing its relationship to the skin*

- dead squamous epithelial cells
- stratified squamous epithelial cells
- Malpighian layer
- Meissner's corpuscle

Muscle spindle

Specialised proprioceptors called muscle spindles have been found in the muscles of mammals, amphibia, crustacea and insects. They respond to changes in tension in the muscles and act as stretch receptors in all activities associated with the control of muscular contraction. The muscle spindle has three main functions, one static and two dynamic:

(1) to provide information to the central nervous system on the state and position of muscles and structures attached to them, a static function;

(2) to initiate reflex contraction of the muscle and return it to its previous length when stimulated by a load, a dynamic function;

(3) to alter the state of tension in the muscle and reset it to maintain a new length, a dynamic function.

The structure and function of the muscle spindle is described in detail in section 17.5.4.

16.5.2 Thermoreceptors

Two types of sense organs found in the dermis are claimed to be responsible for detecting the temperature of the skin. **Organs of Ruffini** are thought to respond to warm temperatures and **bulbs of Krause** are thought to respond to low temperatures. However, it is almost certain that the many free nerve endings in the skin are the major structures detecting temperature (fig 16.30).

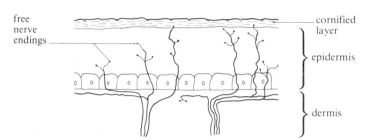

free nerve endings
cornified layer
epidermis
dermis

Fig 16.30 *Free nerve endings in the epidermis and dermis which detect temperature*

16.5.3 Chemoreceptors

The sensations of taste and smell in Man are due to chemical substances exciting specific chemoreceptors and play important roles in feeding, avoiding unfavourable environments and other behavioural activities involving courtship, mating and social organisation.

Taste

Many of the sensations registered as taste are really flavours which are detected both by smell and taste receptors. If a person is blindfolded and pinches his nostrils, preventing chemical stimuli to reach the smell receptors, whilst chewing onion and apple, it is unlikely that the difference between them will be distinguished. This illustrates the lack of sensitivity of taste receptors. Taste or **gustation** is detected by receptor molecules situated in microvilli projecting from sensory cells sunk into goblet-shaped organs known as **taste-buds** found on the top and sides of the tongue (fig 16.31).

There are four 'taste sensations' and the uneven distribution of their receptors may be demonstrated by applying the following stimulating substances to various areas of the tongue: sweet – saccharin; sour – weak acid; salt – sea salt; bitter – quinine. The distribution of these receptor areas is shown in fig 16.31*b*. No correlation has yet been found between the chemical structure of a substance and the taste produced. It is assumed, however, that the production of a generator potential within the receptor cell depends upon substances either penetrating the receptor membrane or attaching to specific receptor sites on the surface of the receptor cell membrane. Taste receptors require higher concentrations of stimulating substances than smell receptors.

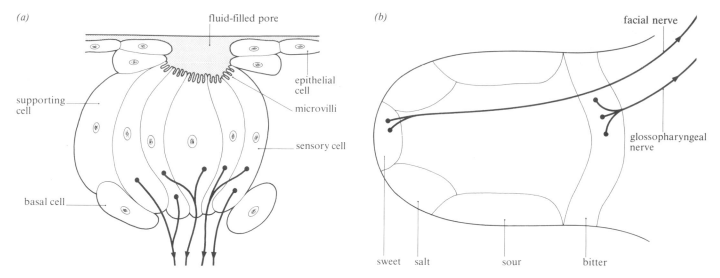

Fig 16.31 (a) Simplified diagram showing the structure of a tastebud. Substances to be tasted dissolve in the fluid surrounding the microvilli and diffuse to receptor cells embedded in the microvilli. (Redrawn and reproduced with permission, from Schmidt, 1978). (b) Diagram showing the symmetrical distribution of taste receptors of the human tongue and their innervation

Smell

The sensation of smell is more acute than that of taste and is due to airborne odoriferous substances dissolving in the layer of mucus and stimulating an area of olfactory epithelium situated high up in the nasal passages. Each nostril has an area of 2.5 cm² containing three types of cells as shown in fig 16.32.

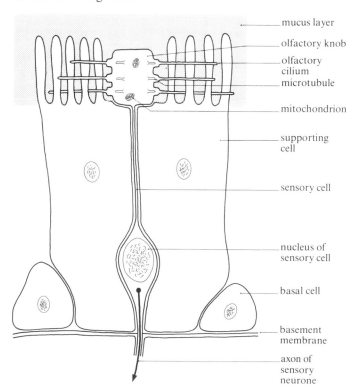

Fig. 16.32 Simplified diagram showing the structure and relationships between sensory cell, supporting cell and basal cell in the olfactory epithelium. Receptor molecules to odoriferous substances are located in the membranes of the olfactory cilia

Amoore in 1963 proposed a stereochemical theory of olfaction that related the properties of receptor sites on the cilia-like projections of the olfactory cells to the shape and dimension of odour-producing molecules. He proposed that there are seven primary odours such as putrid, pungent, peppery etc. and that they each have specific receptor sites. About 10 000 odours can be differentiated, and this is thought to be due to varying degrees of stimulation of these seven types of receptor sites. Water- and lipid-soluble substances produce the strongest sensations of smell.

Taste and smell in insects

The sense of taste in insects is extremely sensitive and has been studied in detail. Taste organs in insects are known as **taste hairs** and they are situated on the antennae, maxillary and labial palps and feet of insects. They consist of a hollow structure containing endings of sensory neurones and are sensitive to both chemical substances and displacement.

In the blowfly, *Calliphora*, there is a taste reflex which extends the proboscis when the legs are in contact with acceptable food substances. The response threshold in blowfly to sucrose is as low as 0.8×10^{-4} M compared with 0.2×10^{-1} M in Man.

Despite these remarkably low thresholds for taste receptors the sensitivity of insects to smell is even greater. The olfactory receptors are usually situated on the antennae and have been extensively studied in moths. Female silk moths, *Bombyx mori*, are capable of attracting males of the same species at distances of several kilometres as a result of releasing a specific chemical substance. Substances, such as this sex attractant, that act as a form of communication within a species are known as **pheromones**. In one experiment a single silk moth female in a muslin cage attracted 40% of a large population of males released 4 km away. Several species that utilise pheromones over great distances have enlarged antennae carrying, in the case of the male polyphemus moth, *Telea polyphemus*, 15 × 10⁴ sensory cells. Molecules of sex attractant are absorbed on to the antennae as air filters through them.

Contrary to popular belief male moths do not fly up concentration gradients to find female moths. Instead they take off into the wind carrying the pheromone and zig-zag across the aerial trail reversing their direction whenever they lose the scent. Once in the immediate vicinity of the female, her exact location is determined by following the concentration gradient.

16.5.4 Mammalian eye

The mammalian eye is a sense organ composed of many sense cells, the rods and cones of the retina, sensory neurones of the optic nerve and a complex array of accessory structures. This arrangement enables the eye to convert light of various wavelengths reflected from objects at varying distances, the **visual field**, into electrical impulses which nerves transmit to the brain where an image of remarkable precision is perceived.

Light travels as waves of electromagnetic radiation and the wavelengths perceived by the human eye occupy a narrow band, the **visible spectrum**, from 380–760 nm (appendix A 1.7). Light is a form of energy and is emitted and absorbed in discrete packets called **quanta** or **photons**. The wavelengths of the visible spectrum carry sufficient energy in each quantum of radiation to produce a photochemical response in the sense cells of the eye.

The camera and the eye work on the same basic principles and these are:
(1) controlling the amount of light entering the structure;
(2) focusing images of the external world by means of a lens system;
(3) registering the image on a sensitive surface;
(4) processing the 'captured' images to produce a pattern which can be 'seen'.

Structure and function of the human eye

The eyes are held in protective bony sockets of the skull called **orbits** by four **rectus** muscles and two **oblique** muscles which control eye movements. Each human eyeball is about 24 mm in diameter and weighs 6–8 g. Most of the eye is composed of accessory structures concerned with bringing the visual field to the photoreceptor cells situated in the innermost layer of the eye, the **retina**. The eye is composed of three concentric layers: the sclera (sclerotic coat) and cornea; the choroid, ciliary body, lens and iris; and the retina, and is supported by the hydrostatic pressure (25 mmHg) of the aqueous and vitreous humours.

The gross structure of the human eye is shown in fig 16.33 and brief notes on the function of the various parts are given below.

Sclera – external covering of eye; very tough, containing collagen fibres, protects and maintains shape of eyeball.

Cornea – transparent front part of the sclera; the curved surface acts as a main structure refracting (bending) light towards the retina.

Conjunctiva – thin transparent layer of cells protecting the cornea and continuous with the epithelium of eyelids; the conjunctiva does not cover the cornea overlying the iris.

Eyelid – protects the cornea from mechanical and chemical damage and the retina from bright light by reflex action.

Choroid – rich in blood vessels supplying the retina and covered with pigment cells preventing reflection of light within the eye.

Ciliary body – junction of sclera and cornea; contains tissue, blood vessels and ciliary muscles.

Ciliary muscles – circular sheet of smooth muscle fibres forming bundles of circular and radial muscles which alter the shape of the lens during accommodation.

Suspensory ligament – attaches the ciliary body to the lens.

Lens – transparent, elastic biconvex structure; provides fine adjustment for focusing light on to the retina and separates the aqueous and vitreous humours.

Aqueous humour – clear solution of salts secreted by the ciliary body, finally draining into the blood through the canal of Schlemm.

Iris – circular, muscular diaphragm containing the pigment giving eye its colour; it separates the aqueous humour region into anterior and posterior chambers and controls the amount of light entering eye.

Pupil – opening in iris; all light enters eye through this.

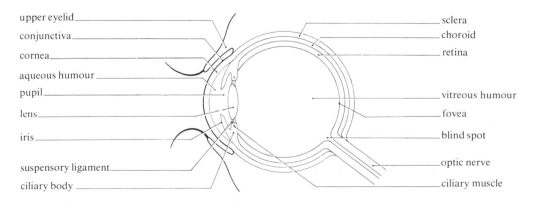

Fig 16.33 *Structure of the mammalian eye*

Vitreous humour – clear semi-solid substance supporting the eyeball.

Retina – contains the photoreceptor cells, rods and cones, and cell bodies and axons of neurones supplying the optic nerve.

Fovea – most sensitive part of retina, contains cones only; most light rays are focused here.

Optic nerve – bundle of nerve fibres carrying impulses from the retina to the brain.

Blind spot – point where the optic nerve leaves eye; there are no rods or cones here, therefore it is not light-sensitive.

16.8 List, in order, the structures through which light passes before striking the retina.

Accommodation

Accommodation is the reflex mechanism by which light rays from an object are brought to focus on the retina. It involves two processes and these will be considered separately.

Reflex adjustment of pupil size. In bright light the circular muscle of the iris diaphragm contracts, the radial muscle relaxes, the pupil becomes smaller and less light enters the eye, preventing damage to the retina (fig 16.34). In poor light the opposite muscular contractions and relaxations occur. The added advantage of reducing the pupil size is that it increases the **depth of focus** of the eye so that any displacement of the sense cells in the retina will not impair the focus.

Refraction of light rays. Light rays from distant objects (> 6 m) are parallel when they strike the eye. Light rays from near objects (< 6 m) are diverging when they strike the eye. In both cases the light rays must be **refracted** or bent to focus on the retina and refraction must be greater for light from near objects. The normal eye is able to accommodate light from objects from about 25 cm to infinity. Refraction occurs when light passes from one medium into another with a different refractive index, and this occurs at the air–corneal surface and at the lens. The degree of refraction at the corneal surface cannot be varied and depends on the angle at which light strikes the cornea (which, in turn, depends upon the distance of the object from the cornea). Most refraction occurs here, and consequently the function of the lens is to produce the final refraction that brings light to a sharp focus on the retina; this is regulated by the ciliary muscles. The state of

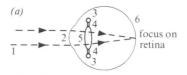

Light from distant object

(a)

focus on retina

1 Parallel light rays reach eye
2 Cornea refracts (bends) light rays
3 Circular ciliary muscle relaxed
4 Suspensory ligament taut
5 Lens pulled out thin
6 Light focused on retina

Light from near object

focus on retina

object

1 Diverging light rays reach eye
2 Cornea refracts (bends) light rays
3 Circular ciliary muscle contracted
4 Suspensory ligament slack
5 Elastic lens more convex
6 Light focused on retina

(b)

Fig 16.35 *Events occurring during accommodation of light rays from objects at various distances, (a) side views of eye, (b) front views of eye*

Table 16.8. Relationship between structures changing the shape of the lens and the degree of refraction

Ciliary muscle	Tension in suspensory ligament	Radius of curvature	Refraction
contracted	no tension	decreased (lens thick)	increased
relaxed	taut	increased (lens thin)	decreased

contraction of the ciliary muscles changes the tension on the suspensory ligaments. This acts on the natural elasticity of the lens which causes it to change its shape (radius of curvature) and thus the degree of refraction. As the radius of curvature of the lens decreases it becomes thicker and the amount of refraction increases. The complete relationship between these three structures and refraction is shown in table 16.8. Fig 16.35 shows the changes occurring in the eye during accommodation to light from distant and near objects.

The image produced by the eye on the retina is inverted and reversed but the mental image is perceived in the correct position because the brain learns to accept an inverted reversed image as normal.

Structure of the retina

The retina develops as an outgrowth of the forebrain called the **optic vesicle**. During the embryonic formation of the eye the photoreceptor cells of the retina turn inwards (invaginate) and lie against the choroid layer. The cells are covered by the cell bodies and axons linking the photoreceptor cells to the brain as shown in fig 16.36.

The retina is composed of three layers of cells each containing a characteristic type of cell. First there is the **photoreceptor layer** (outermost layer) containing the photosensitive cells, the **rods** and **cones**, partially embedded in the microvilli of pigment epithelium cells of the

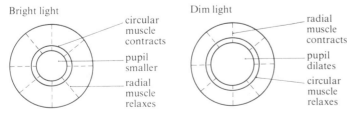

Fig 16.34 *The iris/pupil response to variations in light intensity*

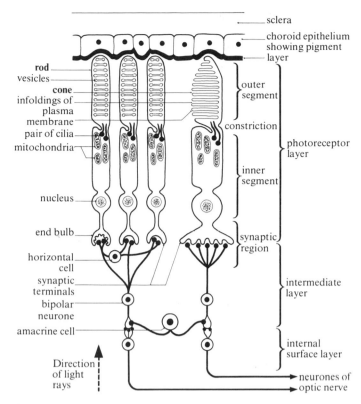

Fig 16.36 *Diagrammatic section through the retina of the eye showing the ultrastructure of a rod and a cone. Connections between the sensory cells and the neurones of the optic nerve are shown in the inner segment. Light rays must pass through the ganglion cells and the intermediate layers before reaching the rods and cones*

choroid. Next is the **intermediate layer** containing bipolar neurones with synapses connecting the photoreceptor layer to the cells of the third layer. Horizontal and amacrine cells found in this layer enable lateral inhibition to occur. The third layer is the **internal surface layer** containing ganglion cells with dendrites in contact with bipolar neurones and axons of the optic nerve.

Structure and function of rods and cones

Rods and cones have an essentially similar structure as shown in fig 16.36 and their photosensitive pigments are attached to the outer surfaces of the membranes in the outer segment. They have four similar regions whose structure and function are summarised below.

Outer segment. This is the photosensitive region where light energy is converted into a generator potential. The entire outer segment is composed of flattened membranous vesicles containing the photosensitive pigments. Rods contain 600–1 000 of these vesicles stacked up like a pile of coins and they are enclosed by an outer membrane. Cones have fewer membranous vesicles and they are formed by repeated infoldings of the outer membrane.

Constriction. The outer segment is almost separated from the inner segment by an infolding of the

outer membrane. The two regions remain in contact by cytoplasm and a pair of cilia which pass between the two. These cilia consist of nine peripheral fibres only, the usual central two being absent.

Inner segment. This is an actively metabolic region. It is packed with mitochondria producing energy for visual processes, and polysomes for the synthesis of proteins involved in the production of the membranous vesicles and visual pigment. The nucleus is situated in this region.

Synaptic region. Here the cells form synapses with bipolar cells. **Diffuse bipolar cells** may have synapses with several rods. This is called synaptic convergence, and whilst it lowers visual acuity it increases visual sensitivity. **Monosynaptic bipolar cells** link *one* cone to *one* ganglion cell and this gives the cones greater visual acuity than rods. **Horizontal cells** and **amacrine cells** link certain numbers of rods together and cones together. This allows a certain amount of processing of visual information to occur before it leaves the retina, for instance these cells are involved in lateral inhibition.

Differences between rods and cones

Rods are more numerous than cones, 120×10^6 as opposed to 6×10^6, and have a different distribution. The thin elongate rods (50×3 µm) are distributed uniformly throughout the retina except at the fovea, where the conical elongate cones (60×1.5 µm) have their greatest concentration (5×10^4 mm^{-2}). Since the cones are tightly packed together at the fovea this gives them higher visual acuity (section 16.4.2). Rods are much more sensitive to light than cones and respond to lower light intensities. Rods only contain one visual pigment, and being unable to discriminate colour are used principally for night vision. Cones contain three visual pigments and these enable the cones to differentiate colours. They are used principally in daylight. The rods have a lower visual acuity because they are less tightly packed together and they undergo synaptic convergence, but this latter point gives them increased collective sensitivity required for night vision.

> **16.9** Explain why synaptic convergence should increase visual sensitivity.
>
> **16.10** Explain why objects are seen more clearly at night by not looking directly at them.

The mechanism of photoreception

Rods contain the photosensitive pigment **rhodopsin** attached to the outer surface of the membranous vesicles. Rhodopsin, or **visual purple**, is a complex molecule formed by the reversible combination of a lipoprotein, **scotopsin**, and a small light-absorbing carotenoid molecule **retinene (retinol)**. The latter is an aldehyde derivative of vitamin A and exists in two isomeric forms according to the light conditions as shown in fig 16.37.

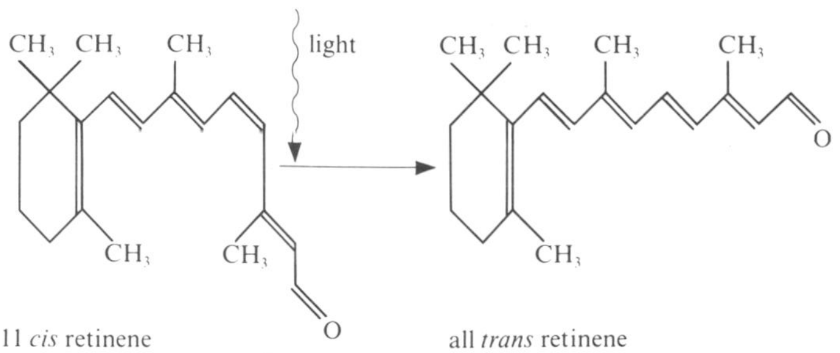

Fig 16.37 *The action of light changes the structure of retinene from the 11 cis isomer to the all trans isomer*

11 *cis* retinene   all *trans* retinene

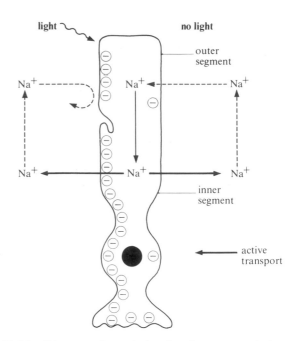

Fig 16.38 *Diagram of a rod showing the proposed changes in sodium permeability of the outer segment produced in the presence of light. The negative charges ⊖ on the right side of the rod indicate the normal resting potential whereas those on the left indicate the hyperpolarisation*

When rhodopsin is exposed to light it is known that one photon of light will produce the above isomeric change. Retinene acts as a prosthetic group and is believed to occupy a certain site on the surface of the scotopsin molecule where it inhibits reactive groups in this molecule involved in initiating electrical activity in the rods. The exact mechanisms of photoreception are not yet known but it is thought that it involves two processes: first the isomeric conversion of 11 *cis* retinene to all *trans* retinene by the action of light, and second the decomposition of rhodopsin via a series of intermediate molecules into retinene and scotopsin, a process known as **bleaching**.

$$\text{rhodopsin} \xrightarrow{\text{bleaching}} \text{retinene} + \text{scotopsin}$$

Rhodopsin is reformed immediately in the absence of further light stimulation. All *trans* retinene is first converted into 11 *cis* retinene in the presence of the enzyme **retinene isomerase**, and is then recombined with scotopsin. This process is called '**dark adaptation**' and in total darkness it takes 30 min for all rods to adapt and the eyes to achieve maximum sensitivity. During the second process, however, the permeability of the outer segment membrane to sodium ions decreases whilst the inner segment continues to pump out sodium ions, thus creating increased negativity within the rod (fig 16.38). This situation gives rise to hyperpolarisation of the rod. This situation is exactly opposite to the effect normally found in sensory receptors where the stimulus produces a depolarisation and not a hyperpolarisation. The hyperpolarisation reduces the rate of release of excitatory transmitter substance from the rod which is released maximally during darkness. The bipolar neurone linked by synapses to the rod cell also responds by producing a hyperpolarisation, but the ganglion cells of the optic nerve supplied by the bipolar neurone respond to this by producing a propagated action potential.

Colour vision

The human eye absorbs light from all wavelengths of the visible spectrum and perceives these as six colours broadly associated with particular wavelengths as shown in table 16.9. There are three types of cones each possessing a different pigment which electrophysiological investigations

Table 16.9. Colours of the visible spectrum and approximate ranges of their wavelength

Colour	Wavelength/nm
red	above 620
orange	590–620
yellow	570–590
green	500–570
blue	440–500
violet	below 440

have shown absorb light of different wavelengths. There are red, green and blue cones.

Colour vision is explained in terms of the trichromacy theory, which states that different colours and shades are produced by the degree of stimulation of each type of cone produced by the light reflected from an object. For example, equal stimulation of all cones produces the colour sensation of white. The initial discrimination of colour occurs in the retina but the final colour perceived involves the integrative properties of the brain. The mixing effect of pigments forms the basis of colour television, photography and painting.

Colour-blindness. The complete absence of a particular cone or a shortage of one type can lead to various forms of colour-blindness or degrees of 'colour-weakness'. For example, a person lacking red or green cones is 'red–green colour-blind', whereas a person with a reduced number of either cones will have difficulty in distinguishing a range of red–green shades. Colour-blindness, or its extent, is determined using test charts, such as the Ishihara test charts, composed of a series of dots of several colours. Some charts bear a number which a person with normal colour vision can perceive, whilst the colour-blind sufferer sees a different number or no number at all.

Colour-blindness is a sex-linked recessive characteristic resulting in the absence of appropriate colour genes in the X chromosome. About 2% of men are red colour-blind, 6% are green colour-blind, but only 0.4% of women show any sign of colour-blindness.

16.11 A person places a green filter over one eye and a red filter over the other eye and looks at an object. Using the data given in table 16.9, describe and explain the apparent colour of the object.

Binocular vision and stereoscopic vision

Binocular vision occurs when the visual fields of both eyes overlap so that the fovea of both eyes are focused on the same object. It has several advantages over monocular vision and these include a larger visual field, damage to one eye being compensated for by the other, for example it cancels the effect of the blind spot, and it provides the basis of stereoscopic vision. Stereoscopic vision depends upon the eyes simultaneously producing slightly different retinal images which the brain resolves as one image. The more frontally the eyes are situated the greater the stereoscopic visual field. For example, Man has a total visual field of 180° and a stereoscopic visual field of 140°. The horse has laterally placed eyes with a limited forward stereoscopic visual field which it uses for viewing distant objects. For nearer objects the horse turns its head and uses monocular vision to examine detail. Frontally placed eyes and centrally situated foveas, producing good visual acuity, are essential for good stereoscopic vision which provides an increased appreciation of size and perception of the depth and distance of objects. Stereoscopic vision is found mainly in predatory animals where it is vital when capturing prey by pouncing or swooping, as shown by members of the cat family, hawks and eagles. Animals which are hunted have laterally placed eyes giving wide visual fields but restricted stereoscopic vision, for instance the rabbit has a total binocular visual field of 360° and frontal stereoscopic vision of 20°. The resolution of the two retinal images produced in stereoscopic vision occurs in two areas of the brain called the **visual cortex**.

Visual pathways and the visual cortex

Nerve impulses generated in the retina are carried by the million or so neurones of the optic nerve to the visual cortex, which is situated in the occipital lobe at the rear base of the brain. Here each minute region of the retina,

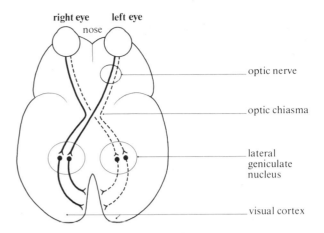

Fig 16.39 *Diagram of the human visual pathway as seen from the underside of the brain*

involving perhaps only a few rods and cones, is represented and it is here that the visual input is interpreted and we 'see'. However, what we see has meaning only after reference to other regions of the cortex and the temporal lobes, where previous visual information is stored and used in the analysis and identification of the present visual input (section 16.2.4). In Man, axons from the left side of the retina of both eyes pass to the left visual cortex and axons from the right side of each retina pass to the right visual cortex. The point where the axons from those regions of the retina closest to the nose cross is called the **optic chiasma** and is included in the visual pathway shown in fig 16.39. About 20% of the optic neurones do not pass to the visual cortex but enter the midbrain, where they are involved in reflex control of pupil size and eye movements.

16.5.5   Arthropod eye

Arthropods have two types of eye: the **simple eye (ocellus)**, which is found in some larval insects, and the more characteristic **compound eye**. The simple eye consists of a single lens covering a few light-sensitive cells and is able to discriminate light and dark but unable to produce images. These eyes are often found in conjunction with the larger, and functionally more important, compound eyes.

Each compound eye is composed of thousands of separate structures called **ommatidia**; for example there are 30 000 in the dragonfly. Each ommatidium is composed of two refractive bodies, a biconvex **lens** formed from cuticle and a **crystalline cone** secreted by **vitrellar cells**. These focus light on to a group of photosensitive **retinulae cells**, whose inner membranes bear microvilli which fuse together to form a structure called a **rhabdome**. The visual pigment is located within the microvilli of the rhabdome where the nerve impulses are set up and pass via the optic nerve to the cerebral ganglia. Each ommatidium is surrounded and isolated from the next by elongate pigment cells (fig 16.40).

Since each ommatidium receives light from a very small area, the image formed by the eye as a whole is made up of a series of separate overlapping points and is known as a

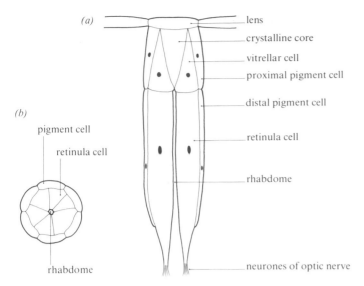

Fig 16.40 *Diagrams of (a) an LS of a single ommatidium and (b) TS of an ommatidium*

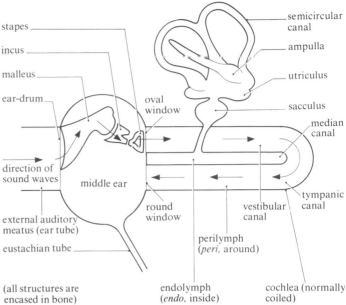

Fig 16.41 *Diagram showing the major structures in the mammalian ear involved in hearing and balance, (not to scale)*

mosaic image. This type of eye lacks the resolution of the mammalian eye but its overlapping images make it very sensitive to movements of objects.

16.5.6 Mammalian ear

The mammalian ear is a sense organ containing mechanoreceptors sensitive to gravity, displacement and sound. Movements and positions of the head relative to gravity are detected by the vestibular apparatus composed of the semicircular canals, the utricle and the saccule. All other structures of the ear are involved in receiving, amplifying and transducing sound energy into electrical impulses and producing the sensation of hearing in the auditory regions of the brain.

Structure and function of the ear

The ear consists of three sections specialising in different functions (fig 16.41). The **outer ear** consists of the **pinna**, strengthened by elastic cartilage, which focuses and collects sound waves into the **ear tube** (external auditory meatus); the sound waves cause the **tympanic membrane** (eardrum) to vibrate. In the **middle ear**, vibrations of the tympanic membrane are transmitted across to the membranous **oval window** by movement of the three ear ossicles, the **malleus, incus** and **stapes** (hammer, anvil and stirrup). A lever system between these three bones and the relative areas of contact of the malleus with the tympanic membrane ($60 \ mm^2$) and the stapes with the oval window ($3.2 \ mm^2$) amplifies the movement of the tympanic membrane 22 times. Damage to the tympanic membrane, due to atmospheric pressure changes, is prevented by a connection between the air-filled middle ear and the pharynx, the **eustachian tube**. Finally there is the **inner ear** which consists of a complex system of canals and cavities within the skull bone containing a fluid called **perilymph**. Within these canals are membranous sacs filled with **endolymph** and sensory receptors. Auditory receptors are found in the cochlea and balance receptors are found in the utricle and saccule and the ampullae of the semicircular canals. The perilymph is enclosed by the membranes of the oval window and round window.

The nature of sound

Sound is produced by the vibration of particles within a medium. It travels as waves consisting of alternating regions of high and low pressure and will pass through liquids, solids and gases. The distance between two identical points on adjacent waves is the **wavelength** and this determines the **frequency** of **vibrations** or **pitch** (whether it sounds high or low). The human ear is sensitive to wavelengths between 40 and 20 000 Hz (cycles per second). The audible range of dogs reaches 40 000 Hz, and that of bats 100 000 Hz. Human speech frequencies vary between 500 and 3 000 Hz, and sensitivity to high frequencies decreases with age.

Tone depends upon the number of different frequencies making up the sound. For example, a violin and trumpet playing the same note, say middle C, produce the same fundamental frequency of 256 Hz but sound different. This is due to overtones or harmonics produced by the instrument which give it its distinctive quality or **timbre**. The same principle applies to the human voice and gives it its characteristic sound.

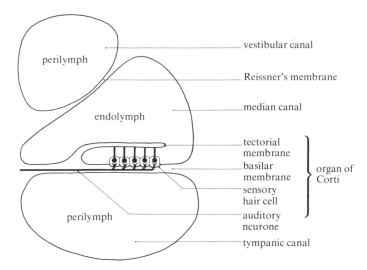

Fig 16.42 *Diagram of a TS cochlea showing the organ of Corti*

The **intensity** (loudness) of a sound depends upon the amplitude of the sound waves produced at the source and is a measure of the energy they contain.

Cochlea and hearing

The cochlea is a spiral canal 35 mm long and subdivided longitudinally by a membranous triangle into three regions as shown in fig 16.42.

Both the vestibular and tympanic canals contain perilymph, and the two canals are connected at the extreme end of the cochlea via a small hole, the **helicotrema**. The median canal contains endolymph. The **basilar membrane** separates the median and tympanic canals and supports sensory hair cells that can be brought into contact with the **tectorial membrane** above. This unit, consisting of basilar membrane, sensory cells and tectorial membrane, is called the **organ of Corti** and is the region where transduction of sound waves into electrical impulses occurs.

Sound waves transmitted from the ear tube to the oval window produce vibrations in the perilymph of the vestibular canal and these are transmitted via **Reissner's membrane** to the endolymph in the median canal. From here they are transferred to the basilar membrane and the perilymph in the tympanic canal, and are finally dissipated into the air of the middle ear as vibration of the round window.

The precise mechanism of transduction of pressure waves into nerve impulses is not known but is believed to involve relative movement of the basilar and tectorial membranes. Vibrations of the basilar membrane, induced by pressure waves, push the sensory hairs against the tectorial membrane and force the two membranes to slide past each other. The distortion produced in the sensory hairs due to the shearing forces causes a depolarisation of the sensory cells, the production of generator potentials and the initiation of action potentials in the axons of the auditory nerve.

Pitch and intensity discrimination

The ability to distinguish the pitch of a sound depends upon the frequency of the vibration producing movement of the basilar membrane and stimulating sensory cells in a specific region of the organ of Corti. These cells supply a particular region of the auditory cortex of the brain where the sensation of pitch is perceived. The basilar membrane becomes broader and more flexible as it passes from the base of the cochlea to its apex and its sensitivity to vibration changes along its length so that only low-frequency sounds can pass to the apex. High-frequency (pitch) sounds stimulate the basilar membrane at the *base* of the cochlea and low frequency sounds stimulate it at the *apical end*. A pure sound, consisting of a single frequency, will only stimulate one small area of the basilar membrane whereas most sounds, containing several frequencies, simultaneously stimulate many regions of the basilar membrane. The auditory cortex integrates the stimuli from these various regions of the basilar membrane and a 'single' blended sound is perceived.

The intensity or loudness of the sound depends upon each region of the basilar membrane containing a range of sensory cells responding to different thresholds of vibration. For example, a quiet sound at a given frequency may only stimulate a few sensory cells, whereas a louder sound at the same frequency would stimulate several other sensory cells having higher thresholds of vibration. This is an example of spatial summation.

Balance

Maintaining balance at rest and during movement of the body relies upon the brain receiving a continual input of sensory information concerning the position of various parts of the body. Information from proprioceptors in joints and muscles indicates the positions and state of the limbs, but vital information related to position and movement of the head is provided by the **vestibular apparatus** of the ear, the **utricle, saccule** and **semicircular canals**.

The basic sensory receptors within these structures consist of cells which have hair-like extensions, **hair cells**, attached to dense structures supported in the endolymph. Movement of the head results in deflection of the hairs and the production of a generator potential in the hair cells.

Regions of the walls of the utricle and saccule called **maculae** contain receptor cells which have their hair-like processes embedded in a gelatinous mass containing granules of calcium carbonate called an **otoconium**. Otoconia respond to the pull of gravity acting at right-angles to the Earth's surface and are mainly responsible for detecting the direction of movement of the head with respect to gravity.

The utricle responds to vertical movements of the head and the otoconia produce maximum stimulation when pulling the receptor hairs downwards, such as when the body is upside down.

The saccule responds to lateral (sideways) movement of the head. The hair cells of the saccule are horizontal when

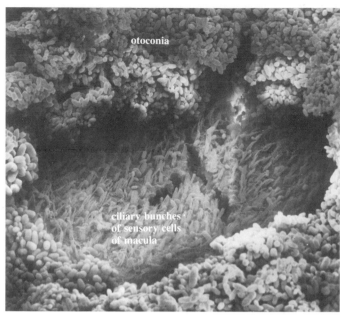

otoconia

ciliary bunches
of sensory cells
of macula

Fig 16.43 *Scanning electron micrographs of the internal structure of the ear. (a) the otoconia and (b) the otoconial layer with a portion removed to show the sensory cells of the macula beneath it*

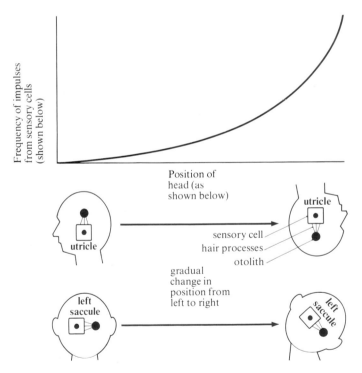

Fig 16.44 *Graph showing the effect of head position on the activity of receptor cells of the utricle and saccule*

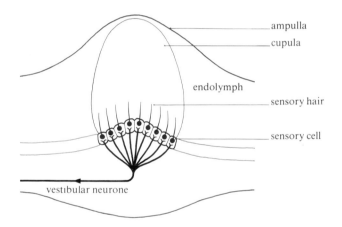

Fig 16.45 *Diagram showing a TS through the ampulla of a semicircular canal*

The three semicircular canals are arranged in three planes at right-angles to each other and detect the direction and rate of change of position of the head. At the base of each canal is a swelling, the **ampulla**, containing a conical gelatinous structure, the **cupula**. This encloses the hair-like projections of the receptor cells. The cupula fully extends across the ampulla (fig 16.45). Rotational movement of the head, semicircular canals and cupula is resisted by the inertia of the endolymph which remains stationary. This produces a relative displacement of the cupula which is bent in the opposite direction to the head movement. The receptor cells respond by producing generator potentials leading to propagated action potentials in the vestibular neurones. The direction and rate of displacement are both detected by the receptor cells. Linear acceleration is detected by both the maculae and cupulae.

the head is upright. Tilting of the head to the left produces a differential response from left and right saccules. The left receives increased stimulation as the otoconia pull downwards on the hairs whereas decreased stimulation occurs on the right. These displacements produce impulses passing to the cerebellum where the orientation of the head is perceived.

16.6   Effectors – the endocrine system

An effector is a differentiated structure, such as a cell, tissue, organ or organ system, performing a specific reaction relative to the environment in response to a stimulus from the nervous system. The most widespread and important effectors are those involved in movement and secretion.

Organisms responding to external stimuli by some form of movement or locomotion may utilise amoeboid, ciliary, flagellate or muscular movements, according to their structure and mode of life, in order to make the response. Details of these mechanisms can be found in chapter 17. In the case of multicellular organisms all types of movement may be involved in response to internal stimuli, and examples include the amoeboid movement of white blood cells through capillary walls to a site of infection in the tissues, the increased movement of cilia in the trachea in response to infection in the lungs, the activation of sperm flagella in response to secretions of the vagina, and reflex contractions of the peristaltic muscles of the oesophagus in response to a food bolus.

Other stimuli, which may be external or internal, bring about a response in the organism involving secretory activity of either an exocrine gland or an endocrine gland (section 8.3.3). For example, exocrine responses may be stimulated by particles of dirt in the eye causing secretion of tears from the tear glands, acidic food in the duodenum causing the release of pancreatic juice and damage to a joint causing an increased production of synovial fluid. Endocrine glands too respond to a variety of stimuli, for example the release of insulin by the cells of the islets of Langerhans in response to rising blood glucose levels, the release of human chorionic gonadotrophin at the beginning of pregnancy by the uterus wall following implantation by a blastocyst and the increased release of thyroxine following prolonged exposure to low temperatures.

16.6.1   The endocrine system

The endocrine and nervous systems function in a coordinated fashion to maintain a homeostatic state within the body. The nervous system transmits nerve impulses whereas the endocrine system utilises the blood as a transport medium. Despite obvious differences in the mechanism of transfer of information, both systems share a common feature in the release of chemical substances as a means of communication between cells. It is believed that these two systems originated and developed side by side as the needs of intercellular communication became more complex due to the increase in the size and complexity of organisms. In both cases the principal role of the systems is the integration, coordination and control of many of the major physiological activities of organisms.

A **gland** is a structure secreting a specific chemical substance, and there are two types of glands in the body; exocrine and endocrine glands. Endocrine glands secrete hormones (*hormon*, to urge on) which are specific chemical substances produced by one part of the body; these then enter the bloodstream and pass to a distant organ, tissue or group of cells where they exert a specific regulatory effect. The major endocrine glands of the body and their hormones and effects are summarised in table 16.10.

Methods of studying glands and hormones

Most of the original information concerning the function of glands and their secretions involved studying the change in body activity associated with overactivity or underactivity of the gland during disease. In some cases the experimental removal of the gland was also used to determine its function. As techniques for the isolation, purification, analysis and synthesis of hormones developed, biologists were able to counteract the symptoms of removing the gland by injecting extracts of the gland or synthetic preparations of the hormone. These techniques clearly established the role of many glands and their secretions but they could not be applied to all glands, for example the liver and kidney. The removal of these glands would produce undesirable conditions other than those connected with their endocrine role.

Radioimmunoassay (RIA) is a technique which is widely used to measure the concentration of hormones, drugs, enzymes, viruses, bacterial and tumour antigens and other organic substances of biological interest in blood, urine or other media. The principle of RIA is simple. The components of the assay consist of a specific anti-serum to the substance (hormone) under investigation, a radioactively labelled form of the substance and the unlabelled substance. The unlabelled substance competes for a limited number of antibody-binding sites with the labelled substance. The amount of inhibition of binding of the labelled substance is proportional to the amount of unlabelled substance present. Measurement of this inhibition is possible by separating (usually precipitating) the antibody-bound material from the unbound, and the technique is made quantitative by comparing the results with a set of tubes containing a *known* concentration of the substance under investigation. This is shown diagrammatically as follows.

$$\text{Ab} + \text{Ag} + \text{Ag}^* \rightleftharpoons \text{Ab.Ag} + \text{Ab.Ag}^*$$

| specific antibody | unlabelled antigen | labelled antigen | unlabelled (antibody–antigen complexes) | labelled |

Current trends in this field are to replace radioactive labels with enzyme-fluorescent or chemiluminescent labels and thus remove the hazards associated with handling radioactive sources.

Mechanisms of hormone action

All vertebrate hormones belong to one of four chemical groups: derivatives of amines, such as **tyrosine**; peptides and proteins; steroids; and fatty acids, as summarised in table 16.11. The mechanisms controlling the release of hormones by glands are as follows.

(*a*) The presence of a specific metabolite in the blood. For

Table 16.10. Summary of the major human endocrines, their functions and the control of their secretion

Gland	Hormone	Functions	Secretion control mechanism
Hypothalamus	Releasing and inhibiting hormones and factors, seven identified, possible number unknown (see table 16.2) Posterior pituitary hormones produced here	Control of specific anterior pituitary hormones	Feedback mechanisms involving metabolite and hormone levels
Posterior pituitary gland	No hormones synthesised here, stores and secretes the following:		Feedback mechanisms involving hormones and nervous system
	Oxytocin	Ejection of milk from mammary gland, contraction of uterus during birth	
	Antidiuretic hormone (ADH) (vasopressin)	Reduction of urine secretion by kidney	Blood osmotic pressure
Anterior pituitary gland	Follicle stimulating hormone (FSH)	In male, stimulates spermatogenesis In female, growth of ovarian follicles	Plasma oestrogen and testosterone via hypothalamus
	Luteinising hormone (LH)	In male, testosterone secretion	Plasma testosterone via hypothalamus
		In female, secretion of oestrogen and progesterone, ovulation and maintenance of corpus luteum	Plasma oestrogen level via hypothalamus
	Prolactin	Stimulates milk production and secretion	Hypothalamic hormones
	Thyroid stimulating hormone (TSH)	Synthesis and secretion of thyroid hormones, growth of thyroid glands	Plasma T_3 and T_4 levels via hypothalamus
	Adrenocorticotrophic hormone (ACTH or corticotrophin)	Synthesis and secretion of adrenal cortex hormones, growth of gland	Plasma ACTH via hypothalamus
	Growth hormone (GH)	Protein synthesis, growth, especially of bones of limbs	Hypothalamic hormones
Parathyroid gland	Parathormone	Increases blood calcium level Decreases blood phosphate level	Plasma Ca^{2+} level, and plasma PO_4^{3-} level
Thyroid gland	Triiodothyronine (T_3) and thyroxine (T_4)	Regulation of basal metabolic rate, growth and development	TSH
	Calcitonin	Decreases blood calcium level	Plasma Ca^{2+} level
Adrenal cortex	Glucocorticoids (cortisol)	Protein breakdown, glucose/glycogen synthesis, adaptation to stress, anti-inflammatory/allergy effects	ACTH
	Mineralocorticoids (aldosterone)	Na^+ retention in kidney, Na^+ and K^+ ratios in extracellular and intracellular fluids, raises blood pressure	Plasma Na^+ and K^+ levels and low blood pressure
Adrenal medulla	Adrenaline (epinephrine)	Increases rate and force of heartbeat, constriction of skin and visceral capillaries Dilation of arterioles of heart and skeletal muscles, raises blood glucose level	Sympathetic nervous system
	Noradrenaline (norepinephrine)	General constriction of small arteries, elevation of blood pressure	Nervous system
Islets of Langerhans	Insulin (beta cells)	Decreases blood glucose level, increases glucose and amino acid uptake and utilisation by cells	Plasma glucose and amino acid levels
	Glucagon (alpha cells)	Increases blood glucose level, breakdown of glycogen to glucose in liver	Plasma glucose level
Stomach	Gastrin	Secretion of gastric juices	Food in stomach
Duodenum	Secretin	Secretion of pancreatic juice Inhibits gastric secretion	Acidic food in duodenum
	Cholecystokinin (pancreozymin)	Emptying of gall bladder and liberation of pancreatic juice into duodenum	Fatty acids and amino acids in duodenum
Kidney	Renin	Conversion of angiotensinogen into angiotensin	Plasma Na^+ level, decreased blood pressure
Ovarian follicle	Oestrogens (17β-oestradiol)	Female secondary sex characteristics, oestrous cycle	FSH and LH
	Progesterone	Gestation, inhibition of ovulation	LH
Corpus luteum	Progesterone and oestrogen	Uterine growth and development	LH
	Progesterone and oestrogen	Foetal development	Developing foetus
Placenta	Chorionic gonadotrophin	Maintenance of corpus luteum	Developing foetus
	Human placental lactogen	Stimulates mammary growth	Developing foetus
Testis	Testosterone	Male secondary sexual characteristics	LH and FSH

Table 16.11. Summary table showing chemical nature of the major hormones of the body

Chemical group		Hormone	Major source
Amines	catecholamines	Adrenaline	Sympathetic nervous system
		Noradrenaline	Adrenal medulla
	tyrosine	Thyroxine	Thyroid gland
		Triiodothyronine	Thyroid gland
Peptides and proteins		Hypothalamic releasing and inhibiting hormones and factors	Hypothalamus
		Follicle stimulating hormone	
		Luteinising hormone	Anterior pituitary gland
		Prolactin	
		Thyroid stimulating hormone	
		Adrenocorticotrophic hormone	
		Growth hormone	
		Oxytocin	Posterior pituitary gland
		Vasopressin (ADH)	
		Parathormone	Parathyroid gland
		Calcitonin	Thyroid gland
		Insulin	Islets of Langerhans (pancreas)
		Glucagon	
		Gastrin	Stomach mucosa
		Secretin	Duodenal mucosa
Steroids		Testosterone	Testis
		Oestrogens	Ovary and placenta
		Progesterone	
		Corticosteroids	Adrenal cortex
Fatty acids		Prostaglandins	Many tissues

example, excess glucose in the blood causes the release of insulin from the pancreas which lowers the blood glucose level.

(b) The presence of another hormone in the blood. For example, many of the hormones released from the anterior pituitary gland are 'stimulating' hormones which cause the release of other hormones from other glands in the body.

(c) Stimulation by neurones from the autonomic nervous system. For example, adrenaline and noradrenaline are released from the cells of the adrenal medulla by the arrival of nerve impulses in situations of anxiety, stress and danger.

In the first two cases the timing of hormone release and the amount of hormone released are regulated by feedback control. Positive and negative feedback mechanisms both operate in endocrine control but positive feedback, since it tends to increase instability, only operates as part of a larger control system. For example, the release of luteinising hormone under the stimulus of oestrogen is an example of positive feedback but its continued release is prevented by the later release of progesterone.

Hormones which are released by the presence of another circulating hormone are usually under the control of the hypothalamus and pituitary glands and the final metabolic or growth effect may involve the secretion of three separate hormones as shown in fig 16.46. This mechanism, known as the **cascade** effect, is significant because it enables the effect of the release of a small amount of initial hormone to become amplified as it passes along the endocrine pathway.

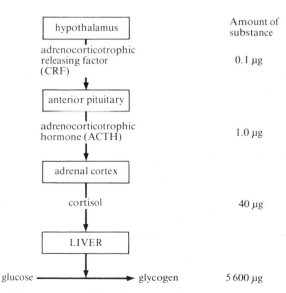

Fig 16.46 *An example of the 'cascade' effect in the control of the conversion of glucose to glycogen as a result of the release of adrenocorticotrophic releasing factor. The total amplification in this example is 56 000 times (data from Bradley, 1976)*

603

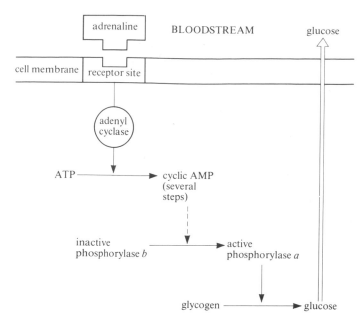

Fig 16.47 *Simplified diagram showing how adrenaline causes the release of glucose from a liver cell. The release of membrane bound adenyl cyclase produces cyclic AMP which activates enzyme systems leading to the breakdown of glycogen to glucose which diffuses out the cells into the blood stream*

Hormones are specific chemical substances and only exert their effects on target cells which possess the specific protein or lipoprotein receptors that interact with the hormone. Non-target cells lack these receptors, therefore there is no response to the circulating hormone. Many hormones have specific regions of their molecular structure for attachment to the receptor, and once attached the hormone may exert its effect at one of the following levels in the cell: (1) the cell membrane, (2) enzymes located in the cell membrane, (3) cellular organelles, and (4) genes. An example of each of these levels follows.

(1) Insulin exerts one of its effects by increasing the uptake of glucose into cells by binding with a receptor site and altering the permeability of the membrane to glucose.

(2) Adrenaline and many peptide hormones bind to receptor sites on the cell membrane and cause the release of a 'second messenger' which initiates a sequence of enzyme mechanisms which produce the appropriate hormonal response. In many cases this 'second messenger' is the nucleotide 3,5–adenosine monophosphate (cyclic AMP) which is formed by the action of the enzyme **adenyl cyclase** on ATP following the enzyme's release from the receptor site. A simplified representation of this mechanism is seen in fig 16.47.

(3) One of the effects of thyroxine is seen at the level of the mitochondrion where it influences the enzymes of the electron carrier system involved with the formation of ATP (section 11.5.4). Much of the energy passing along the electron transport chain in those circumstances is lost as heat.

(4) Steroid hormones, and the insect moulting hormone ecdysone, pass through the cell membrane and bind to a receptor in the cytoplasm. The complex formed passes to the cell nucleus where the hormones exert a direct effect upon the chromosomes by activating genes and stimulating transcription (messenger RNA formation).

In many cases of hormone action hormones appear to exert their effects by influencing enzymes associated with membranes or genetic systems.

16.6.2 The hypothalamus and pituitary gland

Intercellular communication is achieved, as stated earlier, by the activity of nervous and endocrine systems acting independently or together. The major centres in the body for the coordination and integration of the two systems of control are the hypothalamus and pituitary gland. The hypothalamus plays a dominant role in collecting information from other regions of the brain and from blood vessels passing through it. This information passes to the pituitary gland which, by its secretions, directly or indirectly regulates the activity of all other glands.

The hypothalamus

The hypothalamus is situated at the base of the forebrain immediately beneath the thalamus and above the pituitary gland. It is composed of several distinct regions called **nuclei** made up of collections of cell bodies whose axons terminate on blood capillaries in the **median eminence** and **posterior pituitary** as shown in fig 16.48. Many physiological activities such as hunger, thirst, sleep and temperature regulation are regulated by nervous control exercised through nerve impulses passing from the hypothalamus along autonomic neurones. The hypothalamic control of

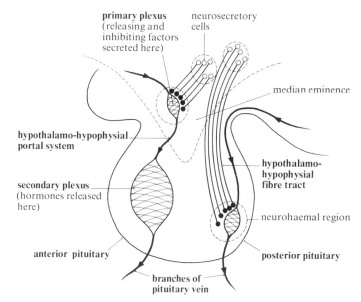

Fig 16.48 *Diagram showing the relationship between neurosecretory cells and blood vessels in the hypothalamus and pituitary gland*

endocrine secretion, however, lies in the ability of the hypothalamus to monitor metabolite and hormone levels in the blood. Information generated this way, together with information from almost all parts of the brain, then passes to the pituitary gland either by the release of 'hormones' into the blood vessels of the median eminence, which supply the pituitary, or by neurones. The information relayed by neurones passes through specialised neurones called **neurosecretory cells**.

All nerve cells release a chemical substance, a transmitter substance, at their terminal synapse, but neurosecretory cells are nerve cells that have developed the secretory capacity to a high level. Chemical substances are produced in the cell bodies of these cells and packaged into granules or droplets before being transported down the axon by axoplasmic streaming. At the terminal end of the neurone these cells synapse on to capillaries into which they release their secretion when stimulated by nerve impulses passing down the axon.

The pituitary gland

The pituitary gland or **hypophysis** (*hypo*, under; *phyein*, to grow) is a small red-grey gland weighing about 0.5 g and connected to the brain by the pituitary stalk (**infundibulum**). It has a dual origin and retains features of those origins in its functions. The two lobes of the pituitary gland are the anterior pituitary and the posterior pituitary.

*Anterior pituitary or adenohypophysis (*aden, gland*).* This is derived from an upgrowth of the glandular roof of the mouth. It is connected to the hypothalamus by blood vessels of the **hypothalamo-hypophysial portal system** which has a capillary bed, the **primary plexus**, in the median eminence of the hypothalamus and a **secondary plexus** in the anterior pituitary.

Nerve terminals from specialised neurosecretory cells release two groups of chemical substances, known as 'releasing factors' and 'inhibiting factors', into the blood capillaries of the primary plexus and these pass to the secondary plexus where they cause the release of six trophic hormones which are produced and stored by the anterior pituitary. These six hormones pass into the blood vessels leaving the pituitary and exert their effects on specific target organs throughout the body, as shown in table 16.12.

The release of the first two hormones is under the dual inhibitory and stimulatory control of the hypothalamus, whereas the release of the other four is regulated by negative feedback of hormones from the target glands acting on receptors in the hypothalamus and anterior pituitary. Pituitary hormones stimulate the release of target gland hormones and as the levels of these rise they inhibit the secretion of hypothalamic and pituitary hormones. When the circulatory level of these target hormones falls below a certain level the hypothalamic and pituitary inhibition ceases allowing the increased secretion from these glands. This control mechanism is described in sections 18.4.4 and 19.6.

*Posterior pituitary or neurohypophysis (*neuro, nerve*).* This is derived from a downgrowth of the floor of the brain. It does not synthesise any hormones but stores and releases two hormones, **antidiuretic hormone** (**ADH** or **vasopressin**) and **oxytocin**. Antidiuretic hormone is released in response to a fall in the water content of plasma and leads to an increase in the permeability to water of the distal and collecting tubules of the nephron so that water is retained in the blood plasma. A reduced volume of hypertonic urine is excreted (section 19.6). Oxytocin causes contraction of the uterus during birth and the ejection of milk from the nipple (section 20.3.8).

ADH and oxytocin are produced by neurosecretory cell bodies lying in the nuclei of the hypothalamus and pass down the nerve fibres attached to carrier protein molecules called **neurophysins**. These neurosecretory cells are much more specialised than those connected with the secretion of releasing factors and they form structures in the posterior pituitary known as **neurohaemal organs**. These are structures consisting of a swollen synapse attached to a capillary and surrounded by connective tissue (fig 16.49).

Table 16.12. Summary table showing the main hypothalamic hormones, the anterior pituitary hormones influenced by them and their target organs

Hypothalamic hormone	Anterior pituitary hormone and response	Site of action
Growth hormone releasing factor (GHRF) Growth hormone release-inhibiting hormone (GHRIH)* (somatostatin)	Growth hormone (GH)	Most tissues
Prolactin releasing factor (PRF) Prolactin inhibiting factor (PIF)	Prolactin (luteotrophin) (LTH) Inhibition of prolactin secretion	Ovary and mammary gland
Luteinising hormone releasing hormone (LHRH)*	Follicle stimulating hormone (FSH) Luteinising hormone (LH)	Ovary and testis
Thyrotrophin releasing hormone (TRH)*	Thyroid stimulating hormone (TSH)	Thyroid gland
Adrenocorticotrophin releasing factor (CRF)	Adrenocorticotrophic hormone (ACTH)	Adrenal cortex

*Releasing factors with an established identity are known as 'hormones'. Luteinising hormone releasing hormone is able to stimulate the release of both FSH and LH.

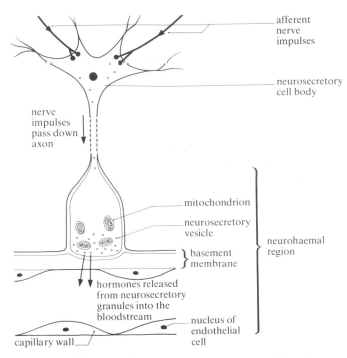

Afferent nerve impulses

neurosecretory cell body

nerve impulses pass down axon

mitochondrion

neurosecretory vesicle

neurohaemal region

basement membrane

hormones released from neurosecretory granules into the bloodstream

nucleus of endothelial cell

capillary wall

Fig 16.49 *Diagram showing a neurosecretory cell and neurohaemal organ, (not drawn to scale)*

Afferent nerve stimuli are relayed to the cell bodies of these neurosecretory cells from other regions of the brain and transmitted down the axons to the neurohaemal organ where secretions stored in vesicles are released into the bloodstream and carried to target organs. The physiological response produced by such a circuit involving the translation of sensory information into hormonal secretions, and eventually a physiological response, is known as a **neuroendocrine response**. Many neuroendocrine responses result in a type of behavioural pattern known as a **neuroendocrine reflex** and many examples of these are associated with courtship and breeding activity.

16.6.3   Pineal gland or epiphysis, (*epi*, upon: *phyein*, to grow)

The pineal gland is an extremely small gland found in the roof of the forebrain (diencephalon) and covered by the corpus callosum and cerebral hemispheres. It is variable in size and weighs about 150 mg. The Romans believed the pineal gland to be the 'seat of the soul' but it is now recognised as an endocrine gland. It has no direct connection with the central nervous system but is richly vascularised and believed to secrete several hormones, including **melatonin**. It is innervated by sympathetic neurones which are stimulated by centres in the brain controlled by light. Exposure to darkness stimulates melatonin synthesis which acts via the brain and modifies the function of the thyroid and adrenal glands and gonads. There is also evidence to suggest that melatonin acts on the brain and influences several physiological processes which are dependent upon time, such as the onset of puberty, ovulation and sleep. Tumours of the pineal gland in young

boys result in precocious sexual development. The pineal gland, then, appears to function as a 'biological clock' and acts as a '**neuroendocrine transducer**' converting cyclic nervous activity, generated by light, into endocrine secretion. Much more research is required to clarify the many functions of this gland.

16.6.4   Parathyroid glands

There are four small parathyroid glands in Man and they are embedded in the thyroid gland. They produce only one hormone called **parathormone** which is a peptide composed of 84 amino acids. Parathormone and the thyroid hormone **calcitonin** work antagonistically to regulate the plasma calcium and phosphate levels. The release of parathormone increases the plasma calcium level to its normal level of 2.5 mmol dm^{-3} and decreases the plasma phosphate level. The activity of the parathyroid glands is controlled by the simple negative feedback mechanism shown in fig 16.50.

Overactivity of the gland, **hyperparathyroidism**, reduces the level of calcium in the plasma and tissues due to calcium excretion in urine. This can lead to a state of tetany in which muscles remain contracted. Also the rate of excretion of phosphate is reduced and the level of phosphate ions in the plasma rises.

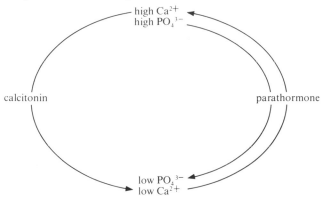

high Ca^{2+}
high PO$_4^{3-}$

calcitonin

parathormone

low PO$_4^{3-}$
low Ca^{2+}

Fig 16.50 *Role of parathormone and calcitonin in the regulation of blood calcium level*

16.6.5   Thyroid gland

The thyroid gland in Man is a bow-tie-shaped structure situated in the neck region with lobes, on each side of the trachea and larynx, connected by a thin band of tissue. The entire gland weighs approximately 25 g and produces three active hormones, **triiodothyronine (T$_3$)**, **thyroxine (T$_4$)** and **calcitonin**. T$_3$ and T$_4$ have a regulatory effect on metabolic rate, growth and development, whilst calcitonin is involved in the regulation of the plasma calcium level.

The structure of the thyroid gland

The thyroid gland is made up of numerous follicles which have a diameter of 0.1 mm and contain a clear colloid composed of the glycoprotein **thyroglobulin**. The wall of each follicle is composed of a single layer of cuboidal cells

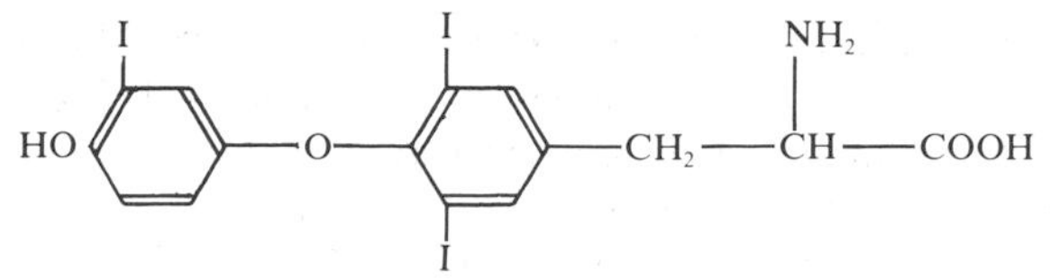

HO — (ring with I at top and I at bottom) — O — (ring with I at top) — CH_2 — CH(NH_2) — COOH

3, 5, 3-triiodothyronine (T_3)

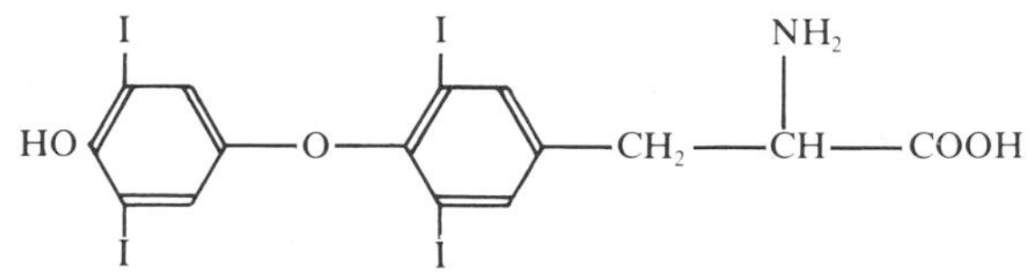

HO — (ring with I at top and I at bottom) — O — (ring with I at top and I at bottom) — CH_2 — CH(NH_2) — COOH

3, 5, 3, 5-tetraiodothyronine (T_4)
thyroxine

Fig 16.51 *Structural formulae of the main thyroid hormones T_3 and T_4*

that become columnar and bear microvilli on their inner surface when the gland is activated by **thyroid stimulating hormone (TSH)** from the anterior pituitary gland.

The formation and release of thyroid hormones

Iodine is taken up by active transport from the plasma, in the numerous capillaries surrounding the follicles, as iodine ions (I^-) and secreted into the lumen of the follicle. Here it is bound to a protein molecule and oxidised to iodine by peroxidase enzymes which form part of a cytochrome enzyme system. The iodine formed reacts with the amino acid tyrosine which is bound to thyroglobulin formed by the follicle cells. Further iodination occurs and subsequent interactions give rise to the two main iodinated amino acid hormones shown in fig 16.51.

The function of T_3 and T_4

Whilst T_3 and T_4 have a major influence upon many metabolic processes, including carbohydrate, protein, fat and vitamin metabolism, their main influence is upon the rate of metabolic processes, an effect known as **calorigenesis**, (*calor*, heat, *genesis*, production). The basal metabolic rate (BMR) in Man, 160 kJ m^{-2} body surface h^{-1}, is maintained at a steady state by the action of thyroxine which promotes the breakdown of glucose and fats into forms which can readily yield energy (section 18.4.2). Further calorigenic effects include increases in the uptake of oxygen by the body and the rate of enzyme reactions involved in the electron transport chain in the mitochondria. This increases the rate of ATP formation and heat production by the tissues. The exact mechanism of this action is not known.

T_3 and T_4 and the growth hormone, **somatomedin**, have a joint stimulatory effect on protein synthesis leading to an increase in growth rate. This effect is clearly seen in frog metamorphosis (section 21.7.4) and in children suffering from a lack of thyroid hormones.

In many of the metabolic processes with which it is involved thyroxine appears to enhance the effects of other hormones such as insulin, adrenaline and glucocorticoids (section 18.5.2).

Control of T_3 and T_4 release

The effects of T_3 and T_4 are longer lasting than those of most other hormones and hence it is homeostatically vital that fluctuations in their secretion be prevented. This is one of the reasons for the storage of T_3 and T_4 within the gland so that it is readily available for release.

The levels of T_3 and T_4 circulating in the blood control their release from the thyroid gland by negative feedback mechanisms involving the hypothalamus and anterior pituitary.

Thyrotrophic releasing hormone (TRH) and TSH release is inhibited by the amounts of T_3 and T_4 in the blood in excess of those required to maintain the metabolic rate at a steady state. Superimposed on these are environmental factors, such as temperature, which influence higher centres of the brain to stimulate the hypothalamus to secrete TRH. This 'sets' the threshold in the pituitary for the negative feedback mechanisms. These mechanisms of control are shown in fig 16.52.

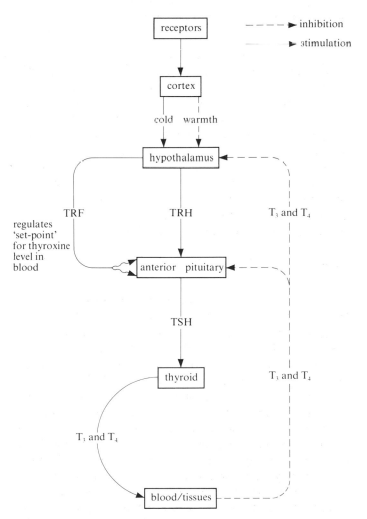

Fig 16.52 *Summary diagram showing the factors regulating thyroxine secretion and leading to homeostatic control of metabolic rate*

Overactivity of the thyroid gland (hyperthyroidism)

Both over- and underactivity of the thyroid gland can produce a swelling in the neck known as a **goitre**. Overactivity may be due to overproduction of thyroxine from an enlarged thyroid gland. The symptoms are increases in heart rate (tachycardia) (section 18.1.5), ventilation rate and body temperature. The basal metabolic rate may increase by 50% with associated increases in oxygen consumption and heat production. Patients become very nervous and irritable and the hands shake when held out. Extreme hyperthyroidism is termed **thyrotoxicosis** and is associated with increased excitability of cardiac muscle which may lead to heart failure unless treated. This may involve the surgical removal of most of the gland or the destruction of the same amount by administering radioactive iodine.

Underactivity of the thyroid gland (hypothyroidism)

A lack of TSH production by the anterior pituitary, iodine deficiency in the diet or failure of enzyme systems involved in thyroxine production may result in hypothyroidism. If there is a deficiency of thyroxine at birth this will lead to poor growth and mental retardation, a condition known as **cretinism**. If the condition is diagnosed at an early stage thyroxine can be given to restore normal growth and development. Thyroxine deficiency in later life gives rise to a condition known as **myxoedema** and the symptoms are a reduction in metabolic rate accompanied by decreased oxygen consumption, ventilation, heart rate and body temperature. Mental activity and movement become slower and weight increases due to the formation and storage of a semi-fluid material under the skin. This causes the face and eyelids to become puffy, the tongue swells, the skin becomes rough and hair is lost from the scalp and eyebrows. All of these symptoms can be eliminated and the condition treated by taking thyroxine tablets.

Calcitonin

In addition to follicular cells the thyroid gland contains other cells known as **C cells**. These secrete a polypeptide hormone **calcitonin** which works antagonistically towards parathormone and lowers blood calcium levels.

16.6.6 Adrenal glands

There are a pair of adrenal (*ad*, to; *renes*, kidneys) glands weighing approximately 5 g each which are situated anterior to the kidneys. Each gland is composed of cells having two different embryological origins, and these cells function independently. The outer cortex is derived from cells of the neural plate and forms 80% of the gland. It is a firm structure and covered by a fibrous capsule and is essential for life. The inner medulla is derived from cells of the neural crest and has retained its close origin with the nervous system. It is not essential for life.

Table 16.13. Summary table showing the main cytological detail, secretion and functions of the three regions of the adrenal cortex

Region	Cytological detail	Secretion	Function	Notes
Zona glomerulosa	Composed of rounded clusters of small cells containing elongated mitochondria	Mineralocorticoids e.g. aldosterone	Control water and electrolyte metabolism by stimulating cation pumps in membranes to conserve Na^+ and Cl^- and remove K^+. Prevent excessive Na^+ loss in sweat, saliva and urine and maintain osmotic concentration of body fluids at a steady state	Renin released from juxtaglomerular apparatus in kidney produces angiotensin. This stimulates release of aldosterone which increases Na^+ uptake by kidney and leads to release of ADH which increases reabsorption of water by kidney tubules. Release is not stimulated by ACTH
Zona fasciculata	2–3 rows of parallel columns of cells arranged at right-angles to the surface of the gland and containing spherical mitochondria	Glucocorticoids e.g. cortisol	(A) Carbohydrate metabolism (1) promote gluconeogenesis (2) promote liver glycogen formation (3) raise blood glucose level (B) Protein metabolism (1) promote breakdown of plasma protein (2) increase availability of amino acids for enzyme synthesis in the liver	Overactivity leads to Cushings' syndrome and patients show abdominal obesity, wasting of muscles, high blood pressure, diabetes and increased hair growth. Overproduction of ACTH by the anterior pituitary is Cushings' disease. Underactivity leads to Addison's disease as shown by muscular weakness, low blood pressure, decreased resistance to infection, fatigue and darkening of the skin
Zona reticularis	Composed of irregularly arranged columns of cells containing elongated mitochondria		(C) Other roles (1) prevent inflammatory and allergic reactions (2) decrease antibody production	

Adrenal cortex

The adrenal cortex has three histologically distinct regions composed of cells grouped around blood capillaries and produces steroid hormones of two types. These regions, their cytological detail, secretions and functions are shown in table 16.13.

All steroids are formed from a common precursor molecule called **cholesterol** which the cortex is able both to synthesise and take up from the circulation following absorption from the diet. The three regions of the cortex then convert it into specific steroid hormones.

Steroids are lipid-soluble substances which diffuse through cell membranes and attach to cytoplasmic receptor proteins. The complexes formed then migrate into the nucleus where they attach to specific areas of the chromosome and de-repress or activate certain genes inducing the formation of messenger RNA.

The size of the adrenal gland is closely linked to the output of ACTH and the ability to withstand stress. During long periods of stress the size of the gland increases. Investigations into the behaviour of organisms under stress have shown that the output of adrenal hormones increases with the rise in number in the population. In organisms where social hierarchies exist, there is a positive correlation between position in the hierarchy and increased size of the adrenal gland.

Control of cortical hormone release

Mineralocorticoid release is stimulated by the activity of **renin** and **angiotensin** as described in table 16.13, whilst glucocorticoids are secreted in response to **adrenocorticotrophic hormone (ACTH)**. The mechanisms of the release of these hormones is shown in fig 16.53.

ACTH is a polypeptide molecule containing 39 amino acids. It attaches to receptors on the surface of the cortical cells and activates adenyl cyclase to convert ATP to cyclic AMP (section 16.6.1). This acts as a cofactor in activating enzymes known as **protein kinases** which stimulate the conversion of cholesterol to pregnenolone. In addition to this ACTH is responsible for the uptake of cholesterol into the cortex, the maintenance of the size of the adrenal cortex and the maintenance of the enzymes involved in steroid production.

Adrenal medulla

The adrenal medulla forms the centre of the adrenal gland. It is a soft tissue composed of strands of cells surrounded by blood capillaries and is richly supplied with nerves. The cells are modified postganglionic sympathetic neurones and when stimulated by preganglionic sympathetic neurones they secrete noradrenaline and adrenaline (section 16.6.1). The adrenal medulla is not essential to life since its function is to augment that of the sympathetic nervous system.

Noradrenaline (norepinephrine) and adrenaline (epinephrine) are formed from the amino acid tyrosine and belong to a group of biologically active molecules called **catecholamines** (fig 16.54). They are both secreted by the cells of the medulla but only noradrenaline is secreted by the postganglionic synapses of the sympathetic nervous system. The effects of both hormones are basically identical as shown in table 16.14, but they differ in their

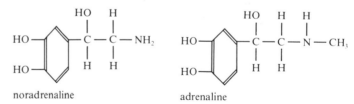

noradrenaline   adrenaline

Fig 16.54 *Molecular structure of noradrenaline and adrenaline*

Table 16.14. Physiological effects of noradrenaline and adrenaline

Dilate pupils of eyes
Cause hair to stand on end
Relax bronchioles thus increasing air flow to lungs
Inhibit peristalsis
Inhibit digestion
Prevent bladder contraction
Increase amplitude and rate of heartbeat
Cause almost general vasoconstriction
Increase blood pressure
Stimulate conversion of liver glycogen to glucose
Decrease sensory threshold
Increase mental awareness

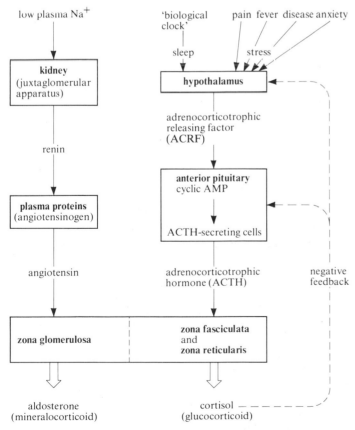

Fig 16.53 *Summary diagram for the control of the main adrenal cortex hormones*

609

effects on blood vessels. Noradrenaline causes vasoconstriction of all blood vessels whereas adrenaline causes vasoconstriction of blood vessels supplying the skin and gut and vasodilation of blood vessels to muscles and the brain. Both of these hormones activate two types of receptor sites on the target tissues known as α and β **adrenergic receptors**. These release adenyl cyclase (cyclic AMP) into the cell and this leads to the specific tissue response as shown in fig 16.53. Most organs have both α- and β-receptors with α-receptors appearing to be more receptive to noradrenaline than adrenaline and vice versa in the case of β-receptors.

The actions of these hormones are widespread throughout the body and prepare the animal for situations of 'fight or flight' and facilitate the response to sudden demands imposed by stress such as pain, shock, cold, low blood sugar, low blood pressure, anger and passion.

16.6.7 Pancreas

The pancreas has both exocrine and endocrine functions and is associated with the alimentary canal (section 10.4). The bulk of this gland is composed of exocrine acinar cells which form rounded structures enclosing a lumen into which the digestive enzymes of the zymogen granules are secreted (section 10.4.9). Interspersed amongst groups of acinar cells are the **islets of Langerhans** containing a small number of large alpha (α) cells, numerous small beta (β) cells and blood capillaries. Alpha cells secrete **glucagon** and beta cells **insulin** and these have antagonistic effects on the blood glucose level.

Insulin

Insulin is a protein composed of 51 amino acids and is released in response to a rise in blood glucose level above $100 \text{ mg } 100 \text{ cm}^{-3}$ blood and a rise in glucagon level. It is carried in the plasma bound to β-globulin and has an important anabolic effect on every organ of the body. Receptor sites on cell membranes bind insulin, and this reaction leads to changes both in cell permeability and the activity of enzyme systems within the cell with the following effects:

(1) increase in the rate of conversion of glucose to glycogen (glycogenesis),
(2) increase in the rate of uptake of glucose by muscle and fat by cell membranes,
(3) increase in the rate of protein and fat synthesis,
(4) increase in the formation of ATP, DNA and RNA.

The secretion of insulin is vital to life since it is the only hormone which lowers the blood glucose level. A deficiency in insulin production leads to the metabolic condition known as **diabetes mellitus** in which the blood glucose reaches such a level that it exceeds that which the kidney can reabsorb, the **renal threshold**, and is excreted in the urine. The involvement of the pancreas in diabetes mellitus has been known for almost a hundred years but it was not until 1921 that the Canadian doctors Banting and Best succeeded in treating the condition with insulin extracted

Table 16.15. Some of the effects of insulin deficiency and excess

Deficiency	Excess
High blood glucose level (hyperglycaemia)	Low blood glucose level (hypoglycaemia)
Breakdown of muscle tissue	Hunger
Loss of weight	Sweating
Tiredness	Irritability
	Double vision

from the pancreas of animals. In 1950 Sanger, in Cambridge, succeeded in determining the primary structure of insulin and opened up the way for its synthetic preparation. The effects of insulin deficiency and excess are summarised in table 16.15.

Glucagon

Glucagon is a peptide composed of 29 amino acids and is released, along with several other hormones, in response to a fall of blood glucose level induced by an increase in metabolic demand. It stimulates the breakdown of proteins and fats to carbohydrates (gluconeogenesis) (section 18.5.2). Receptor sites in the liver cell membrane bind glucagon which causes the release of adenyl cyclase to form cyclic AMP. The action of glucagon is similar to that of adrenaline and both activate phosphorylase enzymes which stimulate the breakdown of glycogen to glucose-6-phosphate as shown in fig 16.47. Glucagon has no effect on muscle glycogen.

Summary diagrams of the role of insulin and glucagon are shown in figs 18.7 and 18.23.

16.6.8 Differences between nervous and endocrine coordination

The nervous and endocrine systems function separately and together in the coordination of many of the body's activities. This chapter describes both situations but it is useful as a summary to examine the differences between the two systems as this highlights the advantage of each system in the light of their roles (table 16.16).

Table 16.16. Differences between nervous and endocrine coordination

Nervous	Chemical
Information passes as electrical impulses along axons (chemical across synapses)	Information passes as a chemical substance through the bloodstream
Rapid transmission	Slow transmission
Response immediate	Response usually slow, e.g. growth
Response short-lived	Response long-lasting
Response very exact	Response usually widespread

16.7   The study of behaviour (ethology)

Behaviour may be defined as the outwardly expressed course of action produced in organisms in response to stimuli from a given situation. The action modifies, in some way, the relationship between the organism and its environment and its adaptive significance is the perpetuation of the species. All living organisms exhibit a variety of forms of behavioural activity determined by the extent to which they are able to respond to stimuli. This varies from the relatively simple action of the growth of a plant stem towards a light source, to the complex sexual behaviour patterns of territory defence, courtship and mating seen in birds and mammals.

Plant behaviour is restricted to movements produced by growth or turgor changes and is stereotyped and predictable. The two main activities associated with plant behaviour are tropisms and nasties and details of these are described in section 15.1.

Animal behaviour is far more complex and diverse than plant behaviour and therefore it is extremely difficult to investigate and account for with any degree of scientific validity. The three main approaches to behavioural studies are the vitalistic, mechanistic and ethological approaches.

Vitalistic approach. This seeks to account for behavioural activities in terms of what animals are seen to do, and attempts to relate this to changes in the environment. It involves the total rejection of any study of the animal outside its natural environment. The technique has its foundations in natural history and has provided a wealth of valuable data, but it is essentially non-scientific since all the observations relate to past events which cannot be tested experimentally.

Mechanistic approach. This is an experimental approach and involves the study of particular aspects of behaviour under controlled conditions in a laboratory. It may be criticised on the grounds of the artificiality of the experimental situation, the nature of the behavioural activities and the way in which the results are interpreted. This technique is, however, used extensively in psychology and was pioneered by Pavlov.

Ethological approach. This is the contemporary approach to behavioural investigations and attempts to explain responses observed in the field in terms of the stimuli eliciting the behaviour. It involves both of the techniques outlined above and was pioneered by Lorenz, von Frisch and Tinbergen.

In all behavioural studies great care has to be taken in interpreting the results of observations in order to eliminate subjectivity. For example, care must be taken to avoid putting oneself in the place of the animal (**anthropocentrism**), or interpreting what is observed in terms of human experience (**anthropomorphism**) or interpreting the cause of the observation in terms of its outcome (**teleology**).

Recent advances in audio-visual technology have assisted the recording of behavioural activities. Infra-red photography has enabled animals to be filmed at night and time-lapse photography and slow-motion cinematography have enabled respectively slow-moving activities, such as moulting in insects, and fast-moving activities, such as bird flight, to be recorded and subsequently seen at speeds more suited to analysis by behaviouralists. The use of miniature cassette tape recorders for recording sounds and their subsequent analysis using sound spectrographs and computers has helped in the study of auditory communication between organisms. The movement of organisms is now studied either using implanted miniaturised signal generators, emitting signals that can be followed using direction-finding equipment, or by the use of tracking radar. The two techniques are employed successfully in following the migrations of mammals, birds and locusts.

Whatever the approach and techniques used in the investigation of behaviour the fundamental explanation of behavioural activity must begin with a stimulus, end with a response and include all the stages occurring at various levels of organisation within the body linking *cause* and *effect*.

Broadly speaking there are two forms of behaviour, **innate behaviour** and **learned behaviour**, but the distinction between the two is not clear-cut and the majority of behavioural responses in higher organisms undoubtedly contain components of both. However, for simplification in this elementary introduction to behaviour, the various aspects of behaviour are considered under these two headings in the next two sections.

16.8   Innate behaviour

Innate behaviour does not involve a single clear-cut category of behaviour but rather a collection of responses that are predetermined by the inheritance of specific nerve or cytoplasmic pathways in multicellular or acellular organisms. As a result of these 'built-in' pathways a given stimulus will produce, invariably, the same response. These behaviour patterns have developed and been refined over many generations (**selected**) and their primary adaptive significance lies in their survival value to the species. Another valuable feature of innate behaviour is the economy it places on nerve pathways within multicellular organisms, since it does not make enormous demands on the higher centres of the nervous system.

There is a gradation of complexity associated with patterns of innate behaviour which is related to the complexity of nerve pathways involved in their performance. Innate behaviour patterns include orientations (taxes and kineses), simple reflexes and instincts. The latter are extremely complex and include biological rhythms, territorial behaviour, courtship, mating, aggression, altruism, social hierarchies and social organisation. All plant behaviour is innate.

Taxes

A taxis or **tactic response** is a movement of the whole organism in response to an external directional stimulus. Tactic movements may be towards the stimulus (**positive,** +), away from the stimulus (**negative,** −), or at a particular angle to the stimulus, and are classified according to the nature of the stimulus. Some examples of types of taxes are shown in table 15.2. In some cases organisms are able to move by maintaining a fixed angle relative to the directional stimulus. For example, certain species of ants can follow a path back to their nest by setting a course relative to the sun's direction. Other organisms orientate themselves so that, for example, their dorsal side is always uppermost. This is called the **dorsal light reaction** and is found in fish such as plaice which maintain their dorsal surface at right-angles to the sky.

Many organisms detect the direction of the stimulus by moving the head, which bears the major sensory receptors, from side to side. This is known as a **klinotactic** response and enables symmetrically placed receptors on the head, such as photoreceptors, to detect the stimulus. If both receptors are equally stimulated the organism will move forwards in approximately a straight line. This type of response is shown by *Planaria* moving towards a food source and by blowfly larvae moving away from a light source. In all cases of klinotaxis it is thought that successive stimulation of receptors on each side of the body is necessary in order to provide the 'brain' with a continuous supply of information since there is no long-term 'memory'.

Kineses

A **kinetic response** is a non-directional movement response in which the *rate* of movement is related to the *intensity* of the stimulus and not the *direction* of the stimulus. For example, the direction of movement of the tentacles of *Hydra* in search of food is random and slow, but if saliva, glutathione or water fleas are placed in the immediate vicinity of the *Hydra* the rate of movement of the tentacles increases.

Both kinetic and tactic responses are observed through the use of woodlice in a **choice chamber** as described in experiment 16.1.

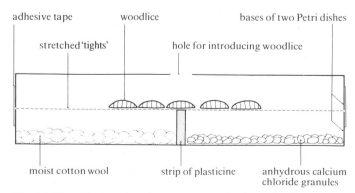

adhesive tape   woodlice   bases of two Petri dishes

stretched 'tights'   hole for introducing woodlice

moist cotton wool   strip of plasticine   anhydrous calcium chloride granules

Fig 16.55 *Choice chamber apparatus for investigating orientation behaviour in woodlice.*

Experiment 16.1: To investigate orientation behaviour in woodlice by the use of a simple choice chamber.

Materials

old pair of tights
bases of 2 Petri dishes
Araldite
hot metal rod
cotton wool
anhydrous calcium chloride
adhesive tape
ten woodlice
plasticine

Method

(1) Cut a circle out of an old pair of tights 10 cm in diameter and stretch over the base of an 8.5 cm Petri dish. Attach with Araldite, held in place by an elastic band until it sets.

(2) Burn out a 1.0 cm hole in the bottom of this Petri dish using a hot metal rod.

(3) Divide the base of another Petri dish in half using a plasticine strip 8.5 cm long, 1.4 cm deep and 0.5 cm wide.

(4) Place cotton wool soaked in water in one half of this Petri dish and granules of anhydrous calcium chloride in the other half.

(5) Attach the Petri dish base prepared in (1) above to the Petri dish base prepared in (4) with adhesive tape as shown in fig 16.55.

(6) Introduce ten woodlice into the apparatus through the hole in the upper Petri dish and record the position and number active at 1 min intervals in a table such as table 16.17.

(7) After 20 min plot a graph of numbers present against time for each environment.

(8) Calculate the percentage number of woodlice active in the dry environment for each minute interval and plot on a graph against time.

(9) Explain the nature of the results obtained in terms of kineses and taxes.

Table 16.17. Specimen arrangement of table of results

	Humid		Dry		
Time/ min	Number present	Number active	Number present	Number active	Percentage active dry side
0	4	1	6	4	40%
1	5	2	5	5	50%
2		etc.		etc.	
3					
.					
.					
.					
20					

In simple experiments of this type the response of organisms to environments having extremes of a given variable can be investigated. Tactic responses are observed by the preference shown by the organisms for a particular environment. For example, woodlice exposed to areas of high and low humidity in a choice chamber congregate in larger numbers in the area of highest humidity, showing them to be **positively hydrotactic**. More complex experiments can be devised using combinations of variables in order to determine which is strongest in eliciting a final response.

Kinetic responses are observed by recording the activity of woodlice at, say, 30 s intervals, in relation to their position in the choice chamber. Results of such investigations show that when first introduced into the choice chamber at the junction of two environments some woodlice move around whilst others remain stationary. After a short time all the woodlice begin moving and the speed of movement and rate of turning is always greatest in the drier side of the choice chamber than in the humid side. The increased, apparently random, moving and turning of the woodlice on the dry side is believed to indicate an attempt to find optimal conditions and, when these are found, the moving and turning response diminishes. These responses are examples of **orthokinesis**. The woodlice move more slowly on the humid side and consequently usually congregate there. The preference shown for the humid side of the choice chamber indicates a positively tactic response to humidity.

Not all orientation behaviour patterns are rigid, and the response shown by an organism may vary depending upon other factors such as the degree of hunger, thirst, light, dark, heat, cold and humidity.

16.8.1 Simple reflexes in vertebrates

A simple reflex is an involuntary stereotyped response of part of an organism to a given stimulus. It is determined by the presence of an inherited pattern of neurones forming spinal and cranial reflex arcs, and the structure and function of these is described in section 16.2.

In terms of behaviour, simple spinal reflexes are either **flexion** responses, involving withdrawal of a limb from a painful stimulus, or **stretch** responses, involving the balance and posture of the organism. Both of these responses are primarily involuntary and most require no integration or coordination outside that found in the spinal cord. However both types of response may be modified by the brain according to circumstances and in the light of previous experience. When this happens innate and learned behaviour patterns overlap and the reflex action is now described as 'conditioned' as described in table 16.18. Many simple cranial reflexes too, may be conditioned, for example blinking in response to a sudden movement.

16.8.2 Instincts

Instincts are complex, inborn, stereotyped behaviour patterns of immediate adaptive survival value to the organism and are produced in response to sudden changes in the environment. They are unique to each species and differ from simple reflexes in their degree of complexity. Konrad Lorenz, a Nobel prize-winning ethologist, defined instincts as 'unlearned species-specific motor patterns'.

Instinctive behaviour is predominant in the lives of invertebrate animals where, in insects in particular, short life cycles prevent modifications in behaviour occurring as a result of trial-and-error learning. Instinctive behaviour in insects and in vertebrates therefore is a 'neuronal economy measure' and provides the organism with a ready-made set of behavioural responses. These responses are handed down from generation to generation and, having undergone successfully the rigorous test of natural selection, clearly have important survival significance.

However, before concluding that instinctive behaviour patterns are completely inflexible as a result of their genetic origin it must be stressed that this is not so. All aspects of the development of an organism, whether anatomical, biochemical, physiological, ecological or behavioural, are the result of the influence of constantly varying environmental factors acting on a genetic framework. In view of this no behavioural pattern can be purely instinctive (that is genetic) or purely learned (that is environmental), and any subsequently described behavioural activity, whilst being either superficially instinctive or superficially learned, is influenced by both patterns. Some authorities prefer the terms **species-characteristic behaviour**, in preference to instinctive behaviour, and **individual-characteristic behaviour**, in preference to learned behaviour. But despite this terminology the same principle of genetic and environmental interaction applies. This point was demonstrated very clearly by Professor W. H. Thorpe in his investigations of chaffinch song. He found that chaffinches whether reared by parents, reared in isolation, or deaf from the time of hatching, all produce sounds clearly identifiable to the human ear as those of a chaffinch. Sound spectrograms show, however, that these are only rudimentary songs, and that chaffinches reared by parents, listening to the songs of their parents and other chaffinches in the population, develop identical sound patterns to the older birds, characteristic of the local population. It was apparent that bird songs within a species have 'local dialects'. Songs of deaf birds or those in isolation remained rudimentary, thus demonstrating that the environment can significantly modify an instinctive pattern.

16.8.3 Motivation

The extent and nature of any behavioural response is modified by a variety of factors that are collectively known as **motivation**. For example, the *same* stimulus does not always evoke the *same* response in the *same* organism. The difference is always circumstantial and may be controlled by either internal or external factors.

Presenting food to a starved animal will produce a different response from that shown by an animal that has been fed. In between the two extremes responses of varying strengths will be produced depending upon the degree of hunger experienced by the organism. However, if the act of feeding would place a hungry animal in danger of being attacked by a predator the feeding response would be curbed until the danger passed. Many behavioural responses associated with reproduction have a motivational element. For example, many female mammals are only receptive to mating attempts by males at certain times of the year. These times coincide with the period of oestrous and have the adaptive significance of ensuring that mating coincides with the optimum time for fertilisation and therefore the production of offspring at the most favourable time of the year. These behavioural patterns are known as **biological rhythms** and are described in section 16.8.5. In many species the degree of motivation, or 'drive', coincides in males and females, but in other species some system of communication between the sexes is essential to express the degree of motivation. In many primate species the timing of oestrus is signalled by a swelling and change of colour of the genital area of the female and this is displayed to the male. Such behaviour reduces the likelihood of a male attempting to mate at a time when the female is not receptive. The signals used to bring about a change in behaviour are known as **sign stimuli** and, depending upon their origin or function, are classified as motivational, releasing or terminating stimuli.

Motivational stimuli. This type of stimulus may be external, for example increasing day length inducing territorial and courtship behaviour in birds, or internal, for example depleted food stores in the body during hibernation results in awakening and food seeking. Motivational stimuli provide the 'drive' or 'goal' preparing the organism for activity which may be triggered off by the second type of sign stimulus.

Releasing stimuli or 'releasers'. A releaser is either a simple stimulus or a sequence of stimuli produced by a member of a species which evokes a behavioural response in another member of the same species. The term 'releaser' was introduced by Lorenz and its role in behaviour was extensively studied by Tinbergen.

The effect of a releaser was demonstrated during an investigation into feeding in herring gulls. Young herring gulls normally peck at a red spot on the yellow lower mandible of the parent's bill to signal the parent to regurgitate fish which the young then swallow. In a series of controlled experiments, carried out by Tinbergen and Perdeck using cardboard models of adult gulls' heads, they found that the releaser of the begging response was the presence of a contrasting colour on the beak. Such was the strength of the releaser that a pointed stick with alternating coloured bands was able to elicit a greater response than the parent bird, as shown in fig 16.57.

Terminating stimuli. Terminating stimuli, as the name implies, complete the behavioural response and may be external or internal. For example, the external visual stimuli of a successfully completed nest will terminate nest building in birds, whereas the internal satisfaction or 'satiety' accompanying ejaculation in the male will terminate copulation and likewise a full stomach will terminate feeding.

Further examples of sign stimuli for a selection of behavioural mechanisms are discussed in sections 16.8.4–16.8.9.

Fig 16.56 *Female chimpanzee signalling to the male that she is sexually receptive*

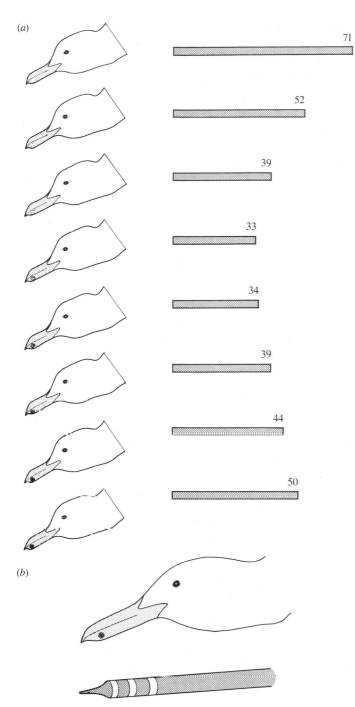

Fig 16.57 (a) The horizontal bars indicate the number of pecking responses made by herring gull chicks to a series of cardboard models of adult herring gull heads having grey bills and spots of varying shade. (From Hinde, R. A. 1966, after Tinbergen, N., 1951)
(b) The artificial bill, coloured red with three white bars evoked 20% more pecks than an accurate three-dimensional model of an adult herring gull head and beak, coloured yellow with a red spot. (From Tinbergen and Perdeck, 1950, Behaviour, 3.1)

16.8.4 Innate releasing mechanisms

Lorenz suggested that there must exist a means of filtering out stimuli which are irrelevant from those that are relevant to producing the correct behavioural response. Investigations suggest that this may occur peripherally at the receptors or centrally within the central nervous system. For example, Schneider found that the chemoreceptors on male moth antennae are only sensitive to the sex-attracting chemicals (pheromones) produced by the female of that species and not to those of other species. Modifications of Tinbergen and Perdeck's experiments on the herring gull have been carried out, and the results suggest, as Lorenz postulated, that centrally situated neurosecretory mechanisms control the response to sign stimuli.

16.8.5 Biological rhythms

Many behavioural activities occur at regular intervals and are known as biological rhythms or **biorhythms**. Well-known examples of these include the courtship displays and nesting behaviour of birds in the spring and the migration of certain bird species in autumn. The time interval between activities can vary from minutes to years depending on the nature of the activity and the species. For example, the polychaete lugworm *Arenicola marina* lives in a U-shaped burrow in sand or mud and carries out feeding movements every 6–7 min. This cyclical feeding pattern has no apparent external stimulus nor internal physiological motivational stimulus. It appears that the feeding pattern rhythm is regulated by a biological 'clock' mechanism dependent, in this case, on a 'pacemaker' originating in the pharynx and transmitted through the worm by the ventral nerve cord.

Rhythms involving an internal clock or pacemaker are known as **endogenous rhythms**, as opposed to **exogenous rhythms** which are controlled by external factors. Apart from examples such as the feeding behaviour of *Arenicola*, most biological rhythms are a blend of endogenous and exogenous rhythms.

In many cases the major external factor regulating the rhythmic activity is **photoperiod**, the relative lengths of day and night. This is the only factor which can provide a reliable indicator of time of year and is used to 'set the clock'. The exact nature of the clock is unknown but the clockwork mechanism is undoubtedly physiological and may involve both nervous and endocrine systems. The effect of photoperiod has been studied extensively in relation to behaviour in mammals, birds and insects and, whilst it is evidently important in activities such as preparation for hibernation in mammals, migration in birds and diapause in insects, it is not the only external factor regulating biological rhythms. Lunar rhythms, too, can influence activity in certain species, such as the palolo worm of Samoa. The polychaete worm swarms and mates throughout the whole South Pacific on one day of the year, the first day of the last lunar quarter of the year, on average

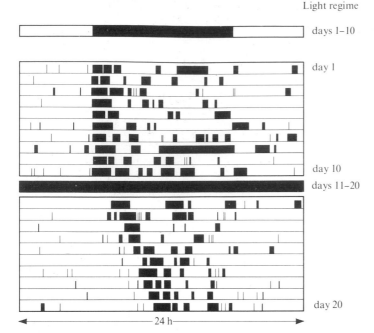

Light regime

days 1–10

day 1

day 10

days 11–20

day 20

◄——— 24 h ———►

Fig 16.58 *Results of cockroach activity over a 20 day period. During days 1–10 the cockroach received a light regime of 12 hour light: 12 hour dark cycle and between days 11–20 the cockroach was kept in constant darkness as indicated in the figure. The black areas shown for each day represent the time and duration of each 'burst' of activity*

2nd November. The influence of lunar rhythms on tidal variations is well known, and these are two exogenous factors which have been shown to impose a rhythmic behaviour pattern on the midge *Clunio maritimus*. The larvae of *Clunio* feed on red algae growing at the extreme lower tidal limit, a point only uncovered by the tide twice each lunar month. Under natural conditions these larvae hatch, the adults mate and lay eggs in their two-hour-long life during which they are uncovered by the tide. In laboratory conditions of a constant 12 h light – 12 h dark photoperiod the larvae continued to hatch at about 15-day intervals, demonstrating the apparent existence of an endogenous clock programmed to an approximately semi-lunar rhythm coinciding with the 14.8-day tidal cycle.

The behaviour of many completely terrestrial insects appears to be controlled by endogenous rhythms related to periods of light and dark. For example, *Drosophila* emerge from pupae at dawn whereas cockroaches are most active at the onset of darkness and just before dawn. These regularly occurring biological rhythms, showing a periodicity of about 24 h, are known as **circadian** (*circa*, about; *dies*, day) rhythms or **diurnal** rhythms. In an investigation of the activity of a cockroach (*Periplaneta*) under two different light regimes (12 h light and 12 h darkness for 10 days followed by total darkness for 10 days), the cockroach restricted its activity in the later regime to a time approximately related to the period of activity associated with the onset of darkness under the former light regime. The results of this investigation are shown in fig 16.58 and

indicate that in the absence of an exernal time-cue the circadian rhythm persisted even though the onset of activity varied by a small amount each day. These results are consistent with the idea that circadian rhythms are controlled by an endogenous mechanism or 'clock', governed or 'set' by exogenous factors.

Circadian rhythms are believed to have many species-specific adaptive significances and one of these involves orientation. Animals such as fish, turtles, birds and some insects which migrate over long distances are believed to use the sun and stars as a compass. Other animals, such as honeybees, ants and sandhoppers use the sun as a compass in locating food and their homes. Compass orientation by sun or moon is only accurate if organisms using it possess some means of registering time so that allowances can be made for the daily movements of the sun and moon. The increasingly familiar concept of 'jet-lag' is an example of a situation where Man's internal physiological circadian rhythm is out of step with the day-and-night rhythm of the destination.

16.8.6 Territorial behaviour

A territory is an area held and defended by an organism or group or organisms against organisms of the same, or different, species. Territorial behaviour is common in all vertebrates except amphibia but is rare in invertebrates. Much research into the nature and function of territoriality has been carried out on birds and groups of primates. In the latter it forms an important part of their social behaviour.

The exact function of territory formation probably varies from species to species, but in all cases it ensures that each mating pair of organisms and their offspring are adequately spaced to receive a share of the available resources, such as food and breeding space. In this way the species achieves optimum utilisation of the habitat. The size of territories occupied by any particular species varies from season to season, according to the availability of environmental resources. Birds of prey and large carnivores have territories several square miles in area in order to provide all their food requirements. Herring gulls and penguins (fig 16.59), however, have territories of only a few square metres, since they move out of their territories to feed and use them for breeding purposes only.

Territories are found, prior to breeding, usually by males. Defence of the area is greatest at the time of breeding and fiercest between males of the same species. There are a variety of behavioural activities associated with territory formation and they involve threat displays between owners of adjacent territories. These threat displays involve certain stimuli which act as releasers. For example, Lack demonstrated that an adult male robin (*Erithacus rubecula*) would attack a stuffed adult male robin displaying a red breast, and a bunch of red breast feathers, but not a stuffed young male robin which did not have a red breast. The level of aggression shown by an

organism increases towards the centre of the territory. The aggressiveness of males is determined partly by the level of testosterone in the body and this can affect territory size. For example, the territory size of a red grouse can be increased by injecting the bird with testosterone. Fig 16.60 shows the changes in territory size of three red grouse treated in this way. The boundary between adjacent territories represents the point where neighbouring animals show equally strong defence behaviour. Despite the apparent conflict and aggression associated with territory formation, actual fighting, which would be detrimental to the species, is rare and is replaced by threats, gestures and postures. Having obtained a territory many species, particularly carnivores, proceed to mark out the boundary by leaving a scent trail. This may be done by urinating or rubbing glandular parts of the body against objects called **scent posts** along the boundary of the territory. Although territorial behaviour involves the sharing of available resources amongst the population there are inevitably some organisms unable to secure and defend a territory. In many bird species, such as grouse, these weaker organisms are relegated to the edges of the habitat where they fail to mate. This appears to be one of the adaptive significances of territoriality as it ensures that only the 'fittest' find a territory, breed and thus pass on their genes to the next generation. Thus a further function of territorial behaviour is associated with **intraspecific competition** and may act as a means of regulating population size.

Fig 16.59 *Aerial photograph showing the territories occupied by penguins*

Fig 16.60 *The solid lines indicate the territories of a group of male red grouse. The dotted lines show changes which occurred after birds **A**, **X** and **Y** had received doses of testosterone. Birds **X** and **Y** had not previously held territories. (After Watson, A (1970). J. Reprod. Fert., Suppl., 11.3.)*

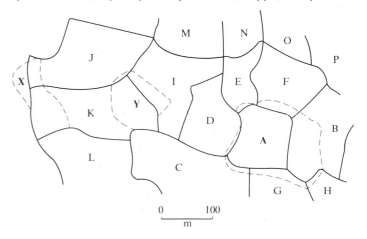

617

16.8.7　Courtship and mating

There are many elaborate and ritualistic species-specific behaviour patterns associated with courtship and mating. In birds, mammals and some fish these two processes often follow the establishment of a territory by the male. Courtship is a complex behaviour pattern designed to stimulate organisms to sexual activity and is associated with pair formation in those species where both sexes are involved in the rearing of offspring, as in thrushes, or in gregarious mixed-sex groups such as baboons. The majority of these species show rhythmic sexual activity of the type described in section 16.8.5.

Courtship behaviour is controlled primarily by motivational and releasing stimuli and leads to mating which is the culmination of courtship. During mating, the behavioural activities are initiated by releasing stimuli and ended by terminating stimuli associated with the release of gametes by the male.

The motivational stimuli for courtship in most species are external, such as photoperiod, and lead to rising levels of reproductive hormones and the maturation of the gonads. In most species this produces striking changes in the secondary sexual characteristics and other behavioural activities including coloration changes, as in the development of a red belly in male sticklebacks; increase in size of parts of the body, as in the plumage of birds of paradise; mating calls, as in nightingales; postural displays, as in grebes (fig 16.61) and the use of chemical sex attractants, as in butterflies and moths.

Of the variety of signals used in courtship to attract members of the opposite sex, sight, sound and smell play important roles. For example, the male fiddler crab, *Uca*, uses a visual display and attracts females by waving an enlarged chela in a bowing movement similar to that of a violinist. The vigour of the movement increases as a female is attracted to the male.

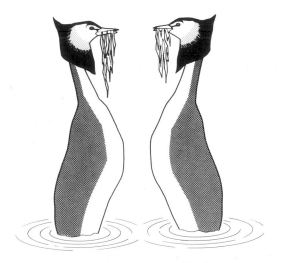

Fig 16.61　*A courtship behavioural activity in great crested grebes. Male and female grebes are shown here presenting nesting material to each other. (After Huxley, J. S. (1914). Proc. Zool. Soc. Lond., 1914 (2), 491–562)*

Many insects, amphibia, birds and mammals use auditory signals in courtship. Some species of female mosquito attract males by the sounds produced by the frequencies of their wing beats whilst grasshoppers, crickets and locusts **stridulate**. This involves either rubbing the hindlegs against each other or the elytron (hardened wing case), or rubbing the elytra together to produce a 'chirping' sound which is species-specific and only produces a response from members of *that* species.

Some species of spiders employ a mechanical means of attracting the opposite sex. Male spiders approach the web of a female sitting at the centre of the web and pluck a thread of the web at a species-specific frequency. The plucking 'serenades' the female and reduces her natural aggressive manner so enabling the male to approach and mate her. Unfortunately, if the male 'woos' a female of the wrong species or 'plays the wrong tune' he is attacked and killed!

The secretion and release by organisms of small amounts of chemical substances, leading to specific physiological or behavioural responses in other members of the same species, is used in courtship and mating and, as described later, the regulation of behaviour within social groups. These substances are called **pheromones** and are usually highly volatile, low relative molecular mass compounds. Many of these compounds function as natural sex attractants and the earliest to be identified were **civetone** from the civet cat and **muscone** from the musk deer. Both of these substances are secretions from the anal glands and are used commercially in the preparation of perfume. Mares, cows and bitches secrete pheromones whilst on 'heat'. This is undetectable by human olfactory epithelium but detectable by the males of the species concerned. **Bombykol**, a pheromone released by eversible glands at the tip of the abdomen of unfertilised adult female silk moths, is capable of attracting males of the same species from considerable distances. The olfactory receptors on the antennae of the male moths detect the presence of the pheromone molecules in great dilutions and the moths make a rheotactic response by flying upwind until they reach the female. Pheromones are used increasingly as a method of **biological control** in insect pest species such as the gypsy moth. In these cases the artificial release of the pheromone, **gyplure**, attracts males to the source of release where they can be captured and killed. This not only immediately reduces the number of male moths in the population but also, in preventing them from breeding, reduces the size of the next generation.

Pheromones are also used to induce mating as in the case of the queen butterfly *Danaus gilippus*. The pheromone is released by the male and brushed on to the female by a pair of brush-like structures, called hairpencils, everted from the tip of the abdomen. The entire courting and mating sequence is shown in fig 16.62.

Courtship in some species is accompanied by conflict behaviour on the part of one or both sexes. In species where individuals normally live a solitary existence,

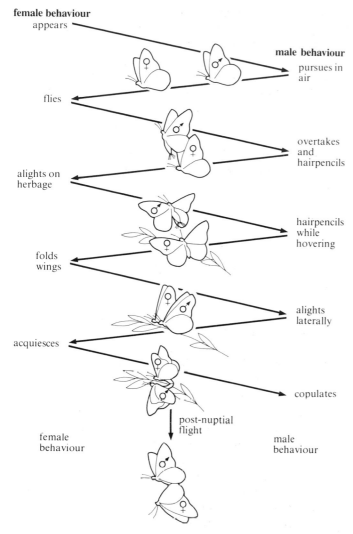

female behaviour
appears

flies

alights on
herbage

folds
wings

acquiesces

male behaviour
pursues in
air

overtakes
and
hairpencils

hairpencils
while
hovering

alights
laterally

copulates

post-nuptial
flight

female
behaviour

male
behaviour

Fig 16.62 *Courtship and copulation in the queen butterfly. (The arrows indicate the stimuli and responses involved in the behavioural activities). (From Brower, L. P., Brower, J. V. Z. and Cranston, F. P. (1965). Zoologica, 50, 18)*

courtship conflict may be associated with changing attitudes to other members of the species as a result of increasing hormone levels. Other significances of this behaviour may be the tightening of the pair bond between the mating pair and the synchronisation of gonadial development so that gametes mature at the same time. In certain species of spider, such as wolf spiders, conflict between male and female only diminishes for the act of copulation which culminates in the female killing the male.

16.8.8 Aggression (agonistic behaviour)

Aggression is a group of behavioural activities including threat postures, rituals and occasionally physical attacks on other organisms, other than those associated with predation. They are usually directed towards members of the same sex and species and have various functions including the displacement of other animals from an area, usually a territory or a source of food, the defence of a mate

or offspring and the establishment of rank in a social hierarchy.

The term 'aggression' is emotive and suggests an existence of unnecessary violence within animal groups; the alternative term '**agonistic**' is preferable. Agonistic behaviour has the adaptive significance of reducing intraspecific conflict and avoiding overt fighting which is not in the best interest of the species. Most species channel their 'aggression' into ritual contests of strength and threat postures which are universally recognised by the species. For example, horned animals such as deer, moose, ibex and chamois may resort to butting contests for which 'ground rules' exist. Only the horns are allowed to clash and they are not used on the exposed and vulnerable flank. Siamese fighting fish, *Betta splendens*, resort to threat postures involving increasing their apparent size as shown in fig 16.63.

The threats issued by two organisms in an agonistic conflict situation are settled invariably by one of the organisms, generally the weaker, backing down and withdrawing from the situation by exhibiting a posture of submission or appeasement. In dogs and wolves an appeasement posture may take the form of the animal lying down on its back or baring its throat to the victor.

During actual physical contact animals often refrain from using their most effective weapons on another member of the same species. For example, giraffes will fight each other using the short horns on their heads, but in defence against other animals they use their very powerful feet.

For agonistic behavioural activities to be most effective they must be stereotyped for any species and Tinbergen demonstrated several of these during investigations carried

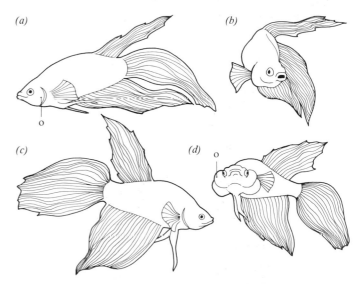

Fig. 16.63 *Stages in threat displays in Siamese fighting fish. (a) and (b) fish not showing threat displays, (c) and (d) operculum, o, and fins erected to increase their apparent size during threat displays. (From Hinde, R. A., 1970, after Simpson, 1968)*

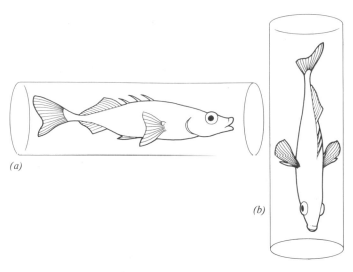

Fig 16.64 *(above) (a) Full threat posture in male stickleback (b) Reduced threat posture when contained in a tube held vertically. (After Tinbergen, N., 1951)*

Fig 16.65 *(below) Models used as releasers of aggressive behaviour in male sticklebacks holding a territory. (a) Accurate model not having a red belly does not elicit aggression from male stickleback. (b)–(c) are models of sticklebacks not having an accurate shape but having a red belly. All these models produced aggressive responses from male sticklebacks. (After Tinbergen, 1951)*

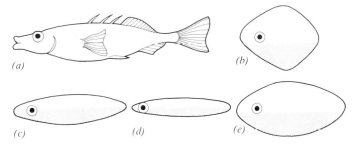

out on sticklebacks. In one series of experiments he demonstrated that the effectiveness of threat posture depended on the stickleback assuming a horizontal position with fins and spines outstretched. When trapped in a specimen tube and kept vertical a male stickleback does not have the same threat potential to ward off other sticklebacks as it has when free-swimming or held horizontally (fig 16.64).

In another series of experiments he demonstrated that agonistic behaviour in male sticklebacks defending a territory is triggered off by 'releasers' which can take the form of almost any object whose underside is coloured red. These objects act as mimics of male sticklebacks whose bellies turn red during the breeding season and who appear to the territory holder as a potential threat (fig 16.65).

At times of stress, for example during conflict situations or during courtship and mating, an organism may perform an action which is trivial and irrelevant to the situation. This is known as **displacement activity** and occurs when motivation is high but two conflicting 'releasers' present themselves. For example, one of a pair of birds involved in a territorial dispute may begin nest-building activities, such as pulling up grass, when presented with a choice between fighting or fleeing. Such displacement activities act as an outlet for pent-up activities. Many activities in Man may be considered displacement activities in certain circumstances, for example fist clenching, fist banging, nail biting, straightening clothes, finger drumming, etc. A similar form of behaviour is called **vacuum activity** which occurs when motivation is high and no releaser presents itself. In this case the normal response is produced but is not directed towards the normal object or situation, and so provides a means of reducing frustration; for example, showing irritation towards someone who is not the cause of the irritation but acts as a substitute.

16.8.9 Social hierarchies

Many species of insects and most vertebrates show a variety of group behavioural activities associated with numbers of individuals living together temporarily or permanently. This is known as **social behaviour** and the coherence and cooperation achieved has the adaptive significance of increasing the efficiency and effectiveness of the species over that of other species. In a social group of this kind a system of communication is essential, and the efficiency of the organisation is further increased by individuals carrying out particular roles within the society. One aspect of social behaviour arising out of these points is the existence of **social hierarchies** or **pecking orders**.

A pecking order is a dominance hierarchy. That is to say that the animals within the group are arranged according to status. For example, in a group of hens sharing a hen-house a linear order is found in which hen A will peck any other hen in the group, hen B will peck all hens other than A and so on. Position in the hierarchy is usually decided by some agonistic form of behaviour other than fighting. Similar patterns of dominance have been observed in other species of birds and in mice, rats, cows and baboons. The institutional organisation of all human societies is based on a pattern of dominance hierarchy.

Pecking orders exist only where animals are able to recognise each other as individuals and possess some ability to learn. The position of an animal within a pecking order usually depends on size, strength, fitness and aggressiveness and, within bird hierarchies, remains fairly stable during the lifetime of the individuals. Lower-order male members can be raised up the hierarchy by injections of testosterone which increase their levels of aggressiveness. The experimental removal of lower-order mice from a hierarchy and subsequent provision of unlimited food for them increases their mass, improves their vigour and can raise their position in the hierarchy when reintroduced to the group. Similarly placing lower-order mice into other groups where they are dominant appears to give them a degree of 'self-confidence' (to use an anthropomorphic term) which stays with them when reintroduced to their original groups and results in their rank increasing.

One advantage of pecking order is that it decreases the amount of individual aggression associated with feeding, mate selection and breeding-site selection. Similarly it avoids injury to the stronger animals which might occur if fighting was necessary to establish the hierarchy. Another advantage of pecking order is that it ensures that resources are shared out so that the fittest survive. For example, if a group of 100 hens is provided with sufficient food for only 50 hens it is preferable, in terms of the species, for 50 hens to be adequately fed and the weaker 50 hens die than for them all to live and receive only half rations, as this might prevent successful breeding. In the short term, social hierarchies increase the genetic vigour of the group by ensuring that the strongest and genetically fittest animals have an advantage when it comes to reproducing.

Social organisation

When animals come together to form a cohesive social group individuals often assume specialised roles, which increases the overall efficiency of the group (fig 16.66). These roles include members specialised or designated for food-finding, reproduction, rearing and defence. Cooperation between members of a society sharing division of labour depends upon stereotyped patterns of behaviour and effective means of communication. These patterns of behaviour and methods of communication vary between species and are vastly different for primate and insect societies. Primate societies are flexible, in that roles are interchangeable between members of the group whereas in insect societies differences in body structure and reproductive potential affect their role within the society, a feature called **polymorphism**.

Ants, termites and bees are social insects living in colonies and have an organisation based on a **caste system**. In the honeybee colony there is a single fertile female queen, several thousand sterile female workers and a few

hundred fertile male drones. Each type of honeybee has a specific series of roles determined primarily by whether it hatched from a fertilised or an unfertilised egg. Fertilised eggs are diploid and develop into females; unfertilised eggs are haploid and develop into males. Secondly, the type of food provided for female larvae determines whether they will become queens or workers. This food is called **royal jelly** and is one example of the importance of chemical substances in the organisation of the society. Information within the colony is transmitted either by chemical odours and pheromones during the many licking and grooming activities called **trophallaxes**, or by particular forms of visual orientation displays known as **dances**.

Karl von Frisch, a German zoologist and Nobel prize-winner, investigated the nature of these dances using marked worker bees in specially constructed observation hives. Worker bees 'forage' for sources of nectar and communicate the distance and direction of the source to other workers by the nature of a dance generally performed on a vertical comb in the hive. If the distance is less than about 90 m the worker performs a **round dance** as shown in fig 16.67a which intimates that the source is less than 90 m from the hive but gives no indication of direction. The **waggle dance** is performed if the source is greater than 90 m and includes information as to its distance from the hive and its direction relative to the hive and the position of the sun. The dance involves the worker walking in a figure-of-eight and waggling her abdomen during which, according to von Frisch, the speed of the dance is inversely related to the distance of the food from the hive, the angle made

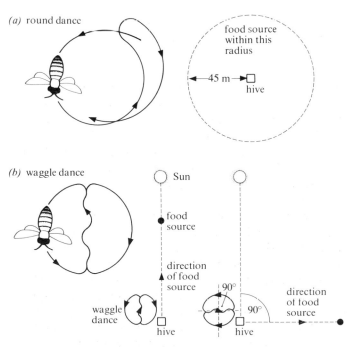

(a) round dance

food source within this radius

45 m — hive

(b) waggle dance

Sun

food source

direction of food source

waggle dance

90°

90°

direction of food source

hive

hive

Fig 16.67 *Honeybee dances*
(a) Round dance is performed when food is less than 90 metres from hive
(b) Waggle dance shows relation between hive, sun and direction of food source

Fig 16.66 *Social grooming in adult chimpanzees provides a means of social cohesion within a group*

between the two loops of the figure-of-eight and the vertical equals the angle subtended at the hive by the sun; and the food source and the intensity of the waggles is related to the amount of food at the source (fig 14.67b). It is thought that allowances for movement of the sun are made by the use of an inbuilt 'biological clock' and that bees orientate on cloudy days by substituting polarised light from the sun for the position of the sun.

Recent evidence has suggested that bees may use high-frequency sound to communicate sources of food to other workers, but whether this is the main means of communication has yet to be demonstrated clearly. This does not, though, invalidate the data and interpretations of von Frisch and may be an associated communication system which augments the visual dance displays. However, it is known that the returning worker may communicate the type of flower visited by feeding the other workers with some of the nectar collected.

16.9   Learned behaviour

16.9.1   Memory

Memory is the ability to store and recall the effects of experience and without it learning is not possible. Past experiences, in the form of stimuli and responses, are recorded as a 'memory trace' or **engram**, and since the extent of learning in mammals is proportional to the extent of the cerebral hemispheres it would appear that these are the site of engram formation and storage.

The nature of the engram is not known and it exists only as a hypothetical concept backed up by conflicting data. Of the two broad areas of thought on the nature of the engram one is based on changes in neuronal structure and organisation within the central nervous system and the other based on permanent changes in brain biochemistry.

Histological examination of brain tissue shows the existence of neurones arranged in loops, and this has given rise to the concept of '**reverberating circuits**' as units of the engram. According to this view these circuits are continuously active carrying the memory information. It is doubtful if this activity could last for any length of time and experiments suggest that memory has greater performance and stability than could be achieved by this mechanism alone. For example, cooling the brains of rats down to 0 °C causes all electrical activity in the nervous system to cease, but on restoring the rats to normal temperatures there is no impairment in memory. However, it is thought that such circuits may play a role in **short-term memory**, that is memory lasting at most for minutes such as memorising six-digit telephone numbers in Man, and in facilitating particular neural pathways. Events associated with short-term memory take longer to be recalled following concussion or amnesia and gradually disappear in old age. Long-term memory is more stable and suggests that some mechanism for permanent change exists in the brain.

Evidence based on the latter observation suggests that memory is a biochemical event involving the synthesis of substances within the brain. Extracts of the 'brains' of trained flatworms or rats injected into untrained flatworms or rats reduce the time taken by the latter organisms to learn the same task as compared with control groups. The active substance in all the experiments appears to be RNA.

Further evidence exists which suggests that the composition of the RNA of neurones changes during learning and that this may result in the synthesis of specific 'memory proteins' associated with the learned behaviour. Investigations have shown that injections of the protein-inhibiting drug, puromycin, also interfere with memory. For example, injecting puromycin into the brains of mice recently trained to choose one direction in a maze destroyed their ability to retain this learning, whereas a control group, injected with saline, retained the learned behaviour.

In conclusion, it would appear that the nature of memory is far from being clarified but it seems probable that changes in electrical properties of neurones, the permeability of synaptic membranes, enzyme production associated with synapses and synaptic transmission are all concerned with the formation of a 'memory trace'. Certainly it seems that memory is associated closely with events occurring at synapses.

16.9.2   Learning

Learning is an adaptive change in individual behaviour as a result of previous experience (fig 16.68). The degree of permanence of newly acquired learned behaviour patterns depends upon memory storing the information gained from the experience. In Man, acquiring or learning 'facts', for example for examinations, may be short lived whereas the ability to carry out coordinated motor activities such as toilet training, riding a bicycle or

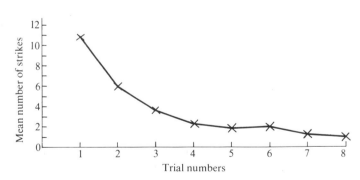

Fig 16.68 *The graph above shows a typical 'learning curve'. The graph shows the results of the number of times a cuttlefish strikes at a prawn kept in a glass tube. The prawn was presented to the cuttlefish on eight successive occasions lasting three minutes each time. As the cuttlefish unsuccessfully attacks the prawn the number of attacks decreases as the cuttlefish 'learns' that it cannot capture the prawn. (The results are based on data obtained from forty cuttlefish, from Messenger, J. B., (1977), Symp. Zoo. Soc. Lond., 38, 347–76)*

swimming, lasts throughout life. Learning is generally thought of in terms of vertebrates, and mammals in particular, but has been demonstrated in all groups of animals except protozoa, coelenterates and echinoderms where neural organisation is absent or primitive. Psychologists have attempted to establish general 'laws of learning' but all attempts so far have failed. It would appear that learning is an individual event and occurs in different ways in different species and different contexts. The classification and features of learned behaviour presented in this chapter are artificial and must be recognised as such. They do, however, cover the spectrum of current thinking on types of learning and are backed up by experimental evidence. A summary of the major types of learned behaviour is given in table 16.18 and is designed to provide only an introduction to the topic of learning.

Table 16.18. Summary of the major types of learned behaviour based on a classification proposed by Thorpe (1963)

Learned behaviour	Features of the learned behaviour
Habituation	Continuous repetition of a stimulus not associated with reward or punishment (reinforcement) extinguishes any response to the stimulus, e.g. birds **learn** to ignore a scarecrow. Important in development of behaviour in young animals in helping to understand neutral elements in the environment, such as movements due to wind, cloud-shadows, wave-action, etc. It is based in the nervous system and is not a form of sensory adaptation since the behaviour is permanent and no response is ever shown to the stimulus after the period of habituation.
Associative learning { Classical conditioning (conditioned reflex)	Based on the research of Pavlov on dogs. It involves the development of a conditioned salivary reflex in which animals **learn** to produce a **conditioned response** (salivation), not only to the natural **unconditioned stimulus** (sight of food) but also to a newly acquired **conditioned stimulus** (ticking of a metronome) which was presented to the dog along with the unconditioned stimulus. Animals learn to **associate** unconditioned stimuli with conditioned stimuli so either produces a response. For example, birds avoid eating black and orange cinnabar moth larvae because of bad taste and avoid all similarly coloured larvae even though they may be nutritious.
Operant conditioning (trial-and-error learning)	Based on the research of Skinner on pigeons. Trial motor activities give rise to responses which are reinforced either by rewarding (positive) or punishment (negative). The **association** of the outcome of a response in terms of reward or punishment increases or decreases respectively future responses. Associative learning efficiency is increased by repetition as shown in investigations carried out on learning in cuttlefish (fig. 16.68).
Latent learning (exploratory learning)	Not all behavioural activities are apparently directed to satisfying a need or obtaining a reward (i.e. appetitive behaviour). Animals explore new surroundings and **learn** information which may be useful at a later stage (hence latent) and mean the difference between life and death. For example in mice, knowledge of the immediate environment of its burrow may help it escape from a predator. At the time of acquiring this knowledge it had no apparent value. This appears to be the method by which chaffinches learn to sing, as described in section 16.8.2.
Insight learning	Probably the 'highest' form of learning. It does not result from immediate trial-and-error learning but may be based on information previously learned by other behavioural activities. Insight learning is based on advanced perceptual abilities such as thought and reasoning. Kohler's work on chimpanzees suggested 'insight learning': when presented with wooden boxes and bananas too high to reach the chimps stacked up the boxes beneath the bananas and climbed up to get them. Observations revealed that this response appeared to follow a period of 'apparent thought' (previous experience of playing with boxes [latent learning] may have increased the likelihood of the response).
Imprinting	A simple and specialised form of learning occurring during receptive periods in an animal's life. The learned behaviour becomes relatively fixed and resistant to change. Imprinting involves young animals becoming associated with, and identifying themselves with, another organism, usually a parent, or some large object. Lorenz found that goslings and ducklings deprived of their parents would follow him and use him as a substitute parent. 'Pet lambs', bottle-fed, show similar behaviour and this may have a profound and not always desirable effect later in life when the animal finds difficulty in forming normal relationships with others of the species. In the natural situation imprinting has obvious adaptive significance in enabling offspring to acquire rapidly skills possessed by the parents, e.g. learning to fly in birds, and features of the environment, e.g. the 'smell' of the stream in which migratory salmon were hatched and to which they return to spawn.

Chapter Seventeen

Movement and support

Movement can occur at the cellular level, for instance cytoplasmic streaming and swimming of gametes, at organ level, such as heartbeat and movement of a limb, or at the level of the organism. Movement of the whole organism from place to place is termed **locomotion**. Plants exhibit cellular and often organ movement, but they do not locomote, that is move from place to place in search of food or water.

Whilst a few animals can survive successfully by remaining attached to one place, the vast majority have complex locomotory systems which presumably evolved to enable them to search for and acquire food. However, even sessile animals exhibit a great degree of mobility of their bodily parts.

Apart from the need for food, some animals use locomotion to avoid capture by predators. It is also used for dispersal purposes and locating new favourable habitats as well as for bringing together individuals for reproductive activity.

Locomotion is the result of the arrangement, interaction and coordination of the nervous, muscular and skeletal systems. Muscles promoting locomotion are attached to the skeleton and are therefore called **skeletal muscles** (section 17.4.1). They act as machines, converting chemical energy into mechanical energy. They have the ability to contract, and when they do they serve to move the systems of levers comprising part of the skeleton. Coordinated movement of the levers enables the animal to move about. The posture of the animal is also maintained by the musculo-skeletal system which is under the overall control of the central nervous system.

Other muscles within the body serve not to move the whole organism but to move materials from place to place within it. Cardiac muscle (section 8.5) of the heart pumps blood round the body, whilst smooth muscle (section 17.5.3) located in the walls of various blood vessels constricts or dilates them and this alters the blood flow. Smooth muscle in the wall of the gut propels food along the intestinal tract by means of peristalsis (section 10.4.11). These are just a few of many such activities constantly occurring within the body.

In this chapter we will be primarily concerned with locomotion, and two systems will be discussed in detail, namely the skeletal and muscle systems. This will be followed by a review of the types of locomotion that occur in a wide variety of organisms.

17.1 Skeletal systems

The vast majority of animals possess some form of supportive structure. It may be from simple rods of strengthening material in the protozoans to the highly complex skeleton of arthropods and vertebrates. Generally speaking, the design of the supporting structure contributes towards the specific shape of the organism. This, in turn, is dictated by the particular requirements of the organism concerned. Structures of different design are needed for aquatic or terrestrial animals, quadripedal or bipedal animals, and for those that move over the ground or through the air.

The general functions of a skeleton are as follows.

(1) **Support**. All skeletons provide a rigid framework for the body and are resistant to compression. They help to maintain the shape of the body. For terrestial organisms the skeleton supports the weight of the body against gravitational force and in many cases raises it above the ground. This permits more efficient movement over the ground. Within the body, organs are attached to, and suspended, from the skeleton.

(2) **Protection**. The skeleton protects the delicate internal organs in those organisms with an **exoskeleton** (arthropods), and parts of the **endoskeleton** are designed for a similar function. For example, in Man the cranium protects the brain and the sense organs of sight, smell, balance and hearing; the vertebral column protects the spinal cord, and the ribs and sternum protect the heart, lungs and large blood vessels.

(3) **Locomotion**. Skeletons composed of rigid material provide a means of attachment for the muscles of the body. Parts of the skeleton operate as levers on which the muscles can pull. When this occurs, movement takes place. Soft-bodied animals rely on muscles acting against body fluids to produce their form of locomotion.

Three major types of skeleton are generally recognised: hydrostatic, exoskeleton and endoskeleton.

17.1.1 Hydrostatic skeleton

This is characteristic of soft-bodied animals. Here fluid is secreted within the body and enclosed by the body wall muscles. The fluid presses against the muscles which in turn are able to contract against the fluid. The muscles are not attached to any structures and thus they can only pull against each other. The combined effect of muscle contraction and fluid pressure serves to maintain the shape and form of the animal. Generally there are two muscle layers, one longitudinal and the other circular in orientation. When they act antagonistically against each other locomotion is effected. If the body of the organism is unsegmented (as in nematodes), when a particular muscle contracts, the pressure on the fluid will be transmitted to all other parts of the body. If the organism is segmented (such as *Lumbricus terrestris*, the earthworm) then such pressure is localised and only certain segments will move or change shape. A detailed account of the function of the hydrostatic skeleton in locomotion is given for the earthworm in section 17.6.5.

17.1.2   Exoskeleton

This is a particular characteristic of the arthropods. Epidermal cells secrete a non-cellular cuticle, or exoskeleton, composed mainly of **chitin**. It acts as a hard outer covering to the animal and is made up of a series of articulated plates or tubes covering or surrounding organs. It also extends into the anterior (stomodeum) and posterior (proctodeum) ends of the alimentary canal, and into the tracheae. Chitin is very tough, light and flexible; however, it can be strengthened by impregnation with 'tanned' (hardened) proteins, and, particularly in the aquatic crustaceans, by calcium carbonate. Where flexibility is required, as at the joints between plates or tubes, chitin remains unmodified. This combination of a system of plates and tubes joined together by flexible membranes provides both protection and mobility.

Arthropods are the only invertebrate group to possess jointed appendages. The joints are hinges, and the levers on either side are operated by flexor and extensor muscles which are attached to inward projections of the exoskeleton (fig 17.1). Chitin is permeable to water and this could lead to desiccation of terrestial animals like insects. This is prevented by the secretion of a thin waxy epicuticle via ducts from gland cells in the epidermis (fig 4.33). Therefore, the exoskeleton supports and protects the delicate inner parts of the animal and in addition prevents their drying up.

The hollow tubular form of the exoskeleton is very efficient as a supporting and locomotive device for small animals, such as most arthropods, and can support a much greater weight without giving way than a solid cylindrical strut of the same mass. However, it loses this efficiency when organisms become bigger and their weight increases. Here, to do the same job just as efficiently, the exoskeleton would have to increase in weight and thickness. The end product would be very heavy and cumbersome.

Growth takes place by **ecdysis** (moulting) in juvenile stages (larvae and nymphs) in insects and throughout adult life in crustaceans. At various times the exoskeleton is shed (ecdysis), thus exposing a new, soft and extensible exoskeleton. Whilst still soft, growth takes place as the

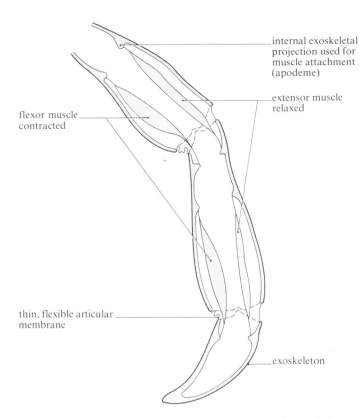

Fig 17.1   *VS of joints and musculature of an arthropod limb*

exoskeleton is extended and moulded into a larger form which often incorporates a change of shape. The new exoskeleton finally hardens. The animal is vulnerable to predators whilst the new exoskeleton is hardening. At this stage the skeleton is unable to support the weight of the animal and movement is virtually impossible. This is less of a problem for aquatic species as their body weight is supported by the water, but aquatic and terrestrial organisms usually hide themselves away during this time in an attempt to decrease their chances of being devoured by predators. Moulting is quite expensive in terms of the energy expenditure involved in building the exoskeleton in the first place and material loss when it is shed.

17.1.3   Endoskeleton

This is found in the protozoan order Radiolaria, where it consists of a skeleton of siliceous spicules, the molluscan class Cephalopoda, where some organisms such as the cuttlefish possess an internal shell, and in vertebrates. Typically the vertebrate skeleton is made either of cartilage or bone, is located within the organism and is internal to the muscles. A further difference between this form of skeleton and the exoskeleton is that the endoskeleton is composed of living tissue and so can grow steadily within the animal thus avoiding the necessity for ecdysis. A number of different types of joint exist and bones that form them are maintained in their correct relative position by elastic ligaments. Skeletal design in quadrupeds and bipeds is essentially the same, but there are slight differences in mobility at the shoulder and the hip. This is correlated with the type of locomotion adopted by the animals concerned and will be discussed in detail later.

17.1.4 The vertebrate skeleton

The vertebrate skeleton is composed either of cartilage or bone. Both tissues provide an internal supporting framework for the body. Only elasmobranch fish (such as dogfish and sharks) possess a wholly cartilaginous endoskeleton. All other vertebrates have a bony skeleton in their adult form, but with cartilage also present in certain regions, such as at the joints or between the vertebrae. In the embryo stage the skeleton of bony vertebrates is initially laid down as hyaline cartilage (section 8.4.4). This is of great biological significance, as cartilage is capable of internal enlargement, and so different parts of the skeleton are able to grow in proportion with each other during the development of the organism. Bone is different from cartilage in this respect as it can grow only by addition of material to its outer surface. If this were to occur during development, the articulating surfaces of bones at joints, and their respective points of muscle attachment would be unable to retain their correct spatial relationships.

17.2 Skeletal tissues

17.2.1 Cartilage

Three types of cartilaginous material are recognisable: **hyaline, white fibrous** and **yellow elastic** cartilage. A detailed account of their histology can be found in section 8.4.4. All types consist of a firm matrix penetrated by numerous connective tissue fibres. The matrix is secreted by living cells called chondroblasts. These later become housed in spaces (lacunae) scattered throughout the matrix. In this condition the cells are termed chondrocytes. Hyaline cartilage is the most common type and is found particularly at the ends of bones articulating to form joints. Its matrix of chondroitin sulphate is compressible and elastic, and is well able to withstand heavy weight and absorb sharp mechanical shocks such as might take place at joints. Within the matrix are embedded fine collagen fibres which provide resistance to tension and compression. Dense connective tissue, called the perichondrium, surrounds the outer surface of this cartilage at all places except where it passes into the cavity of a joint.

White fibrous cartilage contains a dense meshwork of collagen fibres and is found as discs between vertebrae and as a component of tendons. It is very strong yet possesses a degree of flexibility. Yellow elastic cartilage possesses many yellow elastic fibres and is located in the external ear, epiglottis and pharyngeal cartilages.

17.2.2 Bone

Bone is a hard, tough connective tissue composed mainly of calcified material. Details of its histology can be found in section 8.4.4. When a vertical longitudinal section of a long bone, such as a femur, is examined microscopically it is seen to be made up of several distinct components. Such a bone consists of a hollow shaft or **diaphysis**, with an expanded head or **epiphysis** at each end. Covering the entire bone is a sheath of tough connective tissue, the periosteum. The diaphysis is composed of compact bone whilst the epiphyses are composed of spongy bone overlain by a thin layer of compact bone. The layout of the bony material is designed to withstand compression forces and to give maximum strength to the bone (fig 17.2).

Fatty yellow marrow occupies the marrow cavity of the diaphysis, whilst red marrow is present amongst the bony struts (**trabeculae**) of the epiphyses. Numerous small openings penetrate the surface of the bone, through which nerves and blood vessels traverse into the bony tissue and marrow.

Apart from the functions listed earlier in the chapter, a bony skeleton also functions to produce red blood corpuscles and white granulocytes. Further it participates in the maintenance of constant calcium and phosphorus levels in the bloodstream (see chapter 16) by providing a store of calcium and phosphate ions which can be mobilised by the action of parathyroid and calcitonin hormones of the parathyroid and thyroid glands respectively.

> **17.1** Indicate for a bone such as the femur, how its structure, articular cartilage, muscle tendons and ligaments are adapted for the functions they perform.

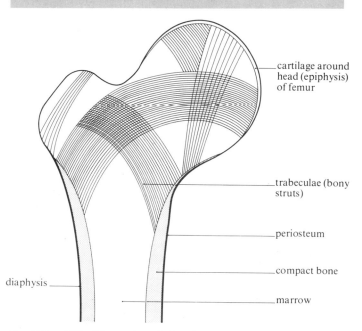

cartilage around head (epiphysis) of femur

trabeculae (bony struts)

periosteum

compact bone

marrow

diaphysis

Fig 17.2 *VS of femur head showing arrangement of trabeculae in spongy bone*

17.2.3 Development of the mammalian bony skeleton

The cartilaginous skeleton of a mammalian embryo is gradually replaced by bone in a growing organism. This involves the removal of existing cartilage, and construction of bone in its place, a process called **ossification**. In a long bone the diaphysis is the first area to be ossified. Here a layer of membrane bone (section 8.4.4) is laid down in the perichondrium forming a complete ring of bone around the diaphysis. When complete, this layer is termed the **periosteum**. Internal to the periosteum, chondrocytes increase in size, the matrix between them becomes calcified and the cells eventually disintegrate. This leads to the appearance of a series of hollow corridors in the cartilage. They are gradually filled by embryonic bone marrow cells and blood vessels arising from the layer of membrane bone in the outlying regions of the diaphysis. Some of the bone marrow cells differentiate into bone forming cells called **osteoblasts**. They position themselves around the remaining bone marrow and secrete layers of bony material. The end product is a strong, hollow tube of bone which surrounds the marrow cavity.

Ossification extends towards the epiphysis, but the cartilage is not completely replaced until the adult structure is attained. Even then, portions of hyaline cartilage remain at the articulating surfaces of the bone. The epiphyses become ossified after the diaphysis. There may be one or several ossification centres present in each epiphysis and they always remain separate from the diaphysis.

Growth in length of the bone occurs at the same time as ossification. It takes place in growth regions towards each end of the bone between the epiphyses and diaphysis. Until the adult form is reached, cartilage continues to be produced and ossified into new bone on either side of these regions. Ultimately growing regions become ossified. When this happens, no further cell division occurs, and growth in length ceases. Increase in girth of the bone is produced by further deposition of bone in the periosteum.

17.2.4 Factors controlling bone deposition

Even after growth is complete, bone absorption, carried out by cells called **osteoclasts**, and bone synthesis and reconstruction still occur. This is important as it permits the shape of the bones to be modified according to the mechanical stresses placed upon them. It is of particular significance in animals that exhibit a marked change in their mode of locomotion during their development into adults. This also generally incorporates a shift in the position of the load that their skeletons have to bear. If continuous pressure is exerted on a specific region of a bone, then that region is absorbed. However, if part of a bone is subjected to periodic stress, bone deposition is stimulated in that region. Such pressures and stresses mould the skeleton into its definitive shape, and in particular, intermittent stresses are responsible for the development of projections and ridges on bones which increase their surface area for muscle attachment. Understressed bone atrophies. This is the subject of much current research because it occurs during prolonged weightlessness in space and presents problems for returning astronauts and cosmonauts. Bone structure may also be weakened by nutritional deficiencies such as lack of vitamins A and D and by lack of growth hormone.

17.2.5 Support in vertebrates

Amphibia evolved from lobe-finned fish and as they migrated from water to land they were faced with the problem of gravity and of holding their bodies off the ground in the absence of any support by the air. As a consequence their vertebrae evolved to become complex structures linked together by interlocking processes. Collectively the vertebrae formed a strong but reasonably flexible girder that supported the weight of the body.

The legs of early amphibians splayed out from the sides of their bodies so that the animals were able to drag themselves over the ground. This type of stance and locomotion is also seen in primitive reptiles (fig 17.3). When in motion most of the muscular energy is used to hold up the trunk from the ground. Such is the effort required to maintain this position that the animals spend the majority of their time whilst on land resting their bellies on the ground.

Later the trend in reptilian evolution was towards bringing the limbs into a position beneath the body and raising the body well clear of the ground (fig 17.3b). This stance provides greater efficiency in locomotion and means that the weight of the body is transmitted through the four relatively straight limbs.

Some reptiles and mammals have evolved a bipedal gait, walking, running or hopping on their hindlimbs. This releases the forelimbs for developing manipulative skills such as feeding, building and cleaning. A special type of locomotion, called **brachiation** characterises some monkeys and apes. These animals swing from tree to tree using

Fig 17.3 *Types of stance in vertebrates:
(a) a primitive amphibian stance – legs projected laterally from body and then down; (b) modern reptilian stance – intermediate between amphibian and mammals; (c) mammalian stance – legs project straight down from beneath the body*

their long arms and elongate hands to grasp the branches. Other animals that climb and move about in trees are too small to brachiate; instead they jump from branch to branch. The most specialised form of aerial locomotion is true flight. This evolved simultaneously during the Jurassic period in the flying reptiles (pterodactyls) and in the first birds (which were descended from reptiles). The forelimbs were modified and adapted into wings. Flying reptiles eventually became extinct, but birds survived and evolved into many highly varied forms.

17.3 Anatomy of the skeleton of a mammal (the rabbit)

All mammalian skeletons possess the same basic divisions. These can be divided into two main groups: the **axial skeleton**, which consists of the skull, vertebral column, ribs and sternum, and the **appendicular skeleton**, which consists of an anterior pectoral and posterior pelvic girdle, attached to each of which is a pair of limbs.

17.3.1 The axial skeleton

The **skull** consists of the cranium to which the upper jaw is fused, and a lower jaw which articulates with the cranium. Muscles connect the lower jaw to the skull and cranium. The **cranium** is composed of a number of flattened bones tightly interlocking forming a series of **immovable joints**. Besides enclosing and protecting the brain, it protects the olfactory organs, middle and inner ear and the eyes. At the posterior end of the cranium are two smooth, rounded protuberances, the **occipital condyles**, that articulate with the atlas vertebra to form a hinge joint which permits the nodding of the head.

The **vertebral column** is the main axis of the body. It consists of a linear series of bones called **vertebrae**, placed end to end, and separated by cartilaginous **intervertebral discs** (fig 17.5). The vertebrae are held together by ligaments which prevent their dislocation, but permit a degree of movement, so that the vertebral column as a whole is flexible. The vertebral column also gives protec-

Table 17.1. Number and types of vertebrae in a range of mammals

Types of vertebra	Region	Number of vertebrae				
		rat	rabbit	cat	cow	Man
cervical	neck	7	7	7	7	7
thoracic	chest	13	12–13	13	13	12
lumbar	abdomen	6	6–7	7	6	5
sacral	hip	4	4	3	5	5
caudal	tail	30±	16	18–25	18–20	4

tion to the spinal cord. On the vertebrae are numerous projections for the attachment of muscles. When the muscles are active, they may bend the vertebral column ventrally, dorsally or from side to side.

The total number of vertebrae varies in different mammals. Nevertheless, in all mammals five regions of the vertebral column can be distinguished. The number and types of vertebrae in a variety of mammals are given in table 17.1.

Vertebrae from different regions of the vertebral column all conform to the same basic design. The structure of a typical vertebra is shown in fig 17.4. Note that two facets (articulating surfaces) called **prezygapophyses** are present at the anterior end of the vertebra, whilst two more, the **postzygapophyses** occur at the posterior end. The prezygapophyses of one vertebra fit against the postzygapophyses of the vertebra immediately anterior to it. This arrangement enables the vertebrae to articulate with each other, but it is not a completely rigid arrangement, for the smoothness of the articulating surfaces permits their slight movement over each other. Below each pre- and postzygapophysis is a small notch. When adjacent vertebrae are fixed closely together the anterior notch of one vertebra is placed against the posterior notch of the vertebra immediately in front of it. This arrangement forms a hole through which a spinal nerve can pass. Other structures characteristic of all vertebrae are the **neural spine** and **transverse processes** for muscle attachment. The **centrum** forms a central rigid body to the vertebra over which the **neural arch** encloses the spinal cord.

Whilst there is a great degree of similarity between vertebrae, their design varies in different regions of the vertebral column. This is because of uneven distribution of body weight along the length of the column, and the vertebrae are modified and adapted to perform those specific functions required by each region.

When a rabbit stands up, its vertebral column is supported by the fore- and hindlimbs, with the bulk of the body weight suspended between them. The centra of the vertebrae withstand compression whilst ligaments and muscles which overlay the dorsal parts of the vertebrae withstand tension (fig 17.5)

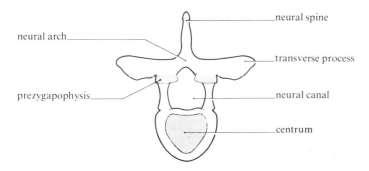

neural spine

neural arch

transverse process

prezygapophysis

neural canal

centrum

Fig 17.4 *Anterior view of a typical mammalian vertebra*

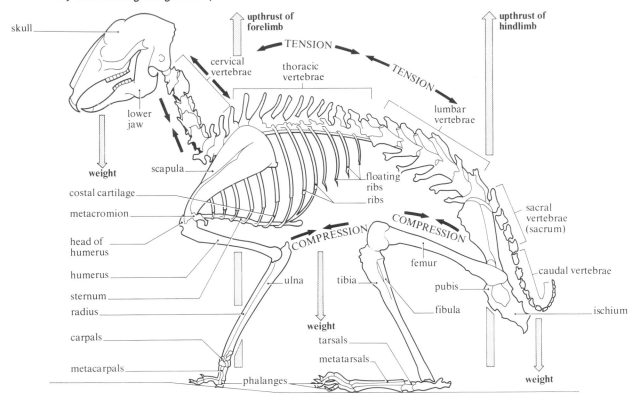

Fig 17.5 *Skeleton of rabbit seen from left side. The centra of the vertebrae serve as compression members whilst the ligaments and muscles which link one vertebra to another form the tension members. The abdominal musculature prevents the weight of the body from forcing the girdles apart*

17.3.2 Structure and functions of the vertebrae of a rabbit

Cervical vertebrae

Cervicals 3–7 are very similar in structure (fig 17.6*a*). They possess a small centrum which is able to withstand compressional forces, and a short neural spine to which the neck muscles are attached. Some of these muscles run from the cervicals to the thoracic vertebrae and are used for holding up the neck, whilst others run to the back of the skull and serve to maintain the head in position. On each side of the centrum is a single hole, the **vertebrarterial canal**, formed by fusion of a cervical rib with the transverse process. As its name implies, it serves as a channel for the vertebral artery to pass through to the brain. Thus this important blood vessel is protected as it traverses the vulnerable region of the neck.

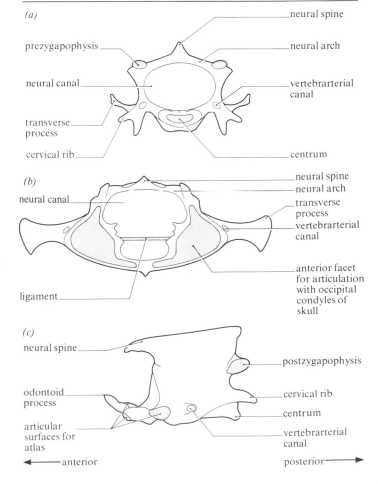

Fig 17.6 *(right) (a) Fifth cervical vertebra of a rabbit, anterior view. Note the characteristic vertebrarterial canal; (b) Anterior view of atlas vertebra of a rabbit. Note absence of centrum and anterior facets; (c) Side view (left) of axis vertebra of a rabbit. Note odontoid process and forwardly projecting neural spine*

630

The first two cervical vertebrae possess a quite different design and are modified to support the head and enable it to move in various directions. The first cervical vertebra is the **atlas** (fig 17.6b). Zygapophyses and a centrum are absent and the neural spine is reduced to a very small crest. On its anterior surface are two concave depressions, the **articular facets** which articulate with the curved convex occipital condyles of the skull to form a hinge joint. This supports the skull and permits it to be nodded up and down. Wide, flattened transverse processes provide a large surface area for the attachment of those muscles that bring about the nodding action.

The second cervical vertebra is the **axis** (fig 17.6c). It possesses a peg-like structure called the **odontoid process** which projects forwards from the centrum. The process is formed by the fusion of the centrum of the atlas to that of the axis, and it fits into the cavity of the atlas below the ligament (fig 17.6b) thus being separated from the neural canal. This arrangement gives a pivot joint which enables the head to be rotated from one side to the other (that is to be shaken). Such activity is brought about by muscles on the left and right sides of the neck. They run forwards from the neural spine of the axis to attach to the transverse processes of the atlas (fig 17.7). No prezygapophyses are present.

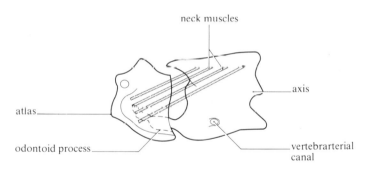

Fig 17.7 *The arrangement of the neck muscles between the atlas and axis vertebrae in a rabbit*

Thoracic vertebrae

These possess long, backwardly pointing neural spines and short transverse processes. Also present on the transverse processes are small, rounded projections called **tubercular facets**. Anterior and posterior half or **demi-facets** are located on the sides of the centrum. Both types of facet are for articulation with the ribs (fig 17.8a). The end of the rib which joins to a thoracic vertebra branches into two projections, one being called the **capitulum** and the other the **tuberculum**. The tuberculum articulates with the facet of the transverse process whilst the capitulum articulates with two demi-facets of the centrum. Here the arrangement is quite complex. When two thoracic vertebrae are closely applied to each other, the anterior demi-facet of one vertebra fits closely to the posterior demi-facet of the

Fig 17.8 *(a) Left side view of thoracic vertebra of a rabbit. Note long neural spine and demi-facets. (b) Lumbar vertebra of a rabbit from left side. No hypapophysis is shown. Where it does occur (first and second lumbar vertebrae) it exists as a small projection from the ventral surface of the centrum. (c) Dorsal view of sacrum of a rabbit*

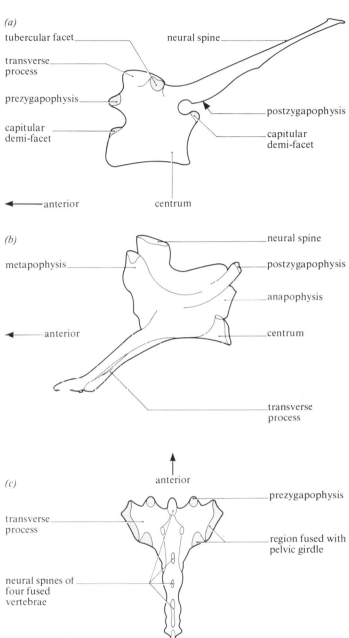

vertebra in front of it to form a common depression. The capitulum of the rib fits into this depression thus effectively articulating with two vertebrae. As a result the thoracic vertebrae serve to support the ribs, but because of the complex arrangement between the vertebrae and ribs, movement between them is strictly limited. Some forward and sideways movement can occur, but in general the thoracic vertebrae are the least flexible of all.

Lumbar vertebrae

The vertebrae of this region are subject to the greatest stress in terms of gravity and locomotion. Not only must they provide rigidity for the body, but they must also permit bending, sideways movement and rotation of the trunk. Therefore, not surprisingly this is the region where the large muscles of the back are attached and where there are many adaptive modifications of the vertebrae. The centrum and neural arch are massive, although the centrum is quite short. This arrangement provides greater flexibility between the lumbar vertebrae. The transverse processes are long and wide. They point forwards and downwards. Extra muscle bearing projections called meta-, ana-, and hypapophyses are present on the vertebrae (fig 17.8b). They also interlock with each other and keep the vertebrae in their correct positions relative to each other when this part of the vertebral column is placed under stress.

Sacral vertebrae (sacrum)

The sacral vertebrae are fused together to form a broad structure, the **sacrum** (fig 17.8c). The most anterior sacral vertebrae possess well-developed transverse processes which are fused to the pelvic girdle. It is through the sacrum that the weight of the body of a stationary animal is transmitted to the pelvic girdle and the legs. When an animal moves forwards, the thrust developed by the hindlimbs is transmitted via the pelvic girdle through the sacrum to the rest of the axial skeleton.

Caudal vertebrae

The number of caudal vertebrae varies greatly from one mammal to another (table 17.1) and is related to different lengths of tails in such mammals. In general, as they pass towards the posterior end of the animal, transverse processes, neural arches and zygapophyses all become reduced in size and gradually disappear. This results in the terminal vertebrae only consisting of small centra. Man possesses four caudal vertebrae which are fused to form the **coccyx**. It is not visible externally.

Ribs and sternum

Each rib is a flattened, curved bone. Its dorsal end is forked into the **capitulum** and **tubercle** which provide points of articulation with the thoracic vertebrae. The joints formed permit movement of the ribs by the intercostal muscles during breathing. All of the ribs, thoracic vertebrae and the sternum form a thoracic cage which protects the heart, lungs and major blood vessels (fig 17.9).

In the rabbit the ventral ends of the first seven pairs of ribs are attached to the **sternum**, a flattened, kite-shaped bone, via **costal cartilages**. These are called true ribs. The next two pairs of ribs are also attached ventrally to the cartilage of the seventh rib. The ventral ends of the remaining three or four pairs of ribs are unattached and are called floating ribs (fig 17.5).

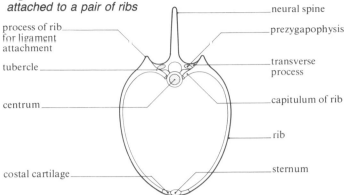

Fig 17.9 *Anterior view of thoracic vertebra of a rabbit attached to a pair of ribs*

- neural spine
- prezygapophysis
- process of rib for ligament attachment
- transverse process
- tubercle
- capitulum of rib
- centrum
- rib
- sternum
- costal cartilage

17.3.3 The appendicular skeleton

Limb girdles

These provide a connection between the axial skeleton and the limbs. The width of the pectoral girdle separates the forelimbs, and that of the pelvic girdle the hindlimbs, and both contribute to the stability of the animal. A number of areas are modified for muscle attachment and articulation with the limb bones.

Pectoral girdle. This is composed of two distinctly separate halves. Each half consists of the scapula, coracoid process and clavicle. It is not fused to the axial skeleton but flexibly attached to it by ligaments and muscles. This arrangement enables the girdle and its associated limbs to be moved through a great variety of planes of movement and angles. The girdle is strong enough to support the majority of the weight of a quadruped when it is stationary. It also acts as a shock absorber when the animal lands at the end of a jump.

The **scapula** is a flat, triangular-shaped bone which overlies a number of the anterior ribs (fig 17.10a). At its apex is a concave depression, the **glenoid cavity**, which articulates with the head of the humerus to form a ball-and-socket joint. A spine runs along the outer surface of the scapula, and at its free end, close to the glenoid cavity are two projections, the **acromion** and **metacromion** which are both used for muscle attachment. The **coracoid process** is all that remains of a small bone, the coracoid, which has fused with the scapula to form a projection above the glenoid cavity.

The **clavicle** is variable in size and shape in different mammals. In Man it is well developed with one end articulating with the acromion process and the other with the sternum. It is used for muscle attachment and aiding the complex movements of the arms. It is sometimes referred to as the collar bone in Man. Its removal has no serious consequences. In quadrupeds it is much smaller and relatively less important. It forms the 'wishbone' in birds.

17.2 What advantages are there to mammals in possessing a flexible connection between the pectoral girdle and vertebral column?

Fig 17.10 (a) Left scapula of a rabbit. (b) Ventral view of pelvic girdle of a rabbit. Note how sacrum is fused to the ilium

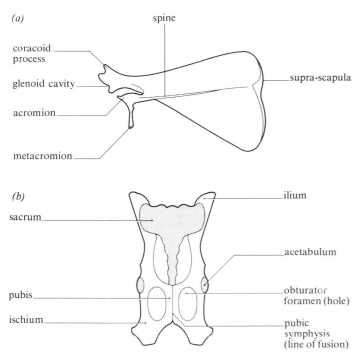

(a)

coracoid process

spine

glenoid cavity

supra-scapula

acromion

metacromion

(b)

sacrum

ilium

acetabulum

pubis

obturator foramen (hole)

ischium

pubic symphysis (line of fusion)

Fig 17.11 Vertebrate pentadactyl limb

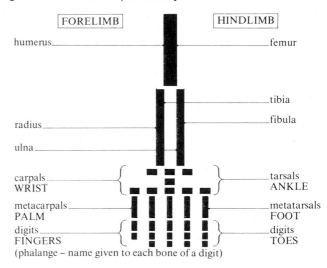

FORELIMB | HINDLIMB

humerus — femur

radius — tibia / fibula

ulna

carpals WRIST — tarsals ANKLE

metacarpals PALM — metatarsals FOOT

digits FINGERS — digits TOES

(phalange – name given to each bone of a digit)

Pelvic girdle. Again this consists of two halves, each half comprising three bones, the ilium, ischium and pubis. They are fused to each other forming a single structure, the **innominate** bone. The **ilium** is fused to the sacrum of the vertebral column on each side. On the outer edge of each half is a depression, the **acetabulum**, which articulates with the head of the femur to form the ball-and-socket hip joint (fig 17.10b). The ilium is above the acetabulum. Dorsally it possesses a large crest to which the thigh muscles are attached.

Between the ischium and pubis is a large hole, the **obturator foramen**. Except for a small aperture through which blood vessels and nerves pass to the legs, it is covered by a sheet of tough inflexible connective tissue which provides yet another surface for muscle attachment. Such a design could be an adaptation to reduce the weight of the pelvic girdle and so lighten the load that has to be supported by the hindlegs.

Ventrally a line of fusion can be seen where the two halves of the pelvic girdle meet. This is the **pubic symphysis**. Flexible cartilage in this region permits a widening of the female's girdle at the time of giving birth.

Limbs

The limbs of all mammals are designed on the same basic plan, that of the **pentadactyl limb**, so named because each limb terminates in five digits (fingers or toes) (fig 17.11). There are numerous variations of the general plan, which are adaptations to the different modes of life of different animals. In some cases the number of digits per limb has been reduced during evolution (section 24.7).

Forelimb. The upper part of the forelimb consists of a single bone, the **humerus**. At its upper end is the head which articulates with the glenoid cavity of the scapula to form a ball-and-socket joint at the shoulder allowing universal movement. Near the head are two roughened projections, the greater and lesser **tuberosities**, between which is a groove, the **bicipital groove**. It is along this groove that the tendon of the biceps muscle passes. At its lower end is the **trochlea** which articulates with the forearm to form a hinge joint at the elbow. A hole, the **supra trochlear foramen**, perforates the humerus just above the trochlea in the rabbit, but is absent in Man. Also visible is the characteristic **deltoid ridge** running anteriorly along the upper half of the humerus (fig 17.12a). The lower part of the forelimb, the forearm, is composed of two bones, the **ulna** and **radius**. The ulna is the longer of the two. A notch, the **sigmoid notch** at its upper end articulates with the trochlea of the humerus. Beyond the elbow joint is a projection, the **olecranon process**. This is a most important structure, for when the arm is straightened it prevents any further backward movement of the forearm; hence dislocation does not occur. On the anterior surface of the humerus, above the trochlea, is a hollow, the **supra trochlear fossa**, into which the radius fits when the arm is bent (fig 17.12b).

The radius is a flattened, slightly curved bone which is relatively simple in design. In Man it is not firmly bound to the ulna; muscles are able to rotate the radius about the ulna so that the palm of the hand can be turned downwards or upwards, contributing to Man's manipulative skills. This freedom of movement is not apparent in the rabbit where both bones are tightly bound and the palm always faces downwards. However, this is not disadvantageous as the limb is in the best position for burrowing and running. Distally the ulna and radius articulate with a number of small **carpal** bones which form the wrist. In turn the carpals articulate with five long **metacarpals** which finally articulate with five digits. The first digit, on the inside of the limb is composed of two **phalanges** whereas all others contain three.

633

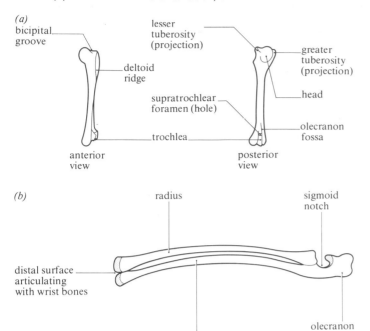

(a)

bicipital groove

lesser tuberosity (projection)

greater tuberosity (projection)

deltoid ridge

head

supratrochlear foramen (hole)

trochlea

olecranon fossa

anterior view

posterior view

(b)

radius

sigmoid notch

distal surface articulating with wrist bones

ulna

olecranon process

Hindlimb. The upper part of the hindlimb consists of a single bone, the **femur**. At its upper end is a large round head which articulates with the acetabulum of the pelvic girdle to form a ball-and-socket joint at the hip (fig 17.13*a*). Three processes called **trochanters** protrude below the head and provide points of attachment for the thigh muscles. The lower end of the femur possesses two curved convex surfaces, called **condyles**, which articulate

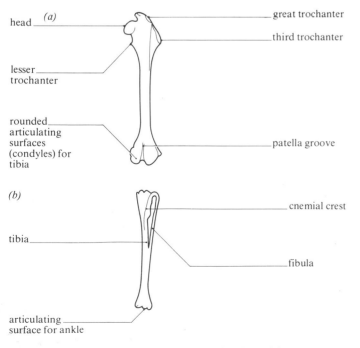

(a)

head

great trochanter

third trochanter

lesser trochanter

rounded articulating surfaces (condyles) for tibia

patella groove

(b)

cnemial crest

tibia

fibula

articulating surface for ankle

17.13 (a) Left femur of a rabbit, anterior view. (b) Anterior view of left tibia and fibula of a rabbit

634

with the tibia to form a hinge joint at the knee. A patella groove separates the two condyles. The patella bone (knee cap) is located here.

The **tibia** and **fibula** bones form the shank of the hindlimb. Two slight depressions at the upper end of the tibia represent the articular surfaces at the knee joint (fig 17.13*b*). The fibula is not a component of this joint. It is a thin bone, and in the rabbit is fused to the tibia at its lower end. At the lower ends of the tibia and fibula are a number of **tarsal** bones. The two longest tarsals, the **astragulus** and **calcaneum** (heel bone), articulate with the tibia and fibula to form the ankle joint. The tarsals articulate distally with long **metatarsal** bones to form the foot, whilst in turn the metatarsals articulate with digits composed of phalanges forming the toes. It is interesting to note that the rabbit hindlimb possesses only four digits.

17.3.4 Joints

In bony vertebrates, where a bone meets another bone, or bones, a joint is formed. Movement of skeletal elements over each other is only possible if there is a joint between them. A variety of different types of joint exist in the mammalian skeleton. They are summarised in table 17.2.

Synovial joints are essentially similar to each other in design. The end surface of each articulating bone is overlain by a smooth covering of hyaline cartilage. Though a living tissue, it contains no blood vessels or nerves. The nutrients and respiratory gases it requires diffuse from the synovial membrane and fluid. The cartilage serves to reduce friction between the bones during movement. Because of its elastic properties, the cartilage also acts as a shock absorber.

The bones of the joint are held in position by a number of ligaments which collectively form a strong fibrous capsule. They run from one side of the joint to the other and are orientated in such a way as to cope effectively with the particular stresses suffered by the joint. The inner surface of the capsule is lined by a thin, cellular synovial membrane which secretes synovial fluid into the synovial cavity (fig 17.4). Synovial fluid, containing mucin, acts as a lubricant

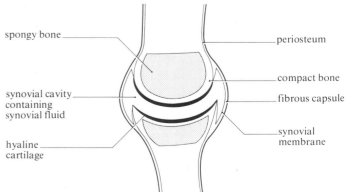

spongy bone

periosteum

compact bone

synovial cavity containing synovial fluid

fibrous capsule

synovial membrane

hyaline cartilage

Fig 17.14 *Diarthrodial/synovial joint of a mammal*

Table 17.2. A variety of joints in the endoskeleton of a mammal

Type of joint	General characteristics	Examples	Function
Immovable/suture/ synarthrodial	A thin layer of fibrous connective tissue exists between the bones, holding them firmly in position	Between bones of skull; between sacrum and ilia of pelvic girdle; between bones of pelvic girdle	Provides strength and support for the body, or protection of delicate structures which cannot withstand any kind of deformation
Partially movable/ amphiarthrodial	Bones are separated from each other by cartilaginous pads		
(a) Gliding		Joints between vertebrae; wrist and ankle bones	Bones glide over each other to a limited extent. Collectively they provide a wide range of movement and confer strength on the limb.
(b) Swivel/rotating/ pivot		Joint between atlas and axis vertebrae	Permits shaking of head from side to side
Freely movable/synovial/ diarthrodial (fig 17.14)	Articulating bone surfaces are covered with cartilage and separated from each other by a synovial cavity containing synovial fluid		
(a) Hinge	Relatively few muscles operate this joint	Elbow, knee and finger joints	Permits movement in one plane about one axis. Capable of bearing heavy loads
(b) Ball and socket	Variety of muscles attached to the bones of the joint	Shoulder and hip joints	Permits movement in all planes, and some rotation. Unable to bear very heavy loads

for the joint surfaces and serves to reduce friction between them. The synovial membrane acts as a waterproof seal preventing escape of synovial fluid. Therefore the joint effectively requires no maintenance.

17.4 The muscle system

Muscles are composed of many elongated cells called **muscle fibres** which are all able to contract and relax. During relaxation they are capable of being stretched, but they exhibit the property of elasticity which permits them to regain their original size and form after being stretched. Muscles are well supplied with blood which conveys to them nutrients and oxygen, and takes away metabolic waste products. The amount of blood arriving at a muscle at any one time is able to be adjusted according to its need. Each muscle possesses its own nerve supply. Histologically three distinct types of vertebrate muscle can be identified.

(1) **Skeletal muscle** (section 17.4.1) (also called striated, striped, voluntary). Muscle which is attached to bone. It is concerned with locomotion, contracts quickly and fatigues quickly. It is innervated by the voluntary nervous system.

(2) **Smooth muscle** (section 17.5.3) (also called unstriated, unstriped, plain, involuntary). Muscle which is found in the walls of tubular organs of the body and is concerned with movement of materials through them.

It contracts slowly and fatigues slowly. It is spontaneously active and innervated by the autonomic nervous system.

(3) **Cardiac muscle**. Muscle found only in the heart. It contracts spontaneously and without fatigue. It is innervated by the autonomic nervous system.

17.4.1 Skeletal muscle in detail

A skeletal muscle is attached to bone in at least two places, namely the **origin**, a firm **non-movable** part of the skeleton, and the **insertion**, a freely movable part of the skeleton. Attachment is by means of tough, relatively inextensible tendons made up of connective tissue comprised almost entirely of collagen (section 5.5). At one end a tendon is continuous with the outer covering of the muscle, while the other end combines with the periosteum of the bone to form a very firm attachment.

As muscles can only produce a shortening force (that is contract), it follows that at least two muscles or sets of muscles must be used to move a bone into one position and back again. Pairs of muscles acting in this way are termed **antagonistic** muscles and they may be classified according to the type of movement they bring about (table 17.3).

It is rare that a movement will involve a single pair of antagonistic muscles. Generally, groups of muscles work together to produce a particular individual movement, and such groups are known as **synergists**.

Table 17.3. Types of movement brought about by pairs of antagonistic muscles

Muscle classification	Type of movement brought about
Flexor	Bends a limb by pulling two skeletal elements towards each other
Extensor	Extends a limb by pulling two skeletal elements away from each other
Adductor	Pulls a limb towards the central long axis of the body
Abductor	Pulls a limb away from the central long axis of the body
Protractor	Pulls distal part of a limb forwards
Retractor	Pulls distal part of a limb backwards
Rotator	Rotates whole or part of a limb at one of its joints

17.4.2 Striated muscle

A striated muscle consists of numerous physiological units called muscle fibres or muscle cells. They are cylindrical in shape and arranged parallel to each other. They are between 0.01 and 0.1 mm in diameter, several centimetres long and multinucleate. The nuclei are located near the surface of each fibre. Bundles of muscle fibres are enclosed by collagen fibres and connective tissue. Collagen also occurs between fibres. At the ends of the muscle the collagen and connective tissue forms tendons which attach the muscle to skeletal elements. Each muscle fibre is enclosed by a membrane, the **sarcolemma**. This is very similar in structure to a typical plasma membrane.

Within the muscle fibres are numerous thin **myofibrils** (*myo*, muscle) which possess characteristic cross striations. Each myofibril is composed of two types of proteinaceous myofilaments, **actin** and **myosin**. Numerous mitochondria are interposed between the myofibrils. The cytoplasm of the myofibril is called **sarcoplasm** and contains a network of internal membranes termed the **sarcoplasmic reticulum**. Running transversely across the fibre and between fibrils is a system of tubules known as the **T system**, which is in contact with the surface of the sarcolemma (fig 17.15). At certain points the T tubules pass between pairs of vesicles which are components of the sarcoplasmic reticulum. A T tubule together with a pair of vesicles is called a **triad**. The tubule and vesicles are held together by membranous cross-bridges. The vesicles are involved in the uptake and release of Ca^{2+} ions. Their activity raises or lowers Ca^{2+} ion concentration in the sarcoplasm, which in turn controls ATPase activity and hence the contractile behaviour of the muscle fibre.

Under a light microscope only the striated nature of the myofibrils can be observed. This is seen as a regular alternation of light and dark bands called the **I and A bands** respectively, traversed by thin, dark lines. Electron microscope studies clearly indicate that the bands are due to the regular arrangement of actin (thin filaments) and myosin (thick filaments). Fig 17.16 shows this clearly.

Traversing the middle of each I band is a dark line called

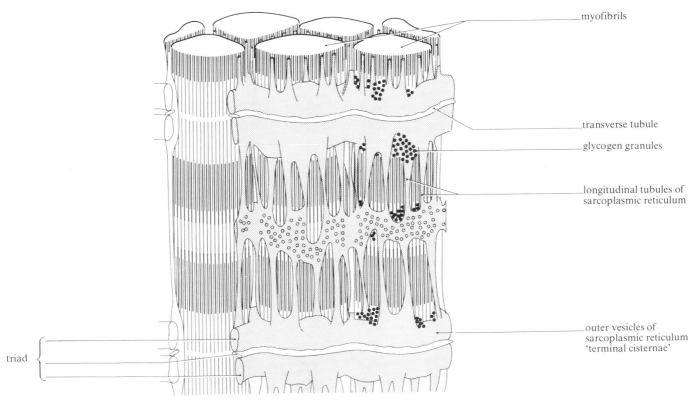

Fig 17.15 *Sarcoplasmic reticulum and T system.*

Labels: myofibrils; transverse tubule; glycogen granules; longitudinal tubules of sarcoplasmic reticulum; outer vesicles of sarcoplasmic reticulum 'terminal cisternae'; triad

Fig 17.16 *Fine structure of skeletal muscle*

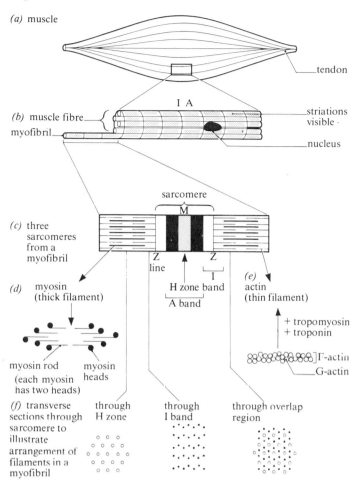

(a) muscle

— tendon

(b) muscle fibre
myofibril

I A

— striations visible

— nucleus

(c) three sarcomeres from a myofibril

sarcomere
M

Z line
Z

H zone band
I
A band

(e) actin (thin filament)

(d) myosin (thick filament)

myosin rod (each myosin has two heads)
myosin heads

+ tropomyosin
+ troponin

]F-actin
G-actin

(f) transverse sections through sarcomere to illustrate arrangement of filaments in a myofibril

through H zone

through I band

through overlap region

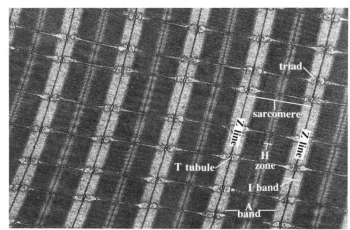

Fig 17.17 *Longitudinal section of fish muscle (roach – Rutilus rutilus). Note the triads and clear myofibrilar structure (× 7 650)*

triad
sarcomere
Z line
T tubule
Z line
H zone
I band
A band

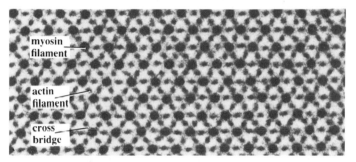

myosin filament
actin filament
cross bridge

Fig 17.18 *Insect flight muscle (giant water bug). Transverse section of fibril in rigor state (× 137 000)*

the **Z line**. The section of a myofibril between two Z lines is called a **sarcomere**. From the Z line actin filaments extend in both directions, whilst in the centre of the sarcomere are found myosin filaments. These are aligned side by side in a hexagonal lattice (fig 17.17 & 17.18). In certain regions of the sarcomere, actin and myosin filaments overlap. Where they do, transverse sections in these regions indicate that six actin filaments surround each myosin filament. This arrangement of actin and myosin filaments results in a number of other bands being recognisable in the sarcomere. Myosin and actin filaments constitute the A band whilst actin filaments alone constitute the I band. The centre of the A band is lighter than its other regions in a relaxed sarcomere as there is no overlap between actin and myosin in this region. It is called the **H band**. The H band itself may be bisected by a dark line, the **M line**. The M line joins adjacent myosin filaments together at a point halfway along their length.

Myosin (thick filaments)

A molecule of myosin consists of two distinct regions, a long rod-shaped region (myosin rod) on one end of which is a globular region. This globular region consists of two similar globular parts, each called a myosin head. The globular heads are regularly spaced and project from the sides of the filament except in a short region halfway along its length. This central portion of the filament, which possesses no heads, is termed the bare zone. Where the actin and myosin filaments overlap the myosin heads can attach to neighbouring actin filaments, and while attached they can generate the force which may cause the muscle to shorten. The energy for this force production is derived from ATP hydrolysis since each myosin head is capable of ATPase activity. As described later, the attachment of myosin heads to actin is controlled by the level of Ca^{2+} ions in the sarcoplasm. The myosin ATPase is activated by attachment of myosin to actin. This activity may be inhibited by Mg^{2+} ions. The importance of this will become evident when we deal with the actual contraction mechanism of the sarcomere.

Actin (thin filaments)

Each actin filament is made up of two helical strands of globular actin molecules (G-actin) which twist round each other. The whole assembly of actin molecules is called F-actin (fibrous actin). It is thought that an ATP molecule is attached to each molecule of G-actin. Neither form of actin exhibits any ATPase activity. Actin filaments consist of F-actin together with two accessory proteins, **tropomyosin** and **troponin**. Tropomyosin is a rod-shaped fibrous

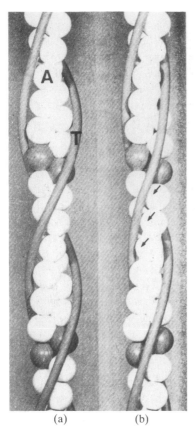

Fig 17.19 *Illustration of changes in actin filament structure (a) 'off' state – low Ca^{2+} level: tropomyosin blocks myosin attachment site. (b) 'on' state – high Ca^{2+} level: tropomyosin moves to expose attachment sites (arrows). A, actin; T, tropomyosin, Troponin, which is not shown, lies nearer to 'grey' actins.*

protein and these rods link end to end to form two helical strands which are wrapped around the F-actin in a longitudinal fashion. Tropomyosin functions to switch on, or off, the contractile mechanism. Troponin is a globular protein with three subunits. Each subunit has a particular function. **Troponin-T** binds troponin to tropomyosin, **troponin-C** is sensitive to, and can reversibly bind to, Ca^{2+} ions, whilst under certain conditions **troponin-I** is able to inhibit any interaction between actin and myosin. Collectively both of these accessory proteins serve to inhibit the actin–myosin interaction in the absence of Ca^{2+} ions (fig 17.19).

17.4.3 The 'all-or-nothing' response

When a skeletal muscle fibre is stimulated by an impulse, the fibre will only contract if the stimulus is at or above a certain threshold level (resting potential). This contraction is maximal for any given set of conditions, and even if the strength of stimulus is considerably increased there will be no increase in the shortening of the muscle or the force that it develops. This phenomenon is referred to as the muscle's 'all-or-nothing' response. A stimulus that is too weak to provoke muscle fibre contraction is referred to as a **subliminal** stimulus.

After response, the muscle endures an **absolute refractory** period when no contraction is possible. This is succeeded by a **relative refractory period**. Only strong stimuli can provoke a response during this time. The refractory period is the time it takes for ionic activity to return the muscle to its resting potential.

17.4.4 Mode of action of vertebrate skeletal muscle

When a muscle is stimulated it exhibits mechanical activity (that is it contracts) and this may either produce a shortening of the muscle, or if the muscle is fixed rigidly at both ends, it may develop tension within the muscle without the muscle changing length. When a muscle shortens against a constant load, this is called **isotonic** contraction, but when there is no change in length, it is **isometric** contraction.

Investigation into the nature of the contractile response of a muscle can be carried out by the use of a **kymograph**. The gastrocnemius muscle of a frog is often used for such investigations. Muscle is excised from a freshly killed frog, placed in a trough on a platform and bathed in a well-oxygenated saline solution. Under these conditions it may perform its contractile activity adequately for several hours. The origin of the muscle is fixed to a rigid station on the platform, whilst its insertion is hooked up to a movable lever. It is then suitably stimulated by an electric current either directly or via a nerve. When the muscle contracts or develops tension it moves the lever, and such movement is recorded as a trace on the revolving drum of the kymograph. The record of events that take place is called a **myogram**. The tension developed by a muscle is a force and is generally measured in terms of grams mass.

17.4.5 Contractile response

Single stimulus. When a single stimulus is applied to a muscle, there is a very short period of about 0.05 s, called the **latent period**, before the muscle responds. Then contraction takes place rapidly and a force is developed. This phase of contraction lasts for about 0.1 s. Following this is a longer period of relaxation where the force declines and the muscle returns to its relaxed state over a period of 0.2 s. A single contraction by a muscle is called a **muscle twitch** (fig 17.20).

Two stimulations. If a long interval of time elapses before a second stimulus is applied, two identical myograms for the muscle are recorded. However, if the time between two stimuli is reduced so that the second stimulus is applied when the muscle is still contracting in response to the first stimulus, a second contraction occurs

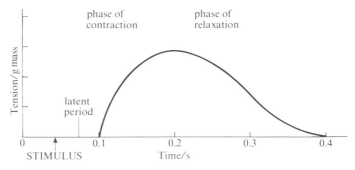

Fig 17.20 *Single muscle twitch of frog gastrocnemius muscle*

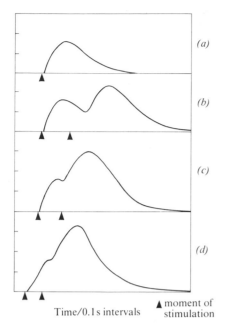

Time/0.1 s intervals ▲ moment of stimulation

Fig 17.21 *Tracings recorded on a kymograph using frog gastrocnemius muscle.*
(a) *Single twitch in response to single stimulus*
(b) ⎡ *Mechanical summation occurring*
(c) ⎨ *when frequency of stimulation*
(d) ⎣ *is increased*

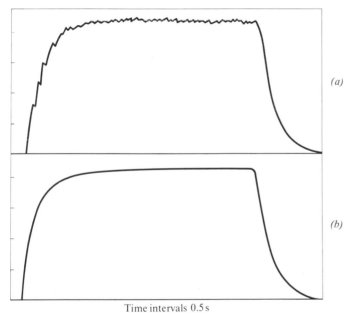

Time intervals 0.5 s

Fig 17.22 *Myogram indicating development of tetany in frog gastrocnemius muscle*
(a) *Unfused tetany, 8 stimulations per 0.5 s*
(b) *Fused tetany, 18 stimulations per 0.5 s*

which is superimposed on the first. This results in a 'bumpy' myogram (fig 17.21). The second contraction also develops a greater force than the first one. This effect is called **mechanical summation**.

Frequent stimulations. If the frequency of stimulation is increased, the bumpiness of the myogram is gradually lost (fig 17.22) and the individual twitches fuse

together (or summate). A smooth trace is drawn which reaches a steady level or plateau and remains there for a relatively long time. When the muscle is in this condition it is said to be in the state of **tetanus**. The plateau of tension developed during tetany is the maximum tension that the muscle can produce. Tetany cannot continue indefinitely as the muscle becomes fatigued.

17.4.6 The sliding filament theory of muscle contraction

In 1954, two independent research groups, namely H. E. Huxley & J. Hanson, and A. F. Huxley & R. Niedergerke, formulated the sliding filament theory of muscle contraction. They discovered independently that the A band of a sarcomere always remained the same length whether the sarcomere was stretched or shortened. This gave rise to the suggestion that there are two interdigitating sets of filaments, actin and myosin, which in some way slide past each other when the sarcomere changes its length. Observations indicated that during contraction the actin filaments move inwards towards the centre of the sarcomere (fig 17.23). The heads of the myosin filaments were thought to operate as 'hooks' attaching to F-actin in a particular way to form cross-bridges, and then changing their relative configuration such that the actin molecules were pulled further into the A band. After the process was completed, the myosin heads detached from the actin and hooked up to another site further along the actin filament. A sarcomere could contract up to 30% of its length, and the cross-bridge attachment/detachment cycles could be repeated many times depending on the speed of shortening. The energy required for this process was provided by the splitting of ATP, one ATP molecule being split for each cross-bridge cycle.

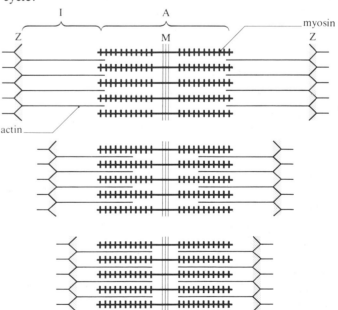

Fig 17.23 *Diagrammatic representation of how a sarcomere contracts by the actin filaments sliding over myosin filaments*

639

Today the theory is almost universally accepted. However, the actual force-generating process, often called the **excitation–contraction–coupling** mechanism, is still little understood and remains one of the major problems to be resolved by muscle physiologists. Much progress has been made in this field and the following section provides an up-to-date picture of sarcomere contraction.

> **17.3** What happens to the length of the A, H and I bands as the sarcomere contracts?
>
> **17.4** Explain how any change in the A, H and I band lengths are brought about in terms of what happens to the actin and myosin filaments.

17.4.7 Excitation–contraction–coupling

At rest a sarcomere possesses Mg^{2+} ions and ATP in certain concentrations, but Ca^{2+} ions are present only in very low concentrations. Under these conditions the actin filament is in the 'off' position. This is achieved by tropomyosin being positioned on each actin molecule in such a way that it blocks the sites on actin to which myosin will attach. Also the myosin heads are held away from actin in a position close to the long axis of the myosin filament.

When a muscle is stimulated by a nerve impulse, the wave of depolarisation spreads over the muscle and passes from the outside of the muscle fibre membrane into the sarcomere along the T system. As the impulse reaches the triad vesicles it stimulates them to release Ca^{2+} ions into the sarcoplasm, and Ca^{2+} ion concentration consequently rises.

Ca^{2+} ions bind to the troponin-C, which in turn interacts with troponin-I and reverses the normally inhibitory effect of the troponin system on actin–myosin interaction. Actin is switched 'on' when the tropomyosin moves to a new position on each actin molecule (fig 17.19) so that the myosin-binding sites are exposed. In some muscle, not vertebrate, the ATPase activity of myosin is also stimulated by the presence of Ca^{2+} ions. It is further enhanced by the presence of actin. In all muscles, when the actin and myosin have been activated, the myosin head moves out from its resting position and links to actin to form an actomyosin cross-bridge. Release of energy by ATP hydrolysis accompanies cross-bridge formation and leads to a change in the angle of the cross-bridge such that the myosin head pulls the actin filament over itself towards the centre of the sarcomere. With all myofilaments acting in this way during sarcomere stimulation the end result is the generation of a force (fig 17.24) which may lead to a shortening of the sarcomere length.

When excitation of the sarcomere ceases, Ca^{2+} ions are actively pumped back into the triad vesicles by an ATP-driven calcium pump. Ca^{2+} ion concentration soon decreases below the threshold for contractile activity and relaxation of the sarcomere begins. The tropomyosin–troponin complex inhibits ATPase activity, cross-bridges are broken, actin and possibly myosin too are switched 'off' and the sarcomere reverts to its normal resting tension.

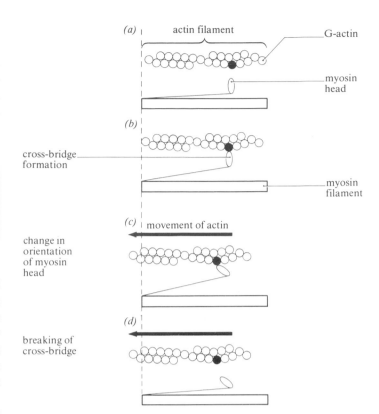

Fig 17.24 *Excitation–contraction coupling. (Tropomyosin and troponin not shown.)*

17.4.8 The energy supply

Within the body the ultimate source of energy for muscle contraction is usually glycogen, but may be fatty acids. When these substrates are metabolised (during respiration), ATP is generated. It is the hydrolysis of ATP that liberates the energy necessary to promote actual muscle contraction:

$$ATP \longrightarrow ADP + P_i + \text{energy for muscle contraction}$$

In resting muscle the level of ATP is low, being sufficient only to power about eight muscle twitches. This condition is maintained by normal aerobic respiration. The ATP is soon used up when a muscle contracts, and has to be quickly restored by other processes.

Restoration of ATP involves a substance located in the muscle called **phosphocreatine** (PCr). The ADP produced during muscle contraction is reconverted to ATP at the expense of phosphocreatine:

$$ADP + PCr \xrightarrow[\text{phosphotransferase}]{\text{creatine}} ATP + Cr$$

This ensures that there is always a constant supply of ATP in the muscle which it can utilise for immediate contraction. At some stage, the phosphocreatine level has to be replenished. This is brought about by oxidation of fatty acids or glycogen. The ATP produced here enables phosphocreatine to be resynthesised from creatine:

$$Cr + ATP \longrightarrow PCr + ADP$$

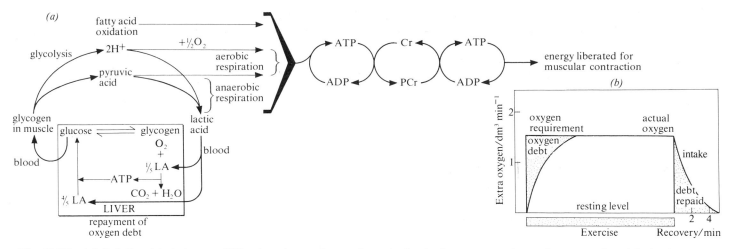

Fig 17.25 (a) Relationship between ATP, phosphocreatine and respiration in the process of muscle contraction. LA, lactic acid. (b) Oxygen requirements during exercise showing the relationship between oxygen intake and oxygen debt

When a muscle becomes very active its oxygen supply rapidly becomes insufficient to maintain adequate oxidative phosphorylation (section 11.3.6) of its respiratory substrates. Under these conditions pyruvic acid, the end-product of glycolysis, is converted to lactic acid by addition of H⁺ ions. This occurs because there is insufficient oxygen present to attach to the H⁺ ions, produced during glycolysis, to form water. Whilst this is happening the muscle is said to be incurring an **oxygen debt**.

$$CH_3COCOOH + 2H^+ \longrightarrow CH_3CHOHCOOH$$
pyruvic acid $\qquad\qquad$ lactic acid

Lactic acid formation is relatively inefficient as an energy-liberating process, yielding only about 7% of the energy available from the complete oxidation of glucose. Lactic acid is toxic and sooner or later has to be removed from the body. This occurs when muscular activity slows down or ceases.

When this happens the oxygen supply once again becomes sufficient to oxidise lactic acid and aid the reconversion of some of it into glycogen. This process generally occurs in the liver where one-fifth of the lactic acid is fully oxidised to carbon dioxide and water, providing energy which is utilised for the conversion of the remaining lactic acid into glucose. Some of the glucose is transported back to the muscle where it is finally transformed to glycogen, whilst the remainder is converted to glycogen and stored in the liver. The time taken for lactic acid to be

fully removed from the body represents the time it takes the body to repay the oxygen debt incurred during strenuous muscular activity (fig 17.25).

17.5 Innervation of skeletal muscle

Each muscle is innervated by many motor nerve fibres, all of which branch to supply a group of muscle fibres. This group, together with its motor supply, is called a **motor unit**, and all muscle fibres in it will contract simultaneously when suitably stimulated. The number of muscle fibres in a motor unit is variable and depends on the sophistication of control that the unit is required to exert. For example, there are about ten in eyeball muscle but over 1 000 in a biceps muscle. The fewer the number of muscle fibres in a unit, the greater the nervous control over them.

Where a motor nerve fibre makes contact with a muscle fibre, a neuromuscular junction, or motor end-plate, is formed. Here the axon of the motor nerve fibre loses its myelin sheath, and its terminal dendrites are sunk into grooves which ramify over the end-plate.

The stimulus for muscle contraction to take place is delivered by the central nervous system (fig 17.26). Impulses are propagated along the motor nerve fibre to the motor end-plate. Here, in response to the nervous signal, acetylcholine is released into the synaptic gap which separates the motor fibre and sarcolemma of the muscle

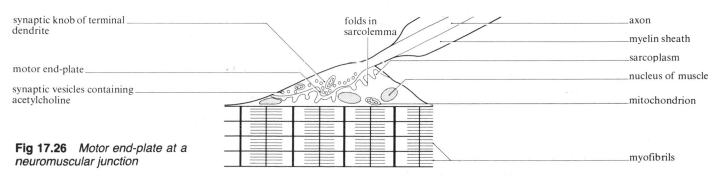

Fig 17.26 Motor end-plate at a neuromuscular junction

641

Table 17.4. Structure, location and general properties of slow and fast skeletal muscle fibres

	Slow/tonic muscle fibres	*Fast/twitch muscle fibres*
Structure	Many mitochondria Poorly developed sarcoplasmic reticulum Red – due to presence of myoglobin and cytochrome pigments Low in glycogen content Capillaries in close contact with fibres to facilitate fast exchange of materials	Few mitochondria Well-developed sarcoplasmic reticulum White – little or no myoglobin or cytochrome pigments Abundance of glycogen granules
Location	Deeply seated inside the limbs	Relatively superficial
Innervation	Associated with small nerve fibres of 5 μm diameter. A number of end-plates are distributed along the length of the fibre. This is called multi-terminal innervation. Velocity of impulse conductance $2–8 \text{ m s}^{-1}$	Associated with large nerve fibres of 10–20 μm diameter. Usually one or possibly two end-plates per fibre $8–40 \text{ m s}^{-1}$

	Slow/tonic muscle fibres	*Fast/twitch muscle fibres*
Excitability	Membrane electrically inexcitable. Each impulse causes release of only small amount of acetylcholine. Therefore amount that membrane is depolarised depends on frequency of stimulation	Membrane electrically excitable. Exhibit 'all-or-none' response when an action potential is elicited.
Response	Slow graded muscular contraction of long duration. Relaxation process slow (up to 100 times slower than twitch fibre)	Fast contraction (3 times faster than slow fibres) Fatigues quite quickly
Physiological activity	Depend on aerobic respiration for ATP production Many continue to function anaerobically if oxygen in short supply in which case lactic acid is formed and an oxygen debt incurred Carbohydrate or fat store mobilised at same rate as respiratory substrate is oxidised Heat transported away from muscle as soon as it is produced Steady state between muscle activity and its needs is set up	Depend on the anaerobic process of glycolysis for ATP supply Oxygen debt quickly built up Glycogen used extensively as respiratory substrate Heat produced is absorbed by the fibres as the circulatory system does not immediately remove it Muscle contraction occurs during a period when the circulatory system has not had time to increase the oxygen supply to the muscle
Function	Enable sustained muscle contractions to occur. This is used for the maintenance of posture by the organism	Immediate, fast muscle contraction is permitted at a time when the circulatory system is still adjusting to the needs of the new level of muscle activity. Therefore of great importance during locomotion.

fibre. What happens at the end-plate is remarkably similar to what happens at a neurone–neurone synapse (section 16.1.2). The acetylcholine diffuses towards the sarcolemma and effects a temporary increase in its permeability to ions, especially Na^+ and K^+. As a result, an end-plate potential is developed and this generates an action potential which passes rapidly along the length of the muscle fibre, also inwards via the T-system, eliciting contraction which is of an all-or-nothing nature.

Acetylcholinesterase, located in large quantities in the region of the sarcolemma, rapidly hydrolyses acetylcholine to choline and ethanoic acid, and thus prevents over-stimulation of the muscle fibre. The motor end-plate rapidly reverts to its resting state once the end-plate potential has passed.

17.5.1 Gradation of response by skeletal muscles

In order for fine control of muscular activity to be exerted, it is important that the degree of tension developed by each muscle should be closely controlled. This is achieved in two ways, either separately or collectively.
(1) The number of muscle fibres that are actually excited at any one time may be varied. It follows that the force generated by a muscle will increase if an increased number of fibres are stimulated, and vice versa. This is what generally happens in vertebrate skeletal muscle.
(2) The frequency of nerve impulses received by muscle fibres may be varied. Repetitive stimulation in this way can increase the force developed by the muscle.

The whole process of muscle contraction within an organism is a smooth, orderly affair. This is achieved by the asynchronous contractions of different groups of muscle fibres in antagonistic muscles.

17.5.2 Types of skeletal muscle fibre

There are two major types of skeletal muscle fibre, each with its own specific physiological properties. They are the slow or **tonic** fibres, and the fast or **twitch** fibres. Table 17.4 indicates their structure, location and general properties. Whilst some muscles may contain purely tonic, or twitch, fibres, some muscles contain proportions of both.

Collectively the two types of fibre endow the organism with the ability to move about and to maintain posture. The twitch fibres enable fast muscle contraction. Predators possess many twitch fibres and use them for fast reactions to capture prey. On the other hand, would-be prey can also react quickly in order to avoid capture by predators. In both cases speed of body movement would influence the probability of survival of the organism concerned. When an animal is still it has to maintain a particular posture. This is achieved by contraction of the tonic muscle fibres. They generate a slower, more sustained contraction, whilst at the same time consuming less fuel than the twitch muscle fibres. The nature of the contraction is usually isometric, and muscles and limbs are held at a constant length, thus resisting the force of gravity.

In Man both types of fibre enter into the composition of all muscles, but one or other usually predominates. The functional significance of this is that the predominantly tonic muscles are suited to long-term slow contractions, and consequently are found in the postural extensor muscles, whilst twitch muscle fibres predominate in the flexor muscles, which are designed to react at speed.

17.5.3 Smooth muscle

Vertebrate smooth muscle is located in the walls of many hollow structures of the body. These include the intestinal tract, bladder, blood vessels, ureter, uterus and vas deferens. The individual cells are uninucleate and spindle-shaped. Connective tissue, consisting largely of collagen, holds them together. They are oriented parallel to each other and form a distinct muscle layer. An example of this is the smooth muscle of the intestine where there is an outer longitudinal, and an inner circular, layer. When the longitudinal muscle contracts, it shortens and dilates the intestinal lumen, whilst contraction of the circular muscle will lengthen and constrict the lumen. Such coordinated activity, called **peristalsis**, aids the movement of the contents of the gut and provides an interesting example of the function of smooth muscle, namely to move along materials within the hollow organs of the body.

Each smooth muscle cell is approximately 50–200 μm long and 2–5 μm in diameter in the extended state. Actin is

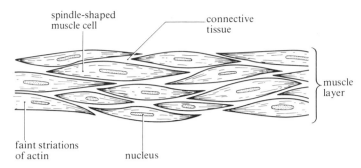

Fig 17.27 *Vertebrate smooth muscle*

arranged in a longitudinal fashion within each cell (fig 17.27). It is now generally accepted that vertebrate smooth muscle has myosin filaments in its normal state, although these may be different from those in striated muscle filaments. Cross-striations are not seen here because the myosin and actin filaments through the cells are not in axial register. It is thought that the contractile mechanism in smooth muscle is essentially similar to that of striated muscle, although regulation of activity may be quite different.

Conduction between cells is relatively slow and this results in prolonged slow contraction of the muscle and an equally slow relaxation period. The muscle is also capable of spontaneous rhythmic contractions and these may vary both in intensity and frequency. Stretching of smooth muscle, caused by the distension of the hollow organ which the muscle surrounds, is generally followed by an immediate contraction of the muscle. This particular property again aids the propulsion of contents within the organ.

The cells are not under voluntary nervous control, but instead are innervated by two sets of nerves from the autonomic nervous system. One set is from the **parasympathetic** and the other from the **sympathetic** system (section 16.2.3). The general opposing effects that they exert on the organs they innervate means that the activity of the organs can be quickly controlled to meet any changing conditions that might occur. Smooth muscle activity may also be modified by adrenaline and other specific hormones.

17.5.4 Muscle spindles and the stretch reflex

Within skeletal muscles are a number of proprioceptors called muscle spindles (fig 17.28). The centre of each muscle spindle is composed of several modified non-contractile muscle fibres called **intrafusal fibres**, enclosed within a connective tissue sheath. These are surrounded by a number of **annulo-spiral nerve endings** which unite to form an afferent nerve which passes to the spinal cord. Surrounding, and in parallel with, the intrafusal fibres are the muscle fibres of the muscle proper (**extrafusal fibres**). The two ends of the spindle consist of contractile muscle fibres innervated by efferent nerves coming from the central nervous system.

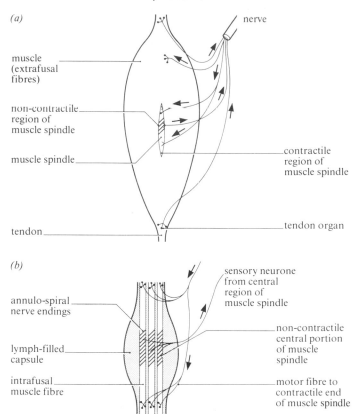

(a)

nerve

muscle (extrafusal fibres)

non-contractile region of muscle spindle

muscle spindle

contractile region of muscle spindle

tendon

tendon organ

(b)

annulo-spiral nerve endings

lymph-filled capsule

intrafusal muscle fibre

sensory neurone from central region of muscle spindle

non-contractile central portion of muscle spindle

motor fibre to contractile end of muscle spindle

When a muscle is stretched, the annulo-spiral nerve endings of the spindle develop a tension and are stimulated to discharge a volley of impulses to the spinal cord via afferent neurones. These synapse directly with efferent neurones which convey impulses to the extrafusal muscle fibres causing a reflex contraction. This is the **stretch reflex**. The greater the degree of stretching incurred by the spindle, the more impulses that are discharged and this leads to a greater degree of muscle contraction. In this way the stretch reflex tries to maintain the constant length of the muscle when the load on it is altered.

Muscle spindles act asynchronously, different ones being active at different times according to the body's needs. There are always some spindles operative at any given time, being stimulated by a constant stream of signals from the central nervous system. This causes a degree of partial muscle contraction within the body called **muscle tone**. Constant use of the muscles, through, for example, physical fitness, is required to maintain good muscle tone.

The two ends of the spindle are important in maintaining muscle tone. When stimulated by impulses from their efferent nerve supply they contract, and this ensures that there is a degree of tension in the muscle before a load is added to it. If the muscle was not maintained in this condition, there would be a danger that it would be overstretched and damaged by the sudden application of such a load.

17.5.5 Inhibitory reflexes

For a limb to be moved to and fro it must be operated by at least two opposing muscles or sets of muscles. When one contracts the other must relax. This is achieved by a simple inhibitory reflex mechanism. It will be recalled that impulses generated by muscle spindles of a muscle arrive at the spinal cord via an afferent neurone and are eventually transmitted to the same muscle causing it to contract. The afferent neurone also synapses with inter-neurones in the grey matter of the spinal cord (fig 17.29). When suitably stimulated, these inhibit the efferent neurones leading to the antagonistic muscle, which is therefore unable to contract and thus remains relaxed.

A good example of this is the mechanism of walking. Initially the limb flexes in order to lift the foot off the ground. During flexion, the antagonistic extensor muscles are stretched but are reflexly inhibited from contracting. After flexion, the limb is straightened and the foot is again brought into contact with the ground. With the flexor muscles no longer contracting, inhibition of the extensor muscles ceases and the stretch reflex now proceeds culminating with the contraction of the extensor muscles. When the limb is straight no stretching in the extensor muscle spindle is detected and the stretch reflex ceases. The whole process is then free to be repeated.

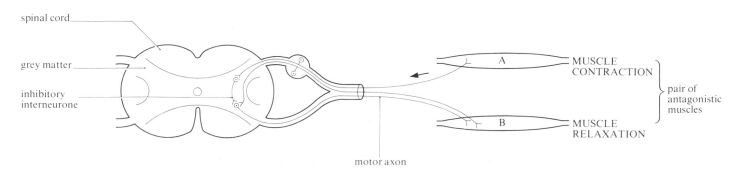

spinal cord

grey matter

inhibitory interneurone

A — MUSCLE CONTRACTION

B — MUSCLE RELAXATION

pair of antagonistic muscles

motor axon

Fig 17.29 *Interneural inhibition. When muscle A contracts, impulses pass to the spinal cord where they meet an inhibitory interneurone. Inhibition of the appropriate motor neurone to muscle B causes it to relax*

17.5.6   Tendon organs

Stretch receptors are also found in tendons. However they only respond when tension becomes severe. Upon stimulation impulses are discharged to the central nervous system where they meet inhibitory interneurones. Stimulation of these causes reflex inhibition of contraction and inhibition of active resistance to stretching. This is significant because it protects the muscle from being damaged when suddenly overloaded, or overcontracting and damaging itself in response to the application of a heavy load.

17.5   Examine fig 17.28 and answer the following questions.

(a) What happens to the muscle spindle when the whole muscle (extrafusal fibres) is stretched?

(b) What happens next when the extrafusal muscle fibres have contracted?

(c) What occurs if the muscle is severely stretched, as when a heavy load is suddenly applied to it?

(d) What occurs when the intrafusal muscle fibres contract?

17.6   Locomotion in a variety of invertebrates

17.6.1   Amoeboid movement

Amoeboid movement is characterised by the formation of temporary projections of the cell called **pseudopodia**. It occurs in protozoans of the class Rhizopoda and in vertebrate white blood cells. During movement the cell produces a definite anterior end which is at the point where new pseudopodia are forming. Analysis of the cytoplasm of an *Amoeba* indicates that there is a peripheral layer of viscous **plasmagel**, the **ectoplasm**, which encloses a more fluid cytoplasm, the **plasmasol** or **endoplasm**. Locomotion is thought to be brought about by alternate changes in the colloidal state of the cytoplasm effected by sol–gel–sol transformations, and the cytoplasmic streaming of plasmasol into the pseudopodia (section 4.1).

Where a pseudopodium is about to form, the plasmagel liquefies into plasmasol. Plasmasol from within the cell now flows towards this point and outwards into the newly forming pseudopodium. Plasmasol in the outer regions of the pseudopodium is rapidly transformed into plasmagel which thus forms a rigid collar around the pseudopodium. At the posterior end of *Amoeba* the plasmagel is rapidly converted to plasmasol which then flows forwards (fig 17.30).

A number of theories exist to explain amoeboid movement. One suggests that the posterior end of the animal contracts and drives plasmasol forwards into the newly forming pseudopodium. It is thought that variations in the viscosity of the cytoplasm accompanied by slight pressure changes in different parts of the cell stimulate streaming of the cytoplasm from one region of the cell to another. A more favoured theory, the '**fountain-zone**' theory, states that the cell is pulled forwards by contraction of the anterior end of the animal. Here, protein molecules in the plasmasol exist in an extended state. When the plasmasol is converted to plasmagel they contract and coil up. As this occurs, protein molecules at the posterior end of the animal are automatically extended, thus being transformed into plasmasol which is then pulled towards the anterior end.

These theories may have to be further modified because it has now been established that the protein molecules actin and myosin are present in all eukaryotic cells and that actin, existing as fine filaments binds reversibly to myosin. This reaction is accompanied by the hydrolysis of ATP. Therefore possibly the whole mechanism of amoeboid movement, and possibly cytoplasmic streaming within cells, may be essentially similar to that of muscle contraction itself.

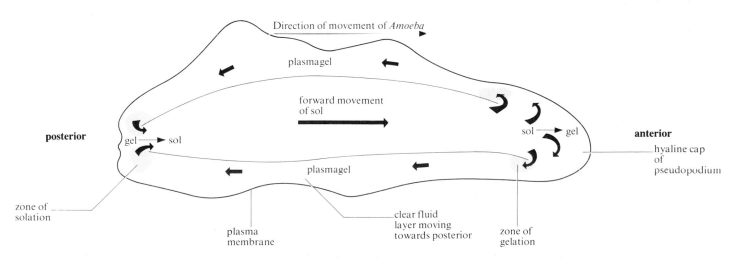

Fig 17.30 *Pseudopodial formation in* Amoeba. *According to the 'fountain-zone' theory, plasmasol gelates and contracts, thus pulling more plasmasol towards it*

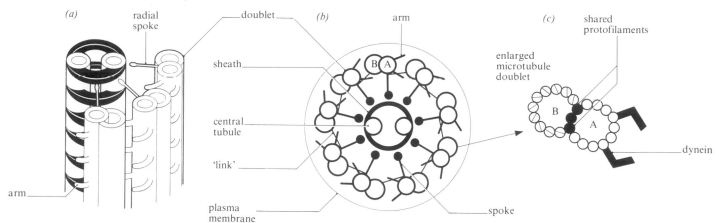

Fig 17.31 *Structure of a cilium or flagellum. (a) An interpretation of the arrangement of tubules and associated material as seen from outside. (b) The structure seen in cross-section. Each doublet consists of an A and a B tubule. Two arms are attached to the A tubule. Note that the A tubule is a complete circle in cross-section, whereas part of the wall of the B tubule is shared with the A. Spokes occur at intervals along the length of each doublet; they connect the doublets to the sheath surrounding the central tubules. (c) An enlarged microtubule doublet.*

17.6.2 Cilia and flagella

Electron micrographs indicate that cilia and flagella possess identical internal structures. Cilia are simply shorter versions of flagella and, unlike flagella, are more commonly found in groups than in isolation. A transverse section of either organelle shows it to consist of a pair of central filaments surrounded by nine peripheral filaments (fig 17.31), the so called '9 + 2' array. This bundle of filaments, called an **axoneme**, is surrounded by a membrane that is continuous with the plasma membrane.

Each peripheral filament is composed of the protein **tubulin** and consists of an A and a B microtubule. Each A microtubule has a pair of 'arms' composed of another protein called **dynein** which is capable of hydrolysing ATP, in other words it is an ATPase. The central filaments are connected to the A microtubules of the peripheral filaments by radial spokes of material.

The end of the cilium or flagellum attached to the cell or organism terminates in a **basal body** which is essentially identical in structure to an axoneme but has a '9 + 0' structure, and is derived from a centriole. It differs from a centriole only in possessing a complex organisation at its basal end known as a **cartwheel structure**. The basal body is thought to act as a template for the assembly of microtubules during development of cilia or flagella. There are often fibres which extend into the cytoplasm from the basal body which act to anchor the basal body in position.

Whilst cilia and flagella possess fundamentally similar internal structures, their mode of action is quite different.

A flagellum possesses a symmetrical beat with several undulations occurring along its length at any given moment (fig 17.32). This wave-like motion may be in one plane, or less commonly such that it beats in a corkscrew (helical) manner which spins the body of the organism about its longitudinal axis as well as propelling it forwards along a helical path (fig 17.33). In some flagellates the flagellum is at the anterior end of the body and beats in such a way as to pull the organism through the water. This sort of flagellum generally possesses minute lateral projections called **mastigonemes** on its surface which aid this type of locomotion. The flagellum itself is sometimes called a '**tinsel**' flagellum. More usually, the flagellum is at the rear of the organism or cell and pushes it through the water, as in the spermatozoan tail. Fig 17.34 shows a summary of the types of movement induced by flagella activity.

The beat of a cilium is asymmetric (fig 17.32), there being an active, fast, straight downstroke followed by a slower, bent, limp recovery action at the end of which the cilium returns to its original position. With so many cilia occurring together it is essential that some sort of mechanism exists to coordinate their activity. In the ciliate *Paramecium*, a traditional view is that this might involve fibres called **neuronemes** which interconnect the basal bodies. Generally the cilia beat in a synchronised fashion which results in

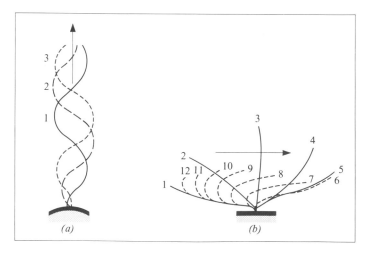

Fig 17.32 *Successive stages in the motion of a flagellum (a) and a cilium (b). The effective stroke of the cilium begins at 1.*

646

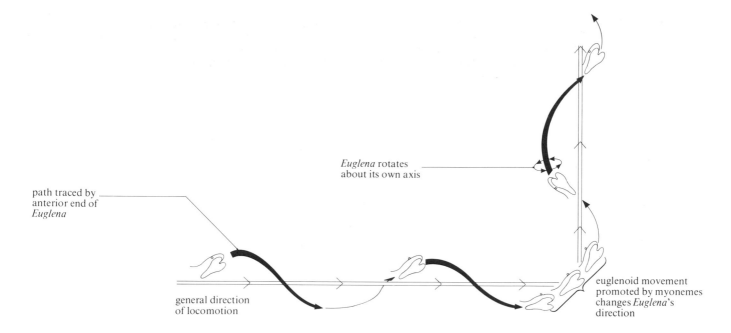

Euglena rotates about its own axis

path traced by anterior end of Euglena

general direction of locomotion

euglenoid movement promoted by myonemes changes Euglena's direction

Fig 17.33 (above) Euglena's path of movement

Fig 17.34 (below) Summary of types of movement induced by flagella activity.

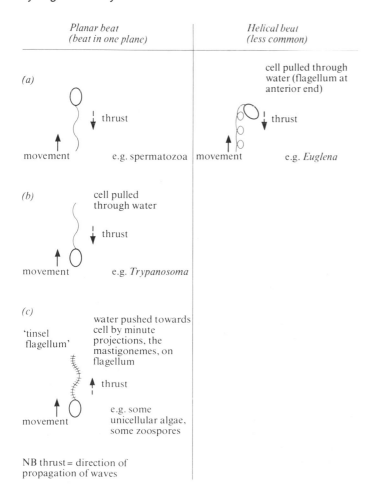

Planar beat (beat in one plane)	Helical beat (less common)
	cell pulled through water (flagellum at anterior end)
(a)	
thrust	thrust
movement	movement
e.g. spermatozoa	e.g. *Euglena*
(b)	cell pulled through water
thrust	
movement	
e.g. *Trypanosoma*	
(c) 'tinsel flagellum'	water pushed towards cell by minute projections, the mastigonemes, on flagellum
	thrust
movement	e.g. some unicellular algae, some zoospores

NB thrust = direction of propagation of waves

waves of ciliary activity passing along the length of the body in one particular direction. This is called **metachronal rhythm**.

There has been much debate concerning the mechanism involved in the actual beat of a cilium or flagellum. Current evidence suggests that a process exists that is essentially similar to that of the sliding filament theory for muscle contraction. A flagellum is said to begin to bend when the two dynein arms of the A microtubule of a peripheral filament link up with an adjacent B microtubule. When this happens ATP is hydrolysed and the A and B microtubules slide over each other causing movement of the flagellum. It is thought that five peripheral filaments on one side operate in this manner to produce the initial movement, whilst the remaining four on the other side slide fractionally later thus inducing the recovery action (fig 17.35). The radial spokes of the cilium tend to resist this sliding process, which instead is converted into a local bending action. It is thought that the central filaments may transmit the signals for sliding from the basal body along the length of the cilium or flagellum. It has also been proved that ciliary activity will only proceed when Mg^{2+} ions are present, and that the direction of the beat of a cilium is dictated by specific levels of intracellular Ca^{2+} ions. Indeed it is interesting to note that the avoiding action of *Paramecium* is controlled in this way. When *Paramecium* encounters an obstacle, it reverses the beat of its cilia before moving forward again. Reversal of ciliary beat is stimulated by a sudden influx of Ca^{2+} ions into the cell due to increased permeability of the organism to Ca^{2+} ions.

Both organelles are used extensively by small eukaryotic organisms to propel themselves through water. The cilia or flagella provide forward propulsion for the organism by thrusting against the surrounding viscous watery medium. Locomotion brought about in this manner is only effective for small organisms which have a much larger surface

Fig 17.35 *The sliding of doublets during motion of a cilium in the gills of a mussel. One of the two tubules of each doublet protrudes further into the tip of the cilium than does the other. Thus, cross-sections at an appropriate constant distance from the tip will show a change in tubule pattern during bending, from all doublets to doublets and single tubules. The entire doublets slide with respect to one another; but the two members of each doublet retain their positions relative to each other. (After P. Satir, from Novikoff & Holtzman.)*

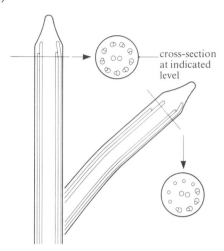

cross-section at indicated level

area:volume ratio than large animals, where the minute forces generated would be quite inadequate. Cilia also frequently occur within the bodies of multicellular organisms where they serve a number of important functions. They may propel fluid through ducts such as in the nephridia of annelids where metabolic waste is removed. They also propel eggs along mammalian oviducts, and move materials over internal surfaces, such as mucus through the respiratory passages, where this activity helps to keep them free from dust particles and other debris. They can also create feeding currents, as in *Paramecium*, from which food particles can be filtered and removed, often by other cilia.

Some bacteria possess flagella, but these differ markedly from eukaryotic flagella, being shorter, thinner and quite stiff. The bacterial flagellum is extracellular (not surrounded by a plasma membrane) and resembles a single microtubule of a eukaryote flagellum. It is moved by forces that emanate from the point where it is joined to the bacterium.

17.6.3   Locomotion in *Euglena*

The locomotory flagellum is at the anterior end of the body and pulls the organism forward. Waves of activity are generated by the flagellum itself, and as they pass in a spiral fashion from its base to its tip they increase in amplitude and velocity. This activity of the flagellum causes the body of *Euglena* to rotate about its axis, at about one complete body turn per second, as well as making it describe a corkscrew pathway through the water. The organism can travel forward at a rate of 0.5 mm s^{-1} which is approximately four times its body length. *Euglena* is able to

change its direction by the action of contractile **myonemes** which lie along the length of its body. When they contract, the shape of the body is changed as well as its direction. This is called **euglenoid motion** (fig 17.33).

17.6.4   Locomotion in *Paramecium*

Surface cilia, arranged in rows, beat diagonally backwards from left to right causing the animal to rotate about its longitudinal axis. At the same time, strongly beating oral groove cilia tend to cause the anterior end of the animal to move in a spiral fashion about its posterior end. The cilia exhibit metachronal rhythm and their coordinated activity may be governed by the **motorium**, a body which is interconnected with the neuronemes and basal bodies. *Paramecium* swims at a speed of about 1 mm s^{-1}, or four times its body length.

17.6.5   Locomotion in the Annelida

An oligochaete, Lumbricus terrestris *(the earthworm)*

The coelom of an earthworm is enclosed by a body wall composed of two antagonistic muscles, an outer circular layer and an inner longitudinal layer. The circular muscle is divided into separate units along the length of the animal by septa between the segments, but the muscle fibres of the longitudinal layer generally extend over several segments. Locomotion is brought about by the coordinated activity of the two muscle layers and those of the **chaetae**.

When an earthworm begins to move forwards, contraction of the circular muscles begins at the anterior end of the body and continues, segment by segment, as a wave along the length of the body. This activity exerts pressure on the coelomic fluid in each segment, stretching the relaxed longitudinal muscle and changing the shape of the segments such that they become longer and thinner. This causes the anterior end of the worm to extend forwards. Chaetae, present in all segments except the first and last, are retracted during the activity of the circular muscles and therefore do not impede the forward movement (fig 17.36).

Whilst the anterior end of the worm is moving forward, longitudinal muscle in more posterior segments contracts, causing this region of the worm to swell and press against the surrounding soil substratum. Chaetae in this region are protruded and help the worm to grip the substratum. This is particularly useful during burrowing for the worm can exert a powerful thrust against the surrounding soil particles during forward locomotion.

Contraction of the circular muscle is quickly followed by contraction of the longitudinal muscles throughout the length of the body, and this means that different parts of the worm may be either moving forward (when the circular muscles contract) or static (when the longitudinal muscles contract) at any given moment. The net effect is a smooth peristaltic wave of activity along the length of the worm as it progresses forwards. The worm is also able to crawl

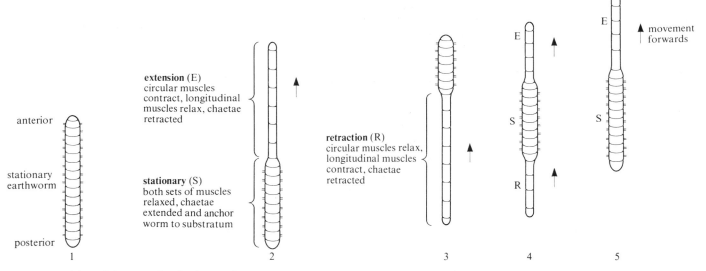

Fig 17.36 (above) *Locomotion in the earthworm*

Fig 17.37 (below) *Segmental innervation of longitudinal muscle in the earthworm (dorsal view). A similar arrangement is present in the circular muscle*

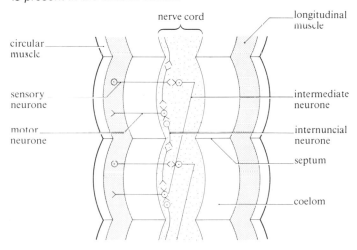

backwards by reversing the direction of contraction of the muscles.

Control of muscle contraction is brought about by a complex network of inter- and intrasegmental neurones. All segments are in contact with the longitudinal nerve cord and also possess their own set of segmental nerves. This means that localised control of each segment is possible, as well as control of overall activity of the animal (fig 17.37).

The ventral nerve cord possesses a **giant axon** which runs centrally along its length and conducts impulses in an anterior-to-posterior direction. Also present in the nerve cord are two longitudinally oriented **lateral fibres** which convey impulses from the tail to the head. When sensory receptors in the head are stimulated, impulses pass along the giant axon stimulating the longitudinal muscles to contract, thus causing the anterior end to be recoiled from the stimulus. If the tail of the worm is similarly stimulated, impulses pass along the lateral fibres from tail to head and cause the tail to be withdrawn. This is the basis of the worm's escape reaction.

A polychaete, Nereis (the ragworm)

In contrast to the earthworm, the longitudinal muscle layer is divided into a pair of dorsal and a pair of ventral muscle blocks (fig 4.26). The circular muscle is relatively weak and segmentally specialised into sets of oblique muscles which run into the **parapodia** and function to move the parapodia and their associated structures. Each parapodium is hollow and ramified by an extension of the coelom which is filled with coelomic fluid. It is subdivided into a dorsal projection, the **notopodium**, and a ventral projection called the **neuropodium**. Both of these structures possess a strengthening rod, the **aciculum**, and a bundle of chaetae.

Interaction between the body wall muscles, parapodia and coelomic fluid brings about several different types of locomotion. Slow creeping movement is achieved by using the parapodia as a system of levers. During its effective stroke a parapodium protrudes its aciculum and chaetae to make contact with the substratum and push against it in a backward direction, thus propelling the animal forwards. Protrusion of these structures is achieved by increased hydrostatic pressure in the coelom of the parapodium. The parapodium moves forward when it lifts from the substratum and its aciculum and chaetae are retracted. Retraction is achieved by contraction of the segmental oblique muscles.

The movements of the right and left parapodia of a segment are coordinated so that whilst one is moving forwards the other is moving backwards. Collectively the parapodia of the worm move as a series of peristaltic waves which pass along the length of the body. In contrast to the earthworm these waves move in a direction from the tail to the head with a group of parapodia on one side all moving generally forwards whilst at the same time their opposite numbers move backwards.

Rapid creeping occurs when the longitudinal muscles on

either side of the body contract alternately throwing the body into a series of lateral undulations. Here the parapodia again come into contact with the substratum. When this occurs, the longitudinal muscles work against these points of contact and effectively pull the animal forwards.

When swimming freely in the water the right and left longitudinal muscles contract alternately to produce waves of lateral movement that pass forward from the tail to the head. The broad, paddle-like parapodia move in a backward direction during their effective stroke. In doing this they push against the water and thrust the animal forwards.

17.6.6 Locomotion in the Arthropoda

Crustacean walking and swimming, Astacus fluviatilis (the crayfish)

The crayfish possesses eight thoracic and six abdominal segments each of which bears appendages of various shapes and sizes which are used for specific functions (fig 4.34). The last four thoracic segments bear walking legs called **pereiopods**, whilst forked paddle-like appendages called **pleopods** are found on abdominal segments 2–5 in the female and 3–5 in the male. The sixth abdominal segment, called the **uropod**, is modified as a flattened tail fin which is most frequently used in swimming.

When walking, the chelipeds of the fourth thoracic segment (section 4.10.1) are raised above the substratum and the abdomen is extended horizontally. Only two legs, one on either side of the body, are out of contact with the ground at any one time, the other six firmly grip the substratum with those of thoracic segments 5–7 pulling the crayfish along while the pair on the eighth thoracic segment push it.

Muscle which promotes movement of the limbs in the crayfish is striated; that in the region of the abdomen is particularly strong. Here thick antagonistic muscles operate to flex and extend the abdomen up and down. When the abdomen is flexed downwards the force exerted on the water by the extended tail is sufficient to cause the crayfish to shoot backwards through the water very quickly. This is the basis of its escape mechanism.

Locomotion in insects

Walking. This is achieved by the coordinated activity of three pairs of legs, one pair being attached to each of the three thoracic segments of the animal. Each leg consists of a series of hollow cylinders whose walls are composed of rigid exoskeletal material. The cylinders are linked together by joints and soft pliable membranes. Where the **coxa** (the basal segment of the insect leg) joins to the body, a form of ball-and-socket joint occurs, but all other joints in the leg are hinge joints. Bending and straightening of the legs is achieved by antagonistic flexor and extensor muscles attached to the inner surface of the exoskeleton on either side of a joint (fig 17.1).

When an insect begins to walk, three legs remain on the ground to support the animal whilst the other three move forward. The first leg on one side pulls the insect, whilst the third leg of the same side pushes. The second leg on the other side serves as a support for this activity. The process is then repeated but with the role of each trio of limbs reversed.

Many insects possess a pair of claws and a sticky pad at the distal ends of their legs. The pad consists of minute hollow tubes which secrete a sticky fluid that helps the insect to adhere to smooth surfaces. Thus, these insects are able to walk up vertical surfaces as well as upside down.

Flight. The wings of insects are flattened extremities of the exoskeleton and are supported by an intricate system of veins. Their movement is controlled by two main groups of muscles, **direct** and **indirect muscles**. In insects with large wings (such as butterflies and dragonflies) the muscles are actually attached to the bases of the wings (fig 17.38); these are the direct muscles. They elevate and depress the wings as well as controlling the angle of the wing stroke during flight. When the angle of one wing is adjusted with respect to the other, turning in the air is accomplished. They are also used to fold up the wings when the insect is stationary.

In insects with smaller wings, the main driving force for flight is developed by two sets of antagonistic, indirect flight muscles; the **dorso-ventrals** are attached to the tergum (roof) and sternum (floor) of the thorax, and the **longitudinals** are attached to the anterior and posterior aspects of the thorax (fig 17.39). There is no direct attachment of the wings to these muscles. However the base of each wing is attached to the tergum and pleura (side) of the thorax. This arrangement acts as a highly efficient lever system, for when either of the indirect muscles shortens fractionally it distorts the shape of the thorax, which in turn produces a large degree of movement by the wings. Because muscle contraction takes place over a very small distance it can be repeated rapidly. This is particularly important for insects that possess very fast wingbeat speeds.

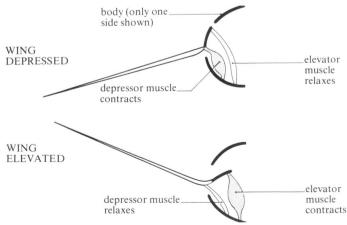

Fig 17.38 *Action of direct flight muscles in a large winged insect, such as a butterfly or dragonfly*

Fig 17.39 *Cross-section of the thorax of an insect from the anterior showing the relationship between wings, pleura, sternum, tergum and muscles during insect flight*

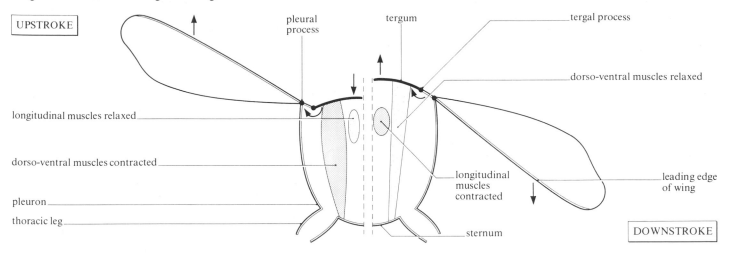

In large, winged insects such as the butterfly and locust the rate of wing beat is between 5–50 beats per second (table 17.5). Here the flight muscles contract each time as a result of a single nerve impulse. Hence impulses are generated at the same rate as the wings beat. Insect flight muscle which responds in this way is called **synchronous muscle**. In the housefly, which has a wing beat frequency of 120–200 beats per second, contraction of the flight muscles is much too fast to be triggered by individual nerve impulses. This muscle is termed **asynchronous** and receives roughly one impulse per 40 wing beats, which is necessary to maintain the muscle in an active state during flight. It can contract further and generate more power than synchronous muscle. Asynchronous muscle can also automatically contract in response to being stretched. This is called the **stretch reflex** and occurs faster than the speed of a nerve impulse.

Table 17.5. Wing speeds of a variety of insects

Wing speeds			
Large butterfly e.g. swallowtail	5 times per second		
Locust	18	,,	,,
Hawkmoth	40	,,	,,
Housefly	120	,,	,, at this speed a humming sound heard
Bee	180	,,	,,
Midge	700–1000	,,	,, at this speed a high pitched whine heard

In general, the smaller the insect the faster it beats its wings.

NB Some insects have two pairs of wings (such as locusts and dragonflies). In some cases both pairs of wings beat together, as in bees; in others the back pair of wings beats slightly ahead of the front pair, for example locusts. Some insects have one pair of wings, such as flies and beetles. In houseflies the hindwings are reduced and modified to form a pair of club-shaped halteres which are sensory in function. They oscillate rapidly during flight, detect aerodynamic forces and provide information for the maintenance of stability in flight. Some insects (very few) have no wings, for example fleas.

The following account of asynchronous flight is based on detailed observations made by Boettiger on the fly *Sarcophaga bullata*. Whilst flying in a straight line the wings describe a pathway through the air in the form of a figure of eight. The downstroke provides the majority of forward thrust and lift for the insect. During this phase each wing beats forward and downward with its anterior margin inclined at a lower level than its posterior one. On the upstroke the wing moves upward and backward with its anterior margin raised above the posterior one. In this position the wings move through the air with minimum resistance whilst at the same time providing more lift for the body.

In order to raise the wings, the dorso-ventral muscles contract. When this occurs the tergum is lowered and the tergal attachment of each wing is pulled into a position below that of its pleural attachment (fig 17.39). During this process the resistance of the tergum to this distortion increases. However, at a critical point the resistance disappears and the wings click into an elevated position. At the same time that this is happening the longitudinal muscles are stretched, considerably stimulating a stretch reflex which makes them contract instantaneously. The tergum now arches upwards and the tergal attachment of the wing is raised above the pleural one. Once again resistance to such a movement is suddenly overcome and the wings click downwards. This action in turn stretches and stimulates the dorsoventral muscles to contract, and the whole cycle is repeated.

17.6 The sarcoplasmic reticulum of insect flight muscle is modified to increase its surface area by being perforated at intervals. Can you suggest a reason for this?

17.7 Would synchronous or asynchronous muscle be expected to contain more sarcoplasmic reticulum? Give a reason for your answer.

Fig 17.40 *Comparison between (a) ostraciform, (b) carangiform and (c) anguilliform locomotion*

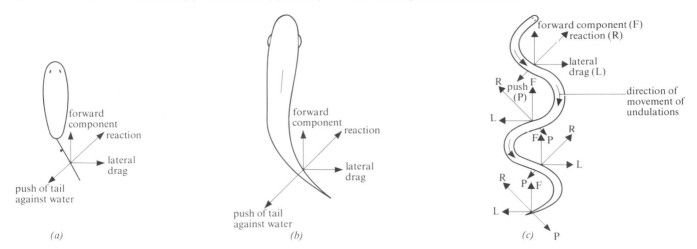

(a)   (b)   (c)

17.7   Locomotion in vertebrates

17.7.1   Swimming in fish

Water, particularly sea water, has a high relative density, many hundreds of times greater than air. As such it represents a comparatively viscous medium to move through. However, its density is made use of by fish as it supports them and also provides a medium against which the fish can thrust during swimming movements.

Any successful organism shows many adaptive features suited to the environment in which it lives and a fish is no exception. The body of most fish is highly streamlined, being tapered at both ends. This means that water flows readily over the body surface and that drag is reduced to a minimum. Apart from the fins no other structures project from a fish, and it seems that the faster the fish, the more perfect is the streamlining. The dermal denticles of cartilaginous fish and the scales of bony fish are moistened by slimy exudation from mucus or oil glands and this also considerably reduces friction between the fish and the water. Other general adaptations possessed by fish for moving efficiently through the water are the fins. Dorsal and ventral, unpaired, median (along the midline of the body) fins help to stabilise the fish, the paired pectoral and pelvic fins are used for steering and balancing the animal, and the caudal or tail fin, in concert with the paired fins, provides the forward movement of the fish through the water. Details of precisely how the fins operate will be discussed later.

17.7.2   Propulsion in fish

Movement is brought about by sets of segmentally arranged antagonistic muscle blocks called **myotomes** located on either side of the vertebral column. Superficially each myotome possesses a zig-zag shape, and internally it traverses the joint formed by two adjacent vertebrae. The vertebral column is a long, flexible rod and, when myotomes on one side of it contract, it bends easily.

The myotomes contract and relax alternately on each side of the vertebral column beginning at the anterior end of the fish and travelling towards its tail. This activity bends the body of the fish into a series of waves, the number increasing the longer and thinner the fish.

Very compact fish such as *Ostracium* (the tunny) show little evidence of this wave-like action with as much as 80% of their forward thrust being achieved purely by the side-to-side lashing of the tail and caudal fin. This locomotion is called **ostraciform**. Longer fish, such as the dogfish and the majority of bony fish, exhibit **carangiform locomotion**; here the posterior half of the fish is thrown into a series of waves. **Anguilliform** locomotion, as demonstrated by eels, is where the body is very long and thrown into many waves so that different parts of the body are moving simultaneously to the left and to the right.

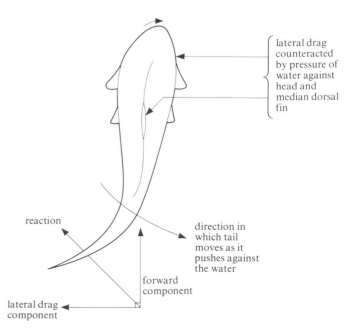

Fig 17.41 *Force components exerted by the caudal fin of a dogfish as it is lashed from side to side*

Fig 17.42 *Action of paired pectoral and pelvic fins and heterocercal tail in the dogfish to provide lift*

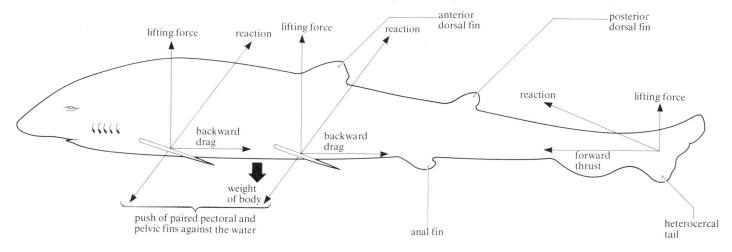

Forward propulsion is generally effected by the side-to-side movement of the tail to which is attached the caudal fin. As the caudal fin is moved in this way it bends slightly and exerts a backward pressure on the relatively viscous water. This force can be resolved into a forward and lateral component. The forward one thrusts the fish through the water whilst the lateral one tends to swing the head of the fish sideways in a direction opposite to that of the tail. This is called **lateral drag** (fig 17.41). Fortunately, it is counteracted by the inertia of the water against the relatively massive anterior end of the body (when compared to the tail) and the large surface area posed by the dorsal median fin. Also it would require a much greater force to move the body laterally through the water than to propel it forwards. The magnitude of the force that the tail and caudal fin apply to the water depends on their speed of action, surface area and the angle at which they are held with respect to the water.

17.7.3 Locomotion in a cartilaginous fish, the dogfish

A dogfish is heavier than sea water and will begin to sink to the bottom if it ceases to swim. To avoid this the paired pectoral and pelvic fins act as **hydrofoils**. They are held at an angle to the long axis of the body, and when the fish wishes to swim up or down in the water their angle is altered accordingly by muscular activity. When held at an angle, the force exerted by the fins can be resolved into an upward component, which forces the head of the fish upwards (positive pitch), and a backward or drag component (fig 17.42). However the drag is considerably less than the forward thrust produced by the tail and is relatively unimportant. The dogfish possesses a **heterocercal** tail, the ventral lobe being proportionately larger than its dorsal counterpart. As the tail thrusts from side to side, once again the force produced by it can be divided into an upwards thrust, termed negative pitch, as well as a lateral component. The positive pitch at the anterior end is balanced by the negative pitch at the rear.

As the fish swims along in a level forward manner it may be subjected to three kinds of displacement or instability. These are **yawing, pitching** and **rolling**. The various fins of the body are generally responsible for maintaining controlled forward locomotion and the way in which they counteract any displacement of the fish can be seen in fig 17.43.

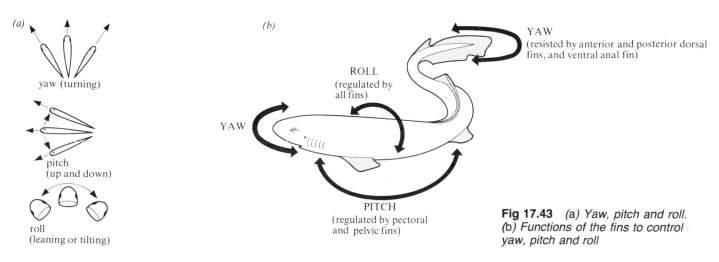

Fig 17.43 *(a) Yaw, pitch and roll. (b) Functions of the fins to control yaw, pitch and roll*

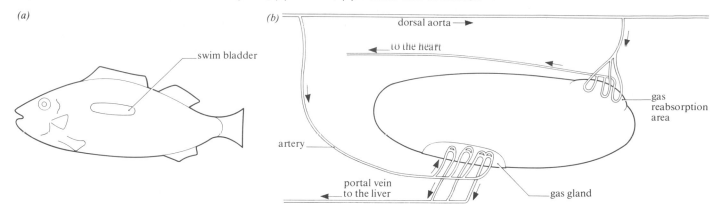

Fig 17.44 *Closed swim bladder of a bony fish; (a) location, (b) bladder and circulation*

The fins respond almost immediately to any form of instability. This is because of the activity of a set of three semicircular canals located on either side of the head of the fish. Should the body yaw, pitch or roll, then the appropriate semicircular canal is stimulated to fire nerve impulses which pass to the brain. The brain, in turn, immediately sends the appropriate motor impulses to the fin muscles which adjust their position accordingly.

17.7.4 Locomotion in a bony fish, the herring

Bony fish possess a structure called the swim or air bladder. Whilst lobe-finned fish used the swim bladder to perfect the air-breathing habit, bony fish adapted it into a hydrostatic device. The swim bladder is a sac lying between the vertebral column and gut and functions to provide the fish with 'neutral buoyancy'. When this occurs the fish possesses a density equal to that of the surrounding water and therefore does not need to expend energy to keep itself from sinking, so concentrating its efforts on moving through the water.

With the development of such a swim bladder in bony fish, the paired fins were released from their lifting function. Now, they are much smaller than those of the dogfish and are used instead as stabilisers or brakes, in the latter case being spread vertically at 90° to the body. Each pectoral fin may be used independently of its opposite number, and in this way they act as pivots round which the fish can turn rapidly. When the fish is swimming in a straight line the paired fins are pressed firmly against the sides of the body thus improving its streamlined shape. Possession of a swim bladder has also permitted the development of a symmetrical **homocercal** tail which transmits most of the force it develops against the water in a forward direction.

Two types of swim bladder exist.

(1) **Open swim bladder** (as in goldfish, herrings). The bladder is connected to the pharynx by a duct. Air is taken in or expelled from the bladder via the mouth and duct, thus decreasing or increasing the relative density of the fish respectively.

(2) **Closed swim bladder** (as in codfish). The bladder has completely lost its connection with the pharynx. By automatically increasing or decreasing the amount of gas in its bladder, the fish can match the density of the surrounding water and thus preserve 'neutral buoyancy'.

The closed swim bladder is under nervous control. At its anterior end is a structure, the **gas gland**, rich in blood capillaries, which secretes gas rich in oxygen into the bladder. Posteriorly is another heavily vascularized region which can absorb gases from the bladder (fig 17.44). In the gas gland, arterial and venous capillaries are interspersed amongst each other. It is here that a countercurrent system operates in order to facilitate secretion of oxygen into the bladder. The gas gland produces lactic acid when gas secretion occurs, and as the acid enters the venous capillaries it reduces the affinity of haemoglobin for oxygen (this is called the root effect). This phenomenon increases the oxygen tension of the blood in the venous capillaries leaving the gas gland, and paradoxically the venous blood

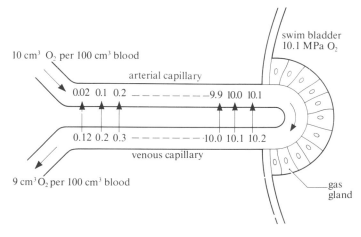

Fig 17.45 *Countercurrent system in the closed swim bladder of a bony fish. The gas gland produces lactic acid which increases the oxygen tension in the venous capillary. Thus gas diffuses from the venous to arterial capillaries, and remains within the loop. As venous blood leaves the gland it contains less oxygen than the incoming arterial blood. NB For simplification only one venous and one arterial capillary are shown. The gas gland itself contains numerous capillaries.*

possesses a higher oxygen tension than that in the arterial capillaries (fig 17.45). Therefore oxygen constantly diffuses from the venous to the arterial capillaries and is secreted into the swim bladder. At the time of gas secretion by the gas gland the blood vessels of the posterior region of the swim bladder are closed off so that no gas can escape from it.

17.8 Summarise the adaptations that fish possess for efficient swimming.

17.7.5 Locomotion in the frog

In the frog the paired limbs are no longer used as fins for stabilising and steering the animal, but are modified to operate as elongated jointed levers, raising the body off the ground whilst at the same time moving the animal over land. The forelimbs are relatively short, with the radius and ulna united. The hindlegs are very long and held underneath the body when the animal is at rest, by being bent at the knee and ankle. The tibia and fibula are fused together and the tarsals greatly elongated. The girdles, which articulate with the limbs, are greatly enlarged when compared with those of fish and support the weight of the animal against the effects of gravity. This is especially true of the pelvic girdle.

When a frog crawls over the substratum its mode of locomotion is effected by diagonally opposite limbs operating in unison with each other. If we begin with a stationary frog with all four limbs on the ground, the following sequence of events takes place when it begins to crawl. The left forelimb retracts at the same time as the right hindlimb extends. Both limbs thrust against the substratum and so propel the animal forwards. This is followed by retraction of the right forelimb and extension of the left hindlimb, the whole process being repeated as long as the animal is crawling. A full explanation is given in fig 17.46.

At take off, during a jump, each joint in the hindlimb is

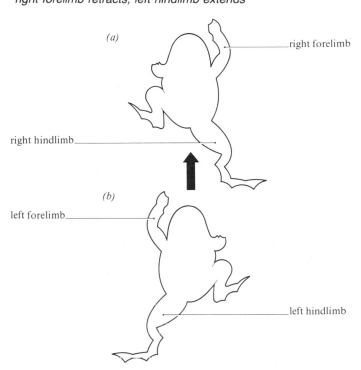

Fig 17.46 *Crawling in a frog viewed dorsally*
(a) Left forelimb retracts, right hindlimb extends, right forelimb extends, left hindlimb placed forwards.
(b) Left forelimb extends, right hindlimb is placed forwards, right forelimb retracts, left hindlimb extends

right forelimb

right hindlimb

left forelimb

left hindlimb

straightened by rapid contraction of strong extensor muscles. The force exerted against the ground during this activity is transmitted from the limbs to the vertebral column via the pelvic girdle and is at least three times greater than the weight of its body. This is sufficient to propel the animal upwards and forwards into the air against the downward pull of gravity. On landing, the short, compact forelimbs, attached in a flexible manner to the pectoral girdle, dampen down the shock of impact (fig 17.47).

Fig 17.47 *The take-off and jump of a frog*

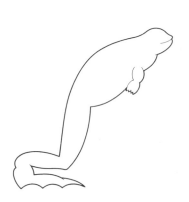
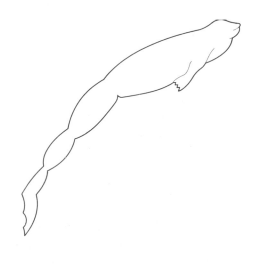

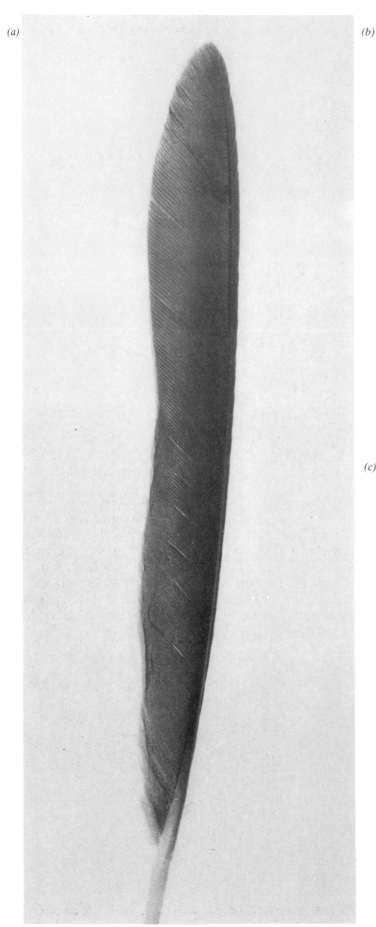

(a)

(b)

(c)

Fig. 17.48 (a) Quill feather, (b) contour feather, (c) down feather

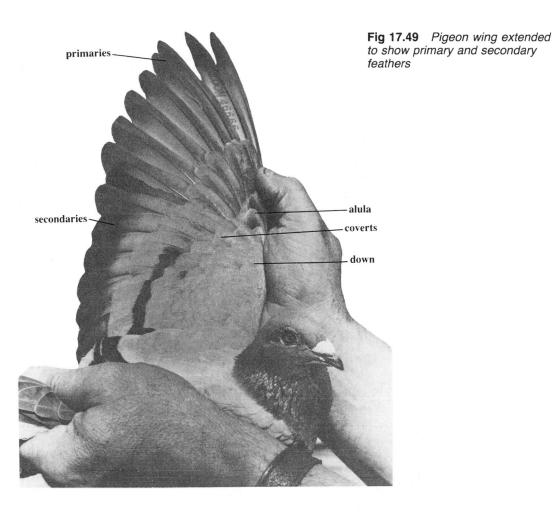

Fig 17.49 *Pigeon wing extended to show primary and secondary feathers*

primaries

secondaries

alula

coverts

down

17.7.6   Bird feathers and flight

The possession of feathers, and considerable modification of their skeleton has enabled most birds to develop structural adaptations which have provided them with the ability to fly, and gain substantial mastery of the air.

Feathers are epidermal structures developed within the skin of birds, evolved from scales of reptiles. Whilst they provide body covering for birds, they are not spread evenly over the body surface. They occur in tracts called **pterylae** (*ptero*, flying) which are separated by featherless areas called **apteria**. Four distinct kinds of feather are recognisable, namely the **quill**, **contour**, **down** and **filoplume**. Details of the structure of each of these can be seen in fig 17.48a–c.

Each bird wing possesses 23 quill feathers called **remiges**. They are positioned in a backward direction over the body and overlap each other. This arrangement provides an upper convex, and lower concave, surface to the wing and therefore enables it to act as an aerofoil, the significance of which will be discussed later. There are 11 remiges attached to the hand (metacarpals and digits), these are called **primaries**, whilst the remaining 12 are attached to the forearm (radius and ulna) and are termed **secondaries** (fig 17.49). The quill feathers of the tail are called **retrices**.

Typically a quill feather is composed of a stiff hollow lower region, the quill, embedded in the skin, and an upper solid **rachis**. The rachis supports the **vane**, which consists of rows of **barbs** on each side, which themselves bear two rows of **barbules**. The barbules interlock with each other by means of small hooks and grooves (fig 17.50) thus providing a firm, strong and light, air-resistant surface to the wing. At the junction between the quill and radius is a smaller tufted structure, the **aftershaft** or afterfeather. It consists of a group of separated barbs.

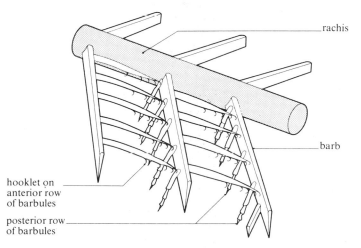

rachis

barb

hooklet on anterior row of barbules

posterior row of barbules

Fig 17.50   *Vane of quill feather showing barbs and barbules*

Contour feathers, though similar in structure, are smaller and more flexible than quill feathers, and their barbs are less firmly attached. They provide the main body covering and wind proof layer of the bird and establish its body outline.

Down feathers are the only body covering of nestlings. In older birds they are closely applied to the skin in amongst the contour feathers. The barbs of these feathers are long and pliable and their barbules do not possess hooks.

Filoplumes are small hair-like structures. There is no vane as such, just a small tuft of flexible barbs and barbules at the tip of the rachis. These feathers are spread all over the bird and help to retain air close to its body.

Apart from the development of feathers, many other modifications associated with flight have taken place within birds. The major ones are summarised below.

(1) The pectoral girdle is well developed and provides a firm base for the wings. There is a sizeable **keeled sternum** providing a large surface area for the attachment of the powerful pectoral flight muscles (fig 17.51). Flight muscles may approach half the body weight in a strong flying bird such as a racing pigeon.

(2) Considerable fusion and elongation of forelimb bones has provided a large wingspan. Three carpals have fused with three metacarpals to form the **carpometacarpus**, a strong supportive structure for the attachment of the primary flight feathers. Only three digits remain. Loss of the others has helped to lighten the wing. The skeleton is rigid in places; for instance some of the vertebrae are fused, and the vertebral column is fused to the pelvic girdle. This transmits the force of the wings more efficiently and provides better lift. The hindlimbs have been lengthened, which means that the wings do not flap against the ground during take-off.

(3) The body is highly streamlined so that when the bird flies through the air its shape provides little resistance. The skull is compact and generally possesses a streamlined, pointed bill. The arrangement of the feathers provides a smooth surface for the air to flow over. The tail is short. This cuts down drag and increases manoeuvrability. The legs of birds are tucked up to the body during flight.

(4) The possession of a number of hollow spongy bones helps to lighten the body. Many of the cavities are filled by air sacs. These also help to improve ventilation in the bird by being able to supply the lungs with fresh air during inspiration and expiration (section 11.6.10). The insides of the bones of large birds have struts for strength. The beak represents toothless, pointed jaws covered with a horny bill. The absence of teeth precludes the need for heavy jaw muscles for grinding food. This function is carried out by the gizzard which is nearer to the centre of gravity of the bird. It has been estimated that in a pelican weighing 11 kg, and standing 1.5 m tall, its skeleton weighs only 0.65 kg, and that the frigate bird (a sea glider) with a wing span of 2 m possesses a skeleton weighing just 110 g. In fact here the feathers weigh more than the skeleton (1.4–1.8 kg)! The sex organs of birds are very small, only developing fully during the breeding season. This again aids flight economy in terms of keeping the body as light as possible.

(5) Birds have a high body temperature and good insulation which combats the cooling effect of the air as the birds move through it. It also ensures more efficient muscle contraction for flight. The heart of a bird is large and strongly beating thus maintaining high blood pressure.

(6) Birds have excellent visual acuity. A third eyelid, the nictitating membrane, is present which removes particles from the eye during flight. Many birds possess a long flexible neck which enables the head to reach the ground for feeding purposes, and permits it to be rotated, providing good all-round vision.

(7) As would be expected, all birds that fly possess remarkable powers of muscular coordination.

17.7.7 Flight in birds

Consider the horizontal flow of air over an inclined wing surface which has its leading edge raised above its trailing edge. In this context the wing acts as an aerofoil. Air flowing over the upper surface meets less resistance than that flowing over the lower surface (fig 17.52) and therefore develops a greater velocity. The combined effect of these two phenomena is to cause air pressure above the wing to be reduced, and that below to be increased, thus providing the wing with a **lifting force**. The power of this lifting effect depends on the size and shape of the wing, the angle at which it is inclined to the long axis of the body (the angle of attack) and the bird's air speed. There is also a force acting on the bird, exerted by the air, which tends to push the wing backward in the direction of the airstream. This is called **drag**. The

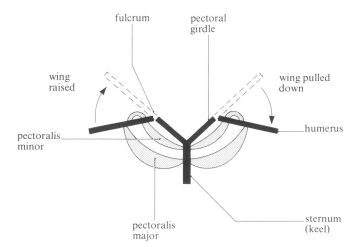

Fig 17.51 *Section of a bird (pigeon) skeleton viewed from the front to show how flight muscles and bones of the wings and pectoral girdle operate together*

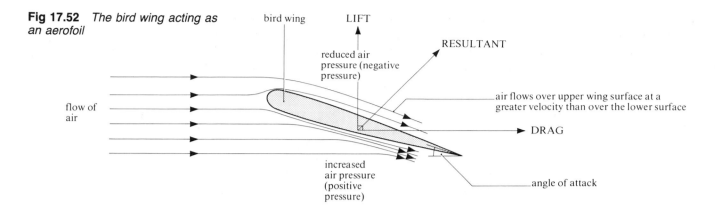

Fig 17.52 *The bird wing acting as an aerofoil*

bird wing

LIFT

RESULTANT

reduced air pressure (negative pressure)

air flows over upper wing surface at a greater velocity than over the lower surface

flow of air

DRAG

increased air pressure (positive pressure)

angle of attack

mechanical efficiency of a wing depends on its ability to develop a big lifting force for a small relative increase in drag.

There are three major types of flight; flapping, gliding and soaring, and hovering.

Flapping flight

In a bird such as the pigeon, which beats its wings two times per second, the main powerstroke is delivered by the downbeat of the wings and is brought about by contraction of the large, powerful **pectoralis major muscles** which are attached at one end to the ventral surface of the humerus and to the keel of the sternum at the other. At take-off the first part of the downstroke is almost vertical with the leading edge of the wing lower than the trailing edge. The primary feathers are bent upwards due to the pressure of the air. They are tightly closed to provide maximum resistance to the air and therefore maximum lift. During the latter part of the downstroke the wing is moved forward

and twists like a propellor so that its front edge is tilted upwards. In this position the wing develops lift for the body. The lifting effect of the air as it moves between the primary feathers tends to separate them and bend them upwards (fig 17.53).

The upstroke starts before the downstroke has been completed. The inner part of the forearm is moved sharply upwards and backwards with its front edge inclined above that of the trailing edge. This action is produced by the **pectoralis minor muscles** attached to the dorsal surface of the humerus and to the sternum. It provides lift for the body. As the wing moves upwards it bends at the wrist and the hand twists round so that the primary feathers are suddenly jerked backwards and upwards until the whole wing becomes more or less straight above the body. On their upward journey the primaries are separated, permitting the air to pass between them thus minimising air resistance. The backward movement of the primaries provides the bulk of the forward propulsive thrust

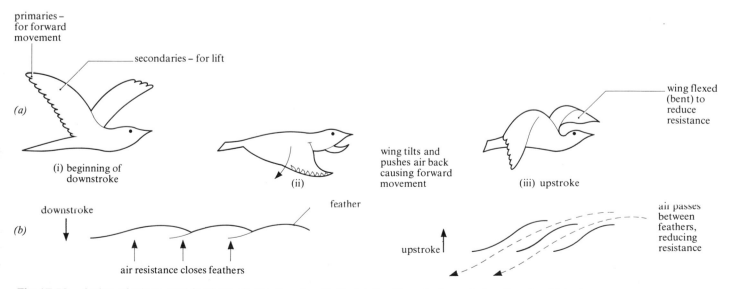

Fig 17.53 *Action of wings and feathers during flapping flight. (a) Position of wings during flapping flight in a pigeon. (b) Position of feathers during downstroke and upstroke of a bird wing during flapping flight*

developed by the animal. Before the primaries have reached their highest point, the pectoralis major muscles begin to contract again, eliciting a new downward beat and the whole process is repeated.

During sustained flapping flight the wing action is considerably modified and requires far less energy than that needed at take-off. Here the wings do not flap so hard, meet each other over the bird's back or move forwards during the latter part of the downstroke. The wings are generally held out straight, and the up and down flapping movements occur mainly at the wrists (junction of lower limb bones and carpals). The active backward lift of the wrist has virtually disappeared and the upstroke is passive, being achieved by air pressure acting against the underside of the wing.

At the end of flight the bird lands by lowering and spreading out its tail. This acts both as a brake and a lifting flap. As lift is achieved, the legs are lowered and the bird comes to rest. The tail is also used to steer the bird in flight, and stability in the air is accomplished by nervous control via the semicircular canals. Impulses are generated here which stimulate accessory muscles to alter the shape and position of the wings and the number of beats of one wing relative to the other.

Different birds fly at different speeds. Such differences are achieved by the shape of the wing, its changing form during flight and the frequency of the wing beat. A comparison of the structure of the wing of a fast flier, the swift, and that of a slow flier, the sparrow, is given in fig 17.54.

Fig 17.54 *Comparison of the structure of the wing of a fast flying bird (such as a swift) and a slow flying bird (such as a sparrow)*

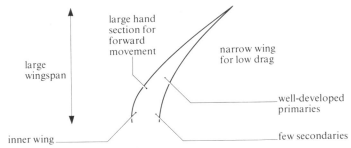

slow flier

short wingspan

wide wing

well-developed secondaries

large inner wing for lift

fast flier

large hand section for forward movement

narrow wing for low drag

large wingspan

well-developed primaries

inner wing

few secondaries

NB wing is flattened for minimum resistance

17.9. List the features which enable the swift to fly so fast.

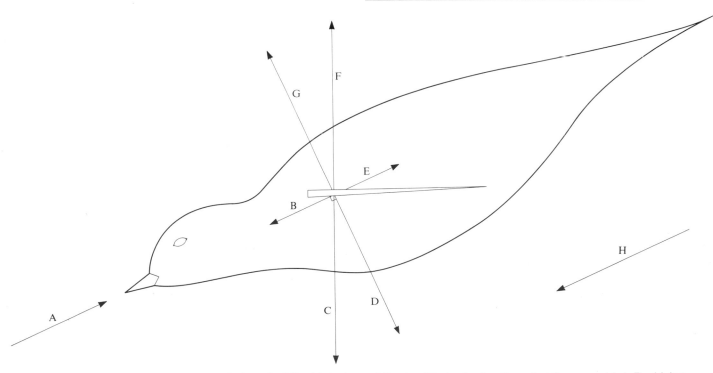

Fig 17.55 *Drawing showing forces exerted against the bird when gliding in still air. A, direction of airflow over bird; B, driving force; C, weight of body; D, sinking force; E, drag; F, resultant aerodyne force; G, lift; H, direction of movement of bird. (Modified after Gray.)*

660

Gliding and soaring

During gliding the wings are held out at more or less 90° to the body and the bird gradually loses height. As it descends, the force acting on it is called the **driving force** (fig 17.55) and the pull of gravity acting in a downward direction is called the **sinking force**. As the gliding speed increases so the lifting force increases and when lift equals the sinking force, and the driving force equals drag, the bird glides through the air at a constant velocity. The speed and angle of the glide depends on the size, shape and angle of attack of the wings and the weight of the bird.

Land birds make use of thermal upcurrents when gliding. They occur when a horizontal wind is deflected upwards on encountering an obstruction such as a mountain (this is known as slope soaring), or when warm air moves upwards and is replaced by colder air, such as over towns. Birds with light bodies and large wings such as buzzards and eagles are good thermal gliders and they manoeuvre gently upwards in a series of small circles. Rising in the air without flapping is called soaring.

Marine birds, such as the albatross, possess a different shape and glide in a different fashion (fig 17.56). The albatross has a large body, and very long narrow wings, and makes use of gusts of wind that arise above the waves. During its upward glide it ascends to a height of about 7–10 m. Then it turns downwind and descends at great speed with its wings angled in a backward direction. At the bottom of the descent the albatross describes an arc as it turns back into the wind and its wings are placed in a more forward position. The new position of the wings and the forward velocity of the body provide the bird with a lifting force which enables it to gain height in preparation for another rapid descent. Albatrosses are also able to glide for long distances close to, and parallel to, wave ridges, using the small upcurrents of wind from the waves as land birds do in slope soaring.

Hovering

Hovering is flapping the wings while at the same time staying in one place. The wings move backwards and forwards at speeds of up to 50 beats per second, and the upward thrust developed counterbalances the bird's weight. Birds that hover possess enormous flight muscles relative to their size ($\frac{1}{3}$ body weight) and are consequently very strong flappers. Their wings can tilt at almost any angle. The majority of the wing feathers are primaries (only six are secondaries) and are used for developing thrust.

17.7.8 Flight in bats

Bats are the only mammals capable of true flight. Each wing is composed of a thin layer of heavily vascularised skin, stretched between the bat's forearm, all fingers of the hand except the thumb, the sides of its body and the ankle of the hindlimb. The wrist bones are fused and give the wing strength whilst those of the forearm and hand are considerably elongated and function as a supportive framework for the wing. The index and middle

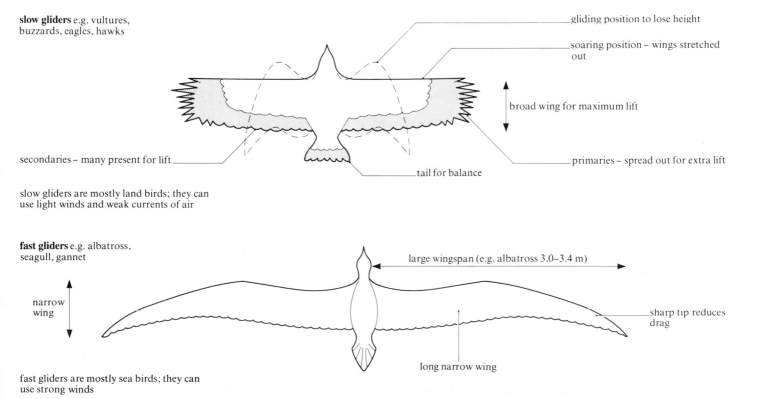

slow gliders e.g. vultures, buzzards, eagles, hawks

gliding position to lose height

soaring position – wings stretched out

broad wing for maximum lift

secondaries – many present for lift

tail for balance

primaries – spread out for extra lift

slow gliders are mostly land birds; they can use light winds and weak currents of air

fast gliders e.g. albatross, seagull, gannet

large wingspan (e.g. albatross 3.0–3.4 m)

narrow wing

sharp tip reduces drag

long narrow wing

fast gliders are mostly sea birds; they can use strong winds

Fig 17.56 *A comparison between the body and wing shapes of slow and fast gliders*

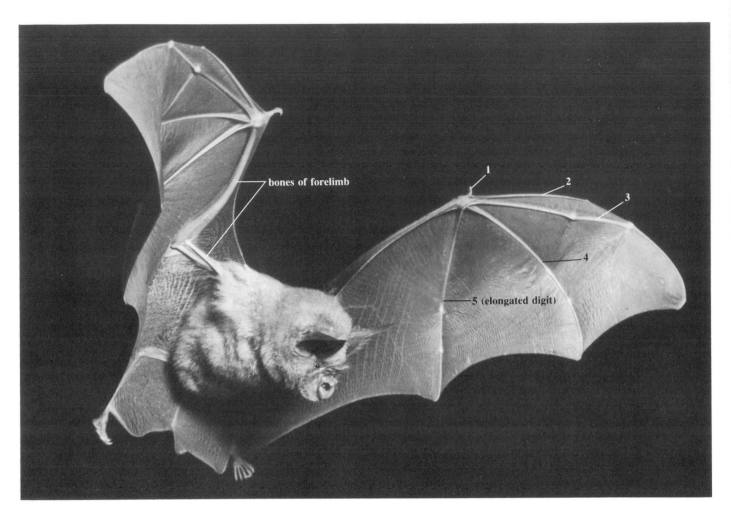

bones of forelimb

1
2
3
4
5 (elongated digit)

fingers of the hand support the leading edge of the wing whilst the other two fingers extend backwards to the trailing edge which eventually links up with the fifth digit of the ankle (fig 17.57). The actual movement of the wings occurs in a similar fashion to the wings of birds, and flight can be powerful and fast.

17.7.9 Locomotion in quadrupeds, the dog

Walking

When a dog walks, its vertebral column remains rigid, and forward movement is achieved by the activity of the hindlimbs. They are moved forwards and backwards by alternate contraction of flexor and extensor muscles respectively.

When its extensor muscle contracts, each hindlimb, acting as a lever, extends and exerts a backward force against the ground, thus thrusting the animal forward and slightly upwards. When the flexor contracts, the limb is lifted clear of the ground and pulled forward. Only one limb is raised at any one time, the other three providing a tripod of support which balances the rest of the body. Beginning with the left forelimb in a stationary dog, the sequence of leg movement is as follows when it walks forward: left forelimb; right hindlimb; right forelimb; left hindlimb; and so on.

Fig 17.57 (above) *Bat wing extended showing attachment of wing to forearm, body and ankle*

Fig 17.58 (below) *Running sequence in a dog (such as a greyhound)*
(a) Backbone fully arched and feet immediately under the body. (b) Backbone fully extended and somewhat concave, limbs fully extended

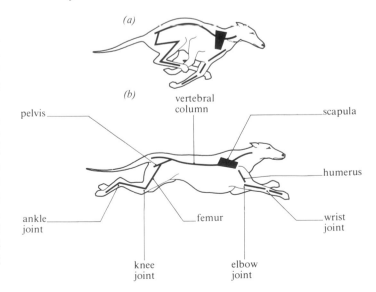

(a)

(b)

pelvis

vertebral column

scapula

humerus

ankle joint

femur

wrist joint

knee joint

elbow joint

662

Running

As a dog begins to run, it loses its tripod means of suspension and develops a type of movement where the forelimbs move together, followed by the hindlimbs. The feet are in contact with the ground for much less time than in walking, and usually one forelimb touches the ground a split second before the other. This also occurs with the hindlimbs. Therefore the sequence of limbs touching the ground is: left forelimb; right forelimb; right hindlimb; left hindlimb.

As the dog reaches maximum speed, leg movement quickens even further, and as they extend, all four legs may be off the ground at the same time. The strong trunk muscles arch the flexible backbone upwards when all four limbs are underneath it, and downwards when the limbs are fully extended. In this way the thrust of the limbs is increased and the stride of the dog considerably lengthened, both of which enable the dog to increase its speed (fig 17.58).

17.7.10 Bipedal gait, Man

In the standing position the weight of the body is balanced over two legs. When a stride is taken by the right limb the first thing to happen is that the right heel is raised by contraction of the calf muscle. This action serves to push the ball of the right foot against the ground and thus exert a forward thrust. The right limb pushes further against the ground as it is pulled forwards, slightly bent at the knee (fig 17.59). As this occurs, the weight of the body is brought over the left foot which is still in contact with the ground and acting as a prop for the rest of the body. When the right limb extends, the heel is the first part of the foot to touch the ground. The weight of the body is gradually transferred from the left side to a position over the right heel, and then as the body continues to move forwards,

Fig 17.59 *Successive positions of the right leg during a single pace*

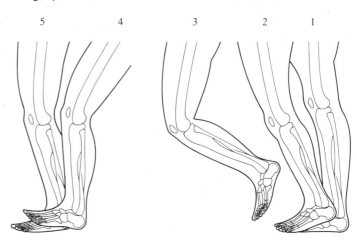

over the right toe, backward pressure against the substratum generally being exerted through the right big toe.

With the weight of the body now over the right leg, the left heel is raised and the whole sequence repeated. This alternating sequence of right and left, heel-and-toe action continues until walking ceases.

17.10 Why do sprinters generally run on their toes?

17.8 Support in plants

Four tissues, the parenchyma, collenchyma, sclerenchyma and xylem contribute towards the support of plants. A full account of their supporting role can be found in chapter 8.

Chapter Eighteen

Homeostasis

An organism may be defined as a physico-chemical system existing in a steady state with its external environment. It is this ability to maintain a steady state within a constantly changing environment that contributes towards the success of living systems. In order to maintain this condition organisms, from the morphologically simplest to the most complex, have developed a variety of anatomical, physiological and behavioural mechanisms designed to achieve the same end, that is the preservation of a constant internal environment. The advantage of a constant internal environment in providing optimal conditions in which organisms can live and reproduce most efficiently was first proposed by the French physiologist Claude Bernard in 1857. Throughout his research he had been impressed by the way in which organisms were able to regulate physiological parameters, such as body temperature and water content, and maintain them within fairly narrow ranges. This concept of self-regulation leading to physiological stability was summed up by Bernard in the now classic statement, 'La fixité du milieu interieur est la condition de la vie libre.' (The constancy of the internal environment is the condition of the free life.)

Bernard went on to distinguish between the **external environment** in which organisms live and the **internal environment** in which individual cells live (in mammals, this is tissue, or interstitial, fluid). He realised the importance of conditions in the latter being continuously stable. For example, mammals are capable of maintaining a constant body temperature despite fluctuations in the external temperature. If it is too cold the mammal may move to warmer or more sheltered conditions; if this is not possible, self-regulating mechanisms operate to raise the body temperature and prevent further heat loss. The adaptive significance of this is that the organism as a whole will function more efficiently because its constituent cells are maintained at optimum conditions. In this respect biological systems are seen to operate not only at the level of the organism but also at the level of the cell. An organism is the sum of its constituent cells and the optimum functioning of the whole depends upon the optimum functioning of its parts.

In 1932 the American physiologist Walter Cannon introduced the term **homeostasis** (*homoios*, same; *stasis*, standing) to describe the mechanisms whereby Bernard's 'constancy of the internal environment' is maintained. Homeostatic mechanisms function to maintain the stability of the cellular environment and in so doing provide the

organism with a degree of independence of the environment which is determined by the effectiveness of the mechanisms. Independence of the environment is used as a criterion of the success of an organism and on this basis mammals are seen as successful since they are able to maintain relatively constant levels of activity despite fluctuations in environmental conditions.

In order to achieve a degree of stability the activities of organisms need to be regulated at all levels of biological organisation, from the molecular to the population. This necessitates organisms employing a range of biochemical, physiological and behavioural mechanisms as are most appropriate to their level of complexity and mode of life. In all these respects mammals are seen to be better equipped than protozoa to cope with changes in environmental conditions.

Investigations have shown that the mechanisms of regulation found in organisms show many features in common with mechanisms of regulation in non-living systems, such as machines. The systems of both organisms and machines achieve stability by some form of control, to which Wiener, in 1948, applied the term **cybernetics** (*cybernos*, steersman). Cybernetics is the science of control mechanisms and is commonly referred to as **control theory**. Plant and animal physiologists have used many of the very precise mathematical models of control theory to explain the functioning of biological control systems, hence before studying some of these self-adjusting mechanisms, such as body temperature regulation, gaseous exchange rates, blood metabolite levels and water and ionic balances, it is necessary to have some appreciation of the theoretical considerations underlying control systems.

18.1 Control systems in biology

18.1.1 Introduction to control systems

The rigorous application of control theory to biology has led to a deeper understanding of the functional relationships between the components of many physiological mechanisms and has clarified many concepts which were previously obscure. For example, living systems are now seen to be **open systems**; that is they require a continuous exchange of matter between the environment and themselves. Living systems are, in fact, in steady state with their environment and require a continuous input of

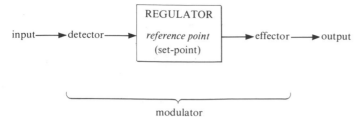

Fig 18.1 *Basic components of a control system*

energy in order to prevent them coming to equilibrium with the environment. This equilibrium is achieved only upon the death of the organism when it becomes thermodynamically stable with respect to its environment. The basic components of any control system are summarised in fig 18.1.

The efficiency of the control system is measured in terms of how little displacement from the reference point (optimal level) occurs and the speed with which the level is restored. Homeostatic mechanisms must be free to fluctuate, as it is the fluctuations themselves which activate the control systems and return the parameter towards its optimal level. Such control systems rely upon their components being linked together so that the output can be regulated in terms of the input, a concept known as **feedback**. In most feedback systems the output and input are identical.

Feedback requires the action of the system to be referred back to a **reference point** or **set-point**, which is the optimal level of the parameter (or **controlled variable**), so that subsequent action may be modified to restore the set-point. There are two forms of feedback, **negative** and **positive**. The former is most common in the homeostatic mechanisms of organisms.

Negative feedback is associated with incrcasing stability of systems (fig 18.2). If the system is disturbed, the disturbance or error sets in motion a sequence of events which counteract the disturbance and tend to restore the system to its original state. The principle of negative feedback may be described in terms of the regulation of

oven temperature by the use of a thermostat. In the electric oven the control system includes an **input** (an electric current flowing through an element which acts as a source of heat), an **output** (the oven temperature) and a thermostat which can be set to a desired level, the set-point. The thermostat acts as a modulator. If the thermostat is set to read 150 °C, an electric current will provide a source of heat which will flow until the oven temperature passes the set-point of 150 °C, then the thermostat will cut out and no more heat will be supplied to the oven. When the oven temperature falls below 150 °C the thermostat will cut in and the electric current will increase the temperature and restore the set-point. In this system the thermostat is functioning as an **error detector** where the error is the difference between the output and the set-point, The error is corrected by increasing the input. This is an example of a steady-state closed-loop system which is typical of many of the physiological control mechanisms found in organisms.

Examples of biological negative feedback mechanisms include the control of gas tensions in the blood, heart rate, arterial blood pressure, hormone and metabolite levels, water and ionic balances, the regulation of pH and body temperature. Fig 18.3 illustrates the role of negative feedback in the control of thyroxine release by the thyroid gland. In this example the modulator has three components, a **detector** (the hypothalamus), a **regulator** (the pituitary gland) and an **effector** (the thyroid gland).

Positive feedback is rare in biological systems since it leads to an unstable situation and extreme states. In these situations a disturbance leads to events which increase the disturbance even further (fig 18.2). For example, during the propagation of a nerve impulse, depolarisation of the neuronal membrane produces an increase in its sodium permeability. Sodium ions pass into the axon through the membrane and produce a further depolarisation which leads to the production of an action potential. In this case positive feedback acts as an amplifier of the response whose extent is limited by other mechanisms as described in section 16.1.1.

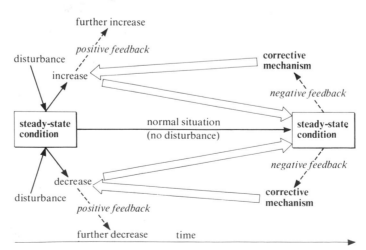

Fig 18.2 *Homeostatic control system. The directions of the lines on the diagram indicate the directions of stimulus and response*

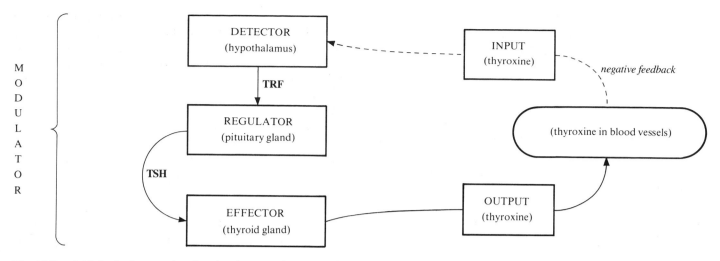

Fig 18.3 *A biological example of a simple control system, the control of thyroxine production. TRF, thyroid releasing factor; TSH, thyroid stimulating hormone; see section 16.6*

There are several control mechanisms in the body which are more complex than those previously described. Broadly they either involve the use of additional detectors (physiological early-warning systems) or effectors ('fail-safe' systems) operating at different levels. For example, temperature detectors situated externally and internally enable homeotherms to maintain an almost constant 'core' body temperature. Temperature receptors in the skin, acting as disturbance detectors of changes in the external environment, send impulses to the hypothalamus which acts as a modulator and initiates corrective measures before any change in blood temperature occurs. Other examples of this system include the control of ventilation during exercise, appetite and thirst. Similarly multiple detectors and effectors provide fail-safe mechanisms for many vital processes, such as regulation of arterial blood pressure where stretch receptors in the carotid sinus and aorta, and baroreceptors in the medulla, respond to blood pressure changes and produce responses in various effectors including the heart, blood vessels and kidneys. Failure of any one of these is compensated for by the others.

18.1.2   The nature and control of the internal environment

The internal environment of an organism and its control may be considered at two levels: the cellular level and the tissue level.

The cell is composed of cytoplasm whose constituents are modulated by the selective permeability of the cell membrane and by enzyme activity under the control of protein synthesis. The cell membrane only permits certain molecules to enter and leave the cell and the rates at which exchange is permitted are strictly controlled by diffusion gradients, osmotic gradients, electrical gradients, active mechanisms involving membrane-bound carrier systems and changes in membrane distribution as shown by pinocytosis and phagocytosis (section 7.2.2). Similarly the

nature and amounts of materials synthesised within the cell are controlled by the rates of protein synthesis. Metabolic activities in cells are determined by enzymes produced by the transcription and translation of the base sequence codes of DNA into the primary structure of proteins which act as enzymes. Regions of DNA carrying the code for a specific protein are known as genes and the 'switching on and off' of genes is thought to be controlled by systems of induction and repression which are described in detail in section 22.7. In terms of control systems the maintenance of a steady state within the cell depends upon the rates of supply and utilisation of cellular material, in other words the input and output, and the activity of the modulators (fig 18.4).

Both single-celled organisms and cells of multicellular organisms control their internal environments as described above. In the case of single-celled organisms their immediate environment is the external surroundings over which they have no control. They may, if they possess locomotory mechanisms, move to more favourable surroundings, but for the most part they are at the mercy of the environment. They adapt to, and tolerate, conditions as best they can. The sheer numbers of these minute species reflect their degree of success in surviving in spite of their structural simplicity.

The immediate environment of the cells of multicellular plants and animals is an extracellular fluid. This is called sap in plants, haemolymph in insects, water in echinoderms and tissue fluid in most other animals. The composition of this extracellular fluid can be regulated by the organisms to varying degrees depending upon the efficiency and effectiveness of their homeostatic organs. In mammals the immediate environment of all living cells is tissue fluid. The mechanism of formation of this remarkably stable fluid is described in chapter 14. Since the time of Bernard, the nature of the extracellular fluid and the mechanisms of its control have been widely studied. It is birds and mammals that show most control over the composition of the fluid

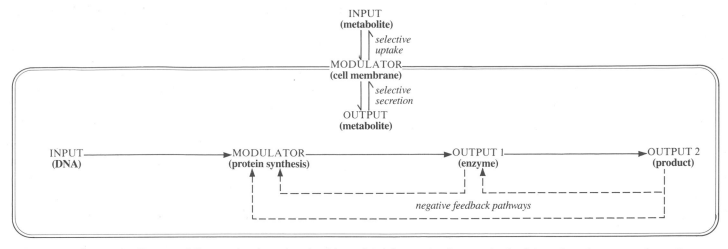

Fig. 18.4 *Summary diagram of the mechanisms involved in maintaining a steady state in the internal environment of a cell*

and its parameters of water, gases, ions, nutrients, hormones, excretory products, pH and temperature. In all cases these parameters have one or several tissues, organs or organ systems to maintain control within narrow limits.

The mechanisms of control in most animals involve responses by endocrine glands, or the nervous system coordinated by control centres in the brain and spinal cord (**regulators**) as shown in fig 18.5.

In conclusion it is worth re-emphasising the adaptive significance of homeostatic mechanisms. All metabolic systems operate most efficiently if maintained within narrow limits either side of optimal conditions. It is the role of homeostatic organs and systems to operate both separately and together to buffer against fluctuations from these optimal conditions caused by variations in the external and internal environments. Some of these mechanisms are discussed in the following sections.

18.1.3 Control of respiratory gases in the blood

The cells of the body require a continuous supply of oxygen from their immediate environment, the tissue fluid, in order to carry out respiration. Carbon dioxide, produced by this process, must not be allowed to accumulate in the cells or in the tissue fluid, as it would upset the equilibria of the reactions involved in respiration

and produce local changes in pH which would affect the rates of enzyme reactions. The body maintains a fine control over the concentration (or tension) of carbon dioxide in the blood despite variations in oxygen availability and metabolic demands which may increase twenty-fold during vigorous activity.

The rate and depth of ventilation (inspiration and expiration) are controlled by **respiratory centres** situated in the pons and the medulla oblongata at the base of the brain (fig 18.6). These centres generate rhythmic impulses to the diaphragm and intercostal muscles which bring about ventilation movements. This rhythm is basically involuntary but can be overridden within limits by higher centres of the brain, as shown by the ability to hold the breath. The rate and depth of ventilation directly governs the composition of the alveolar air which, in turn, determines the oxygen and carbon dioxide tensions in the arterial blood supplied to the body tissues. The mean partial pressures of oxygen and carbon dioxide in alveolar air and the arterial blood are 100 mm Hg and 40 mm Hg respectively in a resting subject at sea level. The maintenance of the above levels is achieved by negative feedback to the respiratory centres in the medulla of impulses from two types of receptors: mechanical stretch receptors (proprioceptors) in the walls of the trachea and lungs, and chemoreceptors in the wall of the aorta, the carotid bodies (situated in the walls of the carotid arteries) and in the medulla itself.

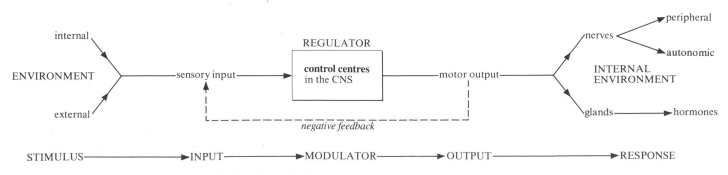

Fig 18.5 *Homeostatic mechanisms for the control of the internal environment*

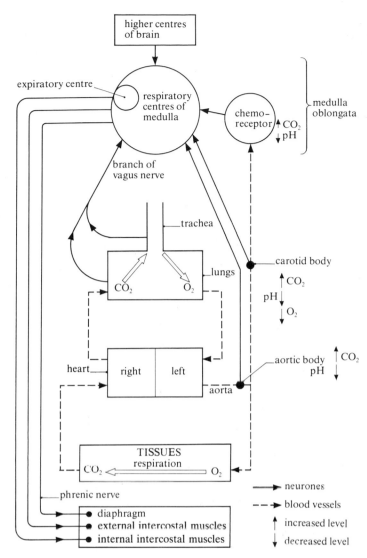

Fig 18.6 *Summary diagram of mechanisms involved in the control of respiratory gases in the blood*

trachea and lungs are no longer stimulated there is no inhibition of the inspiratory respiratory centre and the ventilation cycle repeats. During vigorous activity increased carbon dioxide in the blood stimulates the expiratory centre and impulses pass to the internal intercostal muscles which contract more frequently and this leads to deep or forced breathing.

The rate and depth of ventilation is governed by the activity of chemoreceptors in response to changes in oxygen and carbon dioxide tensions in the blood. Experiments involving subjects breathing air composed of varying concentrations of oxygen and carbon dioxide have shown that the effects of increasing carbon dioxide levels are more important in controlling ventilation than oxygen levels. Reducing the oxygen concentration of air from 20% to 5% produces a doubling of the normal resting ventilation rate, whereas an increase of only 0.2% in carbon dioxide concentration produces the same response.

The influence of carbon dioxide concentrations and reduced blood pH in regulating ventilation rate is mediated almost entirely through chemoreceptors in the aorta, carotid bodies and in the medulla itself. Chemoreceptors in the aorta and carotid bodies are also sensitive to changes in oxygen concentration and are vital when oxygen concentrations are low, because a fall in oxygen concentration depresses activity of the medulla. Increased ventilation facilitates loss of carbon dioxide from the blood by diffusion into the alveolar air which is brought to a new lower equilibrium with atmospheric air. The same effect is achieved by deliberate deep breathing or **hyperventilation**.

> **18.1** Explain why the ventilation rate decreases and subjects feel dizzy and faint after hyperventilating.

At high altitudes (in excess of 3 000 m) the partial pressures of oxygen and carbon dioxide in the atmosphere are reduced. This results in the oxygen and carbon dioxide concentrations in the alveolar air coming to a new equilibrium with those of the atmosphere. Consequently more carbon dioxide is lost from the blood into the alveolar air due to the lower concentration here. As there is insufficient carbon dioxide in the blood to stimulate the carbon dioxide chemoreceptors the stimulus for ventilation cannot be carbon dioxide. Instead, low oxygen concentrations stimulate chemoreceptors in the carotid body which activates the respiratory centres.

There is a close relationship between the respiratory centres and the cardiovascular centre which are both situated in the medulla. Changes in blood pressure, which are maintained by the cardiovascular centre, affect the ventilation rate, for instance ventilation rate increases as the blood pressure falls and vice versa. Equally, changes in respiratory gas concentrations, as monitored by the respiratory centres, will produce changes in blood pressure (section 14.12.6).

Higher centres in the brain can override this feedback and voluntarily inhibit or increase the activity of the respiratory centres, such as during breath-holding, forced breathing, speech, singing, sneezing and coughing.

The effect of impulses from the stretch receptors is mainly concerned with the mechanics of ventilation movements. Impulses generated by the respiratory centres pass down efferent neurones in the spinal cord; some emerge in the cervical region as the phrenic nerves to the diaphragm, other neurones emerge from the thoracic region of the spinal cord as the external intercostal nerves. Together they produce the inspiratory movements. The lungs inflate, and stretch receptors in the walls of the lungs and trachea activate afferent neurones of the vagus which temporarily inhibit the inspiratory respiratory centre, preventing further inspiratory activity. Elastic properties of the lungs produce recoil as the diaphragm relaxes reducing the volume of the thorax and thus expiration of air from the lungs occurs. As the stretch receptors in the

18.1.4 Control of metabolites in the blood

One of the most important metabolites in the blood whose level must be strictly controlled is glucose. This sugar is the principal respiratory substrate and must be continuously supplied to cells. The brain cells are especially sensitive to glucose and are unable to utilise any other metabolites as an energy source. Lack of glucose results in fainting. The normal level of glucose in the blood is about 90 mg 100 cm^{-3} blood, but may vary from 70 to 150 mg 100 cm^{-3} blood during fasting and following a meal, respectively. The sources of blood glucose and its metabolic interrelationships with other metabolites are described in section 18.5.2.

The control of blood glucose level is an example of a complex, endocrine-regulated homeostatic mechanism involving the integrated secretion of at least six hormones and two negative feedback pathways. A rise in blood glucose level (**hyperglycaemia**) stimulates insulin secretion (section 16.6.7) whereas a fall in blood glucose level (**hypoglycaemia**) inhibits insulin secretion and stimulates the secretion of glucagon (section 16.6.7) and other hormones which raise blood glucose levels (hyperglycaemic factors). The control mechanism is summarised in fig 18.7.

18.1.5 Control of heart rate and blood pressure

Variations in heart rate and blood pressure have an indirect effect upon the composition of tissue fluid and enable it to be kept within narrow limits despite fluctuations in the external environment and varying demands imposed on tissues. The mechanisms of control involve the activity of the autonomic system and details of these mechanisms are described in section 14.12.5.

There are two major conditions of abnormal heart rate, tachycardia and bradycardia. **Tachycardia** (*tachys*, swift; *cardia*, heart) is a general term describing an increased heart rate and may be caused by a variety of factors including emotional states, such as anxiety, anger and laughter, and overactivity of the thyroid gland. Severe tachycardia is often the result of changes in the electrical activity of the heart. Regions of the heart, other than the S–A node, can act as foci for the origin of the stimulus producing contraction of the heart muscle and augment the normal heart activity, based on the S–A node, producing tachycardia.

Bradycardia (*bradys*, slow) describes the condition where the heart rate is reduced below the mean level. It is common in athletes who develop an increased stroke volume as a result of training. Therefore, in order to maintain a constant cardiac output at all times their resting heart rate is reduced. Underactivity of the thyroid gland, and changes in the electrical activity of the S–A node and other conductile regions of the cardiac tissue, can also give rise to bradycardia.

The antagonistic regulatory effects of the sympathetic and parasympathetic nervous systems on the S–A node tend to counteract temporary conditions of tachycardia and bradycardia and restore the normal heart rhythm.

Blood pressure is the force developed by the blood pushing against the walls of the blood vessels. It is usually measured in the brachial artery using a **sphygmomano-**

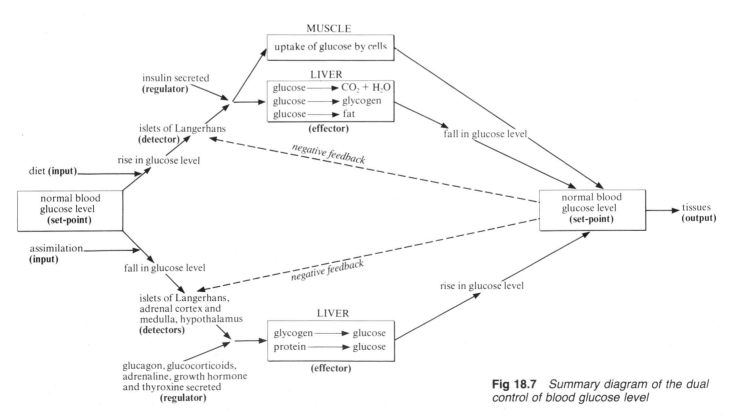

Fig 18.7 *Summary diagram of the dual control of blood glucose level*

meter. The **systolic** pressure is produced by the contraction of the ventricles and the **diastolic** pressure is the pressure in the arteries when the ventricles relax. Blood pressure is affected by age, sex and state of health, and the mean pressures for a healthy young man are 120 mm Hg (systolic) and 80 mm Hg(diastolic). Both pressures are affected by cardiac output and peripheral resistance and indicate the general state of heart and blood vessels. Conditions which lead to narrowing and hardening of the arteries (**atherosclerosis**) or damage to the kidneys may increase the blood pressure, a condition known as **hypertension**, and impose a strain on the heart and blood vessels. This may lead to a weakening of artery walls and their rupture, or the clogging of narrowed vessels by blood clots (thrombosis). These are very serious if they affect the brain or the heart and lead to cerebral haemorrhage (stroke), cerebral thrombosis or coronary thrombosis.

18.1.6 Control of infection

The many mechanisms of defence against infection are homeostatic in that they attempt to maintain a constant internal environment. The skin is the major defence against infection, but viruses, bacteria, protozoa, round worms and flatworms can invade the tissues through natural openings, cuts and by boring through the skin. The presence of pathogens and their toxic waste products in the body evoke several defence mechanisms including the activity of various white blood cells (phagocytes, monocytes and lymphocytes). The mechanisms of blood clotting, wound healing and immunity are described in detail in sections 14.13.5 and 14.14.)

18.2 Temperature regulation

Heat is a form of energy with an important influence upon the maintenance of living systems. All living systems require a continuous supply of heat in order to prevent degradation and cessation of those systems.

The major source of heat for all living organisms is the Sun. Solar radiation is converted into an exogenous (outside the body) source of heat energy whenever it strikes and is absorbed by a body. The extent and effect of this solar radiation depends upon geographical location, and is a major factor in affecting the climate of a region. This, in turn, determines the presence and abundance of species. For example, organisms inhabit regions where the normal air temperatures vary from −40 °C, as in the Arctic, to 50 °C in desert regions. In some of the latter regions the surface temperature may rise as high as 80 °C. The majority of living organisms exist within confined limits of temperature, say 10–35 °C, but various organisms show adaptations enabling them to exploit geographical areas at both extremes of temperature (fig 18.8). This is not the only source of heat available to organisms. Solar radiation of wavelengths within those of the visible spectrum are used by photosynthetic autotrophs and this energy becomes

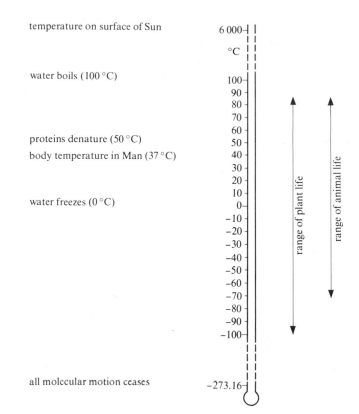

Fig 18.8 *Temperature reference points in living organisms and the ranges of temperature they are able to tolerate*

locked up in the chemical bonds of synthesised organic molecules (chapter 9). This provides an endogenous (within the body) source of heat energy when released by the catabolic reactions of respiration (chapter 11).

Temperature indicates the amount of heat energy in a system and is a major factor determining the rate of chemical reactions in both living and non-living systems. As described in section 6.4.3, heat energy increases the rate at which atoms and molecules move and this increases the probability of reactions occuring between them. The relationship between temperature and the rate of chemical reactions is expressed as the temperature coefficient, or Q_{10}. In living systems temperature has an effect upon enzyme structure which influences the rate of metabolism and exerts the major influence on the distribution and activity of organisms.

18.2.1 The influence of temperature on the growth and distribution of plants

Temperature can act as a limiting factor in the growth and development of plants by influencing the rates of cell division, cell metabolism and photosynthesis. The non-light-requiring reactions of photosynthesis are temperature dependent and control the various metabolic pathways described in chapter 9. The rates of photosynthesis, and the accumulation of sufficient food materials to enable the plant to complete its life-cycle, are factors determining the geographical range of plants.

18.2.2 Adaptations to low temperatures in plants

The flora of northern temperate climates and the tundra show many adaptations enabling plants to take maximum advantage of the short, warm summers. For example, the only plant species found are mosses, lichens, a few grasses and fast-growing annuals. Plants living in extreme northerly or southerly latitudes are subjected to long periods of adverse conditions, such as low light intensity, low temperatures and frozen soil. In order to survive in these conditions, plants shown many anatomical, physiological and behavioural adaptations which may be related to stages in the life cycle. For example, most temperate woody perennials are deciduous and lose their leaves, under the influence of the plant growth regulator substance abscisic acid (ABA), in order to prevent water loss by transpiration and evaporation during periods when soil water uptake is limited by low temperatures (section 15.2.8). Wind and snow damage is also avoided by the shedding of leaves during these periods when the rate of photosynthesis would be severely limited by low light intensities, low temperatures and unavailability of water and salts. Throughout these periods the regions of next year's growth, the buds, are protected by scale leaves and their metabolic activity is suppressed by the presence of a growth regulator substance called **dormin**. This is so called because of its effects. Recent investigations, however, have shown this to be abscisic acid. Many coniferous species dominate the vegetation of the more temperate regions, particularly in northern latitudes. These species have needle-like leaves which reduce the amount of snow which can accumulate on them in winter and have a thick cuticle to prevent water loss in summer. Many species of annuals have short growing periods and survive the winter by producing resistant seeds or organs of perennation. Lower plants survive by producing resistant cysts which may remain viable for hundreds of years, as demonstrated by cysts which have germinated following their removal from the permafrost of Siberia.

Low temperatures are required by many plant species in order to break dormancy and initiate vernalisation. For example, lilac buds develop more quickly after being exposed to low temperatures than to high temperatures. Other examples of the effects of low temperature on plant growth are described in chapter 15 and section 21.6.

18.2.3 Adaptations to high temperatures in plants

In many regions of the world high temperatures are associated with water shortage, and many of the adaptations shown by plants in these regions are related to their ability to resist desiccation and their need to lose water in order to cool themselves.

Plants are unable to escape high temperatures by moving to shaded areas and therefore they have to rely on morphological and physiological adaptations to avoid overheating. It is the aerial parts of plants which are exposed to the heating effect of solar radiation, and the largest exposed surface is that of the leaves. Leaves characteristically are thin structures with a large surface area to volume ratio to facilitate gaseous exchange and light absorption. This structure is ideal for preventing damage by excessive heating. A thin leaf has a relatively low heat capacity and therefore will usually assume the temperature of the surroundings, a phenomenon known as **heterothermism**. This effect is offset in hot regions by the development of a shiny cuticle secreted by the epidermis and which reflects much of the incident light, thus preventing heat being absorbed and overheating the plant. The large surface area contains numerous stomatal openings which permit transpiration. As much as $0.5 \text{ kg m}^{-2} \text{ h}^{-1}$ of water may be lost from plants by transpiration in hot, dry weather, which would account for the loss of approximately 350 W m^{-2} in terms of heat energy. This is nearly half the total amount of energy being absorbed. As a result of these mechanisms plants are able to exercise a considerable degree of control over their temperature. This ability is closely coupled to the relative humidity of the air.

> **18.2** Why do plants suffer permanent physiological damage if exposed to temperatures in excess of 30 °C when the humidity is high?

During hot, sunny days many plants in danger of overheating show a phenomenon known as '**photosynthetic slump**'. This is thought to result from a temporary cessation of metabolic activity as a result of changes in enzyme structure, or the closure of stomata as a result of a build-up of respiratory carbon dioxide within the guard cells. It is possible, however, that the reason for closure of the stomata is simply one of transient lack of water in the leaf. Wilting is a common response to high temperatures and reduced water uptake. An imbalance between the rates of transpiration and water uptake results in an overall loss of turgidity by those plant cells lacking a thickened cell wall, such as parenchyma. The adaptive significance of this response is to reduce the leaf surface area which is exposed to direct sunlight, thereby preventing overheating. **Wilting** may be observed in plants growing in greenhouses in response to the very high temperatures which develop in the leaves, even if adequately supplied with water. Once the temperature begins to fall the plants recover very quickly even if the degree of wilting looks severe.

Plants living in dry conditions are called **xerophytes** and show many morphological adaptations which enable them to survive (section 19.3.2). In most cases these adaptations are primarily concerned with regulating water loss, although the characteristic needle-shaped leaves permit maximum heat dissipation. The mechanisms for withstanding high temperatures, on the other hand, are mainly physiological.

18.2.4 The influence of temperature on the growth and distribution of animals

Temperature influences the metabolic activity of animals and plants primarily through its influence on enzymes and the mobility of atoms and molecules. This directly affects the rate of growth of animals (chapter 21). In addition, temperature may also affect the geographical distribution and ecological preferences of animals through its influence on plants as primary producers in the food chains. The ecological range of most animal species, with the exception of some insects, birds and mammals able to migrate, is determined by local availability of particular food materials. Restricted powers of locomotion limit other organisms to feeding on readily available food sources which are determined by the trophic relationships existing in the ecosystem.

The variety of responses shown by animals to temperature depends upon the degree of thermal stability shown by the environment and the degree of control the organism is able to exercise over its own body temperature. Life is believed to have originated in the marine environment, the environment that poses fewest problems to living organisms. Temperature fluctuations in aquatic environments are slight and the biological significance of this is that aquatic organisms occupy a relatively stable environment with regard to temperature. Most of these organisms, including invertebrates and fish, have a body temperature which varies according to the temperature of the water, though some very active fish such as the tuna are able to maintain body temperatures in excess of that of the water. However, aquatic animals rarely need to exhibit the physiological and behavioural responses shown by terrestrial animals because the physical properties of the water buffer them against sudden and extreme fluctuations. Water has a maximum density at 4 °C and consequently only the surface of the water freezes at 0 °C as ice floats. This enables many aquatic animals to continue to be active at times when most terrestrial organisms would be inactive due to sub-zero conditions.

Air has a relatively low specific heat and therefore air temperature can fluctuate widely over a 24 h period. One of the problems associated with the colonisation of land by animals was adapting to, or tolerating, these temperature fluctuations. This has produced many physiological, behavioural and ecological responses, as well as being a major determinant of geographical distribution. The nature of these responses and examples are described in subsequent sections.

18.2.5 Sources of heat for animals

All animals derive heat from two sources, the external environment and from the release of chemical energy within their cells. The extent to which animals are able to generate and conserve this heat depends upon physiological mechanisms associated with their phylogenetic position. All invertebrates, fish, amphibia and reptiles

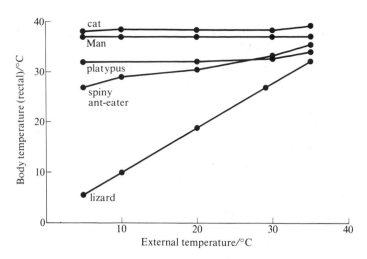

Fig 18.9 *The relationships between external and internal temperatures in vertebrates kept for 2 h at the temperatures indicated*

are unable to maintain their body temperature within narrow limits. Consequently these animals are described as **poikilothermic** (*poikilos*, various; *therme*, heat). Alternatively, because they rely more on heat derived from the environment than metabolic heat in order to raise their body temperature, they are termed **ectothermic** (*ecto*, outside). These animals used to be described as 'cold-blooded' but this is a misleading and inaccurate term.

Birds and mammals are able to maintain a fairly constant body temperature independently of the environmental temperature. They are described as **homeothermic** (or **homoiothermic** – *homoios*, like) or less correctly as 'warm-blooded'. Homeotherms are relatively independent of external sources of heat and rely on a high metabolic rate to generate heat which must be conserved. Since these animals rely on internal sources of heat they are described as **endothermic** (*endos*, inside). Some poikilotherms may, at times, have temperatures higher than those of homeotherms and in order to prevent ambiguity, the terms ectotherm and endotherm are used throughout the text. Fig 18.9 shows the abilities of several vertebrates to regulate their body temperature in various external temperatures.

18.2.6 Body temperature

Whenever reference is made to body temperature in animal studies it usually refers to the **core temperature**. This is the temperature of the tissues below a level of 2.5 cm beneath the surface of the skin. This temperature is normally determined by taking the rectal temperature. Temperatures in other regions of the body can vary tremendously depending upon position and the external temperatures (fig 18.10).

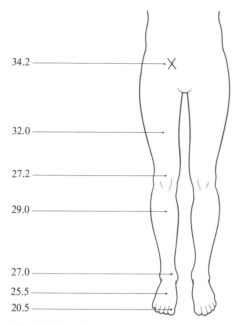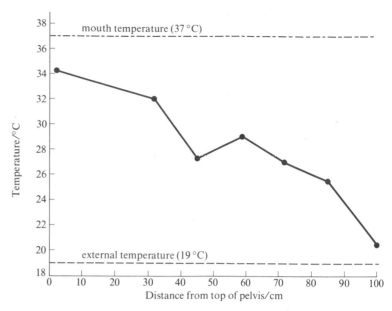

Fig 18.10 *Skin temperatures recorded at various distances from point X at the top of the pelvis. The limb was exposed to an external temperature of 19 °C throughout the period of recording. The low temperature at the knee cap probably reflects the poorer blood supply to this organ*

Whilst the main source of *gaining* heat differs between ectotherms and endotherms, the methods of heat transfer between organism and the environment are the same in both types of organism and these are radiation, convection, conduction and evaporation. Heat can be transferred in either direction by the first three methods depending upon the **thermal gradient** (the direction of the temperature difference from hot to cold) but can only be *lost* from organisms by the latter method.

Radiation. Heat is transferred by electromagnetic waves which lie in the long-wave, infra-red region of the electromagnetic spectrum, beyond the visible spectrum. Bodies do not radiate heat to air, since it is unable to absorb much radiant heat, but transfer it to other bodies at a rate which is proportional to the temperature difference between the two bodies. Radiation accounts for about 50% of the total heat loss in Man and provides the main route for controlled heat loss in animals.

Convection. Heat is transferred between organism and environment by passage through the air. In the case of endotherms, where the ambient (air) temperature is usually lower than body temperature, the air in contact with the organism rapidly becomes warm, rises, and is replaced by cooler air. The rate of heat transfer by this method is linked to the rate of air movement which continually brings cooler air into contact with the body. It may be reduced by materials covering the skin such as feathers, fur, hair and clothing.

Conduction. Heat is transferred by physical contact between two bodies, for instance the organism and the ground. Heat exchange by this means is relatively insignificant for most terrestrial organisms, but may be considerable for aquatic and soil-dwelling organisms.

Evaporation. Heat is lost from the body surface during the conversion of water to water vapour. The evaporation of 1 cm³ of water (1 g) requires the loss of 2.45 kJ from the body. Water loss by evaporation takes place continuously through the skin and from the lungs, as expired air, and this **insensible** water loss cannot be controlled. It is a limiting factor in the distribution of many plant and animal species. **Regulated** evaporative heat loss is controlled and involves water loss by sweating and panting.

18.3 Ectothermic animals

The majority of animals are ectothermic, and their activity is determined by the prevailing environmental temperature. The metabolic rate of ectotherms is relatively low and they lack mechanisms for conserving heat. Aquatic ectotherms live within a restricted temperature range, or **zone of tolerance**, determined by the size of the body of water in which they live. For example, the temperature of a pond can vary considerably throughout the year, whereas that of an ocean may change by only a few degrees. Despite this wide temperature fluctuation in small bodies of water, many insect species have aquatic larval and pupal, or nymphal, stages, since the aquatic temperatures are more stable and less extreme than terrestrial temperatures during the winter months. Mayflies, dragonflies, caddisflies, midges and mosquitoes all have an aquatic diapause (section 21.10.1).

Aquatic invertebrates are able to tolerate greater temperature fluctuations than aquatic vertebrates due to their relatively simple morphology and physiology. Fish have a higher rate of metabolism than aquatic invertebrates but the majority of this endogenous heat is rapidly dissipated around the body and lost to the environment by conduction through the gills and skin. Consequently, fish usually have a body temperature which is at thermal equilibrium with that of the water. Fish cannot maintain a temperature below that of the water but may in some cases, as in the case of tuna fish, retain heat by means of a countercurrent heat-exchanger system. This can raise the temperature of the 'red' swimming muscle to about 12 °C above that of the sea water.

Terrestrial ectotherms have to contend with greater temperature fluctuations than those of aquatic ectotherms, but they have the benefit of living at higher environmental temperatures. This allows them to be more active and show a variety of complex behavioural patterns based upon the prevailing temperature conditions. Many species are able to maintain temperatures slightly above or below air temperature and thereby avoid extremes. The relatively poor thermal conductivity of air reduces the rate of heat loss from organisms whilst water loss by evaporation may be used to cool the organism.

18.3.1 Temperature regulation in terrestrial ectotherms

Heat is gained and lost by terrestrial ectotherms by behavioural and physiological activities. The main sources of heat gain are the absorption of solar radiation and conduction from the air and the ground. The amount of heat absorbed depends upon the colour of the organism, its surface area and position relative to the Sun's rays. For example, a species of Australian grasshopper is dark in colour at low temperatures and absorbs solar radiation thus heating up rapidly. As the temperature rises above a set point, further absorption is reduced by the cuticle lightening in colour. This colour change is believed to be a direct response shown in pigment cells to body temperature. These organisms are known as **basking heliotherms** (*helios*, sun).

Changes in orientation of the organism relative to the Sun's rays vary the surface area exposed to heating. This practice is common in many terrestrial ectotherms including insects, arachnids, amphibia and reptiles. It is a form of behavioural thermoregulation. For example, the desert locust (*Schistocerca*) is relatively inactive at 17 °C but by aligning itself at right-angles to the Sun's rays it is able to absorb heat energy. As the air temperature rises to approximately 40 °C it re-orientates itself parallel to the Sun's rays to reduce the exposed surface area. Further increase in temperature, which may prove fatal, is prevented by raising the body off the ground or climbing up vegetation. Air temperature falls off rapidly over short distances above ground level and these movements enable the locust to secure a more favourable microclimate (section 12.4.4).

Crocodiles too, regulate their body temperature on land by varying their position relative to the Sun's rays and opening their mouths to increase heat loss by evaporation.

If the temperature becomes too high, they move into the water which is relatively cooler. Conversely, at night they retreat to water in order to avoid the low temperatures which would be experienced on land. Thermoregulation mechanisms have been studied most extensively in lizards.

Many different species of lizard have been studied and show a variety of responses to different temperatures. Lizards are terrestrial reptiles and exhibit many behavioural activities in keeping with other ectotherms; but some species employ a number of physiological mechanisms enabling them to raise and maintain their body temperatures above that of the environment, an example is the Australian monitor (*Varanus*). Other species are able to keep their body temperature within confined limits by varying their activity and taking advantage of shade or exposure. In both these respects lizards foreshadow many of the mechanisms of homeothermy shown by birds and mammals.

Surface temperatures in desert regions can rise to 70–80 °C during the day and fall to 4 °C at dawn. In these circumstances most lizards seek refuge, during these extremes, by living in burrows or beneath stones. This response and certain physiological responses are shown by the horned lizard (*Phrynosoma*) which inhabits the deserts of the south-west of the USA and Mexico. In addition to burrowing, the horned lizard is able to vary its orientation and colour, and as the temperature becomes high it can also reduce its body surface area by pulling back its ribs. Other responses to high temperatures involve panting, which removes heat by the evaporation of water from the mouth, pharynx and lungs, eye bulging and the elimination of urine from the cloaca.

The moist skin of amphibia provides an ideal mechanism to enable heat to be lost by evaporation. This water loss, however, cannot be regulated physiologically as in mammals. Amphibia lose water immediately on exposure to dry conditions and, whilst this aids heat loss, it would lead to dehydration if the amphibia did not find moist shaded conditions where the rate of evaporation would be reduced. The marine iguana (*Amblyrhynchus*), a reptile, normally maintains a temperature of 37 °C as it basks on the rocky shores of the Galapagos Islands, but it needs to spend a considerable time in the sea feeding on seaweed at a temperature of approximately 25 °C. In order to avoid losing heat rapidly when immersed in water the iguana reduces the blood flow between surface and core tissues by slowing its heart rate (bradycardia).

18.4 Endothermic animals

Birds and mammals are endothermic and their activity is largely independent of prevailing environmental temperatures. In order to maintain a constant body temperature, which is normally higher than the ambient (air) temperature, these organisms need to have a high metabolic rate and an efficient means of controlling heat loss from the body surface. The skin is the organ of the body in contact with the environment and therefore monitors the changing temperatures. The actual regulation of temperature by various metabolic processes is controlled by the hypothalamus of the brain.

18.4.1 Skin

The term, skin, applies to the outer covering of vertebrate animals and should not be used to describe the outer covering of annelids, molluscs or arthropods. The skin is the largest organ of the body and is made up of connective tissue, blood vessels, sweat glands and sense cells. These enable it to fulfil a great many different functions. The structure of the skin varies in different vertebrate groups and the major differences will be discussed after the basic structure of human skin has been described.

Human skin structure

The skin is composed of two main layers, the epidermis and dermis, that overly the subcutaneous tissue which contains specialised fat-containing cells known as **adipose tissue**. The thickness of this layer varies according to region of the body and from person to person.

Epidermis. The cells of this region are ectodermal in origin and are separated from the dermis by a basement membrane. The epidermis is composed of many layers of cells forming a stratified epithelium (section 8.3.2). The cells above the basement membrane are cuboid epithelial cells (section 8.3.1) and form an actively dividing region known as the **Malpighian layer**. By repeated division of its cells, this region gives rise to all of the cells of the epidermis. The Malpighian layer forms the lower region of the **stratum granulosum**, which is composed of living cells becoming flatter as they approach the outer region of the epidermis, the **stratum corneum**. Cells in this region become progressively flattened and synthesise **keratin**, which is a fibrous sulphur-containing protein

(a)

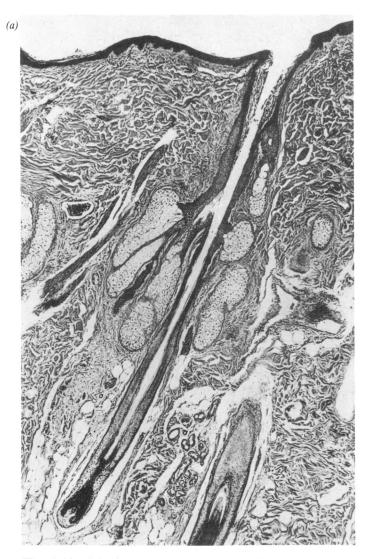

(b)

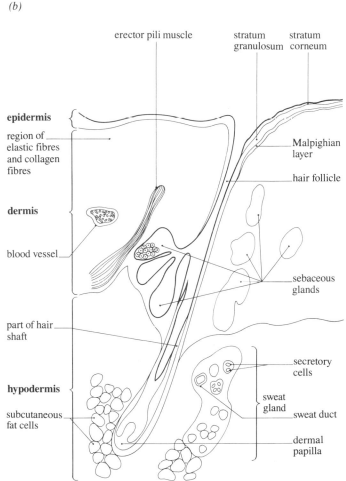

Fig 18.11 (a) VS through human skin. (b) Diagram of skin structure based on (a)

which makes the cells waterproof. As the keratin content of the cells increases they become cornified, their nuclei disappear and the cells die. The thickness of the stratum corneum increases in parts of the body where there is considerable friction, such as the ball of the foot and the bases of the fingers. The outer covering of the skin forms a semi-transparent, thin, tough, pliant, waterproof covering pierced by pores, which are the openings of the sweat glands, and by the hair follicles. The outermost squamous epithelial cells are continually being shed as a result of friction.

The stratum corneum has become modified in many vertebrates to produce nails, claws, hooves, horns, antlers, scales, feathers and hair. Keratin is the main component of all these structures.

Dermis. Most of the cells of the dermis are mesodermal in origin. The dermis is a dense matrix composed of connective tissue rich in elastic fibres and containing blood capillaries, lymph vessels, muscle fibres, sensory cells, nerve fibres, chromatophores (pigment cells), sweat glands and hair follicles.

Hair follicles are epidermal invaginations with a root hair, or papilla, at the base from which the hair shaft develops. Hair is composed of cuboid epithelial cells which become cornified by impregnation with keratin. The outer cortex of the hair contains varying amounts of the pigment melanin which determines hair colour. The medulla of the hair may contain air bubbles, and as the number increases with age and melanin production falls off the hair becomes grey. Blood capillaries supply the growing hair with nourishment and remove waste substances. The upper part of the hair projects beyond the epidermis and is kept supple and prevented from becoming wetted by **sebum**, an oily secretion produced by **sebaceous glands** which open into the hair follicle. Sebum contains fatty acids, waxes and steroids, and spreads along the hair and onto the skin where it keeps the follicle free from dust and bacteria, as well as forming a thin waterproof layer over the skin. This not only prevents water loss from the skin but also prevents water entering the skin.

At the base of the follicle is a smooth muscle, the **erector pili muscle** which has its origin on the basement membrane and its insertion on the hair follicle. Contraction of this muscle alters the angle between the hair and the skin which results in variation of the amount of air trapped above the skin. This is used as a means of thermoregulation and also as a behavioural response to danger in some vertebrates. When the hair 'stands on end' it increases the apparent size of the organism which may be sufficient to frighten off would-be attackers. The distribution of hair in humans in much more restricted than in other mammals.

Sweat glands are coiled tubular exocrine glands situated in the dermis and connected to sweat pores by a duct. They are found over the entire body in Man, but in some mammals are restricted to the pads of the feet. They are absent in birds. Water, salts and urea are brought to the glands by blood capillaries, and the secretory activity of the glands is controlled by the activity of the sympathetic nerve fibres. There are two types of sweat glands, **eccrine** and **apocrine**. The former are the most common (approximately 2.5×10^6 in Man), being found in most regions of the body, and the latter are found in the arm pits, around the nipples, the pubic region, hands, feet and anus. These release an odourless fluid, which may later produce an unpleasant odour due to bacterial activity in this fluid. Certain zinc and aluminium compounds can inhibit the activity of the glands and destroy bacteria. Most anti-perspirants and deodorants contain these compounds.

Blood capillaries are numerous in the dermis and supply the various structures already described. Many of the capillaries form loops and have shunts (fig 18.12) which enable the body to vary the amount of blood flowing through the cutaneous capillaries. This is one of the many ways of regulating body temperature, as described in section 18.4.3.

Motor neurones innervate the muscles and glands in the dermis whilst sensory neurones carry nerve impulses from the many sense cells situated in the dermis. These sense cells detect heat, cold, touch, pain and pressure. Some of the sense cells are simple and consist of free nerve endings, whereas others, such as the Pacinian corpuscle, are encapsulated.

Vertebrate skin structure

The skin of other vertebrates differs in various ways from the structure described above. Fish have well-developed scales or dermal plates and mucus-secreting glands. Amphibia have a smooth skin which is made slippery by the secretion of mucus from the many glands in the dermis. This mucus is watery and keeps the skin moist to facilitate gaseous exchange. In some species, such as toads, the secretion is distasteful to predators. The dermis contains numerous pigment cells enabling amphibia to alter their colouration to blend in with the background, and also to absorb or reflect solar radiation. There are many subcutaneous lymph spaces and the skin is only attached to the underlying muscles at intervals which makes the skin extremely loose.

Reptiles have horny scales covering the body and these form an impermeable layer. The skin is always dry, and the numerous chromatophores in the epidermis enable reptiles to alter their colouration. Birds have developed feathers which are outgrowths from the epidermis. There are different types of feathers carrying specific functions (section 17.7.6) but they all contribute to preventing heat loss from the body. Birds maintain relatively high body temperatures, about 40–43 °C, and as they have a large surface area to volume ratio they need an efficient means of preventing heat loss.

All mammals possess sweat glands and hair, and the number and distribution of these two structures reflect the efficiency of control of heat balance.

Functions of mammalian skin

Skin has four main functions. Temperature regulation is described in detail in section 18.4.3. Further functions are as follows.

Protection. The skin protects the internal organs from damage, dehydration and disease. The cornified epidermis prevents damage by friction, particularly in those regions where pressure and chafing develop. The dermis and subcutaneous tissues prevent mechanical damage from bumps and knocks. Melanin, the dark pigment found in chromatophores, protects the body from excessive harmful ultra-violet light. Variations in hair or fur pigment, giving patterns, provide camouflage against the background of the natural habitat. In several species, such as stoat and the arctic hare, the overall colour changes according to the season and thus helps to protect the organism from attack by predators or recognition by its prey. The cornified layer and sebum prevent uncontrolled water loss by evaporation. Sebum also prevents the fur of aquatic mammals, such as the otter, from wetting, which would destroy the insulatory properties of the air trapped in the hair. The entry of pathogens, including bacteria, viruses, fungi, protozoa, roundworms and flatworms, into the body is greatly hindered by the structure of the skin. Micro-organisms can nevertheless enter through hair follicles and sweat glands and through the bites of insect vectors. The larval stages of many parasitic worms, such as *Schistosoma*, are capable of boring through the skin.

Vitamin production. Ultra-violet radiations from the Sun convert a group of steroids, known as sterols, to vitamin D. This is only a secondary source of the vitamin since most is obtained in the diet (section 10.3.10).

Energy storage. Fat is deposited as adipose tissue in the lower regions of the dermis and also in a subcutaneous position. The secondary effect of this is to provide thermal insulation as described in section 18.4.3. Many mammals build up a store of fat under the skin in preparation for adverse climatic conditions.

18.4.2 Sources of heat

The major source of heat in endotherms is produced from the exothermic biochemical reactions which occur in living cells. This heat is released by the breakdown of molecules derived from the diet, principally carbohydrates and fats. The amount of heat released in a resting fasting organism is known as the **basal metabolic rate** (BMR) and provides a 'base-line' for comparing the energy demands during various activities, and in different organism (see section 11.7.6). The energy content of food required to meet the demands of the basal metabolic rate for an average-sized male human over a 24 h period is approximately 8 000 kJ. The exact amount per individual depends upon size, age and sex, being slightly higher in males.

Most of the metabolic energy which appears as heat energy comes from active tissues such as the liver and voluntary (skeletal) muscle. The rate of energy release is regulated by other factors such as environmental temperature and hormones. Thyroxine, released from the thyroid gland, increases the metabolic rate and therefore heat production. The effects of this hormone are long term, whereas the effects of adrenaline are mostly short-lived. Other sources of metabolic heat energy are initiated by nerve impulses. Repeated stimulation of voluntary muscle by somatic motor neurones produces the shivering response which can increase heat production by up to five times the basal level. During shivering various groups of muscle fibres within a muscle contract and relax out of phase, so that the overall response is an uncoordinated movement. This response may be reinforced by other muscular activity such as rubbing the hands together, stamping the feet and limited forms of exercise. In many mammals there are areas near the thoracic blood vessels which are rich in brown fat cells; stimulation of these by sympathetic neurones causes the rapid metabolism of the numerous fat droplets in the cells. The subsequent release of energy by enzymes in the mitochondria in these cells is particularly important for hibernating animals since it is instrumental in rapidly raising the core temperature during arousal from hibernation (section 21.10.3). The hypothalamus is the centre initiating heat production for most of the mechanisms described above.

18.4.3 Loss of heat

Heat is lost from endotherms by the four mechanisms described in section 18.2.6, that is conduction, convection, radiation and evaporation. In all cases, the rate of loss depends upon the temperature differences between the body core and the skin, and the skin and the environment. The rate can be increased or decreased depending upon the rate of heat production and the environmental temperature.

There are three factors limiting heat loss, as given below.

The rate of blood flow between the body core and skin. The rate of heat loss from the skin by radiation, convection and conduction depends upon the amount of blood flowing through it. If the blood flow is low the skin temperature approaches that of the environment, whereas if the flow is increased the skin temperature then approaches core temperature. The skin of endotherms is richly vascularised and blood can flow through it by any of three routes: through capillary networks in the dermis, through shunt pathways deep in the dermis linking arterioles and venules, and through subcutaneous, small connecting veins linking cutaneous arterioles and veins.

Arterioles have relatively thick muscular walls which can contract or relax altering the diameter of the vessels and the rate of blood flow through them. The degree of contraction is controlled by sympathetic vasomotor nerves from the vasomotor centre in the brain which receives impulses from the thermoregulatory centre in the hypothalamus. The rate

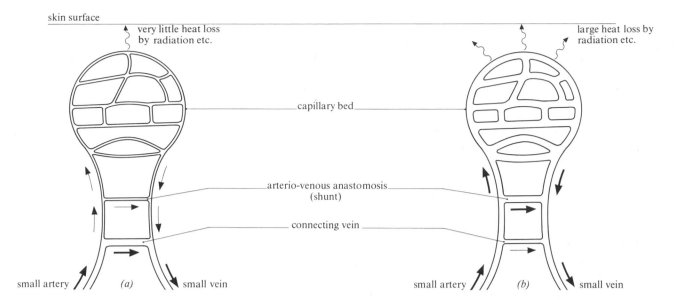

skin surface

very little heat loss by radiation etc.

large heat loss by radiation etc.

capillary bed

arterio-venous anastomosis (shunt)

connecting vein

small artery (a) small vein

small artery (b) small vein

Fig 18.12 *Mechanism of regulation of blood flow through the skin. (a) Blood flow through the skin preventing heat loss. Constriction of the arteriole reduces blood flow through capillaries and shunt. Only sufficient blood passes into the skin to keep the tissues alive. Most of the blood flowing from the body by-passes the skin through the connecting vein and reduces heat loss. (b) Blood flow through the skin increasing heat loss. Dilation of the arteriole increases blood flow through the capillaries and shunt. The capillaries dilate due to the rise in blood pressure within them. Heat is lost from the blood by radiation, convection and conduction and blood flow is increased to the sweat glands*

of blood flow through the skin in Man can vary from less than 1 cm³ min⁻¹ 100 g⁻¹ in cold conditions to 100 cm³ min⁻¹ 100 g⁻¹ in hot conditions, and this can account for an increase in heat loss by a factor of five or six. The 'shunt pathways' are known as **arterio-venous anastomoses** and lie beneath the level of the skin capillary beds. Constriction of these vessels forces blood through the low resistance 'connecting veins' connecting arteries to veins and the bulk of the blood by-passes the capillaries and shunts (fig 18.12). This is a typical response preventing heat loss. Dilation of the shunt vessels encourages blood flow through the capillary beds and shunts and not through the connecting veins. This increases blood flow through the skin and therefore heat is lost more rapidly.

The rate of sweat production and evaporation from the skin. Sweat is a watery fluid containing between 0.1 and 0.4% of sodium chloride, sodium lactate and urea. It is hypotonic to blood plasma and is secreted from tissue fluid by the activity of sweat glands under the control of **sudomotor neurones**. These neurones are part of the sympathetic nervous system and they relay impulses from the hypothalamus. Sweating begins whenever the body temperature rises above its mean value of 36.7 °C. Approximately 900 cm³ of sweat are lost per day in a temperate climate, but the figure can rise as high as 12 dm³ per day in very hot dry conditions, providing that there is adequate replacement of water and salts.

18.3 The latent heat of evaporation of sweat is 2.45 kJ cm⁻³. Calculate the percentage of energy lost by sweating from a coalminer who loses 4 dm³ per day of sweat and has a daily energy uptake of 50 000 kJ.

When sweat evaporates from the skin surface, energy as latent heat of evaporation is lost from the body and this reduces body temperature. The rate of evaporation is reduced by low environmental temperatures, high humidity and lack of wind.

Many mammals have so much hair on their bodies that sweating is restricted to bare areas, for instance pads of the feet of dogs and cats, and the ears of rats. These mammals increase heat loss by licking their bodies and allowing moisture to evaporate, and by panting and losing heat from the moist nasal and buccal cavities. Man, horse and pig are able to sweat freely over the entire body surface.

Experiments have now confirmed that sweating only occurs as a result of a rise in core temperature. Experiments on Man and other animals have shown that lowering the core temperature, by swallowing ice water or cooling the carotid blood vessels with an ice pack around the neck, while at the same time exposing the skin to heat, result in a decrease in the rate of sweating. Opposite effects have been recorded by reversing the environmental conditions. Blood from the carotid vessels flows to the hypothalamus and these experiments have indicated its role in thermoregulation. Inserting a thermistor against the ear-drum gives an acceptable measure of hypothalamic temperature. The relation between changes in temperature in this region and the skin, and rate of evaporation of sweat are shown in fig 18.13. Examine this figure and answer the following questions.

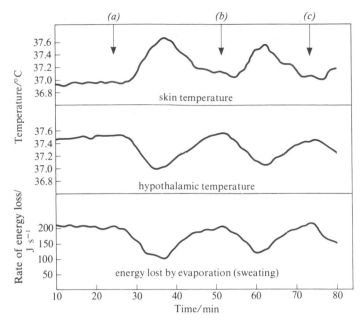

Fig 18.13 *Graphs showing the relation between skin temperature, hypothalamic temperature and rate of evaporation for a Man in a warm chamber (45 °C). Iced water was swallowed at the points labelled (a), (b) and (c)*

18.4 Account for temperature and evaporation rate remaining relatively constant during the first 20 min.

18.5 Describe the relationship between hypothalamic temperature and rate of sweating.

18.6 Suggest why the skin temperature rises shortly after the ingestion of iced water.

The amount of insulation between the core and the environment. Insulation for the body is provided by air trapped outside the skin and by dermal and subcutaneous fat. Feathers, fur and clothes trap a layer of air, known as stagnant air, between the skin and the environment, and because it is a poor conductor of heat it reduces heat loss. The amount of insulation provided by this means depends upon the thickness of the trapped air. Reflex contractions of the erector pili muscles in response to decreasing temperatures increases the angle between the feathers or fur and the skin and thus there is more air trapped. The response is still present in Man but due to the minimal amount of body hair it only produces the effect known as 'goose-flesh' or 'goose-pimples'. Man compensates for the lack of body hair by taking advantage of the insulating effects of clothing. The seasonal accumulation of a thick layer of subcutaneous fat is common in mammals particularly in those species which do not hibernate and manage to withstand cold temperatures. Aquatic mammals, particularly those inhabiting cold waters, such as whale, sea-lion, walrus and seal, have a thick layer of fat known as blubber which effectively insulates them against the cold.

18.4.4 Heat balance and the role of the hypothalamus

The temperature of any body is determined by the following equation:

heat gained by body = heat lost by body

Endothermic animals are able to generate sufficient heat energy and regulate the amount lost so that the two expressions above are always in equilibrium and equal a

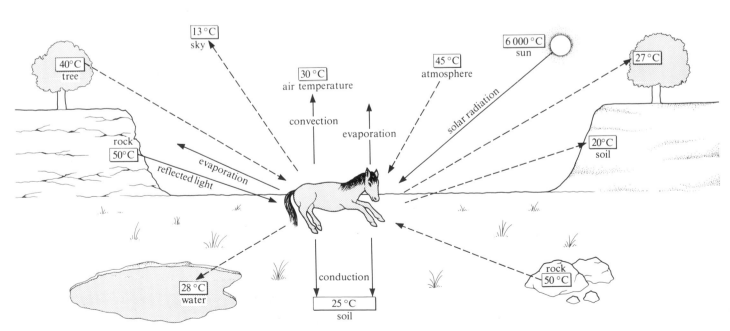

Fig 18.14 *Diagram showing the energy exchanges between a horse, with a body temperature of 38 °C, and the environment on a hot sunny day with an air temperature of 30 °C. The dotted lines represent thermal radiation*

680

constant (fig 18.14). This is known as **homeothermy**. Any mechanism which has an input and an output and is capable of maintaining a constant value must be regulated by a control system as described earlier in this chapter.

Birds and mammals have a well-developed control system involving receptors and effectors and an extremely sensitive control centre, the hypothalamus. This organ monitors the temperature of the blood, which is in equilibrium with the core temperature, flowing through it. If the hypothalamus is to control a constant core temperature, as is the case with endotherms, it is vital that information regarding changes in the external temperature is also transmitted to the hypothalamus. Without such information the body would gain or lose a great deal of heat before changes in core temperature would activate the hypothalamus to take corrective measures. This problem is overcome by having peripheral thermoreceptors, situated in the skin, which detect changes in the environmental temperature and initiate impulses to the hypothalamus in advance of changes in the core temperature. There are two types of thermoreceptors, hot and cold, which **generate** impulses in afferent neurones leading from them when suitably stimulated. Some pass to the hypothalamus and others to the sensory areas of the cortex, where the sensations associated with temperature are registered according to the intensity of stimulation, the duration and the numbers of receptors stimulated. There are estimated to be 150 000 cold receptors and 16 000 heat receptors in Man. This enables the body to make rapid and precise adjustments to maintain a constant core temperature. In the context of control systems, the skin receptors act as disturbance detectors anticipating changes in body temperature. Factors bringing about changes in internal temperature such as metabolic rate or disease will immediately affect the core temperature and in these situations be

Table 18.1 Functions of the heat loss and heat gain centres of the hypothalamus. These are situated in the anterior and posterior hypothalamus respectively and have antagonistic effects

Anterior hypothalamus (heat loss centre)	*Posterior hypothalamus (heat gain centre)*
Activated by increase in the hypothalamic temperature	Activated by impulses from peripheral cold receptors or temperature of the hypothalamus
Increases vasodilation	Increases vasoconstriction
Increases heat loss by radiation, convection and conduction	Decreases heat loss by radiation convection and conduction
Increases sweating and panting	Inhibits sweating and panting
Decreases metabolic activity	Increases metabolic activity through shivering and release of thyroxine and adrenaline
Decreases thickness of air layer by flattening hair or feathers	Increases thickness of air layer by action of hair muscles

detected by thermoreceptors in the hypothalamus. In most cases the activity of both peripheral and hypothalamic receptors is instrumental in controlling body temperature.

Investigations into the thermostatic activity of the hypothalamus have shown that there are two distinct areas concerned with this type of regulation and the functions of these areas are summarised in table 18.1. The interrelationships between the cerebral cortex, the hypothalamic thermoregulatory centres, core temperature, skin temperature and environmental temperatures are shown in fig 18.15 and fig 18.16.

Fig 18.15 *Summary diagram showing the reflex control of body temperature in a mammal involving the environment, hypothalamus and blood temperature*

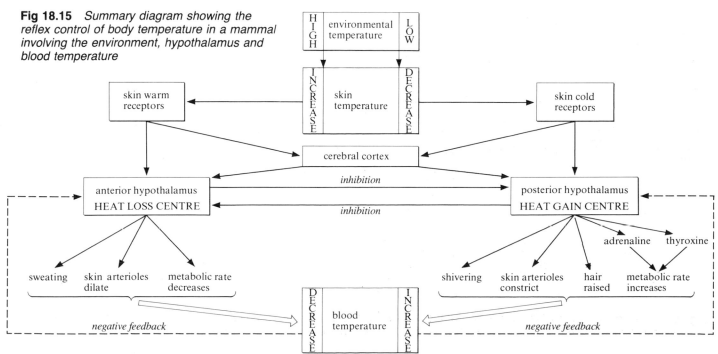

Certain diseases produce an increase in core temperature as a result of the 'thermostat' being set at a higher temperature. It is believed that certain substances known as **pyrogens**, which may be toxins produced by pathogenic organisms or substances released by white blood corpuscles known as neutrophils, directly affect the hypothalamus and increase the set-point. The raised body temperature stimulates the defence responses of the body and aids the destruction of pathogens. Antipyretic drugs such as aspirin lower the set-point and provide relief from the unpleasant symptoms of fever, but probably retard the normal defence mechanisms. In cases of extremely high temperature these drugs are valuable in preventing irreversible damage to the brain.

> **18.7** The onset of fever is often accompanied by shivering and a feeling of cold known as chill. Explain these symptoms in terms of mechanism of control of body temperature.

18.4.5 Adaptations to extreme climates

The size of organs and physiological and behavioural adaptations of organisms vary over their geographical range. The total heat production of endotherms depends upon the volume of metabolically active tissues whilst the rate of heat loss depends upon surface area. The two parameters, surface area and volume, are inversely proportional to each other. For this reason animals living in cold regions tend to be large, for example polar bears and whales, whilst animals living in hot climates are generally smaller, for instance insectivorous mammals. This phenomenon is known as **Bergman's rule** and is observed in many species, including the tiger, which decreases in size with distance from the Poles. There are exceptions to this rule, but the organisms concerned have adaptations favouring survival in these regions. For example, small mammals in temperate or arctic regions have a large appetite enabling them to maintain a high metabolic rate. They have small extremities to reduce heat loss and are forced to hibernate in winter. Large mammals living in hot regions, such as the elephant and hippopotamus, have the opposite problems. The elephant has extremely large ears which are well supplied with blood, and flapping of these ears encourages heat loss by radiation and convection. The hippopotamus lacks sweat glands and adopts a similar behavioural response to temperature as the crocodile in that it moves between land and water in an attempt to minimise the effects on its body of changes in temperature. The size of the external organs also varies according to environmental temperature such that species living in colder climates have smaller extremities than related species in warmer climates. This is known as **Allen's rule** and may be seen in closely related species of, for instance, the fox (fig 18.17).

18.4.6 Adaptations to life at low temperatures

All ectotherms and many endotherms are unable to maintain a body temperature which permits normal activity during cold seasons, and they respond by showing some form of dormancy, as described in section 21.10. Some of these responses are quite startling; for example, the larva of an insect parasite *Bracon*, which invades the Canadian wheat sawfly, is able to survive exposure to temperatures lower than −40.0 °C. This larva accumulates glycerol in its haemolymph. The glycerol acts as an 'antifreeze' and is able to prevent the formation of ice crystals by a process known as 'super-cooling'.

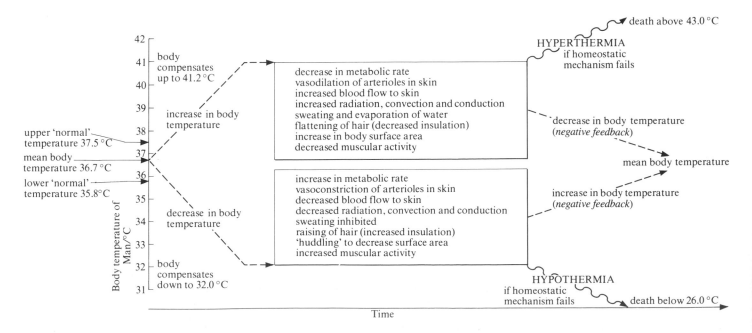

Fig 18.16 *Homeostatic control of body temperature*

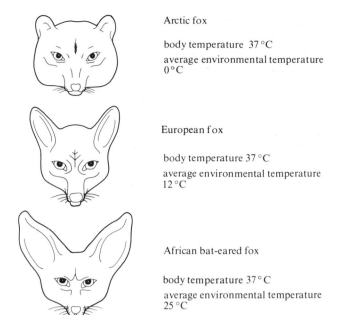

Arctic fox

body temperature 37 °C
average environmental temperature
0 °C

European fox

body temperature 37 °C
average environmental temperature
12 °C

African bat-eared fox

body temperature 37 °C
average environmental temperature
25 °C

Fig 18.17 *Variation in ear length shown by three species of fox (*Lycaon*) which each occupies a different geographical region. This is an example of Allen's rule*

Excessive heat loss to the environment from appendages is prevented in many organisms by the arrangement of blood vessels within the appendages. The arteries carrying blood towards the appendage are surrounded by veins carrying blood back to the body. The warm arterial blood from the body is cooled by the cold venous blood flowing towards the body. Similarly the cold venous blood from the appendage is warmed by the warm arterial blood flowing towards the appendage. Because the blood reaching the appendage is already cooled the amount of heat lost is considerably reduced. This arrangement is known as a **countercurrent heat exchanger** and is found in the flippers and flukes of seals and whales, in the limbs of birds and mammals and in the blood supply to the testes in mammals (fig 18.18).

The countercurrent exchange principle is used for the transfer of materials other than heat, such as respiratory gases and ions (sections 11.7 and 19.5.7).

The induction of a state of hypothermia is being used increasingly in heart surgery since it allows the surgeon to carry out repairs to the heart without the risk of brain damage to the patient. By reducing the body temperature to 15 °C, the metabolic demands of the brain cells are so reduced that blood flow to the brain can be stopped, without any adverse effects, for up to one hour. For operations requiring a longer time than this a heart–lung machine is used, in addition to hypothermia, to maintain blood circulation in the tissues.

18.4.7 Adaptations to life at high temperatures

Animals living in conditions where the air temperatures exceed skin temperature gain heat, and the only means of reducing body temperature is by evaporation of water from the body surface. For climatic reasons hot regions may be, in addition, either dry or humid, and this poses an additional problem. In hot dry regions heat can be lost by the free evaporation of water, but animals in these regions have the problem of finding adequate supplies of water to satisfy the demands of evaporative cooling. In hot humid regions water is freely available to organisms but the humidity gradient between organisms and the environment often prevents evaporation. In the latter case physiological mechanisms of temperature control are often supplemented and there may be behavioural activities which take advantage of the shade and breezes associated with humid forest and jungle habitats.

The **heat load** of an organism is the amount of heat gained by metabolic activities and from the environment, and the latter is approximately proportional to the body

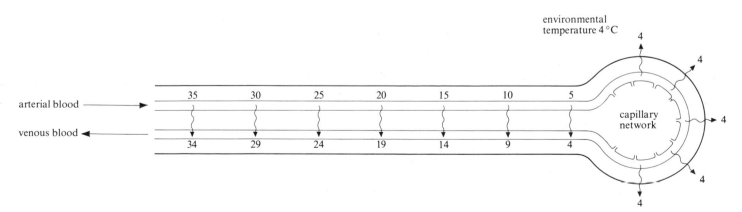

Fig 18.18 *Diagram showing the blood supply between the body of an endotherm with a stable temperature of 35 °C and an appendage in an environment at 4 °C. Heat flows from a warm body to a cool body and the rate of heat loss between the two bodies is proportional to the temperature difference between them. The countercurrent flow shown delivers blood to the capillary network at 5 °C and collects blood from it at 4 °C. The amount of heat lost to the environment is therefore proportional to the temperature difference of 1 °C. Likewise blood returning to the core of the body is only 1 °C cooler than the blood leaving the core. This mechanism prevents the excessive loss of metabolic energy and helps maintain the core temperature at 35 °C*

683

surface area. The majority of animals living in deserts, therefore, are small, such as the kangeroo rat (*Dipodomys*), and have fewer problems than large animals, such as camels. In addition they are able to live in burrows in sand and soil where the microclimate poses fewer problems to life.

A camel in hot dry conditions, with free access to water, is able to regulate its body temperature between about 36 and 38 °C. It is able to do this by losing heat through the evaporation of water from the body surface. If the camel is deprived of water, as say during a journey across the desert lasting several days, the difference in the body temperatures at morning and evening steadily increase according to the degree of dehydration. This diurnal fluctuation can be from 34 °C in the early morning to 41 °C in the late afternoon. By effectively storing up heat during the day the camel does not need to lose this heat by the evaporation of water. It functions in fact, like a storage radiator. In a series of investigations carried out by Schmidt-Nielsen it was found that a 500 kg camel tolerating a 7 °C temperature rise stored approximately 12 000 kJ of heat energy. If this amount of heat were lost by evaporative cooling, in order to maintain a constant body temperature, it would require the loss of 5 dm³ of water. Instead this heat is lost by radiation, conduction and convection during the night. A second advantage of becoming 'partially ectothermic' during the day is that this reduces the temperature difference between the hot desert air and the camel, and therefore reduces the rate of heat gain. The fur of the camel acts as an efficient insulating barrier by reducing heat gain and water loss. In an experiment, in which a camel was shorn, the water loss increased by 50% over that of a control camel. The final significant advantage shown by the camel is its ability to tolerate dehydration. Most mammals cannot tolerate dehydration beyond a loss of body mass of 10–14%, but the camel can survive losses up to 30%, because it is able to maintain its plasma volume even when dehydrated. Heat death as a result of dehydration is due to the inability of the circulatory system to transfer heat from the body core to the surface quickly enough to prevent overheating as a result of a fall in volume of the plasma. Contrary to popular belief, the camel is unable to store water in advance of conditions of water shortage, and there is doubt whether it can obtain water from the metabolism of fat stored in the hump. The camel is, however, able to drink a vast volume of water in a short space of time to rehydrate the body tissues after a period of severe dehydration. For example, a 325 kg camel is known to have drunk 30 dm³ of water in less than ten minutes. This is roughly equivalent to a Man of average build and weight drinking about 7 dm³ (12 pints) of water!

18.5 The mammalian liver

The liver is the largest visceral organ of homeostasis and controls many metabolic activities essential for the maintenance of the composition of blood at a steady state. The liver is derived from an endodermal outpushing of the alimentary canal and many of its functions are associated with the preparation, production and control of substances derived from absorbed food materials. There is a unique dual blood supply to the liver and because of its rich vascularisation it regulates many activities associated with blood and the circulatory system (fig 18.19). Paradoxically, despite the enormous variety of metabolic activities carried out by the liver its histological structure is relatively uniform and simple.

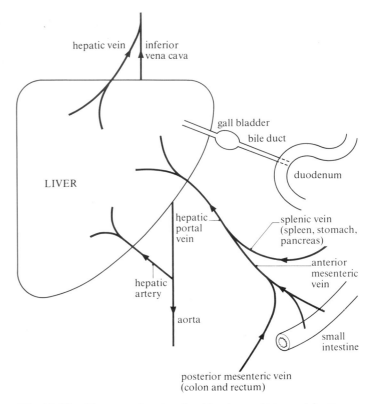

Fig 18.19 *Diagram showing the blood supply to and from the liver and the relative position of the bile duct*

18.5.1 The position and structure of the liver

The human liver is a large organ making up 3–5% of the body weight and lies immediately beneath the diaphragm to which it is attached by the **falciform ligament**. It is made up of several lobes and has a variable shape depending upon the amount of blood present within it. The liver is surrounded by a capsule made up of two layers, the outer layer being a smooth, moist peritoneum and the inner a fibrous covering known as **Glisson's capsule** which surrounds all structures entering and leaving the liver. The fibres of Glisson's capsule form an 'internal skeleton' which supports the rest of the liver.

The cells of the liver are called **hepatocytes** and show no structural or functional differentiation. The only other cells found in the liver are nerve cells and cells associated with blood and lymph vessels. Hepatocytes have prominent nuclei and Golgi apparatus, many mitochondria and

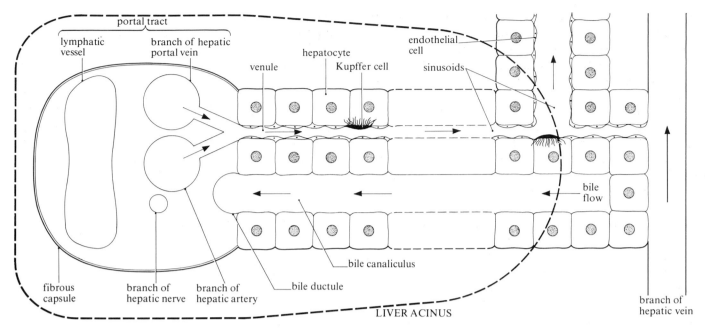

Fig 18.20 *A simplified diagram of a liver acinus showing a transverse section of a portal tract and a longitudinal section through a branch of the hepatic vein*

lysosomes, and are rich in glycogen granules and fat droplets. They are tightly packed together, and where their surface is in contact with blood vessels there are microvilli which are used for the exchange of materials between the two.

The whole internal structure of the liver is complex and not fully understood. It is based upon an arrangement of hepatocytes and two systems of blood vessels which interdigitate with channels called **bile canaliculi**. The hepatic portal vein forms many branches inside the liver and they carry alongside them branches of the hepatic artery, bile duct, nerves, lymphatic vessels and fibrous tissue of Glisson's capsule. This arrangement forms a structure known as a **portal tract**(canal) (fig 18.20). Blood vessels from both the hepatic portal vein, carrying absorbed materials from the alimentary canal, and the hepatic artery, carrying oxygenated blood, join together to form 'venules' which carry blood to the hepatocytes. This arrangement of 'venules' and hepatocytes is believed to form the functional unit of the liver and is known as an **acinus**. Smaller blood vessels called **sinusoids** arise from the 'venules' and form a vast network of capillaries before uniting to carry blood to branches of the hepatic vein. Adjacent sinusoids are separated from each other by 'plates' of hepatocytes which are often only one cell thick. As blood flows along the sinusoids, materials are exchanged between the blood and the hepatocytes. The presence of pores, having a diameter up to 10 nm, in the endothelial lining of the sinusoids, and the microvilli on the hepatocytes where they touch the sinusoids, facilitates the exchange of materials. Bile produced in the hepatocytes does not enter the sinusoids but is secreted into minute bile canaliculi which replace the sinusoids at various points and run between adjacent plates of hepatocytes. These canali-

culi are lined with microvilli and take up bile from the hepatocytes by some form of active transport. The canaliculi form a branching network which unites to form **bile ductules**. These join together in the portal tract to form **bile ducts** and these eventually fuse before leaving the liver as the **common hepatic duct**.

The structure of the liver, as described above, shows it to be a vast network of hepatocytes, blood, blood spaces and bile canaliculi. This produces a structure with an immense surface area where each cell is in direct contact with blood thus facilitating maximum exchange between cell and blood and control of substances in the blood.

The structure of the liver in the pig is much simpler than the human liver but is atypical of other mammals. It is described because its simplicity highlights many of the structural and functional relationships which may not be readily evident from the account of the typical mammalian situation described above. The pig's liver is composed of a large number of discrete units, called **lobules** which are polygonal in transverse section and have a diameter of approximately 1 mm. They form thimble-shaped units about 2–3 mm long and are enclosed in a connective tissue sheath continuous with Glisson's capsule. Between the lobules are the **interlobular blood vessels** consisting of an arteriole of the hepatic artery and a branch of the hepatic portal vein and a bile ductule (as found in the portal tract of other mammals). An **intralobular vein** is situated in the centre of the lobule and receives blood which flows along the sinusoids from the portal vein and artery. Blood from the intralobular veins passes into the hepatic vein. The bulk of the lobule is composed of strands of liver cells running from the periphery of the lobule and converging on the intralobular vein. Exchange of materials between hepatocytes and blood occurs as described previously. The

685

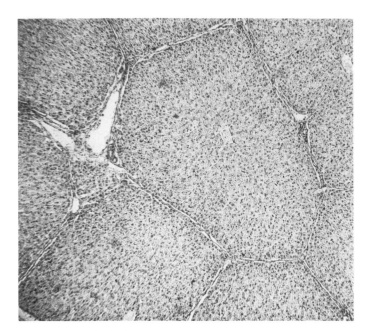

Fig 18.21 *TS pig liver showing lobules*

sinusoids alternate with bile canaliculi which carry bile to the intralobular bile ductule. This relatively simple and regular pattern is shown in figs 18.21 and 18.22.

The functional unit of pig liver is the lobule and its regular structure arises because the intralobular and interlobular blood vessels run parallel to each other. This situation is not generally found in other mammals where lobulation is absent or less definite.

The lymph found in the lymphatic vessels of the portal tract is surprisingly rich in protein and is produced from plasma which escapes from the endothelial pores in the 'venules' and sinusoids.

One other type of cell is found in the liver and it forms part of a more extensive system known as the **reticulo-endothelial system** (see section 14.14). The cells are called **Kupffer cells** and are found attached to the walls of the sinusoids by cytoplasmic projections. They are phagocytic and are involved in the breakdown of old (effete) erythro-cytes and the ingestion of pathogenic organisms.

18.5.2 Functions of the liver

It has been estimated that the liver carries out several hundred separate functions involving thousands of different chemical reactions. These functions are related to the position of the liver in the circulatory system and the vast amount of blood which flows through it at any given time (approximately 20% of the total blood volume). The liver and the kidney between them are the major organs responsible for regulating the steady state of blood metabolites and the composition of the blood tissues. All food materials absorbed from the alimentary canal pass directly to the liver where they are stored or converted into some other form as required by the body at that time.

The functions of the liver therefore fall into two main categories: the storage of food materials and synthesis of their derivatives, and the breakdown of substances not required by the body prior to their excretion. Finally, as a result of the number of metabolic activities occurring within the liver, it may be a source of heat production for animals living in cold climates.

Carbohydrate metabolism

Hexose sugars enter the liver from the gut by the hepatic portal vein, which is the only blood vessel in the body having an extremely variable sugar content. This gives a clue to the role of the liver in carbohydrate metabolism as

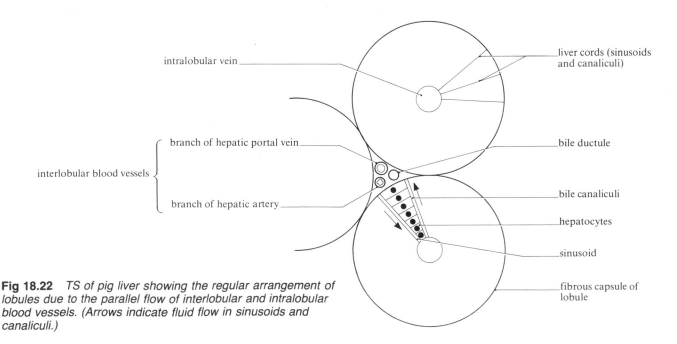

Fig 18.22 *TS of pig liver showing the regular arrangement of lobules due to the parallel flow of interlobular and intralobular blood vessels. (Arrows indicate fluid flow in sinusoids and canaliculi.)*

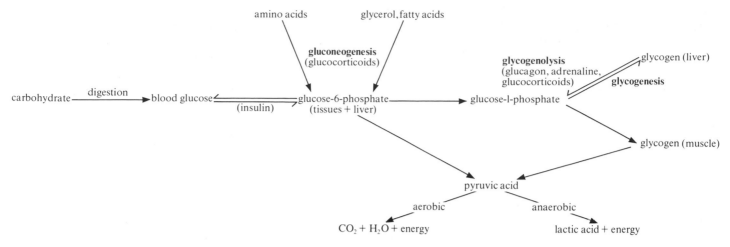

Fig 18.23 *Summary diagram of carbohydrate metabolism*

the organ which maintains the blood glucose level at approximately 90 mg glucose 100 cm^{-3} blood. The liver prevents blood glucose levels from fluctuating according to feeding patterns thus preventing damage to tissues which cannot store glucose, such as the brain. All hexose sugars, including galactose and fructose, are converted to glucose by the liver and stored as the insoluble polysaccharide, glycogen. Up to 100 g of glycogen are stored here but more is stored in muscle. The conversion of glucose to glycogen is known as **glycogenesis** and is stimulated by the presence of insulin:

$$\underset{\text{(phosphorylation)}}{\text{glucose}} \overset{\text{insulin}}{\rightleftharpoons} \text{glucose-6-phosphate} \rightleftharpoons \underset{\text{(condensation)}}{\text{glucose-1-phosphate} \rightleftharpoons \text{glycogen}}$$

Glycogen is broken down to glucose to prevent the blood glucose level falling below 60 mg 100 cm^{-3} blood. This process is called **glycogenolysis** and involves the activation of a phosphorylase enzyme by the pancreatic hormone, glucagon. In times of danger, stress or cold this activity is also stimulated by adrenaline, released by the adrenal medulla, and noradrenaline released by the endings of the sympathetic neurones (section 16.2.3).

$$\underset{\text{(store)}}{\text{glycogen}} \overset{\text{phosphorylase}}{\rightleftharpoons} \text{glucose-1-phosphate} \overset{\text{phosphoglucomutase}}{\rightleftharpoons} \text{glucose-6-phosphate} \overset{\text{glucose-6-phosphatase}}{\rightleftharpoons} \underset{\text{(free)}}{\text{glucose}}$$

Muscle lacks the enzyme glucose-6-phosphatase and cannot convert glycogen directly to glucose via glucose-6-phosphate as shown above. Instead, glucose-6-phosphate is converted into pyruvic acid which is used to produce ATP during aerobic or anaerobic respiration. Lactic acid produced by anaerobic respiration in skeletal muscle can be converted later into glucose and hence glycogen in the liver by a biochemical pathway known as the **Cori cycle**:

lactic acid→pyruvic acid→glucose→glycogen

When the demand for glucose has exhausted the glycogen store in the liver, glucose can be synthesised from non-carbohydrate sources. This is called **gluconeogenesis**. Low blood glucose levels (hypoglycaemia) stimulate the sympathetic nervous system to release adrenaline which helps satisfy immediate demand as described above. Low blood glucose levels also stimulate the hypothalamus to release CRF (section 16.6.2) which in turn releases adrenocorticotrophic hormone (ACTH) from the anterior pituitary gland. This leads to the synthesis and release of increasing amounts of the glucocorticoid hormones, cortisone and hydrocortisone. These stimulate the release of amino acids, glycerol and fatty acids, present in the tissues, into the blood and increase the rate of synthesis of enzymes in the liver which convert amino acids and glycerol into glucose. (Fatty acids are converted into acetyl coenzyme A and used directly in the Krebs cycle.) Carbohydrate in the body which cannot be utilised or stored as glycogen is converted into fats and stored. A summary of carbohydrate metabolism involving the liver, muscles and tissues is shown in fig 18.23.

Protein metabolism

The liver plays an important role in protein metabolism which may be considered under the headings of deamination, urea formation, transamination and plasma protein synthesis.

Deamination. The body is unable to store absorbed amino acids, and those not immediately required for protein synthesis or gluconeogenesis are deaminated in the liver. This involves the enzymic removal of the amino group (–NH$_2$) from the amino acid with the simultaneous oxidation of the remainer of the molecule to form a carbohydrate which is utilised in respiration. The amino group is removed along with a hydrogen atom so that the nitrogenous product of deamination is ammonia (NH$_3$).

For example,

$$2NH_2\!-\!\underset{\underset{H}{|}}{\overset{\overset{R}{|}}{C}}\!-\!COOH \;+\; O_2 \longrightarrow 2\,\underset{\underset{O}{\|}}{\overset{\overset{R}{|}}{C}}\!-\!COOH \;+\; 2NH_3$$

    amino acid   oxygen   keto acid   ammonia

or specifically,

$$2NH_2\!-\!\underset{\underset{H}{|}}{\overset{\overset{CH_3}{|}}{C}}\!-\!COOH \;+\; O_2 \longrightarrow 2\,\underset{\underset{O}{\|}}{\overset{\overset{CH_3}{|}}{C}}\!-\!COOH \;+\; 2NH_3$$

    alanine   oxygen   pyruvic acid   ammonia

This ammonia may be used for the synthesis of certain amino acids or nitrogenous bases, such as adenine and guanine (section 5.6), or excreted.

    Urea formation. Ammonia produced by deamination is converted in the liver into the soluble excretory product urea:

$$2NH_3 \;+\; CO_2 \longrightarrow \underset{NH_2}{\overset{NH_2}{<}}C\!=\!O \;+\; H_2O$$

  ammonia   carbon   urea   water
          dioxide

This occurs by a cyclic reaction known as the **ornithine cycle** which is summarised in fig 18.24.

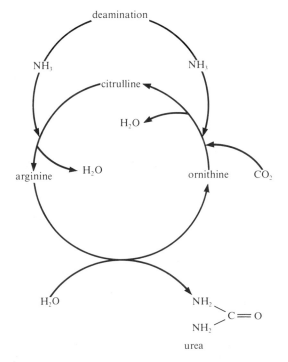

Fig 18.24 *Summary diagram of the ornithine cycle in mammalian liver (ornithine and citrulline are amino acids but are not obtained from the diet)*

Transamination. This is the synthesis of amino acids by the enzymic transfer of the amino group from an amino acid to a carbohydrate in the form of a keto acid (chapter 5). For example the amino acid, glutamic acid, could be synthesised by the following reactions:

$$NH_2\!-\!\underset{\underset{H}{|}}{\overset{\overset{CH_3}{|}}{C}}\!-\!COOH \;+\; O\!=\!\underset{}{\overset{\overset{CH_2COOH}{|}\;\overset{CH_2}{|}}{C}}\!-\!COOH \longrightarrow$$

  alanine   *a*-oxoglutaric acid

$$NH_2\!-\!\underset{\underset{H}{|}}{\overset{\overset{CH_2COOH}{|}\;\overset{CH_2}{|}}{C}}\!-\!COOH \;+\; O\!=\!\underset{}{\overset{\overset{CH_3}{|}}{C}}\!-\!COOH$$

  glutamic acid   pyruvic acid

The general principle underlying these reactions is the mutual exchange of characteristic radicals between the amino acid and the keto acid:

$$NH_2\!-\!\underset{\underset{H}{|}}{\overset{\overset{(A)}{|}}{C}}\!-\!COOH \;+\; O\!=\!\underset{}{\overset{\overset{(B)}{|}}{C}}\!-\!COOH \longrightarrow$$

  amino acid A   keto acid B

$$NH_2\!-\!\underset{\underset{H}{|}}{\overset{\overset{(B)}{|}}{C}}\!-\!COOH \;+\; O\!=\!\underset{}{\overset{\overset{(A)}{|}}{C}}\!-\!COOH$$

  amino acid B   keto acid A

Transamination is the means of producing amino acids which are deficient from the diet, and this is yet another of the liver's homeostatic mechanisms. The 'essential' amino acids, described in section 10.3, cannot be synthesised by transamination in the liver and must be obtained from the diet.

Plasma protein production. Plasma proteins are vital components of plasma and the majority of them are synthesised from amino acids in the liver. Plasma albumin is the commonest protein and about 4 g 100cm^{-3} is normally present in the blood. It plays an important part in exerting a colloid osmotic pressure which opposes the hydrostatic pressure developed in blood vessels. The antagonistic effects of these two factors maintains the balance of fluids inside and outside of blood vessels (section 14.12.1). Albumins also act as transport molecules within the circulatory system, carrying substances such as calcium, tryptophan, bilirubin, bile salts, aspirin and some steroid hormones. Plasma globulins are very large molecules and blood carries about 34 g dm^{-3}. α- and β-globulins transport hormones, including thyroxine and insulin, cholesterol, lipids, iron and the vitamins B$_{12}$, A, D and K. γ-globulins are produced by lymphocytes and the other cells of the reticulo-endothelial tissues, and are involved in the immune response (section 14.14.3). The other main plasma proteins are the blood-clotting factors, prothrombin and fibrinogen, and their functions are described in section 14.13.5.

Fat metabolism

The liver is involved in the processing and transport of fats rather than their storage. Liver cells carry out the following functions: converting excess carbohydrates to fat; removing cholesterol and phospholipids from the blood and breaking them down or, when necessary, synthesising them and producing globulins to transport lipids.

Vitamin storage

The liver stores some of the water-soluble vitamins B and C, especially those of the B group such as nicotinic acid, vitamin B$_{12}$ and folic acid. Vitamin B$_{12}$ (cyanocobalamin) and folic acid are required by the bone marrow for the formation of erythrocytes and deficiency of these vitamins leads to various degrees of anaemia. The main vitamins stored in the liver, however, are the fat-soluble vitamins A, D, E and K. The liver of certain fish contains high concentrations of vitamins A and D, for example cod and halibut. Vitamin K is a vital factor in blood clotting.

Mineral storage

Those elements required in small amounts such as copper, zinc, cobalt and molybdenum (trace elements) are stored in the liver along with iron and potassium. Iron is stored primarily as a compound called **ferritin** which is a complex of iron and β-globulin. Approximately 1 mg g^{-1} dry mass of liver tissue in Man is iron. Most of this iron in the liver is temporary and comes from the breakdown of old erythrocytes and is stored here for later use in the manufacture of new erythrocytes in the bone marrow.

Storage of blood

The blood vessels leaving the spleen and gut join to form the hepatic portal vein and, together with the blood vessels of the liver, contain a large volume of blood which acts as a reservoir, though this is not a static store. Sympathetic neurones and adrenaline from the adrenal medulla can constrict many of these hepatic vessels and make more blood available to the general circulation. Likewise, if the blood volume increases, as for example during a blood transfusion, the hepatic veins along with other veins can dilate to accommodate the excess volume.

Formation of erythrocytes

The liver of the foetus is responsible for erythrocyte production (**erythropoiesis**) but this function is gradually taken over by cells of the bone marrow (section 14.11.2).

Once this process is established the liver takes an opposite role and assists in breaking down erythrocytes and haemoglobin.

Breakdown of haemoglobin

Erythrocytes have a life-span of about 120 days. By this stage they are effete and are broken down by the activity of phagocytic macrophage cells of the reticulo-endothelial system of the liver, spleen and bone marrow. Haemoglobin is broken down into **haem** and **globin**. The globin is reduced to its constituent amino acids and enters the liver's amino acid pool to be used according to demand. The iron is removed from haem and the remaining **pyrrole rings** form a green pigment **biliverdin**. This is converted to **bilirubin**, which is yellow and a component of bile. The accumulation of bilirubin in the blood is symptomatic of liver disease and produces a yellowing of the skin, a condition known as **jaundice**.

Bile production

Bile is a viscous, greenish yellow fluid secreted by hepatocytes. Between 500–1 000 cm^3 of bile are produced each day and it is composed of 98% water, 0.8% bile salts, 0.2% bile pigments, 0.7% inorganic salts and 0.6% cholesterol. It is involved in digestion, the absorption of fats and is a means of excretion of bile pigments.

Bile salts are derivatives of the steroid **cholesterol** which is synthesised in hepatocytes. The commonest bile salts are sodium glycocholate and sodium taurocholate. They are secreted with cholesterol and phospholipids as large particles called **micelles**. The cholesterol and phospholipids hold the polar bile salt molecules together so that all the hydrophobic ends of the molecules are orientated the same way. The hydrophobic ends attach to lipid droplets whilst the other ends are attached to water. This decreases the surface tension of the droplets and enables the lipids to separate, forming an emulsion. These smaller droplets have an increased surface area for attack by pancreatic lipase which converts the lipids into glycerol and fatty acids so that they can then be absorbed from the gut. Bile salts also activate the enzyme lipase, but their action, in all cases, is purely physical. Too little bile salt in bile increases the concentration of cholesterol which may precipitate out in the gall bladder or bile duct as cholesterol gall stones. These can block the bile duct and cause severe discomfort.

Bile pigments have no function and their presence is purely excretory.

Cholesterol is produced by the liver and is the precursor molecule in the synthesis of other steroid molecules. The major source of cholesterol is the diet, and many dairy products are rich in cholesterol or fatty acids from which cholesterol can be synthesised. Thyroxine both stimulates cholesterol formation in the liver and increases its rate of excretion in the bile. Excessive amounts of cholesterol in the blood can lead to its deposition in the walls of arteries leading to **atherosclerosis** (narrowing of the arteries) and the increased risk of the formation of a blood clot which may block blood vessels, a condition known as **arterial thrombosis**. This is often fatal if it occurs in the heart or brain. Cholesterol is often cited as a major cause of cardiovascular disease but, as yet, much of the evidence is contradictory.

Bile is stored and concentrated in the gall bladder by absorption of sodium ions (and water) into surrounding blood capillaries. The stimulus for the release of bile into the duodenum is the presence of the hormone cholecysto-kinin-pancreozymin (CCK-PZ) as described in section 10.5.

Hormone production and breakdown

Whilst the liver is not generally considered as an endocrine gland, it synthesises and releases growth-promoting factors called **somatomedins** under the influence of the hormone **somatotrophin**, released from the pituitary gland. This control of growth is described in more detail in section 21.8.1. The liver destroys almost all hormones to various extents. Testosterone and aldosterone are rapidly destroyed, whereas insulin, glucagon and gut hormones, female sex hormones, adrenal hormones, ADH and thyroxine are destroyed less rapidly. In this way the liver has a homeostatic effect on the activities of these hormones.

Detoxification

This term covers a range of homeostatic activities carried out by the liver so as to maintain the composition of blood at a steady state. Bacteria and other pathogens are removed from the blood in the sinusoids by Kupffer cells but the toxins they produce are dealt with by biochemical reactions in the hepatocytes. Toxins are rendered harmless by one or more of the following reactions: oxidation, reduction, methylation (the addition of a $-CH_3$ group) or combination with another organic or inorganic molecule. Following detoxification these substances, now harmless, are excreted by the kidney. The major toxic substance in the blood though is ammonia, whose fate is described above in this chapter. The detoxification process also includes harmful substances taken in to the body such as alcohol and nicotine. Alcohol taken in excess (in gradually increasing dosage) can result in liver breakdown, such as cirrhosis of the liver in alcoholics.

Some of the metabolic activities of the liver may be potentially harmful and evidence is growing that certain food additives may be converted into poisonous or carcinogenic substances by liver activity. Even the pain killer paracetamol, if taken in excess, is changed into a substance which affects enzyme systems and can cause liver, and other tissue, damage.

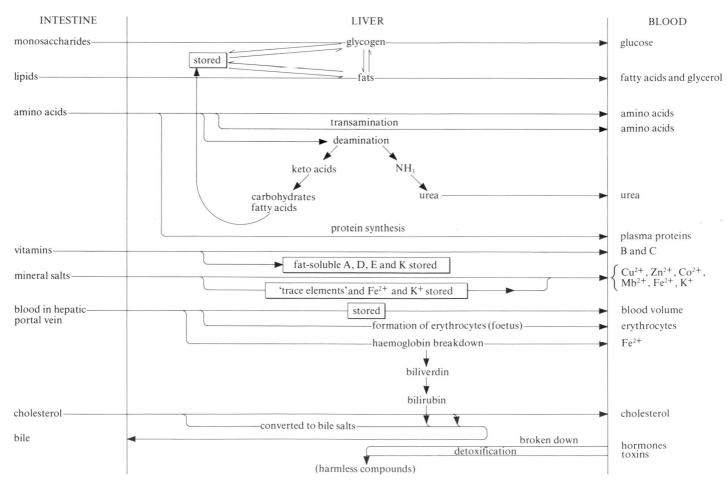

Fig 18.25 *Summary diagram of the functions of the liver*

Heat production

Evidence is accumulating to show that the widespread belief that the metabolic activity of the liver results in it being a major source of heat production in the body of mammals may be false. Many of the liver's metabolic activities are endothermic and therefore require heat energy rather than release it. Under conditions of extreme cold the hypothalamus will increase the ectothermic activity of the liver by its influence on the release of adrenaline by the sympathetic nervous system and the release of thyroxine. In 'normal' temperatures, however, the liver has been shown to be 'thermally neutral' but is usually 1–2 °C hotter than the rest of the body core.

The liver provides yet another example of the intimate relationship which exists in biological systems between structure and function. What is remarkable about the liver is the diversity of function achieved by a highly complex morphological structure which has such a simple, undifferentiated histological structure.

Chapter Nineteen

Excretion and osmoregulation

Excretion and osmoregulation are two important homeostatic processes occurring in living organisms. Each process enables organisms to maintain, to varying degrees, the internal environment at a steady state despite changes in the external environment.

Excretion is the elimination from the body of waste metabolic substances which if permitted to accumulate would prevent the maintenance of a steady state. Many substances which are not metabolic, that is those which have not been synthesised by the organism, are eliminated. To distinguish excretion from these latter functions it is necessary to define them. **Secretion** is the passive or active removal of molecules from cells into the extracellular environment, such as the bloodstream, gastro-intestinal tract or external environment. These molecules have been synthesised *in vivo* (in life), for example hormones and enzymes, and are therefore considered to have been metabolised, but are not regarded as waste substances. Secretion may form part of the process of excretion as is described later in the chapter. **Egestion** is the elimination of waste substances, mainly undigested food, which have never been involved in the metabolic activities of cells.

19.1 The significance of excretion and osmoregulation

Excretion and osmoregulation have a number of functions which may be listed and summarised as follows.

(1) The removal of metabolic waste substances which are often by-products of major metabolic pathways. This is necessary in order to prevent unbalancing the chemical equilibria of reactions. Many metabolic reactions are reversible and the direction of the reaction is determined solely by the relative concentrations of reactants and products in accordance with the law of mass action. For example, in the enzyme-catalysed reaction:

$$A + B \rightleftharpoons C + D$$
$$\text{(reactants)} \qquad \text{(products)}$$

the continued production of C, a vital requirement of metabolism, is ensured by the removal of D, a waste product. This will ensure that the *equilibrium* of the reaction favours the reaction to proceed from reactants to products.

(2) The removal of metabolic waste substances which, if they accumulated, would affect the metabolic activity of the organism. Many of these substances are toxic acting as inhibitors of enzymes involved in metabolic pathways.

(3) The regulation of the ionic content of body fluids. Salts behave as electrolytes and undergo dissociation in the aqueous media of living organisms. For example, sodium chloride, taken in as part of the diet, exists in body fluids as sodium ions (Na^+) and chloride ions (Cl^-). If the balance of these and other ions is not carefully regulated within narrow limits, the efficiency of many physiological and biochemical activities is impaired; for instance a reduction in Na^+ concentration leads to a decrease in nervous coordination. Other important ions whose concentrations must be carefully regulated are K^+, Mg^{2+}, Ca^{2+}, Fe^{2+}, H^+, Cl^-, I^-, PO_4^{3-} and HCO_3^-, as they are vital for many metabolic activities including enzyme activity, protein synthesis, production of hormones and respiratory pigments, membrane permeability, electrical activity and muscle contraction. Their effects on water content, osmotic pressure and pH of body fluids are described below.

(4) The regulation of water content of body fluids. The amount of water within the body fluids and its regulation is one of the major physiological problems faced by organisms in the colonisation of many of the available ecological niches on this planet. The solutions to this problem have produced some of the most important structural and functional adaptations shown by organisms. The mechanisms of obtaining water, preventing water loss and eliminating water are diverse, but they are of great importance in maintaining the osmotic pressure and volume of body fluids at a steady state, as described later in this chapter. Before describing these it is important to emphasise that the osmotic pressure of body fluids depends upon the relative *amounts* of solute and solvent, that is water, present. The mechanisms of regulation of solutes and water are known as **osmoregulation**.

(5) The regulation of hydrogen ion concentration (pH) of body fluids. The nature of pH and methods of its measurement are described in appendix A1.1.5 but the mechanisms of excreting those ions which have a major influence on pH, such as H^+ and HCO_3^-, are considered in this chapter. For example, the pH of urine may vary between 4.5 and 8 in order to maintain the pH of the body fluids at a fairly constant level.

Table 19.1 Summary of the products, sources, functions and fates of the major excretory products

Product	Source	Function/Fate
Oxygen	Photosynthesis in autotrophic organisms	Reactant in aerobic respiration
Carbon dioxide	Aerobic respiration in all organisms Breakdown of urea	Reactant in photosynthesis Decreases pH of body fluids
Water	Aerobic respiration in all organisms Condensation reactions	Solvent in all metabolic activities Reactant in photosynthesis, etc.
Ions (salts)	Nutrient metabolism	Maintenance of osmotic pressures Recycled through ecosystem
Bile salts	Lipid metabolism in liver	Emulsification of fats
Bile pigments	Breakdown of haem in liver	None
Tannins and other organic acids	Nitrogen and carbohydrate metabolism in certain plant species	Bitter substances deter ingestion by animals
Nitrogenous substances	Protein and nucleic acid metabolism	Decompose and recycled through ecosystem

19.1.1 Excretory products

The major excretory products of animals and plants and their sources are summarised in table 19.1. Not all excretory products are waste in the sense of serving no further useful purpose to the body. Indeed, many serve useful purposes prior to their elimination and afterwards, for reasons described in table 19.1.

19.1.2 Excretion in plants

Plants do not have as many problems regarding excretion as do animals. This is because of fundamental differences in the physiology and mode of life between animals and plants. Plants are primary producers and they synthesise all their organic requirements according to the demand for them. For example, plants manufacture only the amount of protein necessary to satisfy immediate demand. There is never an excess of protein and therefore very little excretion of nitrogenous waste substances, produced by the catabolism (breakdown) of proteins, occurs. If proteins are broken down into amino acids, the latter can be recycled into new proteins. Three of the waste substances produced by certain metabolic activities in plants, that is oxygen, carbon dioxide and water, are raw materials (reactants) for other reactions, and excesses of carbon dioxide and water are used up in this way. The only major gaseous excretory product of plants is oxygen. During light periods the rate of production of oxygen is far greater than the plant's demand for oxygen in respiration and this escapes from plants into the environment by diffusion.

Many organic waste products of plants are stored within dead permanent tissues such as the 'heart-wood' or within leaves or bark which are periodically removed. The bulk of most perennial plants is composed of dead tissues into which excretory materials are passed. In this state they have no adverse effects upon the activities of the living tissues. Similarly, many mineral salts, taken up as ions, may accumulate due to the differential use of cations and anions. Organic acids, which might prove harmful to plants, often combine with excess cations and precipitate out as insoluble crystals which can be safely stored in plant cells. For example, calcium ions and sulphate ions are taken up together, but sulphate is used up immediately in amino acid synthesis leaving an excess of calcium ions. These combine freely with oxalic and pectic acids to form harmless insoluble products such as calcium oxalate and calcium pectate. Other ions, such as iron and manganese, and organic acids, such as tannic and nicotinic acids, pass into leaves where they accumulate and contribute to the characteristic autumn tints of leaves prior to their loss during leaf abscission. Substances are not only eliminated through leaf loss but also through petals, fruits and seeds, although this excretory function is not the primary function of their dispersal. Aquatic plants lose most of their metabolic wastes by diffusion directly into the water surrounding them.

19.1.3 Excretion in animals

Any permeable surface which directly connects a region containing excretory products to the external environment is a potential area of excretion. These include the cell membrane of unicellular organisms, the epidermis of lower invertebrates, trachea of arthropods, gills and skin of fish and amphibia and the lungs and skin of higher vertebrates. The cells of organisms having a relatively simple structure are usually in direct contact with the environment and their excretory products are immediately removed by diffusion. As organisms increase in complexity, excretory organs develop to convey excretory products from the body directly or indirectly to the external environment through ducts and pores. In the case of the higher vertebrates specialised excretory structures are present to augment the activity of the vascular system which removes metabolic wastes from cells and transfers them to the excretory organs. The most important excretory organs in these organisms are the skin, lungs, liver and kidney. The roles of the first three only will be described at this stage.

Skin. Water, urea and salts are actively secreted from capillaries in the skin by the tubules of the sweat glands. Sweat is secreted onto the skin where the water evaporates using latent heat of evaporation. In this way heat is lost from the body and this helps to regulate the body temperature.

Lungs. Carbon dioxide and water vapour diffuse from the moist alveolar surfaces of the lungs, which in mammals are the sole excretory organs for carbon dioxide. Some of the water released at the lung surface is metabolic, that is, produced as a waste product of respiration and therefore excretory, but its exact origin is not really important in view of the large volume of water contained within the body.

Liver. Considering the many homeostatic roles of the liver described in section 18.5.2 it is not surprising that these include excretion. Bile pigments are excretory products from the breakdown of the haemoglobin of effete (old) red blood cells. They pass to the duodenum as a constituent of bile for removal from the body along with the faeces, to which they impart a characteristic colour. The most important excretory role of the liver is the formation of nitrogenous waste products by the deamination of excess amino acids (section 18.5.2).

19.2 Nitrogenous excretory products

Nitrogenous waste products are produced by the catabolism of proteins and nucleic acids. The immediate nitrogenous waste product of the deamination of proteins is ammonia, and the basis of this reaction is described in section 18.5.2. Ammonia may be excreted immediately or converted into the major nitrogenous compounds, urea and uric acid, which differ in their solubility and toxicity (fig 19.1). The exact nature of the

Fig 19.1 *Molecular structure of the three main nitrogenous excretory products*

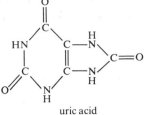

ammonia   urea   uric acid

excretory product is determined by the metabolic capability of the organism (that is, which enzymes are present), the availability of water to the organism (that is, its habitat), and the extent to which water loss is controlled by the organism.

Animals may be classified according to the nature of their major nitrogenous excretory product and, as shown in table 19.2, there is a degree of correlation between excretory product, embryonic environment and adult habitat. The classification of organisms and the correlation with habitats for the majority of organisms may be summarised thus:

ammonia	**ammoniotelic**	aquatic
urea	**ureotelic**	aquatic/terrestrial
uric acid	**uricotelic**	terrestrial

19.2.1 Ammonia

Ammonia is an extremely soluble molecule with a low relative molecular mass (17) and diffuses rapidly through water. It is toxic to animals and cannot be stored in the body. Mammals are very sensitive to ammonia and cannot tolerate concentrations in excess of 0.02 mg 100 cm^{-3} blood. The high solubility of ammonia aids its rapid excretion as ammonium ions (NH_4^+) in most aquatic organisms from protozoa to amphibia before it reaches concentrations which are toxic to the organisms.

19.2.2 Urea

Urea is formed in the liver of vertebrates by the interaction of ammonia, produced by deamination, and carbon dioxide, produced by respiration, in a cyclical reaction known as the **ornithine cycle**. It is less soluble and less toxic than ammonia and is the main nitrogenous excretory substance in elasmobranchs, certain teleost fish, adult amphibia and mammals. The normal level of urea in mammalian blood is 2.5–6.0 mmol dm^{-3} blood. The metamorphosis of the tadpole stage to the adult form in the frog is marked by the change from ammonia excretion to urea excretion.

19.2.3 Uric acid

Uric acid and its salts are ideal excretory products for terrestrial organisms and a pre-requisite for organisms producing a cleidoic egg (shelled egg) (section 19.4.8) since they combine a high nitrogen content with low toxicity and low solubility. They can be stored in cells, tissues and organs without producing any toxic or adverse osmoregulatory effects, and they require a minimal

Table 19.2. Summary of the relationships between excretory products and stages in the life cycle of various animal groups

Animal	Excretory product	Embryonic environment	Adult habitat
protozoan	ammonia	aquatic	aquatic
poriferan	ammonia	aquatic	aquatic
coelenterate	ammonia	aquatic	aquatic
platyhelminth	ammonia	aquatic	aquatic
aquatic crustacean	ammonia	aquatic	aquatic
terrestrial insect	uric acid	cleidoic egg	terrestrial
gastropod mollusc	uric acid	cleidoic egg	terrestrial
echinoderm	ammonia	aquatic	aquatic
elasmobranch	urea	aquatic	aquatic
freshwater teleost	ammonia	aquatic	aquatic
marine teleost	urea, trimethyl-amine oxide	aquatic	aquatic
larval amphibian	ammonia	aquatic	aquatic
adult amphibian	urea	—	semi-terrestrial
reptile	uric acid	cleidoic egg	terrestrial
bird	uric acid	cleidoic egg	terrestrial
mammal	urea	aquatic	terrestrial

amount of water for their excretion. As the concentration of uric acid in the tissue rises it settles out as a solid precipitate. The biochemical details of uric acid formation and excretion are described in section 19.4.5. Uric acid and ammonium urate are the forms in which nitrogenous excretion occurs in insects, lizards, snakes and birds. Man, apes and, because of a kidney defect, the Dalmatian dog excrete small quantities of uric acid but this is produced from the breakdown of nucleic acids and not from the breakdown of proteins. The normal level of uric acid in the blood of Man is 3 mg 100 cm^{-3} blood and approximately 1 g of uric acid is excreted in urine per day.

19.2.4 Other nitrogenous excretory compounds

In addition to the excretory products previously described, excess dietary protein is converted in some marine fishes into another excretory substance, trimethylamine oxide.

$$CH_3$$
$$CH_3 {\Rightarrow} N = O$$
$$CH_3$$

trimethylamine oxide

This is produced by the addition of methyl groups to ammonia, formed by deamination, and the subsequent oxidation of intermediate molecules. Trimethylamine oxide gives fish its characteristic smell.

The only other source of nitrogenous waste substances is nucleic acid. Foods such as yeast, liver and kidney are rich in small cells and have abundant nuclei. The breakdown of these foodstuffs releases significant amounts of the nucleic acid bases, purines and pyrimidines. Spiders and some mammals excrete the purines adenine and guanine directly, but in other organisms these are broken down into uric acid as described later.

Adenine and guanine have a similar structure to uric acid whereas the pyrimidine bases cytosine, thymine and uracil have a structure which enables them to be broken down into a molecule of ammonia and a molecule of amino acid. The amino acid then undergoes deamination and the nitrogenous waste is excreted in the form which is typical of that organism.

Insects, terrestrial reptiles, birds, Man, apes and the Dalmatian dog excrete purines as uric acid. The majority of mammals, however, possess the enzyme uricase in the liver, which converts uric acid directly to the excretory product **allantoin**. Dipteran insects also excrete allantoin. Some teleost fish produce allantoin which oxidises to the excretory product **allantoic acid**.

Creatine and its derivative **creatinine** are other nitrogenous waste products. Creatine is formed in the liver of vertebrates from the amino acids, arginine, methionine and glycine. Approximately 2% of the total amount of creatine in the body is lost each day as creatinine. Some creatine is phosphorylated in the muscles to form creatinine phosphate (phosphagen) where it acts as an energy store for the regeneration of muscle ADP to ATP (section 17.4.8).

A final group of nitrogenous waste compounds results from detoxification processes occurring in the liver. The commonest product is hippuric acid (*hippos*, horse) which was discovered in horse urine and is formed by the conjugation of benzoic acid (from plant foods) and the amino acid glycine. Many other phenolic compounds such as benzoic acid are rendered harmless by similar detoxification reactions.

19.3 Nitrogenous excretion and osmoregulation

The major source of waste nitrogenous substances is the deamination of excess amino acids. This produces ammonia which is extremely toxic and must be eliminated. Being soluble, ammonia can be eliminated from the body rapidly and safely if diluted in a sufficient volume of water. This presents no real problems to organisms which have ready access to water but this applies only to those organisms living in the freshwater environment. Marine and terrestrial organisms have an acute problem of gaining or conserving water respectively, therefore very little is available for the elimination of nitrogenous waste. Table 19.2 reveals that organisms living in these environments have developed alternative means of nitrogen excretion. These involve the development of many anatomical, biochemical, physiological and behavioural mechanisms involving the elimination of nitrogenous waste whilst maintaining the composition of the body fluids at a steady state. Since these may involve excretion and osmoregulation the two processes will be considered together.

Osmoregulation is a homeostatic process by which animals and plants maintain the concentration of their body fluids at a steady state. Body fluids are found within cells (**intracellular**) and outside cells (**extracellular**). For example, the fluid within plant cell vacuoles (cell sap) is intracellular whereas the fluid surrounding the cells of the cortex of a plant stem or root is extracellular. In multicellular animals intracellular fluid is dispersed fairly evenly throughout the cell whereas extracellular fluid exists as plasma and interstitial fluid. The latter is further subdivided in vertebrates into tissue fluid and lymph. It is vital that the composition of these fluids should remain at a steady state in order for the metabolic activities of the cells to work efficiently. The nature of the intra- and extracellular fluids and their regulation in plants is described in section 19.3.2.

Osmoregulation is not a term used simply to describe the control of water balance within an organism. It refers to the control of the composition of body fluids, which in all cases are solutions of varying complexity. Details of the physical and chemical properties of solutions are described in appendix A1.4.

In living systems, even if the osmotic pressures of two solutions are the same (that is they are isotonic), solutes will move if their relative concentrations are different. The movement of water molecules between two solutions, by osmosis, occurs in response to the relative osmotic pressures of the two solutions. Solute molecules move across differentially permeable membranes in a direction determined by their relative concentrations on either side of the membrane and their size in relation to the pores of the membrane. This movement may be **passive** and molecules move down a concentration gradient from a region of their high concentration by **diffusion**, or they may move against the concentration gradient as a result of **active transport** by carrier mechanisms located in the membrane. Membranes, including the plasmalemma (cell or plasma membrane), cytoplasmic tissue layers, body surfaces and gills, can all act as differentially (or selectively) permeable membranes through which water and solutes can pass.

The osmotic concentration of solutions is described in this chapter in terms of **osmotic potential** and expressed either in milli-osmoles per litre (mOsm dm^{-3}) or milli-osmoles per kilogram of water (mOsm kg^{-1}).

For biological purposes involving osmoregulation the concentration of a solution may also be described in terms of the **freezing point depression** of the solution. Pure water freezes at 0 °C, but as solutes are added the freezing point falls below 0 °C and the new freezing point indicates the concentration of solutes in the solution. For example, sea water has an osmotic potential of $-1\,000$ mOsm dm^{-3} and a freezing point depression (Δ) of -1.7 °C.

19.3.1 Osmoregulatory mechanisms

The osmotic relationships between two solutions separated by a differentially permeable membrane can be described in terms of **tonicity** or **osmoticity**. There are important differences between the two terms regarding the nature of solutions and the circumstances in which they are used; however, for simplicity, in this text the relationships between solutions are described in terms of tonicity, that is solutions are either **hypotonic** *to* or **hypertonic** *to* another solution or **isotonic** *with* another solution.

The body fluids of freshwater organisms are usually hypertonic to their aquatic environment whilst those of many marine organisms, particularly vertebrates, are hypotonic to sea water. Many marine invertebrates, on the other hand, are isotonic with the marine environment.

If the concentration of solutes in an aquatic environment increases, or the volume of water decreases, animals respond in either of two ways. An **osmoconformer** would alter the concentrations of its body fluids to equal those of the new surroundings, whilst an **osmoregulator** would maintain its osmotic concentration despite changes in the external environment. In homeostatic terms, osmoconformers are described increasingly as **poikilosmotic** and osmoregulators as **homeosmotic**, in line with the prefixes used in temperature regulation.

19.3.2 Osmoregulation in plants

Plant tissue contains a higher proportion of water than animal tissue, and the effective and efficient functioning of the plant cell and the whole plant depends upon maintaining the water content at a steady state. Plants do not have the same problems of osmoregulation as animals and they can be considered simply in relation to their environment. On this basis plants are classified as outlined below.

Hydrophytes

Freshwater aquatic plants such as Canadian pondweed (*Elodea canadensis*), water milfoil (*Myriophyllum*) and the water lily (*Nymphaea*) are classed as hydrophytes and have fewer osmoregulatory problems than any of the other plant types. Plant cells in fresh water are surrounded by a hypotonic environment and water enters the vacuolar sap by osmosis. The water passes through the freely permeable cell wall and the differentially permeable plasma and tonoplast membranes. As the volume of the vacuole increases due to water uptake, it generates a **turgor pressure**. The cell becomes turgid and a point is reached when the water potential has increased to equal that of the surrounding water (about zero), and no further water enters (see section 14.1.5). This is termed **mechanical osmoregulation**. *Nitella clavata* is a freshwater alga with an extremely hypertonic sap, whose osmoregulatory problems only concern the maintenance of the ionic contents of the sap. This is carried out by active uptake from the surrounding water.

Halophytes

The only plants able to live immersed in sea water are algae and they form the major source of vegetation on the seashore. The distribution of algal species down the shore is determined by many factors, including tolerance to wave

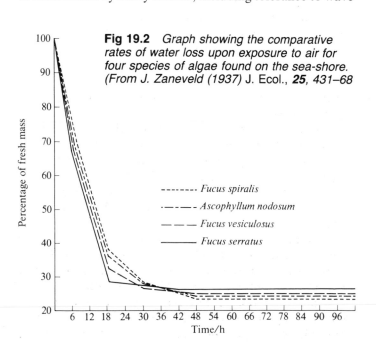

Fig 19.2 *Graph showing the comparative rates of water loss upon exposure to air for four species of algae found on the sea-shore. (From J. Zaneveld (1937) J. Ecol.,* **25**, *431–68*

-------- *Fucus spiralis*

-·-·-·- *Ascophyllum nodosum*

— — — *Fucus vesiculosus*

——— *Fucus serratus*

action, desiccation when exposed by tides and the nature of their photosynthetic pigments. In all cases these species can tolerate increases in salinity and their main osmoregulatory problem is the prevention of water loss by evaporation. Channel wrack (*Pelvetia canaliculata*) occupies the highest algal zone on sheltered rocky shores surrounding the British Isles, and its habitat tolerance is aided by thick cell walls, a thick covering of mucilage and a stipe shaped as a channel. Fig 19.2 shows the rate of water loss and degree of tolerance of four common British species of seaweed which are zoned according to their ability to retain water when exposed to air.

Halophytes, however, are defined as plants inhabiting areas of high salinity such as those encountered in estuaries and salt marshes where salinity is constantly changing and may exceed that of sea water. Whilst the shoot system is not regularly exposed to high salinities, the root system must tolerate the increased salinities of the sand and mud which accompany hot windy periods when the tide is out. It was thought that these plants must tolerate periods of 'physiological drought' when water is unavailable to the tissues due to the hypertonic nature of the environment of the roots. However, this does not seem to be the case and high transpiration rates and high osmotic pressures in root cells enable water to be taken up. Cord grass (*Spartina*) is a common halophyte found low down on estuaries and salt marshes; it has an extensive system of rhizomes for propagation, bearing adventitious roots for anchorage and purposes of water and ion uptake. Other halophytes of estuaries and salt marshes include smaller plants which store water when it is freely available. Common examples of these species are glasswort (*Salicornia*), seablite (*Suaeda maritima*) and sea purslane (*Halimione*). Some species, such as sea milkwort (*Glaux*) and *Spartina* are able to regulate their salt content by excreting salt from glands at the margins of the leaf.

Mesophytes

The majority of angiosperm plant species are mesophytes, and they occupy habitats with adequate water supplies. They are faced with the problem of water loss by evaporation from all aerial parts. Features which help to reduce water loss are both structural (xeromorphic) and physiological, and include the presence of a cuticle, protected stomata whose diameters can be regulated, a variable leaf shape, abscission and an ecological distribution based upon tolerance to dehydration. Further details and examples of these mechanisms are found in section 14.3.

Xerophytes

Plants adapted to life in dry regions and able to survive long periods of drought are called xerophytes. These form the typical flora of desert and semi-desert regions and are common along the strand line of the seashore and in sand dunes. Some plants respond to extreme conditions by surviving in the seed or spore stage. These are known as **drought evaders** and can germinate following rainfall and

grow, flower and complete seed formation in four weeks, for example the Californian poppy (*Escholtzia*). The seeds produced lie dormant until the next rainy spell.

Drought endurers, on the other hand, show many structural (xeromorphic) and physiological adaptations enabling them to survive in extremely dry conditions. Most of the xerophytic species of the British Isles are associated with the strand line and sand dunes, such as saltwort (*Salsola*) and sea sandwort (*Honkenya*) found growing in small mounds of sand on the shore. Sand couch grass (*Agropyron*) and marram grass (*Ammophila*) are dominant species of embryo dunes and have extensive rhizome systems with adventitious roots for obtaining water from well below sand level. *Agropyron* is able to tolerate salt concentrations in the sand up to 20 times that of sea water. Both *Ammophila* and *Agropyron* are important pioneer plants in the development of sand-dune systems.

Xerophytic plant species of desert regions show several adaptations to reducing water loss and obtaining and storing water. Some of these are summarised in table 19.3.

Table 19.3. Summary of methods of conserving water shown by various plant species (see chapters 14 and 16)

Mechanism of water conservation	Adaptation	Example
reduction in transpiration rate	waxy cuticle ⎫ few stomata ⎬ sunken stomata stomata open at night and closed by day surface covered with fine hairs curled leaves	prickly pear (*Opuntia*), pine (*Pinus*), ice plant (*Mesembryanthemum*) marram grass (*Ammophila*)
storage of water	fleshy succulent leaves fleshy succulent stems fleshy underground tuber	*Bryophyllum* candle plant (*Kleinia*) *Raphionacme*
water uptake	deep root system below water table shallow root system absorbing surface moisture	acacia oleander cactus

19.3.3 Processes associated with excretion and osmoregulation

Ultrafiltration is the process by which solvent and solute molecules separate from a solution according to their differential abilities to pass through the pores in a filter. The filter in most animals is the layer separating the circulatory system and the osmoregulatory or excretory organ. The force required to produce filtration is a hydrostatic pressure and comes from the blood pressure. The filtered solution is known as **filtrate**. Most of the contents of blood are removed by ultrafiltration, the exceptions being really large molecules, such as proteins, and cells, such as red blood cells.

Selective reabsorption involves the selective uptake of solute molecules and water in amounts which are useful to the body. Those substances which are metabolic wastes are not reabsorbed, nor are solute and water molecules if their reabsorption would result in their exceeding the normal steady-state composition of the body fluids. Reabsorption occurs initially by passive diffusion until the diffusion gradient levels out, after which further reabsorption occurs by active transport. As solutes are reabsorbed, the filtrate becomes progressively more dilute or hypotonic to the body fluids so that water molecules follow the movement of ions by osmosis to produce a filtrate which is isotonic to the body fluids. A hypotonic filtrate is produced by the further uptake of ions from the filtrate in a region of the osmoregulatory/excretory organ which is impermeable to water.

Secretion occurs by active transport and removes solutes from the body fluids to the filtrate or directly to the environment. It therefore operates in the opposite direction to reabsorption. This mechanism further increases the osmotic pressure of the filtrate and decreases the osmotic pressure of the body fluids.

The net effect of these three mechanisms of ultrafiltration, selective reabsorption and secretion is homeostatic, in that it maintains the composition of the body fluids at a steady state.

There is a range of osmoregulatory or excretory organs and organelles which show variety in morphological structure and anatomical location, yet they all rely for their function on one or more of the mechanisms described above. Some of the structures are relatively non-specialised and share common characteristics within a range of organisms, for example contractile vacuoles, nephridia and kidneys, whereas others are relatively specialised, such as gills, rectal glands and salt glands.

19.3.4 The effect of environment on excretion and osmoregulation

The nature of the environment produces certain osmoregulatory problems in different groups of organisms. Many aquatic organisms living in a hypertonic environment *lose* water by osmosis and *gain* solutes by diffusion. The water loss is replaced in various ways, including drinking and eating, but this increases the solute concentrations of the body fluids and necessitates the removal of excess solute molecules by active transport. Organisms living in a hypotonic environment *gain* water by osmosis and *lose* solutes by diffusion. In order to minimise these exchanges the organisms often have an impermeable outer covering and take up ions from the environment by active transport.

All terrestrial organisms face the problem of water and solute loss from their body fluids to the environment. The intracellular body fluid of these organisms is maintained at a steady state by the regulation of the extracellular body fluid by specialised osmoregulatory/excretory organs, such as Malpighian tubules and kidneys. A balance must be achieved between the amount of water and ions lost and gained. The problems of water balance are described in detail in section 19.4.

Adaptations to severe drought

The kangaroo rat (*Dipodomys*) is quite remarkable among mammals in being able to tolerate drought conditions in the deserts of North America. It flourishes in these conditions by possessing a unique combination of structural, physiological and behavioural adaptations. Water loss by evaporation from the lungs is reduced by exhaling air at a temperature below core temperature. As air is inhaled it gains heat from the nasal passages which assume a lower temperature. During exhalation water vapour in the warm air condenses on the nasal passages and is conserved. The kangaroo rat feeds on dry seeds and other dry plant material and does not drink. Water produced by the chemical reactions of respiration, and that present in minute amounts in its food, are its only sources of water. The classic investigations by Knut Schmidt-Nielsen (summarised in table 19.4) revealed the overall water metabolism balance for a kangaroo rat weighing 35 g metabolising 100 g of barley in experimental surroundings at 25 °C and a relative humidity of 20%. Throughout this period the only source of water was the barley grain.

Table 19.4 Water metabolism for a kangaroo rat under experimental conditions. The absorbed water was the water present in the food

Water gains	cm^3	Water losses	cm^3
oxidation water	54.0	urine	13.5
absorbed water	6.0	faeces	2.6
		evaporation	43.9
Total water gain	60.0	Total water loss	60.0

Finally the kangaroo rat avoids excessive evaporative water losses in the wild by spending much of its time in the relatively humid atmosphere of its underground burrow.

The other spectacular example of water conservation is the camel, whose physiological adaptations are described in section 18.4.7.

19.4 A phylogenetic review of organs and processes of nitrogenous excretion and osmoregulation

Throughout this review the following points should be considered:
(1) the environment influences the nature of the excretory product and the process of osmoregulation,
(2) some groups of organisms have species adapted to life in more than one environment,
(3) some organisms are able to withstand considerable changes in the environment.

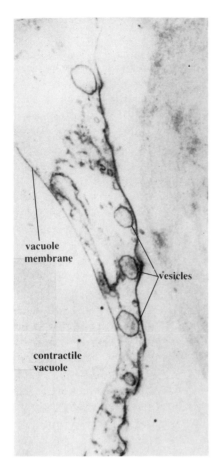

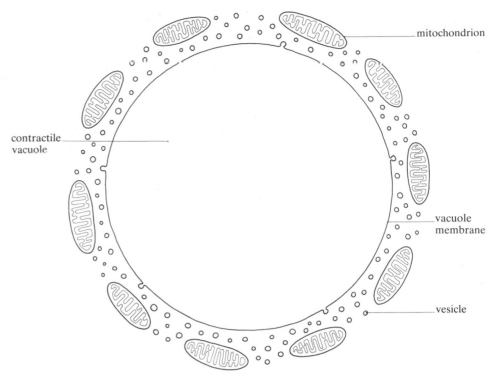

Fig 19.3 *Electron micrograph of contractile vacuole of* Amoeba. *Water is secreted into tiny vesicles which fuse with the membrane of the contractile vacuole discharging water into the vacuole*

19.4.1 Protozoa

Protozoans are found in freshwater and marine habitats and the body fluids of other organisms. The intracellular fluid of a protozoan is separated from the external environment only by a differentially permeable plasma membrane. Excretion of carbon dioxide and ammonia occurs by diffusion over the entire surface of the cell. This has a relatively large surface area to volume ratio which assists the removal of waste substances.

All freshwater species of protozoans are hypertonic to their surroundings and have osmoregulatory organelles known as **contractile vacuoles**. These are necessary to remove water which enters the cell by osmosis from the hypotonic medium through the plasma membrane, and to regulate the volume of the cell and prevent it increasing in size. The exact location and structure of the contractile vacuole is extremely variable. In *Amoeba proteus* a contractile vacuole can form anywhere within the cell and release its fluid into the external environment at any point on its outer surface (fig 19.3). In *Paramecium aurelia* there are two contractile vacuoles with fixed positions (fig 19.4). The method of functioning, however, appears to be similar in all species and involves the movement of water from the cytoplasm into small vesicles which fuse with, and empty their water into, the contractile vacuole. Mitochondria collect around contractile vacuoles, and presumably supply the energy for the 'osmotic' work of filling them.

Investigations carried out into the function of the contractile vacuole in the giant amoeba (*Chaos chaos*) show that the calculated osmotic influx of water based on the osmotic pressure of the intracellular fluid agrees with observed estimates of the volume eliminated by the contractile vacuole. The contents of the contractile vacuole are hypotonic to the intracellular fluid yet hypertonic to the external medium. Several hypotheses have been put forward to account for formation of vacuolar fluid. A probable explanation is shown in fig 19.5.

Many of the marine rhizopod protozoa do not have functional contractile vacuoles because their intracellular fluid composition is isotonic with sea water. This evidence suggests that the primary role of the contractile vacuole is osmoregulation.

19.4.2 Coelenterata

Coelenterates do not appear to possess any excretory or osmoregulatory organs or organelles and the mechanism of osmoregulation is unknown. Carbon dioxide and ammonia are the principal toxic metabolic waste substances and they are removed by diffusion from the cells directly into the water of the extracellular environment.

19.4.3 Platyhelminthes

Most of the metabolic waste products of platyhelminths pass into the much-branched gut and are

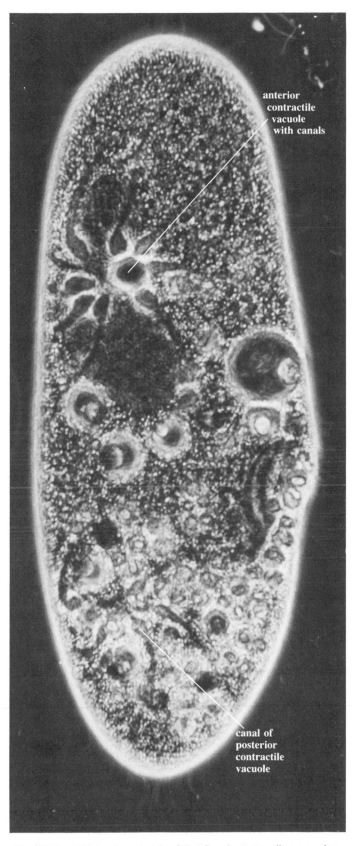

anterior
contractile
vacuole
with canals

canal of
posterior
contractile
vacuole

Fig. 19.4 *Photomicrograph of the fixed contractile vacuoles of* Paramecium

eliminated via the mouth. Some, however, pass into a series of tubules which form a joint excretory and osmoregulatory system. This is a primitive type of nephridium, known as a **protonephridium**, whose principal function is osmoregulation. Protonephridia are found mainly in animals that lack a true body cavity (coelom) such as the platyhelminths and rotiferans. *Planaria* has a pair of protonephridia which run the entire length of the body and open to the exterior via numerous excretory pores (fig 19.6a). Each protonephridium is made up of many tubules which branch and end in enlarged hollow cells from which cilia project into the tubule. If only one cilium is present the cell is known as a **solenocyte** and if several are present it is known as a **flame cell** (fig 19.6b). The cilia of the flame cells undulate, and this movement resembles the flickering of a flame, hence the name. This 'flickering' appears to agitate the fluid in the tubule and propel it along the nephridial ducts towards the excretory pores. The fluid in the flame cell is composed of water and waste substances produced by the tissues. It is thought that some of these wastes are secreted into the tubule by active transport and some by ultrafiltration through the cytoplasm of the flame cell. Water enters the lumen of the flame cell by osmosis. Flame cells are found in some annelids and solenocytes are found principally in the cephalochordate, *Amphioxus*.

19.4.4 Annelida

Annelids have a combined excretory and osmoregulatory organ known as a **metanephridium**, or simply a **nephridium**, which regulates the chemical composition of the body fluids. The exact structure and distribution of nephridia varies in each of the three orders, the Polychaeta, Oligochaeta and Hirudinea, but the basic structure and function is similar in all. Nephridia are unbranched tubules which link the coelom to the exterior. In some species, such as the lugworm (*Arenicola*), the nephridium is formed by the fusion of an ectodermal tubule which opens to the exterior by a pore and a mesodermal tubule or coelomoduct which opens into the coelom. The earthworm (*Lumbricus*) has a pair of nephridia in each segment apart from the first three and the last, but polychaetes and leeches have fewer.

A nephridium consists of a ciliated funnel, the **nephrostome**, which leads via a long ciliated and muscular tubule to a bladder where fluid is stored prior to its release through an external opening, the **nephridiopore**. The waste fluid is called **urine** and is formed by the processes of ultrafiltration, selective reabsorption and active secretion.

Coelomic fluid containing useful and waste substances passes into the nephrostome by pressure created by the beating of cilia (fig 19.7). Fluid passes along the long narrow tube by the action of cilia and muscles but no reabsorption of useful substances occurs here. The cells lining the short middle tube and the longer wide tube reabsorb useful substances into the blood capillaries in their walls, whilst further waste is actively secreted into the

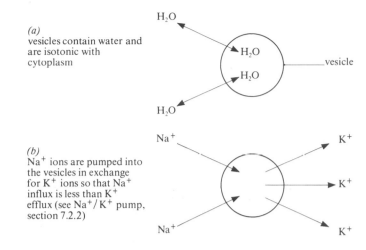

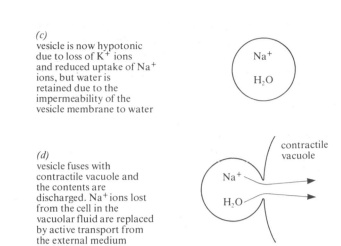

(a) vesicles contain water and are isotonic with cytoplasm

H_2O

H_2O

H_2O

H_2O

vesicle

(b) Na^+ ions are pumped into the vesicles in exchange for K^+ ions so that Na^+ influx is less than K^+ efflux (see Na^+/K^+ pump, section 7.2.2)

Na^+

Na^+

K^+

K^+

K^+

(c) vesicle is now hypotonic due to loss of K^+ ions and reduced uptake of Na^+ ions, but water is retained due to the impermeability of the vesicle membrane to water

Na^+

H_2O

(d) vesicle fuses with contractile vacuole and the contents are discharged. Na^+ ions lost from the cell in the vacuolar fluid are replaced by active transport from the external medium

contractile vacuole

Na^+

H_2O

Fig 19.5 (above) *Diagrammatic explanation of a possible mechanism of water uptake by a contractile vacuole*

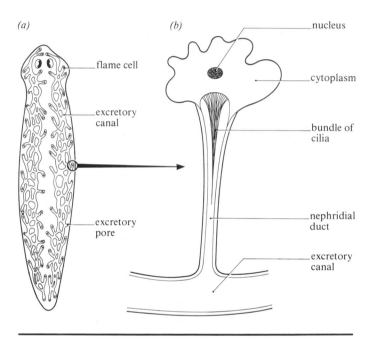

(a) flame cell, excretory canal, excretory pore

(b) nucleus, cytoplasm, bundle of cilia, nephridial duct, excretory canal

Fig 19.6 (left) *Features of the protonephridial excretory system of platyhelminths. (a) Gross structure of the system in Planaria, (b) single flame-cell*

Fig 19.7 (below) *Stages in the formation of urine in the earthworm. Heavy arrows show regions of active secretion of substances. Protein is known to be present in the nephrostome but not in the urine excreted by the nephridiopore. At some stage it is removed from the nephridium but as yet no mechanism is known to account for this uptake. (Graph after Ramsay.)*

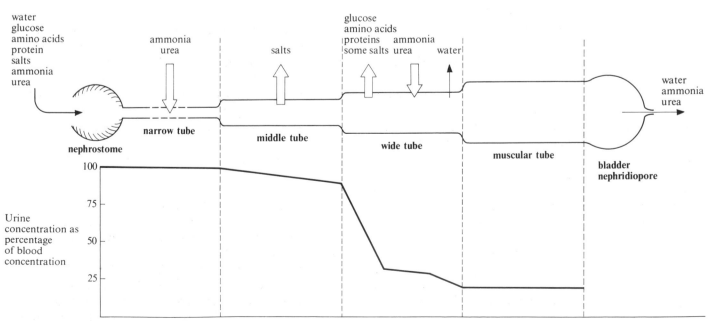

water
glucose
amino acids
protein
salts
ammonia
urea

ammonia
urea

salts

glucose
amino acids
proteins
some salts

ammonia
urea

water

water
ammonia
urea

nephrostome   narrow tube   middle tube   wide tube   muscular tube   bladder nephridiopore

Urine concentration as percentage of blood concentration

100

75

50

25

702

tubule from the capillaries. As substances are reabsorbed the concentration of waste solutes in the urine rises and the urine becomes more dilute. This urine, which is hypotonic to coelomic fluid, is excreted through the nephridiopore. The ability to produce a dilute urine suggests that the nephridium has an osmoregulatory function. Investigations have revealed that *Lumbricus* behaves as a freshwater osmoregulator since, when placed in salt solutions of various concentrations, it remains hypertonic to its environment yet produces a hypotonic urine. Although the natural habitat of the earthworm appears terrestrial, it actually lives in direct contact with the water films that surround the soil particles of the walls of its burrow. Hence it may be considered to be a freshwater organism. The osmoregulatory activities of typically marine polychaete species such as *Nereis diversicolor* are described in section 19.4.6.

19.4.5 Arthropoda

Arthropods are adapted to conditions in a vast range of habitats from marine to fully terrestrial. It is not surprising, therefore, that as a phylum they display a range of excretory and osmoregulatory mechanisms. Adaptations shown by insects to terrestrial life and crustaceans to marine, estuarine and freshwater life have been selected as representative of the range of features shown by arthropods and are described in this section.

One of the major problems of life on land is the prevention of water loss. Insects have an almost impermeable cuticle to reduce water loss from the body surface and spiracles to reduce water loss from the gaseous exchange system of tracheae and tracheoles.

The strong cuticle is composed of a chitinous exo- and endocuticle covered by a thin waterproof layer, the epicuticle (0.3 μm thick) as described in section 4.10.1. Water loss by evaporation is prevented by the impermeable properties of the epicuticle produced by a highly organised monolayer of lipid molecules covered by several layers of irregularly orientated lipid molecules. If these wax or grease lipid layers are abraded by sharp particles, such as sand or alumina, the evaporation rate increases and the insect risks dehydration. Interestingly, as the air temperature surrounding an insect is increased steadily there is a gradual increase in the rate of evaporation until a particular temperature is exceeded after which the evaporation rate increases rapidly. This point is known as the **transition temperature**. If the water loss from the insect is plotted against the insect's surface temperature this transition point can be seen more clearly and marks the temperature at which the ordered orientation of the wax monolayer breaks down, as shown in fig 19.8.

Some insects living on dry food in very dry habitats are able to take up water from the air providing that the relative humidity of the air is above a certain value, such as 90% for the mealworm (*Tenebrio*) and 70% for the house mite (*Dermatophagoides*).

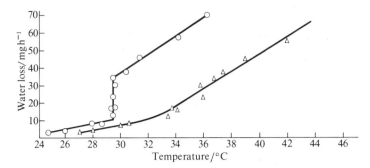

Fig 19.8 (above) Graph showing the water loss from the cuticle of a cockroach at various air temperatures (triangles). The circles indicate water loss plotted against the surface temperature of the cuticle. This shows the dramatic increase in water loss at about 29.5 °C, the **transition temperature**

Fig 19.9 (below) Diagram showing the position of Malpighian tubules in relation to the alimentary canal of Rhodnius prolixus

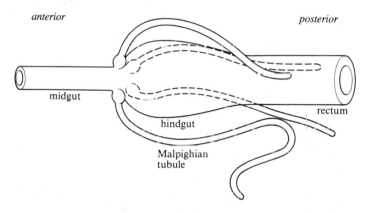

The problem of preventing water loss by excretion is overcome by specialised excretory organs called **Malpighian tubules** which produce and excrete the almost insoluble waste substance **uric acid**.

Malpighian tubules are blind-ending tubules which lie in the intercellular space of the abdomen and are bathed in haemolymph. The number of tubules is variable in insects, some have a pair and others may have several hundred. *Rhodnius*, a blood-sucking hemipteran, has four tubules; in all cases they open into the hindgut at its junction with the midgut and may be long and slender or short and compact (fig 19.9).

Wigglesworth investigated the function of the tubules in uric acid formation in *Rhodnius* and the mechanism appears to be as follows.

The tubule has two histologically distinct regions, an **upper segment** (distal to the gut), composed of a single layer of cells and containing a clear solution, and a **lower segment**. The cells of the lower segment have microvilli on their inner surface and it is here that crystals of uric acid precipitate out of solution (fig 19.10). The contents of the tubule pass into the hindgut or rectum where they mix with waste materials from digestive processes. Rectal glands in the wall of the rectum absorb water from the faeces and uric acid suspension until the waste is dry enough for it to be eliminated from the body as pellets.

Fully terrestrial organisms do not have the same osmoregulatory problems as aquatic or semi-terrestrial organisms. Insects, however, do have to regulate the ionic contents of their haemolymph and this is achieved by maintaining a balance between ions taken up in the diet and those lost through synthesis, egestion and excretion. It is aquatic arthropods such as the freshwater crustacean *Astacus*, the crayfish, and the marine crustacean *Carcinus maenas*, the shore crab, that show most adaptations of their excretory and osmoregulatory organs to their habitats and modes of life.

Astacus lives in freshwater streams which provide a hypotonic environment. Some waste nitrogenous substances and carbon dioxide are deposited in the cuticle of the nymphal stages and shed during moulting, but in the adult, nitrogenous waste is removed as ammonia through specialised excretory/osmoregulatory organs known as **antennal** or **green glands**.

The antennal glands are blind-ending mesodermal structures which lie in the haemocoel just in front of the mouth region and open to the exterior by a pore situated underneath the base of the antennae. Each antennal gland is composed of four regions, a blind-ending sac, a green tube known as the labyrinth, a long white nephridial canal and a thin-walled bladder which opens to the exterior (fig 19.11).

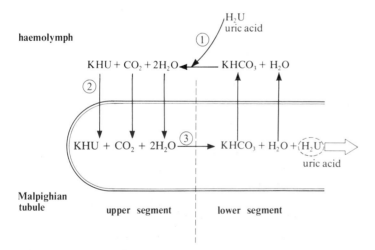

Fig 19.10 *Summary of the suggested mechanism of uric acid excretion by the Malpighian tubule. (1) Uric acid (H$_2$U) produced by the cells of the body is secreted into the haemolymph where it combines with sodium and potassium hydrogencarbonates and water to form sodium and potassium urates (NaHU and KHU), carbon dioxide and water (only potassium is shown in the diagram). (2) These salts are actively secreted into the lumen of the tubule and water follows by osmosis. (3) As these soluble substances pass down the tubule hydrogencarbonates form and these are actively reabsorbed into the haemolymph. Water follows the hydrogencarbonates by osmosis and as the pH in the lower segment fails, due to the reabsorption of hydrogencarbonates, the uric acid precipitates out as crystals*

Water and solutes are filtered from the haemolymph into the end sac by the hydrostatic pressure of the blood. As this filtrate passes through the spaces in the glandular lining of the labyrinth and along the nephridial canal, useful materials are selectively reabsorbed into the haemolymph and further waste substances, including nitrogenous waste, are secreted into the filtrate.

Astacus is hypertonic to its environment and takes in water through any permeable surface especially the gills. Large volumes of urine, which is hypotonic to haemolymph, are produced to counteract this osmotic influx. Most of the nitrogenous waste is lost as ammonia but some urea is also produced.

Carcinus lives in the intertidal zone of the sea-shore, surrounded for most of the time by sea water. It has antennal glands similar to those of *Astacus* which it uses to eliminate waste nitrogenous material, especially ammonia. In common with many other marine species, parts of its surface are permeable to salts and water and the body fluids are isotonic with the sea water. This is an economical measure for marine organisms as they do not need to expend energy in maintaining their body fluids at a higher or lower osmotic potential than their environment. However, even though they are isotonic, the ionic concentration of the body fluids may be maintained at a different level from that of the sea, and energy is required for ionic regulation.

Carcinus is found in a wide range of habitats. It can tolerate the hypertonic conditions which may be encountered in rock pools on sea-shores and salt pans in salt marshes as water evaporates from them on hot days. In these conditions it acts as an osmoconformer and decreases the osmotic pressure of its body fluids by retaining salts which the tissues tolerate. In these conditions the urine is hypertonic to the body fluids. *Carcinus* is able to tolerate the changing conditions found in estuaries and, in keeping with many species found in estuaries, it is euryhaline. As the salt concentration of the water decreases due to the diluting effects of river water or rainfall the body fluids of *Carcinus* become hypertonic to the surrounding medium (fig 19.12). Water tends to enter by osmosis and solutes leave by diffusion. Under these conditions *Carcinus* becomes an osmoregulator and maintains the body fluid composition at a steady state by actively secreting sodium from the urine back into the haemolymph through the cells of the antennal gland. Some water will be retained as the sodium is reabsorbed but the overall volume of the organism is prevented from increasing due to the tough cuticle. In these conditions the urine is isotonic to the body fluids.

19.4.6 Effects of changes in the environment shown by invertebrates

Invertebrates which live in sea water, such as sea anemones, are isotonic with their environment. If placed in diluted sea water they immediately take up water

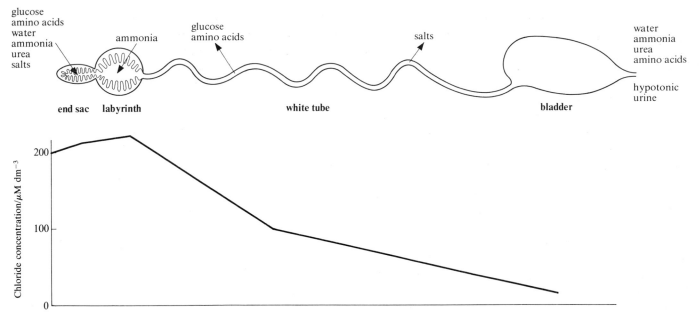

Fig 19.11 *Diagram summarising the structure and function of the antennal (green) gland of* Astacus. *The graph indicates changes in the osmotic potential of the filtrate. (After Peters from Barrington.)*

and lose ions. This is also seen by exposing *Arenicola* to decreasing salinities. After an initial increase in mass the mass returns to normal. This is explained by the fact that water enters by osmosis faster than ions are lost. After a short while conditions become stable due to loss of ions, the body fluids become isotonic with the environment and the mass returns to normal provided the salinity does not fall too low. *Nereis* is normally found in marine conditions in sand and mud but it can osmoregulate down to salinities of 10% sea water and inhabit estuaries. It is an osmoregulator and is able to remain hypertonic to the environment because of the reduced permeability of its body surface and its ability to take up chloride ions from its environment (fig 19.12).

There are some marine species that are hypotonic to sea water, such as the shrimps *Palaemonetes* and *Leander* (fig 19.12). They have overcome problems of water loss and uptake of ions by drinking water and actively secreting ions back into the sea through their gills. These mechanisms of control are so efficient that shrimps are able to maintain their body fluid level at a steady state in external concentrations ranging from 2 to 110% sea water. It is thought that this ability reflects the freshwater ancestry of the species which have secondarily invaded sea water.

The brine shrimp (*Artemia*) is hypotonic to the extremely high salinities of its environment and maintains its body fluids in a hypotonic state by continually removing sodium and chloride ions from the concentrated medium which it drinks. It does this by eliminating them from the haemolymph through the epithelium of the gills. It is also able to maintain its body fluids at a steady state despite fluctuations of 10–1 000% sea water in the external environment.

Some brackish water species, such as the mussel (*Mytilus*), are able to maintain the intracellular composition of their cells at a fairly steady state despite changes in the composition of the external environment and the extracellular fluid. This is thought to be due to regulation of the fluid composition by individual cells.

Many freshwater species, such as *Astacus*, are thought to have developed from marine species via brackish water species by progressive improvements in the efficiency of water and ion regulation.

Small freshwater invertebrate animals have a relatively large surface area to volume ratio. Since they are hypertonic to their environment they tend to take in water and lose salts more rapidly than comparable larger invertebrates, such as *Astacus*, that have a smaller surface area to volume ratio. They have overcome this problem, to a certain extent, by having body fluids with a lower ionic concentration than larger forms.

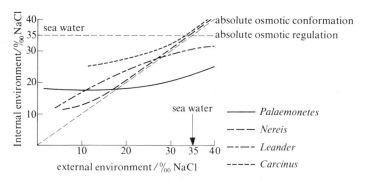

Fig 19.12 *Graph showing the relationship between internal and external environments for osmotic conformers, osmotic regulators and four marine species, the prawns,* Leander *and* Palaemonetes, *the ragworm,* Nereis *and the shore-crab,* Carcinus

19.4.7 Echinodermata

All echinoderms are marine. Nitrogenous waste is removed from the gills and tube-feet by diffusion as ammonia and urea. Echinoderms have a water vascular system containing sea water with which the cells are isotonic. There is no problem of osmoregulation.

19.4.8 Vertebrata

All three nitrogenous waste products are excreted by vertebrates and, with few exceptions, the form of the waste product is related to the environmental availability of water. Osmoregulatory mechanisms in vertebrates are more efficient than in invertebrates because of the reduced permeability of the body surface and the development of the kidney. Biologists are uncertain as to whether the earliest fish originated in the sea or in fresh water. Many biologists favour a marine origin and see the kidney as a later development necessary for survival in the hypotonic conditions of fresh water. In this environment it provides a mechanism for the removal of excess water and the retention of salts. Subsequent development of the kidney is related to the environment of the organism, and shows a progressive increase in complexity throughout the vertebrate classes from the fish to mammals. This increase in complexity is associated with colonisation of the terrestrial environment. The increased efficiency of these mechanisms maintains the internal composition of the body fluids within narrower limits than in the invertebrates.

The basic unit of the kidney is the **nephron**. Nephrons are segmental structures formed from mesodermal nephrotomes (section 21.8) which have become intimately associated with blood vessels from the aorta and are linked to the coelom by a ciliated funnel. The nephrons of fish larvae show their most primitive arrangement where several of them open into the pericardial cavity and form a collective structure known as the **pronephros** (fig 19.13). All adult fish and amphibia lose the pronephros and have a more compact structure made up of many more nephrons and found in the abdominal and tail regions of the organisms. This is called a **mesonephric kidney**. Its nephrons have lost their connections with the coelom and are linked together by a collecting duct which leads to the urinogenital opening. Such a structure is ideal for the production of dilute urine produced predominantly by organisms living in a freshwater environment.

Reptiles, birds and mammals are adapted to life on land where problems of water removal experienced by fish and amphibians are replaced by problems of water retention. These organisms have an even more compact structure, the **metanephric kidney** which contains far more nephrons with longer tubules for water reabsorption. These tubules eventually release concentrated urine into the central cavities of the kidney. From here it passes to the **bladder** by a tube known as the **ureter**. (The detailed structure and function of the mammalian kidney is described in section 19.5.)

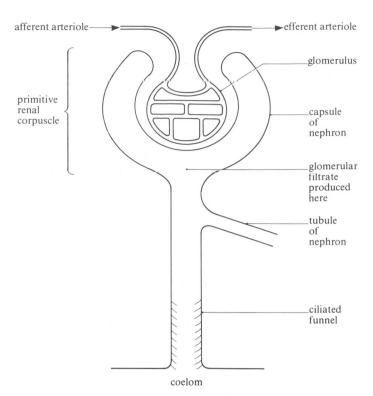

Fig 19.13 *Structure of a primitive nephron. Filtrate produced from the glomerulus passes to the coelom via the ciliated funnel or joins up with other nephrons via connecting tubules*

The vertebrate kidney relies on the principles of ultrafiltration, selective reabsorption and active secretion for the production of urine. **Urine** is a liquid containing nitrogenous waste, water and ions in excess of those required by the body. Ultrafiltration does not discriminate between those substances which are useful to the body and those which are not and energy is expended in reabsorbing 99% of the solutes back into the blood. However, despite the apparent inefficiency in terms of energy, this mechanism gives vertebrates greater flexibility to exploit new habitats since it permits 'foreign' or 'new' substances to be excreted as they are encountered. It does not require the development of new secretory mechanisms to remove these substances.

Pisces

The excretory and osmoregulatory organs of the fish are gills and kidneys. Both structures are permeable to water, nitrogenous waste and ions and have a large surface area to facilitate exchange. The kidney, unlike the gill, is separated from the external environment by the body wall, the body tissues and extracellular body fluid, and can therefore exercise control over the steady-state composition of the body fluids. Despite the fact that fish live in an aquatic environment there are enough differences between the mechanisms of excretion and osmoregulation in freshwater and marine species for them to be described separately.

Freshwater fish. Freshwater teleosts have an internal osmotic concentration of approximately

300 mOsm dm^{-3} and are hypertonic to their environment. Despite having a relatively impermeable outer covering of scales and mucus there is a considerable osmotic influx of water and loss of ions through the highly permeable gills, which also serve as the organs for the excretion of the waste nitrogenous substance ammonia. In order to maintain the body fluids at a steady state, freshwater fish have to continually lose a large volume of water. They do this by producing a large volume of glomerular filtrate from which solutes are removed by selective reabsorption into the capillaries surrounding the kidney tubule. The kidneys produce a large volume of very dilute urine (hypotonic to blood) which contains some ammonia and a number of solutes. Up to one-third of the body mass can be lost per day as urine. Ions which are lost from the body fluids are replaced from food and by active uptake from the external environment by special cells in the gills.

Marine fish. Fish are thought to have originated in the sea and, having successfully invaded the freshwater environment, secondarily re-invaded the sea and given rise to the elasmobranchs and marine teleosts. Whilst in the freshwater environment many of the basic metabolic activities and organ functions evolved based on an osmotic pressure of the body fluids at a level between one-third and one-half that of sea water. On their return to the sea the body fluids retained their ancestral osmotic pressure and this produced problems of maintaining the body fluids at a steady level in a hypertonic environment (fig 19.14).

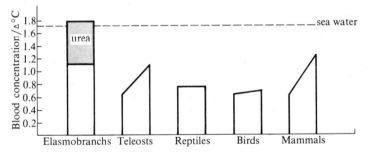

Fig 19.14 *Approximate body fluid concentrations of marine vertebrates. Elasmobranchs are the only vertebrates with a body fluid hypertonic to the environment but as the graph shows the basic osmotic concentration is a little higher than that of teleosts. The retention of urea increases the osmotic pressure to that of sea water, as shown by freezing point depressions ($\Delta °C$ = change in $°C$)*

Elasmobranchs. The basic osmotic pressure of body fluids in elasmobranchs is approximately the same as that of marine teleosts, that is, equivalent to a 1% salt solution. In order to prevent excessive water loss to the hypertonic sea water elasmobranchs have increased the osmotic pressure of their body fluids by synthesising and retaining urea within their tissues and body fluids. The majority of the cells in the body, with the exception of brain cells, appear capable of synthesising urea and their metabolic activities appear not only to depend on its

presence but also to be able to tolerate high levels of it. Investigations carried out on isolated shark hearts have shown that they will only beat if perfused with a balanced salt solution containing urea. The body fluids contain between 2 and 2.5% urea, which is about 100 times the concentration which can be tolerated by other vertebrates. High concentrations of urea normally disrupt the hydrogen bonding between amino acids and denature proteins so inhibiting enzyme activity, but not, for some reason, in elasmobranchs. Urea, together with inorganic ions and another nitrogenous waste substance trimethylamine oxide ($(CH_3)_3N{=}O$) which is less toxic than ammonia, increases osmotic pressure of the body fluids above that of sea water (Δ sea water $-1.7\,°C$, Δ elasmobranchs $-1.8\,°C$) (fig 19.14). Elasmobranchs, being therefore slightly hypertonic to the environment, take in water by osmosis through their gills. This is eliminated along with excess urea and trimethylamine oxide by the kidneys in a urine which is slightly hypotonic to the body fluids. The kidney has long tubules which are used for the selective reabsorption of urea but not for the elimination of salts which enter with the diet. Excess sodium and chloride ions are removed from the body fluids by active secretion into the rectum by the cells of the rectal gland, which is a small gland attached to the rectum by a duct. The gills are relatively impermeable to nitrogenous waste and any which is lost from the body is controlled by the kidney. In this way the osmotic pressure of the body fluids is maintained at a high level.

Marine teleosts. Marine teleosts maintain their body fluids at an osmotic pressure which is hypotonic to sea water (fig 19.14). The body surfaces are relatively impermeable to water and ions due to scales and mucus but the body fluids lose water and gain ions freely through the gills. In order to regulate the composition of the body fluids teleosts drink sea water, and secretory cells in the gut remove salts by active transport into the blood. **Chloride secretory cells** in the gills actively remove chloride ions from the blood into the sea and sodium ions follow to maintain electrochemical neutrality. The other major ions in sea water, magnesium and sulphate, are removed in the small volume of isotonic urine which is produced by the kidneys. The kidneys lack glomeruli and are therefore unable to carry out ultrafiltration. All the contents of the urine – such as the nitrogenous substance trimethylamine oxide which gives fish their characteristic smell – and salts, are secreted into the kidney tubules and water follows by osmosis.

Euryhaline fish. There are several euryhaline fish which not only tolerate slight changes in salinity but are able to adapt totally to freshwater and marine conditions for major periods of their lives. Depending upon the direction in which they move to spawn these fish are described as anadromic or catadromic. **Anadromic** (*ana*, up; *dramein*, to run) species such as the salmon (*Salmo salar*) hatch in fresh water and migrate to the sea where they mature before returning to fresh water to

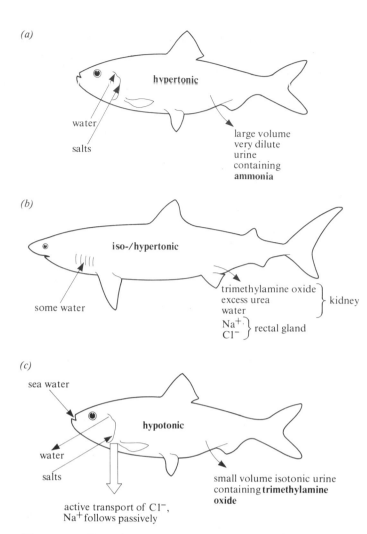

(a)

hypertonic

water

salts

large volume
very dilute
urine
containing
ammonia

(b)

iso-/hypertonic

some water

trimethylamine oxide
excess urea
water } kidney

Na⁺,
Cl⁻ } rectal gland

(c)

sea water

hypotonic

water

salts

small volume isotonic urine
containing **trimethylamine
oxide**

active transport of Cl⁻,
Na⁺ follows passively

Fig 19.15 *Excretion and osmoregulation in (a) freshwater
teleosts, (b) elasmobranchs and (c) marine teleosts*

spawn. **Catadromic** (*cata*, down) species such as the eel
(*Anguilla vulgaris*) move in the opposite direction. They
hatch in sea water and migrate to fresh water where they
mature before returning to the sea to breed. When the eel
moves from fresh water to sea water it loses about 40% of
its body mass in ten hours. To compensate for this and
remain hypotonic it drinks sea water and eliminates ions by
active secretion from the gills. When the eel moves from
sea water to fresh water the mass initially increases as water
enters by osmosis but it is able to achieve an osmotic steady
state after only two days. Whilst in fresh water, salts are
taken up by active transport through the gills.

These two species show that the active transport
mechanisms in the gills are able to work in two directions.
Whether this involves a change in the direction of pumping
of the same cells or the operation of different sets of cells is
not known. It is thought that hormones from the pituitary
gland and the adrenal cortex may influence these mechanisms. In both types of fish a period of 'lying up' is necessary
when they enter freshwater environments to allow their
osmoregulatory mechanisms to adapt to the new surroundings.

Amphibia

Amphibians are believed to have developed from an
ancestral stock of freshwater fish, and have inherited
similar problems of osmoregulation in that their blood
fluids are hypertonic to their freshwater environment. The
skin of a frog is permeable to water, and most of the water
from the environment is absorbed across the skin. The
excess water which enters the body fluids is removed by
ultrafiltration through the many large glomeruli of the
kidney.

The amphibian kidney has been extensively used in
investigating the physiology of the kidney because its large
glomeruli are situated near the surface of the kidney. These
are accessible to micropipettes which can be inserted into
the glomerulus and tubules and the filtrate removed for
analysis. In this way the effectiveness of ultrafiltration and
selective reabsorption can be demonstrated. Amphibia
produce a large volume of very dilute urine (hypotonic to
body fluids). This contains urea which is eliminated by
secretion into the tubule as well as by ultrafiltration. The
advantage of this mechanism is that it allows amphibians, in
dry conditions, to reduce the amount of ultrafiltration by
the glomerulus and thereby reduce water loss in the urine;
at the same time the tubules continue to receive blood from
the renal portal system from which they still actively secrete
urea into the tubule. In this respect the mechanism is
opposite to that seen in elasmobranchs where urea is
actively reabsorbed by the tubule.

Some salts are inevitably lost in the urine and by
diffusion through the skin, but these are replaced from the
diet and by their active uptake from the environment by the
skin which is the main organ of osmoregulation. The larval
stage of the amphibia, the tadpole, is completely aquatic
and excretes ammonia through its gills, but at metamorphosis both the nitrogenous product and the mechanism of
excretion changes, as described earlier in this section.

Frogs are able to store water in their bladders and the
many subcutaneous lymph spaces. This replaces water lost
by evaporation during periods when they are on land.
Toads are able to tolerate dry conditions for longer periods
of time because their skin is less permeable to water and
because their kidneys are able to reabsorb water from the
glomerular filtrate and produce a more concentrated urine.
The permeability of amphibian skin is known to be
controlled by an antidiuretic hormone produced by the
posterior pituitary gland. The mechanism of control of
permeability is thought to be similar to that of the
mammalian kidney tubule.

Water balance in terrestrial organisms

The efficient functioning of animal cells relies on the
maintenance of the steady state of the intracellular fluid of
cells. Homeostatic exchanges in water content between
cells, tissue fluid, lymph, plasma and the environment
present problems to both aquatic and terrestrial forms of
life. Aquatic organisms gain or lose water by osmosis
through all permeable parts of the body surface depending

on whether the environment is hypotonic or hypertonic. Terrestrial organisms have the problem of losing water and many mechanisms are employed to maintain a steady-state water balance as summarised in table 19.5. This steady state is achieved by balancing water loss and water gain, as shown in table 19.6.

Table 19.5. Summary of water conservation mechanisms shown by terrestrial organisms

Organism	Water conservation mechanism
insect	impermeable cuticle trachea and spiracles Malpighian tubules uric acid as nitrogenous waste cleidoic egg
reptile	scales and keratinised skin lungs metanephric kidney uric acid as nitrogenous waste cloacal reabsorption cleidoic egg behavioural responses to heat physiological tolerance to dehydration
bird	feathers lungs metanephric kidney uric acid as nitrogenous waste cleidoic egg cloacal reabsorption
mammal	keratinised skin and hair lungs metanephric kidney hypertonic urine containing urea viviparity behavioural response to heat restricted ecological range physiological tolerance to dehydration

Table 19.6. Summary of water balance mechanisms in terrestrial organisms

water loss from body	=	water gained by body
evaporation from body surface evaporation from gaseous exchange surface water in faeces water in urine water in secretions such as tears		drinking water in food uptake through body surface respiration (metabolic water)

Reptilia

Reptiles are primarily adapted to life in the terrestrial environment and show many morphological, biochemical and physiological adaptations to life on land. However, all three orders, the turtles, lizards and snakes, and crocodiles and alligators, have species which are secondarily adapted to life in the freshwater and marine environments. In all cases the excretory and osmoregulatory mechanisms of these organisms show adaptations to these environments.

Terrestrial reptiles reduce their water loss by having a relatively impermeable skin covered by keratinised scales. The gaseous exchange organs are lungs situated inside the body to reduce water loss. The tissues produce insoluble uric acid which can be excreted without the loss of much water. Excess sodium and potassium ions require water for their removal but, since conservation of water is critical, these combine with uric acid to form insoluble sodium and potassium urates which are excreted with uric acid. The glomeruli are small and produce only enough filtrate to wash out the uric acid from the kidney tubules into the cloaca where more water is reabsorbed. Many terrestrial reptiles have no glomeruli at all.

There is no special mechanism for the removal of salts in terrestrial reptiles and the tissues are able to tolerate increases of up to 50% the normal level of salts following the ingestion of food or when water loss is excessive. Marine reptiles, such as the Galapagos iguana and the edible turtle (*Chelone mydas*) obtain a great deal of salt from their food. Their kidneys are unable to remove the rapid influx of salt from the body fluids and rely on specialised **salt glands** in the head. These glands are able to secrete a concentrated solution of sodium chloride which is several times stronger than sea water. In the turtle the salt glands are found in the orbit of the eye and ducts lead from them to the eyes. They give the impression of 'crying' and produce tears with a very high salt concentration.

The cleidoic egg

An important characteristic of both reptiles and birds which has enabled them to become totally independent of water in their life cycle is the **cleidoic egg** (fig 20.52). This is an egg enclosed in a tough shell which protects the embryo from dehydration. During embryonic development an outgrowth of the hindgut produces a sac-like structure called the **allantois** which stores uric acid produced by the embryo. Since uric acid is insoluble and non-toxic it forms an ideal storage excretory material for the embryo. In the later stages of development the allantois becomes vascularised and pressed up against the shell where it functions as a gaseous exchange organ.

Birds

Birds are believed to have developed from a stock of terrestrial reptiles, such as snakes and lizards, and inherited the same problems. The skin of birds is relatively impermeable to water and the evaporation rate is kept low by the presence of feathers and the absence of sweat glands. However water loss from gaseous exchange surfaces is considerable due to the high ventilation rate and the maintenance of a relatively high body temperature. As a consequence of the increased metabolic rate some small birds may lose up to 35% of their body mass per day.

Nitrogenous waste is eliminated as uric acid in urine which is hypertonic to the body fluids. The urine passes into the cloaca where more water is removed from the urine and faeces before the almost solid residue is released from the body.

The kidney of birds has small glomeruli and all the blood supplying the tubule, where reabsorption of water and secretion of salts occurs, comes from the glomerulus, which relies on a relatively high blood pressure for efficient functioning. Consequently the production of a large volume of glomerular filtrate and the subsequent reabsorption of most of its water and salts have become linked. The surface area of the tubule is increased, to facilitate this reabsorption, by the development of a **loop of Henle**. The physiology of this structure enables the concentration of uric acid in the urine to reach 21% which is approximately three thousand times its concentration in the body fluids.

Some marine birds, such as the penguin, gannet, cormorant and albatross, which feed on fish and sea water, absorb large quantities of salts. These are removed from the body fluids by specialised salt-secreting cells in the **salt**, or **nasal**, **gland**. The nasal glands are similar to those of marine reptiles and are situated in the orbit. They secrete a sodium chloride solution that is four times stronger than that of the body fluids. The nasal glands are composed of many lobules made up of a large number of secretory tubules that open into a central cavity leading to the nasal cavity where the salt is released as large droplets or blown out in a fine spray.

19.5 The mammalian kidney

The kidney is the major excretory and osmoregulatory homeostatic organ of the mammalian body and has functions which include removal of metabolic waste products and 'foreign' molecules; regulation of the chemical composition of body fluids by removal of substances in excess of immediate requirements; regulation of the water content of body fluids, and thus the volume of the body fluids, and regulation of the pH of body fluids.

The kidney has a rich blood supply and regulates the blood composition at a steady state. This ensures that the composition of the tissue fluid, and consequently the cells bathed by it, is maintained at a level which coincides with the optimal conditions of the cells and enables them to function effectively and efficiently at all times.

19.5.1 Position and structure of kidneys

There are a pair of kidneys in Man situated at the back of the abdominal cavity, on either side of the vertebral column, in the region of the thoracic and lumbar vertebrae. Each kidney weighs about 0.5% of the total body mass, and the left kidney lies slightly anterior to the right.

The kidneys receive blood from the aorta via the **renal arteries**, and the **renal veins** return blood to the inferior vena cava. Urine formed in the kidneys passes by a pair of **ureters** to the **urinary bladder** where it is stored until it can be released conveniently via the **urethra**.

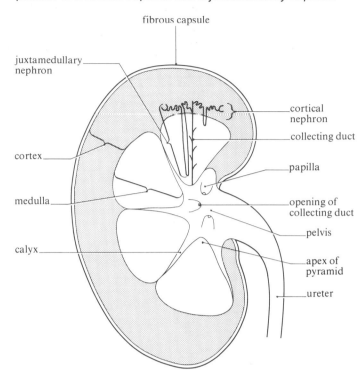

Fig 19.16 *TS through mammalian kidney showing the position of a cortical nephron and a juxtamedullary nephron*

fibrous capsule

juxtamedullary nephron

cortex

medulla

calyx

cortical nephron

collecting duct

papilla

opening of collecting duct

pelvis

apex of pyramid

ureter

A transverse section of the kidney shows two distinct regions, an outer **cortex** and an inner **medulla** (fig 19.16). The cortex is covered by a fibrous capsule, and contains glomeruli which are just visible to the naked eye. The medulla is composed of tubules, collecting ducts and blood vessels grouped together to form **renal pyramids**. The apices of the pyramids are called **papillae**, and they project into the **pelvis** which is the expanded origin of the ureter (fig 19.16). A large number of blood vessels run through the kidney and supply a vast network of blood capillaries.

19.5.2 Nephron – gross structure and blood supply

The basic structural and functional unit of the kidney is the nephron and its associated blood supply. Each kidney, in Man, contains an estimated one million nephrons each having an approximate length of 3 cm. This offers an enormous surface area for the exchange of materials.

Each nephron is composed of six regions having strikingly different anatomical features and physiological functions:
(1) renal corpuscle (Malpighian body), composed of Bowman's capsule and glomerulus,
(2) proximal convoluted tubule,
(3) descending limb of the loop of Henle,
(4) ascending limb of the loop of Henle,
(5) distal convoluted tubule, and
(6) collecting duct.
The structural relationship between these regions is shown in fig 19.17.

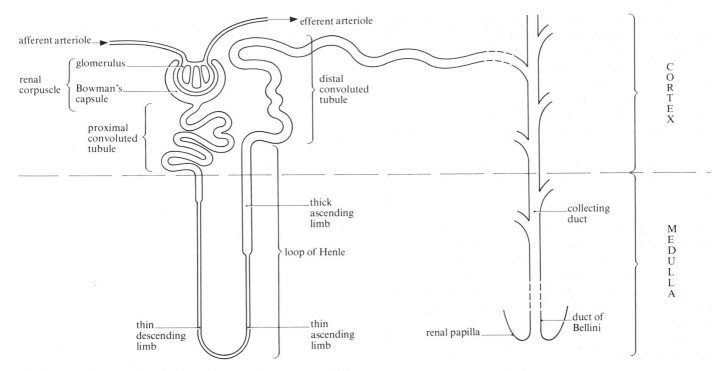

Fig 19.17 *Diagram showing the structure of a nephron. (Not to scale.)*

There are two types of nephrons, cortical nephrons and juxtamedullary nephrons, which differ in their positions in the kidney. **Cortical nephrons** are found in the cortex and have relatively short loops of Henle which just extend into the medulla. **Juxtamedullary nephrons** have their renal corpuscle close to (= *juxta*) the junction of the cortex and medulla. They have long descending and ascending tubules of the loop of Henle which extend deep into the medulla (fig 19.18). The significance of the two types of nephrons relates to differences in their use. Under normal conditions of water availability the cortical nephrons deal with the control of plasma volume, whereas when water is in short

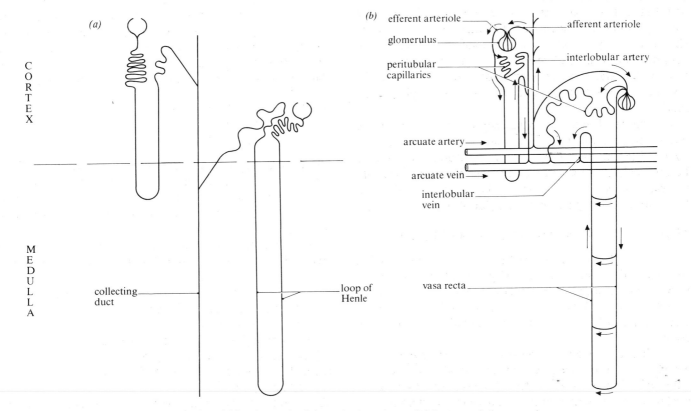

Fig 19.18 *Nephrons and their associated blood supply; (a) cortical nephron, (b) juxtamedullary nephron*

711

supply increased water retention occurs through the juxtamedullary nephrons.

Blood enters the kidney by the renal artery which progressively branches into interlobar arteries, arcuate arteries and interlobular arteries before passing to the glomerulus of the renal corpuscle as an afferent arteriole. A reduced volume of blood leaves the glomerulus by an efferent arteriole and flows through a network of peritubular capillaries in the cortex which surround the proximal and distal convoluted tubules of all nephrons and the loop of Henle of cortical nephrons. Arising from these capillaries are the capillaries of the vasa recta which run parallel to the loops of Henle and the collecting ducts in the medulla. The function of both of these vascular networks is to return blood, containing substances which are useful to the body, to the general circulation. Blood flow through the vasa recta is much less than through the peritubular capillaries and this enables a high osmotic pressure to be maintained in the interstitial tissue of the medulla. This high osmotic pressure is vital in producing a concentrated urine.

19.5.3 The role of the kidney

Apart from their function in the removal of metabolic waste, the kidneys are **homeostatic** organs and maintain the body fluid composition at a steady state despite wide fluctuations in water and salt uptake. A shortage of water, excess water uptake, excessive sweating, a shortage of salts or excess of salts would all have serious consequences for the body if the kidney was unable to adapt its function to these changes. Yet it is only the last two regions of the nephron, the distal convoluted tubule and the collecting ducts, where changes in function occur to regulate the body fluid composition. The rest of the nephron up to the distal convoluted tubule is *stereotyped* and functions in the same way in all physiological states. The waste product of kidney function is urine whose volume and composition varies, reflecting the physiological state of the body. Normally there is a copious supply of dilute urine, but at times when the body is short of water a concentrated urine is produced.

19.5.4 Basic principles of kidney function

A logical explanation of kidney function based on following the course of filtrate through the nephron is made difficult because events in one region of the nephron have important consequences for events in its other regions.

Urine formation and the regulation of the steady state of the body is a dynamic process involving the removal of substances from one part of the nephron to another, such as the collecting duct to ascending limb, and from nephron to capillaries surrounding the nephron.

The purpose of this section is to outline the general principles which underlie nephron function in terms of processes and mechanisms. This provides a background for the detailed study of later sections.

Processes

(1) **Ultrafiltration.** All small molecules, such as water, glucose and urea, are filtered out of the blood plasma in the glomerulus and produce a filtrate in Bowman's capsule which passes into the tubule of the nephron.

(2) **Selective reabsorption.** All substances useful to the body and required to maintain the water and salt composition of the body fluid at a steady state are removed from the filtrate and reabsorbed into the blood capillaries, for example glucose in the proximal convoluted tubule.

(3) **Secretion.** Further substances not required by the body may be secreted into the filtrate, by cells of the nephron, before it leaves the kidney as urine, for example K^+, H^+ and NH_4^+ in the distal convoluted tubule.

Mechanisms

(1) **Active transport.** Molecules and ions are secreted into and out of the filtrate as described in (2) and (3) above, for instance the uptake of glucose into the peritubular capillaries surrounding the proximal tubule and the removal of NaCl from the thick ascending limb.

(2) **Differential permeability.** Various regions of the nephron are selectively permeable to ions, water and urea, for example the proximal tubules are relatively impermeable compared with the convoluted tubule; the permeability of the collecting duct can be modified by hormones.

(3) **Concentration gradients.** A concentration gradient, varying from 300 mOsm kg^{-1} of water in the cortex to 1 200 mOsm kg^{-1} of water at the papillae, is maintained within the interstitial region of the medulla of Man as a result of (1) and (2) above.

(4) **Passive diffusion and osmosis.** Sodium and chloride ions and urea molecules will diffuse either into or out of the filtrate, according to the concentration gradient, wherever the nephron is permeable to them. Water molecules will pass out of the filtrate into a hypertonic interstitial region of the kidney wherever the nephron is permeable to water.

(5) **Hormonal control.** The regulation of water balance in the body and salt excretion is achieved by the effects of hormones acting on the distal convoluted tubule and collecting ducts, such as anti-diuretic hormone, aldosterone and other hormones.

19.5.5 Methods of study of kidney function

Investigations into the functioning of the kidney may be carried out directly on the exposed kidney, as in the case of studying the formation of urine, or indirectly, by analysing the relative composition of plasma and urine.

The American physiologist A. N. Richards showed that the composition of plasma and glomerular filtrate was similar, by inserting micropipettes into the renal corpuscles of amphibian kidneys and removing samples of filtrate for analysis. Amphibian kidneys were used for these studies because their renal corpuscles are relatively large and near to the surface of the kidney. This technique of **renal micropuncture** and withdrawal of fluid has been extended to other parts of the nephron and to mammals where it has yielded much information concerning the functions of these various regions.

Despite these advances there are still many kidney functions which are far from clear, for example the function of the loop of Henle. In these cases current knowledge is only hypothetical and based upon models of how these functions *may* be carried out.

Various techniques, based on the measurement of plasma clearance, have been used to investigate the rates of filtration and reabsorption by the kidney and the rate of blood flow to the kidney. **Plasma clearance** is a measure of the rate at which substances are removed from the plasma by the kidney.

The rate at which plasma is filtered by the glomeruli, the **glomerular filtration rate** (GFR) can be calculated directly from the plasma clearance value for a substance, such as the polysaccharide inulin $(C_6H_{10}O_5)_n$, which is filtered from the blood and not reabsorbed or secreted. For Man the glomerular filtration rate for both kidneys is about 125 cm^3 per minute.

19.5.6 Nephron – structure and function

The **renal corpuscle** consists of a blind-ending tube which invaginates to form a double-walled epithelial capsule called **Bowman's capsule**. This encloses the **glomerulus**, consisting of a knot of about 50 parallel capillaries originating from a single afferent arteriole and rejoining to form an efferent arteriole (fig 19.19). The entire structure of the renal corpuscle is related to its function of filtering blood. The capillary walls are composed of a single layer of endothelial cells with openings between them of diameter 50–100 nm. These cells are pressed up against a **basement membrane** (basal lamina) which completely envelops each capillary and forms the only continuous structure separating the blood in the capillary from the lumen of Bowman's capsule (fig 19.20). The inner layer of Bowman's capsule is composed of cells called **podocytes** (*podos*, foot; *cytos*, cell) and these resemble starfish in having arms (**primary processes**) which give off structures resembling tube-feet called **secondary** or **foot processes**. The foot processes support the basement membrane and capillary beneath it and gaps of 25 nm between the foot processes, called **slit-pores**, facilitate the process of filtration. The outer cells of Bowman's capsule are unspecialised squamous epithelial cells (figs 19.21 and 19.22).

Ultrafiltration is the removal from the blood of all substances with a molecular mass (**RFM**) less than 68 000 and the formation of a fluid called **glomerular filtrate**.

Both kidneys receive a total of about 1 200 cm^3 of

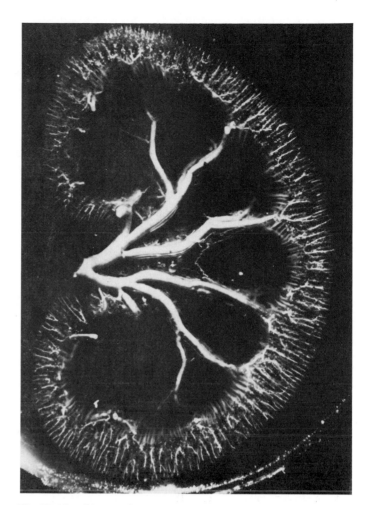

Fig 19.19 *Glomeruli and arterioles of dog kidney injected with silicone rubber. The tissues have been dissolved away*

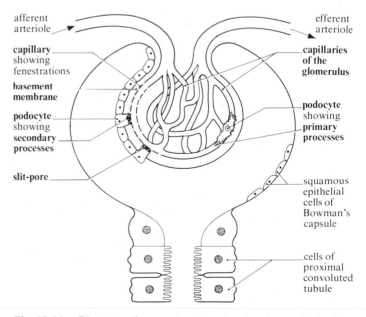

Fig 19.20 *Diagram of a renal corpuscle showing typical cells of the glomerulus and Bowman's capsule*

713

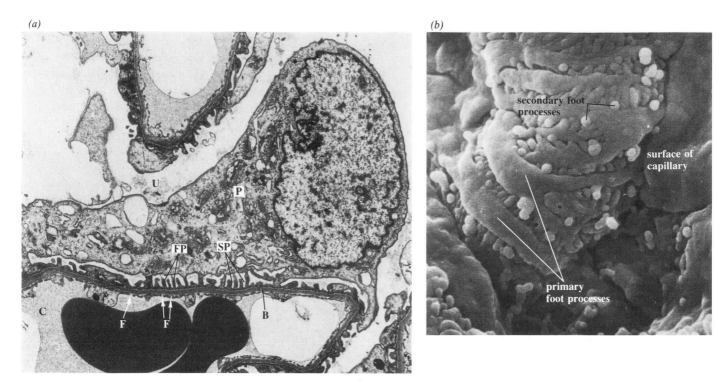

Fig 19.21 (a) Electronmicrograph showing the structure of the glomerular capillary and wall of Bowman's capsule. Lumen of capillary (C) contains plasma which passes through fenestrations in the capillary wall as indicated by the arrows. (B) is the basement membrane which acts as the filter between the capillary (C) and the cavity of Bowman's capsule (U). Foot processes (FP) of a podocyte (P) rest on the basement membrane and slit-pores (SP) can be seen between the foot processes. (b) Scanning electron micrograph of glomerular capillary

Fig 19.22 *Diagram showing the filtration path between the plasma in a glomerular capillary and the filtrate within the lumen of Bowman's capsule*

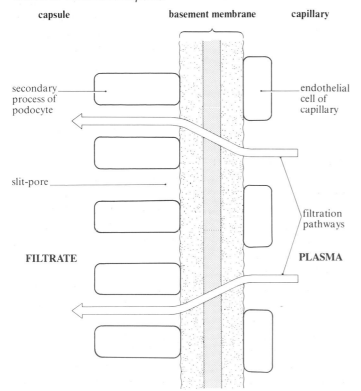

blood per minute which means that all the blood in the circulatory system passes through the kidney every 4–5 minutes. This volume of blood contains 700 cm³ of plasma of which 125 cm³ per minute is filtered out in the renal corpuscle. The substances forced out of the glomerular capillaries pass through the capillary fenestrations, basement membrane and slit-pores by the pressure developed within the capillaries. Most of the pressure is derived from the hydrostatic pressure of the circulating blood, but the effective pressure forcing fluid out of the glomerulus, the **filtration pressure**, is the result of a balance of other pressures shown in fig 19.23 and summarised by the expression:

$$\text{filtration pressure} = \text{hydrostatic glomerular blood pressure} - \left(\text{colloid osmotic pressure} + \text{hydrostatic glomerular filtrate pressure}\right)$$

The blood pressure in the glomerular capillary can be varied by changes in the diameter of the afferent and efferent arterioles which are under nervous and hormonal control. Constriction of the efferent arteriole decreases the blood flow out of the glomerulus, raises the hydrostatic pressure within the glomerulus and, if the condition persists, it leads to substances with molecular masses (RFM) greater than about 68 000 entering the glomerular filtrate.

Glomerular filtrate has a chemical composition similar to

that of blood plasma. It contains glucose, amino acids, vitamins, some hormones, urea, uric acid, creatinine, ions and water. White and red blood corpuscles, platelets and plasma protein molecules, such as albumins and globulins, are prevented from passing out of the glomerulus by the basement membrane which acts as a filter. Blood passing from the glomerulus has an increased colloid osmotic pressure due to the increased concentration of plasma proteins and a reduced hydrostatic pressure.

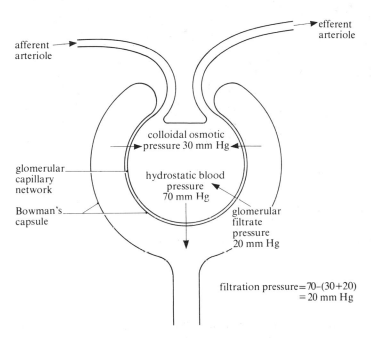

filtration pressure = 70 − (30 + 20) = 20 mm Hg

Fig 19.23 *The direction and magnitude of pressures influencing the filtration pressure in the human glomerulus*

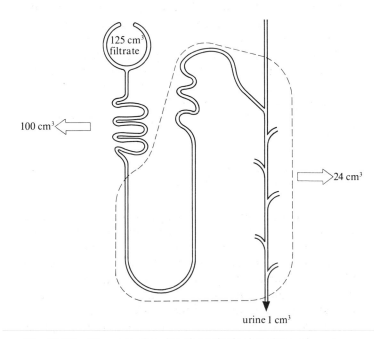

Fig 19.24 *Diagram showing the principal regions of reabsorption of renal filtrate*

The kidney tubules and selective reabsorption and secretion

Ultrafiltration produces a steady supply of glomerular filtrate, about 125 cm³ per minute in Man. If this was removed as urine it would produce 180 dm³ per day. Since only 1 500 cm³ of urine is produced each day, a great deal of reabsorption must occur. In fact, of the 125 cm³ of filtrate produced per minute 124 cm³ is reabsorbed. The main regions of reabsorption are shown in fig 19.24.

Ultrafiltration is an entirely passive and indiscriminate (in terms of substances which are valuable) process. Substances which are useful and vital are removed from the plasma along with excretory and other 'waste' substances. The function of the kidney tubules is to selectively reabsorb substances of further use to the body and those required to maintain the composition of the body fluids at a steady rate. Further waste substances may be added to the tubules by active secretion from the blood capillaries surrounding the tubules.

Proximal convoluted tubule. The proximal convoluted tubule is the longest (14 mm) and widest (60 µm) part of the nephron and conveys filtrate from Bowman's capsule to the loop of Henle. It is composed of a single layer of epithelial cells with extensive microvilli about 1 µm in length forming a brush border on the surface lining the tubule. The outer membrane of the epithelial cell rests on a basement membrane and is invaginated to form a labyrinth of **basal channels**. Adjacent membranes of tubule cells are separated by intercellular spaces and fluid circulates through basal channels and intercellular spaces as shown in fig 19.25. This fluid bathes and links the cells of the proximal convoluted tubule and the surrounding network of peritubular capillaries. The proximal convoluted tubule cells have numerous mitochondria concentrated near the basement membrane where they provide ATP for membrane-bound carrier molecules involved in active transport.

Selective reabsorption. The large surface area, the numerous mitochondria of the proximal convoluted tubule cells and the proximity of the peritubular capillaries are adaptations for the reabsorption of substances from the glomerular filtrate. Over 80% of the glomerular filtrate is reabsorbed here, including all the glucose, amino acids, vitamins, hormones and 85% of the sodium chloride and water. The mechanism of reabsorption occurs as follows. (1) Glucose, amino acids and ions that have diffused into the cells of the proximal convoluted tubule from the filtrate are actively transported out of the cells and into the intercellular spaces and basal channels by carrier mechanisms in the cell membranes. (2) Once in these spaces and channels they enter the extremely permeable peritubular capillaries by diffusion and are carried away from the nephron. (3) The constant removal of these substances from the proximal convoluted tubule cells creates a diffusion gradient between the filtrate in the

Fig 19.25 *Diagram showing the suggested mechanism of reabsorption of glomerular filtrate solutes, such as glucose, from the lumen of the proximal convoluted tubule into the surrounding peritubular capillaries. The carrier molecules of active transport mechanisms are thought to be situated in the basement membrane. The numbers apply to the description of glucose uptake given in the text*

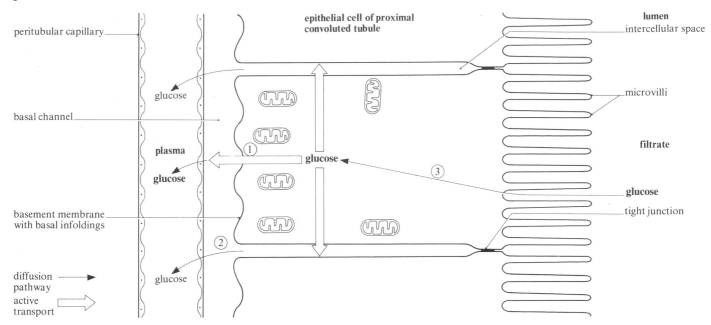

lumen and the cells, down which further substances pass. Once inside the cells they are actively transported into the spaces and channels and the cycle continues.

The active uptake of sodium and accompanying anions reduces the osmotic pressure in the tubular filtrate and an equivalent amount of water passes into the peritubular capillaries by osmosis. Most of the filtered solutes and water are removed from the filtrate at a fairly constant rate. This produces a filtrate in the tubule which is isotonic with blood plasma in the peritubular capillaries.

About 50% of the urea from the filtrate is reabsorbed, by diffusion, into the peritubular capillaries and passes back into the general circulation whilst the remainder is excreted in the urine.

Small molecular mass (RFM) proteins, that is those less than 68 000, passing into the tubule during ultrafiltration are removed by pinocytosis at the base of the microvilli. They are enclosed in pinocytotic vacuoles to which primary lysosomes (section 7.2.8) are attached. Hydrolytic enzymes in the lysosomes digest the proteins to amino acids which are either utilised by the tubule cells or passed on, by diffusion, to the peritubular capillaries.

Finally, active secretion of creatinine and 'foreign' substances occurs in this region. These substances are transported from the interstitial fluid bathing the tubules into the tubular filtrate and eventually removed in the urine.

19.5.7   Urine formation

Urine is formed by the exchange of solutes and water between the filtrate leaving the proximal convoluted tubule and all the structures distal to it (table 19.7).

Table 19.7. The composition of plasma and urine and changes in concentration occurring during urine formation in Man

	Plasma %	Urine %	Increase
water	90	95	—
protein	8	0	—
glucose	0.1	0	—
urea	0.03	2	67×
uric acid	0.004	0.05	12×
creatinine	0.001	0.075	75×
Na^+	0.32	0.35	1×
NH_4^+	0.0001	0.04	400×
K^+	0.02	0.15	7×
Mg^{2+}	0.0025	0.01	4×
Cl^-	0.37	0.60	2×
PO_4^{3-}	0.009	0.27	30×
SO_4^{2-}	0.002	0.18	90×

The ability to produce a hypertonic urine is found only in the two groups of vertebrates, the birds and mammals, which possess a loop of Henle. The concentration of urine produced is directly related to the length of the loop of Henle and the thickness of the medulla relative to the cortex, which both increase progressively in animals living in drier habitats. For example, the beaver (*Castor*), a semi-aquatic mammal, has a thin medulla, a short loop of Henle and produces a large volume of dilute urine (600 mOsm kg^{-1} of water), whereas the desert-dwelling kangaroo rat (*Dipodomys*) and the jerboa (hopping mouse – *Dipus*) have thick medullas, long loops of Henle and produce small volumes of highly concentrated urine (6 000 and 9 000 mOsm kg^{-1} of water respectively).

Descending and ascending limbs of the loop of Henle

Before describing the structure and detailed function of the various regions of the loop of Henle it is necessary to describe its overall function. The loop of Henle, in conjunction with the capillaries of the vasa recta and collecting duct, creates and maintains an increasing osmotic gradient in the medulla from the cortex to the papilla due to the build-up of increasing concentrations of sodium chloride and urea. This, in turn, provides the conditions for the progressive removal of water, by osmosis, from the tubule into the interstitial region of the medulla. The reabsorbed water is then removed from the medulla by the blood vessels of the vasa recta. Consequently a hypertonic urine is produced in the collecting duct.

At present the precise mechanism by which the loop of Henle concentrates sodium chloride towards the papilla of the medulla is not completely understood. The extent of the permeability of the descending tubule to sodium chloride is not yet understood, and whilst this affects the precise details of the mechanism it does not alter what has been described above, or what follows. The movement of ions, urea and water between the loop of Henle, vasa recta and collecting duct is described by the following points which refer to fig 19.26. (1) The first part of the descending limb is short, relatively wide (30 μm) and impermeable to ions, urea and water. It conveys filtrate from the proximal

convoluted tubule to the longer, **thin** (12 μm) **descending limb** which is freely permeable to water. (2) Since the interstitial region of the medulla is hypertonic due to high concentrations of sodium chloride and urea, water is drawn out of the filtrate by osmosis and carried away by the vasa recta. (3) This reduces the volume of the filtrate by 5% and makes it hypertonic. At the apex of the medulla (the papilla) the descending limb of the loop of Henle makes a hairpin turn and becomes the ascending limb which is impermeable to water along its entire length. (4) The first part of the ascending limb, the **thin ascending limb**, is permeable to sodium chloride and urea. Sodium chloride diffuses out of the limb as it passes away from the hypertonic region of the medulla towards the cortex whereas urea diffuses into the limb. (5) The epithelium of the **thick ascending limb** is composed of flattened cuboidal cells with a rudimentary brush border and many mitochondria. These cells are the site of the active transport of sodium and chloride ions out of the filtrate. (6) The loss of sodium and chloride ions from the filtrate increases the hypertonicity of the medulla and results in a hypotonic filtrate passing to the distal convoluted tubule.

The loop of Henle as a countercurrent multiplier

The loop of Henle functions as a countercurrent multiplier for the following reasons:

(1) the close proximity of the descending and ascending limbs,
(2) the permeability of the descending limb to water,
(3) the impermeability of the descending limb to solutes,
(4) the permeability of the thin ascending limb to solutes, and
(5) the active transport mechanisms of the thick ascending limb.

Fig 19.26 *Summary diagram showing the movement of ions, urea and water in the medulla that produce an increasing osmotic gradient within the medulla. The numbers in boxes are the osmotic concentrations in mOsm kg⁻¹ water. The numbers in circles refer to details in the text. The tonicity shown in various regions of the nephron is relative to blood plasma outside the kidney*

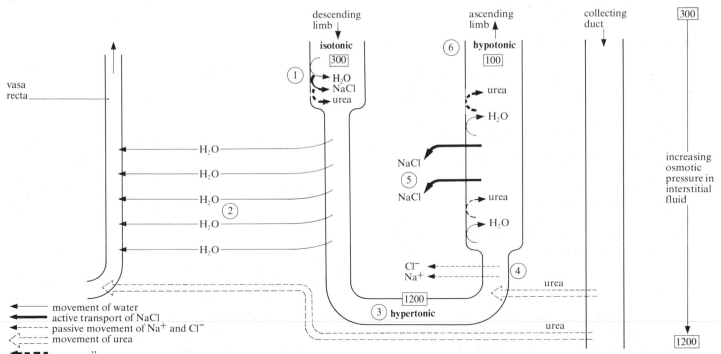

movement of water
active transport of NaCl
passive movement of Na⁺ and Cl⁻
movement of urea

The values for osmotic concentrations of the filtrate in both limbs also suggest that the loop of Henle functions as a countercurrent multiplier. In such a system the concentration difference at any given level between the fluids in the ascending and descending limbs may be slight, but as this is maintained over a long distance, as in the loop of Henle, the difference becomes additive so that the final concentration of filtrate at the base of the loop is much greater than at either end. The longer the loop the greater the concentration difference.

The removal of sodium chloride from the ascending limb increases the concentration of the interstitial region of the medulla and water is drawn out of the descending limb. This water immediately passes into the vasa recta, thereby maintaining high concentrations of solutes in the interstitial region and in the filtrate, as shown in fig 19.27. Filtrate flows around the loop and countercurrent exchange continues. The constant cycling of solutes, both passively and actively, ensures a permanently high concentration of sodium chloride in the medulla. At the same time another system, a **countercurrent exchange** system (see below), operates in the vasa recta, and these two countercurrent mechanisms operate together to ensure the *gradient* of hypertonicity in the medulla.

Fig 19.27 *Model illustrating the countercurrent multiplier formed by the tubules of the loop of Henle. Na^+ and Cl^- ions are actively transported out of the thick ascending limb into the interstitial region. The solute concentration of the interstitial region rises. Water leaves the descending limb. The numbers indicate the osmotic concentration in $mOsm\,kg^{-1}$ water. An arbitrary concentration gradient of $200\,mOsm\,kg^{-1}$ water exists between descending and ascending limbs in the model*

The vasa recta as a countercurrent exchanger

The narrow descending capillary and wider ascending capillary of the vasa recta run parallel to each other and give off branched loops at different levels along their length. They are situated close to the limbs of the loop of Henle but substances are *not* transferred directly from limbs to blood vessels. Instead they pass through the interstitial region of the medulla where, due to the slow rate of blood flow through the vasa recta, sodium chloride and urea are trapped and an osmotic gradient is maintained. The cells of the vasa recta are freely permeable to ions, urea and water, and as the vessels run side by side they function as a countercurrent exchange system. As the descending capillary *enters* the medulla the progressively increasing hypertonic condition of the interstitial region draws water out of the plasma in the capillary by osmosis, and sodium chloride and urea enter by diffusion (fig 19.28). As blood flows *from* the medulla in the ascending capillary the reverse happens and the decreasing osmotic pressure of the interstitial region enables water to re-enter the plasma whilst sodium chloride and urea leave. The adaptive significance of this mechanism is that it allows the osmotic concentration of plasma *leaving* the kidney to remain at a steady state irrespective of the osmotic concentration of plasma *entering* the kidney. Finally, and most importantly, since all the movements of solutes and water are passive, the vasa recta countercurrent exchanger makes no metabolic demand on the kidney.

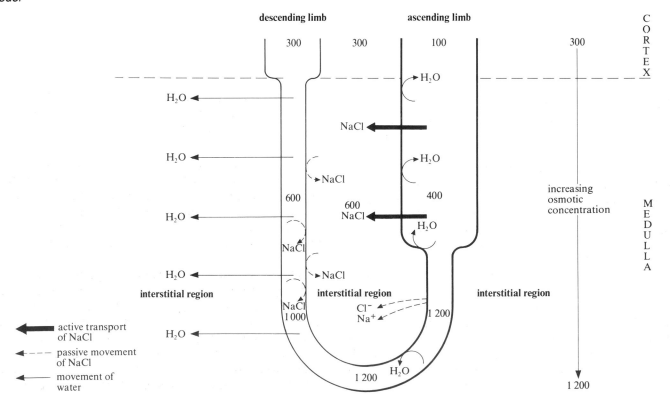

Fig 19.28 *The passive movement of water, ions and urea between adjacent vessels of the vasa recta and between these and the interstitial fluid of the medulla. The vessels of the vasa recta form a countercurrent exchange system. All values are given in mOsm kg⁻¹ water*

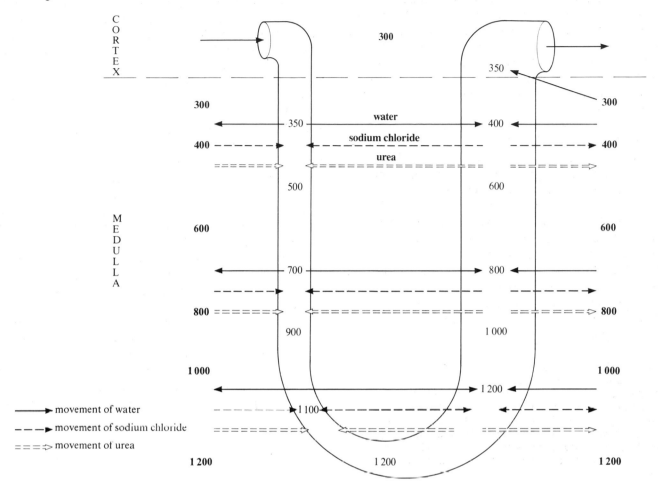

Distal convoluted tubule

The distal convoluted tubule loops backward towards the renal corpuscle and passes through the cortex. The cells of the distal tubule have brush borders and abundant mitochondria and this region is the site of the mechanisms for the fine control of salt, water and pH balance of the blood. The hormonal control of the permeability of the distal convoluted tubule to water is linked to that of the collecting duct; the two are described later. The control of salt and pH balance are described in section 19.7.

Collecting duct

The collecting tubule passes from the distal convoluted tubule in the cortex down through the medulla where it joins up with several other ducts to form larger ducts, the **ducts of Bellini**. The permeability of the walls of the duct to water and urea is controlled by **anti-diuretic hormone (ADH)**, and together with the distal convoluted tubule these structures can produce a hypertonic or hypotonic urine according to the body's demand for water.

19.6 Anti-diuretic hormone (ADH) and the formation of a hypertonic or hypotonic urine

The body maintains the osmotic pressure of the blood at an approximately steady state by balancing water uptake from the diet with water lost in evaporation, sweating, egestion and urine. The precise control of osmotic pressure, however, is achieved primarily by the effect of ADH on the permeability of the distal convoluted tubule and collecting duct.

When small amounts of water are ingested, or excessive sweating occurs, or large amounts of salt are ingested, osmoreceptors in the hypothalamus detect a rise in blood osmotic pressure. Nerve impulses are set up and pass to the posterior pituitary gland where ADH (vasopressin) is released. ADH increases the permeabilities of the distal convoluted tubule and collecting duct, water is withdrawn from the filtrate into the cortex and medulla and a reduced

719

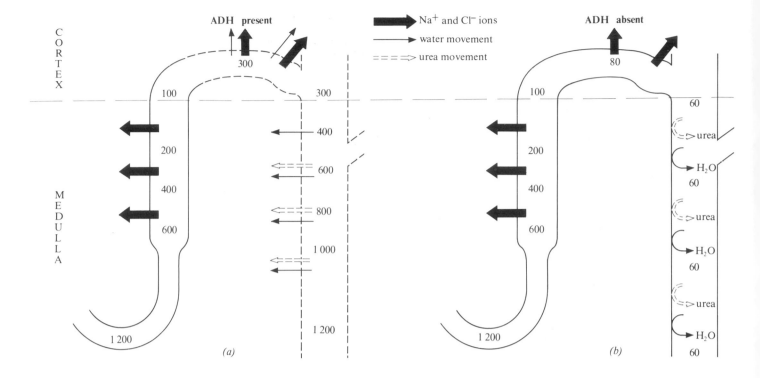

Fig 19.29 *Diagram illustrating the effect of ADH on the permeabilities of the distal convoluted tubule and collecting duct to water and urea*

volume of hypertonic urine (1 000 mOsm kg^{-1} of water) is released from the kidney.

ADH also increases the permeability of the collecting duct to urea, which diffuses out of the urine into the interstitial region of the medulla. Here it increases the osmotic concentration resulting in the removal of an increased volume of water from the thin descending limb (fig 19.29).

When there is a high intake of water and the osmotic pressure of the blood begins to fall ADH release is inhibited, the walls of the distal convoluted tubule and collecting duct become impermeable to water, less water is reabsorbed as the filtrate passes through the medulla and a large volume of hypotonic urine is excreted (fig 19.29).

Table 19.8 shows a summary of the events involved in regulating water balance, and the control mechanisms involved in regulating water and salt balance are shown in fig 19.30.

Failure to release sufficient ADH leads to a condition known as **diabetes insipidus** in which large quantities of hypotonic urine are produced (**diuresis**). The fluid lost in the urine has to be replaced by excessive drinking.

Table 19.8. Summary of the changes produced in the epithelium of the distal convoluted tubule and collecting duct in response to ADH

Blood osmotic pressure	ADH	Epithelium	Urine
rises	released	permeable	concentrated
falls	not released	impermeable	dilute

19.7   Control of blood sodium level

The maintenance of the plasma sodium level at a steady state is controlled by the hormone **aldosterone** which secondarily influences water reabsorption. A decrease in blood volume stemming from a loss of sodium stimulates a group of secretory cells, the **juxtaglomerular complex**, situated between the distal convoluted tubule and the afferent arteriole to release an enzyme, **renin**. Renin activates a plasma globulin, produced in the liver, to form the active hormone **angiotensin** and this releases aldosterone from the adrenal cortex. This stimulates the active uptake of sodium from the filtrate into the plasma in the peritubular capillaries. This uptake for sodium ions causes the reabsorption of an osmotically equivalent amount of water.

19.7.1   Homeostatic control of plasma, water and sodium levels

When the body has free access to water and a normal sodium diet, no ADH or aldosterone is released and the epithelium of the distal convoluted tubule and collecting duct remains impermeable to ions, urea and water and the urine is copious and dilute, a condition known as diuresis. The homeostatic control mechanisms are summarised in fig 19.30.

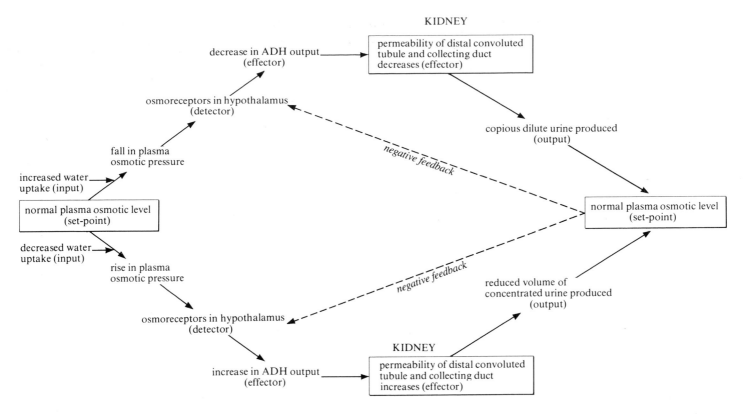

Fig 19.30 *Summary diagram of the control of plasma osmotic pressure*

19.8   Control of blood pH

Hydrogencarbonate and phosphate buffers in the blood prevent excess hydrogen ions (H^+), produced by metabolic activities, from decreasing the pH of the blood. Carbon dioxide released into the blood during respiration is regulated by this system and prevented from causing changes in plasma pH prior to its excretion from the lungs. Excessive changes in blood chemistry which would change the plasma pH from its normal level of 7.4, however, are counteracted by the distal convoluted tubule. This excretes hydrogen ions and retains hydrogencarbonate ions if the pH falls, and excretes bicarbonate ions and retains hydrogen ions if the pH rises. This may produce changes in the pH of the urine from 4.5 to 8.5. A fall in pH also stimulates the kidney cells to produce the base ion ammonia (NH_4^+) which combines with acids brought to the kidney and is then excreted as ammonium salts.

Chapter Twenty

Reproduction

The ability to reproduce, that is to produce a new generation of individuals of the same species, is one of the fundamental characteristics of living organisms. It involves the transmission of genetic material from the parental generation to the next generation, thereby ensuring that the characteristics, not only of the species but also of the parental organisms, are perpetuated. The significance of reproduction in a given species is to replace those members of the species that die, thus ensuring continuity of the species, and also to allow increase in total numbers of the species where conditions are suitable.

A new individual normally has to go through a period of growth and development before it reaches the stage at which it can reproduce itself (chapter 21). Some members of a species will die before they reach reproductive age, due to predation, disease and accidental death, so that a species will only survive if each generation produces more offspring than the parental generation. Population sizes will fluctuate according to the balance between rate of reproduction and rate of death of individuals (section 12.6). There are a number of different reproductive strategies, all with certain advantages and disadvantages which are described in this chapter.

20.1   Asexual and sexual reproduction

There are two basic types of reproduction, asexual and sexual. **Asexual** reproduction is reproduction by a single organism without production of gametes. It usually results in the production of identical offspring, the only genetic variation arising as a result of random mutations among the individuals.

Genetic variation is advantageous to a species because it provides the 'raw material' for natural selection, and hence evolution. Offspring showing most adaptations to the environment will have a competitive advantage over the other members of the species and be more likely to survive and pass on their genes to the next generation. The species therefore has the capacity to change, that is to undergo speciation (section 25.7). Increased variation can be achieved by the mixing of genes from two different individuals, a process known as genetic recombination. This is the essential feature of **sexual** reproduction and occurs in a primitive form in some bacteria (section 2.2.4).

20.1.1   Asexual reproduction

Asexual reproduction is the production of offspring from a single organism without the fusion of gametes. Except in plants with alternation of generations (section 3.3.1), meiosis is not involved and the offspring are identical to the parent. Identical offspring from a single parent are referred to as a **clone**. Members of a clone only differ genetically as a result of random mutation. Higher animals do not naturally reproduce asexually, though recent successful attempts, discussed later, have been made to clone certain species artificially.

There are several types of asexual reproduction. Further details of the process in some of the individuals referred to below are given in the relevant sections of chapters 2, 3 and 4.

Fission

Fission occurs in unicellular organisms and is the division of the cell into two or more daughter cells identical to the parent cell. Replication of DNA and, in the case of eukaryotes, nuclear division precedes cell division. Normally two identical daughter cells are produced, a process called **binary fission**. This occurs in bacteria, many protozoans, such as *Amoeba* and *Paramecium*, and in some unicellular algae, for example *Euglena*. Under suitable conditions it results in rapid population growth, as described in section 2.2.4 for bacteria.

Multiple fission, in which repeated divisions of the parent nucleus are followed by division into many daughter cells, occurs in the Sporozoa, a group of protozoans including the malaria parasite *Plasmodium*. The stage undergoing multiple fission is called the schizont and the splitting process schizogony. In *Plasmodium* schizogony occurs immediately after infection when the parasite enters the liver. About 1 000 daughter cells are released, each capable of invading a red blood cell and producing up to a further 24 daughter cells by schizogony. Such prolific powers of reproduction compensate for the large losses associated with the difficulties of successful transfer between hosts, namely Man and the vector organism, the mosquito.

Spore formation (sporulation)

A spore is a small reproductive unit which is usually microscopic and unicellular, containing a small amount of cytoplasm and a nucleus. Spores are produced by bacteria, protozoans, all groups of green plants and all groups of

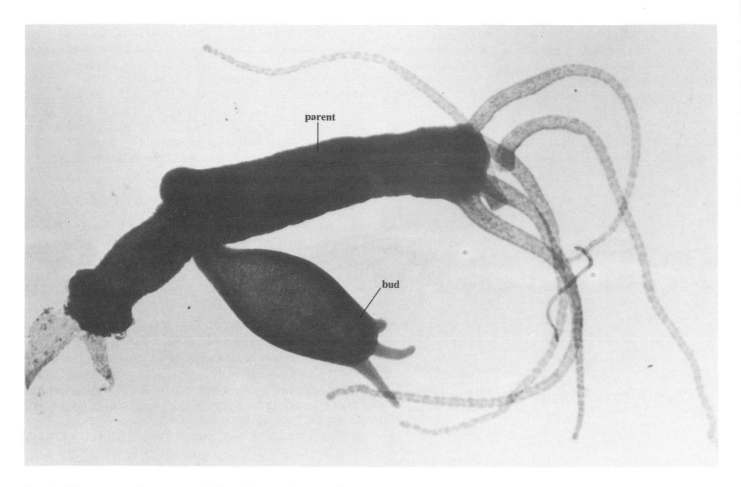

Fig 20.1 (above) *Budding of* Hydra, *a coelenterate*

fungi. They vary in type and function and are often produced in special structures. For example, spores of *Rhizopus* and *Dryopteris* are produced in sporangia; the microspores (pollen) and megaspores (embryo sacs) of seed-bearing plants are produced in sporangia called pollen sacs and ovules respectively.

Often spores are produced in large numbers and are very light, being dispersed easily by air currents as well as by animals, particularly insects. Being small they usually have minimal food stores and there is great wastage as many fail to find a suitable place for germination. In these cases they are primarily a means of rapid multiplication and spread of species, particularly of fungi.

Strictly speaking, the spores of bacteria are not reproductive structures but means of surviving adverse conditions, since each bacterium produces only one spore. Bacterial spores are among the most resistant known. For instance, they will often survive strong disinfectants and boiling in water.

Although this section is concerned with asexual reproduction, it should be pointed out that some spores are sexual spores, that is they take part in sexual reproduction. Examples are the zoospores of *Chlamydomonas* which sometimes function as gametes, and the zygospores of *Rhizopus* and *Spirogyra*. Zygospores are products of sexual reproduction and are relatively large spores with food stores and a protective outer coat. They can remain dormant during periods of adverse conditions.

Fig 20.2 (below) *Asexual reproduction in* Bryophyllum. *Young plantlets are seen along the leaf margins*

724

Note that one organism may produce more than one type of spore, for example *Rhizopus* produces sexual and asexual spores, and higher plants produce micro- and megaspores in an asexual process.

Budding

Budding is a form of asexual reproduction in which a new individual is produced as an outgrowth (bud) of the parent, and is later released as a self-supporting, identical copy of the parent. It takes place in a number of groups of organisms, notably the coelenterates, for example *Hydra* (fig 20.1), and unicellular fungi, such as yeasts. In the latter case budding differs from fission, which also occurs, in that the two parts produced are not of equal size.

An unusual form of budding is shown by the succulent plant *Bryophyllum*, a xerophyte commonly used as a decorative houseplant. It forms miniature plants, complete with small roots, along the margins of its leaves (fig 20.2). These 'buds' eventually fall off and establish themselves as independent plants.

Fragmentation

Fragmentation is the breaking of an organism into two or more parts, each of which grows to form a new individual. Fragmentation occurs in filamentous algae, such as *Spirogyra*. Here breakage into two may occur anywhere along the length of the filament.

Fragmentation also occurs among certain lower animals which, unlike more advanced animals, retain strong powers of regeneration from relatively undifferentiated cells. For example, the bodies of ribbon worms, a group of primitive, mainly marine worms, break up particularly easily into many pieces, each of which can regenerate a new individual. While in this case the process is a natural and controlled one, there are examples of animals that normally only regenerate as a result of accidental fragmentation, such as starfish. These animals have been the subjects of experiments on regeneration, a commonly used example being the free-living flatworm *Planaria*. These experiments have contributed to our understanding of the process of differentiation (section 22.8).

Vegetative propagation (vegetative reproduction)

Vegetative propagation or vegetative reproduction is a form of asexual reproduction in which a relatively large, usually differentiated part of a plant body becomes detached and develops into an independent plant. In essence it is similar to budding. Specialised structures often develop for the purpose, including bulbs, corms, rhizomes, stolons and tubers. Some of these also store food and are means of surviving adverse conditions, such as cold periods or drought. Plants possessing them can therefore survive from one year to the next and are either biennial, flowering and dying in their second year, or perennial, surviving from year to year. The structures are called **perennating organs**, and include bulbs, corms, rhizomes and tubers.

Perennating organs may be stems, roots, or whole shoots (buds), but in all cases the food stored is derived mainly from photosynthesis of the current year's foliage leaves. The food is translocated to the storage organ and then usually converted to an insoluble storage product such as starch. During the period of adverse conditions the aerial parts of the plant die and the perennating organ undergoes a period of dormancy underground. At the beginning of the next growing season the food reserves are mobilised by enzymes and buds become active, growing at the expense of the stored food. If more than one bud grows reproduction has taken place. This sequence of events is synchronised closely with the seasons, being controlled by such factors as day length (photoperiod) and temperature, environmental variables whose profound effects on growth and development are described in chapter 15.

Some of the organs of vegetative propagation and perennation are described below.

Bulb. A modified shoot, for example onion (*Allium*), daffodil (*Narcissus*) and tulip (*Tulipa*). An organ of perennation as well as vegetative propagation.

A bulb has a very short stem and fleshy storage leaves. It is surrounded by brown scaly leaves, the remains of previous year's leaves after their food stores have been used. The bulb contains one or more buds. If more than one grows, each forms a shoot which produces a new bulb at the end of the growing season, this being vegetative propagation. Roots are adventitious, that is they grow from the stem with no tap root.

A typical bulb is illustrated in fig 20.3.

brown **scale leaf,** protective, foliage leaf of season before last

fleshy leaves storing food, swollen bases of last season's foliage leaves

apical bud next season's plant, contains embryo stem, foliage leaves and a flower

apical bud of next season's bulb

axillary bud, may also form a new plant (compare apical bud)

short, flattened **stem**

remains of last season's **adventitious roots**

Fig 20.3 *Diagrammatic section through a dormant bulb*

Corm. A short, swollen, vertical underground stem, as in *Crocus* and *Gladiolus*. An organ of perennation as well as vegetative propagation.

A corm consists of the swollen base of a stem surrounded by protective scale leaves; there are no fleshy leaves, unlike bulbs. Scale leaves are the remains of the previous season's foliage leaves. Roots are adventitious. At the end of the growing season contractile roots pull the new corm down into the soil. The corm contains one or more buds which may result in vegetative propagation (compare bulb).

A typical corm is illustrated in fig 20.4.

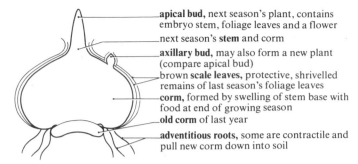

apical bud, next season's plant, contains embryo stem, foliage leaves and a flower

next season's **stem** and corm

axillary bud, may also form a new plant (compare apical bud)

brown **scale leaves,** protective, shrivelled remains of last season's foliage leaves

corm, formed by swelling of stem base with food at end of growing season

old corm of last year

adventitious roots, some are contractile and pull new corm down into soil

Fig 20.4 *Diagrammatic section through a dormant corm*

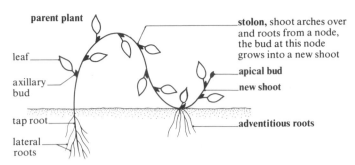

parent plant

leaf

axillary bud

tap root

lateral roots

stolon, shoot arches over and roots from a node, the bud at this node grows into a new shoot

apical bud

new shoot

adventitious roots

Fig 20.6 (above) *Generalised plan of a stolon*

Fig 20.7 (below) *Plan of a strawberry runner*

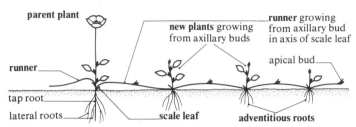

parent plant

runner

tap root

lateral roots

new plants growing from axillary buds

runner growing from axillary bud in axis of scale leaf

apical bud

scale leaf

adventitious roots

Rhizome. A horizontally growing underground stem, such as in *Iris*, Solomon's seal (*Polygonatum*), where it is short and swollen with stored food, and couch grass (*Agropyron repens*), mint (*Mentha*) and Michaelmas daisy (*Aster* spp.) where it is long and thin. It is usually an organ of perennation as well as vegetative propagation.

A rhizome bears leaves, buds, and adventitious roots. The leaves may be scale-like (small and thin, whitish or brownish in colour) as in couch grass, green foliage leaves only as in *Iris*, or a mixture of green and scale leaves as in Solomon's seal, where both types are borne on aerial shoots. An *Iris* rhizome is illustrated in fig 20.5.

Stolon. A creeping, horizontally growing stem that grows along the surface of the ground, for example blackberry (*Rubus*), gooseberry, blackcurrant and redcurrant (all *Ribes* spp.). It is not an organ of perennation. (See also runner below.) Roots are adventitious, growing from nodes.

A plan of a typical stolon is illustrated in fig 20.6.

Runner. A type of stolon that elongates rapidly, as in strawberry (*Fragaria*) and creeping buttercup (*Ranunculus repens*).

A runner bears scale leaves with axillary buds and the buds give rise to adventitious roots and new plants. The runners eventually decay once the new plants are estab-

lished. The runner may represent the main stem or grow from one of the lower axillary buds on the main stem, as illustrated in fig 20.7. In strawberry, scale leaves and axillary buds occur at every node, but roots and foliage leaves arise only at every other node. All axillary buds may give rise to new runners.

Tuber. A tuber is an underground storage organ, swollen with food and capable of perennation. Tubers survive only one year and shrivel as their contents are used during the growing season. New tubers are made at the end of the growing season, but do not arise from old tubers (in contrast to corms, which arise from old corms).

Stem tubers are stem structures produced at the tips of thin rhizomes, as in potato (*Solanum tuberosum*) and artichoke (*Helianthus tuberosum*). Their stem structure is revealed by the presence of axillary buds in the axils of scale leaves. Each bud may grow into a new plant during the next growing season.

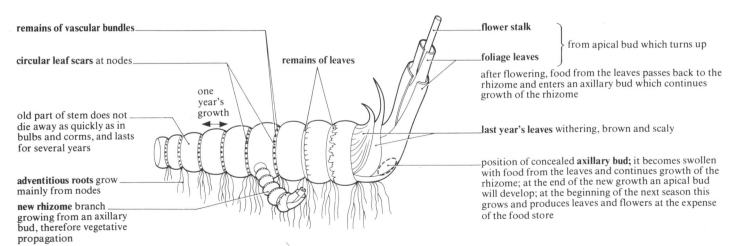

remains of vascular bundles

circular leaf scars at nodes

one year's growth

remains of leaves

old part of stem does not die away as quickly as in bulbs and corms, and lasts for several years

adventitious roots grow mainly from nodes

new rhizome branch growing from an axillary bud, therefore vegetative propagation

flower stalk

} from apical bud which turns up

foliage leaves

after flowering, food from the leaves passes back to the rhizome and enters an axillary bud which continues growth of the rhizome

last year's **leaves** withering, brown and scaly

position of concealed **axillary bud;** it becomes swollen with food from the leaves and continues growth of the rhizome; at the end of the new growth an apical bud will develop; at the beginning of the next season this grows and produces leaves and flowers at the expense of the food store

Fig 20.5 *Diagrammatic structure of an* Iris *rhizome*

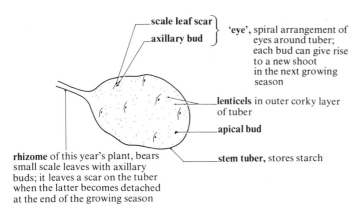

Fig 20.8 (*above*) *Stem tuber of potato*

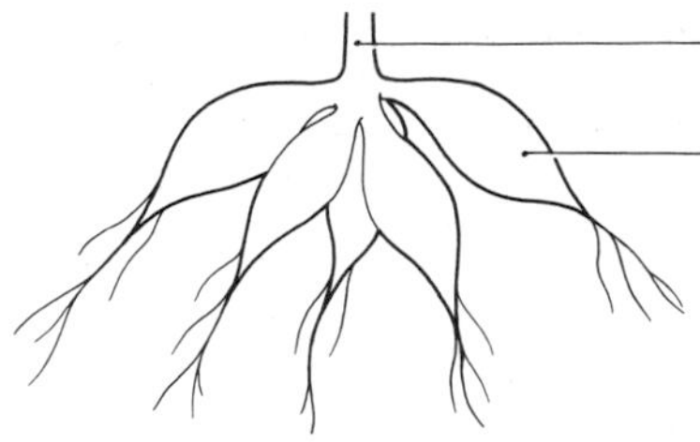

scale leaf scar
axillary bud
'eye', spiral arrangement of eyes around tuber; each bud can give rise to a new shoot in the next growing season
lenticels in outer corky layer of tuber
apical bud
rhizome of this year's plant, bears small scale leaves with axillary buds; it leaves a scar on the tuber when the latter becomes detached at the end of the growing season
stem tuber, stores starch

stem
root tuber swollen adventitious root; stores inulin, a polymer of fructose

Fig 20.9 (*above*) *Root tubers of* Dahlia

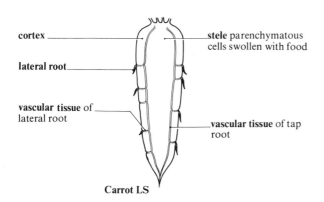

cortex
lateral root
vascular tissue of lateral root
stele parenchymatous cells swollen with food
vascular tissue of tap root

Carrot LS

Fig 20.10 (*below*) *Tap roots of carrot and turnip*

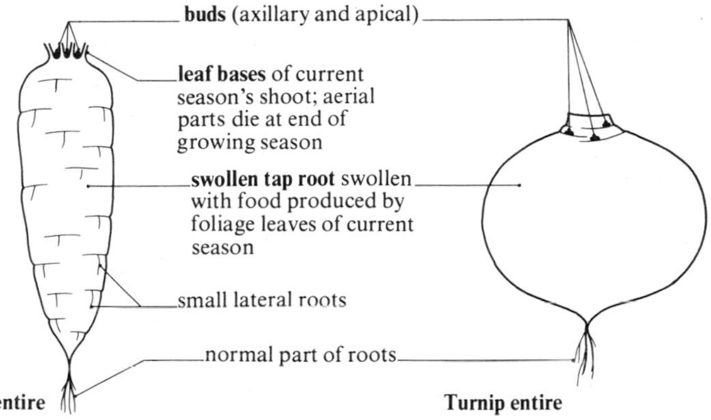

buds (axillary and apical)
leaf bases of current season's shoot; aerial parts die at end of growing season
swollen tap root swollen with food produced by foliage leaves of current season
small lateral roots
normal part of roots

Carrot entire   Turnip entire

Root tubers are swollen adventitious roots, for example *Dahlia* and lesser celandine (*Ranunculus ficaria*). New plants develop from axillary buds at the base of the old stem.

A stem tuber of potato is illustrated in fig 20.8 and root tubers of *Dahlia* in fig 20.9.

Swollen tap roots. A tap root is a main root that has developed from the radicle, the first root of the seedling. Tap root systems are characteristic of dicotyledonous plants. Tap roots may become swollen with parenchymatous food-storing tissue, as in carrot (*Daucus*), parsnip (*Pastinaca*), swede (*Brassica napus*), turnip (*Brassica rapa*) and radish (*Raphanus sativus*). Together with buds at the base of the old stem, just above the tap root, they form organs of perennation and vegetative propagation. Two types of swollen tap root are shown in fig 20.10.

Swollen tap roots are characteristic of biennial plants, plants that grow vegetatively during the first year of growth and survive winter by means of an underground storage organ. They produce flowers and seeds during the second year of growth, at the end of which they die.

Apart from the specialised organs of vegetative propagation described above, some unmodified plant parts have the ability to regenerate new plants if detached from the parent plant, such as the fallen leaves of the succulent plant *Sedum*. The taking of cuttings by gardeners and horticulturalists can be regarded as a form of vegetative propagation.

Cuttings are parts of the plant which, when removed and given suitable conditions, develop roots and leaves and become independent plants. In this way favoured varieties can be artificially propagated without change. A rooting hormone is often added to stimulate rooting. The shoots of *Pelargonium* and *Coleus*, twigs of willow (*Salix* spp.) and *Forsythia* and leaves of *Begonia* and African violet (*Saintpaulia ionantha*) can all be used for successful cuttings.

Another important, commonly used means of artificial propagation is grafting. **Grafting** in plants means the transplantation of part of one plant (a shoot or bud) on to the lower part of the shoot of another plant. The donor plant is called the **scion** and the recipient the **stock**. The stock is cut off above the graft. The resulting plant usually has the root system of the stock and the shoot system, including the flowers and fruit, of the scion. The method is commercially important for the propagation of rose bushes and fruit trees, particularly apple trees. The technique has the twin advantage of combining advantageous features from two different varieties or species, and allowing rapid production of large numbers of the new scion/stock combinations for marketing. Occasionally successful grafts of more than one scion on to a stock have been marketed, an example being apple trees that bear both eating and cooking apples.

Cloning of higher plants and animals

As already mentioned, the production of identical offspring by asexual reproduction is called cloning. Since the early 1960s techniques have been developed which have allowed successful cloning of certain higher plants and animals. These arose from attempts to demonstrate that the nuclei of mature, non-developing cells still contain all the information required to code for an entire organism and that cells become specialised as a result of the switching on and off of genes rather than by the loss of certain genes (section 22.7). The first success was achieved by Professor Steward of Cornell University, who showed that individual cells from a carrot root (the part we eat), when grown in a medium containing suitable nutrients and hormones, could be induced to start dividing again and to produce new carrot plants.

Success with higher animals followed shortly when Gurdon, working at Oxford University, achieved the first successful cloning of a vertebrate. The process does not occur naturally among vertebrates but, by taking a cell from the intestine of a frog and introducing its nucleus into an egg cell whose own nucleus had been destroyed by ultra-violet radiation, he was able to grow a tadpole, and thence a frog, identical to the parent from which the nucleus was transplanted (fig 20.11).

Not only did experiments like these establish that differentiated (specialised) cells still contain all the information needed to make the whole organism, but they suggested that similar techniques might successfully be used in cloning more advanced vertebrates, including Man. The cloning of desirable animals such as prize bulls, racehorses and so on, might be as advantageous as the cloning of plants which it has been noted already takes place. However the application of the technique to Man would be open to serious moral questions. Theoretically any number of genetically identical copies of the same man or woman might be made. Although superficially it might seem that, for example, brilliant scientists or artists might be perpetuated in this way, it has to be remembered that the degree to which environment influences development is not fully known, and any cloned cell would have to go through all the phases of development once again including, in the case of Man, embryo, foetus, baby and childhood.

20.1.2 Sexual reproduction

Sexual reproduction is the production of offspring by the fusion of the genetic material of haploid nuclei. Usually these nuclei are contained in specialised sex cells, or **gametes**, and at fertilisation they unite to form a diploid **zygote** which develops into the mature organism. Gametes are haploid, carrying a set of chromosomes derived by meiosis, and they provide the link between one generation and the next. (Sexual reproduction in flowering plants involves fusion of nuclei rather than cells but generally these nuclei are referred to as gametes.)

Meiosis is an essential feature of life cycles in which sexual reproduction occurs because it provides a mechanism for reducing the amount of genetic material by half. This ensures constancy in the amount of genetic material in each sexually reproducing generation, since fertilisation doubles the amount of genetic information. During meiosis random segregation of chromosomes (**independent assortment**) and exchange of genetic material between homologous chromosomes (**crossing-over**) results in new combinations of genes being brought together in the gamete and this reshuffling increases genetic diversity (section 22.3). The fusion of haploid gametic nuclei is called **fertilisation** or **syngamy** and it results in the production of a diploid zygote, that is a cell containing a set of chromosomes from each parent. This combination of two unique sets of chromosomes (**genetic recombination**) in the zygote forms the genetic basis of variation within species. The zygote grows and develops into the mature organism of the next generation. Sexual reproduction, therefore, involves the alternation, within the life cycle, of diploid and haploid phases, and the form adopted by the organism in each of these phases varies according to species, as shown in fig 20.13, p. 731.

Gametes are usually of two types, male and female, but in some primitive organisms they are of one type only. (See isogamy, anisogamy and oogamy in section 20.2). If the gametes are of two types, they may be produced by separate male and female parents or by a single parent bearing both male and female reproductive organs. Species that have separate male and female individuals are described as **unisexual**, such as *Homo* (Man) and most other animals. Some flowering plants are unisexual and in the case of **monoecious** plants there are separate male and female flowers on the *same* plant, for example *Corylus* (hazel) and *Cucurbita* (cucumber), whilst in **dioecious** plants one plant bears male flowers only and the other female flowers only, as in *Ilex* (holly) and *Taxus* (yew).

Hermaphroditism

Species capable of producing both male and female gametes within the same organism are described as **hermaphrodite**, or **bisexual**. Many protozoans, for example *Paramecium*, coelenterates such as *Obelia*, platyhelminths such as *Taenia* (tapeworm), oligochaetes such as *Lumbricus* (earthworm), crustacea such as *Balanus* (barnacle), molluscs such as *Helix* (garden snail), some fish, lizards and birds, and most flowering plants are hermaphrodite. This is thought to be the most primitive form of sexual reproduction and is seen in many primitive organisms. It represents an adaptation to sessile, slow-moving and parasitic modes of life. One of the advantages of hermaphroditism is the ability to carry out self-fertilisation, an essential for certain endoparasites, such as *Taenia*, which live a solitary existence. However, in the majority of species fertilisation of gametes from different organisms occurs, and many genetic, anatomical and physiological adaptations exist which prevent self-fertilisation and favour cross-

Fig 20.11 *A clone of toads* (Xenopus laevis) *produced by nuclear transplantation.* (above) *A single tail-bud embryo was obtained from a cross between two albino mutants (donor parents). Its cell were dissociated and their nuclei transplanted into u.v.-treated (nucleus destroyed) unfertilised eggs of the wild-type female (recipient) shown.*

(below) The group of 30 toads (nuclear-transplant clone) are all female and albino; they were obtained from a total of 54 nuclear transfers

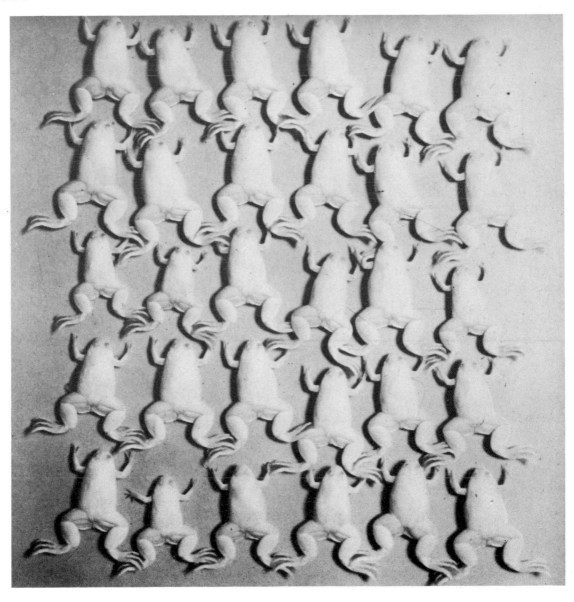

fertilisation. For example, self-fertilisation is prevented in many protozoans by 'genetic incompatability', in many flowering plants by the structure of the androecium and gynaecium and in many animals by the production of eggs and sperm at different times by the same organism.

Parthenogenesis

Parthenogenesis is a modified form of sexual reproduction in which a female gamete develops into a new individual without being fertilised by a male gamete. The process occurs naturally in both animal and plant kingdoms and has the advantage, in some cases, of accelerating the normal reproductive rate.

There are two forms of parthenogenesis, haploid and diploid, depending upon the chromosome number of the female gamete. Many insect species, including ants, bees, and wasps, utilise **haploid parthenogenesis** for the production of specific types of organism within the social group. In these species meiosis occurs and haploid gametes are formed. Some eggs undergo fertilisation and develop normally into diploid females, whereas unfertilised (haploid) eggs develop into fertile haploid males. For example, the queen honeybee (*Apis mellifera*) lays fertilised eggs ($2n = 32$) which develop into females (queens or workers) and unfertilised eggs ($n = 16$) which develop into males (drones) which produce sperm by mitosis and not meiosis. The details of the development of the three types of honeybee are summarised in fig 20.12. In social insects this mechanism has the adaptive significance of controlling the numbers of each type of offspring.

Aphids show **diploid parthenogenesis** in which the egg-producing cells of the female undergo a modified form of meiosis involving total non-disjunction (section 22.3). All the chromosomes enter the egg cell and not the polar bodies. The egg cells develop within the mother and young females are released **viviparously**, that is the parents do not lay eggs but bear live young. This can occur for several generations, particularly during the summer, until a cell undergoes almost complete non-disjunction and produces a cell containing all the autosomes plus a single X chromosome. This cell develops parthenogenically into a male aphid. These autumn stage males and parthenogenically produced females, having undergone meiosis, produce haploid gametes for sexual reproduction. Fertilisation occurs and the diploid eggs laid by the females overwinter and hatch to produce parthenogenic females in the spring. These offspring are viviparous. The parthenogenic generations alternate with a normal sexually reproduced generation which introduces genetic recombination and variation

into the population. The main advantage of parthenogenesis in aphids is the speed with which the population can increase its numbers, since all mature members of the population are egg-layers. This is particularly important at times when the environment is favourable and can support a large population, as during the summer months.

Among plants parthenogenesis occurs widely and takes various forms. One form is called **apomixis**, but it is not strictly a form of sexual reproduction, it only mimics its action. It occurs in some flowering plants in which a diploid cell of the ovule, either from the nucellus or megaspore, develops into a functional embryo in the absence of a male gamete. The rest of the ovule develops into the seed and the ovary into the fruit. In other forms a pollen grain is necessary to trigger parthenogenesis, even though the pollen grain does not grow. In such cases the pollen grain induces the hormonal changes necessary for embryo development, and such cases are, in practice, difficult to distinguish from true sexual reproduction.

20.1.3 The origins of sexual reproduction

Any discussion based upon events occurring at an unknown stage in the history of life is purely speculative and any conclusions which emerge from the discussion must be tentative. The origins of sexual reproduction represent such a situation. It is thought that asexual methods of reproduction represent the primitive form of reproduction which existed as a means of 'copying' generations which were genetically identical. At a later stage, mechanisms are thought to have arisen enabling nucleic acid to be exchanged between organisms. This may have involved the fusion of whole organisms followed by meiosis and, indeed, this possibility would appear to precede the production and fusion of gametes. It is thought that the mechanisms involved in the exchange of genetic material as shown by bacteria and described in section 2.2.4 represent a primitive stage in the development of sex. The advantage of phenotypic variation resulting from meiosis and genetic recombination doubtless played a major role in the development of more complex forms of life and types of gametes, ranging from identical gametes (**isogametes**) to the heterogametic stage of motile male gametes, represented by sperms and antherozoids, and non-motile female gametes, represented by eggs (ova). The fact that every major group of organisms carries out sexual reproduction suggests that it has advantages over asexual reproduction, the latter though rare in animals above the level of platyhelminths, is retained in plants. Indeed the

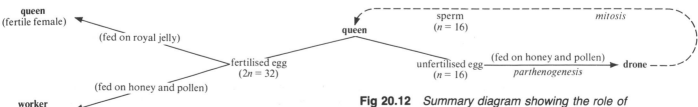

Fig 20.12 *Summary diagram showing the role of parthenogenesis in the life cycle of the honey bee colony*

Table 20.1. Comparison of asexual reproduction with sexual reproduction

Asexual reproduction	Sexual reproduction (omitting bacteria)
One parent only	Usually two parents
No gametes are produced	Gametes are produced. These are haploid and nuclei of two gametes fuse (fertilisation) to form a diploid zygote
Meiosis absent	Meiosis present at some stage in life cycle to prevent chromosome doubling in every generation*
Offspring identical to parent	Offspring are *not* identical to parents. They show genetic variation as a result of genetic recombination
Commonly occurs in plants, lower animals and micro-organisms Absent in higher animals	Occurs in the majority of plant and animal species
Often results in rapid production of large numbers of offspring	Less rapid increase in numbers

*A common source of confusion is the role played by mitosis and meiosis in reproduction. A proper discussion of this depends on a study of different life cycles and the points at which the two types of nuclear division occur in the life cycles. These are shown in fig 20.13 and described in section 20.1.4.

majority of plant species show alternation of asexual and sexual modes of reproduction in their life cycles, as described in section 20.2. One reason for this is that sessile organisms have problems of exchanging gametes and in many cases retain the option of reproducing asexually. Likewise the ecological problem of finding favourable habitats for offspring is aided by parents established in a habitat reproducing asexually. Problems of overcrowding, however, work counter to this and help limit the size of plant populations.

A summary of some of the essential and typical features of asexual and sexual reproduction is given in table 20.1.

20.1.4 Variety of life cycles

The various stages of development through which the members of a species pass from the zygote of one generation to the zygote of the next are called the **life cycle**. Life cycles vary in complexity and in some cases involve two or more generations that differ in their morphology (appearance) and reproduction, a phenomenon sometimes known as **alternation of generations**. This term is better confined to land plants and some advanced algae which show alternation between a diploid, spore-producing generation called the **sporophyte** and a haploid, gamete-producing generation called the **gametophyte** (section 3.3.1). An alternation of asexual and sexual generations also occurs in some coelenterates, but here both generations are diploid and the haploid stage is represented only

A e.g. *Chlamydomonas, Spirogyra, Rhizopus*
The adult (sexual) organism is haploid. The only diploid stage is the zygote. The first nuclear division of the germinating zygote is by meiosis, resulting in a return to the haploid condition.
NB Gametes are *not* produced by meiosis.

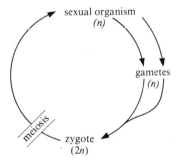

C e.g. *Obelia*
Three different morphological forms occur (polymorphism). All are diploid. The diploid sexual generation alternates with a diploid asexual generation. The only haploid cells are the gametes.
Gametes *are* produced by meiosis.

B e.g. *Fucus*, vertebrates and most other animals

The only haploid cells are the gametes.
Gametes *are* produced by meiosis.

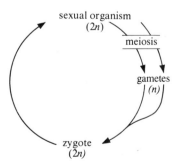

D e.g. *Laminaria* (a brown alga), all land plants i.e. bryophytes, pteridophytes and spermatophytes. Alternation of haploid and diploid generations occurs.
NB Gametes are *not* produced by meiosis.

Fig 20.13 *Representative life cycles. A, B, C, D represent four different, commonly occurring, types of life cycle. Note that meiosis only occurs once in each life cycle. Asexual reproduction of the sexual organism is not shown in A, B and D, though may be possible depending on the species. (n = haploid; 2n = diploid.)*

by the gametes. This form of alternation of generations is sometimes described as **metagenesis** (section 4.4.3). During the life cycle of these coelenterates, different forms of the individuals of the species alternate with each other, a phenomenon known as **cyclic polymorphism**. In *Obelia*, for example, three forms occur in the life cycle, namely two types of polyp and a medusa (fig 4.11). Polymorphism occurs in some other organisms, for example, the primrose (*Primula*) has two types of flower, thrum-eyed and pin-eyed.

The life cycles of parasites are often complex and may involve several generations. Each generation is adapted to a particular situation, either for survival within a host or for transfer between hosts (for example, the life cycle of *Fasciola*, section 4.5.3). The additional generations produced by asexual reproduction (**polyembryony**) serve to increase the numbers of the species. Some representative life cycles are shown in fig 20.13.

Confusion sometimes occurs over the respective roles played by mitosis and meiosis in asexual and sexual reproduction and for this reason the significance of each within the life cycle is described again here in the context of life cycles. Meiosis occurs only in life cycles in which sexual reproduction occurs. When two haploid gametic nuclei fuse, the zygote produced has the diploid number of chromosomes and starts the next life cycle. Unless meiosis occurs somewhere in this life cycle, the gametic nuclei produced will be diploid and the zygote would then be **tetraploid** (have four sets of chromosomes). Meiosis is therefore necessary to prevent chromosome doubling in every generation in those life cycles in which sexual reproduction occurs. It does not necessarily occur immediately before gamete formation, as life cycles A and D in fig 20.13 show. An additional advantage of meiosis is that it contributes to variation by the processes of independent assortment of chromosomes and crossing-over of chromosomes (section 22.3). As a direct result, as in life cycles B and C, or indirectly, as in A and D, the gametes show variation. In the special case of alternation of generations (life cycle D) meiosis occurs in the production of spores and not gametes. Variation therefore occurs among the spores and the gametophytes that develop from the spores. This variation is passed on to the gametic nuclei which are produced in the gametophyte by mitosis. In all cases, however, meiosis can be said to form the basis of sexual reproduction. In life cycles A, B and C, that is life cycles where alternation of generations does *not* occur, asexual reproduction results in the production of genetically identical offspring, and involves mitosis.

20.1 (*a*) Which one of the following statements is true, according to the information given so far in this chapter?
  (i) Asexual reproduction always results in the production of identical offspring.
  (ii) Gametes are always haploid.
  (iii) Gametes are always produced by meiosis.
  (iv) Meiosis always produces haploid cells and mitosis always produces diploid cells.
  (v) Mitosis occurs only in diploid cells.
  (*b*) Give examples of exceptions to the other four statements.

20.2 Sexual reproduction in plants

All green plants that live on land, together with some advanced algae, show alternation of generations in which a haploid gametophyte generation alternates with a diploid sporophyte generation as shown in fig 20.13D. It is the gametophyte which undergoes sexual reproduction, producing gametes by mitosis.

The remaining green plants are all algae, and show a range of types of sexual reproduction which are summarised in section 3.2.3. In the simple types (generally regarded as primitive) the gametes are all identical and the process is called **isogamy**; more complex (or advanced) types show **anisogamy** in which dissimilar gametes are found, the extreme form of anisogamy being **oogamy**, where a motile male gamete swims to a sedentary female gamete.

On leaving water, both plants and animals have evolved strategies over millions of years to cope with dry land. The most advanced groups of plants and animals, namely flowering plants and mammals respectively, owe much of their success to adaptations for sexual reproduction, and certain analogies can be drawn between the two groups. For example, the bringing together of male and female gametes does not rely on gametes being released into water, as it does for example with bryophytes or amphibians, and there is protection and nourishment of the developing embryo by the parent. A fundamental difference is the origin of gametes by mitosis from a gametophyte generation in flowering plants, whereas in mammals there is not alternation of generations and gametes are produced by meiosis from a diploid parent. As will be shown, however, the gametophyte generation of flowering plants is extremely reduced.

20.2.1 The life cycle of flowering plants (angiosperms)

The ways in which flowering plants have adapted to life on land have been described in chapter 3. The major adaptations made in reproduction are the production of seeds and fruits to nourish and protect the embryo plants and to aid in their dispersal, the absence of swimming male gametes, and the extreme reduction of the sexual gametophyte generation. Male gametes are carried inside pollen grains to the female parts of the plant, a process called **pollination** which is followed by the production of a pollen tube carrying male nuclei.

An outline of the life cycle of flowering plants is given in

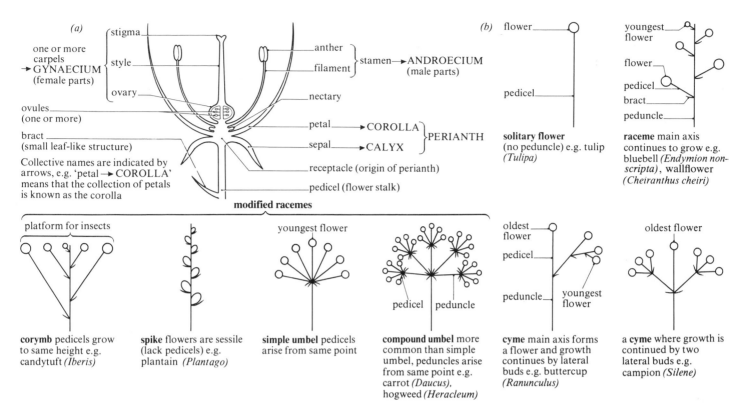

Fig 20.14 *(a) LS of a generalised flower. (b) Arrangement of flowers in groups (inflorescences) or in isolation. Some common types of inflorescence are shown which can be described as racemose or cymose*

fig 3.37, where it is compared with representative life cycles of other plant groups. There is still an alternation of generations in the life cycle, as is shown more simply in fig 20.13D. Since the gametophyte generation is virtually non-existent and is not free-living, it would be difficult to realise that alternation of generations occurs were it not for the comparison that can be made with more primitive ancestors. The life cycle of flowering plants is described in more detail below and, strictly speaking, involves asexual reproduction of the dominant sporophyte generation (the flowering plant) and sexual reproduction of the gametophyte generation.

20.2.2 The structure and functions of the flower

The common use of the term 'flowering plants' to describe the angiosperms is a reference to the uniqueness of this group in producing flowers. Flowers are reproductive structures whose evolutionary origins are unclear, but which are sometimes regarded as collections of highly specialised leaves, analogous to the cones of gymnosperms in that they carry the spore-producing structures. They can be regarded as organs of both asexual and sexual reproduction, asexual because they produce spores (pollen grains and embryo sacs) and sexual because gametes are later produced within the spores. They are commonly referred to simply as organs of sexual reproduction. In areas where there are distinct seasons, flowering is usually synchronised with a particular season and time of

year. Its environmental and hormonal control is described in section 15.5.

The parts of the flower are arranged spirally (in a few primitive flowers) or in whorls around the upper part (receptacle) of a flower stalk (pedicel). A generalised flower and the arrangement of flowers in groups (inflorescences) are shown in fig 20.14, and some of the terms used to describe the flower parts are explained below.

Parts of a flower

The **inflorescence** is a collection of flowers borne on the same stalk, the **peduncle** (see fig 20.14b). A collection of flowers may be more attractive to pollinating insects than a small solitary flower.

The **receptacle** is the end of the flower stalk (**pedicel**) from which the perianth, gynaecium and androecium arise. The receptacle and flower are described as hypogynous if the stamens and perianth are inserted below the gynaecium as in fig 20.14a, epigynous if stamens and perianth are inserted above the ovary, and perigynous if the receptacle is flattened or cup-shaped with the gynaecium at the centre and the stamens and perianth attached round the rim. (See also inferior and superior ovaries under gynaecium below.)

The **perianth** consists of two whorls of leaf-like parts called perianth segments. In monocotyledons the two whorls are usually similar, for instance daffodil (*Narcissus*), tulip (*Tulipa*) and bluebell (*Endymion non-scripta*). In dicotyledons the two whorls are usually different, consisting of an outer whorl of sepals called the calyx and an inner whorl of petals called the corolla.

The **calyx** is the collection of sepals. Sepals are usually green and leaf-like structures that enclose and protect the flower buds. Occasionally they are brightly coloured and petal-like, serving to attract insects for pollination.

Polysepalous – having free (unfused) sepals

Gamosepalous – having sepals that are at least partly fused into a tube.

The **corolla** is the collection of petals. In insect-pollinated flowers the petals are usually large and brightly coloured, serving to attract insects. In wind-pollinated flowers the petals are usually reduced in size and green, or may be entirely absent.

Polypetalous – having free (unfused) petals, for example pea (*Pisum*), rose (*Rosa*) and buttercup (*Ranunculus*)

Gamopetalous or Sympetalous – having petals that are at least partly fused into a tube, for example foxglove (*Digitalis*), primrose (*Primula*), dandelion (*Taraxacum*) and white deadnettle (*Lamium album*)

The **androecium** is the collection of stamens, forming the male reproductive organs of the flower. Each stamen consists of an **anther** and a **filament**. The anther contains the pollen sacs, in which pollen is made. The filament contains a vascular bundle that carries food and water to the anther.

The **gynaecium** or **pistil** is the collection of carpels, forming the female reproductive organs of the flower. A carpel consists of a stigma, style and ovary. The stigma receives the pollen grains during pollination and the style bears the stigma in a suitable position in the flower to receive the pollen. The ovary is the swollen, hollow base of the carpel and contains one or more ovules. Ovules are the structures in which the embryo sacs develop and which, after fertilisation, become seeds. Each is attached to the ovary wall by a short stalk called the funicle and the point of attachment is called the placenta.

The carpels of a flower may be separate and free, the apocarpous condition, as in buttercup, or fused to form a single structure, the syncarpous condition, as in white deadnettle. The ovary formed by fusion of carpels may have a single chamber or loculus (unilocular) or several loculi (multilocular) with one loculus formed by each constituent carpel. The styles of syncarpous flowers may be fused or separate.

Superior ovary – an ovary inserted above the other flower parts on the receptacle, that is the ovary of a hypogynous or perigynous flower

Inferior ovary – an ovary inserted below the other flower parts on the receptacle, that is the ovary of an epigynous flower

The **nectaries** are glandular structures that secrete nectar, a sugary fluid that attracts animals for pollination, usually insects, but also birds and bats in the tropics.

The following terms are applied to whole plants and flowers.

Hermaphrodite (bisexual) plants – male and female sex organs borne on the same plant

Monoecious plants – separate male and female flowers borne on the same plant, such as oak (*Quercus*), hazel (*Corylus*), beech (*Fagus*) and sycamore (*Acer pseudoplatanus*)

Dioecious (unisexual) plants – male and female sex organs borne on separate plants, that is the plants are either male or female, for example yew (*Taxus*), willow (*Salix*), poplar (*Populus*) and holly (*Ilex*)

Hermaphrodite (bisexual) flowers – male and female sex organs in the same flower, such as in buttercup, white deadnettle, bluebell and pea

Unisexual flowers – separate male and female flowers, for example oak, hazel, yew, willow, poplar and holly

Symmetry of flowers

If the flower parts are arranged in radial symmetry around the receptacle, the flower is said to be regular or **actinomorphic**, for instance buttercup and bluebell. If the flower shows bilateral symmetry only, it is said to be irregular or **zygomorphic**, as in white deadnettle and pea.

Representative flowers. Some representative insect-pollinated flowers are illustrated in figs 20.15–20.18. Fig 3.38 illustrates the floral morphology of a typical grass, a wind-pollinated monocotyledon.

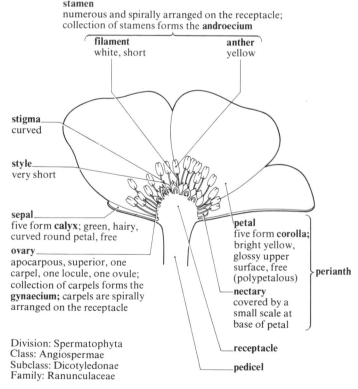

Division: Spermatophyta
Class: Angiospermae
Subclass: Dicotyledonae
Family: Ranunculaceae

Fig 20.15 *Half-flower of meadow buttercup (*Ranunculus acris*), a polypetalous dicotyledon. It is a herbaceous perennial common in damp meadows and pastures. It perennates by means of a rhizome. Flower: actinomorphic and hypogynous. Flowers appear April to September. Pollination: insects such as flies and small bees. Fruit: each carpel contains one seed and forms a fruit called an achene. No special dispersal mechanism*

The structure of a flower is best illustrated by means of a half-flower, a view of the flower obtained by cutting the flower vertically into two equal halves (along the median plane, so as to split the pedicel in two longitudinally) and drawing one half, showing the cut surface as a continuous line.

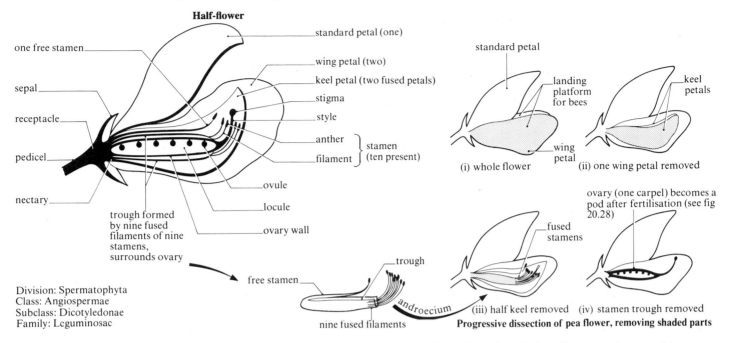

Half-flower

one free stamen

sepal

receptacle

pedicel

nectary

trough formed by nine fused filaments of nine stamens, surrounds ovary

Division: Spermatophyta
Class: Angiospermae
Subclass: Dicotyledonae
Family: Leguminosae

standard petal (one)

wing petal (two)

keel petal (two fused petals)

stigma

style

anther ⎱ stamen
filament ⎰ (ten present)

ovule

locule

ovary wall

free stamen

nine fused filaments

trough

androecium

standard petal

landing platform for bees

keel petals

wing petal

(i) whole flower   (ii) one wing petal removed

ovary (one carpel) becomes a pod after fertilisation (see fig 20.28)

fused stamens

(iii) half keel removed   (iv) stamen trough removed

Progressive dissection of pea flower, removing shaded parts

Fig 20.16   (above) Structure of flower of sweet pea (Lathyrus odoratus), a polypetalous dicotyledon. Flower: actinomorphic and polypetalous. Flowers appear in July. Calyx: five sepals. Corolla: five petals, one standard petal, two wing petals, two fused keel petals interlocking with wing petals. May be white or coloured. Pollination: bees are attracted by colour, scent and nectar. The standard petal is especially conspicuous. The two wing petals act as a landing platform. When a bee lands, its weight pulls them down together with the keel to which they are linked. The style and stigma emerge, striking the undersurface of the bee that may be carrying pollen from another flower. As the bee searches for nectar at the base of the ovary with its long proboscis, the anthers may rub pollen directly on to the undersurface of the style, from where it may be passed to the bee. Self-pollination may also occur. The garden pea (Pisum sativum) is similar, but more commonly self-pollinated. Fruit: a pod consisting of one carpel with many seeds. (See fig 20.28 for self-dispersal.)

Fig 20.17   (below) Half-flower of white deadnettle (Lamium album), a sympetalous dicotyledon. The plant is a herbaceous perennial common in hedgerows and on waste ground. It perennates by means of a rhizome. Flower: zygomorphic (irregular) and hypogynous. Flowers appear in April to June and autumn. Pollination: mainly bumblebees. A bee lands on the lower lip and as it enters the flower its back, which may be carrying pollen, touches the stigma first, thus favouring cross-pollination, although self-pollination is possible. Fruit: four nutlets, each with a hard wall and containing one seed. The fruit is called a carcerulus

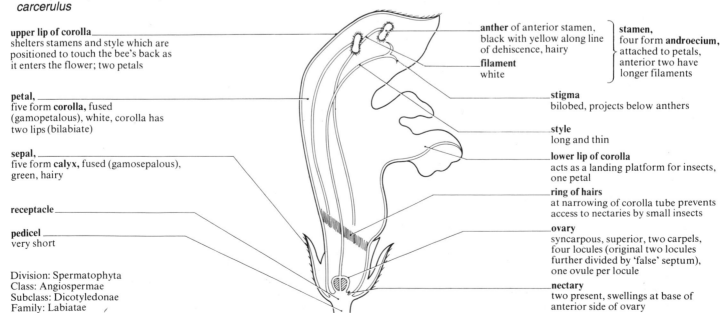

upper lip of corolla
shelters stamens and style which are positioned to touch the bee's back as it enters the flower; two petals

petal,
five form **corolla,** fused (gamopetalous), white, corolla has two lips (bilabiate)

sepal,
five form **calyx,** fused (gamosepalous), green, hairy

receptacle

pedicel
very short

Division: Spermatophyta
Class: Angiospermae
Subclass: Dicotyledonae
Family: Labiatae

anther of anterior stamen, black with yellow along line of dehiscence, hairy

filament
white

stamen,
four form **androecium,** attached to petals, anterior two have longer filaments

stigma
bilobed, projects below anthers

style
long and thin

lower lip of corolla
acts as a landing platform for insects, one petal

ring of hairs
at narrowing of corolla tube prevents access to nectaries by small insects

ovary
syncarpous, superior, two carpels, four locules (original two locules further divided by 'false' septum), one ovule per locule

nectary
two present, swellings at base of anterior side of ovary

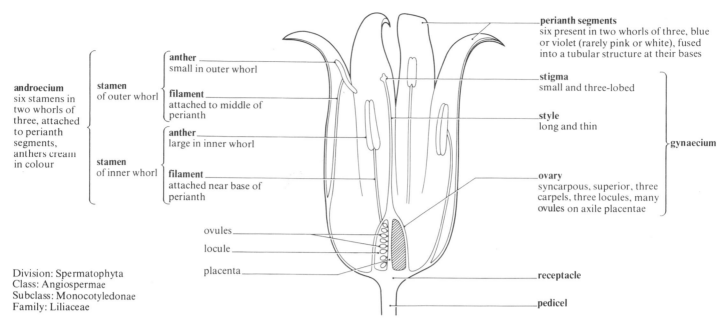

androecium
six stamens in
two whorls of
three, attached
to perianth
segments,
anthers cream
in colour

stamen
of outer whorl

anther
small in outer whorl

filament
attached to middle of
perianth

stamen
of inner whorl

anther
large in inner whorl

filament
attached near base of
perianth

perianth segments
six present in two whorls of three, blue
or violet (rarely pink or white), fused
into a tubular structure at their bases

stigma
small and three-lobed

style
long and thin

gynaecium

ovary
syncarpous, superior, three
carpels, three locules, many
ovules on axile placentae

ovules

locule

placenta

receptacle

pedicel

Division: Spermatophyta
Class: Angiospermae
Subclass: Monocotyledonae
Family: Liliaceae

Fig 20.18 *Half-flower of bluebell (Endymion non-scripta), a monocotyledon. The plant is an herbaceous perennial, common in woods and hedgerows, favouring shady positions and light, acid soils. It perennates by means of a bulb. Flower: actinomorphic and hypogynous. Parts are in threes, as is typical of monocotyledons. Flowers appear in April to May. Pollination: insects such as the honey bee. The flower is slightly scented and nectar is produced at the top of the ovary. Fruit: a capsule dehiscing into three valves*

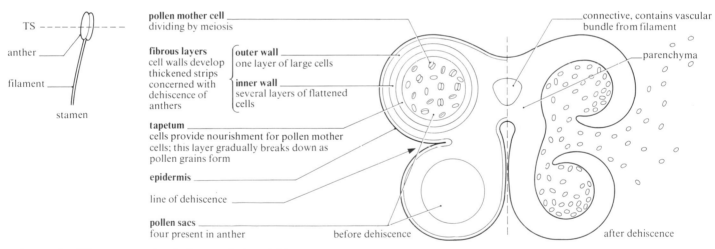

TS

anther

filament

stamen

pollen mother cell
dividing by meiosis

fibrous layers
cell walls develop
thickened strips
concerned with
dehiscence of
anthers

outer wall
one layer of large cells

inner wall
several layers of flattened
cells

tapetum
cells provide nourishment for pollen mother
cells; this layer gradually breaks down as
pollen grains form

epidermis

line of dehiscence

pollen sacs
four present in anther

before dehiscence

connective, contains vascular
bundle from filament

parenchyma

after dehiscence

Fig 20.19 *TS mature anther before and after dehiscence*

Fig 20.20 *Development of pollen grains*

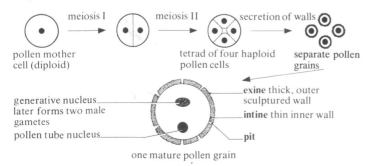

meiosis I

pollen mother
cell (diploid)

meiosis II

tetrad of four haploid
pollen cells

secretion of walls

separate pollen
grains

generative nucleus
later forms two male
gametes
pollen tube nucleus

exine thick, outer
sculptured wall

intine thin inner wall

pit

one mature pollen grain

Development of pollen grains

Each stamen consists of an **anther** in which four pollen sacs produce pollen, and a **filament** which contains a vascular bundle supplying food and water to the anther. Fig 20.19 illustrates the internal structure of an anther, with its four pollen sacs containing spore mother cells. Each spore mother cell undergoes meiosis to form four pollen grains as shown in fig 20.20.

Immediately after meiosis the young pollen grains are seen in tetrads (groups of four). Each grain develops a thick wall, often with an elaborate sculptured pattern characteristic of the species or genus. The outer wall, or **exine**, is

736

made of a substance related to cutin and suberin (sporopollenin) but is more durable than either. It is one of the most resistant substances in nature and allows grain coats to survive unchanged over long periods of time, sometimes millions of years. This fact, together with the ease of identifying the parent genus or species which produced the grain, has given rise to the science of palynology or pollen analysis. By studying pollen grains from a particular time and place it is possible to determine what plants were growing and thus to gain information about, for example, the ecosystems (including animals) and climate of that time. A particularly abundant source of pollen grains is peat, which accumulates to great depths over long periods of time in peat bogs. Cores of peat can be extracted using special peat borers.

> **20.2** How might pollen grains be useful as indicators of (*a*) past climate, (*b*) past activities of Man?

The pollen grain at this stage is equivalent to a microspore, as discussed in chapter 3. Its nucleus divides into two by mitosis to form a generative nucleus and a pollen tube nucleus (fig 20.20). As soon as this happens, the contents of the pollen grain can be regarded as equivalent to a male gametophyte, because male gametes will be formed from the generative nucleus.

20.2.3 Development of the embryo sac and female gamete

Each carpel consists of a stigma, style and ovary. Within the ovary one or more ovules develop, each attached to the ovary wall at a point called the placenta by a short stalk or funicle through which food and water pass to the developing ovule. Often, as it develops, the ovule bends over so that its tip is facing downwards near the base of the funicle. If this occurs, the ovule is described as **anatropous**; if the funicle and ovule remain straight, then the ovule is described as **orthotropous**.

The main body of the ovule is the **nucellus**, enclosed and protected by two sheaths or **integuments**. A small pore is left at one end of the ovule, the **micropyle**. The other end of the ovule, where the funicle joins to the nucellus and integuments, is called the **chalaza**.

Within the nucellus, at the end nearest the micropyle, one spore mother cell develops, known as the embryo sac mother cell. This diploid cell undergoes meiosis and gives rise to a haploid megaspore or embryo sac as shown in fig 20.21. The embryo sac grows and as soon as its nucleus divides by mitosis its contents can be regarded as a female gametophyte. Continued mitotic divisions result in the production of eight nuclei, one of which is the nucleus of the female gamete.

Two polar nuclei migrate to the centre of the embryo sac and fuse to become a single diploid nucleus (in some cases they fuse later at fertilisation). The remaining six nuclei, three at each end, become separated by thin cell walls and only one of these, the female gamete, appears to serve any further function.

The final appearance of the mature carpel at fertilisation is shown in fig 20.22.

20.2.4 Pollination

After formation of pollen grains in the pollen sacs, the cells in the walls of the anther begin to dry and shrink, setting up tensions that eventually result in splitting (dehiscing) of the anther down the sides along two lines of weakness (fig 20.19). The pollen grains are thus released.

The transfer of pollen grains from an anther to a stigma is called **pollination**. This must be achieved if the male gametes, which develop inside the pollen grains, are to reach the female gamete, and special, often elaborate, mechanisms have evolved that ensure successful pollination.

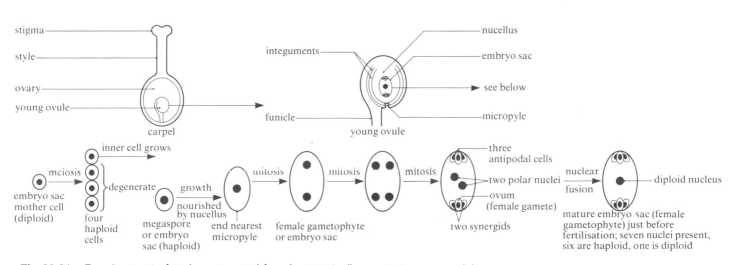

Fig 20.21 *Development of embryo sac and female gamete (in an anatropous ovule)*

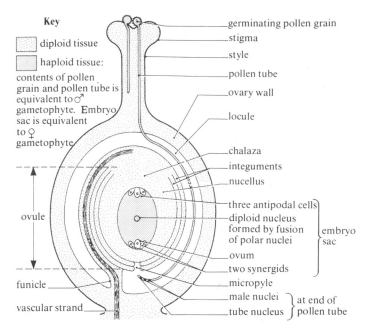

Key

- ☐ diploid tissue
- ▨ haploid tissue:

contents of pollen grain and pollen tube is equivalent to ♂. Embryo sac is equivalent to ♀ gametophyte

germinating pollen grain
stigma
style
pollen tube
ovary wall
locule
chalaza
integuments
nucellus
three antipodal cells
diploid nucleus formed by fusion of polar nuclei } embryo sac
ovum
two synergids
micropyle
male nuclei } at end of
tube nucleus } pollen tube

ovule
funicle
vascular strand

Fig 20.22 *LS carpel at fertilisation. The ovule illustrated is anatropous. Note that the ovule, which becomes the seed after fertilisation, contains both diploid parent tissue and haploid embryo sac tissue*

Transfer from an anther to a stigma of the same flower, or a flower on the same plant, is called **self-pollination**. Transfer of pollen from the anther of one plant to the stigma of another plant is called **cross-pollination**. Cross-pollination leads to cross-fertilisation and has the advantage of increasing the chances of variation. It is thus a form of outbreeding. There are often special features to encourage it, some of which are described below.

Self-pollination leading to self-fertilisation has the advantage of greater reliability, particularly where members of the species are uncommon and are separated by large distances. This is because it is not dependent on an external agency, such as wind or insects, to deliver the pollen. However, self-fertilisation is the extreme form of inbreeding and can result in less vigorous offspring as described in section 25.4. Self-pollination is used in groundsel (*Senecio*) and chickweed (*Stellaria*), which produce no nectar or scent.

Both cross- and self-pollination have advantages and disadvantages and many plants balance the advantages by devices which favour cross-pollination but allow selfing to occur if crossing fails. For example, *some* of the buds produced by violet (*Viola*) and wood sorrel (*Oxalis*) never open, so that self-pollination inside these is inevitable.

Features favouring cross-pollination

Dioecious plants. Self-pollination in dioecious plants is impossible. Monoecious species, where separate male and female flowers occur on the same hermaphrodite plant, also favour cross-pollination but selfing may also occur.

20.3 Dioecious plants are rare, despite the advantages of cross-pollination. Suggest two possible reasons for this.

20.4 Dioecism (separate sexes) is common in animals. Why is the phenomenon more successful in animals than in flowering plants?

Dichogamy. Sometimes anthers mature and stigmas become receptive at different times, a condition known as dichogamy. If the anthers mature first, this is described as **protandry**, if the stigmas mature first it is **protogyny**. Protandrous flowers are much more common, for example white deadnettle, dandelion, rosebay willowherb (*Epilobium angustifolium*); see also sage (*Salvia*) (fig 20.23).

Protogyny occurs in bluebell and figwort (*Scrophularia*). In most cases of dichogamy there is an overlapping period when both anthers and stigmas are ripe, thus allowing selfing if crossing has been unsuccessful. A similar mechanism for ensuring cross-fertilisation exists in some hermaphrodite animals, for instance *Hydra*, where the testes ripen before the ovary.

Self-incompatibility (self-sterility). Even if self-pollination does occur, the pollen grain often does not develop, or develops very slowly, so preventing or discouraging self-fertilisation. In all such cases there is a specific inhibition of pollen penetration of the stigma, or of pollen tube growth down the style, and this is genetically determined by self-incompatibility genes.*

When self-incompatibility occurs, the extent of compatible cross-pollination is variable and again is genetically determined. For most efficient use of the pollen, a high proportion of crosses should be compatible. An extreme example is clover, where all plants are self-incompatible, but cross-incompatibility occurs between less than one in 22 000 pairs. A less efficient system occurs where the compatible types are characterised by differences in floral morphology. An example is the primrose (*Primula*), discussed below.

20.5 Self-incompatibility is controlled by multiple alleles. Assuming (a) that there are three alleles, S_1, S_2 and S_3, and (b) that self-incompatibility occurs if the pollen grain and the style tissue have an allele in common, what proportion of the pollen grains from a plant with the genotype S_1S_2 would be capable of successfully germinating on a plant with the genotype S_2S_3?

---

* The genetics of self-incompatibility and its commercial implications are outside the scope of this book, but are dealt with in *Sexual Incompatibility in Plants*, Institute of Biology, Studies in Biology, No. 110; Lewis, Dan; Arnold, (1979).

Fig 20.23 *A bee entering a flower of meadow sage. The stamens are hinged to a plate and, as the head of the bee pushes against this, the stamens are lowered. This brushes pollen onto the bee's abdomen. The stigma of the flower increases in length as the flower ages. If a bee now enters an older flower, it will come into contact with the stigma and the pollen will be transferred from its abdomen to the stigma. This series of activities causes cross-pollination to take place*

Special floral structures. In most hermaphrodite flowers there are structural features that favour cross-pollination.

In the case of insect-pollinated flowers the stigma is usually borne above the anthers, thus removing the possibility of pollen falling on to the stigma of the same flower. A visiting insect, possibly carrying pollen from another plant, will touch the stigma first as it enters the flower. Later, while the insect is seeking nectar, pollen is either brushed against it or falls on to it before it leaves the flower. This occurs in white deadnettle (fig 20.17). A more primitive mechanism may ensure that the stigma brushes against the insect as it lands, as in pea (see fig 20.16 for details). Such mechanisms are generally reinforced by dichogamy and the flowers are often complex and zygomorphic in shape.

Flowers attract insects by providing a source of food (nectar or pollen) and stimulating the senses of sight and smell of the insects. Those characteristics that enable flowers to do this are discussed below.

In the case of wind-pollinated flowers the stamens, the whole flower, or the inflorescence may hang downwards so that falling pollen will drop clear of the plant before being blown away, for example hazel catkins.

> **20.6** Fig 20.24 shows two types of primrose flower. They occur naturally in roughly equal numbers and differ in length of style (heterostyly) and position of anthers. (*a*) Given that bees collect nectar from the base of the corolla tube, explain how cross-pollination between pin-eyed and thrum-eyed flowers rather than between flowers of the same type, is favoured. (*b*) What is the advantage of such a system?

Although the heterostyly described in question 20.6 and fig 20.24 apparently favours outbreeding, a much more important difference between pin-eyed and thrum-eyed primroses is a self-incompatibility mechanism which is more effective in restricting cross-fertilisation to pin-eye/thrum-eye crosses. The genes that control incompatibility, style length and anther height lie close together on the same chromosome and behave as a single inheritable unit.

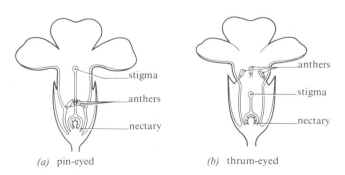

(a) pin-eyed   *(b)* thrum-eyed

Fig 20.24 *Heterostyly in primrose* (Primula) *flowers*

Wind pollination and insect pollination

Pollen grains are spores, but unlike the spores of the non-seed bearing plants they cannot germinate on land and must be transferred to the female parts of either cones, in the case of gymnosperms, or flowers in the case of angiosperms. The original agent of spore dispersal was wind, but this is very inefficient in pollen transfer because the mechanism relies solely on chance interception of the pollen grains by the cones or the flowers. All conifers, and many flowering plants such as grasses and most temperate trees, such as oak and hazel, still rely on wind, but it is at the expense of producing enormous quantities of pollen, a drain on the plant's materials and energy. Insect pollination was rapidly exploited once flowers evolved because the insect is a much more precise agent of dispersal. It can carry a small amount of pollen from the anthers of one flower and deposit it precisely on the stigma of another flower. As a result, special relationships between flowers and insects have evolved, the reward the insects receive from the flowers being food in the form of nectar, and for some, pollen. The insects specialised for flower-feeding appeared at the same time as the flowering plants, and include bees,

Table 20.2. Summary of typical differences between wind- and insect-pollinated flowers

Typical wind-pollinated flower	*Typical insect-pollinated flower*
Small petals not brightly coloured (usually green), or petals absent; flowers therefore inconspicuous	Large coloured petals; flowers therefore conspicuous. If flowers relatively inconspicuous they may be gathered together in inflorescences
Not scented	Scented
Nectaries absent	Nectaries present
Large branched and feathery stigma hanging outside flower to trap pollen	Small stigma, sticky to hold pollen and enclosed within flower
Pendulous stamens hanging outside flower to release pollen	Stamens enclosed within flower
Anthers versatile, i.e. attached only at midpoints to tip of filament so that they swing freely in air currents	Anthers fixed at their bases (basifixed) or fused along their backs to the filaments (dorsifixed) so that they are immovable
Large quantities of pollen owing to high wastage	Less pollen produced
Pollen grains relatively light and small; dry, often smooth, walls	Pollen grains relatively heavy and large. Spiny walls and stickiness help attachment to insect body (fig 20.26)
Flower structure relatively simple	Elaborate structural modifications for particular insects often occur
Flowers borne well above foliage on long stalks (e.g. grasses) or appear before leaves (e.g. many British trees)	Position and time of appearance variable in relation to foliage, though often borne above it for increased conspicuousness

wasps, butterflies and moths. In a few particular cases the insect and the plant it pollinates are so interdependent that neither species can survive without the other, such as the yucca plant and its associated moth.

Insect pollination has the important additional advantage that it encourages cross-pollination and hence cross-fertilisation, so the modifications of flowers to encourage insect pollination described below could be added to the list of features favouring cross-pollination.

In order to attract insects, flowers generally are large, with brightly coloured petals or, if small, are grouped into inflorescences. Insects can see ultra-violet wavelengths that are invisible to Man and so flowers that appear white to Man may, in fact, appear coloured to insects. Often there are markings on the petals such as lines, spots or an increased intensity of colour that guide insects to the nectaries, as in violet and pansy (*Viola*), orchids (*Orchis* and other genera) and foxgloves (*Digitalis*).

More specific than colours are the scents produced by flowers some of which, like lavender and rose, are used by Man in perfumes. Smells of rotting flesh that attract carrion-eating insects are also produced by some plants: the arum lily (*Arum maculatum*) attracts dung flies. Specificity for recognition is also provided by flower shape.

One of the most complex and bizarre mechanisms for ensuring cross-pollination is the sexual impersonation of female wasps by certain orchids. The flower parts mimic the shape, colourings and even the odour of the female wasp, and the impersonation is so convincing that the male wasps attempt to copulate with the flower (fig 20.25). While doing so they deposit pollen and, on leaving the flower, collect fresh pollen to take to the next flower.

A summary of the typical differences between wind-pollinated and insect-pollinated flowers is given in table 20.2.

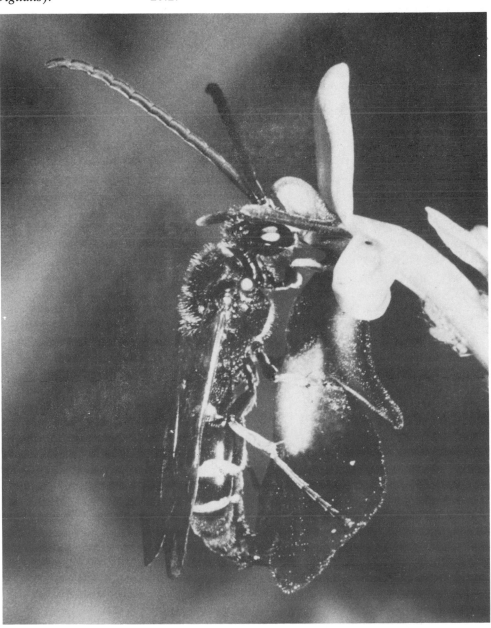

Fig 20.25 *A digger wasp (Argogorytes mystaceus) copulating with the fly orchid (Ophrys insectifera)*

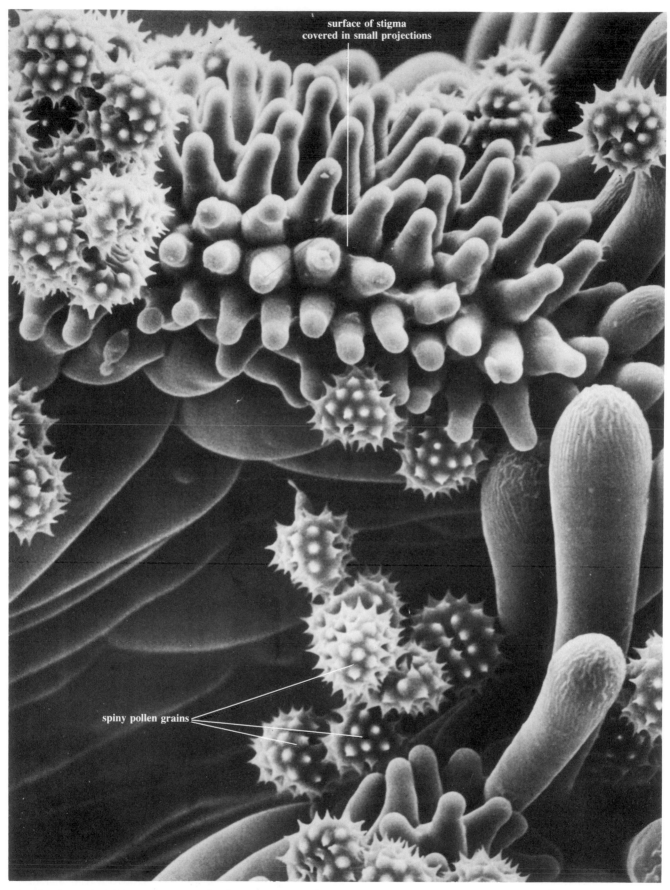

Fig 20.26 *Scanning electron micrograph of pollen grains on the stigma of a flower. The spiked surface of the grains is typical of insect-pollinated flowers*

20.2.5 Fertilisation

Once a pollen grain has landed on the stigma, a sucrose solution secreted by epidermal cells of the stigma stimulates germination of the grain and possibly supplies food (fig 20.26). A pollen tube emerges from one of the pores in the wall of the pollen grain and grows rapidly down the style to the ovary. Its growth involves secretion of digestive enzymes and is controlled by the tube nucleus of the pollen grain, which is found at the growing tip of the tube. Growth is stimulated by auxins produced by the gynaecium, and the pollen tube is directed towards the ovary by certain chemicals, an example of chemotropism. It is probably also negatively aerotropic, that is it grows away from air. Growth depends on compatibility between the pollen and the style tissue as already described.

During growth of the pollen tube the generative nucleus of the pollen grain divides by mitosis to produce two male nuclei that represent the male gametes (fig 20.22). They are non-motile, unlike the sperms of lower plants, and depend on the pollen tube to reach the female gamete which is located in the embryo sac of the ovule. The pollen tube enters the ovule through the micropyle, the tube nucleus degenerates and the tip of the tube bursts, releasing the male gametes in the vicinity of the embryo sac which they enter. One nucleus fuses with the female gamete, forming a diploid zygote, and the other fuses with the two polar nuclei (or diploid nucleus if the latter have already fused) forming a triploid nucleus known as the primary endosperm nucleus. This double fertilisation is unique to flowering plants.

If, as is often the case, more than one ovule is present in the gynaecium, each must be fertilised by a separate pollen grain if it is to become a seed. Thus each seed may have been fertilised by a pollen grain from a different plant.

Experiment 20.1: To investigate the growth of pollen tubes

Stigmas secrete a solution containing sucrose ranging in concentration from about 2 to 45%. This helps to stick pollen grains to the stigma and to promote their germination. The addition of borate to the experimental solution helps to prevent osmotic bursting of pollen tube tips and stimulates growth.

Materials

microscope
cavity slide
flowers containing dehiscing anthers, such as dead-nettle or wallflower
10–20% (w/v) sucrose solution also containing sodium borate to a concentration of 0.01%
acetocarmine or neutral red

Method

Place a drop of sucrose solution in the central depression of a cavity slide and add pollen grains by touching the drop with the surface of a dehisced anther. Observe the slide at intervals over a period of 1–2 hours. The nuclei at the tip of growing tubes may be stained by irrigating with a drop of acetocarmine or neutral red.

20.2.6 Development of the seed to dormancy

Immediately after fertilisation, the ovule becomes known as the **seed** and the ovary the **fruit**.

The zygote grows by mitotic divisions to become a multicellular embryo which consists of a first shoot, the **plumule**, a first root, the **radicle**, and either one or two seed-leaves called **cotyledons** (one in monocotyledons and two in dicotyledons). These cotyledons are simpler in structure than the first true foliage leaves and may become swollen with food to act as storage tissue, as in the pea and broad bean (*Vicia faba*). The plumule consists of a stem, the first pair of true foliage leaves and a terminal bud. The triploid primary endosperm nucleus undergoes repeated divisions (mitotic) to form the **endosperm**, a mass of triploid nuclei which are separated from one another by thin cell walls. In some seeds this remains as the food store, as in maize (*Zea mays*).

If the cotyledons act as a food store they grow at the expense of the endosperm, which may disappear altogether. Some seeds store food in both endosperm and cotyledons.

Thus within the developing seed, both embryo and in some cases the endosperm, grow within the embryo sac. As their growth continues the surrounding nucellus becomes disorganised and breaks down, supplying nutrients for growth. Further nutrients are supplied by the vascular bundle in the stalk (funicle) of the ovule. There are close analogies here with the mammal, where food passes from the parent to the developing embryo via the placenta. As already noted, the term placenta is also used for the point of attachment of the funicle to the ovary wall.

The micropyle remains a small pore in the testa through which oxygen and water will enter when the seed germinates. The testa is a thin but tough protective layer derived from the integuments. The final stages in seed maturation involve a reduction in the water content of the seed from the normal levels for plant tissues of about 90% by mass to about 10–15% by mass. This markedly reduces the potential for metabolic activity and is an essential step in ensuring seed dormancy.

While the seeds develop, the ovary becomes a mature fruit, its wall being known as the **pericarp**. The changes that occur vary with species, but generally the fruit is adapted to protect the seeds and to aid in their dispersal as discussed in section 20.2.8.

The remaining flower parts wither and die and are abscissed in a controlled manner, just as leaves are in deciduous plants. In a few cases structures such as the receptacle, style or sepals are retained and contribute to dispersal. If the receptacle is involved, as in strawberry (*Fragaria*), the structure is called a **false fruit**.

Table 20.3. Summary of the changes that occur after fertilisation in flowering plants

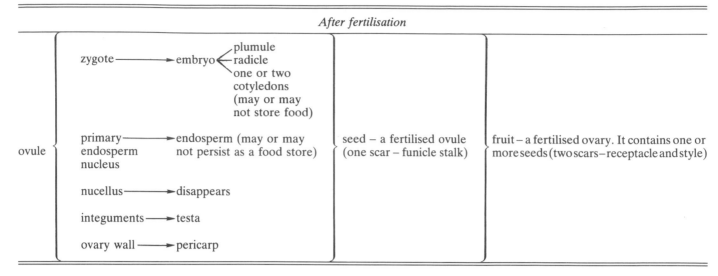

		After fertilisation	
ovule {	zygote ⟶ embryo ← { plumule radicle one or two cotyledons (may or may not store food)		seed – a fertilised ovule (one scar – funicle stalk)	fruit – a fertilised ovary. It contains one or more seeds (two scars – receptacle and style)
	primary endosperm nucleus ⟶ endosperm (may or may not persist as a food store)		
	nucellus ⟶ disappears		
	integuments ⟶ testa		
	ovary wall ⟶ pericarp		

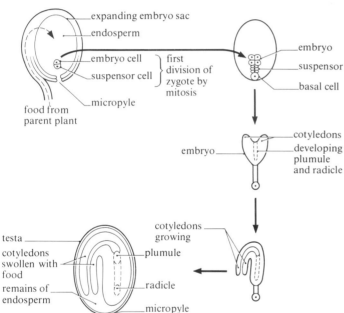

Fig 20.27 *Growth of an embryo in a non-endospermous dicotyledon seed, such as shepherd's purse (Capsella bursa-pastoris)*

The hormonal control of fruit development is discussed in section 15.3.5.

Some of the changes that occur after fertilisation are summarised in table 20.3.

Some stages in the development of the embryo are shown in fig 20.27.

20.2.7 Advantages and disadvantages of reproduction by seed

The seed is the characteristic product of sexual reproduction in the spermatophytes, being defined as a fertilised ovule. It contains an embryo plant with one or more cotyledons, sometimes an endosperm, and is surrounded by a protective testa.

Advantages

(1) The plant is independent of water for sexual reproduction and therefore better adapted for a land environment.
(2) The seed protects the embryo.
(3) The seed contains food for the embryo (either in cotyledons or in the endosperm).
(4) The seed is usually adapted for dispersal.
(5) The seed can remain dormant and survive adverse conditions.
(6) The seed is physiologically sensitive to favourable conditions and sometimes must undergo a period of after-ripening so that it will not germinate immediately (see chapter 15).
(7) The seed is a product of sexual reproduction and therefore has the attendant advantages of genetic variation.

Disadvantages

(1) Seeds are relatively large structures because of the extensive food reserves. This makes dispersal more difficult than by spores.
(2) Seeds are often eaten by animals for their food reserves.
(3) There is a reliance on external agents such as wind, insects and water for pollination. This makes pollination (and hence fertilisation) risky, particularly wind pollination.
(4) There is a large wastage of seeds because the chances of survival of a given seed are limited. The parent sporophyte must therefore invest large quantities of material and energy in seed production to ensure success.
(5) The food supply in a seed is limited, whereas in vegetative reproduction food is available from the parent plant until the daughter plant is fully established.
(6) Two individuals are required in dioecious species

making the process more risky than reproduction in which only one parent is involved. However, dioecious plants are relatively rare.

The information provided above can be used to compare the advantages and disadvantages that seed-bearing plants have compared with non-seed-bearing plants, or to compare the relative merits of sexual reproduction and vegetative propagation within the seed-bearing plants.

20.2.8 Fruit and seed dispersal

After seed development either the entire fruit or the seed(s) contained within it are dispersed from the parent sporophyte. If the pericarp (wall) of the fruit becomes hard and dry it is called a dry fruit and if it becomes fleshy, a succulent fruit. Dry fruits may be dehiscent or indehiscent according to whether they do or do not release seeds by splitting. Alternatively dry fruits may split into a number of one-seeded portions and are then described as schizocarpic.

The further the seeds are dispersed, the less chance there is of competition from the parent plant. There is also more chance of finding a fresh area to colonise, thus increasing in time the overall population size. However, there is an attendant risk of the seed not finding a suitable place for germination if it is dispersed some distance from the parent.

There are three major external agents of dispersal, namely wind, animals and water. In addition self-dispersal mechanisms exist, often involving an explosive release of seeds from the fruit. Examples of all these types of dispersal are given below, fig 20.28, pages 745–8.

Fig 20.28 *Examples of different types of fruit and seed and their methods of dispersal*

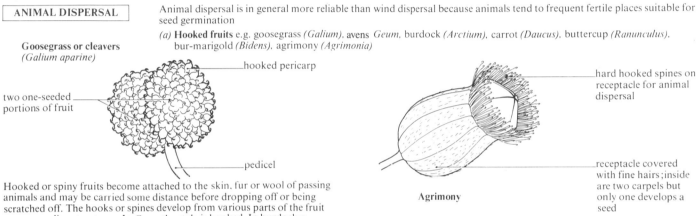

ANIMAL DISPERSAL — Animal dispersal is in general more reliable than wind dispersal because animals tend to frequent fertile places suitable for seed germination

(a) **Hooked fruits** e.g. goosegrass *(Galium)*, avens *Geum*, burdock *(Arctium)*, carrot *(Daucus)*, buttercup *(Ranunculus)*, bur-marigold *(Bidens)*, agrimony *(Agrimonia)*

Goosegrass or cleavers
(Galium aparine)

two one-seeded portions of fruit

hooked pericarp

pedicel

hard hooked spines on receptacle for animal dispersal

receptacle covered with fine hairs; inside are two carpels but only one develops a seed

Agrimony

Agrimony has hard hooked spines on its receptacle.

Hooked or spiny fruits become attached to the skin, fur or wool of passing animals and may be carried some distance before dropping off or being scratched off. The hooks or spines develop from various parts of the fruit or surrounding structures. In *Geum* the style is hooked. In burdock a collection of small fruits is surrounded by hooked bracts (modified leaves) forming one structure. In addition, small stiff hairs break off and penetrate the skin, causing irritation and scratching with consequent removal of the fruits. Goosegrass, carrot and buttercup all have hooked pericarps. In bur-marigold the fruit has a pappus like the dandelion, but with strong barbs.

hooks of the pericarp

pedicel

Scanning electron micrograph of the fruit of goosegrass, showing the numerous small hooks which develop from the pericarp. The hooks cling very effectively to the skin, fur or wool of passing animals (b) **Succulent fruits** e.g. plum *(Prunus)*, blackberry *(Rubus)*, tomato *(Lycopersicum)*, apple *(Malus)*, strawberry *(Fragaria)*

Succulent fruits have fleshy parts that provide food for animals, including birds. They usually attract animals by becoming brightly coloured and scented as they ripen. The fruit is eaten and digested but the seeds are resistant to digestive enzymes and pass unharmed through the gut of the animal, to be deposited in the faeces, often on fertile soil. Nutrients from the decomposition of the faeces may increase the fertility around the seed. Representative examples of different types of fruit structure are illustrated below.

Plum

The plum is an example of a fruit called a **drupe** in which the pericarp has three layers, an **epicarp** (protective skin), a **mesocarp** (succulent) and an inner woody **endocarp**, ('stone') that protects the seed and resists digestion.

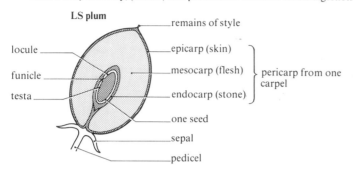

LS plum

- remains of style
- epicarp (skin)
- mesocarp (flesh) } pericarp from one carpel
- endocarp (stone) }
- one seed
- sepal
- pedicel
- locule
- funicle
- testa

Other examples of drupes are peach, cherry and almond (also *Prunus* spp.), elder *(Sambucus)* and coconut *(Cocos nucifera)* (fibrous mesocarp). Almonds sold in shops have normally had the epicarp and mesocarp removed.

Section through blackberry – a collection of drupes formed from one flower

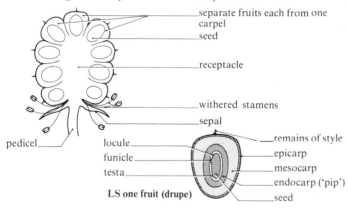

- separate fruits each from one carpel
- seed
- receptacle
- withered stamens
- sepal
- pedicel
- locule
- funicle
- testa
- remains of style
- epicarp
- mesocarp
- endocarp ('pip')
- seed

LS one fruit (drupe)

Tomato

The tomato is an example of a fruit called a **berry**. It resembles a drupe, but the endocarp is fleshy not stony.

LS tomato
fusion of two, three or four carpels

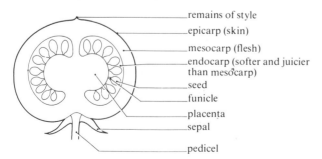

- remains of style
- epicarp (skin)
- mesocarp (flesh)
- endocarp (softer and juicier than mesocarp)
- seed
- funicle
- placenta
- sepal
- pedicel

Other examples of berries are blackcurrant and gooseberry (*Ribes* spp.), marrow *(Cucurbita)*, orange and lemon *(Citrus* spp.), banana *(Musa)*, grape *(Vitis)*, date *(Phoenix dactylifera)* (in date the single seed is woody).

(c) **False succulent fruits**

Sometimes the receptacle becomes swollen and fleshy and itself resembles a fruit. Such fruits are called false fruits. Examples are apple and strawberry.

Apple

The apple is an example of a false fruit called a **pome**. In pomes the flesh of the fruit is formed from the hollow receptacle which surrounds and encloses the carpels. The pericarp of the true fruit becomes the 'core' which contains the seeds ('pips'). Other examples are pear *(Pyrus)* and hawthorn *(Crataegus)*.

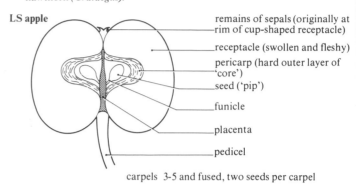

LS apple

- remains of sepals (originally at rim of cup-shaped receptacle)
- receptacle (swollen and fleshy)
- pericarp (hard outer layer of 'core')
- seed ('pip')
- funicle
- placenta
- pedicel

carpels 3-5 and fused, two seeds per carpel

Strawberry

The receptacle becomes swollen and bears on its surface small green fruits called **achenes** ('pips'), each of which contains a single seed.

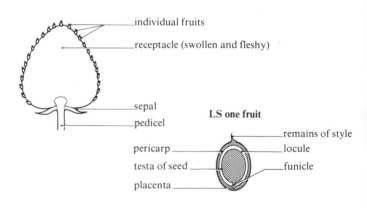

LS strawberry

- individual fruits
- receptacle (swollen and fleshy)
- sepal
- pedicel

LS one fruit

- remains of style
- locule
- funicle
- pericarp
- testa of seed
- placenta

(d) **Nuts** e.g. oak *(Quercus)*, beech *(Fagus)*, chestnut *(Castanea)* Nuts are relatively large, dry fruits that do not split open to allow seed dispersal (indehiscent). The whole fruit is dispersed, often as a result of being collected for food stores by animals, particularly by rodents such as squirrels.

Oak The nut is called an acorn.

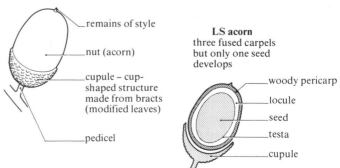

- remains of style
- nut (acorn)
- cupule – cup-shaped structure made from bracts (modified leaves)
- pedicel

LS acorn
three fused carpels but only one seed develops

- woody pericarp
- locule
- seed
- testa
- cupule

(a) **Parachute mechanism** e.g. seeds of willowherb *(Epilobium)*, willow *(Salix)*, cotton *(Gossypium hirsutum)*, fruit of dandelion *(Taraxacum)*, 'old man's beard' *(Clematis)*

Dandelion

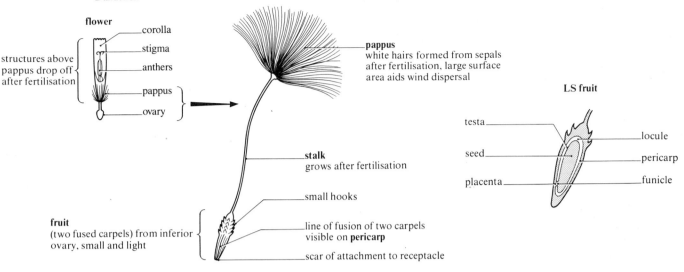

flower

structures above
pappus drop off
after fertilisation

- corolla
- stigma
- anthers
- pappus
- ovary

pappus
white hairs formed from sepals
after fertilisation, large surface
area aids wind dispersal

LS fruit

- testa
- seed
- placenta
- locule
- pericarp
- funicle

stalk
grows after fertilisation

- small hooks
- line of fusion of two carpels visible on **pericarp**
- scar of attachment to receptacle

fruit
(two fused carpels) from inferior
ovary, small and light

(b) **Wings** e.g. seeds of *Pinus* (a gymnosperm), fruit of elm *(Ulmus)*, ash *(Fraxinus)*, sycamore *(Acer)*, hornbeam *(Carpinus)*

Sycamore *(Acer pseudoplatanus)*

- long hairs
- seed

Willowherb

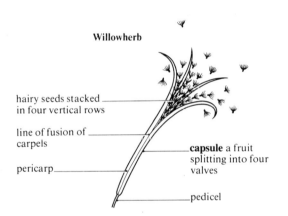

hairy seeds stacked
in four vertical rows

line of fusion of
carpels

pericarp

capsule a fruit
splitting into four
valves

pedicel

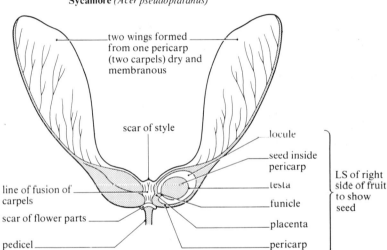

two wings formed
from one pericarp
(two carpels) dry and
membranous

scar of style

- locule
- seed inside pericarp
- testa
- funicle
- placenta
- pericarp

LS of right
side of fruit
to show
seed

line of fusion of
carpels

scar of flower parts

pedicel

One fruit of sycamore Either before or after wind dispersal the fruit separates into two halves along the line of fusion of the carpels (the fruit is described as schizocarpic); as the fruit falls it rotates and is carried by the wind

(c) **Censer mechanism*** e.g. poppy *(Papaver)*, love-in-a-mist *(Nigella)*, foxglove *(Digitalis)*, campion *(Lychnis)* (all these examples have fruits called capsules)

Poppy

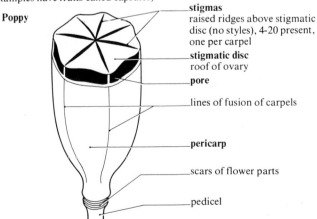

stigmas
raised ridges above stigmatic
disc (no styles), 4-20 present,
one per carpel

stigmatic disc
roof of ovary

pore

lines of fusion of carpels

pericarp

scars of flower parts

pedicel

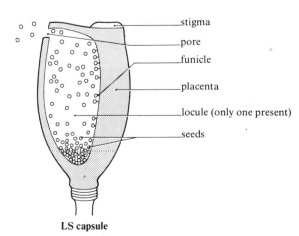

- stigma
- pore
- funicle
- placenta
- locule (only one present)
- seeds

LS capsule

The fruit, called a **capsule**, is borne at the end of a long pedicel which sways in the wind, causing the numerous small seeds to escape from the pores at the top of the capsule (* A censer is a vessel in which incense is burnt and is swayed from side to side as it is carried)

(d) Some plants have extremely small seeds that are light enough to be distributed by wind without the aid of special appendages to increase surface area, e.g. orchids

The most common self-dispersal mechanism involves dehiscent fruits.

Dehiscent fruits

These dry and break open, often by splitting lines of weakness, e.g. pods. Seeds may be forcibly ejected with varying degrees of violence or may simply drop out. The seeds released may also be modified for wind dispersal (e.g. willowherb). Capsules are also dehiscent (see poppy and willowherb under wind dispersal) and some release seeds violently, e.g. violet *(Viola)*.

Pods e.g. pea *(Pisum),* broad bean *(Vicia),* runner bean *(Phaseolus),* gorse *(Ulex)* broom and laburnum *(Cytisus* spp.)
Pods are the characteristic fruits of the legume family (Leguminosae). Pods consist of one carpel containing many seeds. The pericarp splits along two sides.

Broom, laburnum or pea

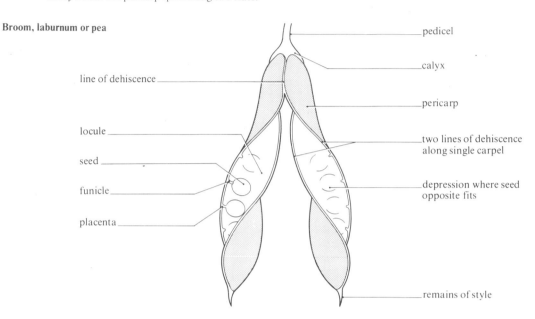

(see also fig 20.16 for earlier stages in development of pea pod)
The pericarp twists on drying due to oblique layers of fibrous tissue. As the twisting tension builds up, the pod may split suddenly along lines of dehiscence, forcibly ejecting some of the seeds. Others are released less forcibly as twisting continues.

WATER DISPERSAL

Few fruits and seeds are specialised for water dispersal, though water may act as a chance agent of dispersal. Those that are specialised are made buoyant by structures possessing air cavities. The coconut *(Cocos nucifera)* is a drupe (compare plum) whose mesocarp is fibrous and contains numerous air spaces. The water lily *(Nymphaea)* has a spongy outgrowth of its seed (the aril) derived from the funicle.

Water lily

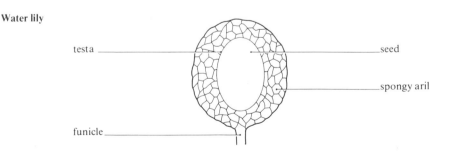

CHANCE DISPERSAL

The categories of wind, animal and self-dispersal are by no means rigid and the degree of specialisation of fruits and seeds for particular methods of dispersal is very variable. An element of chance is therefore bound to be involved in many cases, and more than one of the three dispersal methods could be used by a given fruit or seed. Man is one of the chief agents of chance dispersal, with the possibility of seeds clinging to clothing etc. or being carried in cargoes or by machinery. Contamination of grain crops by weed seeds is a common phenomenon worldwide. Caches of nuts stored by rodents may be forgotten and germinate the following spring. Chance floods, hurricanes, etc. may carry seeds further than usual.

20.3   Sexual reproduction in Man

20.3.1   The human male reproductive system

The male reproductive system is composed of a pair of testes, genital ducts, accessory glands and the penis. The **testis** is an ovoid-shaped compound tubular gland surrounded by a capsule, the **tunica albuginea**, enclosing about 1 000 highly coiled **seminiferous tubules** embedded in connective tissue containing **Leydig cells** (interstitial cells). The tubules of the testis produce the male gametes, **spermatozoa** (commonly referred to as sperm), and Leydig cells produce the male sex hormone **testosterone**. The testes are situated outside the abdominal cavity in the **scrotal sac** and, as a result, temperatures at which sperm develop are 2–3 °C lower than the core temperature. The lower temperature in the scrotal sac is partly due to its position and partly due to the vascular plexus formed by the spermatic artery and vein acting as a countercurrent heat exchange system. The **dartos muscle** of the scrotal sac moves the testes towards or away from the body according to the outside temperature in order to maintain sperm production at an optimum level. Males passing through puberty with undescended testes (a condition called **cryptorchidism**) become permanently sterile and men persistently wearing tight underpants or taking very hot baths may have such a reduced sperm count that it leads to infertility. Whales and elephants are two of the few mammalian species with testes retained in the abdominal cavity.

The seminiferous tubules are approximately 50 cm long and 200 μm in diameter, situated in regions of the testis called **testicular lobules**. Both ends of the tubule are connected to the central region of the testis, the **rete testis**, by short **tubuli recti**. From here 10–20 **vasa efferentia** collect sperm and transfer them to the head of the **epididymis** where they are concentrated by reabsorption of fluid secreted from the seminiferous tubule. Sperm mature in this region of the epididymis before passing 5 m along the coiled tubule to the base of the epididymis where they are stored for a short period before entering the **vas deferens**. The vas deferens is a straight tube about 40 cm long forming, with the spermatic artery and vein, the 'spermatic cord' and conveying sperm to the urethra which traverses the penis. The relationship between these structures and the male accessory glands and penis is shown in figs 20.29 and 20.30.

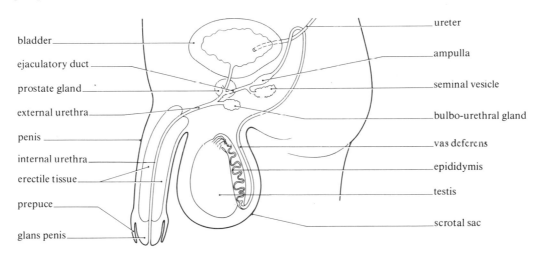

bladder
ejaculatory duct
prostate gland
external urethra
penis
internal urethra
erectile tissue
prepuce
glans penis

ureter
ampulla
seminal vesicle
bulbo-urethral gland
vas deferens
epididymis
testis
scrotal sac

Fig 20.29   (above) *Diagram of the human male reproductive system*

Fig 20.30   (below) *Simplified diagram showing the structure of the human testis and ducts conveying sperm from seminiferous tubules to the urethra*

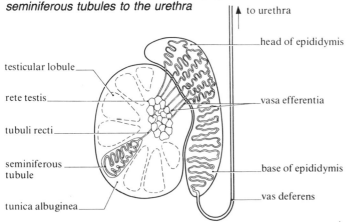

testicular lobule
rete testis
tubuli recti
seminiferous tubule
tunica albuginea

to urethra
head of epididymis
vasa efferentia
base of epididymis
vas deferens

Gamete formation (gametogenesis)

Cells of the germinal epithelium in both male and female gonads undergo a sequence of mitotic and meiotic divisions, called gametogenesis to produce mature male gametes (spermatogenesis) and female gametes (oogenesis). In both cases the process involves three stages, a multiplication stage, a growth stage, and a maturation stage. The multiplication stage involves repeated mitotic divisions producing many spermatogonia and oogonia. Each undergoes a period of growth in preparation for the first meiotic division and subsequent cytokinesis. This marks the beginning of the maturation stage during which the first and second meiotic divisions occur followed by differentiation of the haploid cells and the formation of mature gametes.

749

Development of spermatozoa (spermatogenesis)

Spermatozoa are produced by a sequence of cell divisions called **spermatogenesis** followed by a complex process of differentiation called **spermiogenesis** (fig 20.31). Spermatozoa production takes approximately 70 days and 10^7 spermatozoa are produced per gram of testis per day. The epithelium of the seminiferous tubule consists of an outer layer of **germinal epithelial cells** and about six layers of cells produced by repeated cell divisions of this layer (figs 20.32 and 20.33). These represent successive stages in the development of spermatozoa. Initial divisions of the germinal epithelial cells give rise to many **spermatogonia** which increase in size to form **primary spermatocytes**. These undergo the first meiotic division to form haploid **secondary spermatocytes** and the second meiotic division to form **spermatids**. Between these 'strands' of developing cells are large **Sertoli** or **nurse cells** stretching from the outer layer of the tubule to the lumen.

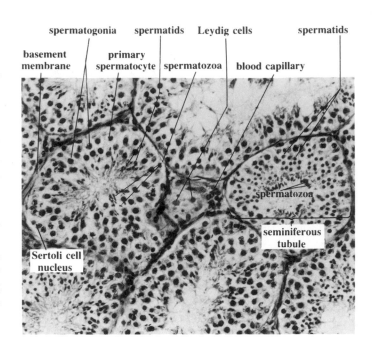

Fig 20.32 (right) *Photomicrographs of a section through the human testis showing seminiferous tubules and Leydig (interstitial) cells*

Fig 20.31 (below) *Summary diagram of the process of spermatogenesis and spermiogenesis in Man, not drawn to scale.*

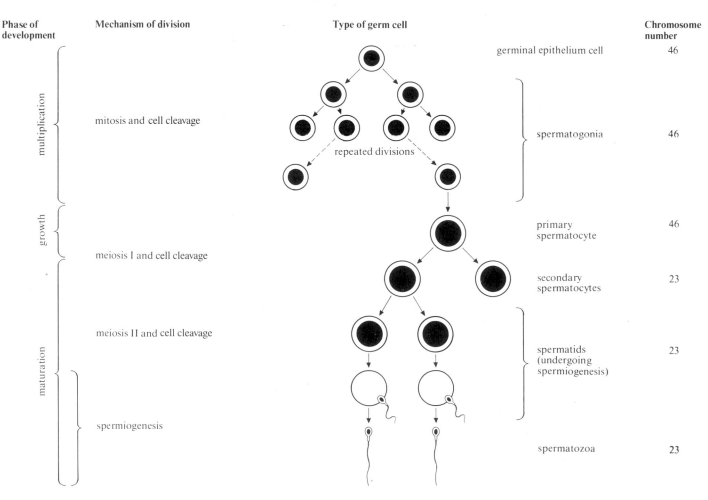

750

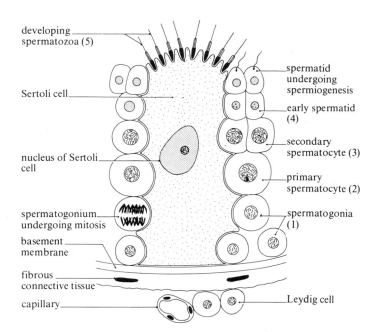

Fig 20.33 Diagram showing the structure of part of the wall of a seminiferous tubule and interstitial cells. Cells in various stages of spermatogenesis and spermiogenesis are shown

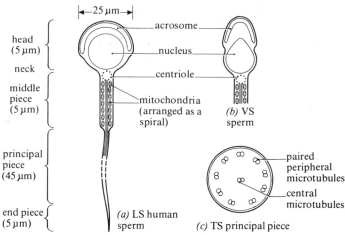

Fig 20.34 Diagram showing the structure of a mature human spermatozoon

20.7 Sertoli cells contain abundant smooth endoplasmic reticulum, Golgi apparatus and many mitochondria and lysosomes. In view of the structure of these cells what can you suggest about their function?

Spermatocytes become embedded in the many invaginations in the lateral margins of the Sertoli cells where they develop into spermatids before passing to the edge of the cell bordering the lumen where they mature as **spermatozoa**. The Sertoli cells are thought to provide mechanical support, protection and nourishment during maturation of the spermatozoa. All nutrients, oxygen and waste substances exchanged between the developing gametes and the blood vessels surrounding the tubules pass through the Sertoli cells. The fluid carrying spermatozoa through the tubules is secreted by the Sertoli cells.

Spermatozoa

Spermatozoa are minute, motile male gametes produced by the male gonads, the testes, and released in millions. They have various shapes according to species but share a common structure. Each spermatozoon is composed of five regions as shown in fig 20.34. The head consists of a nucleus, containing the haploid number of chromosomes, covered by a membrane-enclosed structure, the **acrosome**. This contains hydrolytic enzymes which will be involved in the penetration of the oocyte by the sperm immediately prior to fertilisation. Functionally, therefore, it may be thought of as an enlarged lysosome. The short neck region contains a pair of centrioles lying at right-angles to each other. The microtubules of one of the centrioles elongate

and run the entire length of the rest of the spermatozoon forming the **axial filament** of the flagellum. The middle piece is enlarged by the presence of many mitochondria arranged in a spiral surrounding the flagellum. The energy released by the mitochondria is used in the contractile mechanisms which bring about movement of the flagellum. The principal and end pieces of the spermatozoon are flagellate and in transverse section show the characteristic arrangement of nine pairs of peripheral microtubules surrounding a central pair of microtubules.

Human sperm have a rounded head in plan view and are flattened in a lateral view. Activation of the flagellum is described in section 20.3.2, but it is known that flagellar movement is insufficient to cover the distance from the vagina to the site of fertilisation. The principal locomotory function of sperm is to cluster around the oocyte and to orientate themselves prior to penetration of the oocyte membranes.

Endocrine function of the human testis

The growth, development and maintenance of the testis is controlled by the pituitary gonadotrophins, **follicle stimulating hormone (FSH)** and **luteinising hormone (LH)**. FSH stimulates the development of spermatozoa and LH stimulates the synthesis of the steroid hormone testosterone by the Leydig cells of the testis. LH exerts its influence on the Leydig cells by releasing membrane-bound cyclic AMP (adenosine monophosphate) into the cytoplasm which then passes to the nucleus where it stimulates the synthesis of enzymes involved in the synthesis of testosterone from cholesterol. (LH is sometimes referred to as **interstitial cell stimulating hormone (ICSH)** in males, because of its site of action.)

Testosterone is the principal androgenic hormone and it affects both primary and secondary sexual characteristics. Both testosterone and FSH are required for the successful production of sperm whereas testosterone alone controls the development of the secondary sexual characteristics during puberty and maintains these throughout adult life. These characteristics include the development of the male external genitalia and the accessory glands of the reproductive tract, increased muscle development, enlargement of the larynx producing deepening of the voice, the growth and distribution of hair and behavioural activities associated with mating and parental concern.

20.3.2 The human female reproductive system

Female involvement in reproduction is greater than that of the male and it involves reciprocal interrelationships between the pituitary gland, ovary, uterus and foetus. The female reproductive system is composed of paired ovaries and fallopian tubes, the uterus, vagina and external genitalia (fig 20.35).

The **ovaries** are attached to the wall of the body cavity by a fold in the peritoneum and have the dual function of producing female gametes and secreting female sex hormones. They are about the size and shape of an almond and consist of an outer **cortex** and inner **medulla** surrounded by a connective tissue sheath, the **tunica albuginea**. The outer layer of cells of the cortex is composed of germinal epithelial cells from which gamete cells are produced. The cortex is composed of developing follicles

and the medulla is composed of **stroma**, containing connective tissue, blood vessels and mature follicles (fig 20.38).

The **fallopian tube** is a muscular tube about 12 cm long and conveys female gametes from the ovary to the uterus. The opening of the fallopian tube is expanded and split into **fringes** or **fimbriae** which move nearer to the ovary at ovulation. The lumen of the fallopian tube is lined with ciliated epithelium and female gametes move towards the uterus aided by peristaltic movements of the muscle wall of the fallopian tube.

The **uterus** is a thick-walled organ about 7.5 cm long and 5 cm wide and composed of three main layers. The outer covering is called the **serous coat** and this encloses the middle layer, the **myometrium**, which forms the bulk of the wall. The myometrium is composed of bundles of smooth muscle cells which are sensitive to oxytocin during birth. The inner layer, the **endometrium**, is soft and smooth and composed of epithelial cells, simple tubular glands and spiral arterioles supplying the cells. The cavity of the uterus is capable of extending 500 times during pregnancy, that is from 10 cm^3 to 5 000 cm^3. The lower entrance to the uterus is the **cervix** which separates the uterus from the **vagina**. The vaginal orifice, the urethral orifice and the clitoris are protected by two folds of tissue called the **vulva** composed of the **labia majora** and **labia minora**. The **clitoris** is a small erectile structure which is homologous with the male penis. Within the walls of the vulva are the **vestibular glands** which release mucus when the female is sexually aroused and this helps to lubricate the penis during intercourse.

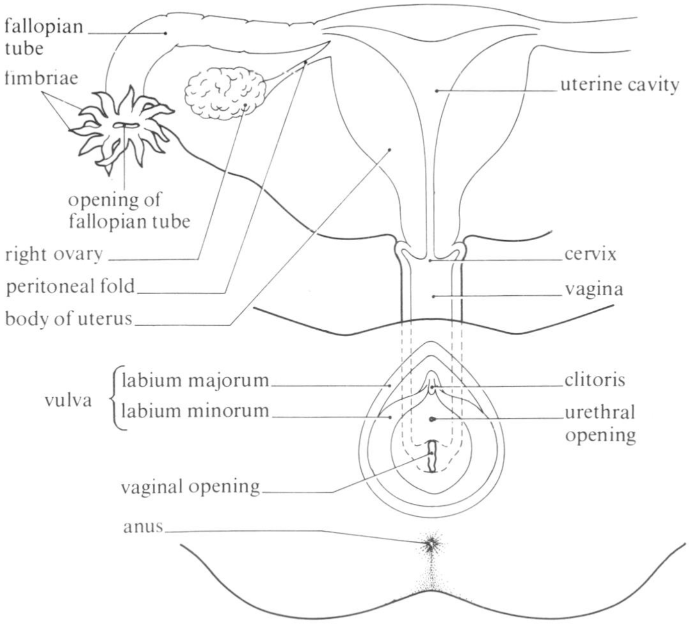

Development of human ova (oogenesis)

Unlike the production of spermatozoa in males which only begins at puberty, the production of ova in females begins before birth and is completed only after fertilisation. The stages in oogenesis are shown in fig 20.36. During foetal development primordial germ cells undergo repetitive mitotic division and produce many larger cells called **oogonia**. These undergo mitosis and form **primary oocytes** which remain at prophase of this stage until just before ovulation. Primary oocytes are enclosed by a single layer of cells, the **membrana granulosa**, and form structures known as **primordial follicles**. Approximately 2×10^6 of these follicles exist in the foetal female just before birth but only about 450 ever develop into secondary oocytes which are released from the ovary during the oestrous cycle. Prior to ovulation the primary oocyte undergoes the first meiotic division to form the haploid **secondary oocyte** and the **first polar body**. The second meiotic division proceeds as far as metaphase but does not continue until a sperm fuses with the oocyte. At fertilisation the secondary oocyte undergoes the second meiotic division producing a large cell, the **ovum**, and a **second polar body**. All polar bodies are small cells. They have no role in oogenesis and they eventually degenerate.

Fig 20.35 *Simplified diagram showing the human female reproductive system. The uterus and vagina are shown in section, and the external genitalia, urethral and anal openings are shown in surface view with the labia parted*

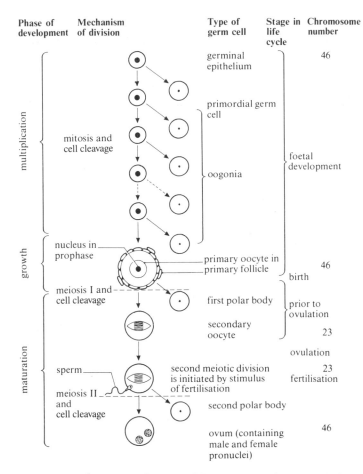

Phase of development	Mechanism of division	Type of germ cell	Stage in life cycle	Chromosome number
		germinal epithelium		46
	mitosis and cell cleavage	primordial germ cell		
		oogonia	foetal development	
	nucleus in prophase	primary oocyte in primary follicle	birth	46
	meiosis I and cell cleavage	first polar body	prior to ovulation	
		secondary oocyte		23
			ovulation	
	sperm	second meiotic division is initiated by stimulus of fertilisation	fertilisation	23
	meiosis II and cell cleavage	second polar body		
		ovum (containing male and female pronuclei)		46

Phases labelled at left: multiplication, growth, maturation.

Fig 20.36 *Summary diagram of the process of oogenesis in Man*

Menstrual cycle

In males, gamete production and release is a continuous process beginning at puberty and lasting throughout life. In females, it is a cyclical activity with a periodicity of approximately 28 days and involves changes in the structure and function of the whole reproductive system. It is called the **menstrual cycle** and can be divided into four

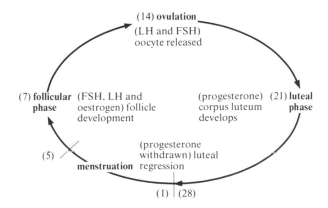

(14) **ovulation**
(LH and FSH)
oocyte released

(7) **follicular phase** (FSH, LH and oestrogen) follicle development

(progesterone) corpus luteum develops (21) **luteal phase**

(5)

(progesterone withdrawn) luteal regression

menstruation

(1) | (28)

Fig 20.37 *Summary of the main phases of the human menstrual cycle. (Figures in brackets indicate days coinciding with phases of the cycle)*

phases as shown in fig 20.37. The events of the menstrual cycle involve the ovaries (the **ovarian cycle**) and the uterus (the **uterine cycle**) and these are regulated by hormones secreted by the ovary which in turn is regulated by pituitary gonadotrophins.

Ovarian cycle

In an adult female the ovarian cycle, which is summarised in fig 20.38, begins with the development of several primary follicles (containing primary oocytes) induced by the release of follicle stimulating hormone (FSH) from the anterior pituitary gland. Only one of these follicles continues to grow whilst the rest break down by a degenerative process known as **follicular atresia**. The cells of the membrana granulosa of the follicle proliferate to produce an outer fibrous layer several cells thick, known as the **theca externa**, and an inner vascular layer, the **theca interna**. The granulosa cells secrete a fluid which collects and forms a space, the **antrum**, within the follicle. Luteinising hormone (LH) released from the pituitary gland stimulates the cells of the thecae to produce steroids, the principal one being **17β-oestradiol**. Increasing levels of oestradiol during the follicular phase feed back negatively on the pituitary gland causing a decrease in FSH levels in the blood (days 4–11); LH levels remain unchanged. Oestrogen levels reach a maximum about three days before ovulation and at this time have a positive feedback action on the pituitary gland causing the release of both FSH and LH.

It is thought that FSH is necessary to stimulate the growth of follicles but that the continued follicular development is controlled mainly by LH. The granulosa cells line the periphery with the ovum displaced to one side of the follicle but still surrounded by a layer of granulosa cells. This mature follicle, known as the **Graafian follicle**, is about 1 cm in diameter and protrudes from the surface of the ovary giving it a warty appearance (fig 20.39). The exact mechanism of ovulation is unknown but LH, FSH and prostaglandins are thought to be involved.

At ovulation the secondary oocyte detaches from the wall of the follicle, is released into the peritoneal cavity and passes into the fallopian tube. Usually only one oocyte is released each month by one of the ovaries so that ovulation alternates between the pair of ovaries. The ovulated oocyte consists of a cell whose nucleus is in metaphase I of meiosis surrounded by a cell layer known as the **zona pellucida** and a layer of granulosa cells known as the **corona radiata** which protects the oocyte up to fertilisation.

Following ovulation, LH levels fall to follicular levels, and in the presence of another gonadotrophin, **prolactin**, the cells of the ruptured follicle change to form the **corpus luteum** (yellow body). This begins to secrete and release another female hormone, **progesterone**, and smaller amounts of oestrogen. These two hormones maintain the structure of the endometrium of the uterus and inhibit FSH and LH release by negative feedback on the hypothalamus.

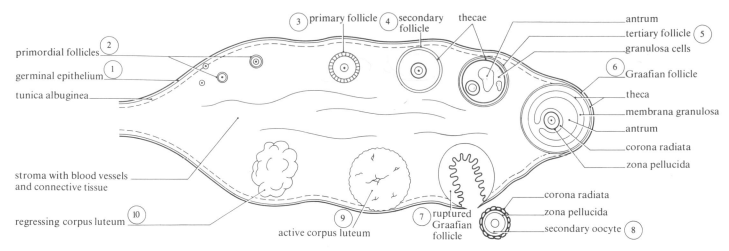

Fig 20.38 (above) Diagrammatic representation of a section through a human ovary showing the stages in the development of a Graafian follicle, ovulation and the formation and regression of the corpus luteum. Not all these stages would be seen together. The numbers indicate the sequence of the stages

Fig 20.39 (below) Photomicrograph of mature human Graafian follicle

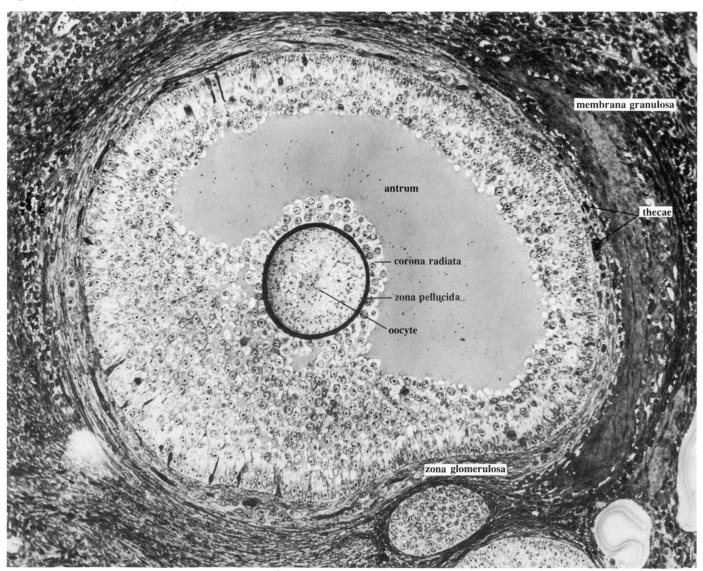

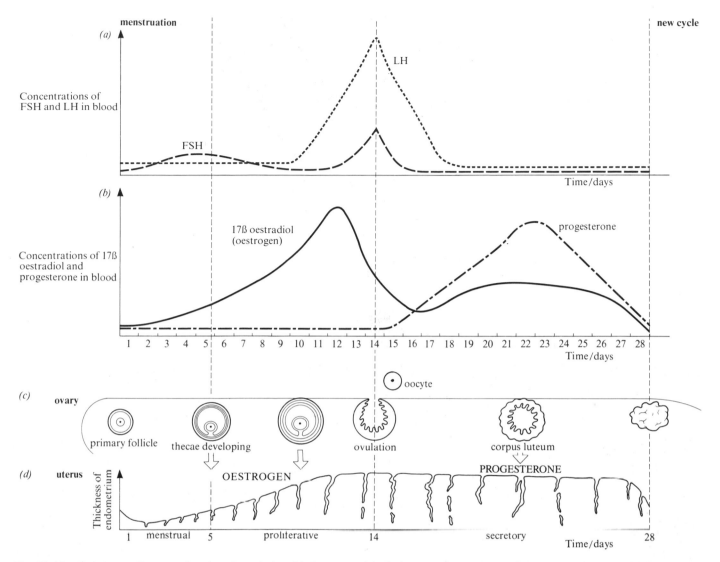

Fig 20.40 *Summary diagram showing the relationship between (a) pituitary gonadotrophins, (b) ovarian steroids, (c) follicle and corpus luteal development and (d) the thickness of the endometrium during the human oestrous cycle*

If fertilisation does not occur factors described later cause the regression of the corpus luteum, which persists as a 'scarred' area, the **corpus albicantus**, and the consequent decrease in progesterone and oestrogen levels. As these levels fall FSH release is no longer inhibited, and as the FSH level rises a new cycle of follicle development occurs. The relationship between the activity of the pituitary gland, ovary and uterus is shown in fig 20.40.

20.8 During a post-mortem carried out on a woman of 22 years of age it was noticed that her ovaries were unequal in size. Analyses of the ovaries revealed the following results:

Smaller ovary	Larger ovary
contained 17 000 follicles	contained 25 000 follicles
" 4 corpora lutea	" 5 corpora lutea
" 10 corpora albicanti	" 48 corpora albicanti

Most of the follicles were small but 219 were over 100 μm in diameter. Five follicles contained two oocytes each and 2% of the oocytes contained two nuclei each. Assuming that each follicle produces a corpus luteum,

(a) (i) at what age did the woman commence ovulation?

(ii) for approximately how many years would ovulation have continued?

(iii) how many potential sets of twins could this woman have produced and what type of twins would they be?

(b) What process accounts for the presence of two nuclei in some of the oocytes (section 22.3)?

Uterine cycle

The uterine cycle consists of three phases represented by structural and functional changes of the endometrium. These are as follows.

Menstrual phase. This is the shedding of the epithelial lining of the endometrium. Just prior to this phase the blood supply to this region is reduced by constriction of spiral arterioles in the wall of the uterus as a result of the fall in the progesterone level in the blood following the regression of the corpus luteum. This leads to the death of the epithelial cells. Following the period of constriction the spiral arterioles then dilate and the increased blood flow detaches the lining of the uterus and it is shed together with a variable amount of blood in the **menstrual flow.**

Proliferative phase. This coincides with the follicular phase of the oestrous cycle and involves the rapid proliferation of endometrial cells causing the thickening of the endometrium under the control of oestrogen from the developing follicle.

Secretory phase. During this phase progesterone from the corpus luteum stimulates the secretion of mucus from tubular glands and this maintains the lining of the uterus in a receptive state for the implantation of a fertilised ovum.

The effect of failure of fertilisation on the oestrous cycle

If fertilisation does not occur within 24 h of ovulation the secondary oocyte undergoes autolysis in the fallopian tube, as do any spermatozoa remaining in the female genital tract. The corpus luteum persists for 10–14 days following ovulation (usually up to day 26 of the cycle) but then it stops secreting progesterone and oestrogen, as a result of inadequate LH circulating in the blood, and undergoes autolysis. Recent evidence has suggested that in some species the wall of the uterus not containing a fertilised ovum produces a factor known as **luteolysin** which is a prostaglandin, **prostaglandin F2α**. This is thought to pass via the bloodstream to the ovary where it causes regression of the corpus luteum, by rupturing lysosomes within the granulosa cells of the corpus luteum, which then undergoes autolysis.

The effect of fertilisation

If fertilisation occurs the zygote develops into a **blastocyst** which embeds itself into the wall of the uterus within eight days of ovulation. The outer cells of the blastocyst, the **trophoblastic cells**, then begin to secrete a hormone, **human chorionic gonadotrophin** (HCG), which has a similar function to LH. This function includes prevention of autolysis of the corpus luteum and the secretion by it of increased amounts of progesterone and oestrogens which cause increased growth of the endometrium of the uterus. Loss of the lining of the endometrium is inhibited and the

absence of menstrual bleeding (the 'period') is the earliest sign of pregnancy. (Chorionic gonadotrophin has an interstitial cell stimulating effect on the male foetus and causes the secretion of testosterone by the foetal testes which induces growth of the male sex organs.) The placenta begins to assume greater importance in about week 10 of pregnancy when it begins to secrete most of the progesterone and oestrogen essential for a normal pregnancy. Premature failure of the corpus luteum before the secretory ability of the placenta is established fully is a common cause of miscarriage at about 10–12 weeks of pregnancy.

During pregnancy HCG may be detected in the urine and this forms the basis of pregnancy testing. The current test used is called the **agglutination-inhibition test** and involves the addition of chorionic gonadotrophin-coated latex particles to a mixture of urine and an antiserum that will agglutinate with chorionic gonadotrophin. If chorionic gonadotrophin is present in the urine it will react with the agglutinating antiserum and not with the latex particles. The absence of agglutination of the latex particles indicates pregnancy and can be used from 14 days after the missed period.

20.3.3 Copulation

Internal fertilisation is an essential part of reproductive cycles in terrestrial organisms and this is facilitated in many organisms, including Man, by the development of an **intromittent** organ, the penis, which is inserted into the vagina and releases gametes as high as possible within the female reproductive tract. Erection of the penis occurs as a result of a local increase in blood pressure in erectile tissue of the penis, due to parasympathetic nervous activity producing constriction of the veins and dilation of the arterioles following some form of sexual excitement. In this state the penis can be inserted into the vagina where the friction, produced by the rhythmic movements of sexual intercourse, increases the tactile stimulation of sensory cells at the tip of the penis. This activates sympathetic neurones which lead to closure of the internal sphincter of the bladder and contraction of the smooth muscle of the epididymis, vas deferens, and the male accessory glands, the seminal vesicle, prostate and bulbo-urethral glands. This action discharges sperm and seminal fluids into the proximal (internal) urethra where they mix to form **semen**. The increased pressure of these fluids in the proximal urethra leads to reflex activity in the motor neurones supplying the muscles at the base of the penis. Rhythmic wave-like contractions of these muscles force semen out through the distal (external) urethra during **ejaculation** which marks the climax of copulation. The other physiological and psychological sensations associated with this climax in both males and females are called **orgasm**. Lubrication is provided during intercourse partly by a clear mucus secreted by the male bulbo-urethral glands following erection but mainly by glands in the vagina and vulva. The secretions of the male accessory glands are alkaline and contain mucus, fructose, vitamin C, citric acid, prostaglandins and various clotting enzymes, and these increase the normally more acidic pH of the vagina to 6–6.5 which is the optimum pH for sperm motility following ejaculation. Approximately 3 cm^3 of semen is discharged during ejaculation of which only 10% comprises sperm. Despite this low percentage, semen contains about 10^8 sperms cm^{-3}.

20.3.4   Fertilisation

Sperm are deposited high up the vagina close to the cervix. Investigations have shown that sperm pass from the vagina through the uterus and to the top of the fallopian tube within five minutes as a result of contractions of the uterus and fallopian tubes. These contractions are thought to be initiated by the release of oxytocin during sexual intercourse and the local action of prostaglandins, present in semen, on the uterus and fallopian tubes. Sperm are viable in the female genital tract for 24–72 h but are only highly fertile for 12–24 h. Sperm can only fertilise the

oocyte after spending several hours in the female genital tract, usually seven hours, during which time they undergo a process known as **capacitation**. This involves a change in the properties of the membrane covering the acrosome and enables fertilisation to proceed. Fertilisation usually occurs high up the fallopian tube.

When a sperm reaches the oocyte (fig 20.41), the outer membrane of the sperm covering the acrosomal region and the membranes of the acrosome rupture enabling **hyaluronidase** and **protease** enzymes stored in the acrosome to 'digest' away the cell layers, including the zona pellucida, surrounding the oocyte. These changes in the sperm head are known as the **acrosome reaction**. Subsequent changes in the sperm head evert the inner membrane of the acrosome allowing penetration of the zona pellucida and the plasma membrane of the oocyte and, in Man, entry of the entire sperm. Once one sperm has entered the oocyte, cortical granules beneath the plasma membrane, beginning at the point of sperm entry, rupture, releasing a substance which causes the zona pellucida to thicken and separate from the plasma membrane. This is called the **cortical reaction** and spreads over the entire surface of the oocyte causing the

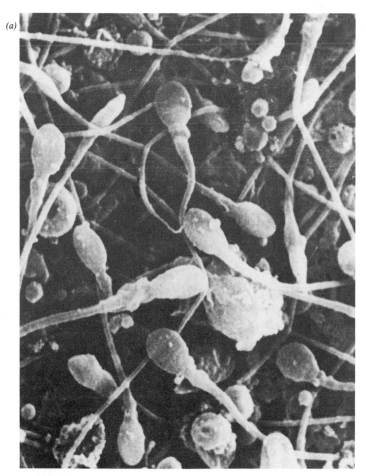

(a)

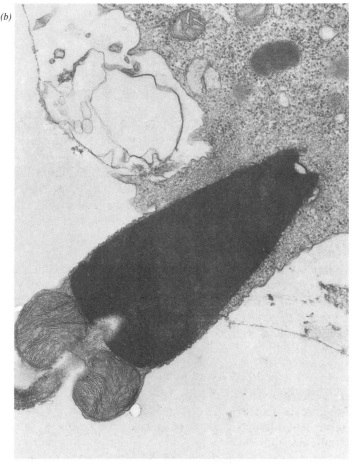

(b)

Fig 20.41   (a) Scanning electron micrograph of human sperms clustered around secondary oocyte
(b) The precise moment of fertilisation as a sperm penetrates the membrane of a sea-urchin's egg. The dark wedge is the head of the sperm, which contains the genetic code. The grey shape behind it is where energy is released that provides power for the tail. The sperm has digested the egg's surface coating of sugary protein and entered. Now the egg's internal fluid welds itself to the outside of the sperm, and draws it in to complete the mating. In some unknown way, the entry of one sperm prevents any others getting in, probably because of rapid changes in the egg's surface coating

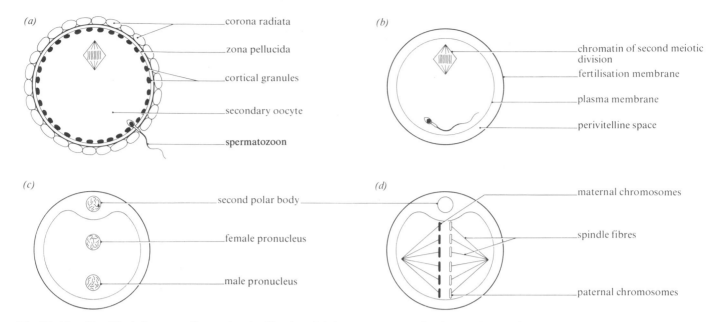

Fig 20.42 *Simplified diagrams illustrating fertilisation. (a) A spermatozoon having undergone capacitation is able to penetrate the zona pellucida of the secondary oocyte and cause the breakdown of cortical granules. (b) The cortical reaction has converted the zona pellucida into the fertilisation membrane which moves off the plasma membrane creating the perivitelline space. (c) The second meiotic division produces the second polar body and is followed by the formation of the female pronucleus and male pronucleus. (d) The nuclear envelopes of the pronuclei break down and maternal and paternal chromosomes align themselves along the equator of the ovum attached to spindle fibres. This is metaphase of the first mitotic division of the zygote*

zona pellucida to form an impenetrable barrier called the **fertilisation membrane** which prevents the entry of further sperm, that is preventing **polyspermy**.

The entry of a sperm acts as the stimulus for completion of the second meiotic division of the secondary oocyte which produces the ovum and the second polar body. The second polar body immediately degenerates, and the tail of the sperm is lost within the cytoplasm of the ovum. Sperm and ovum nuclei form **pronuclei** which are drawn together. The membranes of the pronuclei break down and the paternal and maternal chromosomes attach to spindle fibres which have formed. Both haploid sets of chromosomes by this stage have undergone replication and align themselves as 46 pairs of chromatids along the equator of the spindle as in metaphase of mitosis. This fusion of pronuclear chromosomes is termed **fertilisation**. At this point the diploid number of chromosomes is restored and the fertilised ovum is now called a **zygote**.

Anaphase and telophase of the zygote cell follow and complete the first mitotic division of the zygote. The zygote then undergoes cytokinesis and produces two diploid daughter cells. The process of fertilisation is summarised in fig 20.42.

20.3.5 Implantation

As the zygote passes down the fallopian tube it cleaves by successive nuclear and cell divisions to produce a collection of cells called the **morula**. Cleavage at this stage does not result in an increase in size of the morula because the cells continue to be retained within the zona pellucida. The cleaved cells are called **blastomeres** and they form a wall of cells enclosing a central cavity in the morula, called the **blastocoel**, which fills with liquid from the oviduct. The outer layer of blastomeres is called the **trophoblast** and this differentiates at one point to form a thickened mass of cells, the **inner cell mass**. This stage is called the **blastocyst** and is reached about 4–5 days following ovulation. The structure of the blastocyst is shown in fig 20.43.

When the blastocyst arrives in the uterus it spends about two days in the lumen during which the zona pellucida gradually disappears enabling the cells of the trophoblast to make contact with the cells of the endometrium. The trophoblast cells multiply in the presence of nourishment from the endometrium and between the sixth and ninth days after ovulation the blastocyst becomes embedded

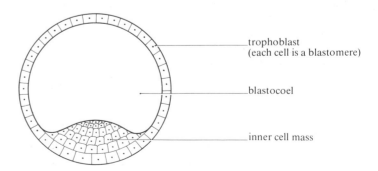

Fig 20.43 *Simplified diagram of a human blastocyst four days after ovulation*

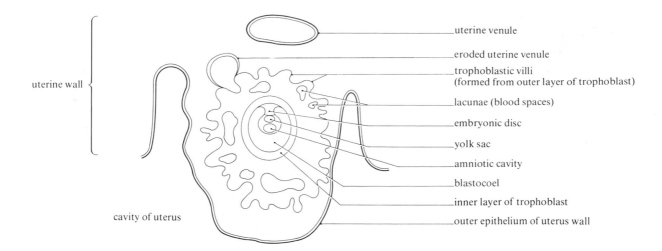

within cells of the endometrium. This process is called **implantation**. The cells of the trophoblast differentiate into two layers and the cell membranes of cells of the outer layer of the trophoblast break down to form the **trophoblastic villi** which grow into the endometrium (fig 20.44). The areas of the endometrium between these villi form interconnecting cavities, called **lacunae**, which give this region of the endometrium a spongy appearance. Hydrolytic enzymes released by this multinucleate structure cause the arterial and venous blood vessels in the endometrium to break down and blood from them fills the lacunae. In the early stages of development of the blastocyst, exchange of nourishment, oxygen and excretory materials between the cells of the blastocyst and the maternal blood in the uterus wall occurs through the trophoblastic villi. Later in development this function is taken over by the placenta.

20.3.6 Early embryonic development

The outer cells of the blastocyst, the trophoblast, grow and develop into an outer membrane called the **chorion** which plays a major role in nourishing and removing waste from the developing embryo. Two cavities appear within the inner cell mass and the cells lining these give rise to two membranes, the **amnion** and the **yolk sac**. The amnion is a thin membrane covering the embryo and has a protective function. Secretion of **amniotic fluid** by the cells of the amnion fill the amniotic cavity between amnion and the embryo. As the embryo increases in size the amnion expands so that it is always pressed up against the uterus wall. The amniotic fluid supports the embryo and protects it from mechanical shock. The yolk sac has no significant function in Man but is important in reptiles and birds for the absorption of food from the yolk and its transfer to the midgut of the developing embryo.

The cells of the inner cell mass, beneath the early amnion, and the yolk sac form a structure called the **embryonic disc**, which gives rise to the embryo. The cells of the disc differentiate at an early stage (when the diameter is less than 2 mm) and form an outer layer of cells, the **ectoderm**, and an inner layer, the **endoderm**. At a later

Fig 20.44 (above) *Simplified diagram showing a recently implanted human blastocyst in the endometrium of the uterus. Enzymes produced by the syncitium of the outer trophoblast break down the blood vessels of the endometrium producing lacunae containing blood which are used in the nourishment and excretion of the blastocyst*

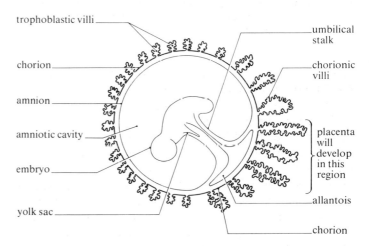

Fig 20.45 *Simplified diagram showing the relationship between the human embryo and extra-embryonic membranes about five weeks after ovulation. The area of the allanto-chorion becomes the placenta*

stage the **mesoderm** is formed and these three germ layers give rise to all the tissues of the developing embryo as described in section 21.8.

During the early stages of embryonic development exchange of materials between embryo and mother across the trophoblastic villi is adequate, but soon a fourth membrane, the **allantois**, develops from the embryonic hindgut. The chorion, amnion, yolk sac and allantois are called **extra-embryonic membranes**, or **foetal membranes** (fig 20.45). The allantois grows outwards until it comes into contact with the chorion where it forms a richly vascularised structure, the **allanto-chorion**, which contributes towards the development of a more efficient and effective exchange structure, the **placenta**.

Placenta

The placenta is a temporary organ found only in eutherian mammals and is the only organ in animals composed of cells derived from two different organisms, the foetus and the mother. It is a point of close association between maternal and foetal circulations and facilitates the transfer of nutrients, oxygen and metabolic waste products between foetus and mother. The placenta is a discrete disc-shaped structure localised in one region of the uterus wall and as it develops it takes over from the trophoblastic villi as the principal site of exchange of materials after 12 weeks.

The foetal part of the placenta consists of connective tissue cells of the chorion which invade the trophoblastic villi in one region of the uterus wall and produce larger projections called **chorionic villi**. The inner regions of the chorionic villi become invaded with looped capillary networks derived from two blood vessels of the foetus, the umbilical artery and umbilical vein. These blood vessels are derived from the allantois and run between foetus and uterus wall in the **umbilical cord** which is a tough structure about 40 cm long covered by cells derived from the amnion and chorion (fig 20.46).

The maternal part of the placenta is composed of outward projections of the outer layers of the endometrium, the **decidua**. Between these and the chorionic villi are lacunae supplied with arterial blood from the uterine arterioles and drained by venules of the uterine vein. The direction of blood flow through the lacunae is determined by the difference in pressure between arterial and venous vessels.

The cell membranes in the wall of the chorionic villi bathed by maternal blood bear microvilli, which increase their surface area, for the exchange of substances by diffusion and other methods of transport. Numerous mitochondria are found in these cells whose membranes contain carrier molecules used in the uptake of materials into the villi by active transport. The presence of numerous small vesicles within the cells of the villi suggests that materials are taken up from the maternal body by pinocytocis (section 7.2.2). A number of mechanisms of uptake are necessary since the distance between foetal and maternal blood is large, for example ten times that across the alveolar membranes of the lung. Water, glucose, amino acids, simple proteins, lipids, mineral salts, vitamins, hormones, antibodies and oxygen pass from mother to foetus, and water, urea and other nitrogenous waste materials, hormones and carbon dioxide pass from foetus to mother across the 'placental barrier'. Potentially harmful substances such as bacteria, viruses, toxins and drugs can pass to the foetus, but this is offset by certain antibodies, globulins, antibiotics and antitoxins passing in the same direction. This ensures that the baby is born with **passive immunity** (section 14.14.5) to certain diseases.

The placental barrier not only protects the foetus from many harmful situations which may occur to the mother but also shields the foetal circulation from the high blood

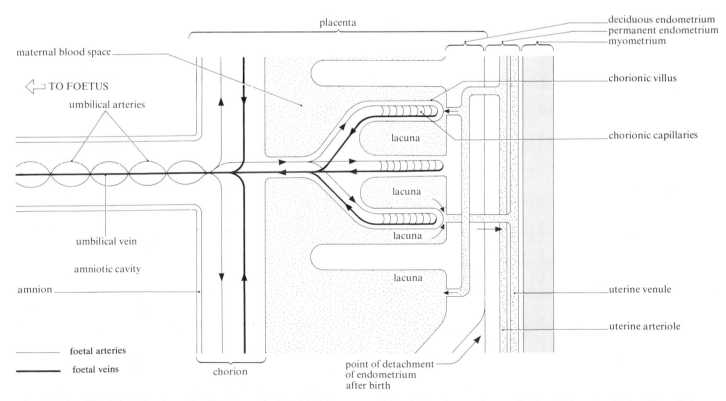

Fig 20.46 *Simplified diagram showing the relationship between umbilical blood vessels, capillaries of the chorionic villi and the blood spaces of the lacunae of the human placenta. This structure forms the link between the circulatory systems of the foetus and the mother*

760

pressure of the maternal circulation. It cannot function, however, as an immunological barrier, and since the foetus carries paternal genes it will produce antigens foreign to the mother who will produce antibodies against them. The mechanisms accounting for the remarkable ability of the foetus (or, in immunological terms, the **homograft**) to resist rejection for the 40 weeks of gestation is not known but is thought to involve the production of immune suppressive substances which circulate in the maternal plasma.

The continual passage of oxygen from mother to foetus is vital to the life and development of the foetus and this is ensured by the difference in affinity for oxygen between foetal and maternal haemoglobins as described in section 14.13.1.

The placenta is an endocrine organ whose major secretions are chorionic gonadotrophin, oestrogens, progesterone and **human placental lactogen**. The latter hormone stimulates mammary development in preparation for lactation. The site of secretion of all these hormones is the connective tissue of the chorion.

Sexual development in the embryo

The genetic sex of the embryo is determined at fertilisation by the sex chromosomes carried by the father's sperm, X in the case of a female and Y in the case of a male. Despite this, it would appear that the basic disposition of the human body is towards being female, largely as a result of the presence of an X chromosome in both sexes. In the early stages of embryonic development a pair of undifferentiated embryonic gonads, the **genital ridges**, and both rudimentary female and male reproductive systems develop in the embryo. As a result of this, all embryos are potentially bisexual up to the sixth week of development.

Recent investigations have revealed a possible mechanism whereby the sex chromosomes determine which of these systems is activated and lead to the phenotypic expression of the embryo's sex.

The X chromosome carries a gene, the **Tfm gene** (**testicular feminisation gene**) which specifies the production of an **androgen-receptor protein molecule** in the cells of the developing reproductive system. Since both male and female embryos carry at least one X chromosome, this molecule is present in both sexes.

The Y chromosome carries a gene called the **Y-linked testis-determining gene** specifying the production of a protein molecule, the **H-Y antigen** which stimulates the cells of the embryonic genital ridges to differentiate into seminiferous tubules and interstitial cells. Testosterone released into the embryonic circulatory system reacts with the androgen-receptor molecules in the target cells of the potential reproductive system. The androgen-receptor/testosterone complex formed passes to the nuclei where it activates genes associated with the development of the tissues. Testosterone will activate only those tissues which give rise to the male reproductive system and therefore an XY embryo will develop into a male foetus. The tissues of the potential female reproductive system are not activated

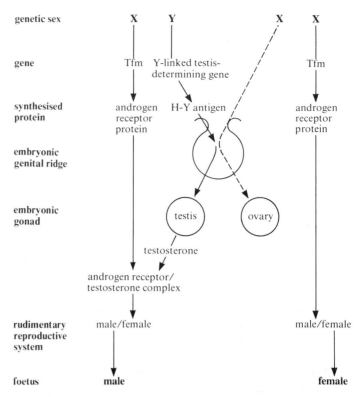

Fig 20.47 *Summary diagram showing the events involved in the differentiation of the embryonic genital ridge and rudimentary reproductive system into the specific gonad and reproductive system of the foetus*

and do not develop. In an XX embryo, the absence of testosterone allows the reproductive system to develop in its inherent direction towards that of female.

Thus it may be concluded that placental influences will direct the development of the embryo in the direction of a female unless diverted by a mechanism initiated by the Y chromosome. A summary of these events is shown in fig 20.47.

20.3.7   Birth

From the beginning of the third month of pregnancy the human embryo is referred to as the **foetus** and it normally completes a total of 40 weeks of development, the **gestation period**, before birth occurs. Most of the major organs are formed by the twelfth week of pregnancy and the remainder of the gestation period is taken up by growth.

Throughout pregnancy oestrogen and progesterone are secreted in progressively greater amounts, first by the corpus luteum and then principally by the placenta. In the last three months of pregnancy oestrogen secretion increases faster than progesterone secretion and, immediately prior to birth, the progesterone level declines and the oestrogen level increases. The functions of these hormones in pregnancy are summarised in table 20.4.

It was thought that hormonal activities within the mother controlled the timing of birth but recent evidence obtained from research on several mammals has suggested there is a

Table 20.4. Summary of major functions of human oestrogen and progesterone during pregnancy

Oestrogen	Progesterone
Growth of mammary glands	Growth of mammary glands
Inhibits FSH release	Inhibits FSH release
Inhibits prolactin release	Inhibits prolactin release
Prevents infection in uterus	Inhibits contraction of myometrium
Increases size of uterine muscle cells	
Increases ATP and creatine phosphate formation	
Increases sensitivity of myometrium to oxytocin	

high degree of foetal involvement in the timing of birth. This would seem to have profound adaptive survival value in ensuring birth of the foetus at a stage in development at which it can lead a relatively independent existence. The initial stages of birth are believed to result from stimuli, as yet undefined, influencing the foetal hypothalamus to release ACTH from the foetal pituitary. One area of current thought concerning the initial birth stimuli is that of 'foetal stress' brought about by an immunological rejection of the mature foetus by the tissues of the mother. As foetal ACTH is released it stimulates the foetal adrenal gland to release corticosteroids which cross the placental barrier and enter the maternal circulation causing a decrease in

progesterone production and an increase in secretion of prostaglandins. The reduction in progesterone level allows the maternal posterior pituitary gland to release the octapeptide hormone, oxytocin, and removes the inhibitory effect on contraction of the myometrium. Whilst oxytocin causes contraction of the smooth muscle of the myometrium, prostaglandins increase the power of the contractions. The release of oxytocin occurs in 'waves' during 'labour' and provides the force to expel the foetus from the uterus. The onset of contractions of the myometrium, so-called 'labour pains', are accompanied by the dilation of the cervix, the rupture of the amnion and chorion releasing amniotic fluid from the cervix, and the stimulation of stretch receptors in the walls of the uterus and cervix. The latter activate the autonomic nervous system and autonomic reflexes induce contraction of the uterus wall. Other impulses pass up the spinal cord to stimulate the hypothalamus to release oxytocin from the posterior pituitary gland. The pressure of the head of the foetus 'engaged' in the pelvis pressing against the cervix with the face towards the mother's anus, irritates the cervix and leads to stronger contractions of the myometrium.

Uterine contractions spread down over the uterus and are strongest from top to bottom, thus pushing the baby downwards. Throughout these contractions the cervix gradually dilates and the time between bouts of contractions decreases. This is the **first stage** of labour and it ends when the cervix has the same diameter as the head. The

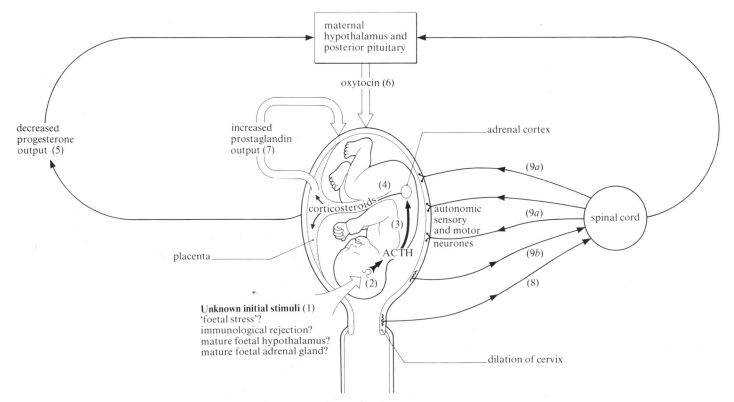

Fig 20.48 *Possible mechanisms associated with birth. Of all the hormonal and nervous mechanisms shown above, only the effect of oxytocin on the uterus wall has been clearly demonstrated. Numbers 1–7 show the possible sequence of events inducing contraction of the uterus wall and 8, 9a and 9b show the possible reflex pathways involved in the control of the contractions*

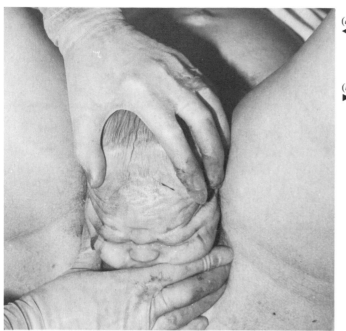

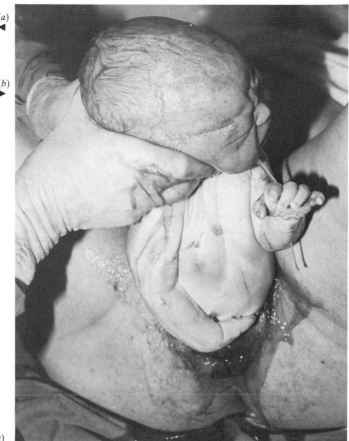

Fig 20.49 (a) (above) The baby's head has been guided through the vagina by the doctor attending the birth and it is now fully emerged. (b) (right) The body of the baby is now partially emerged. The legs are still inside and the umbilical cord remains attached. (c) (below) The baby has been cleaned and is resting on the mother. At this stage the umbilical cord is intact and the baby is still attached to the placenta

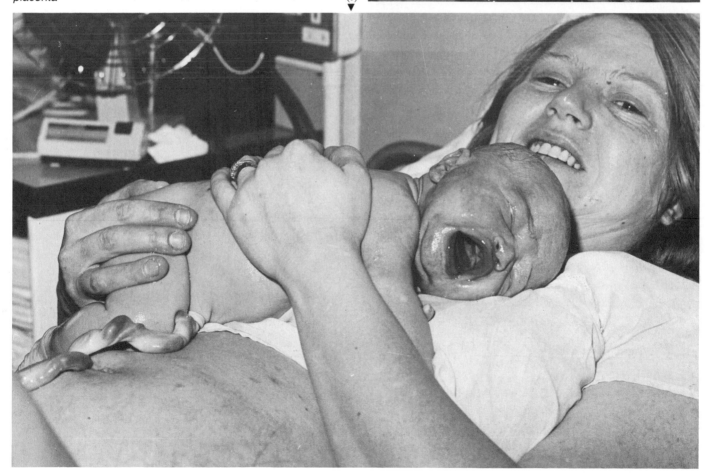

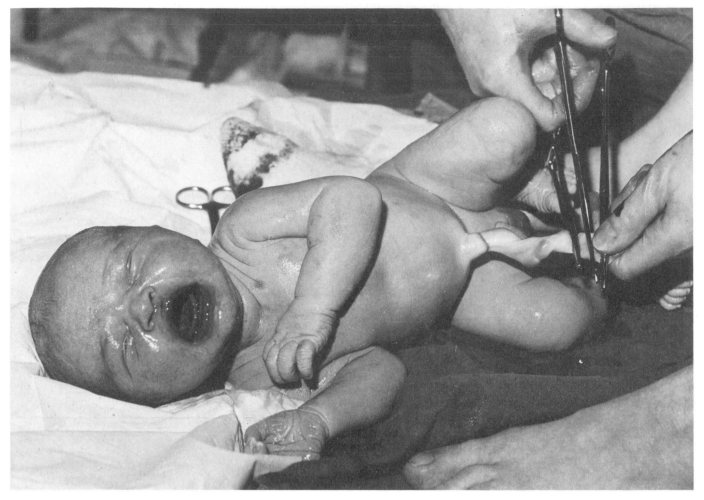

Fig 20.49 *(d) The doctor is now cutting the umbilical cord and the process of birth will then be complete*

second stage of labour involves the passage of the head and body through the vagina and the delivery of the baby. The umbilical cord is ligatured in two places close to the baby and a cut made between the ligatures allowing the baby to be now totally separated from any immediate physiological reliance on the mother. Within 10–45 minutes after birth the uterus contracts dramatically and separates the placenta from the wall of the uterus and the placenta then passes out through the vagina. This is the **third stage** of labour. Bleeding, throughout this period, is limited by contraction of smooth muscle fibres which completely surround all uterine blood vessels supplying the placenta. Average blood loss is kept to about 350 cm^3.

20.3.8 Lactation

The **mammary glands**, or breasts, consist of two types of tissue, glandular tissue and supporting tissue or stroma. Glandular epithelial cells line small sacs called alveoli arranged in 15 lobules within the breast. The alveoli are surrounded by a layer of myoepithelial (contractile) tissue involved in the release of milk. Milk is produced by the glandular cells and passes, via a series of ducts and sinuses which store milk, to separate openings in the nipple.

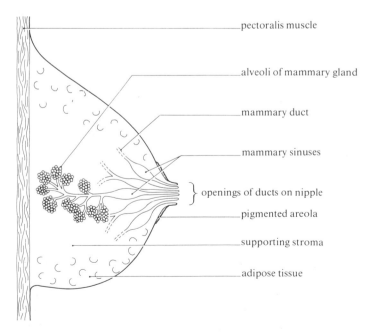

pectoralis muscle

alveoli of mammary gland

mammary duct

mammary sinuses

openings of ducts on nipple

pigmented areola

supporting stroma

adipose tissue

Fig 20.50 *Simplified diagram of the human female breast showing the glandular alveoli where milk is secreted and the ducts and sinuses conveying milk to the nipple.*

During puberty the breasts enlarge due to development of the stroma under the influence of oestrogen and progesterone. Internal changes in the nature of the stroma and secretory ducts, and in the amount of fat in the breasts, occur throughout the menstrual cycle, enlarging slightly during the luteal phase, but during pregnancy there is greater increase in size and activity of the breasts.

The increase in the size of the breasts during pregnancy is due to the development of the secretory areas under the influence of oestrogen, progesterone, corticosteroids, growth hormone, placental lactogen and prolactin. However, throughout pregnancy the presence of progesterone inhibits the formation of milk (**lactogenesis**). At birth, when the progesterone level falls, prolactin is no longer inhibited and it stimulates the alveoli to secrete milk.

Human milk contains fat, lactose (milk sugar) and the proteins lactalbumin and casein which are all easily digestible. The milk is synthesised from metabolites circulating in the blood, such as lactose from glucose under the influence of the enzyme **lactose synthetase**, protein from amino acids, and fats from fatty acids, glycerol and acetates. This food alone is adequate to produce weight gains in the baby of 25–30 g per day.

In between breast feeds prolactin stimulates milk production for the next feed. Oestrogen is necessary for the continued production of milk, but artificially induced high levels of oestrogen have been used to inhibit lactogenesis in mothers not wishing to breast feed. (It is common practice now to use a drug called **bromocriptine** instead of oestrogen.)

The ejection of milk from the nipple involves a simple reflex action, the **milk ejection reflex**. The sucking of the baby on the breast stimulates sensory receptors in the nipple to set up impulses passing via the spinal cord to the hypothalamus which releases oxytocin from the posterior pituitary gland. This causes contraction of the myoepithelial tissue surrounding the alveoli and forces milk through the ducts and sinuses and out of the nipples.

The initial secretion of the breasts, following birth, is not milk but **colostrum**. This has a yellow colour and contains cells from the alveoli and is rich in the protein, globulin, but low in fat. It is believed to be a means of passing antibodies, particularly IgA (section 14.14.3), from mother to baby.

20.3.9   Changes in foetal circulation at birth

Throughout development in the uterus the foetal lungs and digestive tract do not function, since gaseous exchange and nutrition are provided by the mother via the placenta. Most of the oxygenated blood returning to the foetus via the umbilical vein by-passes its liver in a vessel, the **ductus venosus**, which shunts blood into the inferior vena cava and passes it to the right atrium (fig 20.51). Some blood from the umbilical vein flows directly to the liver; blood entering the right atrium, therefore, contains a mixture of oxygenated and deoxygenated blood. From

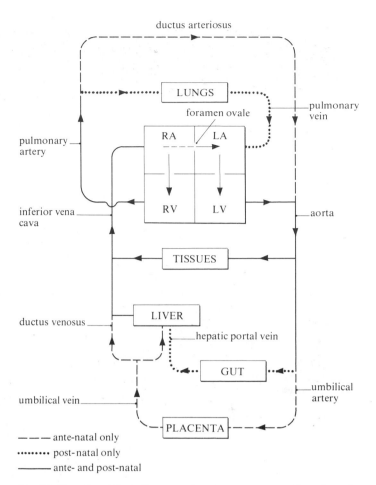

Fig 20.51 *Simplified diagram showing ante-natal (foetal) and post-natal circulatory systems. (The periods when the blood vessels are functional are indicated on the diagram.)*

here most of the blood passes through an opening in the atrial septum, the **foramen ovale**, into the left atrium. Some blood passes from the right atrium into the right ventricle and into the pulmonary artery but does not pass to the lungs. Instead it is shunted via the **ductus arteriosus** directly to the aorta thereby by-passing lungs, pulmonary vein and the atrium and ventricle of the left side of the heart. Blood from the left atrium passes into the left ventricle and into the aorta which supplies blood to the head, upper limbs, trunk and lower limbs and the umbilical artery. Pressure in the foetal circulatory system is greatest in the pulmonary artery and this determines the direction of blood flow through the foetus and placenta.

> **20.9**   Describe a major change that would occur in the foetal circulation if blood pressure were highest in the aorta.

At birth the sudden inflation of the lungs reduces the resistance to blood flow through the pulmonary capillaries and blood flows through them in preference to the ductus arteriosus; this reduces the pressure in the pulmonary artery. Simultaneously the tying of the umbilical cord prevents blood from flowing through the placenta, and this increases the volume of blood flowing through the body of the baby and leads to a sudden increase in blood pressure in the aorta, left ventricle and left atrium. This pressure change causes the small valves guarding the foramen ovale, which open to the left atrium, to close, preventing the short-circuiting of blood from right to left atrium. Within a few months these valves fuse to the atrial septum and close the foramen ovale completely. If this does not occur the baby is left with a 'hole in the heart' and will require surgery to correct the defect.

The increased pressure in the aorta and decreased pressure in the pulmonary artery forces blood backwards along the ductus arteriosus into the pulmonary artery and hence to the lungs, thereby boosting its supply. After a few hours muscles in the wall of the ductus arteriosus constrict under the influence of the rising partial pressure of oxygen in the blood and close off this blood vessel. A similar mechanism of muscular contraction closes off the ductus venosus and increases blood flow through the liver. The mechanism of closing down the ductus venosus is not known but is essential in transforming the ante-natal (before birth) circulation into the post-natal (after birth) condition.

20.4 Phylogenetic review of sexual reproduction in vertebrates

Sexual reproduction occurs in every animal phylum and, whilst the basic processes of gamete formation, fertilisation and zygote formation are common to all groups, there is considerable variation in the anatomical, physiological and behavioural aspects of sexual reproduction. Many examples of the variations shown by the invertebrate phyla are described in chapter 4.

In vertebrates, too, tremendous variation exists in many of the aspects of sexual reproduction, and some of these, together with selected examples, are summarised in table 20.5. The phylogeny of the vertebrates shows a gradual adaptation to life on land. One of the major problems to overcome in making the transition from an aquatic existence to a terrestrial existence involved reproduction. The majority of fish shed their gametes directly into water, fertilisation is external, eggs contain a considerable amount of yolk, larval stages are common and any degree of parental care is rare. In the amphibia there are several examples of adaptations to terrestrial life but few of these involve mechanisms of reproduction. Amphibia have to

Table 20.5. Summary table showing variations in the mechanisms of sexual reproduction in selected vertebrates

Organism	Number of female gametes released per year	Diameter of egg/mm	Site of fertilisation	Site of embryonic development	Degree of parental care
Cod	$3–7 \times 10^6$	0.13	external	Sea as larvae, oviparous*	None, very little yolk in egg
Stickleback	60	2.0	external	Nest, built by male, oviparous	Male occupies territory, courts female; eggs laid and fertilised in nest; young protected in nest
Spotted dogfish (*Scyliorhinus canaliculus*)	144	15.0	internal	Egg case, 'Mermaids purse'; no larval stage, oviparous	Mating occurs near surface of water, large supply of yolk in egg
Frog (*Rana temporaria*)	2 000	2	external	Water, collectively as 'frog spawn', oviparous; larval (tadpole) stage undergoes metamorphosis	Simple courtship, mating occurs; Moderate amount of yolk in egg; no after-care
Sand lizard (*Lacerta agilis*)	6	8.0	internal	Amniote egg in holes in sand or soil, oviparous	Simple courtship, mating occurs; large amount of yolk; no after care
Robin (*Erithacus rubecula*)	5	20.0	internal	Amniote egg in nest built by female, oviparous	Male occupies territory, elaborate courtship, mating occurs, female incubates eggs for 14 days, fledgling fed by both parents, offspring independent after six weeks

*Offspring *laid* or spawned as eggs.

return to water to mate, and the early stages of their development take place there also. There are, however, many amphibian species that show elaborate behavioural patterns associated with parental care. For example, the male *Pipa* toad spreads the fertilised eggs over the back of the female where they stick, become 'embedded' in the skin and develop into tadpoles. After about three weeks they escape from the mother's back and lead an independent existence.

Reptiles were the earliest group of vertebrates to overcome the problems of fertilisation and development on land. Clearly shedding of gametes in a terrestrial situation is impossible, so the first requirement of totally land-dwelling organisms must have been the introduction of male gametes into the female body, that is internal fertilisation. Internal fertilisation occurs in reptiles and the increased chances of fertilisation reduces the numbers of gametes which it is necessary to produce. Once fertilised, the zygote develops within a specialised structure, the **amniote (cleidoic) egg**, which provides the embryo with a fluid-filled cavity in which it can develop on land. The outer shell provides immediate protection from mechanical damage and envelops the four membranes which surround the embryo. These four extra-embryonic membranes, the yolk sac, amnion, chorion and allantois are derived from ectoderm, endoderm and mesoderm and provide the embryo with protection and facilitate many of its metabolic activities including nutrition, respiration and excretion. The **yolk sac** develops as an outgrowth of the embryonic gut and encloses the yolk which is gradually absorbed by the blood vessels of the yolk sac. When the yolk has been used up the yolk sac is withdrawn into the gut. The **amnion** forms from an upgrowth of the cells beneath the embryo and completely encloses the embryo in the **amniotic cavity** which becomes filled with **amniotic fluid** secreted by the cells of the amnion. This provides the embryo with an immediate fluid environment (a replica of the ancestral aquatic environment of the amphibian) in which the

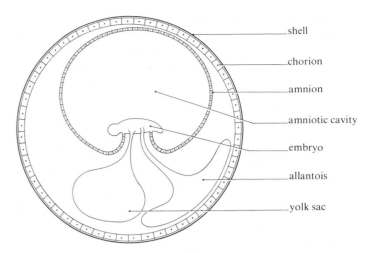

Fig 20.52 *Simplified diagram of the amniote egg*

embryo can develop. All reptiles, birds and mammals have an amnion and are called **amniotes**. As the embryo grows the amnion is pushed out until it fuses with the third embryonic membrane, the **chorion**, which lies immediately within the shell and prevents excessive water loss from the amnion. The **allantois** is an outgrowth of the embryonic hindgut and rapidly expands, in reptiles and birds, to underlie the chorion. Here it functions primarily as a 'bladder' for storing excretory products and as the gas exchange organ of the embryo, facilitating the transfer of respiratory gases between the environmental atmosphere and the amniotic fluid via the porous shell. The structure of the amniote egg is shown in fig 20.52.

Birds and primitive egg-laying mammals called monotremes, such as the duck-billed platypus, *Ornithorhyncus*, all produce an amniotic egg and, whilst the shell of the egg is lost in higher mammals, the four extra-embryonic membranes are retained; two of them, the chorion and allantois, give rise to the placenta in eutherian (placental) mammals (section 20.3.6).

Chapter Twenty-one

Growth and development

Growth is a fundamental characteristic of all living organisms. It is often thought of simply as an increase in size, but careful consideration shows this to be an inadequate definition. For example, the size of a plant cell may increase as it takes up water by osmosis, but this process may be reversible and cannot then be thought of as genuine growth. Also, during cleavage of the zygote and in the early embryo there is an increase in cell numbers without an increase in size (volume or mass). This is the result of cell division without subsequent increase in size of daughter cells. The process is a developmental one and so perhaps should be regarded as growth despite the fact that no increase in size occurs.

The process of development is so closely linked with growth that the phrase 'growth and development' is commonly used to describe the processes which are normally thought of as growth. Starting with an individual cell, growth of a multicellular organism can be divided into three phases:

(1) **cell division (hyperplasia)** – an increase in cell number as a result of mitotic division and cell division;
(2) **cell expansion (hypertrophy)** – an irreversible increase in cell size as a result of the uptake of water or the synthesis of protoplasm;
(3) **cell differentiation** – the specialisation of cells; in its broad sense, growth also includes this phase of cell development.

However, each of these processes can occur at separate points in time. The example of cleavage has already been mentioned above. An increase in volume without change in cell numbers may also occur, as in the region of cell elongation behind the root and shoot tips of higher plants. In the case of single-celled organisms such as bacteria, cell division results in *reproduction* (not growth) of the *individual* and *growth* of the *population*.

All stages of growth involve biochemical activity. Protein synthesis is particularly important since it is the means by which the DNA message is expressed in terms of enzymes synthesised by the cell. Enzymes control cell activities. Changes at the cell level bring about changes in overall form and structure, both of individual organs and of the organism as a whole, and this process is known as **morphogenesis**.

A definition of growth should satisfy the criterion of increase in size that occurs in all organisms from single-celled organisms to the most advanced plants and animals, as well as reflecting the metabolic activity associated with

growth. Growth can therefore be defined as **an irreversible increase in dry mass of protoplasm**. This in turn reflects an increase in the amount of protein which has been synthesised, and the fact that the process of protein synthesis forms the basis of growth.

Growth may be positive or negative. **Positive growth** occurs when anabolism exceeds catabolism, whereas **negative growth** occurs when catabolism exceeds anabolism (chapter 11). For example, in the course of germination of a seed and the production of a seedling various physical parameters increase in magnitude, such as cell number, cell size, fresh mass, length, volume and complexity of form, whilst others such as dry mass may actually *decrease*. From the definition, germination in the latter case is therefore strictly a time of negative growth.

21.1   Measurement of growth

Growth occurs at many levels of biological organisation from the community level down to the molecular level. In all cases if the increase in measurable parameter is plotted against time an S-shaped growth curve is obtained. Fig 21.1 shows a variety of growth curves produced by plotting different parameters such as length, height, mass and surface area, volume and numbers against time. The shape of these curves is described as **sigmoid**, meaning S-shaped.

A sigmoid curve can be divided into four parts. The initial phase is the **lag phase** during which little growth occurs. This leads into the second phase, the **log phase** (grand period of growth) during which growth proceeds exponentially. During this phase the rate of growth is at its maximum and at any point the rate of growth is proportional to the amount of material or numbers of cells or organisms already present.

In all cases of growth the exponential increase declines and the rate of growth begins to decrease. The point at which this occurs is known as the **inflexion point**. The third phase is the **decelerating phase** (self-retarding phase) during which time growth becomes limited as a result of the effect of some internal or external factor, or the interaction of both. The final phase is the **plateau phase** or **stationary phase**. This usually marks the period where overall growth has ceased and the parameter under consideration remains constant. The precise nature of the curve during this phase may vary depending on the nature of the parameter, the

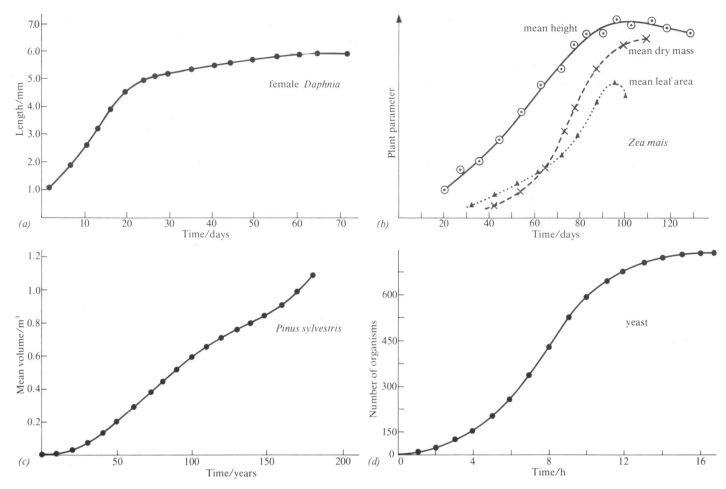

Fig 21.1 (above) Growth curves obtained using six different parameters and four different species. In all cases the curves are sigmoid. ((b) After Kreusler. (c) Indicates growth of trees, after Tischendorf. (d) After Knopf.)

Fig 21.2 (below) A typical sigmoid growth curve showing the four characteristic growth phases and the inflexion point. (a) Lag phase; (b) log phase; (c) inflexion point; (d) decelerating phase; (e) plateau or stationary phase

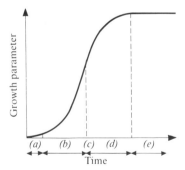

21.1.1 Methods of measuring growth

Growth can be measured at various levels of biological organisation, such as growth of a cell, organism or population. The numbers of organisms in a population at different times can be counted and plotted against time to produce a population growth curve as shown in fig 21.1*d* (section 12.6.3). At the level of the organism there are a variety of parameters which may be measured; length, area, volume and mass are commonly used. In plants, growth curves for roots, stems, internodes and leaf area are often required, and length and area are the parameters chosen. In the case of growth in animals and entire plants length and mass are two commonly measured parameters. With regard to mass there are two values that can be used, namely fresh (wet) mass and dry mass. Of the two, fresh mass is the easier parameter to measure since it requires less preparation of the sample and has the advantage of not causing any injury to the organism, so that repeated measurements of the same organism may be taken over a period of time.

The major disadvantage of using fresh mass as a growth parameter is that it may give inconsistent readings due to fluctuations in water content. True growth is reflected by

species and internal factors. In some cases the curve may continue to increase slightly until the organism dies as is the case with monocotyledonous leaves, many invertebrates, fish and certain reptiles. This indicates **positive growth**. In the case of certain coelenterates the curve flattens out indicating no change in growth whilst other growth curves may tail off indicating a period of **negative growth**. The latter pattern is characteristic of many mammals, including Man, and is a sign of physical senescence associated with increasing age.

changes in the amounts of constituents other than water and the only valid way to measure these is to obtain the dry mass. This is done by killing the organism and placing it in an oven at 110 °C to drive off all the water. The specimen is cooled in a desiccator and weighed. This procedure is repeated until a constant mass is recorded. This is the dry mass. In all cases it is more accurate to obtain the dry mass of as large a number of specimens as is practicable and from this calculate the mean dry mass. This value will be more representative than that obtained from a single specimen.

21.1.2 Types of growth curve

Plotting data obtained from any one of the physical parameters described above, such as dry mass (m), against time (t) produces a growth curve which is known as the **actual** or **absolute growth curve** (fig 21.3). The usefulness of this curve is that it shows the overall growth pattern and the extent of growth. Data from this graph enable the growth curves in figs 21.3–5 to be constructed.

Plotting the change in parameter against time produces an **absolute growth rate curve** (fig 21.4). (The same curve

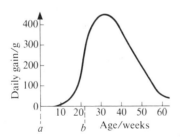

Fig 21.3 *Actual or absolute growth curve obtained by plotting live mass against age for sheep. (Data from L. R. Wallace (1948) J. Agric. Sci.,* **38**, *93 and H. Pálsson & J. B. Vergés (1952) J. Agric. Sci.,* **42**, *93)*

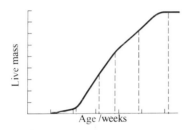

Fig 21.4 *Absolute growth rate curve plotted from data shown in fig 21.3*

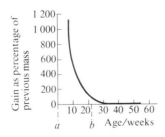

Fig 21.5 *Relative growth rate curve plotted from data shown in fig. 21.3*

could be obtained by calculating the slope of the absolute growth curve $\left(\frac{dm}{dt}\right)$ at various points and plotting these against time).

This curve shows how the rate of growth changes during the time of the study. In particular it shows the period when growth is most rapid and this corresponds to the steepest part of the absolute growth curve. The peak of the absolute growth curve marks the point of inflexion after which the rate of growth decreases as the adult size is attained.

Dividing each of the above values for the absolute rate of growth by the amount of growth at the beginning of each time period $\left(\frac{dm}{dt} \cdot \frac{1}{m}\right)$ and plotting these values against time produces a **relative rate of growth curve** (or **specific rate of growth curve**) (fig 21.5). This is a measure of the efficiency of growth.

A comparison of relative rate of growth curves for organisms grown or reared under different conditions shows clearly the most favourable conditions for rapid growth and for growth over an extended period. In the case of mammals the absolute growth curve is sigmoid but the exact shape of the curve appears to be related to the time taken to reach sexual maturity. In the rat the curve is steep and truly sigmoid since sexual maturity is reached quickly (within 12 months), whereas in Man the absolute growth curve shows four distinct phases of increased growth (fig 21.6).

21.1 What conclusions, regarding growth in Man, may be drawn from the three curves shown in fig 21.6?

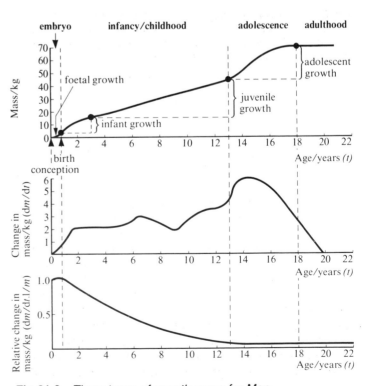

Fig 21.6 *Three types of growth curve for Man*

771

21.2 Patterns of growth

Various patterns of growth occur among organisms.

21.2.1 Isometric and allometric growth

Isometric (*isos*, same; *metron*, measure) growth occurs when an organ grows at the same mean rate as the rest of the body. In this situation change in size of the organism is not accompanied by a change in shape or external form of the organism. The proportions of the two structures remain the same. This type of growth pattern is seen in fish and exopterygote insects, such as locusts (except for wings and genitalia) (fig 21.7). In such cases as these there is a simple relationship between linear dimension, area, volume and mass. The area increases as the square of linear dimension ($A \propto l^2$) whereas volume and mass increase as the cube of linear dimension ($V \propto l^3$ and $M \propto l^3$). Animals showing little change in overall shape

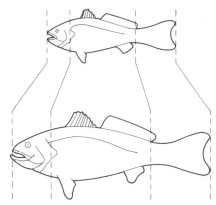

Fig. 21.7 (above) *Development in fish – an example of isometric growth. The external structures retain their shape and spatial relationships as a result of a proportional growth rate. (After Batt (1980)* Influences on animal growth and development, *Studies in Biology, No. 116, Arnold.)*

Fig 21.8 (below) *Development in Man – an example of allometric growth. To show the relative rates of growth from the age of two months to 25 years each stage has been given a constant height. (After Stratz, cited in J. Hammond (ed.) (1955)* Progress in the physiology of farm animals, *2, 431, Butterworths.)*

with time therefore show a marked change in mass: an increase in length of only 10% is accompanied by a 33% increase in mass.

Allometric (*allos*, other; *metron*, measure) growth occurs when an organ grows at a different rate from the rest of the body. This produces a change in size of the organism which is accompanied by a change in shape of the organism. This pattern of growth is characteristic of mammals and illustrates the relationship between growth and development. Fig 21.8 shows how the relative proportions of various structures in Man change as a result of simultaneous changes in patterns of growth and development. In almost all animals the last organs to develop and differentiate are the reproductive organs. These show allometric growth and can be observed only in those organisms with external genital organs, hence they are not seen in many species of fish where growth appears to be purely isometric. Fig 21.9 shows the degree of variation in patterns of growth of different organs of Man. Again it can be seen that the last organs to develop are the reproductive organs.

The shapes of absolute growth curves for whole organisms as represented by length or mass show remarkable similarities and generally conform to the sigmoid shape described in section 21.1. However, several groups of organisms show variations on the general pattern which reflect adaptations to particular modes of life and environments as described in sections 21.2.2–21.2.3.

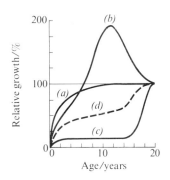

Fig 21.9 (above) *Relative growth rates of (a) brain, (b) thymus and (c) reproductive organs of Man. Each curve is drawn relative to the absolute growth curve of the whole body (d). (After Scammon.)*

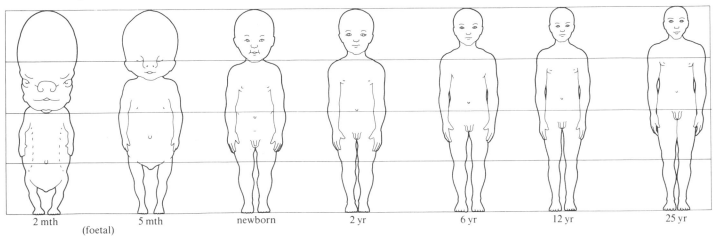

| 2 mth | 5 mth | newborn | 2 yr | 6 yr | 12 yr | 25 yr |

(foetal)

21.2.2 Limited and unlimited growth

Studies of the duration of growth in plants and animals show that there are two basic patterns, called limited (definite or determinate) growth and unlimited (indefinite or indeterminate) growth.

Growth in annual plants is limited and after a period of maximum growth, during which the plant matures and reproduces, there is a period of negative growth or senescence before the death of the plant. If the dry mass of the annual plant is plotted against time then an interesting variation on the sigmoid curve of fig 21.2 is seen, as shown in fig 21.10.

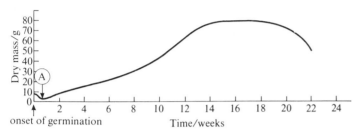

Fig 21.10 *Growth curve of a broad bean (*Vicia faba*) planted in March – an annual plant*

> **21.2** Examine fig 21.10 and answer the following questions, based on your knowledge of the life cycle of an annual plant.
> (*a*) Why is there negative growth initially during the germination of the seed?
> (*b*) Describe the appearance of the seedling when positive growth occurs at A.
> (*c*) What physiological process occurs here to account for positive growth?
> (*d*) Why is the decrease in dry mass after 20 weeks very sudden?

Several plant organs show limited growth but do not undergo a period of negative growth, for example fruits, organs of vegetative propagation, dicotyledonous leaves and stem internodes. Animals showing limited growth include insects, birds and mammals.

Woody perennial plants on the other hand show unlimited growth and have a characteristic growth curve which is a cumulative series of sigmoid curves (fig 21.11), each of which represents one year's growth. With unlimited growth, some slight net growth continues until death.

Other examples of unlimited growth are found among fungi, lower plants, particularly algae, and many animals, particularly invertebrates, fishes and reptiles. Monocotyledonous leaves show unlimited growth.

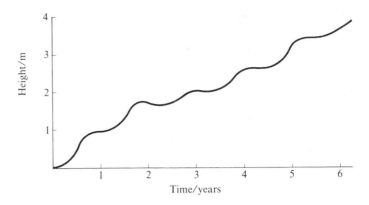

Fig 21.11 *Growth curve of a birch tree – a woody perennial*

21.2.3 Growth in arthropods

A striking and characteristic growth pattern is associated with crustacea and other arthropods, such as hemimetabolous insects and the larvae of holometabolous insects. Due to the inelastic nature of their exoskeletons they appear to grow only in spurts interrupted by a series of moults (**discontinuous growth**). A typical hemimetabolous growth pattern is shown in fig 21.12. It is growth curves such as these, based on length, which do not give a true reflection of growth. If a growth curve is plotted for the same insect, using dry mass as the growth parameter, a normal sigmoid curve is produced demonstrating that true growth, as represented by increase in protoplasm, is continuous.

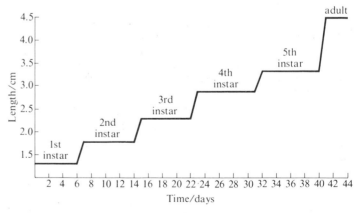

Fig 21.12 *Growth curve showing increase in length of the short-horned grasshopper. (After R. Soper & T. Smith (1979) Modern Biology, Macmillan.)*

21.3 Control of growth and development

The process of growth and development in an organism is controlled ultimately by the information contained in its DNA. Growth, however, is the result of the interaction between the DNA and the internal and external environments of the organism. Important external influences include availability of food, light, heat and water. The internal environment includes chemicals such as hormones and recently discovered cytoplasmic proteins ('transcription factors') that influence gene expression either directly or indirectly. External factors can influence internal factors, for example lack of iodine in the diet of Man leads to an inability to make the hormone thyroxine with a consequent reduction in growth rate.

Table 21.1. Summary of factors inflencing growth and development

External factors	Process affected
Light (intensity, quality and duration)	Photosynthesis – energy source (ch. 9) Photomorphogenesis (ch. 15) Phototropism (ch. 15) Greening (ch. 15) Photoperiodism (chs 15 and 16) Synthesis of vitamin D in Man
Short wavelength electromagnetic radiation (X-rays, γ-rays etc.)	Mutagenesis (ch. 23)
Nutrients	Autotrophic nutrition – carbon dioxide, water, inorganic salts required – deficiency diseases in absence (ch. 9) Heterotrophic nutrition – organic compounds, water and inorganic salts required (ch. 10); deficiency diseases in absence (chs 9 and 10)
Temperature	Affects growth via effect on enzymes (ch. 6 and fig 21.13): thermoperiodism (ch. 15)
Oxygen	Needed by aerobic organisms for respiration: particularly important for active uptake of ions by plant roots and foetal development (ch. 12)
Water	Essential for many processes (ch. 5)
Seasonal influences	Dormancy of buds, seeds and perennating organs (ch. 15) Leaf fall (ch. 15) Reproduction (chs 15, 16 and 20) Photoperiodism and thermoperiodism (chs 15 and 16)
Metabolic waste products	Not normally a problem, but may be inhibitory, e.g. in bacterial colonies

Internal factors	Process affected
Genes	Protein synthesis (ch. 23), hence enzyme synthesis and control of cell chemistry
Hormones and growth substances	Many processes (chs 15 and 16)

Recent experiments involving transplantation of tissues from species with different patterns of growth have revealed the occurrence of a form of control of growth resulting from tissue interaction. If each tissue were to grow at its normal rate discrepancies would occur and the organ would show malformations. Instead the growth rates of both tissues complement each other and growth of the organ is normal. The conclusion drawn from these studies is that one of the tissues determines the growth rate of the other.

Some of the factors affecting growth and development are summarised in table 21.1 (see also fig 21.13).

> **21.3** From the data shown in fig 21.13 explain fully why body mass is at its lowest level at times of maximum food intake.

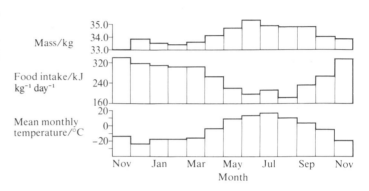

Fig 21.13 *Graphs showing the effects of food intake and temperature on body mass of a husky dog. (Data from J. L. Durrer & J. P. Hannon (1962)* Am. J. Physiol., **202**, *375.)*

21.4 Development

In its broadest sense, growth includes not only an irreversible increase in dry mass as a result of cell division and increase in cell size, but also the subsequent process of development. During development cells become specialised for particular functions within the organism, a process known as **differentiation**. In other words, division of labour occurs among the cells. **Morphogenesis** also takes place, as mentioned earlier. The extent of cell differentiation is linked with the level of phylogenetic organisation as shown in table 21.2.

One of the intriguing problems of differentiation is the mechanism by which it occurs. Cell division is a major contributory factor in growth, and in all multicellular organisms this occurs by mitosis. The implication of this is that every cell derived from the original zygote or spore has an identical genetic composition (genotype) and therefore ought to have identical structure and function. That the latter is not the case in mature organisms is self-evident. What then are the mechanisms bringing about differences between cells, tissues, organs and organ systems? Cell structure and function are determined by the expressed activity of genes, and if cells differ in their structure and

Table 21.2. The approximate numbers of cells and cell types reflecting the degree of differentiation seen at different levels of phylogenetic organisation

Organism	Approximate number of cells	Approximate number of cell types
Protozoa	10^{-1}	10^{-1}
Porifera	$>10^3$	>10
Hydra	10^8	10–20
Annelids	10^{12}	10^2
Insects	10^{12}	10^2
Man	10^{15}	10^3

function this would appear to be due to a differential expression of genes. There are two possible reasons for this. Either cells specialise by losing certain genes, retaining only those needed for the specialised function, or specialisation involves 'switching' on and off different genes in different cells. It became obvious in the early 1960s that the latter was the case, at least in plants. Professor Steward of Cornell University showed that when differentiated cells of a carrot plant, such as phloem cells, were placed in a suitable culture medium they were capable of growing into new carrot plants and therefore still possessed all the relevant information. In 1967 Gurdon, working at Oxford University, showed the same to be true of animals when he transplanted nuclei from the intestinal epithelium of the African clawed toad, *Xenopus*, into eggs of the same species whose own nuclei had been destroyed by ultraviolet radiation. He found that normal development through the tadpole to the adult stage occurred in a small number of these transplants, suggesting that reactivation of genes is possible even in differentiated cells, provided the genes are placed in a suitable environment. Less differentiated cells from an early embryonic stage of development, such as the blastula, gave a higher success rate, and any number of genetically identical frogs can be produced using this technique. Identical offspring from a single parent are referred to as **clones**, and the technique described above is called **cloning** (section 20.1.1).

It is difficult to grow isolated mammalian cells in culture, and even more difficult to induce differentiation. This reflects the highly specialised nature of mammalian cells.

Differentiation may reach such a level of complexity that even growth is prevented. This situation is found in neurones. On the other hand, liver cells remain relatively unspecialised and are able to perform a great many functions (section 18.5). An adult mammalian liver, which has had two-thirds of its mass removed, will regenerate in three weeks to its original size and shape. This evidence not only demonstrates the extent of regenerative growth, but also indicates that the growth of organs and tissues is to a predetermined size and shape.

If nuclei lose none of their genetic potential as a result of differentiation that would suggest that the cytoplasm has a role in regulating differentiation. Spemann and Mangold investigated the influence of cytoplasmic factors on the course of development. By transplanting tissue from a donor embryo into a host embryo they were able to demonstrate that the donor tissue was able to change the course of development of the host. This process is known as **induction** and the areas of the donor which bring about induction are known as **organisers**. A fuller account of the process, and of Spemann and Mangold's experiments, is given in section 22.8.2. The exact way in which the influence is exerted is not entirely clear but it is thought to involve the differential repression and activation of genes in different cells. This is discussed in detail in section 22.8.3.

Another factor affecting differentiation is hormones. Specific examples of growth hormones in plants and a range of animals are described later in this chapter and in chapters 15 and 16. Whilst the action of growth hormones in plants may be variable, there is evidence that certain aspects of growth hormone activity are common to all organisms. Hormones may act directly or indirectly on the genes and exert their influence by 'switching' genes 'on' or 'off' in a sequential manner which determines the pattern of development. Studies carried out on the giant chromosomes from the salivary glands of dipteran fly larvae show 'puffing' in various regions of the chomosomes (sections 22.8.5 and 23.5.1). The positions of these puffs correspond to certain stages in the development of the fly. These regions are genes and are the sites of active messenger RNA synthesis which results in the synthesis of substances vital to certain stages in the life cycle of the fly. Injections of insect growth hormones can induce 'puffing' in larvae which have had their growth-hormone-producing glands removed. Alternatively the injection of supra-optimal levels of growth hormone can alter the normal sequence of 'puffing' and hasten the development of the adult fly form. These studies suggest that hormones sometimes act by 'switching on' genes associated with development.

21.5 Morphogenesis

During the course of development differentiated cells come to occupy specific regions within the organism where they undergo further growth and cell division. This process is part of morphogenesis because it results in cells, tissues and organs, which give form and structure to the mature organism, coming to occupy their characteristic positions. The exact nature of the morphogenic movements is species-specific, but some characteristic examples of morphogenesis in plants and animals are described in the next two sections. The major morphogenic events in plants occur during the development of the stem, root, leaves and flower. In animals there are many spectacular examples of morphogenesis, but those described here are limited to showing the striking changes in form associated with metamorphosis and the increasing tissue complexity which accompanies vertebrate development.

21.6 Growth and development in the flowering plant

21.6.1 Seed dormancy

Certain environmental conditions, namely availability of water, optimum temperature and oxygen, must be present before the embryo of a seed will grow. However, in the presence of these factors, some apparently mature seeds will not germinate and must undergo certain internal changes which can generally be described as **after-ripening**. These changes ensure that premature germination does not occur. For example, seedlings produced immediately from seeds shed in summer or autumn would probably not survive winter. In other words, mechanisms exist which ensure that germination is synchronised with the onset of a season favourable for growth.

These mechanisms often involve the outer layers of seeds, which may contain growth inhibitors, being impervious to water or the passage of oxygen, or being physically strong enough to prevent growth of the embryo as in many legumes. Sometimes physical damage (**scarification**) to the seed coat can remove this restriction, a process which can be induced artificially by removing the testa or simply pricking it with a pin. Under natural circumstances, bacteria may have the same effect. More usually, however, the restriction is removed by some physiological change, involving the following factors.

Growth inhibitors. Many fruits or seeds contain chemical growth inhibitors which prevent germination. Abscisic acid often has this role, for instance in ash seeds. Thorough soaking of the seeds might remove the inhibitor or its effect may be overridden by an increase in a growth promoter such as gibberellin.

Light. The dormancy of some seeds is broken by light after water uptake, a phytochrome-controlled response. This is associated with a rise in gibberellin levels within the seed. Less commonly, germination is inhibited by light, such as in *Phacelia* and *Nigella*. (For a relevant experiment, refer to the foot of Table 15.5, Section 15.4.2.)

Temperature. As noted in section 15.5.1, seeds commonly require a cold period, or **stratification**, before germination will occur. This is common among members of the rose family (Rosaceae) and cereals. It is associated with a rise in gibberellin activity and sometimes a reduction in growth inhibitors.

Exactly how light and cold treatments affect seeds is not clear, but increased permeability of the seed coat, as well as changes in levels of growth substances, may be involved.

> **21.4** Seeds which require a stimulus of light for germination are usually relatively small. What could be the significance of this?

> **21.5** The light which passes through leaves is enriched in green and far-red light relative to the light which strikes the leaf surface.
> (a) Why is this?
> (b) What ecological significance might this have in relation to seeds like lettuce, where germination is a phytochrome-controlled response? (Read section 15.4.2 if necessary.)

21.6.2 Germination

Germination is the onset of growth of the embryo, usually after a period of dormancy. The structure of the seed at germination has been described in section 20.2.

Environmental conditions needed for germination

Water. The initial uptake of water by a seed is by a process called **imbibition**. It takes place through the micropyle and testa and is purely a physical process caused by the **adsorption** of water by colloidal substances within the seed. These include proteins, starch and cell wall materials such as hemicelluloses and pectic substances. The swelling of these substances can lead to strong imbibitional forces sufficient to rupture the testa or pericarp surrounding the seed. Water subsequently moves from cell to cell by osmosis. It is required to activate the biochemical reactions associated with germination, because these take place in aqueous solution. Water is also an important reagent at this stage in the hydrolysis (digestion) of food stores.

Minimum or optimum temperature. There is usually a characteristic temperature range outside which a given type of seed will not germinate. This will be related to the normal environment of the plant concerned and will be within the range 5–40 °C. Temperature influences the rate of enzyme-controlled reactions as described in section 6.4.3.

Oxygen. This is required for aerobic respiration, although such respiration can be supplemented with anaerobic respiration if necessary.

Physiology of germination

A typical seed stores carbohydrates, lipids and proteins, either in its endosperm or in the cotyledons of the embryo. Usually lipids in the form of oils form the major food reserves of the seed, though notable exceptions are the Leguminosae (legumes) and Gramineae (grasses, including cereals) where starch is the major food reserve. These two groups form the principal crops of Man and thus he gets the bulk of his carbohydrates from them. Legumes are also especially rich in proteins, particularly soya bean; hence the use of the latter as a source of protein in new foods. In addition, seeds contain high levels of minerals, notably phosphorus, as well as normal cytoplasmic constituents such as nucleic acids and vitamins.

As a result of imbibition and osmosis the embryo becomes hydrated, and this activates enzymes such as the enzymes of respiration. Other enzymes have to be synthesised, possibly using amino acids provided by the digestion of stored proteins.

Broadly speaking, there are two centres of activity in the germinating seed, the **storage centre** (food reserve) and the **growth centre** (embryo). The main events in the storage centre, with the exception of enzyme synthesis, are catabolic, that is concerned with breakdown.

Digestion of the food reserves proceeds mainly by hydrolysis as below:

$$\text{proteins} \xrightarrow{\text{proteases}} \text{amino acids}$$

$$\text{polysaccharides} \xrightarrow{\text{carbohydrases}} \text{sugars}$$

$$\text{for example starch} \xrightarrow{\text{amylase}} \text{maltose} \xrightarrow{\text{maltase}} \text{glucose}$$

$$\text{lipids} \xrightarrow{\text{lipases}} \text{fatty acids} + \text{glycerol}$$

The soluble products of digestion are then translocated to the growth regions of the embryo. The sugars, fatty acids and glycerol may be used to provide substrates for respiration in both the storage and the growth centres. They may also be used for anabolic reactions in the growth centre, that is, reactions concerned with synthesis. Of particular importance in these reactions are glucose and amino acids. A major use of glucose is for the synthesis of cellulose and other cell wall materials. Amino acids are used mainly for protein synthesis, proteins being important as enzymes and structural components of protoplasm. In addition, mineral salts are required for the many reasons given in table 9.10.

Both storage and growth centres obtain the energy for their activities from respiration. This involves oxidation of a substrate, usually sugar, to carbon dioxide and water. A net loss in dry mass of the seed therefore occurs, since carbon dioxide is lost as a gas, and water does not contribute to dry mass. This loss will continue until the seedling produces green leaves and starts to make its own food (section 21.2.2).

A well-studied example of germination of a polysaccharide-rich seed is the barley grain, where it has been shown that the synthesis of α-amylase and other enzymes takes place in the outer layers of the endosperm in response to gibberellin secreted by the embryo. These outer layers contain stored protein which is the source of amino acids for protein synthesis. The process is described and experimentally investigated in section 15.2.6. Fig 15.21 shows an example of the role of hormones in early germination. The appearance of amylase in germinating barley grains can also be investigated by grinding them in water, filtering and centrifuging to obtain a clear extract and testing the activity of the extract on starch solution. By using samples of barley grains at different times from germination, increase in amylase activity per grain over a period of a week can be determined.

21.6 Explain the results shown in fig 21.14

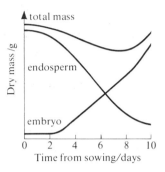

Fig 21.14 *Relative changes in dry mass of endosperm and embryo during germination of barley*

Those seeds which store lipids convert them to fatty acids and glycerol. Each molecule of lipid yields three molecules of fatty acid and one of glycerol (section 5.3.1). Fatty acids are either oxidised directly in respiration or converted to sucrose, which is then translocated to the embryo. The latter involves the glyoxylate cycle (section 11.5.5).

21.7 (This question tests some basic knowledge of chemistry and of the chemistry of lipids. The latter is covered in section 5.3.)

Suppose 51.2 g dry mass of seeds containing 50% fatty acid by mass, converted all the fatty acid to sugar in the following reaction:

$$\underset{\text{fatty acid}}{C_{16}H_{32}O_2} + 11O_2 \longrightarrow \underset{\text{sugar}}{C_{12}H_{22}O_{11}} + 4CO_2 + 5H_2O + \text{energy}$$

(a) Assuming that no other changes occurred which might affect dry mass, calculate the gain or loss in dry mass of the seeds.

(Relative atomic masses: C = 12, H = 1, O = 16.)

(b) What other important change might affect dry mass?

(c) Calculate the volume of carbon dioxide evolved from the seeds at STP (standard temperature and pressure).

(1 mole of gas at STP occupies 22.4 dm³.)

(d) How can fatty acid be obtained from a lipid, and what would be the other component of the lipid?

(e) How many carbon atoms would one molecule of the parent lipid have contained if $C_{16}H_{32}O_2$ was the only fatty acid produced?

(f) What is the identity of the sugar formed in the reaction shown?

(g) How does the oxygen reach the storage tissue?

Respiration in germinating seeds

Respiratory rates in both storage tissues and embryo are high owing to the intense metabolic activity in both regions. Substrates for respiration may differ in each region and may also change during germination. This is revealed by changes in the respiratory quotient (section 11.7.7).

> **21.8** When castor oil seeds were analysed for lipid and sugar content during germination in darkness, the results shown in fig 21.15 were obtained.
>
> The RQ of the seedlings was measured at day 5 and the embryo was found to have an RQ of about 1.0, while the remaining cotyledons had an RQ of about 0.4–0.5.
>
> (a) Suggest as full an explanation of these results as you can (refer to section 21.6.2 for relevant information).
>
> (b) What would you expect the RQ of the whole seedling to be on day 11? Explain very briefly.

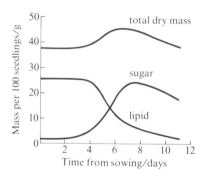

Fig 21.15 *Changes in lipid and sugar content of castor oil seeds during germination in the dark. (Based on data from R. Desveaux & M. Kogane-Charles (1952)* Annls. Inst. natn. Rech. Agron., Paris, **3**, *385–416; cited by H. S. Street & H. Opik (1976)* The physiology of flowering plants *2nd ed., Arnold.)*

> **21.9** The RQ of peas is normally between 2.8 and 4 during the first seven days of germination, but is 1.5–2.4 if the testas are removed. In both cases ethanol accumulates in the seeds, but in much smaller amounts when the testas are removed. Account for these observations.

Growth of the embryo

Within the embryo growth occurs by cell division, enlargement and differentiation. Amounts of proteins, cellulose, nucleic acids and so on increase steadily in the growing regions while dry mass of the food store decreases. The first visible sign of growth is the emergence of the embryonic root, the **radicle**. This is positively geotropic and will grow down and anchor the seed. Subsequently, the embryonic shoot, the **plumule**, emerges and being negatively geotropic (and positively phototropic if above ground) will grow upwards.

There are two types of germination according to whether or not the cotyledons grow above ground or remain below it. In dicotyledons, if that part of the shoot axis, or internode, just below the cotyledons (**the hypocotyl**) elongates, then the cotyledons are carried above ground. This is **epigeal** germination. If the internode just above the cotyledons (the **epicotyl**) elongates, then the cotyledons remain below ground. This is **hypogeal** germination.

In epigeal germination, the hypocotyl remains hooked as it grows through the soil, as shown in fig 21.16 (*b*), thus meeting the resistance of the soil rather than the delicate plumule tip, which is further protected by being enclosed by the cotyledons. In hypogeal germination of dicotyledons the epicotyl is hooked, again protecting the plumule tip, as shown in fig 21.16*c*. In both cases the hooked structure immediately straightens on exposure to light, a phytochrome-controlled response.

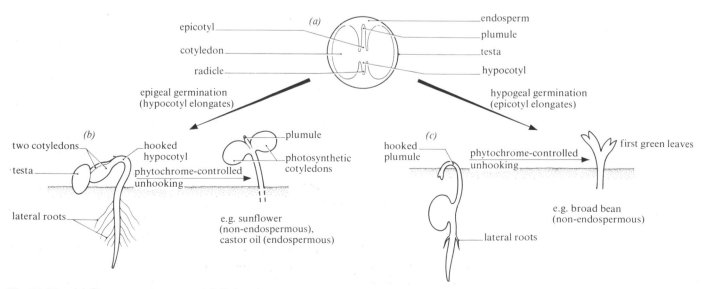

Fig 21.16 (a) *Structure of a seed,* (b) *Epigeal germination,* (c) *Hypogeal germination*

Table 21.3. Types of meristem and their functions

Type of meristem	Location	Role	Effect
Apical	Root and shoot apex	Responsible for primary growth, giving rise to primary plant body	Increase in length
Lateral (cambium)	Laterally situated in older parts of the plant parallel with the long axis of organs, e.g. cork cambium (phellogen), vascular cambium	Responsible for secondary growth. Vascular cambium gives rise to secondary vascular tissue; phellogen gives rise to the periderm, which replaces the epidermis and includes cork	Increase in girth
Intercalary	Between regions of permanent tissue, e.g. at nodes of many monocotyledons, such as bases of grass leaves	Allows growth in length to occur in regions other than tips. This is useful if the tips are susceptible to damage or destruction, e.g. eating by herbivores (grasses), wave action (kelps). Branching from the main axis is not then necessary	Increase in length

In the grasses, which are monocotyledons, the plumule is protected by a sheath called the **coleoptile**, which is positively phototropic and negatively geotropic as described in sectionn 15.1.1. The first leaf grows out through the coleoptile and unrolls in response to light. On emerging into light a number of phytochrome-controlled responses rapidly occur, collectively known as **photomorphogenesis**. The overall effect is a change from etiolation (section 15.4.1) to normal growth. The major changes involved are summarised in table 15.5 and include expansion of the cotyledons or first true foliage leaves, as well as formation of chlorophyll ('greening'). At this point photosynthesis begins and net dry mass of the seedling starts to increase as it finally becomes independent of its food reserves and assumes an autotrophic existence. Once exposed to light, the shoot also shows phototropic responses although these are not phytochrome controlled.

21.6.3 Growth of the primary plant body

Meristems

In contrast to animals, growth in multicellular plants, with the exception of the young embryo, is confined to certain regions known as meristems. A meristem is a group of cells which retain the ability to divide by mitosis, producing daughter cells which grow and form the rest of the plant body. The daughter cells form the permanent tissue, that is, cells which have lost the ability to divide. There are three types of meristem, described in table 21.3. Two types of growth are mentioned in table 21.3, namely primary and secondary growth.

Primary growth is the first form of growth to occur. A whole plant can be built up by primary growth, and in most monocotyledonous plants and herbaceous dicotyledons it is the only type of growth. It is a result of the activity of the apical, and sometimes intercalary, meristems. The anatomy of mature primary roots and stems is dealt with in section 14.3.9.

Some plants continue with **secondary growth** from lateral meristems. This is most notable in shrubs and trees, which are sometimes described as **arborescent** to distinguish them from plants which lack extensive secondary growth,

namely **herbaceous** plants or **herbs**. A few herbaceous plants show restricted amounts of secondary thickening, as in the development of additional vascular bundles in *Helianthus* (sunflower).

Apical meristems and primary growth

A typical apical meristem cell is relatively small, cuboid, with a thin cellulose cell wall and dense cytoplasmic contents. It has a few small vacuoles rather than the large vacuoles characteristic of parenchyma cells, and the cytoplasm contains small, undifferentiated plastids called proplastids. Meristematic cells are packed tightly together with no obvious air spaces between the cells.

The cells are called **initials**. When they divide by mitosis one daughter cell remains in the meristem while the other increases in size and differentiates to become part of the permanent plant body.

21.6.4 Primary growth of the shoot

The structure of a typical apical shoot meristem is illustrated in figs 21.17 and 21.18. Fig 21.18 shows the approximate division of the shoot apex into regions of cell division, cell expansion and cell differentiation. There is more overlap in these zones than in the root. Passing back from the dome-shaped apical meristem, the cells get progressively older, so that different stages of growth can be observed simultaneously in the same apex. Thus it is relatively easy to study developmental sequences of plant tissue.

Three basic types of meristematic tissue are recognised, namely the **protoderm**, which gives rise to the epidermis; the **procambium**, giving rise to the vascular tissues, including pericycle, phloem, vascular cambium and xylem; and the **ground meristem**, producing the parenchyma **ground tissues**, which in the dicotyledons are the cortex and pith. These meristematic types are laid down by division of the initials in the apex. In the zone of expansion, the daughter cells produced by the initials increase in size, mainly by osmotic uptake of water into the cytoplasm and then into the vacuoles. Increase in the length of stems and roots is mainly brought about by elongation of cells during this stage. The process is illustrated in fig 21.19.

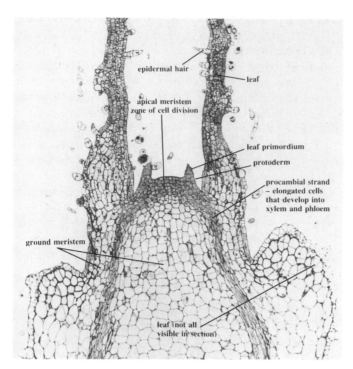

Fig 21.17   (above) The apical meristem

Fig 21.18   (below) LS shoot tip of a dicotyledon showing apical meristem and regions of primary growth. For simplicity, vascular tissue to leaves and buds has been omitted

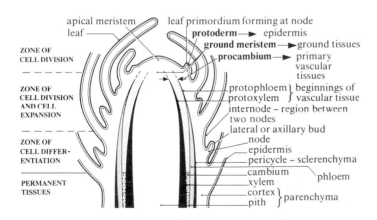

The small vacuoles increase in size, eventually fusing to form a single large vacuole. The turgor pressure developed inside the cells stretches their thin walls and the orientation of cellulose microfibrils in the walls helps to determine the final shape assumed by the cells. The final volume of cytoplasm may not be significantly greater than in the original meristematic cell, but is now confined to the cell periphery by the vacuole. As expansion nears completion, many cells develop additional thickening of the cell walls, either of cellulose or lignin, depending on the type of cell being formed. This may restrict further expansion, but does not necessarily prevent it. Collenchyma cells in the cortex, for example, can continue elongating while extra cellulose is laid down in columns on the inside of the original walls. Thus they can give support to the plant while

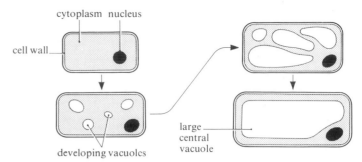

Fig 21.19   Expansion phase of growth of a meristematic cell

still growing. In contrast, developing sclerenchyma cells deposit thick layers of lignin on their walls and soon die. Thus their differentiation does not start until expansion is virtually completed.

The procambium forms a series of longitudinally running strands whose cells are narrower and longer than those of the ground meristem. The first cells to differentiate in the procambium are those of the protoxylem to the inside, and protophloem to the outside. These are the parts of the primary xylem and phloem respectively which form before elongation is complete. The protoxylem typically has only annular or spiral thickenings of lignin on tracheids (section 8.2.1) which, being discontinuous, allow extension and stretching of the cellulose between the thickenings as the surrounding tissue elongates. Both protoxylem and proto-phloem elements soon die and generally get crushed and stretched to the point of collapse as growth continues around them. Their function is taken over by later-developing xylem and phloem in the zone of differentiation.

In the zone of differentiation each cell becomes fully specialised for its own particular function, according to its position in the organ with respect to other cells. The greatest changes occur in the procambial strands, which differentiate into vascular bundles. This involves lignifica-tion of the walls of sclerenchyma fibres and xylem elements, as well as development of the tubes characteristic of xylem vessels and phloem sieve tubes. The final forms of these tissues are described in section 8.2. Sclerenchyma and xylem now supplement the support previously given by collenchyma and turgid parenchyma. Between the xylem and phloem there are cells which retain the ability to divide. They form the vascular cambium, whose activities are described later, with secondary thickening.

Leaf primordia and lateral buds

Development of the shoot also includes growth of leaves and lateral buds. Leaves arise as small swellings or ridges called leaf primordia, shown particularly clearly in fig 21.17. The swellings contain groups of meristematic cells and appear at regular intervals, their sites of origin being called **nodes** and the regions between **internodes**. The pattern of leaf arrangement on the stem varies and is called **phyllotaxis**. Leaves may arise in whorls with two or more leaves at each node, or singly, either in two opposite ranks or in a spiral pattern. Generally, however, they are arranged to minimise overlapping, and hence shading, when fully grown so that they form a **mosaic**.

The primordia elongate rapidly, so they soon enclose and protect the apical meristem, both physically and by the heat they generate in respiration. Later they grow and increase in area to form the leaf blades. Cell division gradually ceases but may continue until they are about half their mature size.

Soon after the leaves start to grow, buds develop in the axils between them and the stem. These are small groups of meristematic cells which normally remain dormant, but retain the capacity to divide and grow at a later stage. They form branches or specialised structures such as flowers and underground structures such as rhizomes and tubers. They are thought to be under the control of the apical meristem (see apical dominance, section 15.3.3).

21.6.5 Primary growth of the root

The structure of the typical apical root system is illustrated in fig 21.20.

At the very tip of the apical meristem is a **quiescent centre**, a group of **initials** (meristematic cells) from which all other cells in the root can be traced, but whose rate of cell division is much slower than their daughter cells in the apical meristem around them. To the outside, the cells of the **root cap** are formed. These become large parenchyma cells which protect the apical meristem as the root grows through the soil. They are constantly being worn away and replaced. They also have the important additional function of acting as gravity sensors, since they contain large starch

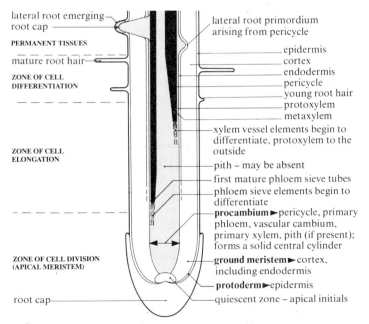

Fig 21.20 *LS apical meristem of a typical root. Xylem differentiation is shown to the right and phloem differentiation to the left. In reality xylem and phloem alternate round the root and would be on different radii. (See fig 14.16). Also, in reality, the zone of elongation would be longer*

grains which act as statoliths, sedimenting to the bottoms of cells in response to gravity. Their role is described in more detail in section 15.2.2.

Behind the quiescent centre, orderly rows of cells can be seen and the meristematic regions already described in the shoot, namely protoderm, ground meristem and procambium, can be distinguished (fig 21.20). In the root the term procambium is used to describe the whole central cylinder of the root, even though at maturity this contains the non-vascular tissues of the pericycle and the pith, if present.

The zone of cell division typically extends 1–2 mm back from the root tip, and overlaps slightly with the zone of cell elongation. Root tips are convenient material for observation of mitosis and a procedure for this is described in section 22.2. Behind this zone, growth is mainly by cell elongation, cells increasing in size in the manner described for the shoot and shown in fig 21.19. The zone of elongating cells extends to a point about 10 mm behind the root tip and their increase in length forces the root tip down through the soil.

Some cell differentiation begins in the zone of cell division, with the development of the first phloem sieve tube elements (fig 21.20). In longitudinal sections, neat files of developing sieve tube elements can be seen, getting progressively more mature further back from the root tip, until they become mature sieve tubes. Development of phloem is from the outside inwards.

Further back in the zone of elongation, the xylem vessels start to differentiate, also from the outside inwards (exarch xylem) in contrast to the stem (endarch xylem). The first-formed vessels are protoxylem vessels, as in the stem, and they show the same pattern of lignification and ability to stretch as cells around them grow. Their role is taken over by metaxylem, which develops later and matures in the zone of differentiation after elongation has ceased. The xylem often spreads to the centre of the root, in which case no pith develops.

Development is easier to examine in roots than in shoots. In the latter procambial strands to the leaves complicate the distribution of developing tissues. Development of xylem, in particular, is easily seen by squashing apical portions of fine roots such as those of cress seedlings and staining appropriately.

After all cells have stopped elongating, further differentiation is completed. This includes the development of root hairs from the epidermis.

Lateral roots

Branching from the main root may occur but not by means of buds, in contrast to the shoot. Instead, a small group of pericycle cells in the zone of differentiation resumes meristematic activity and forms a new root apical meristem. It then grows, forcing its way out through the endodermis, cortex and epidermis as shown in fig 21.20. Such development is termed endarch, compared with exarch development of lateral buds.

781

Adventitious growth

Adventitious structures are those growing in uncharacteristic positions. Adventitious roots and buds may arise in a variety of situations as a result of certain cells resuming meristematic activity. **Adventitious roots** develop independently of the original primary root and form the main rooting system of monocotyledons, arising from nodes on the stem. Rhizomes and runners are stem structures from which adventitious roots arise directly. Adventitious roots are also important in propagation of plants by stem cuttings. Ivy clings by adventitious roots.

Adventitious buds may develop on roots, stems or leaves. For example African violets can be propagated from leaf cuttings, which develop adventitious roots and buds. Trees may develop new branches adventitiously from buds that arise in the trunk.

21.6.6 Lateral meristems and secondary growth

Secondary growth is that growth which occurs after primary growth as a result of the activity of lateral meristems. It results in an increase in girth. It is usually associated with deposition of large amounts of secondary xylem, called **wood**, which completely modifies the primary structure and is a characteristic feature of trees and shrubs.

There are two types of lateral meristem, the **vascular cambium** which gives rise to new vascular tissue, and the **cork cambium** or **phellogen**, which arises later to replace the ruptured epidermis of the expanding plant body.

Vascular cambium

There are two types of cell in the vascular cambium, the **fusiform initials** and the **ray initials**, illustrated in fig 21.21. Fusiform initials are narrow, elongated cells which divide by mitosis to form **secondary phloem** to the outside or **secondary xylem** to the inside. The amount of xylem produced normally exceeds the amount of phloem. Successive divisions are shown in fig 21.22. Secondary phloem contains sieve tubes, companion cells, sclerenchyma fibres and sclereids, and parenchyma.

Ray initials are almost spherical and divide by mitosis to form parenchyma cells which accumulate to form rays between the neighbouring xylem and phloem.

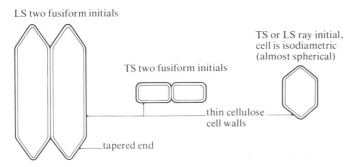

Fig 21.21 *Fusiform and ray initials*

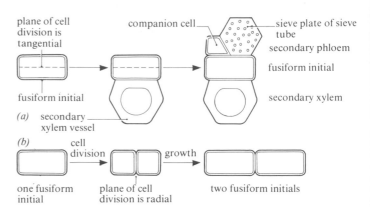

Fig 21.22 (a) *Two successive divisions of a fusiform initial to form xylem and phloem, seen in TS. In reality, differentiation of xylem and phloem to the stages shown would take some time, during which more cells would be produced.* (b) *Division of a fusiform initial to form a new fusiform initial, seen in TS*

Secondary growth in woody dicotyledon stems

The vascular cambium is originally located between the primary xylem and primary phloem of the vascular bundles, its derivation from the apical meristem being shown in fig 21.18. It becomes active very soon after primary cell differentiation is complete. Fig 21.23 summarises the early stages in secondary thickening of a typical woody dicotyledon stem.

Fig 21.23*a* shows the original primary stem structure, omitting the pericycle for simplicity. Fig 21.23*b* shows the development of a complete cylinder of cambium. Fig 21.23*c* shows a complete ring of secondary thickening. Here, fusiform initials have produced large quantities of secondary xylem, and lesser quantities of secondary phloem, while the ray initials have produced rays of parenchyma. As the stem increases in thickness, so the circumference of the cambium layers must increase. To achieve this, radial divisions of the cambial cells occur, as shown in fig 21.22. The original ray initials produce primary medullary rays which run all the way from pith to cortex, unlike the secondary medullary rays produced by later ray initials. The rays maintain a living link between the pith and cortex. They help to transmit water and mineral salts from the xylem, and food substances from the phloem, radially across the stem. Also, gaseous exchange can occur by diffusion through intercellular spaces. The rays may also be used for food storage, an important function during periods of dormancy, as in winter. In three dimensions they appear as radially–longitudinally running sheets because the ray initials occur in stacks one above the other, as shown in fig 21.24. Fig 21.24 illustrates the appearance of wood (secondary xylem) and the rays it contains in the three planes TS, TLS and RLS.

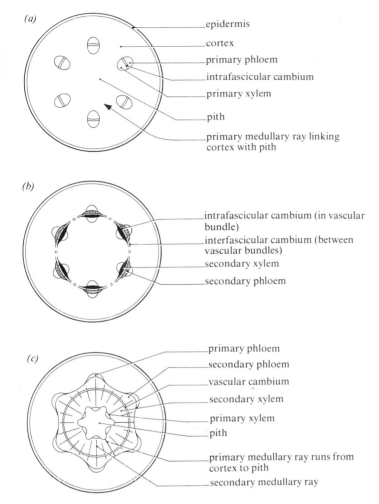

(a)
- epidermis
- cortex
- primary phloem
- intrafascicular cambium
- primary xylem
- pith
- primary medullary ray linking cortex with pith

(b)
- intrafascicular cambium (in vascular bundle)
- interfascicular cambium (between vascular bundles)
- secondary xylem
- secondary phloem

(c)
- primary phloem
- secondary phloem
- vascular cambium
- secondary xylem
- primary xylem
- pith
- primary medullary ray runs from cortex to pith
- secondary medullary ray

Fig 21.23 *Early stages in secondary thickening of a typical woody dicotyledon stem. (a) Primary structure of stem. (b) Cambium forms a complete cylinder as parenchyma cells in the medullary rays become meristematic, spreading outwards from the vascular bundles. Meanwhile secondary xylem and phloem are already being formed by the existing cambium. (c) A complete ring of secondary thickening has developed. Thickening is most advanced at the sites of the original vascular bundles where cambial activity first started*

Fig 21.25 shows part of the stem of a woody dicotyledon in its third year of growth, revealing the large amounts of secondary xylem produced. Fig. 21.26 shows photographs of a three-year-old and a five-year-old stem of *Tilia*, the lime tree.

Annual rings

Each year in temperate climates, growth resumes in the spring. The first vessels formed are wide and thin-walled, being suitable for the conduction of large quantities of water. Water is required to initiate growth, particularly the expansion of new cells, as in developing leaves. Later in the year, fewer vessels are produced and they are narrower with thicker walls. During winter the cambium remains dormant. The autumn wood produced at the end of one year, as growth ceases, will therefore be immediately next to the spring wood of the following year and will differ markedly in appearance. This contrast is seen as the **annual ring** and is clearly visible in fig 21.26. Where vessels are concentrated in the early wood it is said to be **ring porous**, as opposed to **diffuse porous** wood, where they are evenly distributed, and where it is more difficult to see annual rings. In tropical climates, seasonal droughts may induce similar fluctuations in cambial activity.

The width of an annual ring will vary partly according to climate, a favourable climate resulting in production of more wood and hence a greater distance between rings. This has been used in two areas of science, namely dendroclimatology and dendrochronology. **Dendroclimatology** is the study of climate using tree ring data. Applications vary from correlation of recent climatic records with tree growth, of possible interest in a specific locality, to investigations of more distant climatic events several hundreds or even thousands of years in the past. The oldest-known living trees, the bristlecone pines, are about 5 000 years old, and fossil wood of even greater age can be found.

Dendrochronology is the dating of wood by recognition of the pattern of annual rings. This pattern can act as a

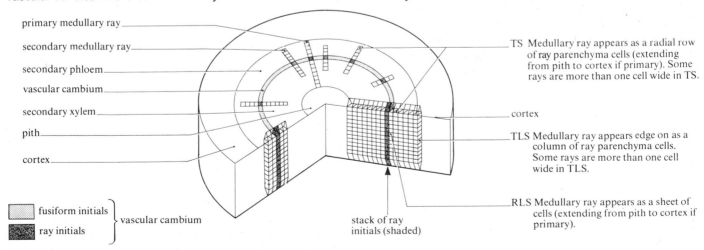

- primary medullary ray
- secondary medullary ray
- secondary phloem
- vascular cambium
- secondary xylem
- pith
- cortex

fusiform initials
ray initials
} vascular cambium

stack of ray initials (shaded)

TS Medullary ray appears as a radial row of ray parenchyma cells (extending from pith to cortex if primary). Some rays are more than one cell wide in TS.

cortex

TLS Medullary ray appears edge on as a column of ray parenchyma cells. Some rays are more than one cell wide in TLS.

RLS Medullary ray appears as a sheet of cells (extending from pith to cortex if primary).

Fig 21.24 *Diagrammatic representation of primary and secondary medullary rays in a typical woody dicotyledonous stem. A primary ray is shown to the right and a secondary ray to the left. (TLS, transverse longitudinal section; RLS, radial longitudinal section.)*

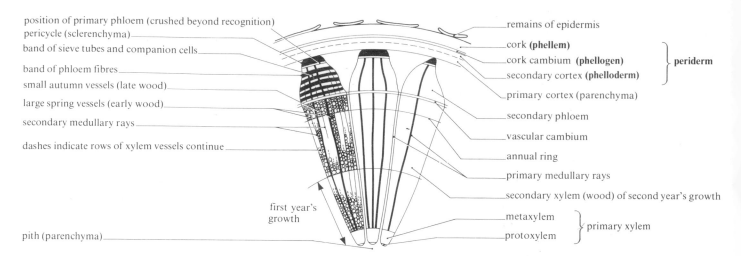

position of primary phloem (crushed beyond recognition)
pericycle (sclerenchyma)
band of sieve tubes and companion cells
band of phloem fibres
small autumn vessels (late wood)
large spring vessels (early wood)
secondary medullary rays
dashes indicate rows of xylem vessels continue
first year's growth
pith (parenchyma)

remains of epidermis
cork **(phellem)**
cork cambium **(phellogen)** ⎫ **periderm**
secondary cortex **(phelloderm)** ⎭
primary cortex (parenchyma)
secondary phloem
vascular cambium
annual ring
primary medullary rays
secondary xylem (wood) of second year's growth
metaxylem ⎫ **primary xylem**
protoxylem ⎭

Fig 21.25 (above) *TS of a typical woody dicotyledonous stem in the third year of growth (age two years), such as* Tilia. *Details of secondary phloem, secondary xylem and secondary medullary rays are shown only in the left-hand sector*

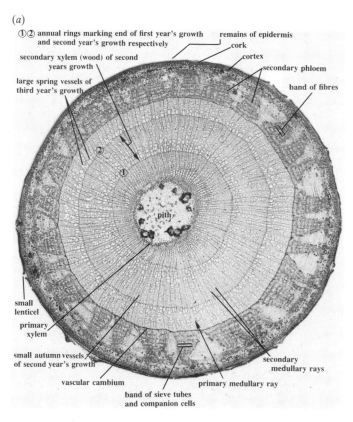

(a)
①② annual rings marking end of first year's growth and second year's growth respectively
secondary xylem (wood) of second years growth
large spring vessels of third year's growth
remains of epidermis
cork
cortex
secondary phloem
band of fibres
pith
small lenticel
primary xylem
small autumn vessels of second year's growth
vascular cambium
band of sieve tubes and companion cells
primary medullary ray
secondary medullary rays

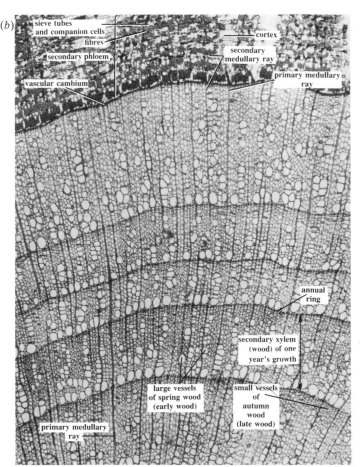

(b)
sieve tubes and companion cells
fibres
secondary phloem
vascular cambium
cortex
secondary medullary ray
primary medullary ray
annual ring
secondary xylem (wood) of one year's growth
large vessels of spring wood (early wood)
small vessels of autumn wood (late wood)
primary medullary ray

Fig 21.26 (a) *TS of a two-year-old (third year) twig of* Tilia vulgaris *(× 2.2). (b) Part of a TS of a five-year-old (sixth year) twig of* Tilia vulgaris *(× 11.5)*

'fingerprint', pinpointing the time during which the wood was growing. Dating of timbers at archaeological sites, in old buildings and ships and so on thus becomes feasible, provided enough data are available.

Heartwood and sapwood

As a tree ages, the wood at the centre may cease to serve a conducting function and become blocked with darkly staining deposits such as tannins. It is called **heartwood**,

whereas the outer, wetter conducting wood is called **sapwood**.

Cork and lenticels

As the secondary xylem grows outwards, so the tissues outside it become increasingly compressed, as well as being stretched sideways by the increasing circumference. This affects the epidermis, cortex, primary phloem and all but the most recent secondary phloem. The epidermis even-

784

tually ruptures and is replaced by cork as the result of the activity of a second lateral meristem, the **cork cambium** or **phellogen**. It generally arises immediately below the epidermis. **Cork** (or **phellem**) is produced to the outside of the cork cambium, while to the inside one or two layers of parenchyma are produced. These are indistinguishable from the primary cortex and form the **phelloderm** or secondary cortex. The phellogen, cork and phelloderm together comprise the periderm (fig 21.25).

As the cork cells mature, their walls become impregnated with a fatty substance called suberin which is impermeable to water and gases. The cells gradually die and lose their living contents, becoming filled either with air or with resin or tannins. The older, dead cork cells fit together around the stem, preventing desiccation, infection and mechanical injury. They become compressed as the stem increases in girth and may eventually be lost and replaced by younger cells from beneath. If the cork layer were complete, the respiratory gases oxygen and carbon dioxide could not be exchanged between the living cells of the stem and the environment, and the cells would die. At random intervals, however, slit-like openings, or **lenticels**, develop in the cork containing a mass of loosely packed, thin-walled dead cells, lacking suberin. They are produced by the cork cambium and have large intercellular air spaces allowing gaseous exchange.

Fig 21.27 shows a diagram of cork and lenticels.

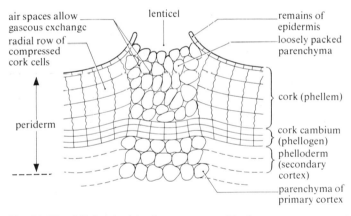

Fig 21.27 *VS lenticel (cell contents omitted)*

Bark

Eventually a woody stem becomes covered with a layer commonly known as bark. The term bark is an imprecise one which is used to refer either to all the tissues outside the vascular system, or more strictly to those tissues outside the cork cambium. Peeling bark from a tree generally strips tissues down to the vascular cambium, a thin layer of cells which is easily ruptured.

It is usual for the cork cambium to be renewed each year as the girth of the stem increases. Often a cork cambium arises in the secondary phloem, in which case the bark will, over a number of years, build up a layered appearance due to alternating layers of secondary phloem and bark.

Secondary growth in roots of dicotyledons

Most dicotyledons that show secondary growth of the stem also show secondary growth of the roots. In the case of plants with storage roots, such as carrots and turnip, it may be more conspicuous than in the stem, although parenchyma predominates in the xylem and phloem of the examples given. The process of secondary growth is summarised in fig 21.28 and is similar in principle to secondary growth in stems.

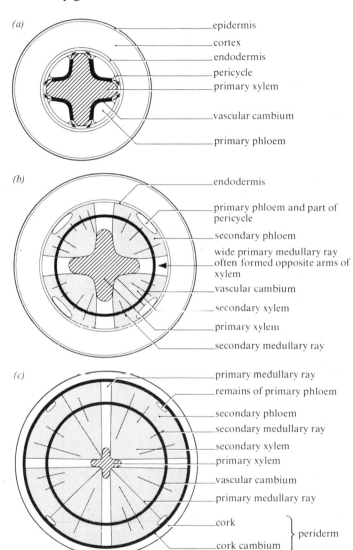

Fig 21.28 *Stages in the secondary growth of a dicotyledonous root. (a) The vascular cambium develops from cells of the procambium (fig 21.23) which have remained meristematic. The cambium continues to grow to form a complete ring (see arrows) as cells of the pericycle outside the xylem arms become meristematic. (b) The cambium produces rows of secondary xylem vessels internally and secondary phloem externally. Growth of secondary xylem starts earlier and is more rapid between the arms of the xylem, until the cambium becomes circular, rather than wavy, in outline. (c) As growth continues, the increasing girth stretches and tears the endodermis, cortex and epidermis, and these are sloughed off. A cork cambium develops from the pericycle. ((c) is drawn to a smaller scale than (a) and (b).)*

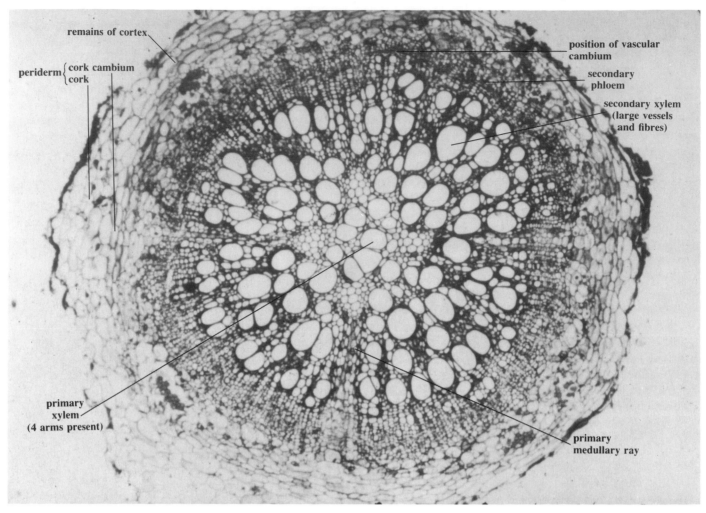

remains of cortex

periderm { cork cambium
             cork

position of vascular cambium

secondary phloem

secondary xylem (large vessels and fibres)

primary xylem (4 arms present)

primary medullary ray

Fig 21.29 *Secondarily thickened root of* Vicia faba *(× 120)*

Development of secondary xylem, secondary phloem and medullary rays is basically similar to that in stems, and annual rings are usually formed as in stems. A cork cambium develops from the pericycle and serves the same function as in the stem. A phelloderm may be produced, but is indistinguishable from the pericycle. As with the stem, the original cork cambium may be replaced at intervals by cork cambium arising further inside the root. Fig 21.29 is a photograph of a transverse section through a root with secondary thickening.

21.7   Metamorphosis

The term metamorphosis (*meta*, between; *morphe*, form) applies to those rapid changes which occur during the transition from larval to adult form. This is the process of postembryonic maturation and is found in many invertebrate groups, especially amongst insects, echinoderms, hemichordates, urochordates, cephalochordates and some fish and amphibian species. Table 21.4 lists various animal groups and names of their larval stages.

Table 21.4. Some larval stages found in the animal kingdom

Animal group	Larval stage
coelenterates	planula
trematodes	miracidium/redia/cercaria
cestodes	hexacanth/cysticercus
polychaetes	trochophore
crustacea	nauplius/cypris/zoaea
insects	caterpillar (maggot, grub) or nymph
molluscs	trochophore/veliger
echinoderms	dipleurula/pluteus
urochordates	ascidian tadpole
lamprey	ammocoete
amphibia	tadpole

21.7.1   Adaptive significance of larval stages

Larvae generally act as a dispersal phase for the distribution of species. This is very important to sessile organisms as it provides a means of preventing overcrowding of the parental organisms by their offspring. Overcrowding would lead to increased competition for food and other resources and this could be harmful to the survival of the species. For example, many sessile marine organisms such as barnacles and mussels produce vast numbers of larvae which are planktonic and are dispersed by ocean currents. At a certain stage they settle on solid objects, a phenomenon known as 'spat-fall', and continue their development.

Larvae usually occupy a different habitat from the adult forms and have different feeding habits, forms of locomotion and behavioural patterns which enable the species to exploit the potential of two ecological niches during the life cycle. This increases the chances of survival of the species between the egg and adult stages. Many species, for example the dragonfly, only feed and grow during their larval stages which form the longest period of their life.

Another feature of larvae is their ability to act as a transition stage during which the species has time to adapt to the new conditions that will be encountered in the adult habitat. Physiological hardiness is another attribute which allows larvae to act as a dormant stage during adverse conditions. For example, some insects overwinter in the soil as larvae but most exist as another metamorphic stage, the pupa, and the physiological changes which accompany these stages are described in section 21.7.3.

A final advantage of larval stages is that they may provide an opportunity for the numbers of larvae to be increased. This is common in the lifecycles of certain platyhelminths (section 4.5.3).

However, larvae should not be thought of as incompletely developed forms. In many cases they are highly developed, as shown by insect larval stages, where the only undeveloped structures are the reproductive organs. An interesting example of a fully developed larval stage which has attained sexual maturity, the axolotl, is described in section 21.7.4.

21.7.2 Characteristics of metamorphosis

The structural and functional changes which occur during metamorphosis prepare the organism for adult life in a new habitat or environment. In some cases these new adaptations may appear whilst the organism still retains the larval form and occupies the larval habitat. In other words metamorphosis is not entirely a response to a change in environment but a *preparation* for a change. For example, tadpoles, living in water where desiccation is not a problem, lose approximately 80% of their nitrogenous waste as ammonia. In the later stages of metamorphosis, whilst still living in water, tadpoles begin to excrete urea. By the time the young frogs are ready to leave the water they are excreting 80% of their nitrogenous waste as urea.

Whilst growth and differentiation may be influenced by hormones, metamorphosis is *entirely* controlled and regulated by endocrine secretions. In some cases metamorphosis is a response to increasing hormone levels and in other cases it is the result of different responses by different target organs to the same level of hormone. These responses may involve either cell death and reduction in size of an organ (involution) or cell division, differentiation and the growth of an organ.

21.7.3 Hormonal control of ecdysis and moulting in insects

The involvement of hormones in ecdysis and moulting was first described by Wigglesworth in Cambridge. In a series of experiments he was able to show that moulting is controlled by a **moulting hormone** (MH) which is released in response to a specific stimulus. The result of the moulting, in terms of stage in the life cycle, may be modified by another hormone, **juvenile hormone** (JH), which prevents the appearance of the adult form.

Wigglesworth chose to investigate insect growth hormone in *Rhodnius prolixus*, a blood-sucking hemipteran from South America. *Rhodnius* is an exopterygote insect with five nymphal stages and no pupal stage. During each nymphal stage only one large blood meal is required and this acts as the stimulus for moulting. Wigglesworth was able to demonstrate that stretch receptors in the abdominal wall, activated by distension, set up nerve impulses which are transmitted to the brain. These impulses initiate a series of coordinated endocrine secretions which result in moulting. In the case of the moult from 4th to 5th instar this occurs within 14 days of feeding at 28°C.

If the insect is decapitated within four days of a blood meal and the wound plugged with wax it will live for 18 months without showing any further growth or development. If decapitation occurs after this four-day period it will continue to grow but no moulting will occur. These observations suggest that it takes four days for impulses from the gut to be passed to the brain and hormones to be released which affect the growth and differentiation of the target tissues, including the epidermal cells.

In his experiments Wigglesworth transplanted the brain from an insect which was just about to moult, into the abdomen of a starved decapitated insect which then proceeded to moult. Transplanting brain tissue from a moulting insect into an insect without head or thorax did not result in moulting. Clearly then, a substance from the brain was influencing a region in the thorax which produced the moulting response. Previous studies on silkworm caterpillars had revealed the presence of a gland in the first thoracic segment, the **prothoracic gland**, which could induce moulting if implanted into the posterior region of a silkworm which was separated from the thorax by a ligature. This suggested that moulting in *Rhodnius* is also controlled by a hormone from the prothoracic gland.

Moulting hormone was isolated in 1953 and is a steroid with a similar structure to cholesterol (section 5.3.6). The hormone was named **ecdysone**, and because of the presence of more hydroxyl groups than cholesterol it is water-soluble. Since then it has been synthesised and produces all the responses normally associated with moulting when injected into insects.

Ecdysone is thought to activate genes controlling the production of enzymes involved in growth. This response is most marked in the epidermal cells, which undergo a series of changes associated with ecdysis and which are described in fig 21.30.

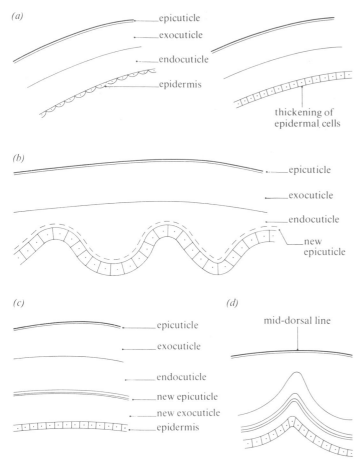

(a)
epicuticle
exocuticle
endocuticle
epidermis

thickening of
epidermal cells

(b)
epicuticle
exocuticle
endocuticle
new
epicuticle

(c)
epicuticle
exocuticle
endocuticle
new epicuticle
new exocuticle
epidermis

(d)
mid-dorsal line

Fig 21.30 *(a) TS* Rhodnius *cuticle. Without blood meal, epidermis thin and flattened. Following blood meal the epidermis starts to thicken out and separate from the endocuticle above. (b) New epicuticle then forms over the epidermis. Chitinase and proteinase enzymes are secreted by epidermis and break down the old cuticle. New cuticle is shielded from enzymes by the formation of a new epicuticle. Old digested endocuticle is absorbed by the epidermis and incorporated into new endocuticle. (c)* Rhodnius *takes in air, expands itself and breaks the old cuticle and moults. The new cuticle is soft and hardens by tanning. (d) Moulting occurs by splitting of the old cuticle along the mid-dorsal line which is specially thinned*

The addition of ecdysone to insect larvae with 'giant chromosomes' produces 'puffing' in specific regions of the chromosomes. These are sites of messenger RNA synthesis and this evidence suggests that ecdysone works directly at the level of genetic transcription.

In a further series of experiments Wigglesworth obtained data which suggested that the head region of *Rhodnius* larvae produces another hormone which promotes the retention of nymphal characteristics, thus preventing development into the adult form. Investigations revealed that a region just behind the brain, the **corpus allatum**, produced this response. Implantation of the corpus allatum from a third- or fourth-stage nymph into a fifth-stage produces a sixth-stage giant nymph and not an adult. Implantation of the corpus allatum of a fifth-stage nymph does not have this effect.

The corpus allatum produces a hormone called **juvenile hormone** or **neotonin**. Growth and metamorphosis in arthropods is now seen to be controlled by the interaction of ecdysone and juvenile hormone. The latter is believed to cause the retention of larval or nymphal characteristics by activating genes responsible for these characters and suppressing genes responsible for producing adult cuticle and structure.

The release of ecdysone and juvenile hormone is controlled by yet another hormone, which is produced by the brain. The mechanism of release may be described with reference to the locust (fig 21.31).

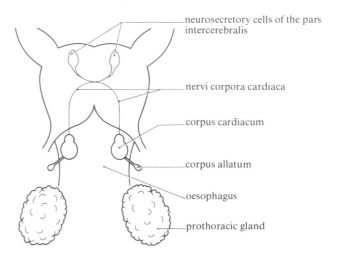

neurosecretory cells of the pars intercerebralis
nervi corpora cardiaca
corpus cardiacum
corpus allatum
oesophagus
prothoracic gland

Fig 21.31 *Moulting glands of the locust*

Neurosecretory cell bodies situated in the **pars intercerebralis** of the brain secrete a hormone, **prothoracicotrophic hormone (PTTH)**, which passes down the axons of the neurosecretory cells through the **nervi corpora cardiaca** possibly by axoplasmic streaming (section 16.6.2). The hormone is stored in a pair of glands, the **corpora cardiaca**, which are situated immediately behind the brain. The stimulus to moult, whatever it may be, sets up nerve impulses in the brain which pass down the nervi corpora cardiaca and cause the release of prothoracicotrophic hormone into the blood (fig 21.32). This passes to the prothoracic gland and ecdysone is released which stimulates, in turn, the epidermal cells to produce a new cuticle.

A similar pattern of events is involved in the control of ecdysis and moulting in *Rhodnius* but the corpora cardiaca and corpora allata are not bilateral structures, having fused together to form single structures situated in the mid-line of the body.

In endopterygote insects the formation of the pupal stage occurs in the presence of a very low level of juvenile hormone whereas the absence of juvenile hormone results in a direct metamorphosis into the adult form. If the corpus allatum is removed from a second, third or fourth nymphal stage of an exopterygote it will moult into a miniature adult. Therefore the increase in size and the attainment of sexual maturity in insects may possibly result from falling

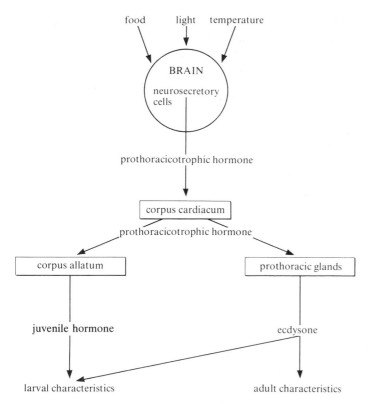

food   light   temperature

BRAIN

neurosecretory
cells

prothoracicotrophic hormone

corpus cardiacum

prothoracicotrophic hormone

corpus allatum   prothoracic glands

juvenile hormone   ecdysone

larval characteristics   adult characteristics

Fig 21.32 *The hormonal control of ecdysis and moulting in insects*

levels of juvenile hormone. The control of growth and metamorphosis in the life cycles of specific endopterygote and exopterygote insects is summarised in fig 21.33.

Once the adult form has been attained in pterygote insects the prothoracic glands atrophy and disappear, preventing any further ecdyses or moults. This does not occur in apterygote insects. In all adult insects the corpus allatum becomes active again and juvenile hormone is secreted. In females it is necessary for the deposition of yolk in the egg and in males it is required for the normal functioning of the accessory glands which produce the **spermatophore**, the capsule used to transfer sperm to the female.

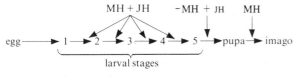

Pieris brassica (cabbage white butterfly) – an endopterygote

MH + JH   – MH + JH   MH

egg → 1 → 2 → 3 → 4 → 5 → pupa → imago

larval stages

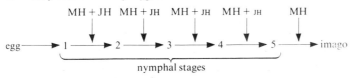

Rhodnius prolixus – an exopterygote

MH + JH MH + JH   MH + JH   MH + JH   MH

egg → 1 → 2 → 3 → 4 → 5 → imago

nymphal stages

Fig 21.33 *The influence of growth hormones on endopterygote and exopterygote insect life cycles (MH moulting hormone, JH juvenile hormone. The height of the letters JH indicates relative concentration.)*

21.7.4   Metamorphosis in amphibia

Metamorphosis in amphibia involves the transition of an aquatic larva into a semi-terrestrial adult. The mechanisms of metamorphosis are controlled by endocrine secretions in an analogous way to those described in insects. Gudernatsch, a German biologist, discovered in 1911 that tadpoles feeding on extracts of mammalian thyroid glands would rapidly change into miniature frogs. This precocious metamorphosis, under the influence of thyroid extract, implicated the hormone thyroxine as the factor responsible for the many anatomical, physiological, biochemical and behavioural changes in the life cycle of the frog. Further investigations involved the removal of the thyroid gland in some animals and the pituitary gland in others. In both cases metamorphosis was prevented but was restored by feeding with thyroxine.

The initial stimulus for metamorphosis is thought to be a change in the environmental conditions such as increase in temperature or daylength. These external stimuli are transmitted to the brain and activate the hypothalamus which secretes **thyrotrophin releasing hormone** (TRH). This enters the blood vessels of the hypothalamico-hypophyseal portal system (section 16.6.2) and passes to the anterior pituitary gland. Here **thyroid stimulating hormone** or **thyrotrophin** (TSH) is released which enters the general circulation and stimulates the thyroid gland to release **thyroxine (tetraiodothyronine)** and **triiodothyronine**. These hormones act directly on all metamorphosing tissue and produce varying responses such as the atrophy of the larval tail and gills, accelerated growth of the limbs and tongue and differentiation of the skin to form gland cells and chromatophores (pigment-containing cells). The direct or local effects of thyroxine on metamorphosis at the tissue and biochemical levels were demonstrated by applying thyroxine in a fatty base to the left side of the tail and the left eye of several tadpoles. Pure fatty base was added to the right side to act as a control. After a few days, regression of the tails on the left side and a change from the larval visual pigment **porphyropsin** to the adult visual pigment **rhodopsin** had occurred in the left eyes. No change had occurred in the control tissues.

The early stages of metamorphosis are controlled by positive feedback, that is to say increasing amounts of thyroxine released by the growing thyroid gland stimulate the further production of thyroxine. As the level of circulating thyroxine increases, different target organs respond by showing cell death, cell division or cell differentiation, as described in the examples quoted above. Once the adult form has been attained thyroxine secretion is controlled by negative feedback (section 16.6.5). The sequence of external morphological changes shown by the tadpole during its metamorphosis is summarised in table 21.5.

The Mexican axolotl, *Amblystoma mexicanum* (fig 21.34), does not normally undergo metamorphosis due to a failure of the pituitary gland to produce thyroid stimulating

Fig 21.34 *The axolotl*

Table 21.5. Changes in external features in frog during metamorphosis. Times and sizes can only be approximate as the rate of metamorphosis depends upon food supply, temperature and internal factors

Time/ weeks	Size/ mm	Stages in development
0	—	Fertilisation
1	7	Hatches from jelly. External gills, tail, mouth with horny jaws. Mucus glands beneath mouth
2	9	External gills begin to atrophy, operculum grows over gills. Eyes prominent
4	12	External gills and mucus gland lost. Spiracle develops. Tail widens to aid swimming
7	28	Hindlimbs appear as buds
9	35	Hindlimbs fully formed but not used for swimming. Head begins to broaden
11–12	35	Left limb emerges through spiracle. Right limb enclosed by operculum. Hindlimbs used for swimming
13	25	Eyes become prominent and mouth widens.
14	20	Tail begins to be reabsorbed
16	15	All external larval features have disappeared. Frog emerges on to land

hormone (TSH). Instead, the axolotl attains sexual maturity whilst retaining larval characteristics such as external gills, tail fins and a light coloration. This is an example of **neoteny**, the attainment of sexual maturity whilst retaining larval characteristics. Neoteny is believed to have played a significant role in the physiological development of many animal groups, for example, the earliest vertebrates, which are thought to have descended from neotenous larval forms of sea-squirts.

The axolotl can be induced to metamorphose by the addition of the correct concentration of thyroxine to the water in which it is living. The visible effects of this are loss of gills and most of the tail fin and the assumption of the shape and features of a close relative, the land salamander.

21.8 Development in vertebrates

The preceding section on metamorphosis in amphibia described the morphological changes which occur during the development of the larval form into the adult form. Whilst these changes are spectacular and have tremendous adaptive significance in preparing the organism to meet the demands of the adult habitat, they appear trivial when compared to the events following fertilisation of the ovum. For example, of the 47 generations of cell division estimated to occur during the development of Man, 42 occur during the period of development which precedes birth. The study of embryonic development is known as **embryology** and the events which occur during this time are fundamentally the same in all animal species. They increase our understanding of the origins and functional relationships between tissues, organs and organ systems. This development is conveniently divided into three main phases, but it should be appreciated that the overall process of embryonic development is continuous and one stage passes imperceptibly into the next. These stages and their main features and implications are as follows.

Cleavage (or *segmentation*) This is the series of mitotic divisions of the zygote nucleus and cytoplasm that follows fertilisation. In the frog, the point of sperm entry into the egg prior to fertilisation imposes symmetry on the future embryo and marks the position of the future dorsal lip of the blastopore. Fertilisation stimulates cleavage which produces daughter cells or **blastomeres** forming a hollow ball of cells, the **blastula**, enclosing a cavity called the **blastocoel**.

By injecting cells with different coloured dyes (a technique known as **intra vitam staining**) the fate of the cells of the blastula can be followed throughout the next two processes of gastrulation and organogeny. Vogt has used this technique and produced **fate maps** which show the **prospective** or **presumptive** fate of cells of different regions, as shown in fig 21.35.

differentiate, and by a series of **morphogenic** movements buckle inwards (*invaginate*) through the blastopore and obliterate the blastocoel forming a new cavity, the **archenteron**. The cells become rearranged as three distinct layers, called **primary germ layers**, within a double-layered structure called the **gastrula**. The germ layers, the ectoderm, mesoderm and endoderm, are now spatially organised so as to undergo organogeny.

Organogeny (organogenesis). Further cell division, growth and differentiation occurs involving many complex morphogenic activities including the formation of the notochord, the formation of the central nervous system and the development of the mesoderm. In vertebrates these give rise to the tissues, organs and organ systems of the embryo as shown in figs 21.36 and 21.37. Organogeny is terminated by the hatching or birth of the embryo.

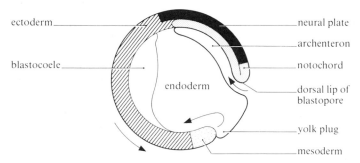

Fig 21.35 *VS of developing gastrula showing presumptive areas. Later growth and cell migration of the ectoderm and mesoderm is indicated by arrows. Mesoderm spreads inwards and occupies a position beneath the ectoderm*

Gastrulation. The onset of gastrulation is marked by the appearance of a circular opening, the **blastopore**. In the frog, cells of the blastula divide rapidly,

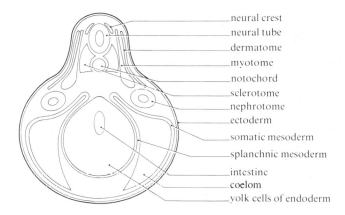

Fig 21.36 *Diagram of TS of newly hatched frog tadpole showing derivatives of the germ layers shown in fig 21.37. The tadpole is still dependent upon food provided by yolk since the ectoderm has not differentiated sufficiently to form the complete alimentary canal*

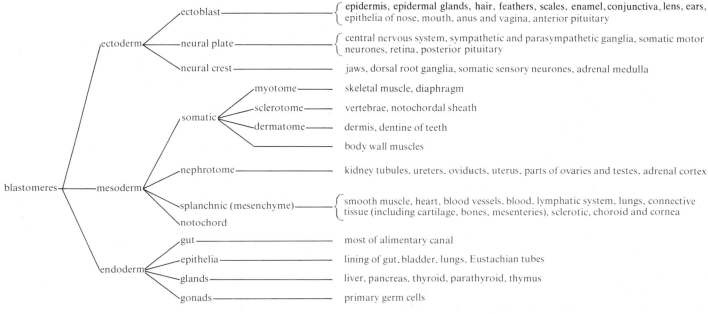

Fig 21.37 *The embryological fate of the three germ layers in vertebrates*

21.8.1 Mammalian growth hormones

There are four glands which secrete hormones influencing growth and development; they are the thyroid, liver, adrenal cortex and gonads. In all cases these glands secrete hormones under the control of other hormones released from the pituitary gland. The pituitary gland in turn is under the influence of specific releasing and inhibiting factors produced by the hypothalamus (section 16.6.2). Examples of these three levels of hormonal control are described with reference to the release of the growth hormone, **somatomedin** by the liver.

During the early part of this century numerous experiments involving ablation (removal) of the pituitary gland and replacement therapy confirmed the role of the pituitary in determining the rate and extent of growth in animals. A pituitary extract was isolated which increased body mass when injected into animals. This substance was called 'growth hormone'. Subsequent research has revealed that this growth hormone is a trophic hormone, **somatotrophin**, which is released from the pituitary gland under the influence of two other hormones produced by the hypothalamus. These are **somatostatin**, a peptide made up of 40 amino acids and **growth hormone-releasing factor** (GH-RF). These two hormones are thought to have an antagonistic effect, with somatostatin being an inhibitor and GH-RF a stimulator of somatotrophin release. The former is thought to have a dominant influence over the latter.

Human somatotrophin is a protein of 190 amino acids. It acts via receptor sites in the hepatocytes of the liver, and stimulates synthesis and release of somatomedin into the hepatic vein. Somatomedin stimulates growth throughout the body by increasing the synthesis of nucleic acids in preparation for mitosis and increasing the amino acid uptake into cartilage and muscle. It also produces a rise in the intracellular levels of potassium, phosphorus, calcium and sodium, and changes in blood glucose and lipid levels aimed at providing extra metabolites for cell synthesis and growth.

21.9 Repair and regeneration

Cell growth does not cease with the attainment of adult size. The loss of cells and tissues as a result of ageing, damage sustained by disease, accident or attack by other organisms can act as a stimulus for cell division and differentiation, resulting in the healing, repair and replacement of damaged or missing tissues.

Many tissues in mammals, such as skin, gut epithelial cells and blood cells, are continuously replaced throughout life at a steady rate determined by the normal rate at which they are lost. Other tissues, for example the liver, thyroid and pancreas, normally show a very low rate of cell division in the adult stage. If any part of these organs is lost in any way, the remaining tissues will undergo rapid cell division

and differentiation to restore the size of the organ. This process is known as **compensatory hypertrophy**. The cells of the central nervous system, on the other hand, are incapable of regeneration if damaged or lost.

Regeneration is the replacement, by growth, of parts of an organism lost for one of the reasons stated above. It is common in plants, particularly in the angiosperms where whole plants can be grown from cuttings which involve no more than a single leaf and its petiole, such as *Tradescantia*. The regenerative power of plants is used as a means of vegetative propagation (section 20.1.1).

The degree to which animals are able to regenerate new structures appears to be related to their structural complexity. Sponges, coelenterates and flatworms have remarkable powers of regeneration. Sponges and some coelenterates, such as *Hydra*, are capable of being macerated and regenerating complete organisms. *Planaria* can be cut in half longitudinally or transversely and then regenerate new halves. Another flatworm, *Dugesia* can completely regenerate from a small piece cut from an adult. Most species of annelids are able to regenerate missing regions of the body, for example the earthworm can regenerate the first five segments if they are lost and a substantial portion of the posterior end. Crustacea, insects and echinoderms can regenerate new limbs and arms, just as amphibia and lizards are able to regenerate limbs and tails as a result of attack by others of the species or predators. Lizards with their long tails are able to shed them if attacked. The wriggling movements of the detached tail act as a diversion enabling the lizard to escape. This ability to voluntarily shed limbs is shared by lobsters and crabs and is called **autotomy**.

21.10 Dormancy

During their life cycle many plants and animals undergo periods when metabolic activity is reduced to a minimum and growth ceases. This is **dormancy**. It is a physiologically determined behavioural response and may involve the adult organism, a development stage such as the pupa, or a specialised reproductive body such as a spore. Dormancy is induced by environmental changes and has the biological significance of enabling the species to survive periods when the supply of energy is inadequate for normal growth and metabolism.

Most plant species of tropical and temperate zones, and all arctic plant species, exhibit dormancy in response to changing light, temperature and moisture conditions. The mechanisms of control of dormancy by plant growth regulator substances are described in section 15.5.

Animals show three forms of dormancy involving physiological adaptations which enable them to tolerate environmental extremes, and these are considered here. Some animals though, because of well-developed mechanisms of locomotion, are able to avoid unfavourable environmental conditions by moving to more favourable regions, such as by migration. These responses, although coordinated by physiological mechanisms, are strictly behavioural and are described in section 16.8.

21.10.1 Diapause

Diapause is a form of arrested development shown by insects, but this term is also used to describe the period of inactivity shown by protozoan cysts and the winter eggs of many freshwater aquatic organisms. Insect life cycles are adapted to produce offspring at times when food is plentiful for the larval and nymphal stages. Diapause is a means of coordinating these two events. Development can be arrested at any stage in the life cycle, egg, larva, pupa or adult, and for any species the exact stage or stages is determined genetically. Some insects always undergo a period of diapause known as **obligatory diapause**, for example the locust *Nomadacris*, whereas others enter diapause only if conditions become unfavourable, such as the locust *Schistocerca*, and this is termed **facultative diapause**.

The main factor inducing diapause in all species is daylength (photoperiod), but food availability, temperature and moisture may be influential. In order for diapause to be effective, the factor inducing diapause must act *in advance* of the adverse conditions. Therefore the mechanism of synchronisation often acts on a stage preceding that which undergoes diapause. For example, diapause in the egg stage of the silkworm, *Bombyx mori*, is the result of the photoperiod experienced by the female parent during development of the egg. Adult diapause, on the other hand, is induced by light conditions occurring during the early larval stages.

Light is thought to have a direct effect upon the brain which, in turn, influences the activity of the neurosecretory system. In aphids, light is thought to act directly on neurosecretory cells. In the case of the giant silkworm, *Hyalophora cecropia*, the short photoperiod of autumn inactivates neurosecretory cells in the brain which produce prothoracicotrophic hormone. This prevents the release of ecdysone from the thoracic glands and, in the absence of further development, the species overwinters in the pupal stage. Normal secretion and further development is only restored after an extended period of exposure to low temperatures. Paradoxically, it is the adverse conditions themselves, which diapause avoids, which act as the stimulus to break the period of dormancy (fig 21.38).

> **21.10** Using the experimental data presented in fig 21.38, account for the mechanisms which terminate diapause.

Most species of insect exposed to long periods of daylight undergo continuous growth and development and produce several generations per year, for example the black bean aphid, *Aphis fabae*. These species do not undergo diapause if artificially maintained in conditions of long daylength.

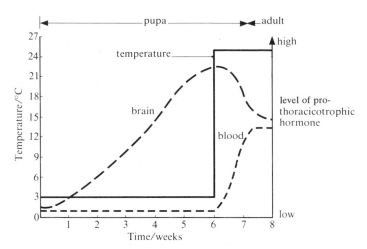

Fig 21.38 *Graph showing the relationship between the levels of prothoracicotrophic hormone in the brain and blood of silkworm at 3 °C and 25 °C*

They show a **long-day response** and only enter diapause if exposed to periods of short daylength. Other species, such as the silkworm, *Bombyx mori*, which has an embryonic diapause (egg stage), grow and develop normally during periods of short daylength and only enter diapause following exposure to periods of long daylength. This is a **short-day response**. Diapause eggs of the silkworm begin to grow and develop during the short daylengths of spring, and the adult emerges during early summer. As development occurs during periods of short daylength the eggs laid by these adults hatch and develop during the summer *without* entering diapause. However, the eggs laid by these summer silkworms enter diapause in preparation for winter. Since long photoperiods induce diapause in this type of insect this limits the number of generations per year. In the case of the silkworm there are two, as shown in fig 21.39.

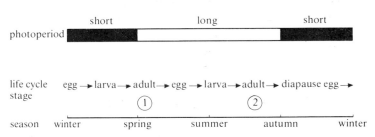

Fig 21.39 *Diagram showing the relationship between daylength, diapause and stages in the life cycle of* Bombyx mori. *This is an example of a short-day response*

Investigations have revealed the existence of a **diapause hormone** in *Bombyx* which determines whether or not the egg will undergo diapause. The long photoperiods of summer stimulate the brain to release a diapause hormone from a pair of neurosecretory cells situated in the suboesophageal ganglion. This has a direct effect on the ovary which releases darkly pigmented eggs which undergo diapause. Silkworms which develop during the short

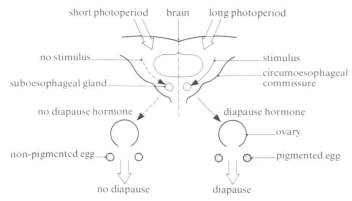

no stimulus — — stimulus

circumoesophageal
commissure

suboesophageal gland —

no diapause hormone   diapause hormone

— ovary

non-pigmented egg —○ ○   ◎ ◎— pigmented egg

no diapause   diapause

Fig 21.40 *Diagram showing the effects of photoperiod on the production of eggs in* Bombyx mori

photoperiods of later winter and spring do not release diapause hormone and lay non-pigmented eggs which do not undergo diapause (fig 21.40).

21.10.2   Aestivation

Aestivation (*aestas*, summer) is a particular form of dormancy found in certain fish and amphibia in response to hot dry periods. In such cases the organisms bury themselves in mud whilst it is still soft and undergo a period of metabolic inactivity which enables them to survive conditions of extreme dehydration. During this time they breathe atmospheric air. Normal metabolic activities are restored only when the river, pool or lake floods again following the period of drought. Two of the three genera of lungfish, *Lepidosiren* in South America and *Protopterus* in Africa, are able to aestivate for at least six months when the rivers they inhabit dry up.

21.10.3   Hibernation

Hibernation (*hiber*, winter) is a period of relatively low metabolic activity associated with periods of low temperature. This enables hibernating species of amphibia, reptiles, birds and mammals to survive at times when food is in short supply by reducing their energy demands to a low level. This is especially important in the case of homeotherms, which normally require a high metabolic rate to maintain their core temperature. True hibernation involves a fall in body temperature to that of the environment (the ambient temperature) and a reduction in heart rate, ventilation rate, metabolic rate, growth and development. In such conditions animals become almost poikilothermic. Examples of organisms showing true hibernation include insectivores such as shrews and hedgehogs: rodents including marmots, ground squirrels, dormice and hamsters: insectivorous bats and a few birds. Most other species which show some form of hibernation are in fact in a state of **torpor**, sleep or pseudohibernation. These include snakes, lizards, tortoises, salamanders, toads, newts and frogs. During this period the organism

may wake up, if the environmental temperature rises, in order to feed on supplies kept in the burrow or to urinate and defaecate.

The onset of hibernation is related to decreasing environmental temperature and photoperiod and the accumulation of adequate supplies of stored food. There is some experimental evidence that suggests a metabolite is present in the blood which could trigger hibernation, since blood taken from a hibernating ground squirrel induced hibernation in a non-hibernating squirrel within 48 h. Likewise hibernation has been induced in ground squirrels at times of the year when they are normally active by injecting blood from a hibernating squirrel. Some species such as the woodchuck, *Arctomys*, enter hibernation within a few hours whereas other species allow their core temperature to fall steadily over a period of several nights before achieving their hibernation temperature.

As the body temperature falls to about 1–2 °C above the environmental temperature the heart rate may fall from 400 to 8 beats per minute, as in the ground squirrel, and the basal metabolic rate may fall to less than 2% of the non-hibernating rate. Hibernating animals are unable to withstand a considerable drop in temperature, but they avoid freezing conditions by hibernating in nests or burrows where the microclimate is several degrees above freezing. Curling up the body aids in reducing the body surface area and conserving heat, as does burying the nose and mouth into the fur. If conditions become severe and body temperature falls to about 2 °C there is a danger of tissue damage by frost. The animal prevents this either by waking up and becoming active, thereby raising its temperature, or by increasing its metabolic rate without waking.

Many hibernating animals store energy as lipid droplets in a special type of adipose tissue known as **brown fat**. These cells contain many spherical mitochondria, and it is the presence of these that gives the cells their characteristic colour. Lipids in these cells are stored throughout the cytoplasm as droplets and not as a solid. Throughout hibernation stored lipids are used up steadily, but as animals come out of hibernation the metabolic activity of these cells rises sharply. This release of energy enables the animal to shiver vigorously and generate heat, which is dispersed by the blood system as the heart rate increases. The heart, brain and lungs receive this heat first as a result of vasoconstriction of blood vessels to other parts of the body. This is initiated by the sympathetic nervous system. Gradually the whole body warms up and normal metabolic and physiological activities are resumed.

Some small birds and mammals with large surface area to volume ratios have extremely high metabolic rates, and in order to survive they lower their body temperatures at night when they are unable to feed. This is known as **diurnal hibernation** and is seen in humming birds and small insectivorous bats.

Chapter Twenty-two

Continuity of life

The development of the cell theory by Schleiden and Schwann is described at the beginning of chapter 7. Rudolph Virchow extended this theory in 1855 by declaring that *omnis cellula e cellula* ('every cell is from a cell'). Recognition of the continuity of life stimulated further workers throughout the later part of the nineteenth century to investigate the structure of the cell and the mechanisms involved in cell division. Improved techniques of staining and better microscopes with increased resolution revealed the importance of the nuclei, and in particular the chromosomes within them, as being the structures providing continuity between one generation of cells and another. In 1879 Boveri and Flemming described the events occurring within the nucleus leading to the production of two identical cells, and in 1887 Weismann suggested that a specialised form of division occurred in the production of gametes. These two forms of division are called mitosis and meiosis respectively. The basic processes are almost identical but the outcome is entirely different.

Mitosis is the process by which a cell nucleus divides to produce two daughter nuclei containing identical sets of chromosomes to the parent cell. It is usually followed immediately by an equal division of the cytoplasm, the re-formation of a cell (plasma) membrane and cell wall (plants), or cell (plasma) membrane only (animals), and separation of the two daughter cells. This process is known as cell division. Mitosis with cell division results in an increase in cell numbers and is the method by which growth, replacement and repair of cells occurs in all higher animals and plants. In unicellular organisms, mitosis provides the mechanism of asexual reproduction leading to an increase in their numbers.

Meiosis is the process by which a cell nucleus divides to produce four daughter nuclei each containing half the number of chromosomes of the original nucleus. An alternative name for meiosis is **reduction division** since it reduces the number of chromosomes in the cell from the diploid number ($2n$) to the haploid number (n). The significance of the process lies in the fact that it enables the chromosome number of a sexually reproducing species to be kept constant from generation to generation. Meiosis occurs only during gamete formation in animals and during spore formation in plants showing alternation of generations (section 20.2), and produces haploid nuclei that fuse together during fertilisation to restore the diploid number of chromosomes.

Chromosomes are the most significant structures in the cell during division since they are responsible for the transmission of hereditary information from generation to generation and have a regulatory role in cell metabolism (section 23.2). The chromosomes of eukaryotic cells are composed of DNA, proteins and small amounts of RNA (section 5.6). In non-dividing cells the chromosomes are extremely long and thin and are dispersed throughout the nucleus. Individual chromosomes cannot be seen, but the chromosomal material may stain with certain basic dyes (appendix A2.4.2.) and is known as **chromatin** (coloured threads). During cell division the chromosomes shorten and the stain intensifies so that individual chromosomes can be seen. In their extended form the chromosomes are involved in controlling the synthesis of all materials in the cell, but during cell division this function ceases.

In all forms of cell division the DNA of each chromosome undergoes replication so that two identical polynucleotide chains of DNA are produced (section 22.4.2). These become 'surrounded' by a protein 'coat' and at the onset of cell division appear as two identical strands lying side by side. Each strand is called a **chromatid** and they are attached to each other by a non-staining region called the **centromere (kinetochore)**.

22.1 The cell cycle

The sequence of events which occurs between the formation of a cell and its division into daughter cells is called the cell cycle. It has three main stages.

(1) **Interphase.** This is a period of intense synthesis and growth. The cell produces many materials required for its own growth and carrying out all the functions peculiar to it. DNA replication occurs during interphase.

(2) **Mitosis.** This is the process of nuclear division involving the separation of chromatids and their redistribution as chromosomes into daughter cells.

(3) **Cell division.** This is the process of division of the cytoplasm into two daughter cells.

The entire cycle is laid out in fig 22.1.

The length of the cycle depends on the type of cell and external factors such as temperature, food and oxygen supply. Bacteria may divide every 20 min, epithelial cells of the intestine wall every 8–10 h, onion root-tip cells may take 20 h, whilst many cells of the nervous system never divide.

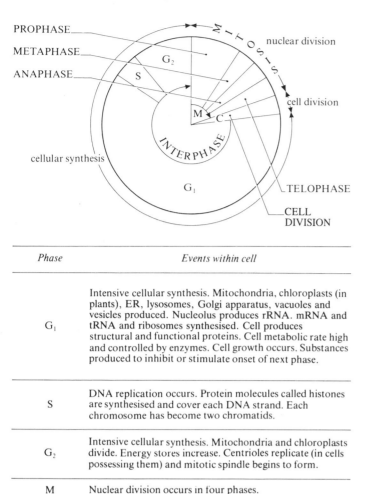

Phase	Events within cell
G_1	Intensive cellular synthesis. Mitochondria, chloroplasts (in plants), ER, lysosomes, Golgi apparatus, vacuoles and vesicles produced. Nucleolus produces rRNA. mRNA and tRNA and ribosomes synthesised. Cell produces structural and functional proteins. Cell metabolic rate high and controlled by enzymes. Cell growth occurs. Substances produced to inhibit or stimulate onset of next phase.
S	DNA replication occurs. Protein molecules called histones are synthesised and cover each DNA strand. Each chromosome has become two chromatids.
G_2	Intensive cellular synthesis. Mitochondria and chloroplasts divide. Energy stores increase. Centrioles replicate (in cells possessing them) and mitotic spindle begins to form.
M	Nuclear division occurs in four phases.
C	Equal distribution of organelles and cytoplasm into each daughter cell.

Fig 22.1 *The cell cycle*

Experiment 22.1: To investigate the phases of mitosis

Chromosomes can normally be observed only during nuclear division. The apical meristem of roots (root tips) of garlic ($2n=16$), onion ($2n=16$) and broad bean ($2n=12$) provide suitable material for the experiment. The material is set up so that root development is initiated and the root tips are removed, fixed, stained and macerated so that the chromosomes may be observed under the microscope.

Materials

pins	pair of fine needles
test-tube containing water	several sheets of
scalpel	blotting paper
small corked tube	clove of garlic
forceps	distilled water
2 Petri dishes	acetic alcohol
water bath and test-tube	molar hydrochloric acid
microscope slide	Feulgen stain
cover-slip	

Method

(1) Place a pin through a clove of garlic and suspend in a test-tube full of water so that the base of the clove is covered with water. Leave for 3–4 days without any disturbance as this is likely to inhibit cell division temporarily.

(2) When several roots have grown 1–2 cm, remove the clove and cut off the terminal 1 cm of the root.

(3) Transfer the roots to a small corked tube containing acetic alcohol and leave overnight at room temperature to fix the material.

(4) Remove the root tips with forceps by grasping the cut end of the root, transfer to a Petri dish containing distilled water and wash for a few minutes to remove the fixative.

(5) Transfer the root tips to a test-tube containing molar hydrochloric acid which is maintained at 60 °C for 3 min (6–10 min for onion, peas and beans). This breaks down the middle lamellae holding the cells together and hydrolyses the DNA of the chromosomes to form deoxyribose aldehydes which will react with the stain.

(6) Pour the root tips and acid into a Petri dish. Remove the roots into another Petri dish containing distilled water and wash to remove the acid. Leave for 5 min.

(7) Transfer the roots to a small tube containing Feulgen stain and cork. Leave in a cool dark place (preferably a refrigerator) for a minimum of 2 h.

(8) Remove a root tip and place in a drop of acetic alcohol on a clean microscope slide.

(9) Cut off the terminal 1–2 mm of the root tip and discard the rest of the root.

(10) Tease out the root tip using a pair of fine needles and cover with a cover-slip. Place the slide on a flat surface, cover with several sheets of blotting paper and press down firmly over the cover-slip with the ball of the thumb. Do not allow the cover-slip to move sideways.

(11) Examine the slide under the low and high powers of the microscope and identify cells showing different phases of mitosis.

(12) Draw and label nuclei showing the various phases.

22.2 Mitosis

The events occurring within the nucleus during mitosis are usually observed in cells which have been fixed and stained (appendix A2.4.2). Whilst this shows the phases through which chromosomes pass during cell division, it fails to reveal the continuity of the process. The use of the phase-contrast microscope and time-lapse photography has enabled the events of nuclear division to be seen in the living cell as they happen. By speeding up the film, mitosis is seen as a continuous process which occurs in four active stages. The changes occurring during these stages in an animal cell are described in fig 22.2.

Interphase

Often mistakenly called **resting stage**. Variable duration depending upon function of the cell. Period during which cell normally carries out synthesis of organelles and increases in size. The nucleoli are prominent and actively synthesising ribosomal material. Just prior to cell division the DNA & histone of each chromosome replicates. Each chromosome now exists as a pair of **chromatids** joined together by a **centromere**. The chromosomal material will stain and is called **chromatin** but structures are difficult to see.

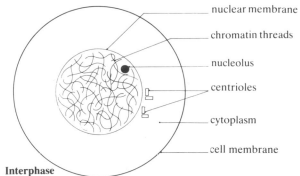

Prophase

Usually the longest phase of division. Chromatids shorten (to 4% of their original length) and thicken by **spiralisation** and condensation of the DNA protein coat. Staining shows up the chromatids clearly but the centromeres do not stain. The position of the centromere varies in different chromatid pairs. In animal cells and lower plants the **centrioles** move to opposite poles of the cell. Short **microtubules** may be seen radiating from the centrioles. These are called **asters** (*astra*, a star). The **nucleoli** decrease in size as their nucleic acid passes to certain pairs of chromatids. At the end of prophase the nuclear membrane disintegrates and a spindle is formed.

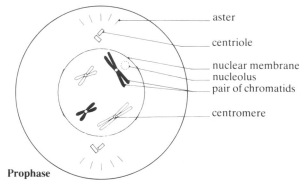

Metaphase

The pairs of chromatids become attached to the spindle by **spindle fibres** (microtubules) at their centromeres. The chromatids move upwards and downwards along the spindle until their centromeres line up across the '*equator*' of the spindle and at right-angles to the spindle axis.

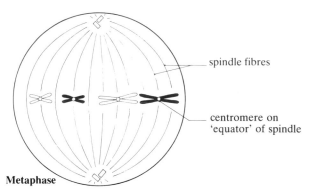

Anaphase

This stage is very rapid. The centromeres split into two and the spindle fibres pull the daughter centromeres to opposite poles. The separated chromatids, now called **chromosomes** are pulled along behind the centromeres.

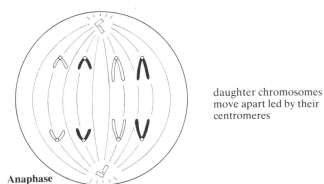

Telophase

The chromosomes reach the poles of the cell, uncoil, lengthen and lose the ability to be seen clearly. The spindle fibres disintegrate and the centrioles replicate. A nuclear membrane forms around the chromosomes at each pole and the nucleoli reappear. Telophase may lead straight into **cytokinesis** (cell division).

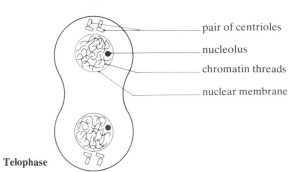

Fig 22.2 *Summary notes and diagrams of the stages of mitosis in an animal cell*

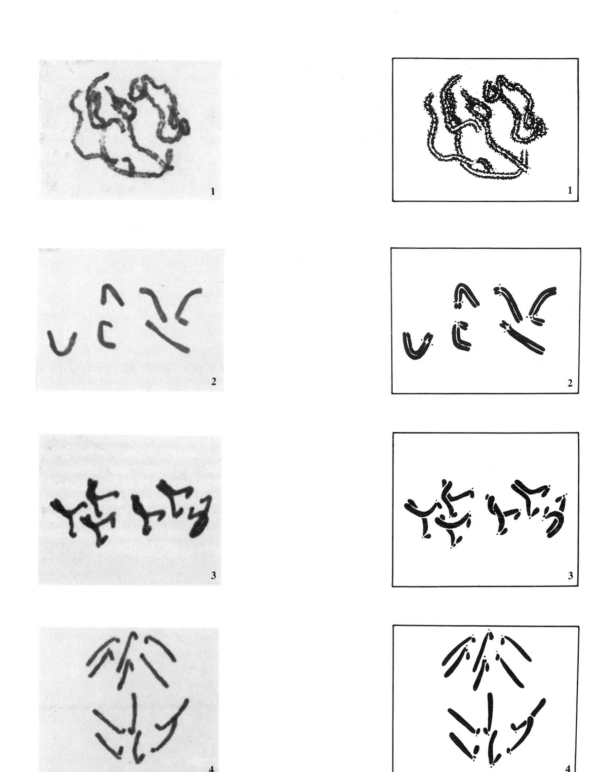

Mitosis

Four stages of mitotic cell division from root-tip cells of the plant Crocus balansae (2n = 6). These are from squash preparations with only the stained chromosomes showing clearly. Details of nucleoli, spindles and cytoplasm are unstained and not visible

At the start of division (1) the chromosomes are long, thin, but visibly double. They coil up and shorten. When fully contracted the nuclear membrane breaks down and the chromosomes become orientated on the spindle (2: polar view). After a while, spindle fibre activity on the centromeres (dotted in drawings) pulls the sister chromatids apart (3). Spindle fibres pull centromeres and chromatids to the poles (4) with the formation of two identical polar groups. Following cell division these form the nuclei of the two daughter cells

Fig 22.2 (continued) Photomicrographs and drawings based on them showing the stages in mitosis in plant cells. (Courtesy of Dr S. A. Henderson, Department of Genetics, University of Cambridge)

22.2.1 Centrioles and spindle formation

Centrioles are organelles situated in the cytoplasm close to the nuclear envelope in animal and lower plant cells. They occur in pairs and are double structures which lie at right-angles to each other.

Each centriole is approximately 500 nm long and 200 nm in diameter and is composed of nine groups of microtubules arranged in triplets. Adjacent triplets are believed to be attached to each other by fibrils (fig 22.3).

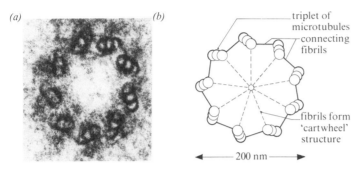

Fig 22.3 (a) Electron micrograph of a TS of a centriole from embryonic chick pancreas. (b) Diagram of TS through a centriole as seen under the electron microscope

Centrioles also occur at the bases of cilia and flagella, where they are known as **basal bodies** (section 17.6.2).

Spindle fibres are tubular and have a diameter of approximately 25 nm. They form during mitosis and meiosis, and are composed of microtubules made up of the protein **tubulin** and other protein molecules. At one time it was thought that the function of the centrioles was to act as organisers of the spindle fibres, but this is not now thought to be the case. The majority of plant cells lack centrioles but are capable of producing spindle fibres made up of microtubules identical to those found in animal cells. Some spindle fibres run from pole to pole, others are bound to the centromeres in bundles. It is thought that the relative movement of these spindle fibres accounts for the separation of daughter chromosomes during anaphase of mitosis. Electron microscopy provides evidence of the presence of cross-bridges between the two types of fibre. These **cross-bridges** suggest that the fibres may slide past each other during nuclear division using a ratchet-type mechanism similar to that associated with the movement of muscle fibrils (section 17.4.6).

The addition of **colchicine** (section 23.9.1) to actively dividing cells inhibits spindle formation and the chromatid pairs remain in their metaphase positions. This technique enables the number and structure of chromosomes to be examined under the microscope.

22.2.2 Cell division

Cytokinesis is the division of the cytoplasm. This stage normally follows telophase and leads into the G_1 phase of interphase. In preparation for division, the cell

organelles become evenly distributed towards the two poles of the telophase cells along with the chromosomes. In animal cells the cell membrane begins to invaginate during telophase towards the region previously occupied by the spindle equator. Microfilaments in the region are thought to be responsible for drawing in the cell membrane to form a continuous furrow around the equatorial circumference of the cell. The cell membranes in the region of the furrow eventually join up and completely separate the two cells.

In plant cells the spindle fibres begin to disappear during telophase everywhere except in the region of the equatorial plane. Here they move outwards in diameter and increase in number to form a barrel-shaped region known as the **phragmoplast**. Microtubules, ribosomes, mitochondria, endoplasmic reticulum and Golgi apparatus are attracted to this region and the Golgi apparatus produces a number of small fluid-filled vesicles. These appear first in the centre of the cell and, guided by microtubules, coalesce to form a **cell plate** which grows across the equatorial plane (fig 7.23). The contents of the vesicles contribute to the new middle lamella and cell walls of the daughter cells, whilst their membranes form the new cell membranes. The spreading plate eventually fuses with the parent cell wall and effectively separates the two daughter cells. The new cell walls are called **primary cell walls** and may be thickened at a later stage by the deposition of further cellulose and other substances such as lignin and suberin to produce a **secondary cell wall** (fig 22.4). In certain areas the vesicles of the cell plate fail to fuse and cytoplasmic contact remains between the daughter cells. These cytoplasmic channels are lined by the cell (plasma) membrane and form structures known as **plasmodesmata**.

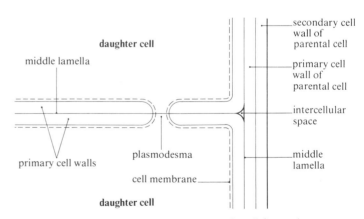

Fig 22.4 The structure of the plant cell wall formed as a result of the cytokinesis of a parental cell

22.2.3 Mitosis in animal and plant cells

The most important event occurring during mitosis concerns the equal distribution of duplicate chromosomes between the two daughter cells. This process is almost identical in animal and plant cells but there are a number of differences, and these are summarised in table 22.1.

Table 22.1. Differences between mitosis in plant and animal cells

Plant	Animal
No centriole present	Centrioles present
No aster forms	Asters form
Cell plate forms	No cell plate forms
No furrowing of cytoplasm at cytokinesis	Furrowing of cytoplasm at cytokinesis
Occurs mainly at meristems	Occurs in tissues throughout the body

The rate of mitosis varies in different organisms and tissues, being greatest in bacteria and embryonic stages of multicellular organisms and least in highly differentiated cells. Isolated cells taken from plants or animals and grown in nutrient culture solutions providing optimum conditions for cell division show the highest rate of mitosis. Such a population of cells derived from a single parent cell is known as a **clone** (section 20.1.1). The cells found in a clone need not be identical in structure or function. For example, single cells taken from an organism can give rise to a new organism or to a new tissue identical to that from which it was taken, such as a single lung cell giving rise to lung tissue having alveoli and ducts.

22.2.4 Significance of mitosis

The following points outline the main significances of mitosis.

Genetic stability. Mitosis produces two nuclei which have the same number of chromosomes as the parent cell. Moreover, since these chromosomes were derived from parental chromosomes by the exact replication of their DNA, they will carry the same hereditary information in their genes. Daughter cells are genetically identical to their parent cell and no variation in genetic information can therefore be introduced during mitosis. This results in genetic stability within populations of cells derived from parental cells, as in a clone.

Growth. The number of cells within an organism increases by mitosis (a process called **hyperplasia**) and this is a basic component of growth (chapter 21).

Asexual reproduction, regeneration and cell replacement. Many animal and plant species are propagated by asexual methods involving the mitotic division of cells. These methods of vegetative reproduction are described more fully in section 20.1.1. In addition to asexual reproduction, regeneration of missing parts, such as legs in crustacea, and cell replacement occurs, to varying degrees, in multicellular organisms.

22.3 Meiosis

Meiosis (*meio*, to reduce) is a form of nuclear division involving a reduction from the diploid number ($2n$) of chromosomes to the haploid number (n). In its simplest terms it involves a single duplication of chromosomes (DNA replication, as in mitosis) in the parent cell followed by two cycles of nuclear divisions and cell divisions (the **first meiotic division** and the **second meiotic division**). Thus a single diploid cell gives rise to four haploid cells as shown in outline in fig 22.5.

Meiosis occurs during the formation of sperm and ova (gametogenesis) in animals (sections 20.3.1 and 2) and during spore formation in most plants (those showing alternation of generations, section 20.2.2). Some lower plants do not show alternation of generations and meiosis occurs here at gamete formation. The stages of meiosis can be seen in spermatocyte nuclei from the testes of locust or grasshopper or nuclei in immature pollen sacs of *Crocus*.

Like mitosis, meiosis is a continuous process but is conveniently divided into prophase, metaphase, anaphase and telophase. These stages occur once in the first meiotic division and again in the second meiotic division. The behaviour of chromosomes during these stages is illustrated in fig 22.6, which shows a nucleus containing four chromosomes ($2n=4$), that is two homologous pairs of chromosomes.

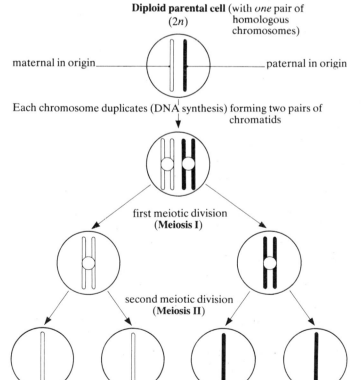

Fig 22.5 *The basic characteristics of meiosis showing one chromosome duplication followed by two nuclear and cell divisions*

Interphase

Variable length depending upon species. Replication of cell organelles and increase in size of cell. Most of the DNA and histone is replicated in premeiotic interphase but some is delayed and prolonged into early meiotic prophase I. Each chromosome now exists as a pair of chromatids joined together by a centromere. Chromosomal material will stain but no structure clear except prominent nucleoli, (see Fig. 22.2 as for mitosis).

Prophase I

The longest phase. It is often described in five stages called **leptotene**, **zygotene**, **pachytene**, **diplotene,** and **diakinesis** but will be considered here as a progressive sequence of chromosomal changes.

(*a*) Chromosomes shorten and become visible as single structures. In some organisms they have a beaded appearance due to regions of densely stained material called **chromomeres** alternating with non-staining regions. Chromomeres are regions where the chromosomal material is tightly coiled.

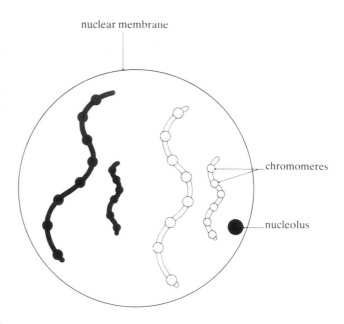

(a) *early prophase I*

(*b*) Chromosomes derived from maternal and paternal gamete nuclei come together and pair up. These are **homologous chromosomes**. Each pair is the same length, their centromeres are in the same positions and they usually have the same number of genes arranged in the same linear order. The chromomeres of the homologous chromosomes lie side by side. The pairing process is called **synapsis** and it may begin at several points along the chromosomes which then completely unite as if zipped up together. The paired homologous chromosomes are often described as **bivalents**. The bivalents shorten and thicken. This involves both molecular packaging and some visible coiling (or **spiralisation**). Each chromosome and its centromeres can now be seen clearly.

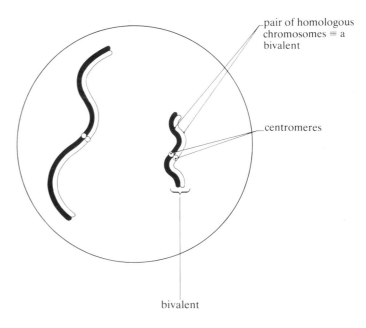

(b) *prophase I*

Fig 22.6 (a) – (k) *Summary notes and diagrams of the stages of meiosis in an animal cell.*

(*c*) The homologous chromosomes of the bivalents now fall apart and appear to repel each other partially. Each chromosome is now seen to be composed of two **chromatids**. The two chromosomes are seen to be joined at several points along their length. These points are called **chiasmata** (chiasma, a cross). It can be seen that each chiasma is the site of an exchange between chromatids. It is produced by breakage and reunion between two of the four strands present at each site. As a result, genes from one chromosome (e.g. paternal, **A**, **B**, **C**) become attached to genes from the other chromosome (maternal, **a**, **b**, **c**) leading to new gene combinations in the resulting chromatids. This is called **genetic crossing over.** The two chromosomes do not fall apart after crossing over (chiasma formation) because sister chromatids (of *both* chromosomes) remain firmly associated until anaphase.

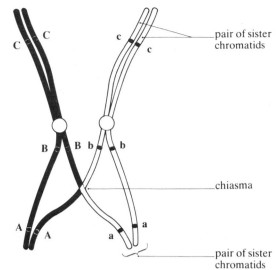

(c) *crossing over during prophase 1*

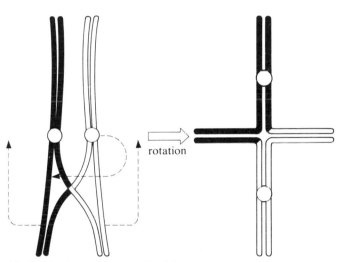

(d) (i) *Bivalent with a single chiasma*
Rotation of arms usually occurs during diplotene so that the X-shaped chiasma at the start of chiasma formation ends up looking like an open cross.

(*d*) The chromatids of homologous chromosomes continue to repel each other and bivalents assume particular shapes depending upon the number of chiasmata. Bivalents having a single chiasma appear as open crosses, two chiasmata produce a ring shape and three or more chiasmata produce loops lying at right angles to each other. By the end of prophase I, all chromosomes are fully contracted and deeply stained. Other changes have occurred within the cell including: the centrioles (if present) migrate to the poles, the nucleoli and nuclear membrane break down and then the spindle fibres form.

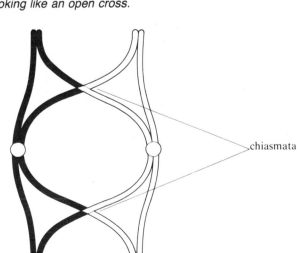

(d) (ii) *Bivalent with double chiasmata*
Rotation of the arms produces a ring shape.

803

Metaphase I

The bivalents become arranged across the equatorial plate of the spindle. Their centromeres (though often visibly double) behave as though single and organise spindle fibres pointing towards only one of the poles. Gentle pulling from these fibres places each bivalent on the equator, with each centromere equidistant above and below it.

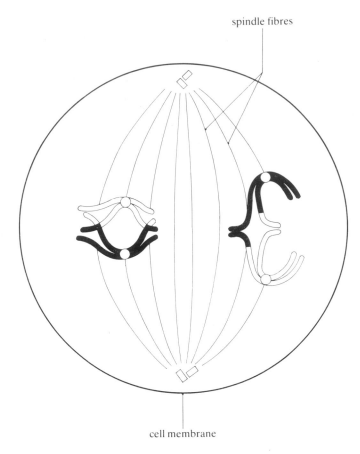

(e) *late metaphase I*

Anaphase I

The two centromeres of each bivalent do not divide, but sister chromatid adhesion ends. Spindle fibres pull whole centromeres, each attached to two chromatids, towards opposite poles of the spindle. This separates the chromosomes into two haploid sets of chromosomes in the daughter cells.

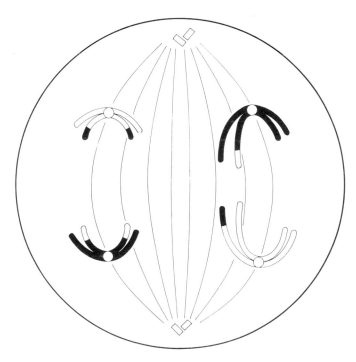

(f) *anaphase I*

Fig 22.6 (*continued*)

Telophase I

The arrival of homologous centromeres and their pairs of chromatids at opposite poles marks the end of the first meiotic division. Reduction of chromosome number has occurred but each pole possesses chromosomes composed of two chromatids.

As a result of crossing over, or chiasma formation, these chromatids are *not* genetically identical and must be separated in the second meiotic division. Spindles and spindle fibres usually disappear.

In animals and some plants the chromatids usually uncoil and a nuclear membrane forms at each pole and the nucleus enters interphase. Cleavage (animals) or cell wall formation (plants) then occurs as in mitosis. In many plants there is no telophase, cell wall formation or interphase and the cell passes straight from anaphase I into prophase of the second meiotic division.

Interphase II

This stage is present usually only in animal cells and varies in length. There is no S-phase and no further DNA replication occurs. The processes involved in the second meiotic division are mechanically similar to those of mitosis. They involve separation of the chromatids of both daughter cells produced during the first meiotic division. The second meiotic division differs from mitosis mainly in that (a) these sister chromatids are often widely separated at metaphase II of meiosis and (b) the haploid number of chromosomes is present.

Prophase II

This stage is absent from cells omitting interphase II. The length of the stage is inversely proportional to the length of telophase I. The nucleoli and nuclear membranes break down and the chromatids shorten and thicken. Centrioles, if present, move to opposite poles of the cells and spindle fibres appear. The chromatids are arranged with their axes at right angles to the spindle axis of the first meiotic division.

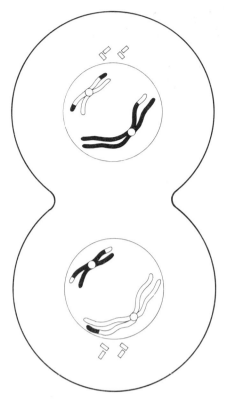

(g) *telophase I in an animal cell*

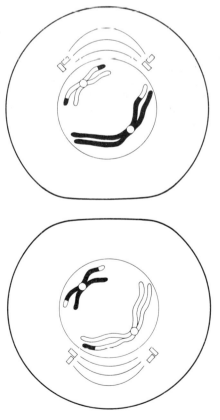

(h) *prophase II*

Metaphase II

At this division the centromeres now behave as structurally double. They organise spindle fibres on each side to *both* poles and hence become aligned on the equator of the spindle.

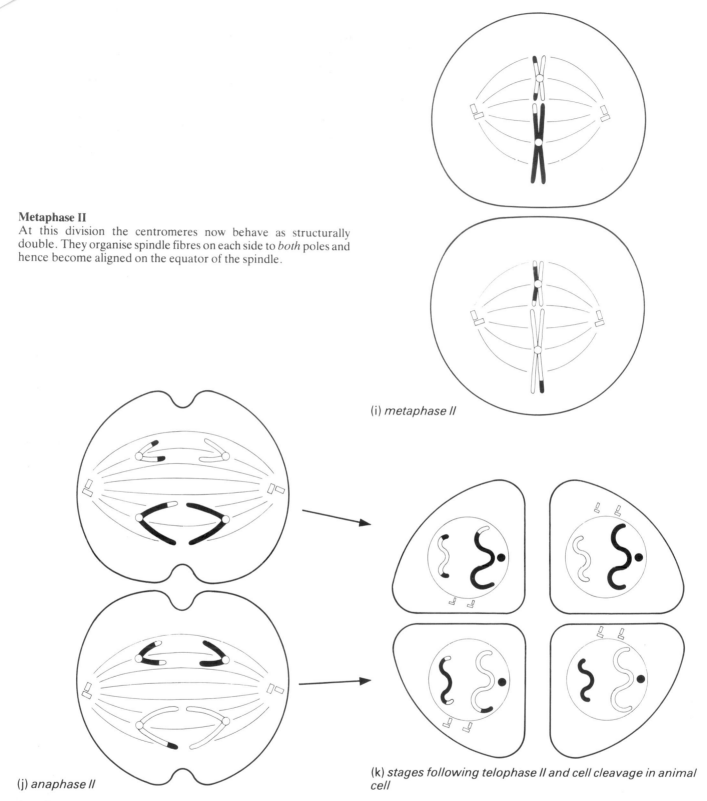

(i) *metaphase II*

(j) *anaphase II*

(k) *stages following telophase II and cell cleavage in animal cell*

Anaphase II

The centromeres divide and the spindle fibres pull the centromeres to opposite poles. The separated chromatids, now called chromosomes, are pulled along behind the centromere.

Telophase II

This stage is very similar to that found at mitosis. The chromosomes uncoil, lengthen and become very indistinct. The spindle fibres disappear and the centrioles replicate. Nuclear membranes re-form around each nucleus which now possesses half the number of single chromosomes of the original parent cell (haploid). Subsequent cleavage (animals) or cell wall formation (plants) will produce four daughter cells from the original single parent cell.

Fig 22.6 (*continued*)

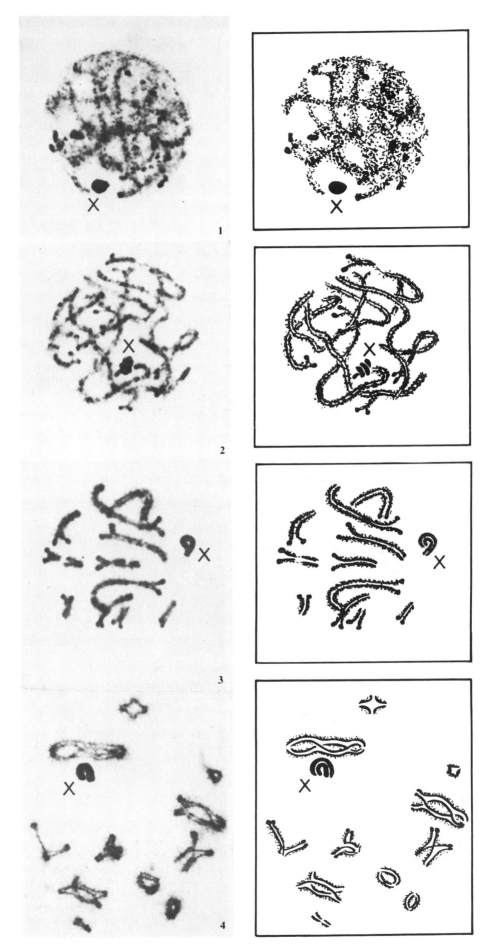

Fig 22.7 (a) Eight stages of meiosis from spermatocytes of the desert locust Schistocerca gregaria (2n = 22 + **X** ♂). As at mitosis, these are from squash preparations with only the stained chromosomes showing clearly. Details of nucleoli, spindles and cytoplasm are unstained and not visible. At the start of the first meiotic division (1) the chromosomes are long, thin, fuzzy and not clearly visible, while the **X** is deeply staining. Pairing of homologous (maternal and paternal) chromosomes takes place with the formation of the haploid number (11) of **bivalents** and the **X** (2,3). Molecular exchange occurs between maternal and paternal chromosomes when intimately paired. They then fall apart along their length except at points where exchanges took place (4). These are called **chiasmata**. (part (b) overleaf)

807

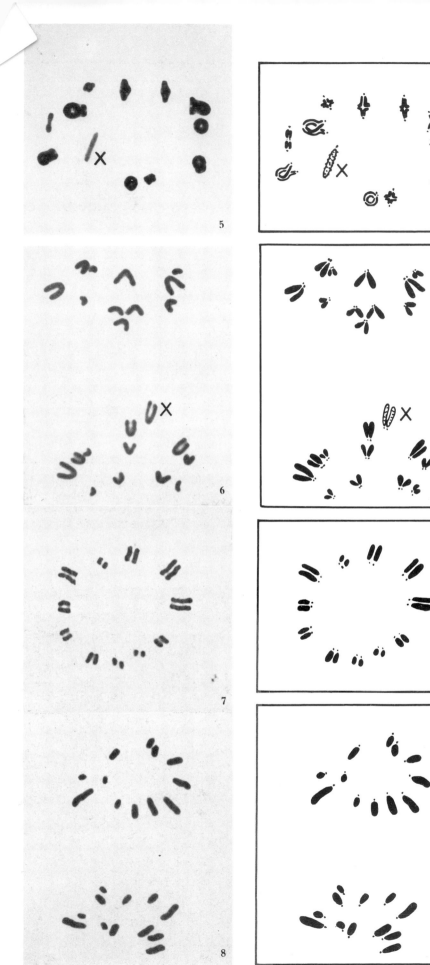

Fig 22.7 (b) Further contraction produces short, fat bivalents which, following breakdown of the nuclear membrane, become attached to the spindle by their centromeres (5: polar view). Spindle fibre activity pulls the haploid number of chromosomes apart (6: side view). The **X**, which is now weakly staining, goes undivided to one pole. At the second meiotic division the haploid number of chromosomes lie on the equatorial plate (7: polar view) and single chromatids are pulled to the poles by spindle fibre activity (8: side view) (Photomicrographs and drawings by courtesy of Dr S. A. Henderson, Department of Genetics, University of Cambridge)

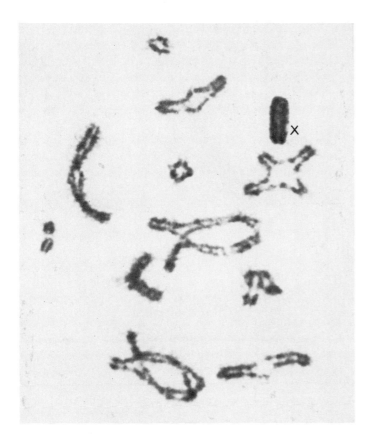
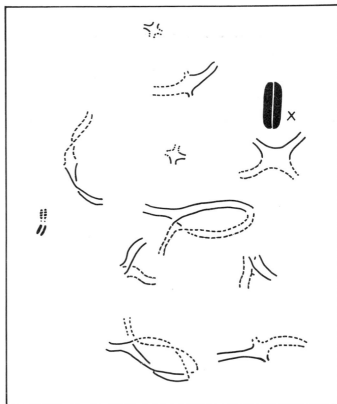

Fig 22.8 *Diplotene (prophase I) showing chiasmata. The chromosomes from a single cell at diplotene in the locust* Locusta migratoria, *showing bivalents with one or two chiasmata. Maternal and paternal chromosomes are represented by solid and dotted lines in the drawing. At each chiasma a genetic exchange has occurred. The shape of the bivalent will vary from rod-shaped, to cross-shaped or ring-shaped, depending on the number and position of chiasmata. The unpaired* **X** *chromosome is deeply staining at this stage (Dr S. A. Henderson)*

Fig 22.9 *Meiosis in living cells. Pairing and cell division at meiosis in living spermatocytes of the locust locust Locusta migratoria. These preparations are photographed with an optical technique known as Nomarski interference contrast, which uses polarised light and produces images of remarkably 3–D appearance in living, unstained cells. Two cells show chromosome pairing in early prophase I nuclei, with chromomere alignment (arrowed). The other two cells are at the end of the first meiotic division. It can be seen that, after the two polar groups have formed, cleavage of the cell takes place and two approximately equal daughter cells are produced. The fibrous structures stretching between the two polar groups, pinched in two like a wheat sheaf at cleavage, are the mitochondria*

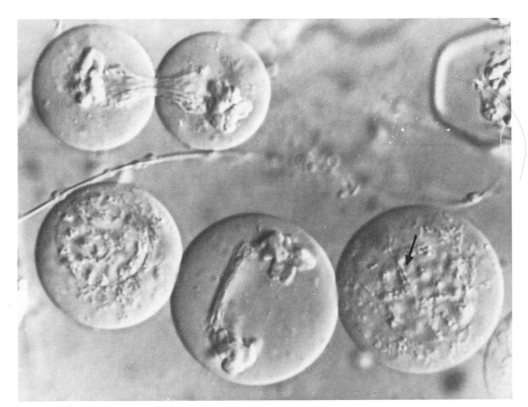

22.3.1 Significance of meiosis

The following points outline the main significances of meiosis.

Sexual reproduction Meiosis results in the formation of four daughter cells, each with half the number of chromosomes of the parent cell in all organisms carrying out sexual reproduction. During fertilisation the nuclei of the two gamete cells fuse and produce a zygote which has a fixed number of chromosomes for each species. In all organisms this number of chromosomes represents the diploid condition ($2n$). If meiosis did not occur fusion of gametes would result in a doubling of the chromosomes for each successive sexually reproduced generation. (An exception to this is shown in polyploidy which is described in section 23.9.) This situation is prevented in the life cycle of all sexually reproducing organisms by the occurrence, at some stage, of cell division involving a reduction in the diploid number of chromosomes ($2n$) to the haploid number (n).

> **22.1** The amount of DNA present per cell during several nuclear divisions is represented diagrammatically in fig 22.10.
> (*a*) Which type of nuclear division is represented by fig 22.10?
> (*b*) What phases are represented by the dashed lines W, X and Y?
> (*c*) What type of cells are represented by the line Z?

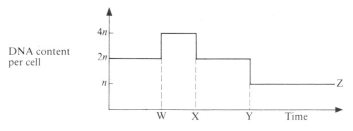

Fig 22.10 *Diagram for use in question 22.1*

Genetic variation Meiosis also provides opportunities for new combinations of genes to occur in the gamete cells. This leads to genetic variation in the genotype and phenotype of offspring produced by the fusion of gametes. The mechanisms of meiosis that contribute to this variation may be summarised as follows:
(1) The reduction of chromosomes from the diploid to the haploid number segregates (separates) alleles so that each gamete cell carries only one allele for a particular gene locus (section 23.2).
(2) The orientations on the equatorial spindle of bivalents during metaphase I and of chromosomes in metaphase

II are random. The subsequent separation of these during anaphase I and II respectively produces new allelic recombinations in gamete cells. This is called **independent assortment** and results in the random assortment of maternal and paternal chromosomes between daughter nuclei. This is the basis of Mendel's second law (section 23.1.3).
(3) As a result of chiasmata, crossing over of segments of chromatids occurs between homologous chromosomes during prophase I, leading to the formation of new combinations of alleles on chromosomes of the gamete cells. This breaks established linkage groups and produces new ones.

The significance of these three mechanisms in the process of inheritance and the production of variation is described in detail in section 23.8.4.

22.3.2 Similarities and differences between mitosis and meiosis

The main similarities between mitosis and meiosis involve the mechanisms by which the chromosomes and other cell organelles replicate and are manoeuvred within the cell prior to and during cell division. The mechanism of cell division, too, is similar in mitosis and meiosis.

The differences between the two processes are shown in table 22.2.

Differences between males and females, animals and plants
The above description of meiosis applies in a general way to all animals and plants, and males and females, but there are important differences also.

(*a*) **Males**
In *animals*, cleavage occurs at the end of both first and second meiotic divisions and the daughter cells separate immediately and behave independently thereafter. All four meiotic products survive, form spermatids and develop into spermatozoa. In *plants*, cell wall formation occurs and the daughter cells remain associated at the end of the first meiotic division to form a **diad**, and at the second division, to form a **tetrad**. All products again survive to give rise to pollen grains.

(*b*) **Females**
Female meiosis in both plants and animals ends up with three of the four meiotic products lost – only one survives to form an egg nucleus.

In *animals*, first division cleavage is unequal and results in the production of a primary oocyte and a polar body. Second division is also unequal and the oocyte gives rise to a secondary oocyte and a second polar body (the first polar body may also divide and all three polar bodies abort). Only one functional oocyte is produced. In *plants*, a linear meiosis results in four nuclei lying in the embryo sac. Three abort and only one remains to give rise to the embryo sac nuclei and the egg nucleus.

Table 22.2. Differences between stages of mitosis and meiosis

	Mitosis	Meiosis
Prophase	Chromomeres not visible Homologous chromosomes remain separate No chiasmata formation No crossing over	Chromomeres visible Homologous chromosomes pair up Chiasmata occur Crossing over may occur
Metaphase	Pairs of chromatids line up on the equator of the spindle Centromeres line up in the same plane on the equator of the spindle	Pairs of chromatids line up on the equator only in second meiotic division Centromeres lie equidistant above and below the equator in the first meiotic division
Anaphase	Centromeres divide Chromatids separate Separating chromatids identical	Centromeres divide only during second meiotic division Chromatids separate only in the second meiotic division. In the first division whole chromosomes separate. Separating chromosomes may not be identical due to crossing over
Telophase	Same number of chromosomes present in daughter cells as parent cells Both homologous chromosomes present in daughter cells if diploid	Half the number of chromosomes present in daughter cells Only one of each pair of homologous chromosomes present in daughter cells
Occurrence	May occur in haploid, diploid or polyploid cells Occurs during the formation of somatic cells and some spores. Also occurs during the formation of gametes in plants with alternation of generations	Only occurs in diploid or polyploid cells In formation of gamete cells or spores

22.4 The structure of chromosomes

Histochemical and cytological analyses of chromosomes of eukaryotic cells have shown them to be composed of deoxyribonucleic acid (DNA) and protein, with small amounts of chromosomal RNA. The 'chromosomes' of prokaryotic cells (bacteria and blue-green algae) are composed of DNA only and strictly should not be called chromosomes. DNA has negative charges distributed along its length, and positively charged (basic) protein molecules called **histones** are bonded to it. This DNA protein complex is called **chromatin**. The protein molecules increase the diameter of the chromosome and may act as an outer protective coat for the DNA. The exact structural relationship between the DNA and histones in a chromosome is still far from certain, but it would appear that a chromosome is not simply a single molecule of DNA surrounded by a layer of histones, but something much more. Several models of the structure of chromosomes have been proposed.

The diameter of a single DNA double helix is 2 nm, whereas the thinnest chromosomes seen with the light microscope are between 100 and 200 nm in diameter. The explanation may be either that a chromosome contains several DNA double helices or that one long DNA double helix is tightly coiled. Electron micrographs taken of lampbrush chromosomes (so-called because of their resemblance to brushes used to clean the glass of oil lamps) of amphibian oocytes during metaphase show that each chromatid appears to be composed of a tightly coiled axis with several lateral loops made up of a single DNA double helix (fig 22.11). These loops may represent DNA which

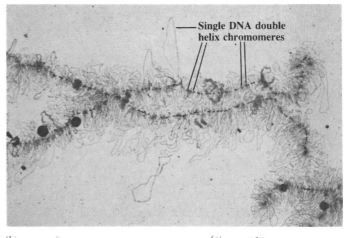
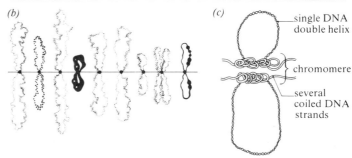

Fig 22.11 (a) Lampbrush chromosomes of amphibian oocyte showing centromere and three chiasmata. (b) and (c) The effects of stretching lampbrush chromosomes to show the central filament of DNA and the loops of DNA where mRNA synthesis takes place. The dense regions are thought to be chromomeres. Each chromomere and its associated loop is thought to be associated with a specific gene locus. (From H. G. Callan (1963) Int. Rev. Cytology, **15**, 1.)

has been exposed for the purpose of transcription (section 22.6.6). Recent investigations into the structure of chromosomes suggest that the DNA helix combines with groups of eight histone molecules to form structures known as **nucleosomes** having the appearance of 'beads on a string'. These nucleosomes, and the DNA strands linking them, are packed closely together to produce a 3 nm diameter helix with about six nucleosomes per turn which has the dimensions and other features of a chromosome. The proposed structure of the chromosome is shown in fig 22.12.

In the chromosomes of sperm of some species, such as salmon and herring, protamines replace histones as the proteins bound to the DNA.

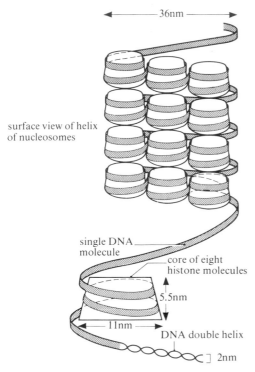

Fig 22.12 *Proposed structure of the nucleosome and its relationship to the chromosome and the DNA molecule. (From E. J. Du Praw School of Medicine, University of Maryland, (metaphase chromosome).)*

22.4.1 Evidence for the role of DNA in inheritance

Following the proposal by Sutton and Boveri at the beginning of this century that chromosomes were the structures by which genetic information passed between generations (section 23.2), it took many years to clarify whether the genetic material was the DNA or the protein of the chromosomes. In a series of experiments, Alfred Mirsky demonstrated that all the somatic cells of a given species contain the same amount of DNA, and this is double the amount found in gamete cells. However, the same applies to the protein content of the chromosomes so this knowledge did little to clarify the nature of the genetic material.

Table 22.3. Results of Griffith's experiments

Injected form of Pneumococcus	*Effect*
Live non-capsulated	mice live
Live capsulated	mice die
Heat-killed capsulated	mice live
Heat-killed capsulated + live non-capsulated	mice die

It was suspected that protein might be the only molecule with sufficient variety of structure to act as genetic material.

Frederick Griffith, an English bacteriologist, made an observation in 1928 which was later to prove significant in resolving the problem. In the days before the development of antibiotics, pneumonia was often a fatal disease. Griffith was interested in developing a vaccine against the bacterium *Pneumococcus* which causes one form of pneumonia. Two forms of *Pneumococcus* were known, one covered with a gelatinous capsule and virulent (disease-producing) and the other non-capsulated and non-virulent. The ability of these bacteria to cause pneumonia appeared to be related to the presence of the gelatinous capsule. Griffith hoped that by injecting patients with the non-capsulated, or heat-killed encapsulated forms, their bodies would produce antibodies which would afford protection against pneumonia. In a series of experiments Griffith injected mice with both forms of *Pneumococcus* and obtained the results shown in table 22.3. Post mortems carried out on the dead mice revealed the presence within their bodies of live encapsulated forms. On the basis of these results Griffith concluded that something must be passing from the heat-killed encapsulated forms to the live non-capsulated forms which caused them to develop capsules and become virulent. However, the nature of this **transforming principle**, as it was known, was not isolated and identified until 1944. For ten years Avery, McCarty and McCleod analysed and purified the constituent molecules of heat-killed encapsulated pneumococcal cells and tested their ability to bring about transformation in live non-encapsulated cells. Removal of the polysaccharide capsule and the protein fraction from the cell extracts had no effect on transformation, but the addition of the enzyme deoxyribonuclease (DNAase), which breaks down (hydrolyses) DNA, prevented transformation. The ability of extremely purified extracts of DNA from encapsulated cells to bring about transformation finally demonstrated that Griffith's principle was in fact DNA. Despite this evidence many scientists still refused to accept that DNA, not protein, was the genetic material. In the early 1950s a wealth of irrefutable evidence, based upon the study of viruses, eventually demonstrated the ubiquitous nature of DNA as the carrier of hereditary information.

Viruses became one of the major experimental materials in genetic research in the 1940s and since then experiments involving their use have become as classic as those involving the garden pea, the fruit fly and, as will be described later, the bread mould *Neurospora*. Virus particles have an extremely simple structure consisting of a mainly protein coat enclosing a molecule of nucleic acid, either DNA or RNA (section 2.5.2). As such they provided ideal research material to investigate whether protein or nucleic acid is the genetic material. In 1952 Hershey and Chase began a series of experiments involving a particular type of virus which specifically attacks bacterial cells and is called a **bacteriophage**. Bacteriophage T_2 attacks the colon bacillus *Escherichia coli* (*E. coli*) and causes it to produce large numbers of T_2-phage particles in a very short time. The essence of Hershey and Chase's experiment involved growing T_2-phage particles in *E. coli* which had been grown on a medium containing radioactive isotopes of either sulphur (^{35}S) or phosphorus (^{32}P). The phage particles formed in *E. coli* labelled with radioactive sulphur had incorporated this into their protein coats, whereas those formed in phosphorus-labelled *E. coli* contained radio-actively labelled ^{32}P DNA. This selective distribution of isotopes is due specifically to the fact that proteins do not contain phosphorus and nucleic acids do not contain sulphur. The labelled T_2-phage particles were allowed to infect non-radioactively labelled *E. coli* and after a few minutes the cells were agitated in a blender or liquidiser which stripped off the phage particles from the bacterial walls. The bacteria were then incubated and examined for radioactivity. The results are shown in fig 22.13.

On the basis of these results Hershey and Chase concluded that it was the phage DNA which entered the bacterial cell and gave rise to large numbers of phage progeny. These experiments had demonstrated that DNA is the hereditary material. Confirmatory evidence that only the DNA contained within the phage is introduced into the bacterial cell has been provided by electron microscopy and increased knowledge of the life cycle of viruses. (The life cycle of virus and phage particles is described in sections 2.5.3 and 2.5.4.)

22.4.2 DNA replication

The double helical structure of DNA, as determined by Watson and Crick, is described in section 5.6.3. One of its most attractive features is that it immediately suggests a method by which replication could occur. Watson and Crick proposed that the two strands were capable of unwinding and separating, and acting as templates to which a complementary set of nucleotides would attach by base pairing. In this way each original DNA molecule would give rise to two copies with identical structures.

In 1956 Kornberg succeeded in demonstrating the in vitro synthesis of a DNA molecule using a single strand of

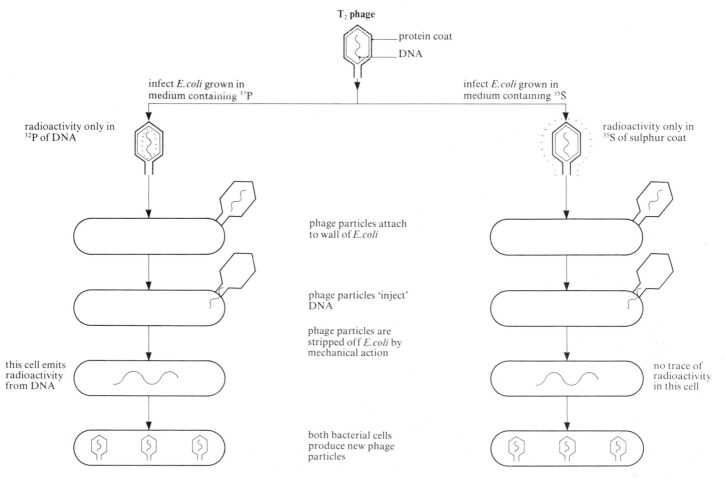

Fig 22.13 *Summary diagrams of Hershey and Chase's work on T$_2$ phage and* E. coli

DNA as a template. (This technique was used by later researchers to investigate the nature of the genetic code (section 22.5).) Kornberg extracted and purified an enzyme from *E. coli* which was capable of linking free DNA nucleotides, in the presence of ATP as an energy source, to form a complementary strand of DNA. This enzyme he named **DNA polymerase**. In subsequent experiments Kornberg used nucleoside triphosphates (ATP, GTP, TTP, CTP) instead of nucleotides and ATP, and they too produced a complementary strand of DNA. Later evidence confirmed that this is the form in which nucleotides readily attach themselves to the DNA template and each other. As the nucleoside triphosphates link up, the two terminal phosphate groups are broken off. The remaining phosphate group of the nucleotide and the energy released are used to form the ester linkage between the $5 \rightarrow 3$ carbon atoms of the sugar molecules of adjacent nucleotides (fig. 22.14).

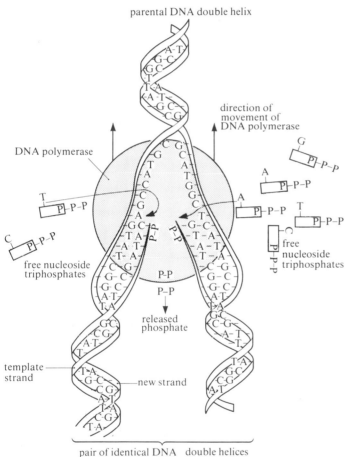

Fig 22.14 *Replication of the DNA double helix. The parental DNA helix unwinds and the complementary strands separate due to the breaking of weak hydrogen bonds between complementary bases. The DNA polynucleotide chains do not break due to the strength of their phosphodiester linkages. Base pairing occurs between the bases of the template strands and free nucleoside triphosphates link up to form a polynucleotide chain. In this way two identical DNA molecules are produced. The enzyme DNA polymerase is involved in the separation of the parental strands and the formation of the new polynucleotide chain but other enzymes are also thought to influence replication*

Kornberg later demonstrated, in 1967, that DNA polymerase only adds nucleotides to the strand running in the $5 \rightarrow 3$ direction. Since the two DNA strands lie in opposite directions, that is are anti-parallel as shown in fig 22.12, DNA polymerase can only continuously produce one new DNA molecule at a time. Short sections of the other daughter DNA molecule are produced by the action of DNA polymerase moving in the opposite direction. These short sections of newly synthesised polynucleotide chains are joined together by the action of another enzyme called **DNA ligase** (fig. 22.15). DNA molecules produced by in vitro synthesis in the presence of DNA ligase are biologically active and can be used in protein synthesis. Those DNA molecules produced in 1956 by Kornberg, whilst having the correct DNA structure, were biologically inactive due to the failure of sections of the synthesised $5 \rightarrow 3$ chain to connect up.

The method of DNA replication proposed by Watson and Crick and shown in fig 22.16 is known as **semi-conservative replication** since each new double helix retains one strand of the original DNA double helix. The evidence for this mechanism was provided by a series of classic experiments carried out by Meselsohn and Stahl in 1958. *E. coli* has a single circular chromosome, and when cultures of these cells were grown for many generations in a medium containing the heavy isotope ^{15}N all the DNA became labelled with ^{15}N. These cells containing DNA labelled with ^{15}N were transferred to a culture medium containing the normal isotope of nitrogen (^{14}N) and allowed to grow. After periods of time corresponding to the generation time for *E. coli* (50 min at 36 °C) samples were removed and the DNA extracted and centrifuged at 40 000 times gravity for 20 h in a solution of caesium chloride (CsCl). During centrifugation the heavy caesium chloride molecules began to sediment to the bottom of the centrifuge tubes producing an increasing density gradient from the top of the tube to the bottom. The DNA settles out where its density equals that of the caesium chloride solution. When examined under ultra-violet light the DNA appeared in the centrifuge tube as a narrow band. The positions of the bands of DNA extracted from cells grown in ^{15}N and ^{14}N culture media and the interpretation of their structure are shown in fig 22.16. These experiments conclusively demonstrated that DNA replication is semi-conservative.

22.2 There were three hypotheses advanced to explain the process of DNA replication. One of these is known as semi-conservative and is described above and in fig 22.14. The other hypotheses are known as conservative replication and dispersive replication and are summarised in fig 22.17.

Draw diagrams to show the distribution of the different types of DNA in a density gradient which Meselsohn and Stahl would have found in the first two generations if these latter hypotheses had been correct.

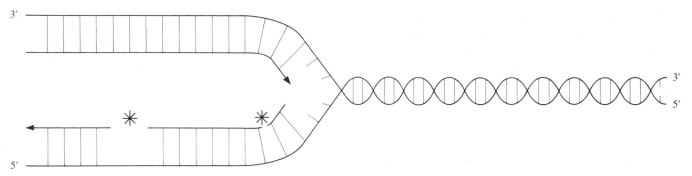

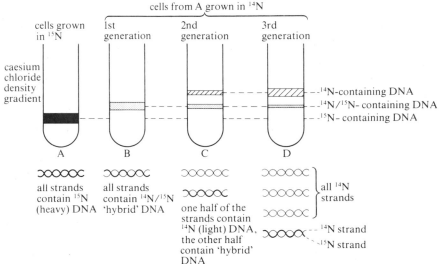

Fig 22.15 (above) *The role of DNA ligase in DNA replication. The arrows show the direction in which DNA polymerase moves in producing new DNA double helices. DNA ligase is active in joining short sections of polynucleotide chains at the points labelled with an asterisk*

Fig 22.16 (right) *The results and interpretation of Meselsohn and Stahl's experiment into the process of DNA replication. The widths of the DNA bands in the centrifuge tubes reflect the proportions of the various types of DNA molecules as shown in the diagrams (right). In C the ratio of the width is 1:1 and in D the ratio is 3:1*

Fig 22.17 (below) *Diagrams explaining two further theories of DNA replication*

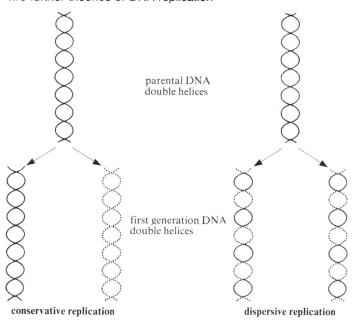

22.5   The nature of genes

The **particulate** nature of heredity has always been a feature of the study of inheritance. Mendel proposed in 1866 that the characteristics of organisms were determined by hereditary units called '**elementes**'. These were later termed **genes** and shown to be located on, and transmitted from generation to generation by chromosomes (section 23.2).

Despite our current knowledge of chromosomes and the structure and function of DNA, it is still extremely difficult to give a precise definition of a gene. Investigations into the nature of the gene have so far produced three possible definitions of a gene and these are outlined below, since they have implications in the fields of genetics and evolution.

A unit of recombination. From his studies of chromosome mapping in *Drosophila* (section 23.3), Morgan postulated that a gene was **the shortest segment of a chromosome which could be separated from adjacent segments by crossing-over**. This definition regards the gene as a large unit, a specific region of the chromosome determining a distinct characteristic in the organism.

A unit of mutation. Investigations into the nature of mutations revealed that changes in characteristics occurred as a result of random and spontaneous alterations in the structure of a chromosome, a sequence of bases or even a single base (section 23.9). It seemed therefore that a gene might be as small as a single pair of complementary bases in the nucleotide sequence of DNA, that is **the shortest segment of a chromosome which could undergo mutation**.

A unit of function. Since genes were known to determine structural, physiological and biochemical characteristics of organisms it was suggested that a gene was **the shortest segment of a chromosome responsible for the production of a specific product**.

The third definition is the most acceptable but it lacks precision concerning the nature of the specific product. In some cases one 'gene' is known to affect several characteristics (section 23.1.1) whilst in other cases several 'genes' (polygenes) may determine one specific characteristic (section 23.7.6).

It was, however, as a result of research carried out by Beadle and Tatum that the third definition of the gene gained recognition. This became known as the **one gene, one enzyme hypothesis** and was largely substantiated by the development of a new field of biology called **molecular genetics**. (Subsequent research has narrowed this functional concept to that of the one cistron, one polypeptide hypothesis (section 22.5.1).)

22.5.1 Genes and enzymes

The relationship between genes and enzymes was first suggested, although not in those terms, by an English physician, Sir Archibald Garrod in 1908. Garrod postulated that certain 'inborn errors of metabolism' were the result of the failure of the body to produce certain important chemical substances which, in turn, were determined by hereditary mechanisms. It was almost 40 years later that the full extent of this hypothesis was demonstrated and found to be true as a result of the pioneer work in molecular genetics.

Initial investigations in molecular genetics involved establishing the various compounds and enzymes of metabolic pathways. Certain metabolic disorders produce defects in organisms which behave as though controlled by single genes. They may appear spontaneously, as in the case of mutations, or be inherited according to conventional genetic mechanisms. For example, the amino acids phenylalanine and tyrosine are normally used in the manufacture of cell proteins and other structural and physiological compounds, and the excess is broken down into carbon dioxide, water and nitrogenous wastes. In all cases their fate is determined by simple metabolic pathways involving a series of enzymes. Defective enzymes or lack of enzymes at four points in these pathways produce the metabolic disorders **phenylketonuria**, **goitrous cretinism**, **albinism** and **alkaptonuria**. In all four cases these disorders are inherited in such a way as to suggest that they are each controlled by a single recessive gene.

Further important evidence supporting the one gene, one enzyme hypothesis was gained from work begun by Beadle and Tatum in 1941, investigating the mechanisms of inheritance of enzymes in the pink bread-mould *Neurospora crassa*. In common with Mendel and Morgan they were careful in their choice of experimental organism.

Neurospora is an ascomycete fungus and has the following advantages for genetic research:
(1) it is easy to grow,
(2) it can be bred in large numbers,
(3) it has a very short life cycle (10 days),
(4) it has a haploid vegetative stage.

The latter point is very significant. Since only one set of chromosomes is present for most of the life cycle there is no masking of recessive genes. If a mutation arises and produces a recessive gene the effects of the mutation will be seen immediately. *Neurospora* normally produces asexual spores (**conidia**) which germinate and give rise to a **mycelium**. Segments of mycelia of opposite mating strains may fuse and produce a diploid zygote. This immediately undergoes a meiotic division followed by a single mitotic division to form an **ascus** or fruiting body containing eight haploid **ascospores**, four of these ascospores being derived from each parental strain. Each ascospore may germinate and produce a new mycelium. A mycelium can therefore arise from an asexually produced conidium or a sexually produced ascospore (fig 22.18).

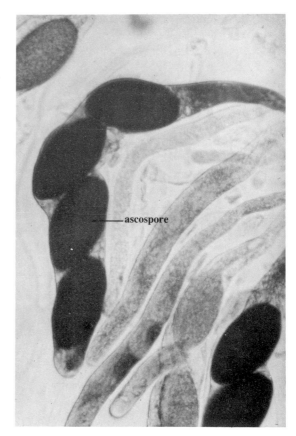

Fig 22.18 *Ascospores in an ascus*

Neurospora can grow on a culture medium containing only agar, sugars, salts and the vitamin biotin. This is known as **minimal medium**. Growth under these conditions demonstrates that *Neurospora* is able to synthesise all the carbohydrates, fats, amino acids and vitamins essential for its growth using enzymes produced by its cells.

Beadle and Tatum carried out the following procedure in their investigations:

(1) Conidia were exposed to X-rays in order to increase the mutation rate.

(2) These conidia were transferred to **complete medium** (containing all the necessary amino acids and vitamins for normal growth) and grown.

(3) The mycelia which formed were then crossed with mycelia from conidia not exposed to X-rays ('wild type').

(4) The asci produced contained four ascospores from each parental mycelial strain (mutant and wild type).

(5) The ascospores were dissected out and separately transferred to complete medium where they all grew.

(6) Samples of mycelia were placed on vitamin-enriched minimal medium. In some cases no growth occurred.

(7) The strains which did not grow were unable to synthesise certain amino acids. In order to determine which amino acids could not be synthesised, these strains were then transferred to a series of minimal media cultures each containing a single different amino acid.

(8) The specific medium in which growth occurred therefore contained the amino acid which the strain of *Neurospora* was unable to synthesise. In this way mutant strains of *Neurospora* were identified. Analysis of the results showed that in all cases where half of the ascospores from a given ascus produced a mutant strain, the other half were able to grow in minimal medium.

This suggested that the mutant gene behaved as a single recessive gene and was transmitted according to the rules of normal Mendelian inheritance. Beadle and Tatum interpreted these results as demonstrating that, in each case, the X-rays had induced a mutation in one gene controlling the production of one enzyme necessary in the synthesis of an amino acid. This formed the basis of their 'one gene, one enzyme' hypothesis (fig 22.19).

This early work established the experimental procedure of using minimal media which has been used and modified in microbial genetics to produce a vast amount of information concerning the role of genes.

It is now clearly established that genes exercise control within the cell by the synthesis of enzymes and other proteins. These enzymes in turn direct the synthesis of all other materials within the cell.

Over the years, however, the exact definition of the gene has been modified. Research carried out by Benzer in 1955 into the structure of genes in the bacteriophage T$_4$ gave rise to the concept of the cistron as a unit of function. A **cistron** is a region of DNA carrying information for the production of a polypeptide chain. This may function on its own as a biologically active molecule or may form part of a larger macromolecule. Current views on the nature of the gene have moved from the 'one gene, one enzyme' concept to the '**one cistron, one polypeptide**' concept.

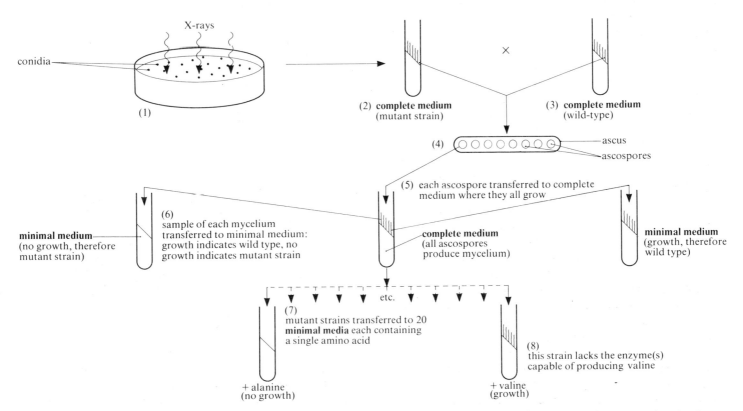

Fig 22.19 *Flow diagram illustrating the main steps in identifying mutant alleles controlling the synthesis of enzymes involved in amino acid production. Full details are given in the text. (The numbers on the diagram correspond with those in the text.)*

22.5.2 The genetic code

When Watson and Crick proposed the double helical structure for DNA in 1953 they also suggested that the genetic information which passed from generation to generation, and which determined cell metabolism, might reside in the sequence of bases of the DNA molecule. Once it had been demonstrated that DNA only specified the production of protein molecules it became clear that the DNA nucleotide base sequence must determine the amino acid sequence of protein molecules. This relationship between bases and amino acids is known as the **genetic code**. The problems remaining were to demonstrate that a nucleotide code existed, to break the code and determine how the code is translated into the amino acid sequence of a protein molecule.

22.5.3 The code

There are four nucleotide bases in the DNA molecule, **adenine** (A), **guanine** (G), **thymine** (T) and **cytosine** (C) (section 5.6). They are arranged as a polynucleotide strand that can be indicated by the initial letters of the bases. This 'alphabet' of four letters is responsible for carrying the code that results in the synthesis of a potentially infinite number of different protein molecules. If one base determined the position of a single amino acid in the primary structure of a protein, the protein could only contain four amino acids. If a combination of pairs of bases coded for each amino acid then 16 amino acids could be specified into the protein molecule.

22.3 Using different pairs of the bases A, G, T and C list the 16 possible combinations of bases that can be produced.

Only a code composed of three bases could incorporate all 20 amino acids into the structure of protein molecules. Such a code would produce 64 combinations of bases.

22.4 If four bases used singly would code for four amino acids, pairs of bases code for 16 amino acids and triplets of bases code for 64 amino acids, deduce a mathematical expression to explain this situation.

Evidence for the existence of a **triplet code** was provided by Francis Crick in 1961 by producing mutations involving the addition or deletion of bases in T$_4$ phages. These additions and deletions which produced **frame-shifts** in the code, as shown in fig 22.20, were expressed in T$_4$ phages as mutations. These frame-shifts produced base triplet sequences which failed to result in the synthesis of protein molecules with the original amino acid sequence (primary structure). Only by adding a base and deleting a base at specific points could the original base code sequence be restored. Restoring the original base sequence prevented the appearance of mutants in the experimental T$_4$ phages. These experiments also demonstrated that the code is **non-overlapping**, that is to say, each triplet is discrete. No base of a given triplet contributes to part of the code of the adjacent triplet (fig 22.21).

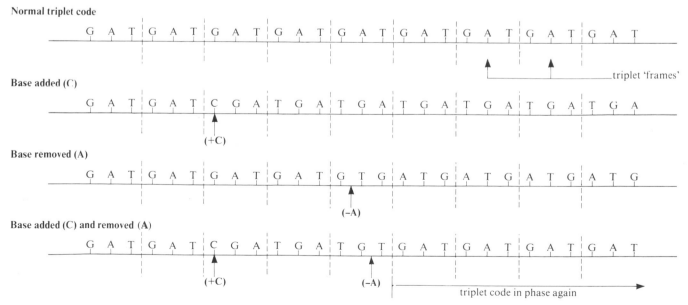

Fig 22.20 *Diagrammatic explanation of the effect of adding and deleting bases to the triplet code. The addition of the base C produces a frame shift which makes the original message GAT, GAT, . . . read as TGA, TGA, . . . The deletion of the base A produces a frame shift changing the original message from GAT, GAT, . . . to ATG, ATG, . . . The addition of the base C at the point indicated and the deletion of the base A at the point indicated restores the original message GAT, GAT. (After F. H. C. Crick (1962) The genetic code I, Scientific American Offprint No. 123, Wm. Saunders & Co.)*

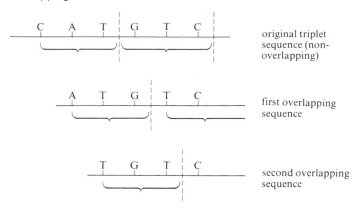

original triplet sequence (non-overlapping)

first overlapping sequence

second overlapping sequence

22.5 Using repeated sequences of the triplet GTA and the base C show that the sequence of triplets can only be restored by adding or deleting three bases. (Set out your answer as shown in fig 22.20.)

22.5.4 Breaking the code

In order to understand the experimental procedures used to determine which triplet base sequence codes for which amino acid (that is, break the genetic code) it is necessary to appreciate, in outline, the mechanism by which the triplet code is translated into the structure of a protein molecule.

Protein synthesis involves the interaction of two types of nucleic acid, deoxyribonucleic acid, DNA and ribonucleic acid, RNA. There are three kinds of RNA: messenger RNA (**mRNA**), ribosomal RNA (**rRNA**) and transfer RNA (**tRNA**). Apart from a number of organelles such as mitochondria and chloroplasts, DNA is confined to the nucleus where its base sequence is copied (**transcribed**) on to strands of messenger RNA (mRNA) which leave the nucleus. These become attached to ribosomes in the cytoplasm where the base sequence of mRNA is **translated** into an amino acid sequence. Specific amino acids become attached to tRNA molecules which link up with complementary triplet bases on the mRNA. Adjacent amino acids brought together in this way react together to form a polypeptide chain. The process of protein synthesis, therefore, depends upon the presence of DNA, mRNA, ribosomes, tRNA, amino acids, ATP as an energy source and various enzymes and cofactors which catalyse each stage in the process.

Nirenberg used this information and various research techniques which had been developed during the late 1950s and designed a series of experiments to break the code. The essence of his experiments involved using a known base sequence of mRNA as a coded message and analysing the amino acid sequence of the polypeptide chain produced from it. Nirenberg was able to synthesise a mRNA molecule that consisted of the same triplet (UUU)

repeated many times. This was called **polyuridylic acid** (poly-U) and acted as a code. A series of 20 test-tubes was prepared, each containing cell-free extracts of *E. coli* including ribosomes, tRNA, ATP, enzymes and a different radioactive labelled amino acid. Poly-U was added to each test-tube and left to allow in vitro synthesis of polypeptides to occur. Analysis of the contents of the test-tubes showed that a polypeptide had been formed only in the test-tube containing the amino acid phenylalanine. Thus the genetic code had been partly solved. Nirenberg had shown that the base triplet of the mRNA, or **codon**, UUU, determines the position of phenylalanine in a polypeptide chain. Nirenberg and his co-workers then set about preparing synthetic polynucleotide molecules of all 64 possible codons and by 1964 had translated the codes for all 20 amino acids (table 22.4).

As can be seen from table 22.4 some amino acids have several specified codons. This type of code where the number of amino acids is less than the number of codons is termed **degenerate**. Analysis of the code also shows that for many amino acids only the first letters appear to be significant. Three of the codons shown in table 22.4 act as 'full stops' in determining the end of the code message. These presumably mark the end-point of a functional unit of the DNA, a cistron. In all of these experiments involved in breaking the genetic code, mRNA was used as the source of triplet bases. The 'genetic code', however, is transmitted from cell to cell and between generations by the triplet base sequence of DNA. Since mRNA is formed directly on the DNA polynucleotide strand by the method of complementary base pairing, the inheritable DNA genetic code is the complement of the mRNA code. This code can be obtained by translating the RNA bases into their complementary DNA bases according to the rules shown in table 22.5.

22.6 Write out the base sequence of mRNA formed from a DNA strand with the following sequence

A T G T T C G A G T A C C A T G T A A C G

One of the remarkable features of the genetic code is that it is thought to be universal. All living organisms contain the same 20 common amino acids and the same five nitrogenous bases, A, G, T, C and U. Nirenberg demonstrated that introducing mRNA from species A into a cell-free system from species B produced the same polypeptide as would normally be produced in species A. For example, mammalian haemoglobin molecules have been synthesised in cell-free extracts of *E. coli* supplied with mammalian haemoglobin mRNA.

Certain codons act as 'start signals' for the initiation of polypeptide chains, such as AUG (methionine), whereas others, such as UAA, are 'nonsense' codons and do not code for amino acids but act as 'stop signals' for the termination of polypeptide chains.

Table 22.4. The base sequences of the triplet code and the amino acids for which they code

NB These are **codons**, i.e. base sequences of mRNA and not DNA. The DNA genetic code would have complementary bases and T would replace U.

	Second base				
First base	**U**	**C**	**A**	**G**	**Third base**
U	UUU ⎱ phe / UUC ⎰ UUA ⎱ leu / UUG ⎰	UCU / UCC / UCA / UCG ⎫ ser	UAU ⎱ tyr / UAC ⎰ UAA c.t.* UAG c.t.*	UGU ⎱ cys / UGC ⎰ UGA c.t.* UGG trp	U C A G
C	CUU / CUC / CUA / CUG ⎫ leu	CCU / CCC / CCA / CCG ⎫ pro	CAU ⎱ his / CAC ⎰ CAA ⎱ gln / CAG ⎰	CGU / CGC / CGA / CGG ⎫ arg	U C A G
A	AUU ⎱ AUC ⎰ ileu AUA ⎰ AUG met	ACU / ACC / ACA / ACG ⎫ thr	AAU ⎱ asn / AAC ⎰ AAA ⎱ lys / AAG ⎰	AGU ⎱ ser / AGC ⎰ AGA ⎱ arg / AGG ⎰	U C A G
G	GUU / GUC / GUA / GUG ⎫ val	GCU / GCC / GCA / GCG ⎫ ala	GAU ⎱ asp / GAC ⎰ GAA ⎱ glu / GAG ⎰	GGU / GGC / GGA / GGG ⎫ gly	U C A G

*c.t., chain termination codon, equivalent to a full stop in the message.

Table 22.5. The RNA bases which are complementary to those of DNA

DNA bases	Complementary RNA bases
A (adenine)	U (uracil)
G (guanine)	C (cytosine)
T (thymine)	A (adenine)
C (cytosine)	G (guanine)

Advances in molecular biology have reached the point now where it is becoming possible to determine the base sequences for whole genes, and the genetic code for an entire organism, the phage ΦX174, has been determined. This represented a major landmark and whole genes can now be synthesised artificially, a practice which is of use in genetic engineering (section 2.3.6).

The main features of the genetic code are summarised below.

(1) A **triplet** of bases in the polynucleotide chain of DNA is the code for the incorporation of one amino acid into a polypeptide chain.

(2) It is **universal**: the same triplets code for the same amino acids in all organisms.

(3) It is **degenerate**: a given amino acid may be coded for by more than one codon.

(4) It is **non-overlapping**: for example, an mRNA sequence beginning AUGAGCGCA is not read AUG/UGA/GAG . . . (an overlap of two bases) or AUG/GAG/GCG . . . (an overlap of one base). (However, recent studies have shown overlapping of certain genes in the bacteriophage ΦX174. This seems likely to be exceptional and may be an economy measure since it has very few genes.)

22.6 Protein synthesis

From the information given so far in this chapter it may be seen that the only molecules capable of being synthesised directly from the hereditary material of the cell are proteins. These may have a structural role, such as keratin and collagen, or a functional role, as in insulin, fibrinogen and most importantly enzymes, which are responsible for controlling cell metabolism. It is the particular range of enzymes in the cell which determines what type of cell it becomes. The 'instructions' for the manufacture of these enzymes and all other proteins are located in the DNA, which is generally confined to the nucleus; but, as was shown in the early 1950s, the actual synthesis occurs in the cytoplasm and involves ribosomes. This led to the realisation that a mechanism had to exist for carrying the genetic information from nucleus to cytoplasm. In 1961 two French biochemists, Jacob and Monod, postulated, on theoretical grounds, the existence of a specific form of RNA functioning as an intermediate molecule in the synthesis of protein. This compound was identified later as mRNA.

22.6.1   The role of RNA

RNA exists as a single-stranded molecule in all living cells. It differs from DNA in possessing the pentose sugar ribose instead of deoxyribose and the pyrimidine uracil instead of thymine. Analysis of the RNA content of cells has shown the existence of three types of RNA which are all involved in the synthesis of protein molecules. These are messenger RNA (mRNA), transfer RNA (tRNA) and ribosomal RNA (rRNA). All three types are synthesised directly on DNA, which is said to act as a template for RNA production, and the amount of RNA in each cell is directly related to the amount of protein synthesis.

22.6.2   Messenger RNA

Analyses of cells have shown that 3–5% of the total RNA of the cell is mRNA. This is a single-stranded molecule formed on a single strand of DNA by a process known as **transcription**. In the formation of mRNA only one strand of the DNA molecule is copied. As yet the mechanism determining which strand is to be copied has not been demonstrated. It may involve the activity of a promoter gene and operator gene (section 22.7.1). RNA nucleotides are attracted to the DNA strand according to the rules of base pairing and link up to form an mRNA polynucleotide strand under the influence of the enzyme **RNA-polymerase**. The base sequence of mRNA is a complementary copy of the template DNA strand and varies in length according to the length of the polypeptide chain for which it codes. The smallest mRNA molecule is approximately 300 nucleotide units long. Most mRNA exists within the cell for a short time. In the case of bacteria this may be a matter of minutes whereas mammalian reticulocytes, which lose their nuclei as they become red blood cells, may continue to produce haemoglobin for several days.

22.6.3   Ribosomal RNA

Ribosomal RNA was the first RNA to be identified, and it makes up approximately 80% of the total RNA of the cell. It is synthesised by genes present on the DNA of several chromosomes found within a region of the nucleolus known as the **nucleolar organiser**. The base sequence of rRNA is similar in all organisms from bacteria to higher plants and animals. It is found in the cytoplasm where it is associated with protein molecules which together form the cell organelles known as ribosomes (see section 7.2.6).

Ribosomes are the site of protein synthesis. Here the mRNA 'code' is **translated** into a sequence of amino acids in a growing polypeptide chain. Ribosomes are often found in clusters linked together by a strand of mRNA. This complex is known as a polyribosome or **polysome** and enables several molecules of the same polypeptide to be produced simultaneously.

22.6.4   Transfer RNA

The existence of transfer RNA (tRNA) (or soluble RNA (sRNA) as it is sometimes referred to) was postulated by Crick and demonstrated by Hoagland in 1955. Each amino acid has its own tRNA molecule which transfers amino acids present in the cytoplasm to the ribosome. Consequently it acts as an intermediate molecule between the triplet code of mRNA and the amino acid sequence of the polypeptide chain. It constitutes about 15% of the total RNA of the cell and, having on average 80 nucleotides per molecule, it is the smallest of all the RNAs. There are more than 20 different tRNA molecules (60 have so far been identified) carrying specific amino acids. All tRNA molecules have the same basic structure as shown in fig 22.22.

The 5′-end of the tRNA always ends in the base guanine whilst the 3′-end always ends in the base sequence of CCA. The nucleotide sequence of the rest of the molecule is variable and may include some 'unusual bases' such as inosine (I) and pseudouracil (ψ). The triplet base sequence at the anticodon (fig 22.22) is directly related to the amino acid carried by that tRNA molecule. Each amino acid is attached to its specific tRNA by its own form of the enzyme **amino-acyl-tRNA synthetase**. This produces an amino acid–tRNA complex with sufficient energy in the bond between the terminal A nucleotide (of CCA) and the amino acid to later form a peptide bond with the carboxyl group of the adjacent amino acid. In this way a polypeptide

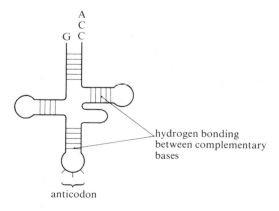

Fig 22.22 *A proposed model for the structure of transfer RNA (tRNA). The whole molecule is composed of 80 nucleotides but only 20 show complementary base pairing*

chain is synthesised. Experiments using ribosomes from rat liver cells in a cell-free extract of *E. coli* have shown that *E. coli* proteins can be manufactured despite the presence of 'foreign' ribosomes. This demonstrates the universal nature of coding mechanisms involving mRNA, tRNA and rRNA in the production of proteins.

22.6.5 The mechanism of protein synthesis

Information from various sources and involving a variety of experimental techniques carried out on a range of organisms from viruses to mammals has shown that protein synthesis is a two-stage process which may be summarised by fig 22.23.

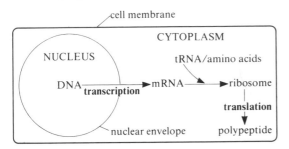

Fig 22.23 *Summary diagram of the main steps involved in protein synthesis*

22.6.6 Transcription

Transcription is the mechanism by which the base sequence of a cistron of a DNA strand is converted into the complementary base sequence of mRNA. The histone coat protecting the DNA double helix in the region of the cistron is thought to be stripped away, exposing the polynucleotide sequences of the DNA molecule. The double helix unwinds by breakage of the relatively weak hydrogen bonds between the bases of complementary strands exposing single strands of DNA. By some mechanism, as yet not understood, one of these strands is selected as a **template** for the formation of a complementary single strand of mRNA. This molecule is formed by the linking of free ribonucleotides under the influence of RNA polymerase and according to the rules of base pairing between DNA and RNA (table 22.5 and fig 22.24).

The exact nature of the copying of DNA bases into RNA bases has been demonstrated using synthetic DNA composed solely of thymine nucleotides (TTT). When introduced into a cell-free system containing RNA polymerase and all four nucleotides (A, U, C and G) the messenger RNA formed was composed entirely of adenine nucleotides.

When the mRNA molecules have been synthesised they leave the nucleus via the nuclear pores and carry the genetic code to the ribosomes. When sufficient numbers of mRNA molecules have been formed from the cistron the RNA polymerase molecule leaves the DNA, the two strands 'zip' up re-forming the double helix and the protective protein coat is added again.

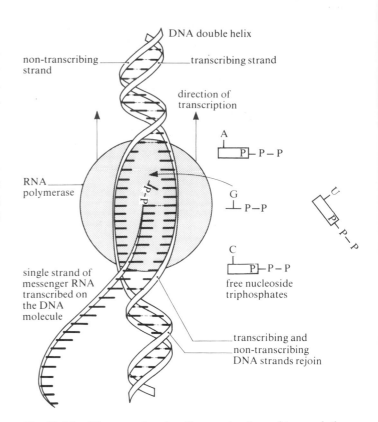

Fig 22.24 *Diagram showing the mechanism of transcription. In the presence of RNA polymerase the DNA double helix unwinds by breakage of the hydrogen bonds between complementary bases, and a polynucleotide strand of mRNA is formed from free RNA nucleoside triphosphates which link up opposite complementary DNA bases on the transcribing strand of template DNA. (After E. J. Ambrose & D. M. Easty (1977) Cell biology, 2nd ed., Nelson.)*

22.6.7 Translation

Translation is the mechanism by which the triplet base sequences of mRNA molecules are converted into a specific sequence of amino acids in a polypeptide chain. This occurs on ribosomes. Several ribosomes may become attached to a molecule of mRNA like beads on a string and the whole structure is known as a **polysome**. These structures, which can be seen under the electron microscope (fig 22.25) have a common strand with a diameter of 1.5 nm. This is the diameter of a single strand of mRNA. The advantage of such a complex is that it allows several polypeptides to be synthesised simultaneously (section 22.6.3). Each ribosome is composed of a small and a large subunit, resembling a 'cottage loaf' (fig 7.18). Messenger RNA is thought to form a reversible attachment to the surface of the small subunit in the presence of magnesium ions (Mg^{2+}). Having become attached to the ribosome it is thought that two mRNA codons are exposed to the larger ribosome subunit. The first codon binds the tRNA molecule having the complementary anticodon and which is carrying the first amino acid (usually methionine) of the polypeptide being synthesised. The second codon then attracts a tRNA–amino acid

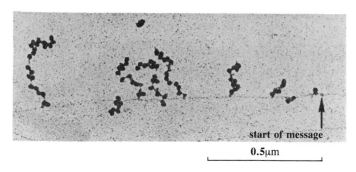

start of message

0.5μm

(b)

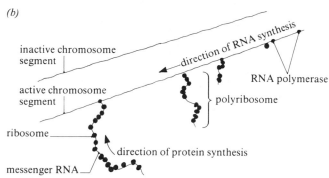

inactive chromosome segment

direction of RNA synthesis

active chromosome segment

RNA polymerase

polyribosome

ribosome

direction of protein synthesis

messenger RNA

Fig 22.25 *Transcription and formation of a polysome in bacteria. (a) Electron micrograph of a chromosome segment showing stages in the development of mRNA and the attachment of ribosomes. (b) Diagrammatic representation of the structure shown in the electron micrograph in (a)*

complex showing the complementary anticodon (figs 22.26*a* and *b*). The function of the ribosome is to hold in position the mRNA, tRNA and the associated enzymes controlling the process until a peptide bond forms between the adjacent amino acids.

Once the new amino acid has been added to the growing polypeptide chain the ribosome moves along the mRNA to enclose a new codon. The tRNA molecule which was previously attached to the polypeptide chain now leaves the ribosome and passes back to the cytoplasm to be reconverted into a new tRNA–amino acid complex (fig 22.26*c*).

This sequence of the ribosome steadily 'reading' and 'translating' the mRNA code continues until it comes to a codon signalling 'stop'. These terminating codons are UAA, UAG and UGA. At this point the polypeptide chain, now with its primary structure as determined by the DNA cistron, leaves the ribosome and translation is complete. The main steps involved in translation may be summarised under the following headings:
(1) binding of mRNA to ribosome,
(2) amino acid activation and attachment to tRNA,
(3) polypeptide chain initiation,
(4) chain elongation,
(5) chain termination,
(6) fate of mRNA,
and the process is summarised in fig 22.27.

As the polypeptide chains leave the ribosome they may immediately assume either secondary, tertiary or quaternary structures (section 5.5.3).

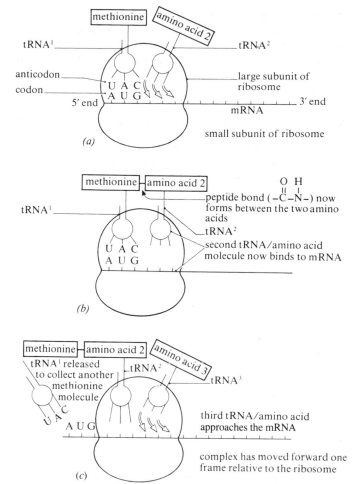

Fig 22.26 *(a) and (b) Consecutive stages in the attachment of tRNA/amino acid complexes by their anticodons to the codons on mRNA and the formation of a peptide bond between adjacent amino acids. (c) The relative movements of mRNA and ribosome exposing a new triplet (frame) for the attachment of the tRNA/amino acid complex. The initial tRNA molecule is now released from the ribosome and cycles back into the cytoplasm to be reactivated by enzymes to form a new tRNA/amino acid complex*

Evidence that it is the complementary base pairing between the mRNA codon and the tRNA anticodon which determines the incorporation of an amino acid into the polypeptide chain, and not the amino acid, was demonstrated by the following experiment. The tRNA–cysteine complex normally pairs up, via its anticodon ACA, with the mRNA codon UGU. Exposure of this tRNA–cysteine complex to a catalyst, Raney nickel, converted the cysteine to the amino acid alanine. When the new tRNA–alanine complex (carrying the tRNA–cysteine anticodon) was placed in a cell-free system containing poly-UGU–mRNA the polypeptide chain formed contained only alanine. This experiment demonstrated the importance of the role of the mRNA-codon–tRNA-anticodon mechanism in translating the genetic code.

The whole sequence of protein synthesis occurs as a continuous process and is summarised in fig 22.28.

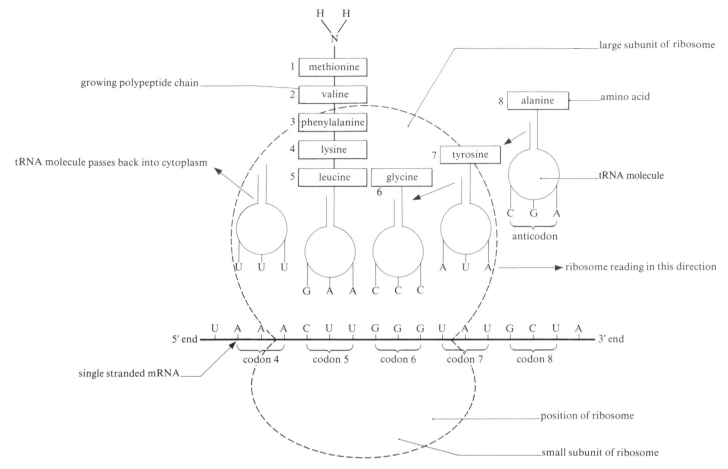

Fig 22.27 *Diagrammatic representation of translation. The anticodon of each specific tRNA/amino acid complex pairs with its complementary bases of the mRNA codon in the ribosome. In the example above a peptide bond would form between leucine and glycine and in this way an additional amino acid would be added to the growing polypeptide chain*

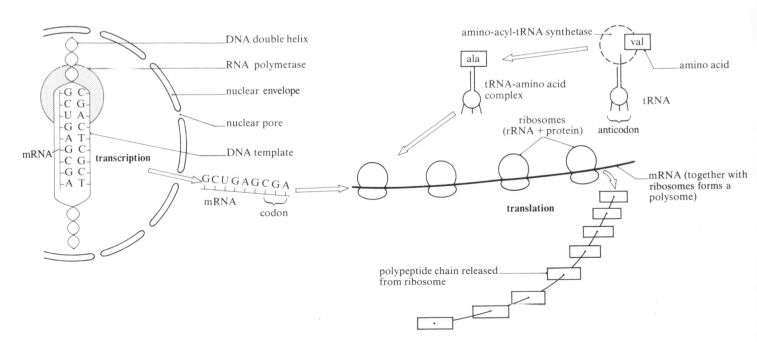

Fig 22.28 *Simplified summary diagram of the major structures and processes involved in protein synthesis in the cell*

22.7 Genetic control

In this chapter the mechanisms whereby cells transfer genetic material from generation to generation have been described. The structure and methods of functioning of the genetic material are now known in considerable detail, but there are still many areas of genetics where there are many questions and few answers. Genetic research has come a long way in the last 30 years and produced many answers to fundamental questions. The major breakthroughs were undoubtedly the discovery of the structure of DNA and the breaking of the genetic code. Both of these provided inspiration and incentive to other scientists to delve deeper into understanding the apparent mysteries of molecular genetics. Most of these unsolved problems which face molecular geneticists are concerned with the mechanisms by which gene activity is controlled in the processes of metabolism, development and differentiation.

Classical genetics has demonstrated that all somatic cells of an organism carry the same genetic complement, that is they contain the same number of chromosomes carrying the same alleles. Despite this, cells in a multicellular organism show wide variation in structure and function. Even within a single cell the rate at which certain protein molecules are synthesised varies according to circumstances and demand. Evidence for the mechanism by which genes are regulated within the cell was first obtained from studies into the control of enzyme synthesis in *E. coli*.

In 1961 Jacob and Monod carried out a series of experiments to investigate the nature of induction of enzyme synthesis in *E. coli*. Of the 800 enzymes thought to be synthesised by *E. coli* some are synthesised continuously and are called **constitutive enzymes**; others are synthesised only in the presence of an inducer compound, which may not be the substrate, and are called **inducible enzymes**. One of the latter enzymes is called β-**galactosidase**.

E. coli will grow rapidly on a culture medium containing glucose. When transferred to a medium containing lactose instead of glucose it will not grow immediately but after a short delay begins to show the same growth rate as seen on a glucose medium. Investigations revealed that growth on lactose medium required the presence of two substances not normally synthesised, called β-galactosidase, which hydrolyses lactose to glucose and galactose, and **lactose permease**, which enables the cell to take up lactose. This is an example of where a change in environmental conditions, lactose instead of glucose, has induced the synthesis of a particular enzyme. Other experiments involving *E. coli* showed that high concentrations of the amino acid **tryptophan** in the culture medium suppressed the production of the enzyme **tryptophan synthetase** used to synthesise tryptophan. β-galactosidase synthesis is an example of **enzyme induction**, whereas the suppression of tryptophan synthetase is an example of **enzyme repression**. On the basis of these observations and experiments, Jacob and Monod proposed a mechanism to account for induction and repression, the mechanism by which genes are 'switched on and off'.

22.7.1 The Jacob–Monod hypothesis of genetic control

The genetic blueprint determining the amino acid sequence of the proteins described above is located on **structural genes**, those for β-galactosidase and lactose permease being closely linked on the same chromosome. The activity of these genes is controlled by another gene called a **regulator gene** which is thought to prevent the structural genes from becoming active. This may be situated some distance from the structural genes. Evidence for the existence of a regulator gene comes from studies of mutant *E. coli* which lack this gene and as a consequence produce β-galactosidase continuously. The regulator gene carries the genetic code which results in the production of a **repressor molecule** that prevents the structural genes from being active. The repressor molecule does not directly affect the structural genes but is thought to influence a gene immediately adjacent to the structural genes known as the

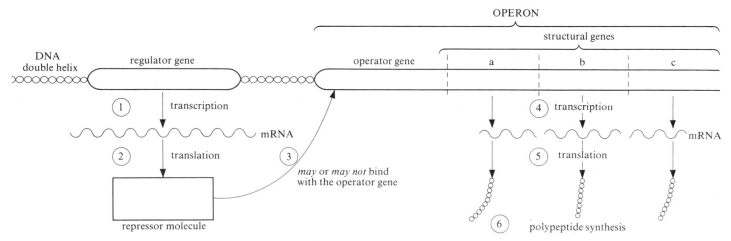

Fig 22.29 *The basic structures and processes involved in the control of protein synthesis according to the hypothesis produced by Jacob and Monod. The numbers indicate the sequence of events*

operator gene. The operator and structural genes are collectively known as the **operon** (fig 22.29).

The repressor molecule is thought to be a particular type of protein known as an **allosteric protein** which can either bind with the operator gene and suppress its activity ('switch it off') or not bind and permit the operator gene to become active ('switch it on'). When the operator gene is 'switched on' the structural genes carry out transcription and mRNA is formed which the ribosomes and tRNA translate into polypeptides. When the operator gene is 'switched off' no mRNA is formed and no polypeptides are formed (fig 22.29).

The mechanism controlling whether or not the allosteric protein binds to the operator gene is simple, yet sensitive to varying intracellular conditions. It is thought that the repressor molecule has at least two active sites to which either an inducer molecule or a co-repressor molecule may become attached, depending upon their relative concentrations at any given time, as described in section 22.7.4.

22.7.2 Enzyme induction

The binding of an inducer molecule to its active site on the repressor molecule alters the tertiary structure of the repressor (allosteric effect) (section 6.6) so that it cannot bind with the operator gene and repress it.

The operator gene becomes active and 'switches on' the structural genes.

In the case of *E. coli* grown on glucose medium, the regulator gene produces a repressor substance which combines with the operator gene and switches it 'off'. The structural genes are not activated and no β-galactosidase and lactose permease are produced. When transferred to a lactose medium the lactose is thought to act as an inducer of protein synthesis by combining with the repressor molecule and preventing it combining with the operator gene. The structural genes become active, mRNA is produced and proteins are synthesised. Lactose is thus an inducer of its own breakdown (fig 22.30).

22.7.3 Enzyme repression

If a co-repressor molecule binds with its active site on the repressor molecule it reinforces the normal binding response of the repressor molecule with the operator gene. This inactivates the operator gene which, in effect, prevents the structural genes from being 'switched on'.

E. coli synthesises the amino acid tryptophan in the presence of the enzyme tryptophan synthetase. When the cell contains an excess of tryptophan some of it acts as a co-repressor of enzyme synthesis by combining with the

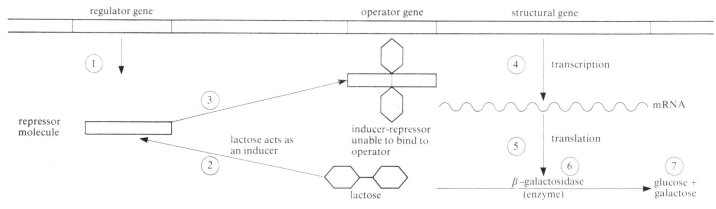

Fig 22.30 (above) *The method of induction of β-galactosidase synthesis according to the Jacob–Monod hypothesis. The numbers indicate the sequence of events*

Fig 22.31 (below) *The mechanism of repression of tryptophan synthetase synthesis according to the Jacob–Monod hypothesis. The numbers indicate the sequence of events. Solid lines indicate actual processes. The dotted lines represent repressed stages*

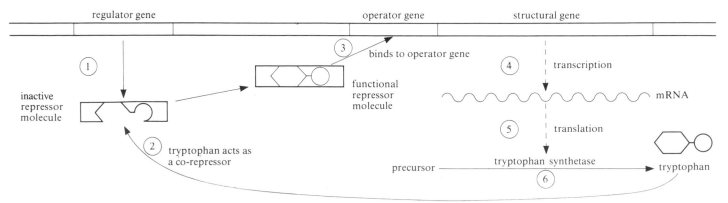

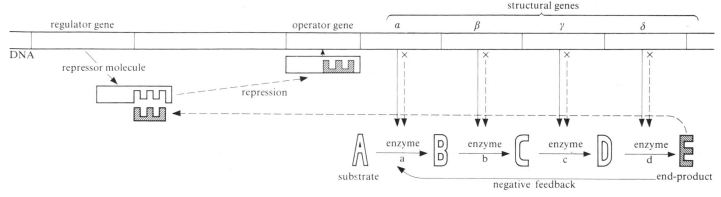

Fig 22.32 *Mechanisms of control of the metabolic pathways A→E. The solid lines represent the mechanism operating during negative feedback. The dotted lines represent the mechanisms operating during repression. X represents blocks in the enzyme synthesis*

repressor molecule. Co-repressor and repressor molecules combine with the operator gene and inhibit its activity. The structural genes are 'switched off', no mRNA is produced and no further tryptophan synthetase is synthesised. This is an example of feedback inhibition acting at the gene level (fig 22.31).

22.7.4 Control of metabolic pathways

This dual mechanism enables the cytoplasm and nucleus to interact in a delicate control of cell metabolism. In the case of a simple metabolic pathway as shown in fig 22.32 the initial substrate and final product can act as inducer and co-repressor respectively. This mechanism enables the cell to produce the amount of enzyme required at any given time to maintain the correct level of product. This method of metabolic control is highly economical. Negative feedback involving the inactivation of the initial enzyme (*a*) by combination with the end-product (*E*) would rapidly halt the pathway but would not prevent the continued synthesis of the other enzymes (*b*, *c* and *d*). In the system proposed by Jacob and Monod, the end-product (*E*), by combining with the repressor molecule to increase its repressive effect on the operator gene, would prevent the synthesis of all enzymes (*a*, *b*, *c* and *d*) and halt the pathway.

22.7.5 Modification to the 'operon' hypothesis

Since 1961 when Jacob and Monod suggested a mechanism by which genes are 'switched on and off', further evidence has accumulated which has helped to clarify aspects of the mechanism. Genetic evidence has suggested the existence of a **promoter gene** situated adjacent to the operator gene which acts between it and the regulator gene. It is thought to have two functions. First the promoter gene is the site to which RNA polymerase binds before moving along the DNA to begin the transcription of mRNA on the structural genes. This movement will, of course, depend upon whether the operator gene is

'operational' or not. Secondly, the base sequence of the promoter gene determines which strand of the DNA double helix attracts the RNA polymerase. In this way the promoter gene determines which strand of the DNA double helix acts as the template for mRNA transcription.

22.8 The genetic control of development

The life cycle of the majority of multicellular animals and plants begins with a single cell, the zygote. This undergoes repeated mitotic and cytoplasmic divisions to give rise to a complex and highly differentiated organism. This process is known as **growth and development** and includes the process of **differentiation**. Differentiation, that is the process whereby cells assume particular structures which enable them to carry out a restricted number of particular functions more efficiently, is one of the remarkable events of development. Why should the cells of an organism produced by repeated cell divisions and containing identical genetic material show the range of diversity which typifies higher multicellular organisms? The answer is far from clear but must involve the induction and repression of genes, perhaps by mechanisms similar to those described in the previous section. Evidence has suggested that there are three factors which act together in various ways to bring about differentiation. They are the nucleus, the cytoplasm and the environment.

22.8.1 The role of the nucleus

The importance of the nucleus as the storage site of the genetic material and its primary role in determining phenotypic characteristics has been appreciated for a long time. The German biologist Hammerling was one of the earliest workers to demonstrate the primary role of the nucleus. He chose as his research organism the unusually large acellular marine alga *Acetabularia*. There are two closely related species, *A. mediterranea* and *A. crenulata*, which differ only in the shape of their 'head' region (fig 22.33).

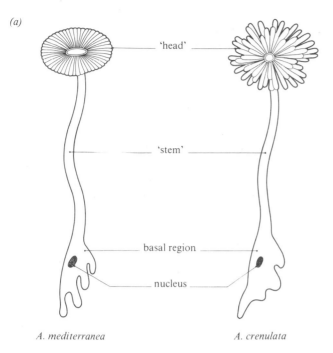

(a)

'head'

'stem'

basal region

nucleus

A. mediterranea

A. crenulata

Fig 22.33 *The marine alga* Acetabularia *used by Hammerling to demonstrate the role of the nucleus. (a) Two species of* Acetabularia. *(b) Transplant and excision experiments carried out by Hammerling*

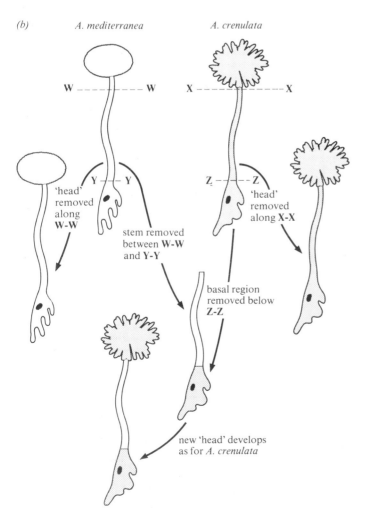

(b)

A. mediterranea

A. crenulata

W ———— W   X ———— X

Y — Y   Z — Z

'head' removed along **W-W**

'head' removed along **X-X**

stem removed between **W-W** and **Y-Y**

basal region removed below **Z-Z**

new 'head' develops as for *A. crenulata*

In a series of experiments, including some that involved separating the 'head' region from the 'basal' region (which contained the nucleus), he was able to demonstrate the necessity of the nucleus for normal development. Further experiments involving the reciprocal grafting of the nucleus-containing 'basal' region of one species to the enucleate stalk region of the other species always produced hybrids that developed the 'head' which was characteristic of the nucleate portion of the graft.

However, in considering this model of nuclear control, due regard must be taken of the primitive nature of the organism used. Later experiments performed by two American scientists, Briggs and King, in 1952, made use of the technique of grafting but in this case they used cells from the frog *Rana pipiens*. The nuclei were removed from unfertilised egg cells and replaced with nuclei from late blastula cells which showed signs of differentiation. In most cases the recipient cells developed and grew into normal adult frogs.

22.7 What did the results of the above experiments demonstrate?

22.8.2 The role of the cytoplasm

Further evidence for the role of the cytoplasm is provided by embryological studies. From an early stage in the embryological development of many organisms from algae to mammals the egg cytoplasm is not homogeneous. The cytoplasm appears to be stratified, with less dense material at the upper pole and dense granular material at the lower pole. In those species, where the early cleavage planes are vertical, such as amphibia, all resulting cells, if separated, give rise to normal offspring. In other species where early cleavage planes are horizontal, such as molluscs, the cells, if separated, do not undergo normal development. In the former case all cells contain an equal distribution of the different layers of cytoplasm, whereas in the latter there is an unequal distribution of cytoplasm. Eggs where the cytoplasm is differentiated in this way in order to give rise to certain regions of the embryo are known as **mosaic eggs**. In all cases the nuclei of the cells contain the same genetic complement. Differential developments would therefore appear to result from some form of cytoplasmic influence on the genes.

In a series of now classic embryological experiments, Spemann and Mangold demonstrated in 1924 that differentiation is largely controlled by the cytoplasmic influence which one cell type has over another. In one of their experiments, they removed tissue from the dorsal lip of the blastopore of an amphibian gastrula (fig 22.34) and implanted it into a ventral region of another gastrula (the host). The cells of the dorsal lip normally develop into the notochord, mesodermal somites (myotomes) and neural tube. The host gastrula in this experiment developed a secondary notochord, extra myotomes and a neural tube in

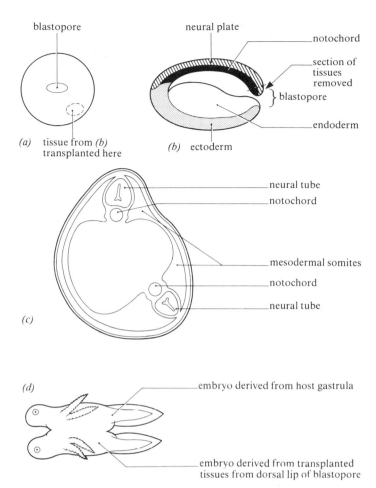

(a) tissue from (b) transplanted here

(b) ectoderm

(c)

neural tube
notochord

mesodermal somites
notochord
neural tube

(d)

embryo derived from host gastrula

embryo derived from transplanted tissues from dorsal lip of blastopore

Fig 22.34 *Technique and results of Spemann and Mangold's experiments on embryonic induction. (a) Surface view of the developing gastrula showing the blastopore. (b) LS through gastrula of an amphibian showing the region of the dorsal lip of the blastopore which is excised and transplanted into gastrula (a). (c) TS through the developing embryo showing the development of two identical groups of embryological tissues. (d) 'Siamese' embryos produced by transplanting tissue from the dorsal lip of the blastopore*

the region of the transplant which gave rise to a second tadpole as shown in fig 22.34.

On the basis of these observations Spemann and Mangold advanced a hypothesis of differentiation known as **embryonic induction**. According to this hypothesis certain cells act as **organisers** of other cells described as **competent** (or **determined**). Organisers are capable of inducing competent cells to develop into cell types having a structure and function different from those which would appear in the absence of organisers. These misplaced structures are described as **atopic** (*a*, without; *topos*, place).

In the embryological development of organisms a certain region known as the **primary organiser** determines the entire further course of development. In the case of amphibia this is the dorsal lip of the blastopore, whereas in birds it is a region known as the primitive streak. These primary organisers establish the **embryonic axis** and induce

other tissues to act as secondary and tertiary organisers and so on until all the organs and organ systems of the embryo have differentiated and developed in their normal positions.

22.8.3 The nature of the organiser

Experiments have been carried out involving the removal of a tissue known to act as an organiser and placing it on a piece of agar for several hours. Implantation of the agar into regions known to be competent has induced them to differentiate as directed by the organiser tissue. This technique demonstrates that the organiser is a chemical substance which has diffused into the agar. Attempts to isolate the substance have so far produced no clear-cut result. Steroids, proteins and nucleic acids have all been suggested as likely organiser substances. Paul and Gilmour have observed that DNA molecules in different tissues are differentially 'coated' with histone and non-histone proteins. They suggest that histones 'cover' those regions of the DNA which are non-functional, that is their genes are irreversibly repressed, whilst non-histone proteins 'cover' those genes which are to be transcribed. This idea fits in well with the situation in mosaic eggs where a distribution of histones throughout the cytoplasm would lead to the production of cells with different regions of DNA 'blocked off'. In this way various genes would be effectively 'switched off' in different cells and this would provide a possible mechanism of differentiation.

22.8.4 The role of the environment

It is largely as a result of experiments such as those of Jacob and Monod that the extent of environmental influence can be seen on development. For example, lactose is an environmental factor that has a direct influence on the functioning of genes in *E. coli*. Light, temperature, water, nutrients and gas supplies can all influence the extent of development and growth in plants and animals as described in chapters 9, 10, 15, 16 and 21. The effect of the environment on differentiation is probably normally through an intermediate influence on the cytoplasm which in turn has a direct effect on the genes.

22.8.5 The role of genes in development

The relationship between specific regions of the DNA molecule and morphological development has been studied extensively in organisms possessing **giant chromosomes**. These are found, for example in the salivary glands of many dipteran larvae, including *Drosophila*. The reasons for the size of these **polytene chromosomes** are given in section 23.5.1. They are relatively easy to see under the light microscope and show distinct banding patterns when stained with Feulgen stain. During metamorphosis the *Drosophila* larvae pass through several stages, or instars, each separated by a period of intense cellular activity called ecdysis followed by moulting of the

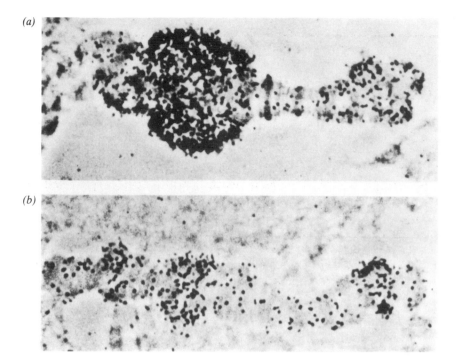

Fig 22.35 *The relationship between puffing and mRNA synthesis is clearly demonstrated by these autoradiograms of chromosome IV of the midge* Chironomus tentans. *The black dots indicate the position of radioactive uridine taken up during mRNA synthesis. (a) shows that RNA synthesis is closely related to the region of puffing. (b) Very little puffing and uridine uptake has occurred following the addition of small amounts of actinomycin D which inhibits mRNA synthesis. (From W. Beerman & U. Clever (1964) Chromosome puffs, Scientific American Offprint No. 180. Wm. Saunders & Co)*

old cuticle. The final two ecdyses are the most dramatic and produce the pupal stage and the imago (adult) stage. These are stages of intense metabolic activity and differentiation. Metamorphosis is controlled by hormones as described in section 21.4. During metamorphosis 'bands' along the chromosomes enlarge and form structures known as **chromosome puffs** or **rings of Balbiani** (after the scientist who first observed them in 1890). Specific stains which show up RNA, and autoradiographic studies involving labelled RNA nucleotides have shown these 'puffs' to be regions of RNA synthesis. The size of the 'puffs' has also been shown to be directly related to the rate of RNA synthesis. The puffing effect is thought to be produced by the unwinding of DNA molecules, the separation of complementary strands and the formation of mRNA during transcription.

There is a definite sequence of puffing during metamorphosis and this is induced by the moulting hormone ecdysone. During the various larval stages and the pupal stage different regions of the chomosomes show 'puffing', suggesting that the puffs correspond to the structural genes postulated in the Jacob–Monod hypothesis. Evidence that regions of puffing correspond to regions of genetic activity was produced by Beerman using two species of midge belonging to the genus *Chironomus*. Certain cells in the salivary gland of one species are granulated whereas those of the other species are non-granulated. Genetic mapping based upon crosses between these two species has shown that the alleles determining these characteristics are situated near the centromere of one of the chromosomes and the allele for granulated cells is dominant. Examination of the chromosomes of these species showed that puffing is only seen in the region where this gene is located in the species producing granulated cells. Furthermore, in the case of midges which are heterozygous for this

characteristic, puffing at this locus is only seen in the chromosome carrying the dominant allele.

Further evidence for the link between chromosome puffs and mRNA synthesis is provided by the effect of injecting the drug actinomycin D into organisms having giant chromosomes. Actinomycin D inhibits transcription by preventing the synthesis of mRNA, and no puffing is seen in organisms treated in this way (fig 22.35).

Another factor influencing growth and development in plants and animals is hormones. In many cases this occurs at the level of transcription of mRNA. The exact way in which a given hormone affects transcription and protein synthesis is extremely variable, but some are thought to exert their influence on receptor sites on the cell membrane. Following binding of the hormone on to the receptor site, thought to be the enzyme **adenylate cyclase**, cyclic AMP is released into the cytoplasm and this acts as a second messenger which induces transcription. Further details of this mechanism are described in section 16.6.1.

This chapter has attempted to describe some of the processes associated with the continuity of life. Living systems appear to require both short-term genetic stability and long-term genetic flexibility. Genetic stability is seen to be achieved by the mechanisms of mitosis, whereas the mechanisms of meiosis introduce an enormous amount of genetic variation, enabling organisms to adapt to changing environment.

Having established the cytological mechanisms of inheritance, research has shifted to considerations of the nature of the genetic material and the mechanisms involved in its control of cellular activities such as development, growth and differentiation. The next chapter describes the ways in which characteristics are inherited, the rules governing these processes and the way variations are introduced into populations.

Chapter Twenty-three

Variation and genetics

Genetics may rightly be claimed to be one of the most important branches of biology. For thousands of years, Man has used the techniques of genetics in the improvement of domestic animals and crops without having any real knowledge of the mechanisms which underlie these practices. Various pieces of archaeological evidence dating back 6 000 years suggest that Man understood that certain physical characteristics could be transmitted from one generation to another. By selecting particular organisms from wild stocks and interbreeding these, Man has been able to produce improved varieties of plants and animals to suit his needs.

It is only since the beginning of this century, though, that scientists have begun to appreciate fully the principles and mechanisms of heredity. Whilst advances in microscopy have revealed that the sperm and the ova transmitted the hereditary characteristics from generation to generation, the problem nevertheless remained of how minute particles of protoplasm could carry the vast number of characteristics that make up an individual organism.

The first really scientific advance in the study of inheritance was made by the Austrian monk Gregor Mendel who published a paper in 1866 which laid the foundations for the present-day science of genetics. He demonstrated that characteristics do not blend but pass from parents to offspring as discrete units. These units, which appear in the offspring in pairs, remain discrete and are passed on to subsequent generations by the male and female gametes which each contain a single unit. The Danish botanist Johannsen called these units **genes** in 1909, and the American geneticist Morgan, in 1912, demonstrated that they are carried on the chromosomes. Since the early 1900s the study of genetics has made great advances in explaining the nature of inheritance at both the level of the organism and at the level of the gene.

23.1 Mendel's work

Gregor Mendel was born in Moravia in 1822. In 1843 he joined an Augustinian monastery at Brünn in Austria (now Brno, in Czechoslovakia) where he took Holy Orders. From there he went to the University of Vienna where he spent two years studying natural history and mathematics before returning to the monastery in 1853. This choice of subjects undoubtedly had a significant influence on his subsequent work on inheritance in pea plants. Whilst in Vienna, Mendel had become interested in the process of hybridisation in plants and, in particular, the different forms in which hybrid progeny appear and the statistical relationships between them. This formed the basis of Mendel's scientific investigations on inheritance which he began in the summer of 1856.

Mendel's success was due, in part, to his careful choice of experimental organism, the garden pea, *Pisum sativum*. He ascertained that it had the following advantages over other species:
(1) There were several varieties available which had quite distinct characteristics.
(2) The plants were easy to cultivate.
(3) The reproductive structures were completely enclosed by the petals so that the plant was normally self-pollinating. This led to the varieties producing the same characteristics generation after generation, a phenomenon known as **pure breeding**.
(4) Artificial cross-breeding between varieties was possible and resulting hybrids were completely fertile. From the 34 varieties of garden pea, Mendel selected 22 varieties which showed clear-cut differences in characteristics and used these in his breeding experiments. The seven basic characteristics, or **traits**, that Mendel was interested in were length of stem, shape of seed, colour of seed, shape and colour of pod, position and colour of flower.

Many scientists before Mendel had performed similar experiments on plants but none had produced results which had the accuracy and detail of Mendel's, nor were they able to explain their results in terms of a mechanism of inheritance. The reasons for Mendel's success may be taken as a model of how to carry out a scientific investigation. They may be summarised as follows:
(1) Preliminary investigations were carried out to obtain familiarity with the experimental organism.
(2) All experiments were carefully planned so that attention was focussed on only one variable at any time, thus simplifying the observations to be made.
(3) Meticulous care was taken in carrying out all techniques, thus preventing the introduction of contaminating variables (see below for details).
(4) Accurate records were kept of all the experiments and the results obtained.
(5) Sufficient data were obtained to have statistical significance.
As Mendel stated,

'The value and utility of any experiment are

determined by the fitness of the material to the purpose for which it is used.'

However, it is worth stating that there was an element of luck in Mendel's choice of experimental organism. The characters chosen by Mendel lacked many of the more complex genetic features which were later discovered, such as incomplete dominance (section 23.7.1), characteristics controlled by more than one pair of genes (section 23.7.6) and linkage (section 23.3).

23.1.1 Monohybrid inheritance and the principle of segregation

Mendel's earliest experiments involved selecting plants of two varieties which had clearly differentiated characteristics, such as flowers distributed along the main stem (axial) or flowers at the tip of the stem (terminal). These plants, showing a single pair of contrasted characteristics, were grown for a number of generations. Seeds collected from axial plants always produced plants with axial flowers, whilst those from terminal plants always produced terminal flowers. This demonstrated to Mendel that he was using pure-breeding plants. With this information he was in a position to carry out hybridisation experiments (experimental crosses) using these plants. His experimental technique involved removing the anthers from a number of plants of one variety before self-fertilisation could have occurred. These he called 'female' plants. Pollen was then transferred, by means of a brush, from the anthers of another plant of the same variety to the stigmas of the 'female' plant. The experimental flowers were then enclosed in a small bag to prevent pollen from other plants reaching their stigmas. **Reciprocal crosses** were carried out by transferring pollen grains from axial plants to terminal plants and pollen grains from terminal plants to axial plants. In all cases the seeds subsequently collected from both sets of plants gave rise to plants with axial flowers. This characteristic, 'axial flower', shown by these first generation hybrid plants (subsequently called the **first filial generation** or F_1 **generation** by Bateson and Saunders in 1902) was termed **dominant** by Mendel. None of the F_1 plants produced terminal flowers.

The F_1 plants then had their flowers enclosed in bags (to prevent cross-pollination occurring) and were left to self-pollinate. The seeds collected from these F_1 plants were counted and planted the following spring to produce the **second filial generation** or F_2 **generation**. (An F_2 generation is always the result of allowing the F_1 generation to inbreed or, as in this case, to self-pollinate.) When these plants flowered, some bore axial flowers and others terminal flowers. In other words, the characteristic 'terminal flower', which was absent in the F_1 generation, had reappeared in the F_2 generation. Mendel reasoned that the terminal characteristic must have been present in the F_1 generation but as it failed to be expressed in this generation he termed it **recessive**. Of the 858 F_2 plants that Mendel obtained, 651 had axial flowers and 207 had terminal flowers. Mendel carried out a series of similar experiments involving in each case the inheritance of a single pair of contrasting characteristics. Seven pairs of contrasting characteristics were studied and the results of the experimental crosses are shown in table 23.1. In all cases the analyses of the results revealed that the ratios of dominant to recessive characteristics in the F_2 generation were approximately 3:1.

The example quoted above is typical of all Mendel's experiments involving the inheritance of a single characteristic (**monohybrid inheritance**) and may be summarised as follows.

Observations

Parents   axial flowers × terminal flowers
F_1 all axial flowers
F_2 651 axial flowers   207 terminal flowers
F_2 *ratio*   3   :   1

On the basis of these, and similar results, Mendel drew the following conclusions.

(1) Since the original parental stocks were pure breeding, the axial variety must have possessed *two* axial factors and the terminal variety *two* terminal factors.
(2) The F_1 generation possessed *one* factor from **each** parent which were carried by the gametes.
(3) These factors do not blend in the F_1 generation but retain their individuality.

Table 23.1 The results of Mendel's experiments on the inheritance of seven pairs of contrasted characteristics. (The observed ratio of dominant to recessive characteristics approximates to the theoretical value of 3:1.)

Characteristic	Parental appearance		F_2 appearance		Ratio
	(*dominant*)	(*recessive*)	(*dominant*)	(*recessive*)	
length of stem	tall	dwarf	787	277	2.84:1
shape of seed	round	wrinkled	5 474	1 850	2.96:1
colour of seed	yellow	green	6 022	2 001	3.01:1
shape of pod	inflated	constricted	882	299	2.95:1
colour of pod	green	yellow	428	152	2.82:1
position of flower	axial	terminal	651	207	3.14:1
colour of flower	red	white	705	224	3.15:1
total			14 949	5 010	2.98:1

(4) The axial factor is dominant to the terminal factor which is recessive.

The separation of the pair of parental factors, so that one factor is present in each gamete, became known as **Mendel's first law**, or the **principle of segregation**. This states that

> the characteristics of an organism are determined by internal factors which occur in pairs. Only one of a pair of such factors can be represented in a single gamete.

We now know that these factors determining characteristics, such as flower position, are regions of the chromosome known as **genes**.

The foregoing experimental procedure carried out by Mendel in the investigation of the inheritance of a *single* pair of contrasted characteristics is an example of a **monohybrid cross**. This may be represented in terms of symbols and placed in a modern context of gamete formation and fertilisation. By convention, the initial letter of the dominant characteristic is used as the genotypic symbol and its capital form (e.g. **A**) represents the dominant allele and the lower case (e.g. **a**) represents the recessive allele. All of the terms and symbols described above are used in genetics and arc summarised in table 23.2.

Fig 23.1 shows the correct way to describe a monohybrid cross or arrive at the solution to a genetics problem involving the inheritance of a single pair of contrasted characteristics.

The ratio of dominant phenotypes to recessive phenotypes of 3:1 is called the **monohybrid ratio**. Mendel's conclusions regarding the transfer of a single characteristic by each gamete and the genotypic appearance can be demonstrated by mathematical probability. The probability of a gamete cell from a heterozygous F_1 parent containing either the dominant allele **A** or the recessive allele **a** is 50% or $\frac{1}{2}$. If each gamete is represented by $\frac{1}{2}$, the

Let:

    A represent axial flower (dominant)
    a represent terminal flower (recessive)

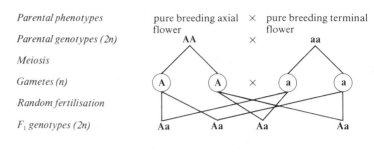

F_1 phenotypes   all heterozygous axial flower (the alleles **A** and **a** remain distinct in spite of the dominance of **A**)

The F_1 generation were self-pollinated

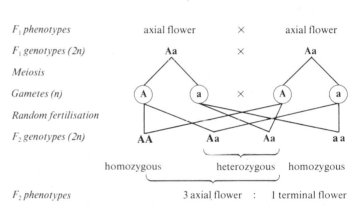

F_2 phenotypes   3 axial flower : 1 terminal flower

Fig 23.1 *Full genetic explanation of one of Mendel's monohybrid crosses. (2n represents the diploid condition, n represents the haploid condition; see section 22.3.)*

Table 23.2 Glossary of common genetic terms with examples based on fig 23.1.

Genetic term	Explanation	Example
gene	The basic unit of inheritance for a given characteristic	flower position
allele	Alternative forms of the same gene responsible for determining contrasting characteristics	**A** or **a**
locus	Position of an allele on a chromosome	
homozygous	The diploid condition where both alleles are identical	**AA** or **aa**
heterozygous	The diploid condition where different alleles are present	**Aa**
phenotype	The physical or chemical expression of a characteristic	axial, terminal
genotype	The genetic expression of a characteristic in terms of alleles	**AA, Aa, AA**
dominant	The allele which influences the appearance of the phenotype when present in the homozygous or heterozygous condition	**A**
recessive	The allele which only influences the appearance of the phenotype when present in the homozygous condition	**a**
F_1 generation	The generation produced by crossing two parental stocks	
F_2 generation	The generation produced by crossing two F_1 organisms	

number of possible combinations of F_2 genotypes is represented by $\frac{1}{2} \times \frac{1}{2} = \frac{1}{4}$. Hence there are four possible F_2 genotypes. The statistical probability of the **A** and **a** containing gametes combining by random fertilisation is shown in fig 23.2 As a result of dominance the phenotpyic appearance will be 3 dominant phenotypes : 1 recessive phenotype. The results of Mendel's breeding experiments bear out this theoretical ratio as shown in table 23.1.

Let the probability of the alleles **A** and **a** appearing in the heterozygote **(Aa)** = 1,
    therefore $A = \frac{1}{2}$
              $a = \frac{1}{2}$

Using these values the probability of each genotype and phenotype appearing in the F_2 generation can be demonstrated as shown below:

F_1 *genotypes (2n)*   **Aa**   ×   **Aa**

Meiosis

Gametes (n)   Ⓐ Ⓐ × Ⓐ Ⓐ

(In terms of probability)   (½)(½) × (½)(½)

Random fertilisation

F_2 *genotypes (2n)*   ¼ **AA**   ¼ **Aa** + ¼ **Aa**   ¼ **aa**

F_2 *phenotypes*   ¾ dominant: ¼ recessive
                     i.e. 3 dominant: 1 recessive

Fig 23.2 *Explanation of the 3:1 Mendelian monohybrid ratio in terms of probability*

23.1 If a pure strain of mice with brown-coloured fur are allowed to breed with a pure strain of mice with grey-coloured fur they produce offspring having brown-coloured fur. If the F_1 mice are allowed to interbreed they produce an F_2 generation with fur colour in the proportion of three brown-coloured to one grey.
(*a*) Explain fully these results.
(*b*) What would be the result of mating a brown-coloured heterozygote from the F_2 generation with the original grey-coloured parent?

23.1.2   Backcross or test cross

The genotype of an F_1 organism, produced by the breeding of homozygous dominant and homozygous recessive parents, is heterozygous but shows the dominant phenotype. An organism displaying the recessive phenotype must have a genotype which is homozygous for the recessive allele. In the case of F_2 organisms showing the dominant phenotype the genotype may be either homozygous or heterozygous. It may bc of interest to a breeder to know the genotype and the only way in which it can be determined is to carry out a breeding experiment. This involves the use of a technique known as **testcross** or **backcross**. By crossing an organism having an unknown genotype with a homozygous recessive organism it is possible to determine an unknown genotype within *one* breeding generation. For example in the fruit fly, *Drosophila*, long wing is dominant to vestigial wing. The genotype of a long wing *Drosophila* may be homozygous (**LL**) or heterozygous (**Ll**). In order to establish which is the correct genotype, the fly is testcrossed with a double recessive (**ll**) vestigial wing fly. If the testcross offspring are all long wing the unknown genotype is homozygous dominant. A ratio of 1 long wing : 1 vestigial wing indicates that the unknown is heterozygous (fig 23.3).

23.2 Why is it not possible to use a homozygous dominant organism (such as **TT**) in a backcross experiment to determine the genotype of an organism showing the dominant phenotype? Illustrate your answer fully using appropriate genetic symbols.

23.1.3   Dihybrid inheritance and the principle of independent assortment

Having established that it was possible to predict the outcome of breeding crosses involving a single pair of contrasted characteristics, Mendel turned his attention to the inheritance of two pairs of contrasted characteristics. Since two pairs of alleles are found in

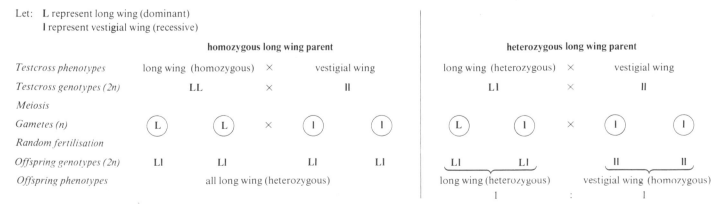

Let: **L** represent long wing (dominant)
      l represent vestigial wing (recessive)

	homozygous long wing parent				heterozygous long wing parent			
Testcross phenotypes	long wing (homozygous)	×		vestigial wing	long wing (heterozygous)	×		vestigial wing
Testcross genotypes (2n)	**LL**	×		**ll**	**Ll**	×		**ll**
Meiosis								
Gametes (n)	Ⓛ Ⓛ	×	Ⓛ	Ⓛ	Ⓛ Ⓛ	×	Ⓛ	Ⓛ
Random fertilisation								
Offspring genotypes (2n)	**Ll** **Ll**		**Ll**	**Ll**	**Ll** **Ll**		**ll**	**ll**
Offspring phenotypes	all long wing (heterozygous)				long wing (heterozygous) 1	:	vestigial wing (homozygous) 1	

Fig 23.3 *A full genetic explanation of how to determine the genotype of an organism showing a dominant characteristic. This technique is known as a testcross, and produces offspring phenotypes as shown*

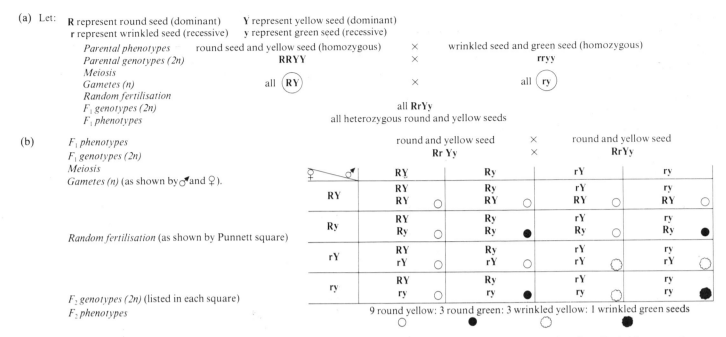

Fig 23.4 (a) Stages in the formation of F₁ phenotypes from homozygous parents. This is an example of a dihybrid cross since two characteristics are being considered (b) Use of Punnett square to show all possible combinations of gametes to form F₂ genotypes

the heterozygotes, this condition is known as **dihybrid inheritance.**

In one of his experiments Mendel used pea shape and pea cotyledon colour as the characteristics. Using the same techniques as described in section 23.1.1, he crossed pure-breeding (homozygous) plants having round and yellow peas with pure-breeding plants having wrinkled and green peas. The F₁ generation seeds were round and yellow. Mendel knew that these characteristics were dominant from earlier monohybrid breeding experiments but it was the nature and number of organisms of the F₂ generation produced from the self-pollination of the F₁ plants that now interested him. He collected a total of 556 F₂ seeds from the F₁ generation which showed the following characteristics:

> 315 round and yellow,
> 101 wrinkled and yellow,
> 108 round and green and
> 32 wrinkled and green.

The proportions of each phenotype approximated to a ratio of 9:3:3:1. This is known as the **dihybrid ratio.** Mendel made two deductions from these observations.

(1) Two new combinations of characteristics had appeared in the F₂ generation: wrinkled and yellow, and round and green.

(2) The ratios of each pair of allelomorphic characteristics (phenotypes determined by different alleles) appeared in the monohybrid ratio of 3:1, that is 423 round to 133 wrinkled, and 416 yellow to 140 green.

On the basis of these results Mendel was able to state that the two pairs of characteristics (seed shape and colour),

whilst combining in the F₁ generation, separate and behave independently from one another in subsequent generations. This forms the basis of **Mendel's second law** or the **principle of independent assortment** which states that,

> any one of a pair of characteristics may combine with either one of another pair.

The above experiment can be written out in terms of our present knowledge of genetics as shown in fig 23.4a. As a result of separation (segregation) of alleles (**R**, **r**, **Y** and **y**) and their independent assortment (rearrangement or **recombination**) four possible arrangements of alleles can be found in each of the male and female gametes. In order to demonstrate all the possible combinations of gametes that occur during random fertilisation a **Punnett square** is used. This is a grid named after the Cambridge geneticist R. C. Punnett and its value lies in minimising the errors which can occur when listing all possible combinations of gametes. It is advisable when filling in the Punnett square to enter all the 'male' gametes first in the vertical squares and then enter all the 'female' gametes in the horizontal squares. Likewise, when determining the F₂ phenotypes, it is advisable to mark off identical phenotypes in some easily identifiable way, as shown in fig 23.4b. From figs 23.4a and b, which are based on Mendel's first and second laws, it can be seen that each F₁ male and female genotype can give rise to gametes with the following combination of alleles;

R can only be present with **Y** or **y** (not **r**), that is **RY** or **Ry**,

r can only be present with **Y** or **y** (not **R**), that is **rY** or **ry**.

Thus there is a 1 in 4 chance of any gamete containing any of the four allele combinations shown above.

From a consideration of monohybrid inheritance, where $\frac{3}{4}$ of the F_2 phenotypes show the dominant allele and $\frac{1}{4}$ the recessive allele, the probability of the four alleles appearing in any F_2 phenotype is as follows:

round (dominant) $\quad \frac{3}{4}$
yellow (dominant) $\quad \frac{3}{4}$
wrinkled (recessive) $\frac{1}{4}$
green (recessive) $\quad \frac{1}{4}$

Hence the probability of the following combinations of alleles appearing in the F_2 phenotypes is as follows:

round and yellow $\quad = \frac{3}{4} \times \frac{3}{4} = \frac{9}{16}$
round and green $\quad = \frac{3}{4} \times \frac{1}{4} = \frac{3}{16}$
wrinkled and yellow $= \frac{1}{4} \times \frac{3}{4} = \frac{3}{16}$
wrinkled and green $= \frac{1}{4} \times \frac{1}{4} = \frac{1}{16}$

The results of Mendel's breeding experiments with two pairs of contrasted characteristics approximated to the theoretical values shown above.

23.3 In the guinea pig, (*Cavia*), there are two alleles for hair colour, black and white, and two alleles for hair length, short and long. In a breeding experiment all the F_1 phenotypes produced from a cross between pure-breeding, short black-haired and pure-breeding, long white-haired parents had short black hair. Explain (*a*) which alleles are dominant, and (*b*) the expected proportions of F_2 phenotypes.

23.4 Flower colour in sweet pea plants is determined by two allelomorphic pairs of genes (**R,r**, and **S,s**). If at least one dominant gene from each allelomorphic pair is present the flowers are purple. All other genotypes are white.

If two purple plants, each having the genotype **RrSs**, are crossed, what will be the phenotypic ratio of the offspring?

23.1.4 Summary of Mendel's hypotheses

The following summary includes terms taken from our present knowledge of the nature of genetics.
(1) Each characteristic of an organism is controlled by a pair of alleles.
(2) If an organism has two unlike alleles for a given characteristic, one may be expressed (the dominant allele) to the total exclusion of the other (the recessive allele).
(3) During meiosis each pair of alleles separates (segregates) and each gamete receives one of each pair of alleles (*the principle of segregation*).
(4) During gamete formation in each sex, either one of a pair of alleles may enter the same gamete cell (combine randomly) with either one of another pair (*the principle of independent assortment*).

(5) Each allele is transmitted from generation to generation as a discrete unchanging unit.
(6) Each organism inherits one allele (for each characteristic) from each parent.
NB The mechanism of dihybrid inheritance, the examples quoted in this section and the typical dihybrid ratio of 9:3:3:1 only apply to characteristics controlled by genes on *different* chromosomes. Genes situated on the *same* chromosome may not show this pattern of independent assortment as described in section 23.3.

23.2 The chromosomal basis of inheritance

Mendel published his research data and hypotheses in 1866 in a journal, *The Proceedings of the Brünn Natural History Society*, which was sent to most of the learned scientific societies throughout the world. In all cases they failed to appreciate the importance of his findings, possibly because scientists at the time were unable to relate them to any physical structures in the gametes by which the hereditary factors might be transmitted from parent to offspring.

By 1900, as a result of improvements in the optical properties of microscopes and advances in cytological techniques, the behaviour of chromosomes in gametes and zygotes had been observed. In 1875 Hertwig noted that during the fertilisation of sea urchin eggs two nuclei, one from the sperm and one from the egg, fused together. Boveri, in 1902, demonstrated the importance of the nucleus in controlling the development of characteristics in organisms, and in 1882 Flemming clarified the chromosomal events involved in mitosis.

In 1900 the significance of Mendel's work was realised almost simultaneously by three scientists, de Vries, Correns and Tschermak. In fact, it was Correns who summarised Mendel's conclusions in the familiar form of two principles and coined the term '**factor**', Mendel having used the term '*elemente*' to describe the hereditary unit. It was an American, William Sutton, however, who noticed the striking similarities between the behaviour of chromosomes during gamete formation and fertilisation, and the transmission of Mendel's hereditary factors. These have been summarised in table 23.3.

On the basis of the evidence suggested above, Sutton and Boveri proposed that chromosomes were the carriers of Mendel's factors, the so-called **chromosome theory of heredity**. According to this theory, each pair of factors is carried by a pair of homologous chromosomes, with each chromosome carrying one of the factors. Since the number of characteristics of any organism vastly outnumbers the chromosomes, as revealed by microscopy, each chromosome must carry many factors.

The term **factor** as the basic unit of heredity was replaced by Johannsen, in 1909, with the term **gene**. Whilst gene is used to describe the unit of heredity, it is the alternative

Table 23.3 A summary of the similarities between events occurring during meiosis and fertilisation and Mendel's hypotheses.

Meiosis and fertilisation	Mendel's hypotheses
Diploid cells contain *pairs* of chromosomes (homologous chromosomes)	Characteristics are controlled by *pairs* of factors
Homologous chromosomes *separate* during meiosis	Pairs of factors *separate* during gamete formation
One homologous chromosome passes into each gamete cell	Each gamete receives *one* factor
Only the *nucleus* of the male gamete fuses with the egg cell nucleus	Factors are transmitted from generation to generation as *discrete units*
Homologous pairs of chromosomes are restored at fertilisation, each gamete (♂ and ♀) contributing *one* homologous chromosome	Each organism inherits *one* factor from each parent

forms of the gene or **alleles** which determine the expression of the gene. Alleles are the alternative forms in which a gene may exist and they occupy corresponding positions or **loci** (singular **locus**) on **homologous chromosomes**, as shown in fig 23.5.

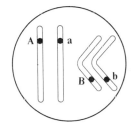

Fig 23.5 *A cell showing two pairs of homologous chromosomes. The positions of two different gene loci are indicated by circles. In this example two gene loci are shown situated on different pairs of homologous chromosomes and each gene is present as two alleles*

Mendel's principle of segregation of factors could now be explained in terms of the separation (segregation) of homologous chromosomes which occurs during anaphase I of meiosis and the random distribution of alleles into gamete cells. These events are summarised in fig 23.6.

23.2.1 Chromosomal explanation of independent assortment

Mendel's principle of independent assortment may also be explained in terms of the movement of chromosomes during meiosis. During gamete formation the distribution of each allele from a pair of homologous chromosomes is entirely independent of the distribution of alleles of other pairs. This situation is described in fig 23.7. It is the random alignment or assortment of homologous chromosomes on the equatorial spindle during metaphase I of meiosis, and their subsequent separation during metaphase I and anaphase I, that leads to the variety of allele recombinations in the gamete cells. It is possible to predict the number of allele combinations in either the male or female gamete using the general formula 2^n, where n = haploid number of chromosomes. In the case of Man, where $n = 23$, the possible number of different combinations is $2^{23} = 8\ 388\ 609$.

> **23.5** The deposition of starch in pollen grains in maize is controlled by the presence of one allele of a certain gene. The other allele of that gene results in no starch being deposited. Explain why half the pollen grains produced by a given maize plant contain starch.
>
> **23.6** Calculate the number of different combinations of chromosomes in the pollen grains of the crocus (*Crocus balansae*) which has a diploid number of six ($2n = 6$).

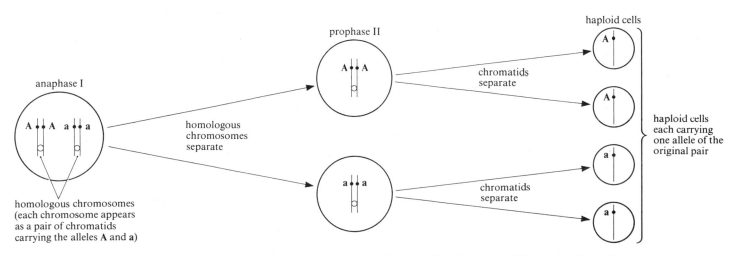

Fig 23.6 *Mendel's principle of segregation of factors (alleles)* **A** *and* **a** *described in terms of the separation of homologous chromosomes which occurs during meiosis*

837

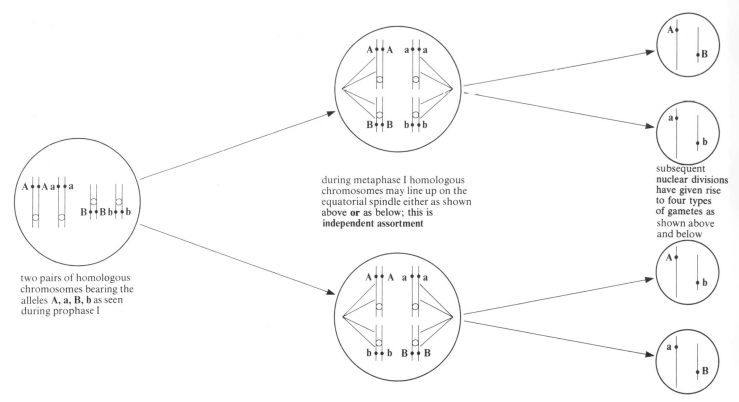

Fig 23.7 *Mendel's principle of independent assortment of factors (alleles)* **A, a, B, b,** *described in terms of the separation of homologous chromosomes which occurs during meiosis*

23.3 Linkage

All the situations and examples discussed so far in this chapter have dealt with the inheritance of genes situated on different chromosomes. Cytological studies have revealed that Man possesses 46 chromosomes in all the somatic (body) cells. Since Man possesses thousands of characteristics such as blood group, eye colour and the ability to secrete insulin, it follows that each chromosome must carry a large number of genes.

Genes situated on the same chromosome are said to be **linked**. All genes on a single chromosome form a **linkage group** and usually pass into the same gamete and are inherited together. As a result of this, genes belonging to the same linkage group usually do not show independent assortment. Since these genes do not conform to Mendel's principle of independent assortment they fail to produce the expected 9:3:3:1 ratio in a breeding situation involving the inheritance of two pairs of contrasted characteristics (dihybrid inheritance). In these situations a variety of ratios are produced which may be explained quite simply now that we possess a basic understanding of the mechanisms of inheritance as revealed by Mendel. (At this point it is worth re-emphasising Mendel's good fortune in choosing to study the inheritance of pairs of characteristics located on *different* chromosomes.) In *Drosophila* the genes for body colour and wing length have the following **allelomorphs** (phenotypic characteristics determined by different alleles): grey and black body, and long and vestigial (short) wings. Grey body and long wing are dominant. If pure-breeding grey-bodied long-winged *Drosophila* are crossed with black-bodied vestigial-winged *Drosophila*, the expected F_2 phenotypic ratio would be 9:3:3:1. This would indicate a normal case of Mendelian dihybrid inheritance with random assortment resulting from the genes for body colour and wing length being situated on non-homologous chromosomes. However this result is not obtained. Instead the F_2 show an approximately 3:1 ratio of parental phenotypes. This may be explained by assuming that the genes for body colour and wing length are found on the same chromosome, that is they are linked, as shown in fig 23.8.

In practice, though, this 3:1 ratio is never achieved and four phenotypes are invariably produced. This is because **total** linkage is rare. Most breeding experiments involving linkage produce approximately equal numbers of the parental phenotypes and a significantly smaller number of phenotypes showing new combinations of characteristics, also in equal numbers. These latter phenotypes are described as **recombinants**. From this it is possible to produce the following definition of linkage.

Two or more genes are said to be linked when phenotypes with new gene combinations (recombinants) occur less frequently than the parental phenotypes.

The events leading to the discovery of linkage by the American Thomas H. Morgan may be summarised in one

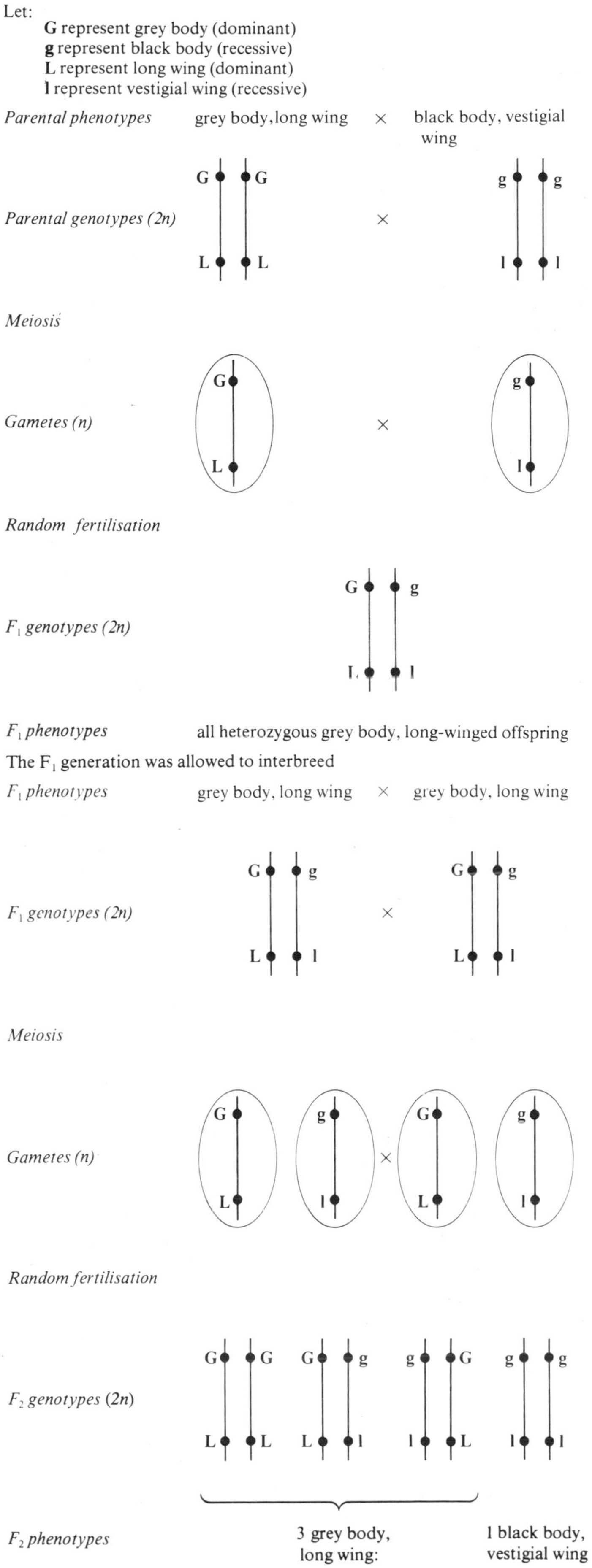

Let:
G represent grey body (dominant)
g represent black body (recessive)
L represent long wing (dominant)
l represent vestigial wing (recessive)

Parental phenotypes grey body, long wing × black body, vestigial wing

Parental genotypes (2n)

G G   g g

L L   l l

×

Meiosis

Gametes (n)

G   g

L   l

×

Random fertilisation

F_1 genotypes (2n)

G g

L l

F_1 phenotypes all heterozygous grey body, long-winged offspring

The F_1 generation was allowed to interbreed

F_1 phenotypes grey body, long wing × grey body, long wing

F_1 genotypes (2n)

G g   G g

L l   L l

×

Meiosis

Gametes (n)

G   g   G   g

L   l   L   l

×

Random fertilisation

F_2 genotypes (2n)

G G   G g   g G   g g

L L   L l   l L   l l

F_2 phenotypes   3 grey body, long wing :   1 black body, vestigial wing

Fig 23.8 *Genetic explanation of the 3:1 ratio produced in F_2 phenotypes as a result of linkage*

of his experiments in which he predicted the results of a backcross between heterozygous grey-bodied long-winged *Drosophila* (the F_1 generation of the experimental cross shown in fig 23.8) and homozygous recessive black-bodied vestigial-winged *Drosophila*. The two possible outcomes were predicted as follows:

(1) If the four alleles for grey and black body, and long and vestigal wings, were on different pairs of chromosomes (that is *not* linked) they should show independent assortment and produce the following phenotypic ratios:

1 grey body, long wing: 1 grey body, vestigial wing: 1 black body, long wing: 1 black body, vestigial wing.

(2) If the alleles for body colour and wing length were situated on the same pair of chromosomes (that is linked) the following phenotypic ratio would be produced:

1 grey body, long wing:1 black body, vestigial wing.

An explanation of these predictions is given in fig 23.9.

Morgan carried out this backcross several times and never obtained either of the predicted outcomes. Each time he obtained the following results:

41.5% grey body long wing
41.5% black body vestigial wing
8.5% grey body vestigial wing
8.5% black body long wing

On the basis of these results he postulated that:
(1) the genes were located on chromosomes,
(2) both the genes were situated on the same chromosome, that is linked,
(3) the alleles for each gene were on homologous chromosomes,
(4) alleles were exchanged between homologous chromosomes during meiosis.

The reappearance of recombinant alleles in 17% of the offspring was explained in terms of point (4). This is known as **crossing-over**.

> **23.7** A homozygous purple-flowered short-stemmed plant was crossed with a homozygous red-flowered long-stemmed plant and the F_1 phenotypes had purple flowers and short stems. When the F_1 generation was testcrossed (backcrossed) with a double homozygous recessive plant the following progeny were produced.
>
> 52 purple flower, short stem
> 47 purple flower, long stem
> 49 red flower, short stem
> 45 red flower, long stem
>
> Explain fully these results.

(a) If the four alleles are situated on different pairs of chromosomes

Testcross phenotypes   grey body, long wing × black body, vestigial wing
(heterozygous)   (homozygous)

Testcross genotypes (2n)   **GgLl**   ×   **ggll**

Meiosis

Gametes (n)
(as shown by
♂ and ♀)

♀ \ ♂	GL	Gl	gL	gl
gl	GL gl	Gl gl	gL gl	gl gl

Random fertilisation
(as shown in Punnett
square)

Offspring genotypes (2n)
(listed in each square)

Offspring phenotypes   1 grey body, long wing: 1 grey body, vestigial wing:
                         1 black body, long wing: 1 black body, vestigial wing

(b) If the four alleles are situated on the same pair of chromosomes

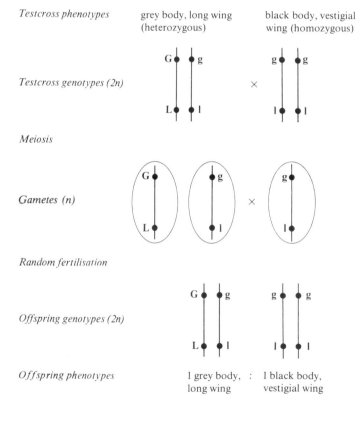

Testcross phenotypes   grey body, long wing   black body, vestigial
(heterozygous)   wing (homozygous)

Testcross genotypes (2n)

Meiosis

Gametes (n)

Random fertilisation

Offspring genotypes (2n)

Offspring phenotypes   1 grey body, : 1 black body,
                    long wing   vestigial wing

Fig 23.10 *(right) Genetic explanation of crossing-over and the appearance of recombinant genotypes. The recombination frequency can be calculated by counting the number of individuals showing recombination and the total number of individuals and applying the following formula:*

$$\text{recombination frequency (\%)} = \frac{x}{y} \times 100$$

Fig 23.9 *(left) (a) and (b) Genetic explanation of Morgan's predictions*

23.3.1 Crossing-over and crossover values

In 1909 the Belgian cytologist Janssens observed **chiasmata formation** during prophase I of meiosis (section 22.3). The genetic significance of this process was clarified by Morgan who proposed that crossing-over of alleles occurred as a result of the breakage and recombination of homologous chromosomes during chiasmata. Subsequent research based on the microscopic examination of cells and recombinant phenotypic ratios has confirmed that crossover of genetic material occurs between virtually all homologous chromosomes during meiosis. The alleles of parental linkage groups separate and new associations of alleles are formed in the gamete cells, a process known as **genetic recombination**. Offspring formed from these gametes showing 'new' combinations of characteristics are known as **recombinants**. Thus crossing-over is a major source of observable genetic variation within populations.

The behaviour of a pair of homologous chromosomes in *Drosophila*, carrying the alleles grey body and long wing (both dominant) and black body and vestigial wing (both recessive), during formation of chiasmata may be used to illustrate the principle of crossing-over. A cross between a male homozygous grey-bodied long-winged *Drosophila* and a female homozygous black-bodied vestigial-winged *Drosophila* produced heterozygous F_1 offspring with grey bodies and long wings as shown in fig 23.10.

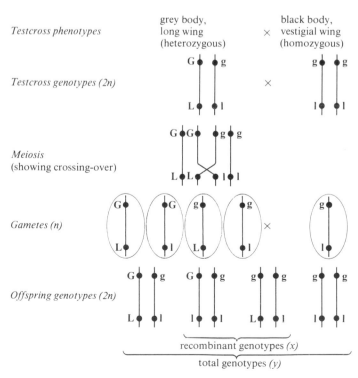

Testcross phenotypes   grey body, long wing (heterozygous) × black body, vestigial wing (homozygous)

Testcross genotypes (2n)

Meiosis
(showing crossing-over)

Gametes (n)

Offspring genotypes (2n)

recombinant genotypes *(x)*
─────────────────────
total genotypes *(y)*

Backcrossing the F_1 generation flies with homozygous double recessive flies produced the following results.

Parental phenotypes $\left\{\begin{array}{ll} \text{grey body, long wing} & 965 \\ \text{black body, vestigial wing} & 944 \end{array}\right.$

Recombinant phenotypes $\left\{\begin{array}{ll} \text{black body, long wing} & 206 \\ \text{grey body , vestigial wing} & 185 \end{array}\right.$

These results indicate that the genes for body colour and wing length are linked. (Remember that a dihybrid cross between an F_1 heterozygote and a double homozygous recessive would have produced a 1:1:1:1 phenotypic ratio if the genes had been situated on different chromosomes and therefore had undergone random assortment.) Using the figures obtained from the above cross it is possible to calculate the recombination frequency of the genes for body colour and wing length.

The **recombination frequency** is calculated using the formula

$$\frac{\text{number of individuals showing recombination}}{\text{number of offspring}} \times 100$$

From the example above the recombination frequency (%) is

$$\frac{(206 + 185)}{(965 + 944) + (206 + 185)} \times 100$$

$$= \frac{391 \times 100}{2300}$$

$$= 17\%.$$

This value indicates the number of crossovers which have occurred during gamete formation. A. H. Sturtevant, a student of Morgan, postulated that the recombinant frequency or **crossover frequency (crossover value (COV))** demonstrated that genes are arranged linearly along the chromosome. More importantly, he suggested that the crossover frequency reflects the relative positions of genes on a chromosome because the further apart linked genes are on the chromosomes, the greater the possibility of crossing-over occurring between them, that is the greater the crossover frequency (fig 23.11).

Fig 23.11 *Three gene loci represented by A, B and C are shown on the chromosome. Crossing-over and separation of genes is more likely to occur between A and C than between B and C or A and B since the frequency of crossing-over is related to the distance between the genes*

23.8 The diagram below shows the gene loci of 12 alleles situated on a pair of chromosomes. Their relative distances from the centromere are shown.

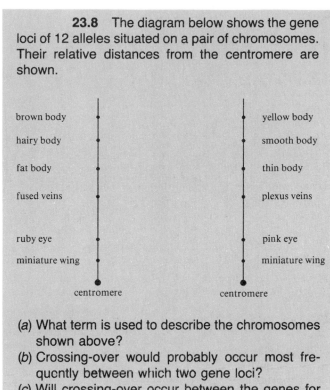

(a) What term is used to describe the chromosomes shown above?
(b) Crossing-over would probably occur most frequently between which two gene loci?
(c) Will crossing-over occur between the genes for eye colour and antenna shape? Explain your answer.

23.4 Gene mapping

The major significance of calculating cross-over frequencies is that it enables geneticists to produce maps showing the relative positions of genes on chromosomes. Chromosome maps are constructed by directly converting the crossover frequency or value between genes into hypothetical distances along the chromosome. A crossover frequency or value (COV) of 4% between genes A and B means that those genes are situated 4 units apart on the same chromosome. A COV of 9% for a pair of genes A and C would indicate that they were 9 units apart, but it would not indicate the linear sequence of the genes, as shown in fig 23.12.

Fig 23.12 *Possible gene loci of A, B and C on the basis of the data presented*

In practice it is usual to determine crossover values for at least three genes at once, as this **triangulation** process enables the sequence of the genes to be determined as well as the distances between them. Consider the following crossover values as determined by a series of breeding experiments involving four genes **P**, **Q**, **R** and **S**.

$$P - Q = 24\%$$
$$R - P = 14\%$$
$$R - S = 8\%$$
$$S - P = 6\%$$

To calculate the sequence and distances apart of the genes, a line is drawn representing the chromosome and the following procedure carried out.

(1) Insert the positions of the genes with the least COV in the middle of the chromosome, that is $S - P = 6\%$ (fig 23.13a).
(2) Examine the next largest COV, that is $R - S = 8\%$, and insert both possible positions of **R** on the chromosome, relative to S (fig 23.13b).
(3) Repeat the procedure for the next largest COV, that is $R - P = 14\%$. This indicates that the right-hand position of **R** is incorrect (fig 23.13c).
(4) Repeat the procedure for the COV for $P - Q = 24\%$ (fig 23.13d). The position of **Q** cannot be ascertained without additional information. If, for example, the COV for $Q - R = 10\%$ this would confirm the left-hand position for gene **Q**.

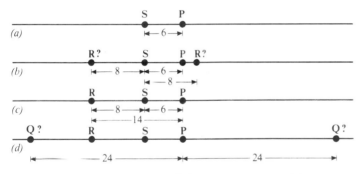

Fig 23.13 *Use of the triangulation process to establish the positions of genes* **P**, **Q**, **R** *and* **S** *on a chromosome*

A problem which arises in preparing chromosome maps is that of **double crossover**, particularly when considering genes which are widely separated, since the number of apparent crossovers will be less than the actual number. For example, if crossovers occur between alleles **A** and **B** and **B** and **C** in fig 23.14, **A** and **C** will still appear linked, but the chromosome will now carry the recessive allele **b**.

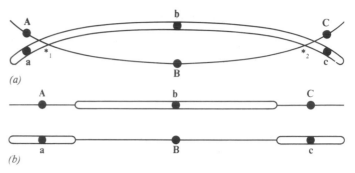

Fig 23.14 *(a) A pair of homologous chromatids, one carrying the dominant alleles* **A**, **B** *and* **C** *and the other carrying the recessive alleles* **a**, **b** *and* **c**. *Crossing-over occurs at two points* $*_1$ *and* $*_2$. *(b) The result of separation of the chromatids in which the sequences of alleles are different, although the sequences of gene loci and the distances between them remain the same*

23.9 In maize the genes for coloured seed and full seed are dominant to the genes for colourless seed and shrunken seed. Pure-breeding strains of the double dominant variety were crossed with the double recessive variety and a backcross of the F_1 generation produced the following results.

coloured, full seed	380
colourless, shrunken seed	396
coloured, shrunken seed	14
colourless, full seed	10

Calculate the distance in units between the genes for coloured seed and seed shape on the chromosomes.

23.5 Linkage groups and chromosomes

Much of the evidence presented in this chapter so far has shown how our knowledge of the mechanics of inheritance has gradually increased. Most of the research into genetics in the early part of this century involved establishing the role of genes in inheritance. Morgan's research with the fruit fly (*Drosophila melanogaster*) established that the majority of phenotypic characteristics were transmitted together in four groups and these were called **linkage groups**. It was observed that the number of linkage groups corresponded to the number of pairs of chromosomes.

Studies on other organisms produced similar results. Breeding experiments using a variety of organisms revealed that some linkage groups were larger then others (that is they carried more genes). Examination of chromosomes in these organisms showed that they varied in length. Morgan demonstrated that there was a distinct relationship between these observations. This provided further confirmatory evidence that genes were located on chromosomes.

23.5.1 Giant chromosomes and genes

In 1913 Sturtevant began his work on mapping the positions of genes on the chromosomes of *Drosophila* but it was 21 years before there was a possibility of linking visible structures on chromosomes with genes. In 1934, it was observed that the chromosomes in the salivary gland cells of *Drosophila* were about 100 times larger than chromosomes from other body cells. For some reason these chromosomes duplicate without separating until there are several thousand lying side by side. When stained they can be seen with the light microscope and appear to be made up of alternating light and dark bands. Each chromosome has its own distinctive pattern of bands (fig 23.15). It was originally thought, or rather hoped, that these bands were genes, but this is not the case. Phenotypic abnormalities may be artificially induced in *Drosophila* and these correlate with changes in chromosomal banding patterns, as observed with the microscope. These phenotypic and chromosomal abnormalities in turn correlate with gene loci shown on chromosome maps which have been constructed on the basis of crossover values obtained from breeding experiments. Therefore it is possible to say that the bands on the chromosomes indicate the *positions* of genes but are not themselves genes.

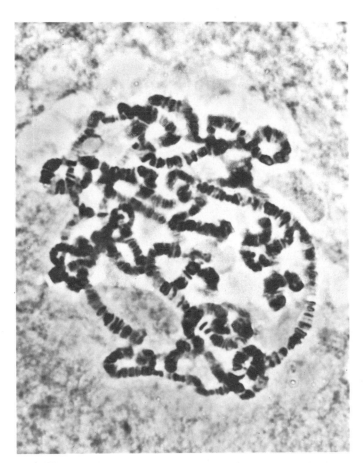

Fig 23.15 *Giant chromosomes from the salivary glands of* Drosophila melanogaster. *Four pairs of chromosomes are shown joined at their centromeres*

23.6 Sex determination

The technique of relating phenotypic characteristics of organisms to the structure of their chromosomes, as described in earlier sections, is seen most clearly in the determination of sex. In *Drosophila* the observed phenotypic differences between the two sexes appear to be related to the differences in the size of their chromosomes, as shown in fig 23.16. Examination of the chromosome structure of a range of animals revealed that males and females showed certain chromosomal differences. Pairs of

Fig 23.16 *Structure of chromosomes in male and female* Drosophila melanogaster. *Four pairs of chromosomes are shown. The sex chromosomes are numbered I*

chromosomes (homologous chromosomes) are found in all cells, but one pair of chromosomes always shows differences between the sexes. These are the **sex chromosomes** or **heterosomes**. All other chromosomes are known as **autosomal chromosomes** or **autosomes**. As can be seen in fig 23.16, *Drosophila* has four pairs of chromosomes. Three pairs appear identical in both sexes (numbers II, III and IV), but the other pair, whilst appearing identical in the female, differ in the male. The chromosomes are known as X and Y chromosomes, and the genotype of the female is XX and that of the male is XY (fig 23.17). These characteristic sex genotypes are found in most animals, including Man; but in the case of birds (including poultry), moths and butterflies the sex genotypes are reversed: the females are XY and the males are XX. In some insects, such as the grasshopper, the Y chromosome may be absent entirely and so the male has the genotype XO.

Fig 23.17 *Human sex chromosomes as they appear during metaphase of mitosis*

Fig 23.18 Genetic explanation of the sex ratio in humans

Parental phenotypes	female ($\female$)		$\times$		male ($\male$)
Parental genotypes (2n)	XX		$\times$		XY

Meiosis

Gametes(n)	(X)	(X)	$\times$	(X)	(Y)

Random fertilisation

Offspring genotypes (2n)	XX	XY		XX	XY
Offspring phenotypes	$\female$	$\male$		$\female$	$\male$

sex ratio 1 female : 1 male

In the production of gametes the sex chromosomes segregate in typical Mendelian fashion. For example, in mammals each ovum contains an X chromosome; in males one half of the sperms contains an X chromosome and the other half contains a Y chromosome as shown in fig 23.18. The sex of the offspring depends upon which type of sperm fertilises the ovum. The sex having the XX genotype is described as **homogametic** as it produces gamete cells containing only X chromosomes. Organisms with the XY genotype are described as **heterogametic** since half their gametes contain the X chromosome and half the Y chromosome. In humans, the genotypic sex of an individual is determined by examining non-dividing cells. One X chromosome always appears in the active state, which has the normal appearance. If another is present, it is seen in a resting state as a tightly coiled dark-staining body called the **Barr body**. The number of Barr bodies is always one less than the number of X chromosomes present, that is male (XY) = 0, female (XX) = 1. The function of the Y chromosome appears to vary according to species. In Man the presence of a Y chromosome controls the differentiation of the testis which subsequently influences the development of the genital organs and male characteristics (section 20.3.1). In most organisms, however, the Y chromosome does not carry genes concerned with sex. In fact it is described as **genetically inert** or **genetically empty** since it carries so few genes. In *Drosophila* it is thought that the genes determining male characteristics are carried on the autosomes and their phenotypic effects are masked by the presence of a pair of X chromosomes. Male characteristics, on the other hand, appear in the presence of a single X chromosome. This is an example of **sex-limited inheritance**,

as opposed to sex-linked inheritance and in humans is thought to cause suppression of the genes for growth of beard in females.

Morgan and his co-workers noticed that inheritance of eye colour in *Drosophila* was related to the sex of the parent flies. Red eye is dominant over white eye. A red-eyed male crossed with a white-eyed female produced equal numbers of F_1 red-eyed females and white-eyed males (fig 23.19a). A white-eyed male, however, crossed with a red-eyed female produced equal numbers of F_1 red-eyed males and females (fig 23.19b). Inbreeding these F_1 flies produced red-eyed females, red-eyed males and white-eyed males but *no* white-eyed females, (fig 23.19c). The fact that male flies showed the recessive characteristic more frequently than female flies suggested that the white eye recessive allele was present on the X chromosome and that the Y chromosome lacked the eye colour gene. To test this hypothesis Morgan crossed the original white-eyed male with an F_1 red-eyed female (fig 23.19d). The offspring included red-eyed and white-eyed males and females. From this Morgan rightly concluded that only the X chromosome carries the gene for eye colour. There is no gene locus for eye colour on the Y chromosome. This phenomenon is known as **sex linkage**.

23.10 In *Drosophila* the genes for wing length and for eye colour are sex-linked. Normal wing and red eye are dominant to miniature wing and white eye.

(a) In a cross between a miniature wing, red-eyed male and a homozygous normal wing, white-eyed female, explain fully the appearance of (i) the F_1 and (ii) the F_2 generations.

(b) Crossing a female from the F_1 generation above with a miniature wing, white-eyed male gave the following results:

normal wing, white-eyed males and females	35
normal wing, red-eyed males and females	17
miniature wing, white-eyed males and females	18
miniature wing, red-eyed males and females	36

Account for the appearance and numbers of the phenotypes shown above.

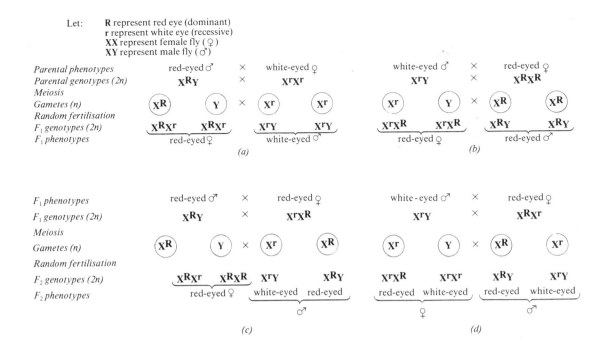

Fig 23.19 *(a) and (b) Morgan's reciprocal experimental crosses between red-eyed and white-eyed Drosophila. Note the low frequency of appearance of white eyes. (c) Morgan's confirmatory inbreeding experimental cross between an F₁ red-eyed male and an F₁ (heterozygous) red-eyed female. (d) The experimental cross between a white-eyed male and an F₁ (heterozygous) red-eyed female. Note the appearance of the white-eyed characteristic only in homozygous white-eyed female flies*

23.6.1 Sex linkage

Genes carried on the sex chromosomes are said to be sex-linked. In the case of the heterogametic sex there is a portion of the X chromosome for which there is no homologous region of the Y chromosome (fig 23.20).

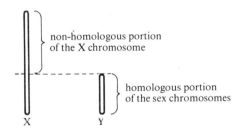

Fig 23.20 *Homologous and non-homologous regions of the sex chromosomes*

Characteristics determined by genes carried on the non-homologous portion of the X chromosome therefore appear in males even if they are recessive. This special form of linkage explains the inheritance of **sex-linked traits** such as red–green colour blindness, premature balding and haemophilia. Haemophilia or 'bleeder's disease' is a sex-linked recessive condition which prevents the formation of factor VIII, an important factor in increasing the rate of blood clotting. The gene for substance VIII is carried on the non-homologous portion of the X chromosome and can appear in two allelomorphic forms: normal (dominant) and mutant (recessive). The following possible genotypes and phenotypes can occur.

genotype	phenotype
$X^H X^H$	normal female
$X^H X^h$	normal female (carrier)
$X^H Y$	normal male
$X^h Y$	haemophiliac male

In all sex-linked traits, females who are heterozygous are described as **carriers** of the trait. They are phenotypically normal but half their gametes carry the recessive gene. Despite the father having a normal gene there is a 50% probability (probability $\frac{1}{2}$) that sons of carrier females will show the trait. In the situation where a carrier haemophiliac female marries a normal male they may have children with phenotypes as shown in fig 23.21.

Let: **H** represent normal allele for blood clotting (dominant)
h represent allele for haemophilia (recessive)
XX represent female chromosomes
XY represent male chromosomes

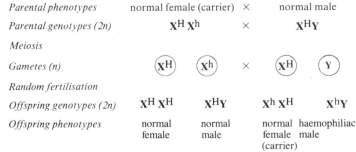

Fig 23.21 *Mechanism of inheritance of the sex-linked allele for haemophilia*

845

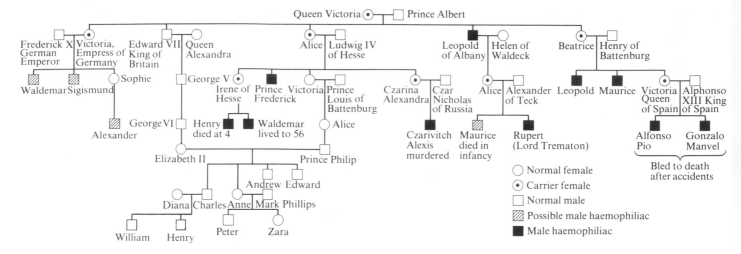

One of the best-documented examples of the inheritance of haemophilia is shown by the descendants of Queen Victoria. It is thought that the gene for haemophilia arose as a mutation in Queen Victoria or one of her parents. Fig 23.22 shows how the haemophilia gene was inherited by her descendants.

Fig 23.22 *Transmission of haemophilia in the descendants of Queen Victoria. In the diagram only those descendants involved in the transmission and appearance of haemophilia have been shown. The ancestry of the British Royal Family has been given to show why haemophilia is absent from seven generations of Queen Victoria's descendants*

23.11 Body colour in cats and magpie moths is controlled by a sex-linked gene on the X chromosome. The following data were obtained in two breeding experiments where the homogametic sex was homozygous for body colour in the parental generation.

	Magpie moth (normal colour dominant to pale colour)	Cat (black colour dominant to yellow colour)
Parental phenotypes	pale male × normal female	black male × yellow female
Offspring phenotypes	1 normal male : 1 pale female	1 yellow male : 1 black female

Which is the heterogametic sex in each of these organisms?

23.7 Gene interactions

The topics in this chapter so far have represented the simpler aspects of genetics: dominance, monohybrid and dihybrid inheritance, linkage, sex determination and sex linkage. There are many situations in genetics where genes interact in ways other than those already described and it is probable that the majority of phenotypic characteristics in organisms result from these. Several types of gene interaction will now be considered.

23.7.1 Incomplete dominance

There are several conditions where two or more alleles do not show complete dominance or recessiveness due to the failure of any allele to be dominant in the heterozygous condition. This state of **incomplete dominance (co-dominance or blending)** is an exception to the situation described by Mendel in his monohybrid breeding experiments. It is fortunate that he did not select organisms which show this condition as it may have unnecessarily complicated his early work.

Incomplete dominance is found in both plants and animals. In most cases the heterozygote has a phenotype which is intermediate between the homozygous dominant and recessive conditions. An example is the production of blue Andalusian fowls by crossing pure-breeding black and splashed white parental stocks. The presence of black plumage is the result of the possession of an allele for the production of the black pigment melanin. The splashed white stock lack this allele. The heterozygotes show a partial development of melanin which produces a blue sheen in the plumage.

As there are no accepted genotypic symbols for alleles showing incomplete dominance, the importance of specifying symbols in genetic explanations is apparent. For example, in the case of the Andalusian fowl, the following genotypic symbols may be used to illustrate the alleles: black – **B**; splashed white – **b**, **W**, **B^W** or **B^{BW}**. The results of a cross between black and splashed white homozygous fowl are shown in fig 23.23.

Let:
B represent the black allele
B^W represent the splashed white allele

Parental phenotypes	black (homozygous)	×	splashed white (homozygous)
Parental genotypes (2n)	**BB**	×	**B^{W}B^W**
Meiosis			
Gametes (n)	(B) (B)	×	(B^W) (B^W)
Random fertilisation			
F$_1$ genotypes (2n)	**BB^W** **BB^W**		**BB^W** **BB^W**
F$_1$ phenotypes	all 'blue' heterozygotes		

Fig 23.23 *The production of F$_1$ hybrids of Andalusian fowl*

If the F$_1$ generation are allowed to interbreed, the F$_2$ generation shows a modification of the normal Mendelian phenotypic monohybrid ratio of 3:1. In this case a phenotypic ratio of 1:2:1 is produced where half the F$_2$ generation have the F$_1$ genotype (fig 23.24). This ratio of 1:2:1 is characteristic of examples of incomplete dominance. Other examples are shown in table 23.4.

F$_1$ phenotypes	blue	×	blue
F$_1$ genotypes (2n)	**BB^W**	×	**BB^W**
Meiosis			
Gametes (n)	(B) (B^W)	×	(B) (B^W)
Random fertilisation			
F$_2$ genotypes (2n)	**BB** **BB^W**	**BB^W**	**B^{W}B^W**
F$_2$ phenotypes	black 1	blue 2	splashed white 1

Fig 23.24 *The production of F$_2$ hybrids of Andalusian fowl*

Table 23.4 Examples of incomplete dominance.

Characteristic	*Alleles*	*Heterozygous phenotype*
Antirrhinum flower (snapdragon)	red × white	pink
Mirabilis flower (four-o'clock flower)	red × white	pink
Short-horn cattle	red × white	roan
Angora and rex rabbits	long hair and short hair	intermediate silky fur

23.7.2 Multiple alleles

In all the cases studied so far, each characteristic has been controlled by a gene which may have appeared in one of two forms or alleles. There are several conditions where a single characteristic may appear in several different forms controlled by three or more alleles, of which any two may occupy the same gene loci on homologous chromosomes. This is known as the **multiple allele** (or **multiple allelomorph**) condition and it controls such characteristics as coat colour in mice, eye colour in mice and blood group in Man.

Inheritance of blood groups

Blood group is controlled by an autosomal gene. The gene locus is represented by the symbol **I** (which stands for isohaemagglutinogen) and there are three alleles represented by the symbols **A**, **B** and **O**. The alleles **A** and **B** are equally dominant and **O** is recessive to both. The genotypes shown in table 23.5 determine the phenotypic appearance of blood groups. The presence of a single dominant allele results in the blood producing a substance called agglutinin which acts as an antibody. For example, the genotype **I^{A}I^O** would give rise to the agglutinogen **A** on the red blood cell membrane, and the plasma would contain the agglutinin **anti-B** (the blood group would be A). Blood-grouping is described in section 14.14.6.

Table 23.5 Human blood group genotypes.

Genotype	Blood group (phenotype)
I^{A}I^A	A
I^{A}I^O	A
I^{B}I^B	B
I^{B}I^O	B
I^{A}I^B	AB
I^{O}I^O	O

23.12 In cats, the genes controlling the coat colour are carried on the X chromosomes and are incompletely dominant (co-dominant). A black-coat female mated with a ginger-coat male produced a litter consisting of black male and tortoiseshell female kittens. What is the expected F$_2$ phenotypic ratio? Explain the results.

23.13 (*a*) Explain, using appropriate genetic symbols, the possible blood groups of children whose parents are both heterozygous, the father being blood group A and the mother B.
(*b*) If these parents have non-identical twins, what is the probability that both twins will have blood group A?

Fig 23.26 *Variation in comb shape in domestic fowl* (top left) *single comb,* (top right) *pea comb,* (bottom left) *rose comb,* (bottom right) *strawberry comb*

23.7.3 Lethal genes

There are several examples of conditions where a single gene may affect several characteristics, including mortality. In the case of Man and other mammals a certain recessive gene may lead to internal adhesions of the lungs resulting in death at birth. Another example involving a single gene affects the formation of cartilage and produces congenital deformities leading to foetal and neonatal death.

In chickens which are homozygous for an allele controlling feather structure called 'frizzled', several phenotypic effects result from the incomplete development of the feathers. These chickens lack adequate feather insulation and suffer from heat loss. To compensate for this they exhibit a range of structural and physiological adaptations, but these are largely unsuccessful and there is a high mortality rate.

The effects of a lethal gene are clearly illustrated by the inheritance of fur colour in mice. Wild mice have grey-coloured fur, a condition known as agouti. Some mice have yellow fur. Cross-breeding yellow mice produces offspring in the ratio 2 yellow fur : 1 agouti fur. These results can only be explained on the basis that yellow is dominant to agouti and that all the yellow coat mice are heterozygous. The atypical Mendelian ratio is explained by the foetal death of *homozygous* yellow coat mice (fig 23.25). Examination of the uteri of pregnant yellow mice

Let:
Y represent yellow fur (dominant)
y represent agouti fur (recessive)

Parental phenotypes	yellow fur		×		yellow fur
Parental genotypes (2n)	**Yy**		×		**Yy**
Meiosis					
Gametes (n)	Ⓨ ⓨ		×		Ⓨ ⓨ
Random fertilisation					
Offspring genotypes (2n)	**YY**	**Yy Yy**			**yy**
Offspring phenotypes	1 yellow fur:	2 yellow fur :			1 agouti fur
	die before birth				

Fig 23.25 *Genetic explanation of fur colour inheritance in mice showing the lethal genotype **YY***

from the above cross revealed dead yellow foetuses. Similar examination of the uteri of crosses between yellow fur and agouti fur mice revealed no dead yellow foetuses. The explanation is that this cross would not produce homozygous yellow (**YY**) mice.

23.7.4 Gene-complex

The presence of a pair of alleles occupying a given gene locus and controlling the production of a single phenotypic characteristic is true in some cases only and exceptional in most organisms. Most characteristics are determined by the interaction of several genes which form a '**gene-complex**'. For example, a single characteristic may

be controlled by the interaction of two or more genes situated at different loci. In the case of the inheritance of the shape of the comb in domestic fowl there are genes at two loci situated on different chromosomes which interact and give rise to four distinct phenotypes, known as pea, rose, walnut and single combs (fig 23.26). The appearance of pea comb and rose comb are each determined by the presence of their respective dominant allele (**P** or **R**) and the absence of the other dominant allele. Walnut comb results from a modified form of incomplete dominance in which at least one dominant allele for pea comb and rose comb is present (that is **PR**). Single comb appears only in the homozygous double recessive condition (that is **pprr**). These phenotypes and genotypes are shown in table 23.6.

The F_2 genotypes and F_2 phenotypic ratios resulting from crossing a pure-breeding pea-comb hen with a pure-breeding rose-comb cock are shown in fig 23.27.

Table 23.6 Phenotypes and possible genotypes associated with comb shape in poultry.

Phenotype	Possible genotypes
pea	**PPrr, Pprr**
rose	**RRpp, Rrpp**
walnut	**PPRR, PpRr, PPRr, PpRR**
single	**pprr**

23.14 In poultry, the allele for white feather (**W**) is dominant over the allele for black feather (**w**). The alleles for pea comb, **P**, and rose comb, **R**, produce the phenotypes stated. If these alleles are present together they produce a phenotype called walnut comb and if their recessive alleles are present in the homozygous condition they produce a phenotype called single comb.

A cross between a black rose-comb cock and a white walnut-comb hen produced the following phenotypes:
3 white walnut-comb, 3 black walnut-comb, 3 white rose-comb, 3 black rose-comb, 1 white pea-comb, 1 black pea-comb, 1 white single-comb and 1 black single-comb.

What are the parental genotypes? Show clearly how they give rise to the phenotypes described above?

23.7.5 Epistasis

A gene is said to be **epistatic** (*epi*, over) when its presence suppresses the effect of a gene at another locus. Epistatic genes are sometimes called '**inhibiting genes**' because of their effect on the other genes which are described as **hypostatic** (*hypo*, under).

Fur colour in mice is controlled by a pair of genes occupying different loci. The epistatic gene determines the

Let:
  P represent presence of pea comb (dominant)
  p represent absence of pea comb (recessive)
  R represent presence of rose comb (dominant)
  r represent absence of rose comb (recessive)

Parental phenotypes	pea comb	×	rose comb
Parental genotypes (2n)	**PPrr**	×	**RRpp**
Meiosis			
Gametes (n)	(Pr)	×	(Rp)
Random fertilisation			
F₁ genotypes (2n)		all **PpRr**	
F₁ phenotypes		all walnut comb	
F₁ phenotypes	walnut comb	×	walnut comb
F₁ genotypes (2n)	**PpRr**	×	**PpRr**
Meiosis			

Gametes (n) (as shown by ♂ and ♀)

♀ \ ♂	PR	Pr	pR	pr
PR	PR PR ○	Pr PR ○	pR PR ○	pr PR ○
Pr	PR Pr ○	Pr Pr □	pR Pr ○	pr Pr □
pR	PR pR ○	Pr pR ○	pR pR △	pr pR △
pr	PR pr ○	Pr pr □	pR pr △	pr pr ◌

Random fertilisation

F₂ genotypes (2n) (shown in Punnett square)

F₂ phenotypes 9 walnut comb : 3 pea comb : 3 rose comb : 1 single comb
Offspring symbols ○   □   △   ◌

Fig 23.27 *Genetic explanation of comb inheritance in fowl*

Let:
  A represent agouti fur (dominant)
  a represent black fur (recessive)
  C represent coloured fur (dominant)
  c represent albino fur (recessive)

Parental phenotypes	agouti	×	albino
Parental genotypes (2n)	**AaCc**	×	**Aacc**
Meiosis			

Gametes (n) (as shown by ♂ and ♀)

♀ \ ♂	AC	Ac	aC	ac
Ac	AC Ac ○	Ac Ac □	aC Ac ○	ac Ac □
ac	AC ac ○	Ac ac □	aC ac △	ac ac □

Random fertilisation

Offspring genotypes (2n) (as shown in Punnett square)

Offspring phenotypes 3 agouti : 4 albino : 1 black
Offspring symbols ○   □   △

Fig 23.28 *A genetic explanation of how unusual phenotypic ratios can be produced in the case of epistatic genes*

presence of colour and has two alleles, coloured (dominant) and albino (white) (recessive). The hypostatic gene determines the nature of the colour and its alleles are agouti (grey) (dominant) and black (recessive). The mice may have agouti or black fur depending upon their genotypes, but this will only appear if accompanied by the allele for coloured fur. The albino condition appears in mice that are homozygous recessive for colour even if the alleles for agouti and black fur are present. Three possible phenotypes can occur and they are agouti, black and albino. A variety of phenotypic ratios can be obtained depending on the genotypes of the mating pair (fig 23.28 and table 23.7).

Table 23.7 Some examples of the range of phenotypic ratios which can be produced as a result of epistatic gene interactions (see fig 23.28 for explanation of alleles).

Parental phenotypes	Genotypes	Phenotypic ratios
agouti × agouti	**AaCc × AaCc**	9 agouti : 3 black : 4 albino
agouti × black	**AaCc × aaCc**	3 agouti : 3 black : 2 albino
agouti × albino	**AaCc × Aacc**	3 agouti : 1 black : 4 albino
agouti × albino	**AaCc × aacc**	1 agouti : 1 black : 2 albino
agouti × albino	**AACc × aacc**	1 agouti : 1 albino
agouti × black	**AaCc × aaCC**	1 agouti : 1 black
albino × black	**AAcc × aaCC**	all agouti
albino × black	**AAcc × aaCc**	1 agouti : 1 albino

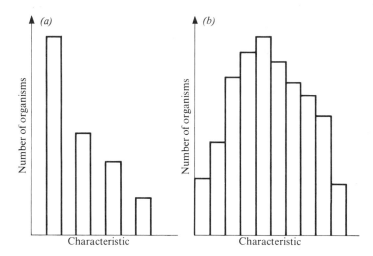

Fig 23.29 *Histograms representing frequency distribution in the case of (a) discontinuous variation and (b) continuous variation*

23.7.6 Polygenic inheritance

Many of the most obvious characteristics of organisms are produced by the combined effect of many different genes. These genes form a special gene complex known as a **polygenic system**. Whilst the effect of each gene alone is too small to make any significant impression on the phenotype, the almost infinite variety produced by the combined effect of these genes (**polygenes**) has been shown to form the genetic basis of **continuous variation**, which is described further in section 23.8.2.

23.8 Variation

The term variation describes the difference in characteristics shown by organisms belonging to the same natural population or species. It was the amazing diversity of structure within any species that caught the attention of Darwin and Wallace during their travels. The regularity and predictability with which these differences in characteristics were inherited formed the basis of Mendel's research. Whilst Darwin recognised that particular characteristics could be developed by selective breeding, as described in section 24.4.2, it was Mendel who explained the mechanism by which selected characteristics were passed on from generation to generation.

Mendel described how hereditary factors determine the genotype of an organism which in the course of development becomes expressed in the structural, physiological and biochemical characteristics of the phenotype. Whilst the phenotypic appearance of any characteristic is ultimately determined by the genes controlling that characteristic, the extent to which certain characteristics develop may be influenced by the environment.

A study of phenotypic differences in any large population shows that two forms of variation occur, discontinuous and continuous. Studies of variation in a character involve measuring the expression of that characteristic in a large number of organisms within the population, such as height in Man. The results are plotted as a histogram or a graph which reveals the **frequency distribution** of the variations of that characteristic within the population. Typical results obtained from such studies are shown in fig 23.29 and they highlight the difference between the two forms of variation.

23.8.1 Discontinuous variation

There are certain characteristics within a population which exhibit a limited form of variation. Variation in this case produces individuals showing clear-cut differences with no intermediates between them, such as blood groups in Man, wing length in *Drosophila*, melanic and light forms in *Biston betularia*, style length in *Primula* and sex in animals and plants. Characteristics showing discontinuous variation are usually controlled by one or two major genes which may have two or more allelic forms and their phenotypic expression is relatively unaffected by environmental conditions.

Since the phenotypic variation is restricted to certain clear-cut characteristics, this form of variation is alternatively known as **qualitative inheritance**, as opposed to **quantitative inheritance** which is characteristic of continuous variation.

23.8.2 Continuous variation

Many characteristics in a population show a complete gradation from one extreme to the other without any break. This is illustrated most clearly by characteristics such as mass, linear dimension, shape and colour of organs and organisms. The frequency distribution for a characteristic exhibiting continuous variation is a **normal distribution curve** (section A2.7.3). Most of the organisms in the population fall in the middle of the range with approximately equal numbers showing the two extreme forms of the characteristic. Characteristics exhibiting continuous variation are produced by the combined effects of many genes (polygenes) and environmental factors. Individually each of these genes has little effect on the phenotype but their combined effect is significant.

23.8.3 Environmental influences

The ultimate factor determining a phenotypic characteristic is the genotype. At the moment of fertilisation the genotype of the organism is determined, but the subsequent degree of expression allowed to this genetic potential is influenced greatly by the action of environmental factors during the development of the organism. For example, Mendel's tall variety of garden pea normally attained a height of six feet. However, it would only do so if provided with adequate light, water and soil conditions. A reduction in the supply of any of these factors (**limiting factors**) would prevent the gene for height exerting its full effect. It was the Danish geneticist Johanssen who demonstrated the effect of the interaction of genotypic and environmental factors on phenotype. In a series of experiments on the mass of dwarf bean seeds he selected the heaviest and lightest seeds from each generation of self-pollinating dwarf bean plants and used these to produce the next generation. After repeating these experiments for several years he found only small differences in the mean mass of seeds from the same selected line, that is heavy or light, but large differences in mean mass of seeds from different selected lines, that is heavy and light. This suggested that both heredity and environment were influencing the phenotypic appearance of the characteristic. From these results it is possible to describe continuous phenotypic variation as being '**the cumulative effect of varying environmental factors acting on a variable genotype**'. The results also indicated that the extent to which a characteristic is inherited is determined primarily by the genotype. In the development of human characteristics such as personality, temperament and intelligence, there is evidence to suggest that both **nature** (hereditary factors) and **nurture** (environmental factors) interact to varying degrees in different individuals to influence the final appearance of the characteristic. It is these genetic and environmental differences which act to produce phenotypic differences between individuals. There is no firm evidence, as yet, to suggest that one factor is universally more influential than the other, but the environment can never increase the extent of the phenotype beyond that determined by the genotype.

23.8.4 Sources of variation

It will be appreciated that, as a result of the interaction between discontinuous and continuous variations and the environment, no two organisms will possess identical phenotypes. Replication of DNA is so nearly perfect that there is little possibility of variation occurring in the genotypes of asexually reproducing organisms. Any apparent variation between these organisms is therefore almost certainly the result of environmental influences. In the case of sexually reproducing organisms there is ample opportunity for genetic variation to arise. Two processes occurring during meiosis and the fusion of gametes during fertilisation provide the means of introducing unlimited genetic variation into the population. These may be summarised as follows:

(1) Reciprocal crossing-over of genes between chromatids of homologous chromosomes may occur during prophase I of meiosis. This produces new linkage groups and so provides a major source of genetic recombination of alleles (section 23.3 and 22.3).

(2) The orientation of the chromatids of homologous chromosomes (bivalents) on the equatorial spindle during metaphase I of meiosis determines the direction in which the pairs of chromatids move during anaphase I. This orientation of the chromatids is random. During metaphase II the orientation of pairs of chromatids once more is random and determines which chromosomes migrate to opposite poles of the cell during anaphase II. These random orientations and the subsequent independent assortment (segregation) of the chromosomes gives rise to a large calculable number of different chromosome combinations in the gametes (section 23.2.1)

A third source of variation in sexual reproduction results from the fact that the fusion of male and female gametes containing complementary sets of haploid chromosomes to produce a diploid zygotic nucleus is completely random (at least in theory). Thus, any male gamete is potentially capable of fusing with any female gamete.

These sources of genetic variation account for the routine '**gene reshuffling**' which is the basis of continuous variation. The environment acts on the range of phenotypes produced and those best suited to it thrive. This leads to changes in allele and genotypic frequencies as described in chapter 25. However, these sources of variation do not generate the major changes in genotype which are necessary in order to give rise to new species as described by evolutionary theory. These changes are produced by mutations.

23.9 Mutation

A mutation is a change in the amount or the structure of the DNA of an organism. This produces a change in the genotype which may be inherited by cells derived by mitosis or meiosis from the mutant cell. A mutation may result in the change in appearance of a characteristic in a population. Mutations occurring in gamete cells are inherited, whereas those occurring in somatic cells can only be inherited by daughter cells produced by mitosis. The latter are known as **somatic mutations**.

A mutation resulting from a change in the amount or arrangement of DNA is known as a **chromosomal mutation** or **chromosomal aberration**. Some forms of these affect the chromosomes to such an extent that they may be seen under the microscope. Increasingly the term mutation is being used to describe a change in the structure of the DNA at a single locus and this is known as a **gene mutation** or **point mutation**.

The concept of mutation as the cause of the sudden appearance of a new characteristic was first proposed by the Dutch botanist Hugo de Vries in 1901, following his work on inheritance in the evening primrose *Oenothera lamarckiana*. Nine years later T. H. Morgan began a series of investigations into mutations in *Drosophila* and, with the assistance of geneticists throughout the world, identified over 500 mutations.

23.9.1 Mutation frequency and causes of mutation

Mutations occur randomly and spontaneously; that is to say that any gene can undergo mutation at any time. The rates at which mutations occur vary between organisms.

As a result of the work of H. J. Müller in the 1920s it was observed that the frequency of mutation could be increased above the spontaneous level by the effects of X-rays. Since then it has been shown that the mutation rates can be significantly increased by the effects of high energy electromagnetic radiation such as ultra-violet light, X-rays and gamma rays. High-energy particles, such as α and β particles, neutrons and cosmic radiation, are also **mutagenic**, that is cause mutations. A variety of chemical substances, including mustard gas, caffeine, formaldehyde, colchicine, certain constituents of tobacco and an increasing number of drugs, food preservatives and pesticides, have been shown to be mutagenic.

23.9.2 Chromosome mutations

Chromosomal mutations may be the result of changes in the number or structure of chromosomes. Certain forms of chromosomal mutation may affect several genes and have a more profound effect on the phenotype than gene mutations. Changes in the number of chromosomes are usually the result of errors occurring during meiosis but they can also occur during mitosis. These changes may involve the loss or gain of single chromosomes, a condition called **aneuploidy**, or the increase in entire haploid sets of chromosomes, a condition called **euploidy (polyploidy)**.

Aneuploidy

In this condition half the daughter cells produced have an extra chromosome $(n + 1)$, $(2n + 1)$ and so on, whilst the other half have a chromosome missing $(n - 1)$, $(2n - 1)$ and so on. Aneuploidy can arise from the failure of a pair, or pairs, of homologous chromosomes to separate during anaphase I of meiosis. If this occurs, both sets of chromosomes pass to the same pole of the cell and separation of the homologous chromosomes during anaphase II may lead to the formation of gamete cells containing either one or more chromosomes too many or too few as shown in fig 23.30. This is known as **non-disjunction**.

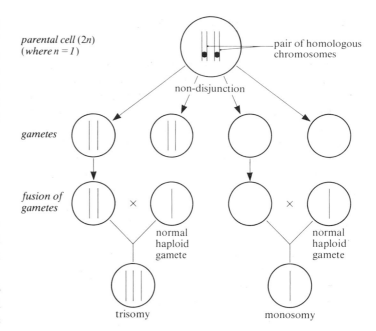

Fig 23.30 *Non-disjunction in gamete cell formation and the results of fusion of these abnormal gametes with normal haploid cells. The resulting cells may show a form of polysomy where the chromosome number may be (2n + 1) trisomy, (2n + 2) tetrasomy, (2n + 3) pentasomy etc., or monosomy (2n − 1) depending upon the number of homologous chromosomes which fail to separate normally*

Fusion of either of these gametes with a normal haploid gamete produces a zygote with an odd number of chromosomes.

Zygotes containing less than the diploid number of chromosomes usually fail to develop, but those with polysomic chromosomes may develop. In most cases where this occurs in animals it produces severe abnormalities. One of the commonest forms of chromosomal mutation in Man resulting from non-disjunction is a form of trisomy is called **Down's syndrome** $(2n = 47)$. The condition, which is named after the doctor who first described it in 1866, is due to the non-disjunction of the G21 chromosomes (fig 23.31). The symptoms of Down's syndrome include mental retardation, reduced resistance to disease, congenital heart abnormalities, a short stocky body and thick neck, and the characteristic folds of skin over the inner corner of the eye which produce a superficial facial similarity to Mongolians. The syndrome is commonly, but rather cruelly, termed mongolism. Down's syndrome and other related chromosomal abnormalities occur more frequently in children born to older women. The exact reason for this is unknown but appears to be related to the age of the mother's egg cells.

Non-disjunction of the male and female sex chromosomes may also occur and produce aneuploidy affecting secondary sexual characteristics, fertility and, in some cases, intelligence (table 23.8).

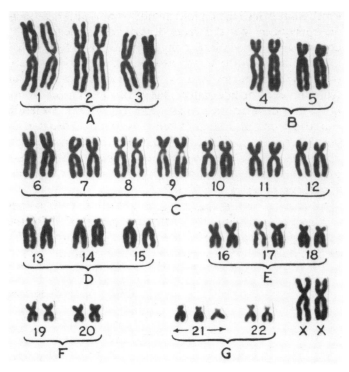

Fig 23.31 *The chromosomes of a female suffering from Down's syndrome. The non-disjunction of chromosomes G21 in one of the gametes has led to these chromosomes being trisomic in this female. A photograph, such as the one above, shows a complete set of chromosomes for an individual known as a karyotype*

Table 23.8 Phenotypic abnormalities resulting from non-disjunction of the sex chromosomes.

Condition/ Genotype	Symptoms	Frequency in Western populations
Klinefelter's syndrome (XXY)	♂, possessing some ♀ secondary sexual characteristics, sterile, testes very small, little facial hair, breasts may develop, usually low intelligence	0.02%
Turner's syndrome (XO)	♀, lacking normal secondary sexual characteristics and very short, nipples close together	0.03%
XXX	♀, normal appearance, fertile, but mentally retarded	0.12%
XYY	♂, tall, variable intelligence, may possess psychopathic traits or tendency for petty criminal acts	0.1%

Euploidy (polyploidy)

...matic cells containing multiples of the ...romosomes are called **polyploids**, and ...a-, and so on, indicate the extent of ...nple 3n is triploid, 4n is tetraploid, 5n is

pentaploid and so on. Polyploidy is much more common in plants than in animals. For example, approximately half the 300 000 known species of angiosperms are polyploid. The relatively low occurrence in animals is explained by the fact that the increased number of chromosomes in polyploids makes normal gamete formation during meiosis much more prone to error. Since most plants are capable of propagating themselves vegetatively they are able to reproduce despite being polyploid. Polyploidy is often associated with advantageous features such as increased size, hardiness and resistance to disease. This is called **hybrid vigour** (section 25.4.2). Most of our domestic plants are polyploids producing large fruits, storage organs, flowers or leaves.

There are two forms of polyploidy, autopolyploidy and allopolyploidy.

Autopolyploidy. This condition may arise naturally or artificially as a result of an increase in number of chromosomes within the same species. For example, if chromosomes undergo replication (during interphase) and the chromatids separate normally (during anaphase) but the cytoplasm fails to cleave (during cytokinesis), a **tetraploid** (4n) cell with a large nucleus is produced. This cell will undergo division and produce tetraploid cells. The amount of cytoplasm in these cells increases to preserve the nucleo-cytoplasmic volume ratio and leads to an increase in the size of the whole plant or some part of it. Autopolyploidy can be induced by the use of a drug called **colchicine** which is extracted from the corm of the autumn crocus (*Colchicum*). Concentrations of the order of 0.01% inhibit spindle formation by disrupting microtubules so that the chromatids fail to separate during anaphase. Colchicine and related drugs have been used in the breeding of certain varieties of economically important crops such as tobacco, tomatoes and sugarbeet. Autopolyploids can be as fertile as diploids if they have an even number of chromosome sets.

A modified form of polyploidy can occur in animals and give rise to cells and tissues which are polyploid. This process is called **endomitosis** and involves chromosome replication without cell division. The giant chromosomes in the salivary glands of *Drosophila* and tetraploid cells in the human liver are produced by endomitosis.

Allopolyploidy. This condition arises when the chromosome number in a sterile hybrid becomes doubled and produces fertile hybrids. F_1 hybrids produced from different species are usually sterile since their chromosomes cannot form homologous pairs during meiosis. This is called **hybrid sterility**. However, if multiples of the original haploid number of chromosomes, for example $2(n_1 + n_2)$, $3(n_1 + n_2)$ and so on (where n_1 and n_2 are the haploid numbers of the parent species) occur, a new species is produced which is fertile with polyploids like itself but infertile with both parental species.

Most allopolyploid species have a diploid chromosome number which is the sum of the diploid numbers of their parental species; for example rice grass (*Spartina anglica* (2n = 122) is a fertile allopolyploid hybrid produced from a cross between *Spartina maritima* (*stricta*) (2n = 60) and *Spartina alterniflora* (2n = 62). (The F₁ hybrid formed from the latter two species is sterile and is called *Spartina townsendii* (2n = 62)). Most allopolyploid plants have different characteristics from either parental species, and include many of Man's most economically important plants. For example, the species of wheat used to make bread, *Triticum aestivum* (2n = 42), has been selectively bred over a period of 5 000 years. By crossing a wild variety of wheat, einkorn wheat (2n = 14), with 'wild grass' (2n = 14) a different species of wheat, emmer wheat (2n = 28), was produced. Emmer wheat has crossed with another species of wild grass (2n = 14) to produce *Triticum aestivum* (2n = 42) which actually represents the hexaploid condition (6n) of the original einkorn wheat. Another example of interspecific hybridisation involving crossing the radish and cabbage is described in section 25.9.

Allopolyploidy does not occur in animals because there are fewer instances of cross-breeding between species. Polyploidy does not add new genes to a gene pool (section 25.1.1) but gives rise to a new combination of genes.

Structural changes in chromosomes

Crossing-over during prophase I of meiosis involves the reciprocal transfer of genetic material between homologous chromosomes. This changes the allele sequence of parental linkage groups and produces recombinants, but no gene loci are lost. Similar effects to these are produced by the structural changes in chromosomes known as inversions and translocations. In other forms of change, such as deletions and duplications, the number of gene loci on chromosomes is changed, and this can have profound effects on the phenotypes. Structural changes in chromosomes resulting from inversion, deletion and duplication, and in some cases from translocation, may be observed under the microscope when homologous chromosomes attempt to pair during prophase I of meiosis. Homologous genes undergo synapsis (pairing) (section 22.3) and a loop or twist is formed in one of the homologous chromosomes as a result of the structural change. Which chromosome forms the loop and the arrangement of its genes depends upon the type of structural change.

Inversion occurs when a region of a chromosome breaks off and rotates through 180° before rejoining the chromosome. No change in genotype occurs as a result of inversion but phenotypic changes may be seen (fig 23.32). This suggests that the order of gene loci on the chromosome is important; a phenomenon known as the **position effect**.

Translocation involves a region of a chromosome breaking off and rejoining either the other end of the same chromosome or another non-homologous chromosome (fig 23.32). The position effect may again be seen in the phenotype. Reciprocal translocation between non-homologous chromosomes can produce two new homologous pairs of chromosomes. In some cases of Down's

syndrome, where the diploid number is normal, the effects are produced by the translocation of an extra G21 chromosome onto a larger chromosome, usually D15.

The simplest form of chromosomal mutation is **deletion**, which involves the loss of a region of a chromosome, either from the ends or internally. This results in a chromosome becoming deficient in certain genes (fig 23.33). Deletion can affect one of a homologous pair of chromosomes, in which case the alleles present on the non-deficient chromosome will be expressed even if recessive. If deletion affects the same gene loci on both homologous chromosomes the effect is usually lethal.

In some cases a region of a chromosome becomes duplicated so that an additional set of genes exists for the region of **duplication**. The additional region of genes may be incorporated within the chromosome or at one end of

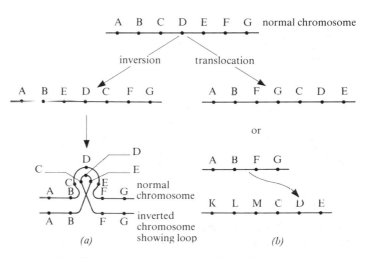

Fig 23.32 *Diagrammatic representation of inversion and translocation and their effects on the positions of genes A–G. (a) Looping in prophase due to inversion. (b) Part of the chromosome carrying genes C, D and E has broken off and become attached to the chromosome carrying genes K, L and M*

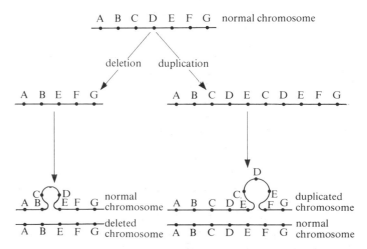

Fig 23.33 *Diagrammatic representations of deletion and duplication and their effects on the positions of genes A–G. In both cases looping can be seen*

855

the chromosome, or become attached to another chromosome (fig 23.33).

23.9.3 Gene mutations

Sudden and spontaneous changes in phenotype, for which there are no conventional genetic explanations or any microscopic evidence of chromosomal mutation, can only be explained in terms of changes in gene structure. A **gene mutation** or **point mutation** (since it applies to a particular gene locus) is the result of a change in the nucleotide sequence of the DNA molecule in a particular region of the chromosome. Such a change in the base sequence of the gene is transmitted to mRNA during transcription and may result in a change in the amino acid sequence of the polypeptide chain produced from it during translation at the ribosomes (section 22.6).

There are a variety of forms of gene mutation involving the addition, loss or rearrangement of bases in the gene. These mutations take the form of the **duplication**, **insertion**, **deletion**, **inversion** or **substitution** of bases. In all cases they change the nucleotide sequence and result in the formation of a modified polypeptide. For example, deletion causes a **frame shift** and the implications of this are described in section 22.5.

Gene mutations occurring during gamete formation are transmitted to all the cells of the offspring and may be significant for the future of the species. Somatic gene mutations which arise in the organism are inherited only by those cells derived from the mutant cells by mitosis. Whilst they may affect that organism, they are lost on the death of the organism. Somatic mutations are probably very common and go unnoticed, but in some cases they may produce cells with an increased rate of growth and division. These cells may give rise to a tumour which may be **benign** and not affect other tissues, or **malignant**, which lives parasitically on healthy cells, a condition known as *cancer*.

The effects of gene mutation are extremely variable. Most minor gene mutations pass unnoticed in the phenotype since they are recessive, but there are several cases where a change in a single base in the genetic code can have a profound effect on the phenotype. **Sickle cell anaemia** in Man is an example of **base substitution** mutation affecting a base in one of the genes involved in the production of haemoglobin. The respiratory pigment haemoglobin of adults is made up of four polypeptide chains (two α chains and two β chains) attached to the prosthetic group haem. The polypeptide chains influence the oxygen-carrying capacity of the haemoglobin molecule. A change in the base sequence of the triplet coding for one particular amino acid out of the 146 in the β chains gives rise to the production of sickle cell haemoglobin (HbS). The amino acid sequences for the normal and abnormal β chains differ in the substitution of **valine** for **glutamic acid** at one point in the abnormal polypeptide chains of **haemoglobin S**. Such a minor change causes haemoglobin S to crystallise at low oxygen concentrations. The histological effect of this is to cause haemoglobin-S-containing red blood cells to distort and appear sickle-shaped. The physiological effect is to lower the amount of oxygen which can be carried by these cells, leading to acute anaemia. This not only causes physical weakness, but may lead to heart and kidney failure and an early death in individuals homozygous for the mutant allele. In the heterozygous condition individuals show the **sickle cell trait**. The red blood cells appear normal and only about 40% of the haemoglobin is abnormal. This produces only mild anaemia and in parts of the world where malaria is endemic, Africa and Asia in particular, it prevents carriers of the trait from contracting the disease. This is because the protozoan *Plasmodium*, which causes malaria, cannot live in red blood cells containing the abnormal haemoglobin (section 25.1.5).

23.9.4 Implications of mutation

The effects of chromosome and gene mutations are very variable. In many cases the mutations are lethal and prevent development of the organism, for example in humans about 20% of pregnancies end in natural abortion before 12 weeks and of these about 50% exhibit a chromosome abnormality. Some forms of chromosome mutation may bring certain gene sequences together, and that combined effect may produce a 'beneficial' characteristic. Another significance of bringing certain genes closer together is that they are less likely to be separated by crossing-over and this is an advantage with beneficial genes.

Gene mutation may lead to several alleles occupying a specific locus. This increases both the heterozygosity and size of the gene pool of the population and leads to an increase in variation within the population. Gene reshuffling as a result of crossing-over, independent assortment, random fertilisation and mutations, may increase the amount of continuous variation but the evolutionary implications of this are often short-lived since the changes produced may be rapidly diluted. Certain gene mutations, on the other hand, increase discontinuous variation and this has the more profound effect on changes in the population. Most gene mutations are recessive to the 'normal' allele which has come to form genetic equilibrium with the rest of the genotype and the environment as a result of successfully withstanding selection over many generations. Being recessive the mutant alleles may remain in the population for many generations until they come together in the homozygous condition and are expressed phenotypically. Occasionally a dominant mutant allele may arise in which case it will appear immediately in the phenotype (section 25.5, *Biston betularia*).

The information provided in this chapter accounts for the origins of variation within populations and the mechanisms by which characteristics are inherited, but it does not explain how the amazing diversity of living organisms described in chapters 2–4 may have arisen. Possible answers to this problem form the basis of the next two chapters.

Chapter Twenty-four

Evolution – history of life

The nature of life, its origin, the diversity of living organisms and the unifying structural and functional relationships which underlie this diversity form a focal point within the study of biology.

This chapter attempts to describe and discuss the many theories concerning the origin of life and the possible ways in which species have originated. Traditionally the study of the history of life has been fraught with allegations of indoctrination. Indoctrination may be defined as a conscious effort to inculcate an unshakeable commitment to a belief or doctrine. Such an approach is not only anti-scientific but also intellectually dishonest, and efforts to avoid this have been made in this text. A brief outline of the main theories on the origin of life is presented in this chapter so that students are aware that there is diversity of opinion as to the nature of this event. Much of the evidence on which these theories are based is metaphysical, that is to say it is impossible to repeat the exact events of the origin of life in any demonstrable way. This is true of both scientific and theological accounts. However, one theory, evolution, is increasingly being seen not as a single metaphysical theory but as a collection of individual scientific hypotheses each of which is capable of being tested, as described in section A2.1.

In this chapter, and in chapter 25, scientific facts have been selected to produce a coherent account of the processes underlying the origins and diversity of forms of life. Because of the necessity to be selective this account lacks absolute objectivity; indeed, this is inevitably true of any account, be it historical, scientific or metaphysical. However, by stressing the limitations and assumptions associated with the evidence presented here, this account may have a degree of objectivity and tentativeness which characterises good scientific writing. It must be stressed that the evidence presented in this chapter, and the conclusions drawn from it, represent current views. These are constantly under review and their validity is limited by the knowledge available to us at any given time.

24.1 Theories of the origin of life

Theories concerned with the origin of the Earth, and indeed the Universe, are diverse and uncertain. Steady-state cosmologists maintain that the Universe never had an origin. Other hypotheses suggest that it may have begun as a ball of neutrons, exploded in a 'big bang', emerged from one of several black holes, or may be the design of a Creator. Science, contrary to popular belief, cannot contradict the idea of a divine origin for the early universe, nor do theological views necessarily dismiss the view that during the origins of life, life acquired those characteristics explained by the natural laws of science.

The major theories accounting for the origin of life on Earth are:

(1) life was created by a supernatural being at a particular time (**special creation**);
(2) life arose from non-living matter on numerous occasions (**spontaneous generation**);
(3) life has no origin (**steady-state**);
(4) life arrived on this planet from elsewhere (**cosmozoan**);
(5) life arose according to chemical and physical laws (**biochemical evolution**).

24.1.1 Special creation

This theory is upheld by most of the world's major religions and civilisations and attributes the origin of life to a supernatural event at a particular time in the past. Archbishop Ussher of Armagh calculated in 1650 that God created the world in October 4004 BC, and finished with Man at 9.00 a.m. on the morning of the 23rd. He achieved this figure by adding up the ages of all the people in the biblical genealogies from Adam to Christ (the 'begats'). Whilst the arithmetic is sound, it places Adam as having lived at a time when archaeological evidence suggests that there was a well-established urban civilisation in the Middle East.

The traditional Judaeo-Christian account of creation, given in Genesis 1:1–26, has attracted, and continues to attract, controversy. Whilst all Christians would agree that the Bible is God's word to Man, there are differences of interpretation concerning the length of the 'day' mentioned in Genesis. Some believe that the world and all species were created in six days of 24 hours duration. They reject any other possible views and rely absolutely on inspiration, meditation and divine revelation. Other Christians do not regard the Bible as a scientific textbook and see the Genesis account as the theological revelation of the Creation of all living things through the power of God, described in terms understandable to men in all ages. For them the Creation account is concerned with answering the question 'Why?' rather than 'How?'. Whilst science broadly relies on observation and experiment to seek truth, theology draws its insights from divine revelation and faith.

'Faith is the substance of things hoped for, the

evidence of things not seen . . . by faith . . . we understand that the universe was created by God's word, so that what can be seen was made out of what cannot be seen.' (Hebrews 11:1, 3)

Faith accepts things for which there is no evidence in the scientific sense. This means that logically there can be no intellectual conflict between scientific and theological accounts of creation, since they are mutually exclusive realms of thought. Scientific truth to the scientist is tentative, but theological truth to the theist is absolute.

Since the process of special creation occurred only once and therefore cannot be observed, this is sufficient to put the concept of special creation outside the framework of scientific investigation. Science concerns itself only with observable phenomena and as such will never be able to prove or disprove special creation.

24.1.2 Spontaneous generation

This theory was prevalent in ancient Chinese, Babylonian and Egyptian thought as an alternative to special creation, with which it coexisted. Aristotle (384–322 BC), often hailed as the founder of biology, believed that life arose spontaneously. On the basis of his personal observations he developed this belief further in relating all organisms to a continuum, a *scala natura* (ladder of life).

'For nature passes from lifeless objects to animals in such unbroken sequence, interposing between them, beings which live and yet are not animals, that scarcely any difference seems to exist between neighbouring groups, owing to their close proximity.' (Aristotle)

In stating this he reinforced the previous speculations of Empedocles on organic evolution. Aristotle's hypothesis of spontaneous generation assumed that certain 'particles' of matter contained an 'active principle' which could produce a living organism when conditions were suitable. He was correct in assuming that the active principle was present in a fertilised egg, but incorrectly extrapolated this to the belief that sunlight, mud and decaying meat also had the active principle.

'Such are the facts, everything comes into being not only from the mating of animals but from the decay of earth . . . And among plants the matter proceeds in the same way, some develop from seed, others, as it were, by spontaneous generation by natural forces; they arise from decaying earth or from certain parts of plants.' (Aristotle)

With the spread of Christianity, the spontaneous generation theory fell from favour, except among those who believed in magic and devil-worship, although it remained as a background idea for many more centuries.

Van Helmont (1577–1644), a much-acclaimed and successful scientist, described an experiment which gave rise to mice in three weeks. The raw materials for the experiment were a dirty shirt, a dark cupboard and a handful of wheat grains. The active principle in this process was thought to be human sweat.

24.1 What did Van Helmont omit from his experiment?

In 1688 Francesco Redi, an Italian biologist and physician living in Florence, took a more rigorous approach to the problem of the origin of life and questioned the theory of spontaneous generation. Redi observed that the little white worms seen on decaying flesh were fly larvae. By a series of experiments he produced evidence to support the idea that life can arise only from pre-existing life, the concept of **biogenesis**.

'Belief would be vain without the confirmation of experiment, hence in the middle of July, I put a snake, some fish, some eels of the Arno and a slice of milk-fed veal in four large, wide-mouthed flasks; having well closed and sealed them, I then filled the same number of flasks in the same way, leaving only these open.' (Redi)

Redi reported his results as follows.

'It was not long before the meat and the fish, in these second vessels (the unsealed ones), became wormy and the flies were seen entering and leaving at will; but in the closed flasks I did not see a worm, though many days had passed since the dead fish had been put in them.'

24.2 What do you consider was Redi's basic assumption?

These experiments, however, did not destroy the idea of spontaneous generation and, whilst the old theory took a setback, it continued to be the dominant theory within the secular community.

Whilst Redi's experiments appeared to refute the spontaneous generation of flies, the pioneer work in microscopy by Anton van Leeuwenhoek appeared to reinforce the theory with regard to micro-organisms. Whilst not entering the debate between biogenesis and spontaneous generation, his observations with the microscope provided fuel for both theories and finally stimulated other scientists to design experiments to settle the question of the origin of life by spontaneous generation.

In 1765 Lazzaro Spallanzani boiled animal and vegetable broths for several hours and sealed them immediately. He then removed them from the source of heat. After being set aside for several days, none of them, on examination, showed any signs of life. He concluded from this that the high temperature had destroyed all forms of living organisms in his vessel and without their presence no life could appear.

24.3 Suggest another reason why Spallanzani's experiment might have prevented the growth of organisms.

In 1860 Louis Pasteur turned his attention to the problem of the origins of life. By this stage he had demonstrated the existence of bacteria and found the solutions to the economic problems of the silk and wine industries. He had also shown that bacteria were ubiquitous and that non-living matter could easily become contaminated by living matter if all materials were not adequately sterilised.

24.4 What were Pasteur's basic assumptions about the origins of life?

In a series of experiments based upon those of Spallanzani, Pasteur demonstrated the theory of biogenesis and finally disproved the theory of spontaneous generation.

The validation of biogenesis however raised another problem. Since it was now clear that a living organism was required in order to produce another living organism, where did the first living organism come from? The steady-state hypothesis has an answer for this but all the other theories imply a transition from non-living to living at some stage in the history of life. Was this a primeval spontaneous generation?

Experiment 24.1: To investigate the origin of micro-organisms in terms of spontaneous generation and biogenesis

The objectives of this experiment are to repeat the experiments of Spallanzani and Pasteur and carry out further guided experiments which take into account the criticisms of their experimental techniques, and to evaluate objectively the hypotheses of spontaneous generation and biogenesis.

Materials

8 × 30 cm^3 boiling tubes	straight glass tubing
boiling tube rack	0.5 × 6 cm
120 cm^3 nutrient broth	air-lock (S-shaped) glass
5 cotton wool plugs	tubing 0.5 × 10 cm
aluminium foil	access to: autoclave,
water bath	incubator set at 32 °C

Method

(1) Autoclave eight boiling tubes.
(2) Place 15 cm^3 of nutrient broth into each of these boiling tubes, labelled 1–8.
(3) Set up tubes 1–8 as outlined below.

Pair A
Tube 1 – Leave unplugged, do not heat.
Tube 2 – Plug with cotton wool and cover top with aluminium foil. Do not heat.

Pair B
Tube 3 – Leave unplugged. Heat in a boiling water bath for 10 min.
Tube 4 – Plug with cotton wool and cover top with aluminium foil. Heat in a boiling water-bath for 10 min.

Pair C
Tube 5 – Leave unplugged. Autoclave at 15 lb pressure for 20 min.

Tube 6 – Plug with cotton wool and cover top with aluminium foil. Autoclave at 15 lb pressure for 20 min.

Pair D
Tube 7 – Surround straight glass tubing with cotton wool and plug boiling tube. Autoclave at 15 lb pressure for 20 min.
Tube 8 – Surround S-shaped glass tubing with cotton wool and plug boiling tube. Autoclave at 15 lb pressure for 20 min.

(4) Place all boiling tubes in an incubator at 32 °C.
(5) Examine all boiling tubes every two days for ten days. Record observations in the form of a table.
(6) After ten days remove a drop of broth from each tube using sterile techniques and examine under the high power of the microscope. Record observations in the form of a table.
(7) Draw conclusions from these observations.

24.5 Clearly state the hypothesis which would account for the appearance of micro-organisms in the nutrient broth.

24.6 List the variables (factors) which may influence the appearance of micro-organisms in the broth.

24.7 Which variable differs between each of the tubes 1 and 2, 3 and 4, 5 and 6, and 7 and 8?

24.8 Which variable differs between the pairs of tubes A, B, C and D?

24.9 Which tubes repeat the experiments of Spallanzani and Pasteur?

24.10 Which tubes act as controls?

24.11 Do you consider that the experiments carried out above meet all the criteria of a scientific investigation, and what degree of validity would you attach to your conclusions?

24.1.3 Steady-state theory

This theory asserts that the Earth had no origin, has always been able to support life, has changed remarkably little, if at all, and that species had no origin.

Estimates of the age of the Earth have varied greatly from the 4004 BC calculation of Archbishop Ussher to the present-day values of $5\,000 \times 10^6$ years based on radioactive decay rates. Improved scientific dating techniques (Appendix 5) give increasing ages for the Earth, and extrapolation of this trend provides advocates of this theory with the hypothesis that the Earth had no origin. Whilst generally discrediting the value of geochronology in giving a precise age for the Earth, the steady-state theory uses this as a basis for supposing that the Earth has always existed. This theory proposes that species, too, never originated, they have always existed and that in the history of a species the only alternatives are for its numbers to vary, or for it to become extinct.

The theory does not accept the palaeontological evidence that presence or absence of a fossil indicates the origin or extinction of the species represented and quotes, as an example, the case of the coelacanth, *Latimeria*. Fossil evidence indicates that the coelacanths died out at the end of the Cretaceous period, 70 million years ago. The discovery of living specimens off the coast of Madagascar has altered this view. The steady-state theory claims that it is only by studying living species and comparing them with the fossil record that extinction can be assumed and then there is a high probability that this may be incorrect. The palaeontological evidence presented in support of the steady-state theory describes the fossil's appearance in ecological terms. For example, the sudden appearance of a fossil in a particular stratum would be associated with an increase in population size or movement of the organism into an area which favoured fossilisation. Most evidence for this theory is based on discredited aspects of evolutionary theory such as the gaps in the fossil record and is best studied, in detail, alongside it.

24.1.4 Cosmozoan theory

This theory does not offer a mechanism to account for the origin of life but favours the idea that it had an extraterrestrial origin. It does not therefore, constitute a theory of origin as such, but merely transposes the problem to elsewhere in the Universe.

The theory states that life could have arisen once or several times, at various times and in various parts of the Galaxy or Universe. Its alternative name is the theory of **panspermia**. Repeated sightings of UFOs, cave-drawings of rocket-like objects and 'spacemen' and reports of encounters with aliens provide the background evidence for this theory. Russian and American space probes have provided evidence that the likelihood of finding life within our Solar System is remote but cannot comment on the nature of life outside our Solar System. Research into meteoritic and cometary materials has revealed the presence of many pre-vital organic molecules, such as cyanogen and hydrocyanic acid, which may have acted as 'seeds' falling on a barren Earth. There are several claims that objects bearing resemblances to primitive forms of life on Earth have been found in meteorites but they have yet to gain any real credibility in scientific circles.

24.1.5 Biochemical evolution

It is generally agreed by astronomers, geologists and biologists that the Earth is some $4.5–5.0 \times 10^9$ years old.

Many biologists believe that the original state of the Earth bore little resemblance to its present-day form and had the following probable appearance: it was hot (about $4\,000–8\,000\ °C$) and as it cooled carbon and the less volatile metals condensed and formed the Earth's core; the surface was probably barren and rugged as volcanic activity, continuous earth movements and contraction on cooling, folded and fractured the surface.

The atmosphere is believed to have been totally different in those days. The lighter gases hydrogen, helium, nitrogen, oxygen and argon would have escaped because the gravitational field of the partially condensed planet would not contain them. However, simple compounds containing these elements (amongst others) would have been retained, such as water, ammonia, carbon dioxide and methane, and until the earth cooled below 100 °C all water would have existed as vapour. The atmosphere would appear to have been a 'reducing atmosphere', as indicated by the presence of metals in their reduced form (such as iron(II)) in the oldest rocks of the Earth. More recent rocks contain metals in their oxidised form (for example iron(III)). The lack of oxygen in the atmosphere would probably be a necessity, since laboratory experiments have shown, paradoxically, that it is far easier to generate organic molecules (the basis of living organisms) in a reducing atmosphere than in an oxygen-rich atmosphere.

In 1923 Alexander Oparin suggested that the atmosphere of the primeval Earth was not as we know it today but fitted the description given above. On theoretical grounds he argued that organic compounds, probably hydrocarbons, could have formed in the oceans from more simple compounds, the energy for these synthesis reactions probably being supplied from the strong solar radiation (mainly ultra-violet) which surrounded the Earth before the formation of the ozone layer, which now blocks much of it out. Oparin argued that if one considered the multitude of simple molecules present in the oceans, the surface area of the Earth, the energy available and the time scale, it was conceivable that oceans would gradually accumulate organic molecules to produce the 'primeval soup', in which life could have arisen. This was not a new idea, indeed Darwin himself expressed a similar thought in a letter he wrote in 1871:

'It is often said that all the conditions for the first production of a living organism are now present, which could ever have been present. But if, (and oh what a big if) we could conceive of some warm little pond, with all sorts of ammonia and phosphoric salts, light, heat, electricity, etc., present that a protein compound was chemically formed ready to undergo still more complex changes, at the present day, such matter would be constantly devoured or absorbed, which could not have been the case before living creatures were formed.'

In 1953 Stanley Miller, in a series of experiments, simulated the proposed conditions on the primitive Earth. In his experimental high-energy chamber (fig 24.1) he successfully synthesised many substances of considerable biological importance, including amino acids, adenine and simple sugars such as ribose. More recently Orgel at the Salk Institute has succeeded in synthesising nucleotides six units long (a simple nucleic acid molecule) in a similar experiment.

It has since been suggested that carbon dioxide was present in relatively high concentrations in the primeval

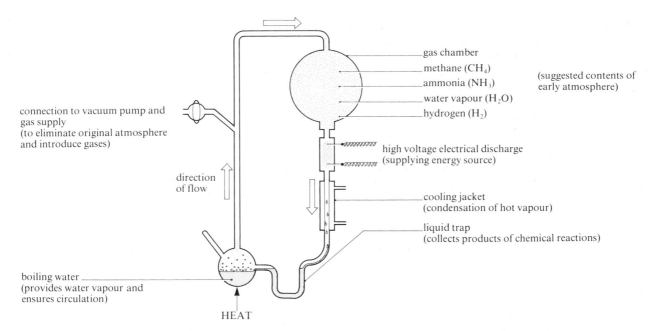

Labels in figure:

gas chamber
methane (CH₄)
ammonia (NH₃)
water vapour (H₂O)
hydrogen (H₂)

(suggested contents of early atmosphere)

connection to vacuum pump and gas supply
(to eliminate original atmosphere and introduce gases)

direction of flow

high voltage electrical discharge
(supplying energy source)

cooling jacket
(condensation of hot vapour)

liquid trap
(collects products of chemical reactions)

boiling water
(provides water vapour and ensures circulation)

HEAT

atmosphere. Recent experiments using Miller's apparatus but containing mixtures of carbon dioxide and water and only traces of other gases have produced similar results to those of Miller. Oparin's theory has been widely accepted, but major problems remain in explaining the transition from complex organic molecules to simple living organisms. This is where the theory of a process of biochemical evolution offers a broad scheme which is acceptable to the majority of contemporary biologists. However, there is no agreement as to the precise mechanism by which it may have occured.

Oparin considered that protein molecules were crucial to the transformation from inanimate to animate. Because of the zwitterionic nature of protein molecules they are able to form colloidal hydrophilic complexes which attract, and become surrounded by, envelopes of water molecules. These bodies may separate from the body of the liquid in which they are suspended (aqueous phase) and form a type of emulsion. Coalescence of these structures produces a separation of colloids from their aqueous phase, a process known as **coacervation** (*coacervus*, clump or heap). These colloid-rich coacervates may have been able to exchange substances with their environment and selectively concentrate compounds within them, particularly crystalloids. The colloid composition of a coacervate would depend on the composition of the medium. The varying composition of the 'soup' in different areas would lead to variation in the chemical composition of coacervates, producing the raw material for 'biochemical natural selection'.

It is suggested that substances within the coacervates may have undergone further chemical reactions and, by absorbing metal ions into the coacervates, formed enzymes. The alignment of lipid molecules (complex hydrocarbons) along the boundary between the coacervates and the external medium would have produced a primitive cell membrane which conferred stability on the coacervates. Thus the incorporation of a pre-existing molecule capable

Fig 24.1 *Stanley Miller's apparatus in which he synthesised amino acids from gases under conditions thought to have been present in the primeval atmosphere. The gases and vapours were circulated under pressure and exposed to a high voltage for one week. At the end of the period the liquid products in the trap were analysed by paper chromatography. A total of 15 amino acids was isolated including glycine, alanine and aspartic acid*

of self-replication into the coacervate, and an internal rearrangement of the lipid-coated coacervate, may have produced a primitive type of cell. Increase in size of coacervates and their fragmentation possibly led to the formation of identical coacervates which could absorb more of the medium and the cycle could continue. This possible sequence of events would have produced a primitive self-replicating heterotrophic organism feeding on an organic-rich primeval soup.

Whilst this account of the origin of life is widely accepted by many scientists, the astronomer Sir Fred Hoyle has recently argued that the probability of random molecular interactions giving rise to life as described above is

'as ridiculous and improbable as the proposition that a tornado blowing through a junk yard may assemble a Boeing 747'.

24.2 The nature of the earliest organisms

Current evidence suggests that the first organisms were heterotrophs as these were the only organisms capable of utilising the external supplies of available energy locked up within the complex organic molecules present in the 'soup'. The chemical reactions involved in synthesising food substances appear to have been too complex to have arisen within the earliest forms of life.

As more complex organic molecules arose through 'biochemical evolution', it is assumed that some of these were able to harness solar radiation as an energy source and use it to synthesise new cellular materials. Incorporation of these molecules into pre-existing cells may have enabled the cells to synthesise new cellular materials without the need for them to absorb organic molecules, hence becoming autotrophic. Increasing numbers of heterotrophs would have reduced the available food resources in the primeval soup and this competition for resources would hasten the appearance of autotrophs.

The earliest photosynthetic organisms, whilst utilising solar radiation as their energy source, lacked the biochemical pathways to produce oxygen. At a later stage, it is believed that oxygen-evolving photosynthetic organisms developed, similar to existing blue-green algae (section 3.2), and this resulted in the gradual build-up of oxygen in the atmosphere. The increase in atmospheric oxygen and its ionisation to form the ozone layer would reduce the ultra-violet radiation striking the Earth. Whilst decreasing the rate of synthesis of new complex molecules, the decreasing radiation would confer some stability on otherwise successful forms of life. A study of the physiology of present-day organisms reveals a great diversity in biochemical pathways associated with energy capture and release, which may mirror many of nature's early experiments with living organisms.

Despite the simplified account given above, the problem of the origin(s) of life remains. All that has been outlined is speculative and, despite tremendous advances in biochemistry, answers to the problem remain hypothetical. The above account is a simplified amalgam of present-day hypotheses. No 'ruling hypothesis' has yet achieved the status of an all-embracing theory (section A2.1). Details of the transition from complex non-living materials to simple living organisms remain a mystery.

24.3 Summary of the 'theories' of the origin of life

Many of these 'theories' and the way they explain the existing diversity of species cover similar ground but with varying emphases. Scientific theories may be ultra-imaginative on the one hand and ultra-sceptical on the other. Theological considerations too, may fit into this framework depending upon one's religious views. One of the major areas of controversy, even before the days of Darwin was the relationship between scientific and theological views on the history of life.

Diagrams (a)–(e) in fig 24.2 represent straightforward descriptions of theories, hypotheses or beliefs on the history of life, whereas (f) represents an attempt to combine certain aspects of three theories (b), (c) and (d) into an alternative acceptable to many people. The practices of science and religion are not therefore necessarily mutually exclusive as witnessed by the number of scientists who hold religious beliefs.

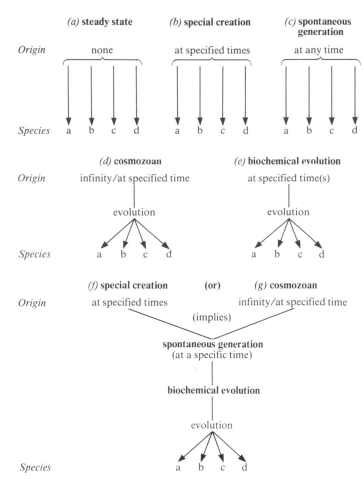

Fig 24.2 *Diagrammatic representation of various theories of the origin of life and the formation of species*

24.4 The theory of evolution

The term 'evolution' has a special place in the study of the history of life. It has become the unifying concept which underpins the whole study of biology. Evolution implies an overall gradual development which is both ordered and sequential. In terms of living organisms it may be defined as **'the development of complex organisms from pre-existing simpler organisms over the course of time'**.

The concept of evolution did not begin with Darwin and the publication of *On the Origin of Species*. Long before Darwin, Man's attempts to explain the obvious diversity of living organisms which surround him had, paradoxically, led him to consider the basic structural and functional similarities which exist between organisms. Evolutionary hypotheses had been proposed to account for this and these ideas have themselves 'evolved' since the time of Darwin as knowledge has advanced.

The historical background to the development of the theory of evolution, as outlined in table 24.1, shows that the concept of continuity or gradual development of more complex species from pre-existing simpler forms had

Table 24.1 The history of evolutionary thought.

Ancient Chinese

Confucius	Life originated from a single source through a gradual unfolding and branching

Greek and Mediaeval period

Diogenes	All things are differentiations of the same thing and are the same thing
Empedocles	Air, earth, fire and water are the four roots of all things. Life arose by the action of the forces of attraction and repulsion on the four elements. Explained origin of Universe, plants, animals and Man (Produced the germ of the idea of organic evolution.)
Democritus	Living things arose by spontaneous generation from the slime of the Earth
Anaxogoras	Organisms sprang from atmospheric germs
Thales (640–546 BC)	All life came from water
Anaximander	Plants, then animals, and finally Man arose from the mud of the emerging Earth
Aristotle (384–322 BC)	Proposed theory of continuous and gradual evolution from lifeless matter, based on his observations of animals. Recognised a 'scala natura' for animals
Dark Ages (400–1400 AD)	All theories based on those above or acceptance of special creation

Age of speculation (1400–1790)

John Ray (1627–1705)	Developed concept of species
Carl Linnaeus (1707–78)	Formalised 'binomial classification' system. Suggested genera were created separately and species were variants of them
Buffon (1707–88)	Suggested different types of animals had different origins at different times. Recognised influence of external environment. Believed in acquired inheritance
James Hutton (1726–97)	Theory of uniformitarianism. Gave age of Earth in millions of years

Age of formulation (1790–1900)

Erasmus Darwin (1731–1802)	Life arose from one 'filament' made by God. Did not accept the preformation of Man. The filament evolved by acquired characteristics
Jean-Baptiste Lamarck (1744–1829)	Inheritance of acquired characteristics. Environment acts on organisms. Phenotype changes are passed on. Concept of use and disuse of organs
Georges Cuvier (1769–1832)	Established palaeontological evidence. Fossils the results of 'catastrophes' by which new species arose
William Smith (1769–1838)	Opposed Cuvier's theory of catastrophism on basis of continuity of similar species in related strata
Charles Lyell (1797–1875)	Demonstrated the progressive history of fossil evidence
Charles Darwin (1809–82)	Influenced by Lyell and Malthus. Established a theory of evolution by means of natural selection
Alfred Russel Wallace (1823–1913)	Similar theory to Darwin, but excepted Man from his theory
Hugo de Vries (1848–1935)	Recognised existence of mutations which were heritable as a basis for discontinuous variation and regarded species as arising by mutation
August Weismann (1834–1914)	Showed that the reproductive cells of animals are distinct and therefore unaffected by the influences acting on somatic tissues
Gregor Mendel (1822–84)	Work on genetics (published 1865) only came to light after 1900. Laws of inheritance

Developments in twentieth century (neo-Darwinism)

W. L. Johannsen	Phenotype characteristics are determined by genotype and environmental factors
T. Henry Morgan	Developed chromosome theory of heredity on basis of cytological evidence
H. J. Muller (1927)	Genotype can be altered by X-rays: induced mutation
R. A. Fisher (1930)	No difference between change investigated by geneticists and change shown in the fossil record
G. W. Beadle and and E. L. Tatum (1941)	Demonstrated the genetic basis of biochemical synthesis (following A. E. Garrod (1909) and J. B. S. Haldane (1935))
J. Lederberg and A. D. Hershey (1951)	Demonstrated value of using bacteria in studying changes in genotype
J. D. Watson and F. H. C. Crick (1953)	Proposed molecular structure of DNA and its mechanism of replication
F. Jacob and J. Monod (1961)	Proposed a mechanism for regulation of gene activity

occurred to several philosophers and natural historians before the formal declarations of evolutionary hypotheses were advanced in the early nineteenth century.

24.4.1 Lamarckian evolution

The French biologist Lamarck proposed, in 1809, a hypothesis to account for the mechanism of evolution based on two conditions: the use and disuse of parts, and the inheritance of acquired characteristics. Changes in the environment may lead to changed patterns of behaviour which can necessitate new or increased use (or disuse) of certain organs or structures. Extensive use would lead to increased size and/or efficiency whilst disuse would lead to degeneracy and atrophy. These traits acquired during the lifetime of the individual were believed to be heritable and thus transmitted to offspring.

According to Lamarckism, as the theory came to be known, the long neck and legs of the modern giraffe were the result of generations of short-necked and short-legged ancestors feeding on leaves at progressively higher levels of trees. The slightly longer necks and legs produced in each generation were passed on to the subsequent generation, until the size of the present-day giraffe was reached. The webbed feet of aquatic birds and the shape of flat fish could be explained similarly. In aquatic birds the constant spreading of the toe bones and the skin between them in order to swim to find food and escape predators gave rise to their webbed feet. Likewise adaptations resulting from fish lying on their sides in shallow water were proposed to explain the shape of flat fish. Whilst Lamarck's theory helped prepare the way for acceptance of the concept of evolution, his views on the mechanism of change were never widely accepted.

However, Lamarck's emphasis on the role of the environment in producing phenotypic changes in the individual was correct. For example, body-building exercises will increase the size of muscles, but these acquired traits, whilst affecting the phenotype, are non-genetic, and having no influence on the genotype cannot be inherited. To demonstrate this, Weismann cut off the tails of mice over many successive generations. According to Lamarckism, the enforced disuse of tails should have led to progeny with smaller tails. This was not the case. Weismann postulated that somatic (body) acquired characteristics (resulting in phenotypic changes) did not directly affect the germ (gamete) cells which were the means by which characteristics are passed on to the next generation. His theory of the 'Continuity of the Germ-Plasm' was a historical necessity before the inheritance of genetic characteristics by sexual reproduction could be accepted.

24.4.2 Darwin, Wallace and the origin of species by natural selection

Charles Darwin was born in 1809, the son of a wealthy doctor, and like many great people he had an undistinguished academic career. In 1831 he accepted an unpaid post as naturalist on the survey ship H.M.S. *Beagle*, which spent the next five years at sea charting the East Coast of South America. The *Beagle* returned to Falmouth in October 1836 via the coast of Chile, the Galapagos Islands, Tahiti, New Zealand, Tasmania and South Africa. For most of this time Darwin was concerned with studying geology, but during a five-week stay on the Galapagos Islands he was struck by the similarities shown by the flora and fauna of the islands and mainland. In particular he was intrigued by the characteristic distributions of species of tortoises and finches (section 24.7.2). He collected a great deal of biological data concerned with variation between organisms which convinced him that species were not immutable. On his return home his work on the selective breeding of pigeons and other domestic animals gave him a clue to the concept of artificial selection, but he was unable to appreciate how this could operate in the wild. An earlier *Essay on the Principles of Population* by the Reverend Thomas Malthus, published in 1778, had highlighted the consequences of the reproductive potential of Man. Darwin applied this to other organisms and saw that despite this the numbers within populations remained relatively constant. Having collated a vast amount of information he began to realise that under the intense competition of numbers in a population, any variations which favoured survival in a particular environment would increase that individual's ability to reproduce and leave fertile offspring. Less favourable variations would be at a disadvantage and organisms possessing them would therefore have their chances of successful reproduction decreased. These data provided Darwin with the framework to formulate, by 1839, a theory of evolution by natural selection, but he did not publish his findings at that time. Indeed Darwin's greatest contribution to science was not so much to show that evolution occurs but how it might occur.

In the meantime, another naturalist, Alfred Russel Wallace, who had travelled widely in South America, Malaya and the Eastern Indian archipelago, and also read Malthus, had come to the same conclusions as Darwin regarding natural selection.

In 1858, Wallace wrote a 20-page essay outlining his theory and sent it to Darwin. This stimulated and encouraged Darwin and in July 1858, Darwin and Wallace presented papers on their ideas at a meeting of the Linnean Society in London. Over a year later, in November 1859, Darwin published *On the Origin of Species by Means of Natural Selection*. All 1 250 printed copies were sold on the day of publication and it is said that this book has been second only to the Bible in its impact on Man's thinking.

24.5 Natural selection

Darwin and Wallace proposed that natural selection is the mechanism by which new species arise from pre-existing species. This hypothesis/theory is based on three observations and two deductions which may be summarised as follows.

Observation 1: Individuals within a population have a great reproductive potential.

Observation 2: The numbers of individuals in a population remain approximately constant.

Deduction 1: Many individuals fail to survive or reproduce. There is a 'struggle for existence' within a population.

Observation 3: Variation exists within all populations.

Deduction 2: In the 'struggle for existence' those individuals showing variations best adapted to their environment have a 'reproductive advantage' and produce more offspring than less well-adapted organisms.

Deduction 2 offers a hypothesis called natural selection which provides a mechanism accounting for evolution.

24.5.1 Evidence for natural selection

Observation 1: It was Malthus who highlighted the reproductive potential of Man and observed that human populations are able to increase exponentially (section 12.6.3). The capacity for reproduction is basic to all living organisms, and is a fundamental drive which ensures continuance of the species. This applies to other organisms as shown in table 24.2. If every female gamete was fertilised and developed to maturity, the Earth would be totally overcrowded in a matter of days.

Table 24.2 Reproductive potential of selected species.

Crassostrea virginica	American oyster	1.0×10^6 eggs per season
Lycoperdon sp.	giant puff ball	7.0×10^{11} spores
Papaver rhoeas	poppy capsule	6.0×10^3 seeds
Carcinus maenas	shore crab	4.0×10^6 eggs per season

Observation 2: All population sizes are limited or checked by various environmental factors, such as food availability, space and light. Populations tend to increase in size until the environment supports no further increase and an equilibrium is reached. The population fluctuates around this equilibrium, as discussed in section 12.6.3. Hence population sizes generally remain approximately constant over a period of time related to the length of the organism's life cycle.

Deduction 1: The continuous competition between individuals for environmental resources creates a 'struggle for existence'. Whether this competition occurs within a species (**intraspecific competition**) or between members of different species (**interspecific competition**) may be immaterial in affecting the size of the individual population (section 12.6.5), but it will still imply that certain organisms will fail to survive or reproduce.

Observation 3: Darwin's study of beetles whilst an undergraduate at Cambridge, his subsequent journey in the *Beagle* and his knowledge gained through the selective breeding of certain characteristics in pigeons convinced

him of the importance of intraspecific variation. Likewise the adaptive significance of the interspecific variation seen in Galapagos finches (genus *Geospiza*) gave Darwin a clue to his second deduction. Data collected by Wallace in the Malayan archipelago provided further evidence of variation between populations. Darwin and Wallace, however, were unable to account for the sources of the variation. This was not to be clarified until Mendel's work on the particulate nature of inheritance demonstrated how genetic variation is conserved.

Deduction 2: Since all individuals within a population exhibit variation and a 'struggle for existence' has been clearly established, it follows that some individuals possessing particular variations will be more suited to survive and reproduce. The key factor in determining survival is adaptation to the environment. Any variation, however slight, be it physical, physiological or behavioural, which gives one organism an advantage over another organism will act as a **selective advantage** in the 'struggle for existence'. (The term 'selective advantage' is less emotive than that coined by the social philosopher, Herbert Spencer, who described natural selection as 'survival of the fittest'. The term 'fit' has irrelevant human connotations, which have given an erroneous impression of natural selection.) Favourable variations will be inherited by the next generation. Unfavourable variations are 'selected out' or 'selected against', their presence conferring a **selective disadvantage** on that organism. In this way natural selection leads to increased vigour within the species and, in phylogenetic terms, ensures the survival of that species (assuming environmental conditions remain constant). The whole of Darwin's and Wallace's hypothesis of natural selection is summed up most succinctly in Darwin's own words:

> 'As many more individuals of each species are born than can possibly survive, and as, consequently, there is a frequently recurring struggle for existence, it follows that any being, if it vary however slightly in any manner profitable to itself, under the complex and sometimes varying conditions of life, will have a better chance of surviving and thus be naturally selected. From the strong principle of inheritance, any selected variety will tend to propagate its new and modified form.' (Darwin, 1859)

Many misconceptions have grown up around the theory of evolution as outlined by Darwin and they may be summarised as follows.

(1) Darwin made no attempt to describe how life originated on the Earth: his concern was with how new species might arise from pre-existing species.

(2) Natural selection is not simply a negative, destructive force, but can be a positive mechanism of innovation within a population (section 25.5). The 'struggle for existence' described by Darwin was popularised by the coining of unfortunate terms such as 'survival of the fittest' and 'elimination of the unfit' by the philosopher Herbert Spencer and the press of the day.

(3) The misconception that Man was 'descended from the apes' by some process of linear progression was over-sensationalised by the press and offended both the religious and secular communities. The former saw this as an insult to their belief that Man was created in the 'image of God', whilst the latter were outraged by the apparent undermining of Man's 'superior' position within the animal kingdom.

(4) The apparent contradiction between the Genesis six-day Creation account and that of a progressive origin for species was exacerbated by the meeting of the British Association for the Advancement of Science in June 1860. Bishop Samuel Wilberforce of Oxford vehemently attacked the conclusions of Darwin as outlined in *On the Origin of Species* but not being a biologist his address lacked accuracy. In concluding, he turned to Professor Thomas Henry Huxley, a proponent of Darwin's theory, and asked whether he claimed his descent from a monkey through his grandfather or grandmother. Huxley replied by expounding the more important ideas of Darwin and correcting the misconceptions of Bishop Wilberforce. In conclusion he implied that he would prefer to have a monkey for an ancestor than 'to be connected with a man who used great gifts to obscure the truth'. This unfortunate controversy has continued as the Genesis versus Evolution debate. Professor R. J. Berry has summarised the extremes of the debate as:

(*a*) those who are awed by scientists and believe that the Bible has been disproved;

(*b*) those who cling to the inspiration of Scripture and their own interpretations of it, and shut their eyes to the fact that God's work can be studied by scientific methods.

24.6 Modern views on evolution

The theory of evolution as proposed by Darwin and Wallace has been extended and elaborated in the light of contemporary evidence from genetics, molecular biology, palaeontology, ecology and ethology and is known as **neo-Darwinism** (*neo*, new, adding to the notion of). This may be defined as *the theory of organic evolution by the natural selection of genetically determined characteristics*.

The term 'evolution' may mean the result, or the process, of the above and different types of evidence support different aspects of this theory. In order to accept neo-Darwinian evolutionary theory, as defined above, for the historical development of life it is necessary to:

(1) establish the fact of change through time (**past evolution**);

(2) demonstrate a mechanism which produces evolutionary change (**natural selection of genes**);

(3) observe evolution happening today ('**evolution in action**').

Evidence for past evolution comes from many sources based on geology, such as fossils and stratigraphy. Evidence for a mechanism is found in the experimental and observational data of the natural selection of heritable characteristics, such as the selection of shell colour in *Cepaea* (section 25.5.1), and the mechanism of inheritance demonstrated by Mendelian genetics, as in Mendel's work on peas. Finally, evidence for the action of these processes occurring today is provided by studies of present populations, such as speciation in the herring gull (section 25.8.4), and the results of artificial selection and genetic engineering, as in the cultivation of wheat and the production of monoclonal antibodies.

There are no laws of evolution, only well-corroborated hypotheses which collectively add together to form a well-attested theory. The premature acceptance of current concepts as dogmatic truths at Advanced level, as at any level of scientific inquiry, may stifle intellectual growth and the search for truth. The uncritical acceptance of evolutionary theory is a case in point. Some of the events presented as evidence for evolutionary theory can be reproduced under laboratory conditions, but that neither implies nor confirms that they did take place in the past; it merely indicates the possibility that these events occurred. Contemporary scientific debates on evolution are not concerned that evolution takes place but that it takes place according to natural selection of randomly generated mutations.

24.7 Evidence for the theory of evolution

Evidence associated with current views on the theory of evolution, is provided from many sources, the main ones being palaeontology, geographical distribution, classification, plant and animal breeding, comparative anatomy, adaptive radiation, comparative embryology and comparative biochemistry.

Much of the evidence presented in this chapter was unavailable to Darwin and Wallace at the time of publication of their papers on the origin of species by natural selection. Whilst great scientists are often characterised more by their powers of induction than those of deduction based on observation and experiment, Darwin and Wallace appear to have had a judicious blend of both. Darwin sums up both of these approaches in his statement:

'In October 1838, that is, 15 months after I had begun my systematic enquiry, I happened to read, for amusement, Malthus on Population, and being well prepared to appreciate the struggle for existence which everywhere goes on from long-continued observation of the habits of animals and plants, it at once struck me that under these circumstances favourable variations would tend to be preserved, and unfavourable ones to be destroyed. The result of this would be the formation of new species. Here, then, I had at last got a theory by which to work.'

The evidence presented here largely, but tentatively, supports the theory of evolution by natural selection as

Table 24.3 Types of fossils, their formation and examples

Fossil	Fossilisation process	Examples
Entire organism	Frozen into ice during glaciation	Woolly mammoths found in Siberian permafrost
,, ,,	Encased in the hardened resin (amber) of coniferous trees	Insect exoskeletons found in Oligocene rocks in Baltic coast
,, ,,	Encased in tar	'Mummies' found in asphalt lakes of California
,, ,,	Trapped in acidic bogs: lack of bacterial and fungal activity prevents total decomposition	'Mummies' found in bogs and peat in Scandinavia
Hard skeletal materials	Trapped by sedimentary sand and clay which form sedimentary rocks, e.g. limestone, sandstone and silt	Bones, shells and teeth (very common in British Isles)
Moulds and casts	Hard materials trapped as above. Sediments harden to rock. The skeleton dissolves leaving its impression as a mould of the organism. This can be infilled with fine materials which harden to form a cast. Great detail is thus preserved	Gastropods from Portland Stone, Jurassic. Casts of giant horsetails (*Calamites*) of Carboniferous forests. Internal casts of mollusc shells showing muscle attachment points
Petrifaction	Gradual replacement by water-carried mineral deposits, such as silica, pyrites, calcium carbonate or carbon. Slow infilling as organism decomposes producing fine detail	Silica replacements of the echinoderm *Micraster*
Impressions	Impressions of remains of organisms in fine-grained sediments on which they died	Feathers of *Archaeopteryx* in Upper Jurassic. Jellyfish in Cambrian found in British Columbia. Carboniferous leaf impressions
Imprints	Footprints, trails, tracks and tunnels of various organisms made in mud are rapidly baked and filled in with sand and covered by further sediments	Dinosaur footprints and tail scrapings indicate size and posture of organisms
Coprolites	Faecal pellets prevented from decomposing, later compressed in sedimentary rock. Often contain evidence of food eaten, e.g. teeth and scales	Cenozoic mammalian remains

outlined in section 24.5. It draws on data obtained from many sources, and in all cases is interpreted in terms that assume the validity of the concept of evolution. Much of the evidence is also supportive of other sources of evidence. Circular arguments and exceptions to the evidence abound and alternative interpretations can be found, but the broad concept of evolution is backed up by a wealth of scientific evidence which, at this level, is difficult to present in a form which is comprehensible yet not indoctrinatory.

24.7.1 Palaeontology

Palaeontology is the study of fossils. Fossils are any form of preserved remains thought to be derived from a living organism. They may include the following: entire organisms, hard skeletal structures, moulds and casts, petrifactions, impressions, imprints and coprolites (fossilised faecal pellets) (table 24.3).

Fossil evidence alone is inadequate to uphold an evolutionary theory, but it supports a theory of progressive increase in complexity of organisms and denies the fixity of species. Fossils were well known before evolution was generally accepted. They were interpreted either as the remains of former creations or as artefacts inserted into the rocks by God. Most of the remains found so far can be classified into the same taxonomic groups (phyla and classes) as living species, but whether they represent the ancestors of present-day forms can only be debated, not proved.

The oldest fossil-bearing rocks contain very few types of fossilised organisms and they all have a simple structure. Younger rocks contain a greater variety of fossils with increasingly complex structures. Throughout the fossil record many species which appear at an early stratigraphic level disappear at a later level. This is interpreted in evolutionary terms as indicating the times at which species originated and became extinct.

Geophysical evidence suggests that geographical regions and climatic conditions have varied throughout the Earth's history. Since organisms are adapted to particular environments, the constantly changing conditions may have favoured a mechanism for evolutionary change that accounts for the progressive changes in the structure of organisms as shown by the fossil record. Ecological considerations also fit in with the fossil evidence. For example, plants appeared on land before animals, and insects appeared before insect-pollinated flowers.

One of the major criticisms of using fossil evidence in support of an evolutionary theory is the lack of a continuous fossil record. Gaps in the fossil record ('missing links') are taken as strong evidence against a theory of descent by

Fig 24.3 *Photograph of trilobite fossil in Cambrian rocks*

modification. However, there are several explanations for the incompleteness of the fossil record. These include the facts that:

(1) dead organisms decompose rapidly;
(2) dead organisms are eaten by scavengers;
(3) soft-bodied organisms do not fossilise easily;
(4) only a small fraction of living organisms will have died in conditions favourable for fossilisation;
(5) only a fraction of fossils have been unearthed.

Support for an evolutionary process increases as more and more possible 'missing links' are discovered, either as fossils, such as *Seymouria* (amphibia/reptile), *Archaeopteryx* (reptile/bird) and *Cynognathus* (reptile/mammal), or as living organisms representing groups with close structural similarities, such as *Peripatus* (fig 24.18) and *Latimeria*.

Alternatively, there exists the possibility that new species appeared so suddenly that intermediate forms in the lineage do not exist. Eldredge and Gould have proposed a process called '**punctuated equilibria**' which accounts for the sudden appearance of species. This depends upon the fact that evolutionary rates are variable and that certain new species arise rapidly with the palaeontological consequence of an incomplete fossil record. These apparent 'jumps' in the evolutionary sequence have given rise to the term '**saltatory evolution**' (*saltare*, to jump). Darwin himself considered this possibility and stated as much in the *Origin of Species*:

'I do not suppose that the process (speciation) . . . goes on continuously; it is far more probable that each form remains for long periods unaltered, and then again undergoes modification.'

The fossil history of the horse

The history of the horse provides one of the best examples of phylogeny based on an almost complete fossil record found in North American sedimentary deposits from the early Eocene to the present.

The earliest recognisable perissodactyls (odd-toed, hoofed mammals) appeared about 54×10^6 years ago and present-day perissodactyls include horses, tapirs and rhinoceroses. The oldest recognisable horse-like fossils belong to a genus called *Hyracotherium* which was widely distributed throughout North America and Europe during the early Eocene. By the beginning of the Oligocene it was extinct everywhere except North America. It was a small animal, lightly built and adapted for running. The limbs were short and slender and the feet elongated so that the digits were almost vertical. There were four digits in the forelimbs and three digits in the hindlimb. The incisors were small and the molars had low crowns with rounded cusps covered in enamel.

The probable course of development of horses from *Hyracotherium* to *Equus* involved at least twelve genera and several hundred species. The major trends seen in the development of the horse were concerned with locomotion and feeding. They represent adaptations to changing environmental conditions and may be summarised as follows:

(1) increase in size,
(2) lengthening of limbs and feet,
(3) reduction of lateral digits,
(4) increase in length and thickness of the third digit,
(5) straightening and stiffening of the back,
(6) better-developed sense organs,
(7) increase in size and complexity of the brain associated with point (6) above,
(8) increase in width of incisors,
(9) replacement of premolars by molars,
(10) increase in tooth length,
(11) increase in crown height of molars,
(12) increased lateral support of teeth by cement,
(13) increased surface area of cusps by exposure of enamel ridges.

A dominant genus from each geological epoch of the Cenozoic has been selected to show the progressive development of the horse in fig 24.4. However there is no evidence that the forms illustrated are direct relatives of each other.

The significance of the fossil sequence shown in fig 24.4 is that it supports a theory of progressive change based on homologous structures such as limbs and teeth. Each of the species shown in fig 24.4 represents a stage of development which was successful for several million years (as judged by the abundance of fossils) before becoming extinct. The extinction of a species did not, however, represent the disappearance of the family line. The fossil evidence reveals that another closely related species always superseded its extinction. As all the species in the sequence show structural and ecological similarities, this gives support to a theory of descent with modification. Other fossils found in the same rock strata suggest changing climatic conditions which, together with other evidence, indicates that each species was adapted to prevailing conditions.

The history of the horse does not show a gradual transition regularly spaced in time and locality, and neither is the fossil record totally complete. It would appear that several offshoots occurred from the line represented in fig 24.4, but they all became extinct. All modern horses appear to be descended from *Pliohippus*. The modern genus *Equus* arose in North America during the Pleistocene and migrated into Eurasia and Africa where it gave rise to zebras and asses as well as the modern horse. Paradoxically, having survived in North America for millions of years, the horse became extinct there several thousand years ago, at a time which coincided with the arrival of Man. Cave-paintings from other parts of the world suggest that the earliest use for the horse was as a source of food. The horse was absent from North America until its reintroduction by the Spaniards almost 500 years ago.

24.7.2 Geographical distribution

All organisms are adapted to their environment to a greater or lesser extent. If the abiotic and biotic factors (section 12.2) within a habitat are capable of supporting a particular species in one geographical area, then one might assume that the same species would be found in a similar habitat in a similar geographical area, for example lions in the savannah of Africa and the pampas of South America. This is not the case. Plant and animal species are discontinuously distributed throughout the world. Ecological factors often account for this discontinuous distribution, but evidence from the successful colonisation of habitats by plant and animal species introduced there by Man suggests that factors other than those of ecological adaptation are involved. Rabbits are not endemic (naturally occurring) species in Australia, yet their rapid increase in numbers following their introduction by Man indicates the suitability of the Australian habitat. Similar examples of this principle are illustrated by the spread of domestic animals and plants by Man, such as sheep, corn, potatoes and wheat. A rational explanation for the discontinuous distribution of organisms is based on the concept of species originating in a given area and their subsequent dispersal outwards from that point. The extent of the dispersal will depend upon the success of the organisms, the efficiency of the dispersal mechanism and the existence of natural barriers such as oceans, mountain ranges and deserts. Wind-blown spores and seeds and flying animals would appear to have the best adaptations for dispersal over land and sea.

In contrast to, and despite the general principle of organisms being naturally confined to certain parts of the world, many related forms are found in widely separated regions, for example the three remaining species of lungfish (order Dipnoi) are found separately in tropical areas of South America (*Lepidosiren*), Africa (*Protopterus*) and Australia (*Neoceratodus*); camels and llamas (family Camelidae) are distributed in North Africa, Asia and

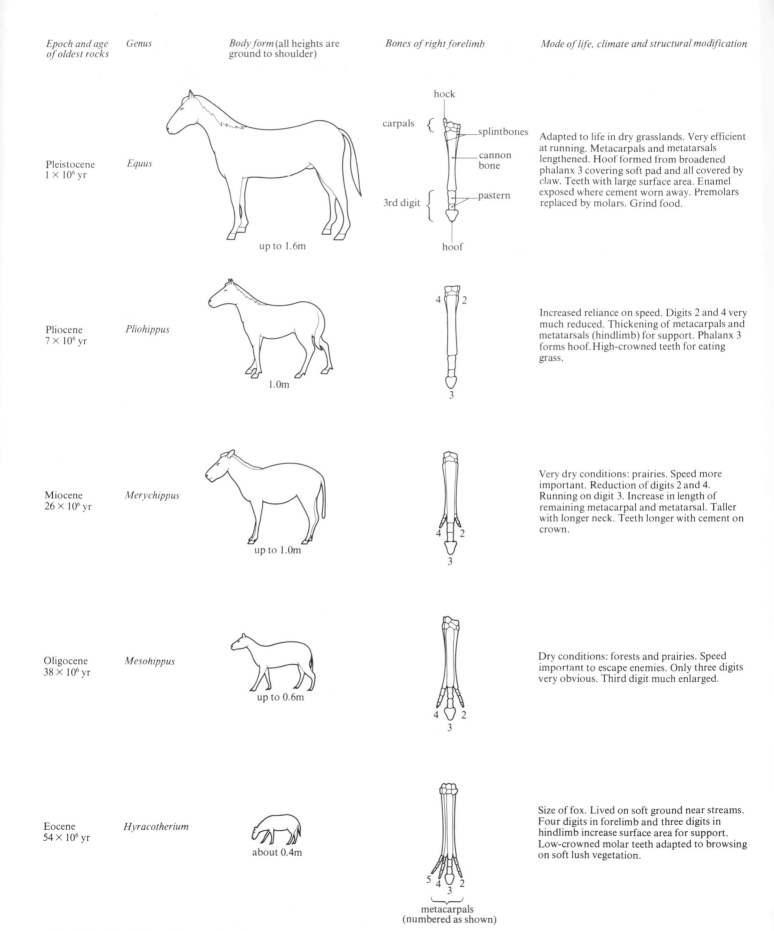

Epoch and age of oldest rocks	Genus	Body form (all heights are ground to shoulder)	Bones of right forelimb	Mode of life, climate and structural modification
Pleistocene 1×10^6 yr	Equus	up to 1.6m	hock / carpals / splintbones / cannon bone / 3rd digit / pastern / hoof	Adapted to life in dry grasslands. Very efficient at running. Metacarpals and metatarsals lengthened. Hoof formed from broadened phalanx 3 covering soft pad and all covered by claw. Teeth with large surface area. Enamel exposed where cement worn away. Premolars replaced by molars. Grind food.
Pliocene 7×10^6 yr	Pliohippus	1.0m	4 2 / 3	Increased reliance on speed. Digits 2 and 4 very much reduced. Thickening of metacarpals and metatarsals (hindlimb) for support. Phalanx 3 forms hoof. High-crowned teeth for eating grass.
Miocene 26×10^6 yr	Merychippus	up to 1.0m	4 2 / 3	Very dry conditions: prairies. Speed more important. Reduction of digits 2 and 4. Running on digit 3. Increase in length of remaining metacarpal and metatarsal. Taller with longer neck. Teeth longer with cement on crown.
Oligocene 38×10^6 yr	Mesohippus	up to 0.6m	4 2 / 3	Dry conditions: forests and prairies. Speed important to escape enemies. Only three digits very obvious. Third digit much enlarged.
Eocene 54×10^6 yr	Hyracotherium	about 0.4m	5 4 2 / 3 / metacarpals (numbered as shown)	Size of fox. Lived on soft ground near streams. Four digits in forelimb and three digits in hindlimb increase surface area for support. Low-crowned molar teeth adapted to browsing on soft lush vegetation.

Fig 24.4 *Evolution of the modern horse*

South America; and racoons are widely found in North and South America and a small area of south-east Asia. Fossil evidence indicates that the distribution of these organisms was not always as seen today and that in the past they were more widely distributed.

Whilst none of this evidence has any immediate significance for evolutionary theory, it does point to the fact that the distribution of land masses was not always as it is today, as explained below.

It used to be believed that the world had always been as it now is and that the present continents and oceans had never changed positions. Early geologists, such as Hutton and Lyell (table 24.1), accounted for the existence of sedimentary rocks in terms of the periodic rise and fall of the sea. Later it was suggested that there were once two large continental masses, one in the Northern Hemisphere called Laurasia and one in the Southern Hemisphere called Gondwanaland, linked by extensive land bridges across which animals and plants could migrate and disperse. Subsequent geological research has modified this idea and favours the hypothesis of **continental drift**, based on the concept of **plate tectonics**. The hypothesis of continental drift was first proposed by Snider in 1858 but developed by Taylor in America and Wegener in Germany in the late 1800s. Wegener proposed that, during Carboniferous times, Laurasia and Gondwanaland formed one large land mass called Pangaea (Greek, all earth) which floated on the denser molten core of the Earth. It is now believed, though, that continents have drifted apart as a result of convection currents within the Earth spreading upwards and outwards, dragging plates on which the continents float. This hypothesis would account for the continuous movements of land masses and the present distribution of species such as those of the lungfishes (fig 24.5).

Fig 24.5 *(a) Relative positions of South America, Africa and Australia during early stages of continental drift, indicating proximity of areas where lungfish may have originated. (b) Present distribution of species of lungfish*

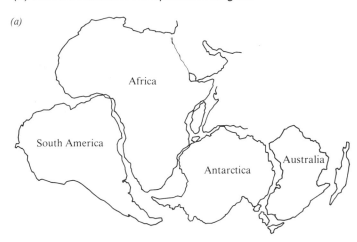

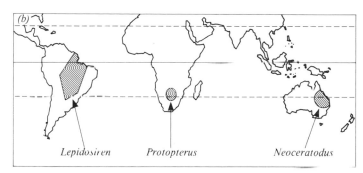

In the case of the camels and llamas it is believed that they arose from a common ancestor which fossil evidence suggests had its origin in North America. During the Pleistocene this ancestor spread southwards into South

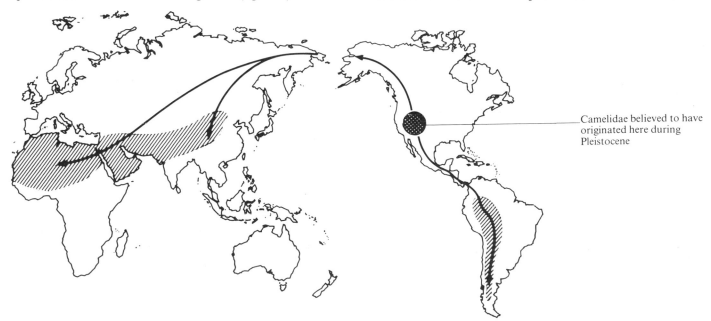

Camelidae believed to have originated here during Pleistocene

Fig 24.6 *Map of the world showing distribution of present members of the family Camelidae, the camels in North Africa and Asia and the llamas in South America. During Pleistocene times the Camelidae were distributed throughout North and South America and much of Asia and North Africa. This distribution is based on fossil evidence. Solid black lines indicate possible migration routes. (Based on Matthews (1939) Climate of evolution, Vol. 1, 2nd ed., NY Acad. of Sci.)*

America via the Isthmus of Panama, and northwards into Asia before changes in sea-level separated it from North America (fig 24.6). Throughout this time it is thought that progressive changes within the Camelidae occurred, producing the two genera *Camelus* and *Lama* at the extremes of their Pleistocene migration. Forms intermediate between the present camels and llamas exist in the fossil record throughout North America, Asia and North Africa. The fossil record indicates that other animals of the Camelidae in other parts of the world became extinct at the close of the last Ice Age.

Another example of discontinuous distribution as a result of geographical isolation is provided by the monotremes and marsupials of Australasia. Australasia is believed to have broken away from the other land masses during the late Jurassic, just after the appearance of primitive mammals. The mammals are divided into three orders: Monotremata, Marsupialia and Eutheria. In Australasia only the monotremes and marsupials developed. Here they coexisted and underwent adaptive radiation to produce the characteristic Australasian fauna represented by the monotremes *Tachyglossus* and *Zaglossus* (the spiny anteaters) and *Ornithorhynchus* (the duck-billed platypus), and 45 genera of marsupials. Elsewhere in the world the more advanced eutherian (placental) mammals also developed. As they spread out over the continents it is believed that they ousted the more primitive monotremes and marsupials from their ecological niches, except where geographical barriers disrupted their dispersal, as into Australasia.

These points may be summarised as:
(1) species originated in a particular area;
(2) species dispersed outwards from that area;
(3) dispersal could only occur for most species where land masses were close enough together to permit dispersal;
(4) the absence of more advanced organisms from a region usually indicates the prior separation of that region from the area of origin of those organisms.

Whilst none of the evidence presented above indicates the mechanism by which species are thought to have originated, it does suggest that various groups have originated at various times and in various regions. Fossil evidence reveals the ways in which these organisms have undergone gradual modification, but again gives no indication of the possible mechanism.

Evidence for a possible mechanism of the origin of species by natural selection is supplied by the distribution of plants and animals on oceanic islands. Both Wallace and Darwin were struck by the amazing diversity of species found on such islands, such as the Hawaiian and the Galapagos groups. Geological evidence indicates that these islands were formed by oceanic volcanic activity which thrust them up above sea level, so that they have never had any direct geographical links with any land mass. Plant species must have arrived on the islands by wind dispersal as spores and seeds, or water dispersal as floating seeds and masses of vegetation. Aquatic and semi-aquatic

organisms are believed to have been carried there by ocean currents, whilst terrestrial organisms may have been carried clinging to logs or floating masses of vegetation. Birds, bats and flying insects would have fewer problems of dispersal to these islands.

The Galapagos Islands are situated in the Pacific Ocean on the equator almost 1 000 km west of Ecuador and form an archipelago described further in section 25.8.3. When Darwin visited the islands in 1835, he noticed the similarity of the species found there to those on the nearest mainland, a fact he had also observed on the Cape Verde Islands off the coast of West Africa. However, the plant and animal species on oceanic islands were noticeably larger in most cases. This may be accounted for by the lack of competition from larger, and more dominant, advanced species which were absent from the islands, but which co-habited with smaller related species on the mainland. For example, the giant tortoise (*Geochelone elephantopus*), nearly 2 m long and weighing 260 kg, feeding on the plentiful vegetation found on the islands presumably attained this size due to the absence of competition from various mammalian species which existed on the mainland. Darwin noticed too that iguana lizards on the Galapagos Islands were abundant and again much larger than related mainland species. Lizards are terrestrial reptiles, but on the Galapagos Islands, where two species were found, one was aquatic. The aquatic form, *Amblyrhyncus cristatus*, fed on marine algae and showed adaptations for locomotion in water such as a laterally-flattened tail and well-developed webs of skin between the toes of all four limbs (fig 24.7). Competition for food, space and a mate within the terrestrial form is thought to have exerted a selection pressure on the lizards and favoured those showing variations with aquatic adaptations. This mechanism of environmental factors operating on a variable genotype is called **natural selection** and is described above. It could have been the process

Fig 24.7 *Giant aquatic lizard of the Galapagos Islands*

Types of finch	Beak shape	Food source	Habitat	Number of species
large ground finch (ancestral)	typical main land type: short and straight	crushing seed	coastal	1
ground finches	various, but short and straight as above	seeds/insects	coast/lowlands	3
cactus ground finches	long slightly curved, split-tongue	nectar of prickly-pear cactus	lowland	2
insectivorous tree finches	parrot-like	seeds/insects	forest	3
vegetarian tree finch	curved, parrot-like	fruit/buds/soft fruit	forest	1
warbler finch	slender	insects in flight	forest	1
woodpecker finches	large, straight, (uses cactus spine or stick to poke insects out of holes in wood)	larvae insect	forest	2

which gradually gave rise to the aquatic species. It was, however, the diversity of adaptive structure shown by the 13 species of finches found within the archipelago which had the greatest influence on Darwin's thinking on the mechanism of the origin of species. Only one type of finch existed on the mainland of Ecuador and its beak was adapted to crushing seeds. On the Galapagos Islands, six major beak types were found, each adapted to a particular method of feeding. The various species, their feeding methods and numbers of species are summarised in fig 24.8.

Darwin postulated that a group of finches from the mainland colonised the islands. Here they flourished, and the inevitable competition produced by increase in numbers, and the availability of vacant ecological niches, favoured occupation of niches by those organisms showing the appropriate adaptive variations. Differences between species relate to small differences in body size, feather colour and beak shape. Several species of finch are found on all the bigger islands. The ground and warbler finches, thought to be the most primitive types, are found on most islands. The tree and vegetarian/tree finches are missing from the outlying islands, and the woodpecker finches are confined to the central group of islands. The actual species distribution is interesting and has been explained by Lack on the basis of adaptive radiation and geographical isolation. For example, on the central islands there are

Fig 24.8 (a) Adaptive radiation of Darwin's finches. (After Lack) (b) A male cactus finch (Geospiza scandens)

(b)

873

many species of several different types of finch, such as ground, tree warbler and woodpecker, rather than several species of the same type. Even where several species of only one type of finch are present, as on the outlying islands, each species differs in its ecological requirements. This fits in with the Gaussian exclusion principle (section 12.6) which states that two or more closely related species will not occupy the same area unless they differ in their ecological requirements.

24.7.3 Classification

The system of classification described in Appendix 3 was proposed by Linnaeus before the time of Darwin and Wallace, but has implications for the origin of species and evolutionary theory. Whilst it is possible to conceive that all species, both living and extinct, were created separately at a specific time or had no origin, the structural similarities between organisms, which forms the basis of a natural system of **phylogenetic classification**, suggest the existence of an evolutionary process. These similarities and differences between organisms may be explained as the result of progressive adaptation by organisms within each taxonomic group to particular environmental conditions over a period of time.

Numerical taxonomists, working mainly from comparative phenotypic characters have found it possible to construct a **phenetic classification** system (Appendix 3) which is consistent, to the extent of present knowledge, with the concept of evolution. These systems of classification are capable of standing in their own right as a basis for biological organisation, but they also strongly suggest that an evolutionary process has occurred.

24.7.4 Plant and animal breeding

One of the earliest features of Man's civilisation was his cultivation of plants and domestic animals from ancestral wild stocks. By selecting those members of a species which showed a favourable variation, such as increased size or improved flavour, and artificially breeding them by selective mating, selective propagation or pollination, the desired characteristics were perpetuated. Continued selective breeding by Man has produced the varieties of domestic animals and plants of agricultural importance seen today. It is known from archaeological remains that early Man was proficient in rearing cattle, pigs and fowl, and cultivating cereal crops and certain vegetables. Until the revelation of Mendel's work on genetics the theoretical basis of inheritance and breeding was not clear, but this had not limited Man's practical endeavours. In terms of genetics, Man is preserving those genes which are considered desirable and eliminating those which are undesirable for his purposes. This selection exploits naturally occurring gene variation, together with any fortuitous mutations which occur from time to time.

Whilst varieties of dogs, cats, birds, fish and flowers have been produced for sporting or decorative purposes, it is

Fig 24.9 *The result of selective breeding. The wild pig (a) is native to Europe, Asia and Africa but has been selectively bred to produce a variety of breeds, of which the English Large White pig (b) with its high quality of meat yield, is an example*

economically important varieties of animals and plants which have been studied most by plant and animal breeders (fig 24.9). Some specific examples of phenotypic characteristics which have been artificially selected are shown in table 24.4. A recently developed form of artificial selection is the selection for resistance to antibiotics, pesticides and herbicides shown respectively by pathogens, pests and weeds. A vicious circle is produced as new strains of organisms become immune to the ever-increasing number of chemical substances produced to contain and control them.

Table 24.4 Selected phenotypic characteristics and examples of them.

Phenotypic characteristic	Example
Hardiness	Sweetcorn grown in England
Size	Potato, cabbage
Increased yield	Milk, eggs, wool, fruit
Earlier maturity	Cereal crops (two per season)
Lengthened season	Strawberries
Taste/eating quality	Apples, seedless grapes
Harvesting ease	Peas
Length of storage	Beans/peas for freezing
Increased ecological efficiency	Protein from plants, e.g. soyabean
Resistance to disease	Rust and mildew (fungi)-resistant wheat

Since characteristics can be 'produced' by Man's ability to selectively breed, as in the case of breeds of dogs or pigeons, Darwin used this as evidence for a mechanism by which species might arise 'naturally'. In the latter case the environment rather than Man was believed to act as the agent of selection. Artificially selected forms probably would not have arisen in the 'wild'; in most cases they are unable to compete successfully with closely related non-domesticated forms.

24.7.5 Comparative anatomy

Comparative study of the anatomy of groups of animals or plants (morphology) reveals that certain structural features are basically similar. For example, the basic structure of all flowers consists of sepals, petals, stamens, stigma, style and ovary; yet the size, colour, number of parts and specific structure are different for each individual species. Similarly, the limb-bone pattern of all tetrapods from amphibia to mammals has the same structural plan: it is called the **pentadactyl limb** (fig 17.11). This basic structure has been modified in several ways as illustrated in fig 24.10. In each case, the particular structure is adapted to a certain method of locomotion in a particular environment.

Organs having a similar basic structure, a similar topographic relationship as structures in other species, the same histological appearance and a similar embryonic development are said to be **homologous**, a term introduced in 1843 by Richard Owen.

Homologous structures showing adaptations to different environmental conditions and modes of life are examples of adaptive radiation. The ecological significance of these processes is considered in section 24.7.6. The specific functions that these structures carry out may vary in different organisms. These differences reflect the particu-

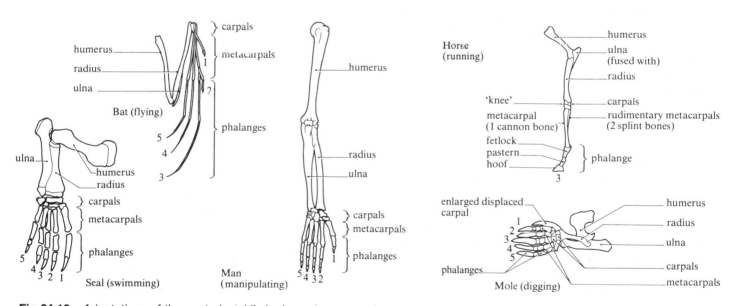

Fig 24.10 *Adaptations of the pentadactyl limb shown by mammals*

lar ways the organisms are adapted to their environments and modes of life. Other examples of homology are given below.

Branchial arches/Ear ossicles. Certain bones of the jaw in fish can be traced through other vertebrates, where they are involved in jaw suspension, to mammals where they appear as the ear ossicles, the malleus, incus and stapes (fig 24.11).

Halteres. The hind pair of wings typical of most insects have been modified in the Diptera into little rods, the halteres, which serve as gyroscopic organs helping to maintain balance in flight.

Pericarp. The ovary wall in flowering plants becomes modified, following fertilisation of the ovules, in a variety of ways to aid seed dispersal (figs 20.28 and 24.12).

Whilst homology does not prove that evolution has occurred, the existence of homology within a group of organisms is interpreted as evidence of their descent from a common ancestor and indicates close phylogenetic relationships.

Linnaeus used homology as the basis for his system of classification. The more exclusive the shared homologies, the closer two organisms are related and hence the lower the rank of the taxonomic group in which they are placed.

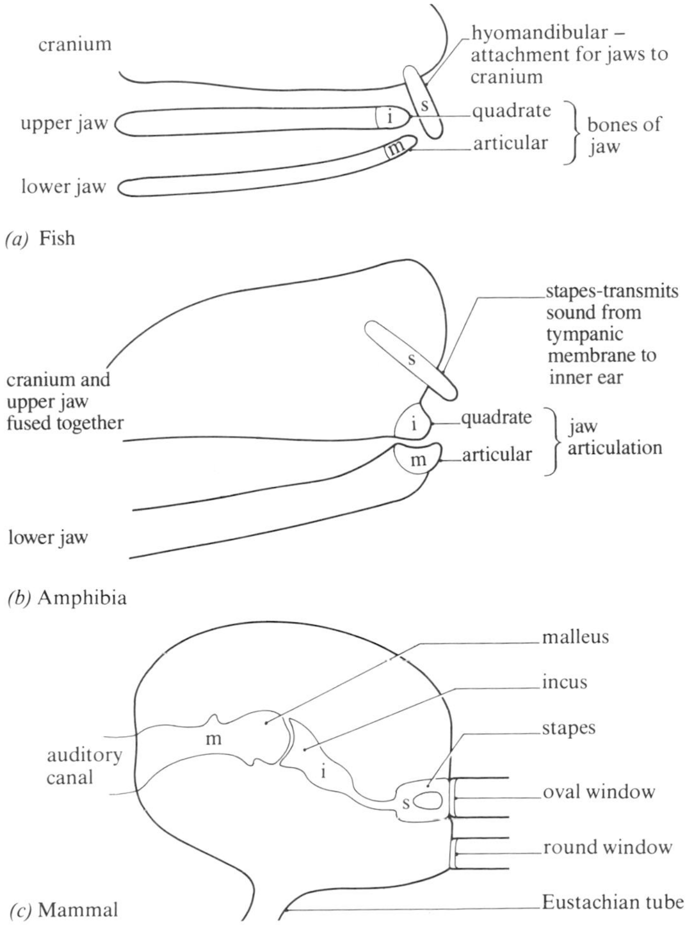

Fig 24.11 *Relative positions and functions of bones of the mammalian ear ossicles as seen in fish and amphibia*

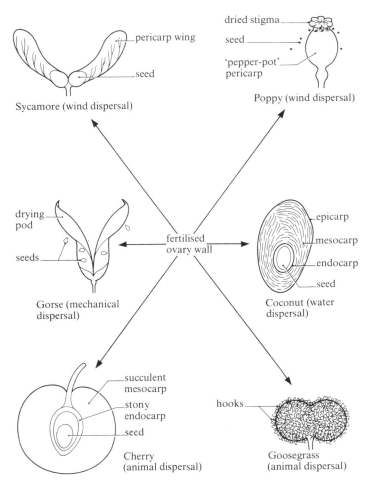

Fig 24.12 *Variation in pericarp structure for different methods of seed dispersal*

For example, butterflies and moths belong to the same order (Lepidoptera) whereas wasps and bees belong to another order (Hymenoptera).

Certain homologous structures in some species have no apparent function and are described as **vestigial organs**. The appendix of Man, although not concerned with digestion, is homologous with the functional appendix of herbivorous mammals. Likewise, certain apparently non-functional bones in snakes and whales are thought to be homologous with the hip bones and hindlimbs of quadruped vertebrates. The vertebrae of the human coccyx are thought to represent vestigial structures of the tail possessed by our ancestors and embryos. It would be very difficult to explain the occurrence of vestigial organs without reference to some process of evolution.

24.7.6   Adaptive radiation

When a group of organisms share a homologous structure which is differentiated to perform a variety of different functions, it illustrates a principle known as **adaptive radiation**. Adaptive radiation may be demonstrated within all taxonomic groups higher than the species. For example, all organisms belonging to a particular class share a number of diagnostic characteristics. Additionally, variations between different species within the class enable them to have modes of life adapted to particular habitats. For instance, the mouthparts of insects consist of the same basic structures: a labrum (upper lip), a pair of mandibles, a hypopharynx (floor of mouth), a pair of maxillae and a labium (fused second pair of mandibles, lower lip). Insects are able to exploit a variety of food materials, as shown in fig 24.13, because some of the above structures are enlarged and modified, others reduced and lost. This produces a variety of feeding structures.

The relatively high degree of adaptive radiation shown by insects reflects the adaptability and utility of the basic features of the group. It is this 'evolutionary plasticity' which has permitted them to occupy such a range of ecological niches. This is one of a group of related criteria used to describe the biological success of a taxonomic group, such as a phylum or class. Other criteria include the evolutionary age of the group and the number of species within the group.

The presence of a structure or physiological process in an ancestral organism, which has become greatly modified in more advanced, apparently related organisms, may be interpreted as indicating a process of descent by modification which is the basis of evolutionary theory as defined in section 24.4.2. The significance of adaptive radiation is that

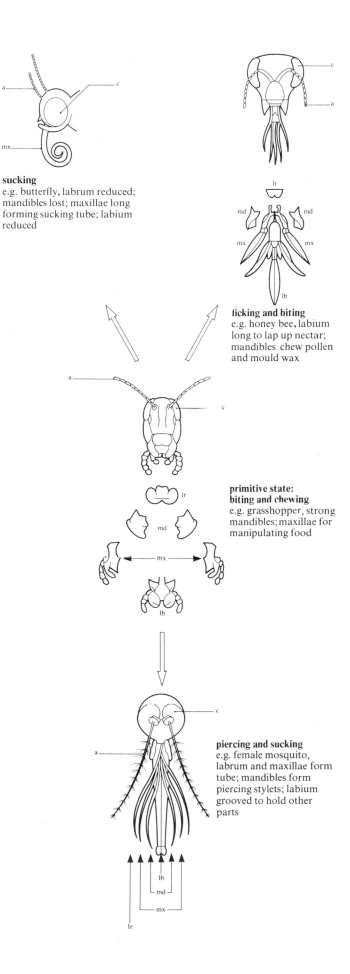

sucking
e.g. butterfly, labrum reduced; mandibles lost; maxillae long forming sucking tube; labium reduced

licking and biting
e.g. honey bee, labium long to lap up nectar; mandibles chew pollen and mould wax

primitive state: biting and chewing
e.g. grasshopper, strong mandibles; maxillae for manipulating food

piercing and sucking
e.g. female mosquito, labrum and maxillae form tube; mandibles form piercing stylets; labium grooved to hold other parts

Fig 24.13 *Adaptive radiation of insect mouthparts; a, antennae; c, compound eye; lb, labium; lr, labrum; md, mandibles; mx, maxillae*

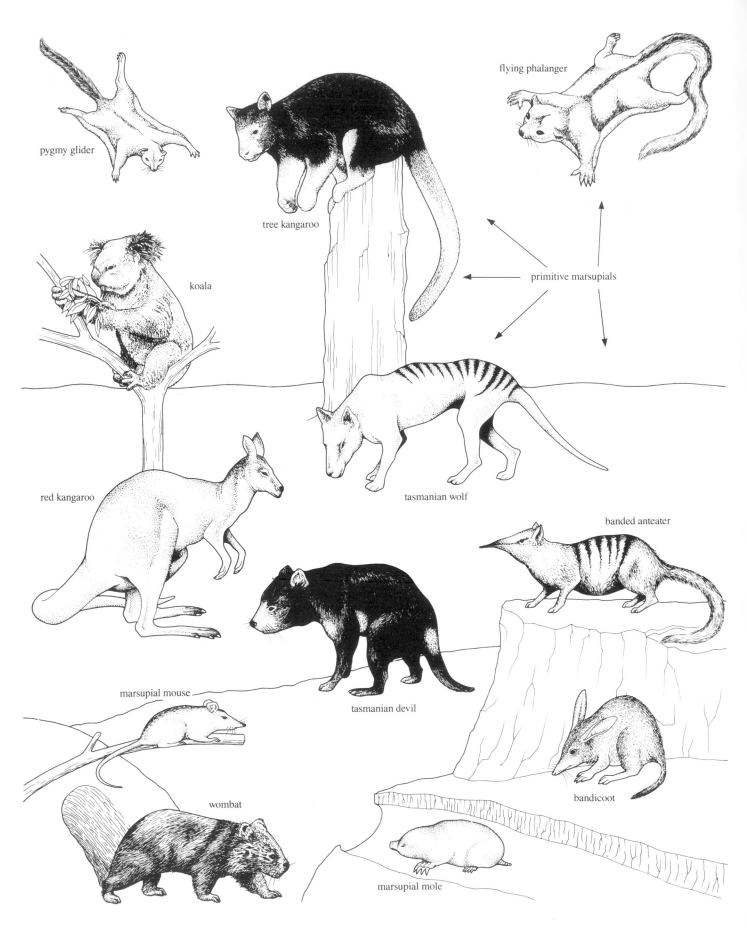

Fig 24.14 *Adaptive radiation of marsupials in Australia (from a variety of sources)*

it suggests the existence of divergent evolution based on modification of homologous structures.

Similar structures, physiological processes or modes of life in organisms apparently bearing no close phylogenetic links but showing adaptations to perform the same functions are described as **analogous**. Examples include the eyes of vertebrates and cephalopod molluscs, the wings of insects and bats, the jointed legs of insects and higher vertebrates, the presence of thorns on plant stems and spines on animals, and the existence of vertebrate neuroendocrines, such as acetylcholine, 5-hydroxy-tryptamine and histamine, in nettle stings. Analogous structures only bear superficial similarities. For example, the wings of insects are supported by toughened veins composed of cuticle, whereas both bats and birds have hollow bones for support. Likewise the embryological development of the cephalopod and vertebrate eyes is different. The former produces an erect retina with photoreceptors facing the incoming light, whereas the latter has an inverted retina with photoreceptors separated from incoming light by their connecting neurones (fig 16.33). Thus the vertebrate eye has a blind spot, which is absent in cephalopods.

The existence of analogous structures suggests the occurrence of **convergent evolution**. Convergent evolution may be explained in terms of the environment, acting through the agency of natural selection, favouring those variations which confer increased survival and reproductive potential on those organisms possessing them.

The significance of divergent evolution, suggesting an evolutionary process, and convergent evolution, suggesting an evolutionary mechanism, is highlighted by the **parallel evolution** of marsupial and placental mammals. Both groups are thought to have undergone convergent evolution and come to occupy identical ecological niches in different parts of the world (fig 24.14 and table 24.5).

Table 24.5 Examples of parallel evolution shown by marsupial and placental mammals.

Marsupial mammals (Australasia)	Placental mammals (elsewhere)
Marsupial mole	Mole
Marsupial mouse	Mouse
Banded anteater	Anteater
Wombat	Prairie dog
Kangaroo	Antelope
Bandicoot	Rabbit
Flying phalanger	Flying squirrel
Koala	Sloth
Tasmanian wolf	Hyena

Fig 24.15 *Stages in embryological development as shown by examples from three vertebrate classes*

24.7.7 Comparative embryology

A study of the embryonic development of the vertebrate groups by Von Baer (1792–1867) revealed striking structural similarities occurring in all the groups, particularly during cleavage, gastrulation and the early stages of differentiation (section 21.5). Haeckel (1834–1919) suggested that this had an evolutionary significance. He formulated the principle that 'ontogeny recapitulates phylogeny', that is the developmental stages through which an organism passes repeats the evolutionary history of the group to which it belongs. Whilst this principle over-generalises the situation, it is attractive and has a degree of demonstrable validity. Examination alone of the embryos and foetal stages of all the vertebrate groups reveals that it is impossible to identify the group to which they belong. Fig 24.15 shows that it is only in the later stages of development that they begin to assume some similarity to their adult form. At comparable stages the vertebrate embryos all possess the following.

(1) External branchial grooves (visceral clefts) in the pharyngeal region and a series of internal paired gill pouches. These join up in fishes to form the gill slits involved in gaseous exchange. In the other vertebrate groups the only perforation that develops in adults becomes the Eustachian tube and auditory canal involved in hearing.

(2) Segmental myotomes are evident in the tail-like structure which is retained in certain species only.

(3) There is a single circulation which includes a two-chambered heart showing no separation into right and left halves, a situation retained completely only in fishes.

As development proceeds in the vertebrate embryo, changes occur which produce the characteristics of fish, amphibian, reptile, bird or mammal depending upon the embryo's parentage. The interpretation placed on these

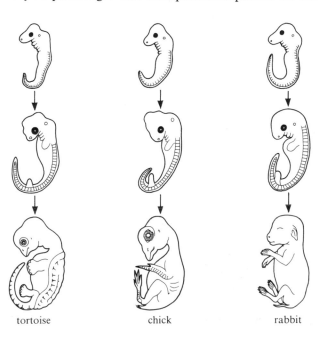

tortoise   chick   rabbit

observations is that these embryos, and hence the groups to which they belong, had a common ancestor. There seems little point in an organism having developmental structures which are apparently non-functional in the adult unless they are the remaining stages of ancestral structures. However the principle of recapitulation cannot be accepted entirely since no living organisms can show all the features of their proposed evolutionary ancestors. What appears to be probable is that organisms retain the inherited developmental mechanisms of their ancestors. Hence at various stages in development it is likely that an organism will show structural similarities to the embryos of its ancestors. Subsequent adaptations to different environmental conditions and modes of life will modify later stages of the developmental process. Observation reveals that the closer the organisms are classified on the basis of common adult homologous structures the longer their embryological development will remain similar. Organisms showing adaptations to certain modes of life and environments not typical of the major group to which they belong show fewer similarities to other members of the group during their embryonic development. This is clearly seen in the development of the parasitic platyhelminths (flatworms) *Fasciola* and *Taenia*, where a series of larval stages showing adaptations to secondary hosts exist which do not appear in the development of the free-living turbellarian platyhelminths, such as *Planaria*. Similarly, the terrestrial earthworm *Lumbricus* does not possess the ciliated trochophore larva which is typical of more primitive annelids. This evidence highlights the limitations of Haeckel's principle of recapitulation.

Study of the embryological development of major groups of organisms reveals structural similarities evident in the embryonic and larval stages which are not apparent in the adult stages. These observations are interpreted as suggesting phylogenetic relationships between various groups of organisms and the implication underlying this is that an evolutionary process exists. On the basis of the cleavage patterns of the zygote and the fate of the blastopore, triploblastic animals may be divided into two groups, the protostomes and deuterostomes. **Protostomes**

show spiral cleavage and their blastopore becomes the mouth of the adult. This pattern of development is seen in the annelids, molluscs and arthropods. **Deuterostomes** show radial cleavage and their blastopore becomes the anus of the adult. The echinoderms and chordates show this pattern of development. These differences are shown in fig 24.16. It is evidence such as this which has helped clarify problems of the phylogenetic affinities of the echinoderms. The adult structure of echinoderms suggests that they are an invertebrate phylum, but their deuterostomic embryological development confirms their affinities with the chordate line of development. This example illustrates the principle that phylogenetic relationships should not be decided purely on evidence of adult homologous structures.

Evidence of the progressive development of various groups on the basis of embryological evidence can be seen within the plant kingdom, but examples are less well documented than for the animal kingdom. The early gametophyte of mosses and ferns, as represented by the protonema produced by germination of the spores, has a similar structure, physiology and pattern of growth to the filamentous green algae from which they are therefore thought to have developed. The principle of alternation of generations in plant life cycles, and the homologous variations upon it reflecting adaptations to various environmental conditions, may be interpreted as examples of homology and provide further evidence for evolutionary relationships between plant groups.

The gymnosperms represent a group of plants which show features intermediate between those plants adapted to a terrestrial existence and those plants which still require water for the transfer of gametes. In the order Cycadales the male gametophyte resembles the light dry microspore (pollen grain) of the angiosperms in that it is distributed by wind. As the male gametophyte develops, a pollen tube is formed as in angiosperms, but instead of this conveying a non-motile male gamete to the archegonium the terminal (antheridial) cell gives rise to two flagellated antherozoids (sperms) which swim to the ovule to bring about fertilisation (fig 24.17). The cycads therefore appear to represent an intermediate group between the lower plants and the angiosperms and this suggests that a phylogenetic continuum exists within the plant kingdom. The existence of a group of organisms possessing features common to two other groups showing different levels of complexity or adapted to different environments, may be interpreted as

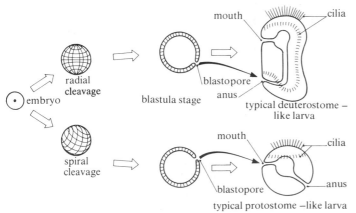

Fig 24.16 *Early developmental stages of deuterostomes and protostomes*

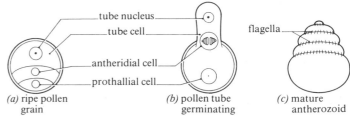

Fig 24.17 *Development of motile male gametes from pollen grain in* Cycas

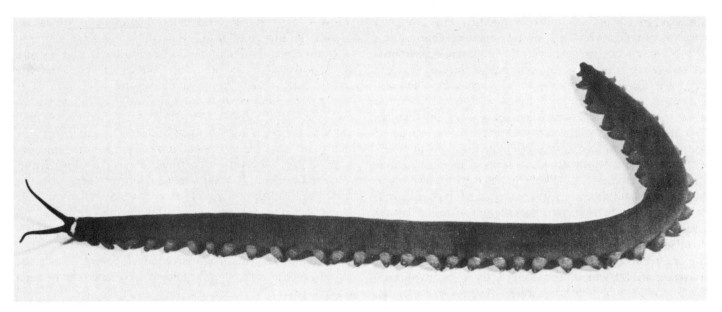

Fig 24.18 *The primitive arthropod* Peripatus

suggesting phylogenetic continuity between the three organisms based on the descent of one group (such as the angiosperms) from the other (the lower plants) via the intermediate form (the cycads). Many of these intermediate forms are extinct and it is only by studying the fossil record that a progressive developmental sequence can be deduced. In many cases intermediate forms have not been found. These are equivalent to the 'missing links' that appear as gaps in the fossil record. It may be that these links do not exist according to the hypothesis of punctuated equilibria (section 24.7.1). However if one accepts the adage '*Natura non facit saltum*' ('Nature does not make leaps'), their absence may be explained by the possibility that they did not fossilise, have not yet been found, or even did not exist. In the case of the phylogenetic link between the annelids and the arthropods there is one group of organisms, the Onychophora, characterised by the genus *Peripatus*, which has features of both annelids and arthropods (fig 24.18). The annelid features include a body wall containing circular and longitudinal muscles, non-jointed parapodia-like limbs, segmental nephridia-like excretory tubules and a double ventral nerve cord. The arthropod features include a chitinous cuticle, spiracles and tracheae and an open blood system. Another 'living fossil' intermediate form is represented by the Dipnoi (lungfish) which suggest a link between fish and amphibians.

Whilst much of this evidence suggests that some form of evolutionary process has occurred, it must be appreciated that there is no conclusive proof that it did occur.

24.7.8 Comparative biochemistry

As techniques of biochemical analysis have become more precise, this field of research has shed new light on evolutionary ideas. The occurrence of similar molecules in a complete range of organisms suggests the existence of biochemical homology in a similar way to the anatomical homology shown by organs and tissues. Again, this evidence for an evolutionary theory is supportive of other evidence rather than confirmatory in its own right. Most of the research which has been carried out on comparative biochemistry has involved analyses of the primary structure of widely distributed protein molecules, such as cytochrome c and haemoglobin, and more recently of nucleic acid molecules, particularly ribosomal RNA. Slight changes in the genetic code as a result of gene mutation produce subtle variations in the overall structure of a given protein or nucleic acid. This forms a basis for determining phylogenetic relationships if the following assumption is made: the fewer the differences in the molecular structure, the fewer the mutations which have occurred and the greater the affinity between organisms containing the molecule. Large differences in the molecular structure represent large differences in the DNA and predictably this situation exists in organisms showing fewer anatomical homologies.

Cytochromes are respiratory proteins situated in the mitochondria of cells and are responsible for the transfer of electrons along the respiratory pathway which produces water and liberates the energy required to synthesise ATP molecules (section 11.5.4). Cytochrome c is one such protein from the pathway. It is a conjugated protein composed of an iron-containing prosthetic group surrounded by a polypeptide chain containing between 104 and 112 amino acids, depending upon species. Modern techniques of computerised mass spectrometry have enabled the primary structure of the cytochrome c polypeptide chain to be worked out for a range of

Table 24.6 Cytochrome *c* amino acid sequences for 21 species.

Species	70	1	2	3	4	5	6	7	8	9	80	1	2	3	4	5	6	7	8	9	90	1	2	3	4	5
Man	D	T	L	M	E	Y	L	E	N	P	K	K	Y	I	P	G	T	K	M	I	F	V	G	I	K	K
Rhesus monkey	D	T	L	M	E	Y	L	E	N	P	K	K	Y	I	P	G	T	K	M	I	F	V	G	I	K	K
Horse	E	T	L	M	E	Y	L	E	N	P	K	K	Y	I	P	G	T	K	M	I	F	A	G	I	K	K
Pig, bovine, sheep	E	T	L	M	E	Y	L	E	N	P	K	K	Y	I	P	G	T	K	M	I	F	A	G	I	K	K
Dog	E	T	L	M	E	Y	L	E	N	P	K	K	Y	I	P	G	T	K	M	I	F	A	G	I	K	K
Grey whale	E	T	L	M	E	Y	L	E	N	P	K	K	Y	I	P	G	T	K	M	I	F	A	G	I	K	K
Rabbit	D	T	L	M	E	Y	L	E	N	P	K	K	Y	I	P	G	T	K	M	I	F	A	G	I	K	K
Kangaroo	D	T	L	M	E	Y	L	E	N	P	K	K	Y	I	P	G	T	K	M	I	F	A	G	I	K	K
Chicken, turkey	D	T	L	M	E	Y	L	E	N	P	K	K	Y	I	P	G	T	K	M	I	F	A	G	I	K	K
Penguin	D	T	L	M	E	Y	L	E	N	P	K	K	Y	I	P	G	T	K	M	I	F	A	G	I	K	K
Pekin duck	D	T	L	M	E	Y	L	E	N	P	K	K	Y	I	P	G	T	K	M	I	F	A	G	I	K	K
Snapping turtle	E	T	L	M	E	Y	L	E	N	P	K	K	Y	I	P	G	T	K	M	I	F	A	G	I	K	K
Bullfrog	D	T	L	M	E	Y	L	E	N	P	K	K	Y	I	P	G	T	K	M	I	F	A	G	I	K	K
Tuna	D	T	L	M	E	Y	L	E	N	P	K	K	Y	I	P	G	T	K	M	I	F	A	G	I	K	K
Screwworm fly	D	T	L	F	E	Y	L	E	N	P	K	K	Y	I	P	G	T	K	M	I	F	A	G	I	K	K
Silkworm moth	D	T	L	F	E	Y	L	E	N	P	K	K	Y	I	P	G	T	K	M	I	F	A	G	L	K	K
Wheat	N	T	L	Y	D	Y	L	L	N	P	K	K	Y	I	P	G	T	K	M	V	F	A	G	L	K	K
Fungus (*Neurospora*)	N	T	L	F	E	Y	L	E	N	P	K	K	Y	I	P	G	T	K	M	V	F	A	G	L	K	K
Fungus (*baker's yeast*)	N	N	M	S	E	Y	L	T	N	P	K	K	Y	I	P	G	T	K	M	V	F	P	G	L	K	K
Fungus (*Candida*)	P	T	M	S	D	Y	L	E	N	P	K	K	Y	I	P	G	T	K	M	A	F	G	G	L	K	K
Bacterium (*Rhodospirillum*)	A	N	L	A	A	Y	V	K	N	P	K	A	F	V	L	E	S	K	M	T	F	K	-	L	T	K

Amino acid sequence

Key to amino acids

A	alanine	F	phenylalanine	K	lysine	P	proline	T	threonine
C	cysteine	G	glycine	L	leucine	Q	glutamine	V	valine
D	aspartic acid	H	histidine	M	methionine	R	arginine	W	tryptophan
E	glutamic acid	I	isoleucine	N	asparagine	S	serine	Y	tyrosine

After Dayhoff, M. O. and Eck, R. V. (1967–8) *Atlas of protein sequence and structure*, National Biomedical Research Foundation, Silver Spring, Md.

---

organisms, including bacteria, fungi, wheat, screwworm fly, silkworm, tuna, penguin, kangaroo and primates. The similarity in cytochrome *c* amino acid sequence between 21 organisms studied in this way is surprisingly high. In 20 out of the 21 organisms studied, ranging from the athlete's-foot fungus to Man, the amino acids in positions 78–88 were identical (table 24.6). The amino acid sequence for cytochrome *c* of Man and chimpanzee is identical and differs from the rhesus monkey by only one amino acid. Computer studies, based on amino acid sequences of cytochrome *c*, have produced plant and animal phylogenetic trees which show close agreement with phylogenetic trees based on anatomical homologies.

Similar results have been obtained from the study of the globin proteins, haemoglobin and myoglobin, involved in oxygen transport and storage. The similarities and differences between the haemoglobin molecules of four primate species are shown in table 24.7. The relationships between the various globins, based on amino acid sequences, and their occurrence in organisms is shown in fig 24.19. Variations in the amino acid sequence of cytochrome *c* and the globins are thought to have arisen by mutations of ancestral genes.

Immunological research has also produced evidence of phylogenetic links between organisms. Protein molecules,

Table 24.7 Similarities and differences between the polypeptide chains of haemoglobin in four primate species.

	Polypeptide chains		
Species	α-haemoglobin (*141 amino acids*)	β-haemoglobin (*146 amino acids*)	γ-haemoglobin
Man	+	+	+
Chimpanzee	+	+	1
Gorilla	1	1	1
Gibbon	3	3	2

Haemoglobin is composed of four polypeptide chains, made up of α, β, and γ polypeptides. + indicates no difference in amino acid sequence from that of Man, figures indicate number of amino acid differences.

present in serum, act as antigens when injected into the bloodstream of animals that lack these proteins. This causes the animal to produce antibodies against them which results in an antigen/antibody interaction (section 14.14). This immune reaction depends upon the host animal recognising the presence of foreign protein structures in the serum. Human serum injected into rabbits sensitises them to human serum and causes them to produce antibodies against human serum proteins. After a period of time, if human serum is added to a sample of

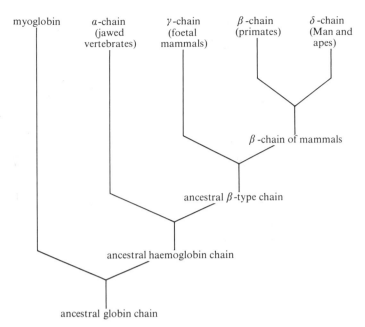

myoglobin   α-chain (jawed vertebrates)   γ-chain (foetal mammals)   β-chain (primates)   δ-chain (Man and apes)

β-chain of mammals

ancestral β-type chain

ancestral haemoglobin chain

ancestral globin chain

Fig 24.19 *Supposed origins of myoglobin and vertebrate globin polypeptide chains. All five types are found in Man. (After V. M. Ingram, (1963) Haemoglobins in genetics and evolution, Columbia University Press.)*

sensitised rabbit serum, antigen/antibody complexes form which settle out as a precipitate that can be measured. Adding serum from a variety of animals to samples of rabbit serum containing antibodies against human serum produces varying amounts of precipitate. Assuming that the amounts of precipitate are directly related to the amounts of 'foreign' protein present, this method can be used to establish affinities between animal groups as shown in table 24.8.

This technique of comparative serology has been used extensively to corroborate phylogenetic links. For example, zoologists were uncertain as to the classification of the king crab (*Limulus*). When various arthropod antigens were added to *Limulus* serum the greatest amount of precipitate was produced by arachnid antigens. This evidence reinforced morphological evidence, and *Limulus* is now firmly established in the class Arachnida. Similar

Table 24.8 Amounts of precipitate produced by adding serum from the following mammals to rabbit serum containing anti-human antibodies against human serum (amount of precipitate produced with human serum taken as 100%).

Man	100%
Chimpanzee	97%
Gorilla	92%
Gibbon	79%
Baboon	75%
Spider monkey	58%
Lemur	37%
Hedgehog	17%
Pig	8%

work has clarified many phylogenetic uncertainties amongst the mammals.

The separation of animal phyla into protostomes and deuterostomes on the basis of embryological development has been reinforced by analysis of the phosphate-containing storage molecules found in muscle and used in the synthesis of ATP. Protostomes, represented by annelids, molluscs and arthropods contain arginine phosphate, whilst deuterostomes represented by echinoderms and chordates, contain creatine phosphate.

A final example of biochemical homology is provided by the presence of similar or identical hormones in vertebrates where they carry out a range of different functions. For example, a hormone similar to mammalian prolactin occurs in all vertebrate groups where it is produced by the pituitary gland. Although it has been reported that there may be 90 distinct effects of prolactin, these can be arranged under two broad headings, reproduction and osmoregulation (table 24.9).

Table 24.9 Action of prolactin in vertebrates.

Group	Reproduction	Osmoregulation
Bony fish	Secretion of skin mucus	Increases urine production
Amphibia	Secretion of 'egg jelly'	Increases skin permeability to water
Reptiles	Suppresses egg production	Stimulates water loss in turtles
Birds	Production of 'crop milk'	Increases water uptake
Mammals	Mammary development and lactation	ADH-like activity

24.7.9 Conclusion

Neo-Darwinian evolutionary theory is based on evidence from a broad range of sources and supported by a mass of otherwise unrelated observations. This constitutes to the scientist the strongest type of evidence for the 'validity' of the theory. Evolution is widely accepted amongst scientists but there is still much work to be done in refining the theory and its application to all observed circumstances.

All scientific accounts, hypotheses and theories of the history of life are tentative and, as long as Man remains objective in his search for truth, will remain so.

Since evolution forms a focal point within the study of biology it would be remiss to conclude this chapter without relating evolution to the perspective of the natural world. To do this it is fitting to quote from Darwin's final paragraph of the *Origin of Species*,

'There is a grandeur in this view of life, with its several powers, having been originally breathed by the Creator into a few forms or into one; and that, whilst this planet has gone cycling on according to the fixed law of gravity, from so simple a beginning endless forms most beautiful and most wonderful have been and are evolving.'

Chapter Twenty-five

Mechanisms of speciation

The previous chapter described how Darwin came to appreciate that heritable variations occurred in natural populations as well as in artificial breeding situations. He perceived that these heritable variations were significant in evolutionary theory but had no means of accounting for the mechanism by which variations could appear and characteristics remain discrete. It was only with the reappearance of the work of Mendel on inheritance, and the appreciation of its importance in the understanding of evolutionary theory, that many of these problems could be resolved. Modern explanations of variation between organisms are a blend of evolutionary theory based on the work of Darwin and Wallace and genetic theory based on principles expounded by Mendel. Variation, inheritance and evolutionary theory may now be explained by evidence from a branch of biology known as **population genetics**.

25.1   Population genetics

A population is a group of organisms of the same species usually found in a clearly defined geographical area. Darwin was concerned how natural selection worked at the level of the individual organism in bringing about evolutionary change. Following the rediscovery of Mendel's demonstration of the particulate nature of inheritance, the importance of the genotype became significant in the study of variation, inheritance and evolutionary change. Bateson, the scientist who introduced the term 'genetics' in 1905, saw genetics as

'the elucidation of the phenomena of heredity and variation'.

It is the study of population genetics which forms the basis of modern views of evolutionary theory, a theory called **neo-Darwinism**, or the **synthetic theory of evolution**.

Genes acting independently, or in conjunction with environmental factors, determine the phenotypic characteristics of organisms and produce variation within populations. Phenotypes adapted to the environmental conditions or 'ecological framework' are '**selected for**', whereas nonadaptive phenotypes are '**selected against**' and eventually eliminated. Whilst natural selection operating on the phenotypic characteristics of individual organisms determines the fate of its genotype, it is the collective genetic response of the whole population that determines not only the survival of the species but also the formation of new species. Only those organisms which successfully reproduce before dying contribute to the future of the species. The fate of an individual organism is relatively insignificant in the history of a species.

25.1.1   Gene pool

A gene pool is the total variety of genes and alleles present in a sexually reproducing population, and in any given population the composition of the gene pool may be constantly changing from generation to generation. New combinations of genes produce unique genotypes which, when expressed in physical terms as phenotypes, undergo environmental selection pressures which continually select and determine which genes pass on to the next generation.

A population whose gene pool shows consistent change from generation to generation is undergoing evolutionary change. A static gene pool represents a situation where genetic variation between members of the species is inadequate to bring about evolutionary change.

25.1.2   Allele frequency

The appearance of any physical characteristic, for example coat colour in mice, is determined by one or more genes. Several forms of each gene may exist and these are called alleles (table 23.2). The number of organisms in a population carrying a particular allele determines the **allele frequency** (which is sometimes, less correctly, referred to as the **gene frequency**). For example, in humans the frequency of the dominant allele for the production of pigment in the skin, hair and eyes is 99%. The recessive allele, which is responsible for the lack of pigment, a condition known as **albinism**, has a frequency of 1%. It is usual in population genetic studies to represent gene or allele frequencies as decimals rather than percentages or fractions. Hence this dominant allele frequency is 0.99 and the recessive albino allele frequency is 0.01. Since the total population represents 100% or 1.0 it can be seen that:

dominant allele frequency + recessive allele frequency = 1
0.99   +   0.01   = 1

In terms of Mendelian genetics the dominant allele would be represented by a letter, say N (for normal pigmentation), and the recessive allele would be represented by n (the albino condition). In the example above, $N = 0.99$ and $n = 0.01$.

Population genetics has borrowed two symbols from the mathematics of probability, p and q, to express the frequency with which a pair of dominant and recessive alleles appear in the gene pool of the population. Therefore,

$$p + q = 1$$

where p = dominant allele frequency, and q = recessive allele frequency.

In the case of pigmentation in humans, $p = 0.99$ and $q = 0.01$,

$$\text{since} \qquad p + q \quad = 1$$
$$0.99 + 0.01 = 1$$

The value of the above equation lies in the fact that if the frequency of either allele is known, the frequency of the other may be determined. For example, if the frequency of the recessive allele is 25% then $q = 25\%$ or 0.25.

$$\text{Since} \qquad p + q \quad = 1$$
$$p + 0.25 = 1$$
$$p \quad = 1 - 0.25$$
$$p \quad = 0.75$$

That is, the frequency of the dominant allele is 0.75 or 75%.

25.1.3 Genotype frequencies

The frequencies of particular alleles in the gene pool are of importance in calculating genetic changes in the population and in determining the frequency of genotypes. Since the genotype of an organism is the major factor determining its phenotype, calculations of genotype frequency are used in predicting possible outcomes of particular matings or crosses. This has great significance in horticulture, agriculture and medicine.

The mathematical relationship between the frequencies of alleles and genotypes in populations was developed independently in 1908 by an English mathematician G. H. Hardy and a German physician W. Weinberg. The relationship known as the **Hardy–Weinberg equilibrium** is based upon a principle which states that

'the frequency of dominant and recessive alleles in a population will remain constant from generation to generation provided certain conditions exist.'

These conditions are:
(1) the population is large;
(2) mating is random;
(3) no mutations occur;
(4) all genotypes are equally fertile, so that no selection occurs;
(5) generations do not overlap;
(6) there is no emigration or immigration from or into the population, that is, there is no gene flow between populations.

Any changes in allele or genotype frequencies must therefore result from the introduction of one or more of the conditions above. These are the factors that are significant

in producing evolutionary change, and when changes occur the **Hardy–Weinberg equation** provides a means of studying the change and of measuring its rate.

25.1.4 The Hardy–Weinberg equation

Whilst the Hardy–Weinberg equation provides a simple mathematical model of how genetic equilibrium can be maintained in a gene pool, its major application in population genetics is in calculating allele and genotype frequencies.

Starting with two homozygous organisms, one dominant for allele **A** and one recessive for allele **a**, it can be seen that all offspring will be heterozygous (**Aa**).

Let	**A** = dominant allele		
	a = recessive allele		
Parental phenotypes	homozygous dominant	×	homozygous recessive
Parental genotypes (2n)	**AA**	×	**aa**
Meiosis			
Gametes (n)	Ⓐ Ⓐ	×	ⓐ ⓐ
Random fertilisation			
F₁ genotypes (2n)	**Aa** **Aa**		**Aa** **Aa**
F₁ phenotypes	all heterozygous		

If the presence of the dominant allele **A** is represented by the symbol p and the recessive allele **a** by the symbol q, the nature and frequency of the genotypes produced by crossing the F₁ genotypes above are seen to be:

F₁ phenotypes	heterozygous	×	heterozygous
F₁ genotypes (2n)	**Aa**	×	**Aa**
Meiosis			
Gametes (n)	Ⓐ ⓐ	×	Ⓐ ⓐ

Random fertilisation		**A** (p)	**a** (q)
	A (p)	**AA** (p^2)	**Aa** (pq)
	a (q)	**Aa** (pq)	**aa** (q^2)
F₂ genotypes (2n)	**AA** (p^2)	**2Aa** ($2pq$)	**aa** (q^2)
F₂ phenotypes	homozygous dominant,	heterozygous,	homozygous recessive

Since **A** is dominant, the ratio of dominant to recessive genotypes will be 3:1, the Mendelian monohybrid cross ratio. From the cross shown above it can be seen that the following genotypes can be described in terms of the symbols p and q:

$$p^2 = \text{homozygous dominant}$$
$$2pq = \text{heterozygous}$$
$$q^2 = \text{homozygous recessive}$$

The distribution of possible genotypes is statistical and based on probability. Of the three possible genotypes resulting from such a cross it can be seen that they are represented in the following frequencies:

AA 2Aa aa
$\frac{1}{4}$ $\frac{1}{2}$ $\frac{1}{4}$

In terms of genotype frequency the sum of the three genotypes presented in the above population equal one, or, expressed in terms of the symbols p and q, it can be seen that the genotypic probabilities are:

$$p^2 + 2pq + q^2 = 1$$

(In mathematical terms $p + q = 1$ is the mathematical equation of probability and $p^2 + 2pq + q^2 = 1$ is the binomial expansion of that equation (that is $(p + q)^2$)).

To summarise, since

p = dominant allele frequency
q = recessive allele frequency
p^2 = homozygous dominant genotype
$2pq$ = heterozygous genotype
q^2 = homozygous recessive genotype

it is possible to calculate all allele and genotype frequencies using the expressions:

allele frequency $p + q = 1$, and
genotype frequency $p^2 + 2pq + q^2 = 1$.

However, in most populations it is only possible to estimate the frequency of the two alleles from the proportion of homozygous recessives, as this is the only genotype that can be identified directly from its phenotype.

For example, one person in 10 000 is albino, that is to say that the albino genotype frequency is 1 in 10 000. Since the albino condition is recessive, that person must possess the homozygous recessive genotype and in terms of probability it can be seen that

$$q^2 = \frac{1}{10\ 000}$$
$$= 0.0001$$

Knowing that $q^2 = 0.0001$ the frequencies of the albino allele (q), the dominant pigmented allele (p), the homozygous dominant genotype (p^2) and the heterozygous genotype ($2pq$) may be determined in the following manner.
Since

$$q^2 = 0.0001$$
$$q = \sqrt{0.0001}$$
$$= 0.01,$$

the frequency of the albino allele in the population is 0.01 or 1%.
Since

$$p + q = 1$$
$$p = 1 - q$$
$$= 1 - 0.01$$
$$= 0.99,$$

the frequency of the dominant allele in the population is 0.99 or 99%.
Since

$$p = 0.99$$
$$p^2 = (0.99)^2$$
$$= 0.9801,$$

the frequency of the homozygous dominant genotype in the population is 0.9801, or approximately 98%.
Since

$$p = 0.99 \text{ and } q = 0.01,$$
$$2pq = 2 \times (0.99) \times (0.01)$$
$$= 0.0198,$$

the frequency of the heterozygous genotype is 0.0198, or approximately 2% of the population carry the albino allele either as heterozygotes or albino homozygotes.

These calculations reveal a surprisingly high value for the frequency of the recessive allele in the population considering the low number of individuals showing the homozygous recessive genotype.

Heterozygous individuals showing normal phenotypic characteristics but possessing a recessive gene capable of producing some form of metabolic disorder when present in homozygous recessives are described as **carriers**. Calculations based on the Hardy–Weinberg equation show that the frequency of carriers in a population is always higher then would be expected from estimates of the occurrence of the disorder in the phenotype. This is shown in table 25.1.

Table 25.1 Some metabolic disorders and the frequencies of homozygous recessive and heterozygous genotypes.

Metabolic disorder	Approximate frequency of homozygous recessive genotype (q^2)	Frequency of 'carrier' heterozygous genotype ($2pq$)
albinism (lack of pigmentation in body)	1 in 10 000 (in Europe)	1 in 50
alkaptonuria (urine turns black upon exposure to air)	1 in 1 000 000	1 in 503
amaurotic family idiocy (leads to blindness and death)	1 in 40 000	1 in 100
diabetes mellitus (failure to secrete insulin)	1 in 200	1 in 7.7
phenylketonuria (may lead to mental retardation if not diagnosed)	1 in 10 000 (in Europe)	1 in 50

25.1 Cystic fibrosis of the pancreas occurs in the population with a frequency of 1 in 2 000. Calculate the frequency of the carrier genotype.

25.1.5 Implications of the Hardy–Weinberg equation

The Hardy–Weinberg equation shows that a large proportion of the recessive alleles in a population exist in carrier heterozygotes. In fact, the heterozygous genotypes maintain a substantial potential source of genetic variability. As a result of this, very few of the recessive alleles can be eliminated from the population in each generation. Only the alleles present in the homozygous recessive organism will be expressed in the phenotype and so be exposed to environmental selection and possible elimination. Many recessive alleles are eliminated because they confer disadvantages on the phenotype. This may result from the death of the organism prior to breeding or **genetic death**, that is the failure to reproduce. Not all recessive alleles, however, are disadvantageous to the population. For example, in human blood groups the commonest phenotypic characteristic in the population is blood group O, the homozygous recessive condition. This phenomenon is also clearly illustrated in the case of sickle-cell anaemia. This is a heritable disease of the blood common in certain populations in Africa, India, certain Mediterranean countries and amongst North American negroes. Homozygous recessive individuals usually die before reaching adulthood thereby eliminating two recessive alleles from the population. Heterozygotes, on the other hand, do not suffer the same fate. Studies have revealed that the sickle-cell allele frequency has remained relatively stable in many parts of the world. In some African tribes the genotype frequency is as high as 40%, and it was thought that this figure was maintained by the appearance of new mutants. Investigations have revealed that this is not the case, and in many parts of Africa where malaria is a major source of illness and death, individuals possessing a single sickle-cell allele have increased resistance to malaria. In malaria regions of Central America the selective advantage of the heterozygous genotype maintains the sickle-cell allele in the population at frequencies between 10 and 20%. The maintenance of a fairly constant frequency for a recessive allele which may be potentially harmful is known as **heterozygote advantage**. In the case of North American negroes who have not been exposed to the selection effect of malaria for 200–300 years the frequency of the sickle-cell allele has fallen to 5%. Some of this loss may be accounted for by increased gene flow resulting from black–white marriages, but an important factor is the removal of the selection pressure for the heterozygote due to the absence of malaria in North America. As a result of this the recessive allele has slowly been eliminated from the population. This is an example of evolutionary change in action. It clearly shows the influence of an environmental selection mechanism on changes in allele frequency, a mechanism which disrupts the genetic equilibrium predicted by the Hardy–Weinberg principle. It is mechanisms such as these that bring about the variations in populations which lead to evolutionary change.

25.2 Factors producing changes in populations

The Hardy–Weinberg equilibrium principle states that given certain conditions the allele frequencies remain constant from generation to generation. Under these conditions a population will be in genetic equilibrium and there will be no evolutionary change. However the Hardy–Weinberg equilibrium principle is purely theoretical. Few natural populations show the conditions necessary for the Hardy–Weinberg equilibrium to exist (section 25.1.3).

The four major sources of genetic variation within a gene pool were described in detail in section 23.8.4, and they are crossing-over during meiosis, independent segregation during meiosis, random fertilisation and mutation. The first three sources of variation are often collectively referred to as **sexual recombination**, and they account for **gene reshuffling**. These processes however, whilst producing new genotypes and altering genotype frequencies, do not produce any changes in the existing alleles, hence the allele frequencies within the population remain constant. Many evolutionary changes, however, usually occur following the appearance of new alleles and the major source of this is mutation.

Other situations in which the conditions for the Hardy–Weinberg equilibrium principle do not exist are when there is non-random breeding, when the population is small and leads to genetic drift, when genotypes are not equally fertile so there is genetic load, and when gene flow occurs between populations. These situations are discussed below.

25.2.1 Non-random breeding

Mating in most natural populations is non-random. Sexual selection occurs whenever the presence of one or more inherited characteristics increases the likelihood of bringing about successful fertilisation of gametes. There are many structural and behavioural mechanisms in both plants and animals which prevent mating from being random. For example, flowers possessing increased size of petals and amounts of nectar are likely to attract more insects and increase the likelihood of pollination and fertilisation. Colour patterns in insects, fishes and birds, and behavioural patterns involving nest-building, territory possession and courtship, all increase the selective nature of breeding.

An experimental investigation with *Drosophila* illustrated the effect of non-random mating on genotype and allele frequencies. A culture of fruit flies containing equal numbers of red-eyed and white-eyed males and females was set up and within 25 generations all white-eyed fruit flies were eliminated from the population. Observation revealed that both red-eyed and white-eyed females preferred mating with red-eyed males. Thus sexual selection, as a mechanism of non-random mating, ensures that certain individuals within the population have an increased reproductive potential so their alleles are more likely to be passed on to the next generation. Organisms with less favourable characteristics have a decreased reproductive potential and the frequency of their alleles being passed on to subsequent generations is reduced.

25.2.2 Genetic drift

This refers to the fact that variation in gene frequencies within populations can occur by chance rather than by natural selection. Random genetic drift or the **Sewall Wright effect** (named after the American geneticist who realised its evolutionary significance) may be an important mechanism in evolutionary change in small or isolated populations. In a small population not all the alleles which are representative of that species may be present. Chance events such as premature accidental death prior to mating of an organism which is the sole possessor of a particular allele would result in the elimination of that allele from the population. For example, if an allele has a frequency of 1% (that is $q = 0.01$) in a population of 1 000 000 then 10 000 individuals will possess that allele. In a population of 100 only one individual will possess that allele so the probability of losing the allele from a small population by chance is much greater.

Just as it is possible for an allele to disappear from a population it is equally possible for it to drift to a higher frequency simply by chance. Random genetic drift, as its name implies, is unpredictable. In a small population it can lead to the extinction of the population or result in the population becoming even better adapted to the environment or more widely divergent from the parental population. In due course this may lead to the origin of a new species by natural selection. Genetic drift is thought to have been a significant factor in the origin of new species on islands and in other reproductively isolated populations.

A phenomenon associated with genetic drift is the **founder principle**. This refers to the fact that when a small population becomes split off from the parent population it may not be truly representative, in terms of alleles, of the parent population. Some alleles may be absent and others may be disproportionally represented. Continuous breeding within the **pioneer** population will produce a gene pool with allele frequencies different from that of the original parent population. Genetic drift tends to reduce the amount of genetic variation within the population, mainly as a result of the loss of those alleles which have a low frequency. Continual mating within a small population decreases the proportion of heterozygotes and increases the number of homozygotes. Examples of the founder principle were shown by studies carried out on the small populations of religious sects in America who emigrated from Germany in the eighteenth century. Some of these sects have married almost exclusively amongst their own members. In these cases they show allele frequencies which are uncharacteristic of either the German or American populations. In the case of the Dunkers, a religious sect in Pennsylvania, each community studied was made up of about 100 families, a population so small as to be likely to lead to genetic drift. Blood group analyses produced the following results:

	Blood group A
Pennsylvanian population	42%
West German population	45%
Dunker population	60%

These values would appear to be the result of genetic drift occurring within small populations.

Whilst genetic drift may lead to a reduction in variation within a population it can increase variation within the species as a whole. Small isolated populations may develop characteristics atypical of the main population which may have a selective advantage if the environment changes. In this way genetic drift can contribute to the process of speciation.

25.2.3 Genetic load

The existence within the population of disadvantageous alleles in heterozygous genotypes is known as **genetic load**. As mentioned in section 25.1.5, some recessive alleles which are disadvantageous in the homozygous genotype may be carried in the heterozygous genotype and confer a selective advantage on the phenotype in certain environmental conditions, such as the sickle-cell trait in regions where malaria is endemic. Any increase in recessive alleles in a population as a result of deleterious mutations will increase the genetic load of the population.

25.2.4 Gene flow

Within the gene pool of a given cross-fertilising population there is a continual interchange of alleles between organisms. Providing there are no changes in allele frequency as a result of mutation, gene reshuffling will confer genetic stability or equilibrium on the gene pool. If a mutant allele should arise it will be distributed throughout the gene pool by random fertilisation.

Gene flow is often used loosely to describe the movement of alleles within a population as described above, but strictly speaking it refers to the movement of alleles from one population to another as a result of interbreeding between members of the two populations. The random introduction of new alleles into the **recipient** population and their removal from the **donor** population affects the allele frequency of both populations and leads to increased genetic variation. Despite introducing genetic variation into populations, gene flow has a conservative effect in terms of evolutionary change. By distributing mutant alleles throughout all populations, gene flow ensures that all populations of a given species share a common gene pool, that is it reduces differences between populations. The interruption of gene flow between populations therefore is a prerequisite for the formation of new species.

The frequency of gene flow between populations depends upon their geographical proximity, and the ease with which organisms or gametes can pass between the two populations. For example, two populations may be situated so close together that interbreeding is continuous and they may be considered in genetic terms as being one population since they share a common gene pool, for example two snail populations in adjacent gardens separated by a privet hedge.

It is relatively easy for flying animals and pollen grains to be actively or passively dispersed into new environments. Here they may interbreed or cross with the resident population, thereby introducing genetic variation into that population.

25.3 Selection

This is a mechanism that can be thought of as occurring at two interrelated levels, at the level of the organism and at the level of the alleles.

Selection is the process by which those organisms which appear physically, physiologically and behaviourally better adapted to the environment survive and reproduce; those organisms not so well adapted either fail to reproduce or die. The former organisms pass on their successful characteristics to the next generation, whereas the latter do not. Therefore selection can be seen to operate through the processes of **differential mortality** and **differential reproductive potential**. Selection has an adaptive significance in perpetuating those organisms most likely to ensure survival of the species and depends upon the existence of phenotypic variation within the population.

When a population increases in size, certain environmental factors become limiting, such as food availability in animals and light in the case of plants. This produces competition for resources between members of the population. Those organisms exhibiting characteristics which give them a competitive advantage will obtain the resource, survive and reproduce. Organisms without those characteristics are at a disadvantage and may die before reproducing. Both environmental limiting factors and population size operate together to produce a **selection pressure** which can vary in intensity.

Therefore, selection is the process determining which alleles are passed on to the next generation by virtue of the

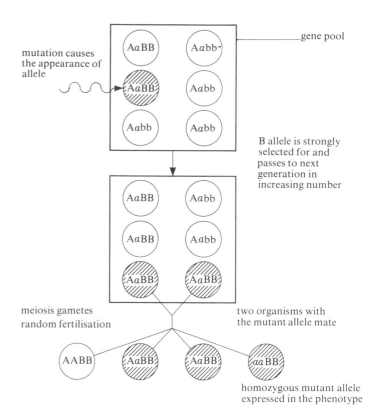

Fig 25.1 *Diagram showing the increased rate of spreading of a mutant allele (α) through a population if linked to a dominant allele (B) which is strongly selected for*

differential advantages they exhibit when expressed as phenotypes. Selection pressure can then be seen as a means of increasing or decreasing the spread of an allele within the gene pool and these changes in allele frequency can lead to evolutionary change. Major changes in genotype arise from the spread of mutant alleles through the gene pool.

The extent and timing of selection will depend upon the nature of the mutant allele and the degree of effect it has upon the phenotypic trait. If the allele is dominant, it will appear in the phenotype and be selected for or against. If the allele is recessive, as is the case with most mutants, it will not undergo selection until it appears in the homozygous state. The chances of this occurring immediately are slight and the allele may be 'lost' from the gene pool before appearing in the homozygous condition. An allele which is recessive in a given environment may persist until changes in the environment occur where it may have a dominant effect. These effects would probably appear first in the heterozygote and selection would favour its spread throughout the population, as in the case of sickle-cell anaemia.

A recessive mutant allele may spread rapidly through a population if it occupies a position (locus) on a chromosome very close (linked) to a functionally important dominant allele which is strongly selected for. In this 'linked' condition the chances of the mutant allele combining with another mutant allele to produce the homozygous condition are increased (fig 25.1).

The influence of a given mutant allele can vary. Those mutations affecting alleles controlling important functions are likely to be lethal and removed from the population immediately. Evolutionary change is generally brought about by the gradual appearance of many mutant alleles which exert small progressive changes in phenotypic characteristics.

There are three types of selection process occurring in natural and artificial populations and they are called stabilising, directional and disruptive. They may be best explained in terms of the normal distribution curve associated with the continuous phenotypic variation found in natural populations (fig 25.2).

25.3.1 Stabilising selection

This operates when phenotypic features coincide with optimal environmental conditions and competition is not severe. It occurs in all populations and tends to eliminate extremes from the population. For example, there is an optimum wing length for a hawk of a particular size with a certain mode of life in a given environment. Stabilising selection, operating through differential reproductive potentials will eliminate those hawks with wing spans larger or smaller than this optimum length.

Karn and Penrose carried out a study on the correlation between birth weight and post-natal mortality on 13 730 babies born in London between 1935 and 1946. Of these 614 were still-born or died within one month of birth. Fig 25.3 shows that there is an optimum birth weight of about 3.6 kg. Babies heavier or lighter than this are at a selective disadvantage and have a slightly increased rate of

mortality. From these results it is possible to calculate the intensity of selection pressure.

If 614 babies died at birth or within one month this represents a mortality of 4.5%. Even at the optimum birth weight 1.8% of babies died. Hence the selection pressure for weight at birth for babies of 3.6 kg is 4.5% −1.8% = 2.7% or 0.027. At a birth weight of 1.8 kg there is a 34% mortality giving an intensity of selection pressure at this weight of approximately 30% or 0.3. It should be pointed out, however, that advances in paediatric medicine have considerably reduced post-natal mortality since 1946.

Stabilising selection pressures do not promote evolutionary change but tend to maintain phenotypic stability within the population from generation to generation.

25.3.2 Directional selection

This form of selection operates in response to gradual changes in environmental conditions. It operates on the range of phenotypes existing within the population and exerts selection pressure which moves the mean phenotype towards one phenotypic extreme. Once the mean phenotype coincides with the new optimum environmental conditions stabilising selection will take over.

This kind of selection brings about evolutionary change by producing a selection pressure which favours the increase in frequency of new alleles within the population. Directional selection forms the basis of artificial selection where the selective breeding of phenotypes showing desirable traits increases the frequency of those phenotypes within the population (section 25.4). In a series of experiments, D. S. Falconer selected the heaviest mice

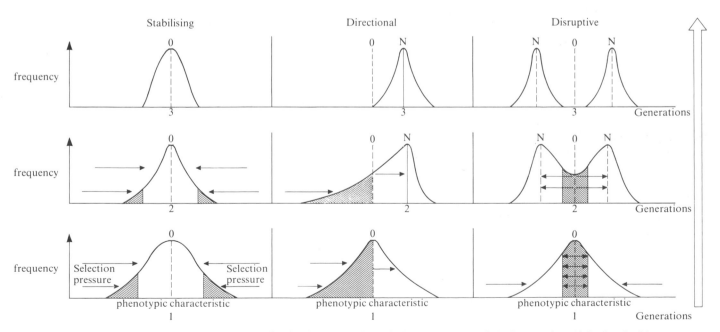

Fig 25.2 *Diagrams showing the three types of selection operating within populations. O indicates the original coincidence between optimum phenotype and optimum environmental conditions; N indicates the new position of coincidence of optimum phenotype and optimum environmental conditions. Organisms possessing characteristics in the shaded portions of the normal distribution are at a selective disadvantage and are eliminated by selection pressure. (The numbers 1–3 indicate the order of generations.)*

891

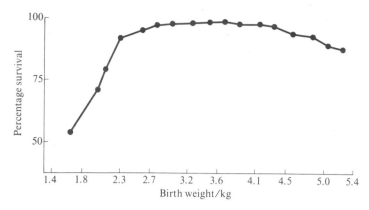

Fig 25.3 *The relationship between percentage survival and birth weight in human babies. (After M. N. Karn & L. S. Penrose (1951) Ann. Eugen., London, 16, 147–64.)*

from a population at six weeks and let them inbreed. He also selected the lightest mice and allowed them to inbreed. This selective breeding according to mass resulted in the production of two populations, one increasing in mass and the other decreasing (fig 25.4). After termination of selective breeding neither group returned to the original population mass of approximately 22 g. This suggested that the artificial selection of phenotypic characteristics led to some genotypic selection and some loss of alleles from each population. Many classic examples of natural directional selection can be seen in evidence today and they are discussed in section 25.5.

25.3.3 Disruptive selection

This is probably the rarest form of selection but can be very important in bringing about evolutionary change. Fluctuating conditions within an environment, say associated with season and climate, may favour the presence of more than one phenotype within a population. Selection pressures acting from within the population as a result of increased competition may push the phenotypes away from the population mean towards the extremes of the population. This can split a population into two sub-populations. If gene flow between the subpopulations is prevented, each population may give rise to a new species. In some cases this form of selection can give rise to the appearance of different phenotypes within a population, a phenomenon known as **polymorphism** (*poly*, many; *morphos*, form), and is discussed in section 25.5.1. Within a species organisms with different phenotypes, or **ecotypes**, may show adaptations to particular environmental conditions (section 25.6.2). When a species occupies an extremely large geographical range, organisms distributed along it may show local changes in phenotypic characteristics which are intermediate between those at the extremes of the range. This continuous gradation of characteristics along a geographical range is usually a phenotypic response to climate and/or edaphic (soil) variables and is known as a **cline** (section 25.6.3).

25.3.4 Intensity of selection pressure

The intensity of selection pressure within a population varies at different times and in different places and may be produced by changes in external or internal factors. External factors may include an increase in numbers of predators or pathogens or competition from other species (**interspecific competition**) for food and breeding space in the case of animals, and light, water and mineral salts in the case of plants. Changes in climatic conditions or the state of the habitat in which organisms live may exert new selection pressures. Internal factors such as a rapid increase in the size of the population can result in increased competition for environmental resources (**intraspecific competition**). As the population size increases, so do the numbers of parasites and predators. Pathogens, too, are more easily transmitted from organism to organism as the host population rises and diseases spread very rapidly. All of these factors may not only affect the intensity of the selection pressure but also the direction of the pressure. 'New' phenotypes (and genotypes) are selected for, and poorly adapted organisms are eliminated from, the population. The organisms to be eliminated first are those at the non-adaptive extremes of the phenotypic range.

One result of increased selection pressure is that it may cause organisms to become **specialised** to certain modes of life or narrower environmental conditions. This may be a disadvantage for the future of that species. Increased uniformity and dependency by a species increases the likelihood of that species becoming extinct should environmental conditions change. The fossil record contains many extinct organisms that were bizarre and overspecialised.

> **25.2** How might a knowledge of selection pressure and mode of life be useful in the eradication of a **named** parasite?

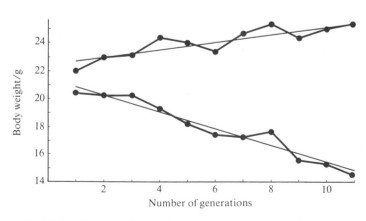

Fig 25.4 *Changes in weight in two mouse populations in successive generations undergoing selection for body weight. (After D. S. Falconer (1953) J. Genetics, 51 470–501.)*

From what has been said it can be seen that increased selection pressure is a conservative mechanism selecting for the phenotype best adapted to the prevailing environmental condition (the optimum phenotype).

A reduction in the intensity of selection pressure usually has the opposite effects to those described above. It may be produced by an absence of predators, pathogens, parasites and competing species or an increase in optimum environmental conditions. These conditions are usually found when an organism is introduced into a new environment. It is conditions such as these which are believed to have favoured the diversity of finch species found on the Galapagos Islands.

25.4 Artificial selection

Man has practised artificial selection in the form of the domestication of animals and plants since the earliest times of his civilisation. Darwin used evidence from artificial selection to account for the mechanism whereby changes in species could arise in natural populations, that is natural selection. The basis of artificial selection is the isolation of natural populations and the selective breeding of organisms showing characteristics or traits which have some usefulness to Man. In the case of cattle, the Hereford and Aberdeen Angus breeds have been selected for the quality and quantity of their meat, whereas Jersey and Guernsey cows are favoured for their milk yield. Hampshire and Suffolk sheep mature early and produce a good

quality meat but lack the hardiness and foraging ability of the Cheviot and Scotch Blackface. The latter examples show that no single breed has all the characteristics necessary for the best economic yield under all conditions and therefore a planned programme of selective breeding is often practised to increase the quality of the breed and the yield.

In artificial selection Man is exerting a directional selection pressure which leads to changes in allele and genotype frequencies within the population. This is an evolutionary mechanism which gives rise to new breeds, strains, varieties, races and subspecies. In all cases these groups have isolated gene pools, but they have retained the basic gene and chromosomal structure which is characteristic of the species to which they still belong.

25.4.1 Inbreeding

This involves selective reproduction between closely related organisms, for example between offspring produced by the same parents, in order to propagate particularly desirable characteristics. Inbreeding is a particularly common practice in the breeding of 'show' animals such as cats and dogs. It was used by livestock breeders to produce cattle, pigs, poultry and sheep with high yields of milk, meat, eggs and wool respectively, but for reasons stated below inbreeding is not now widely practised.

Prolonged inbreeding can lead to a reduction in fertility and this is a particular problem in the breeding of livestock.

(a) (b)

Fig 25.5 *An example of hybrid vigour. Photograph (a) shows two parental maize stalks which when interbred produce the hybrid shown in the centre of the photograph. The ear shown in the centre of the photograph (b) was produced by hybridisation of parental stocks with ears A and B as shown on the left and right of the photograph. (Photograph by D. F. Jones, Connecticut Agricultural Experiment Station.)*

Intensive inbreeding reduces the variability of the genome (the sum of all the alleles of an individual) by increasing the number of homozygous genotypes at the expense of the number of heterozygous genotypes. In order to overcome these problems breeders resort to outbreeding after several generations of inbreeding. For example, a dairy farmer may use his own bull and successive generations of his own cows to produce cows with a high milk yield. Before the cattle begin to show signs of decreased resistance to disease and reduced fertility, the farmer will use another bull or artificially inseminate his breeding cows with semen acquired from a cattle-breeding centre. This introduces new alleles into the herd, thereby increasing the hetero-zygosity of the breeding population.

25.4.2   Outbreeding

This is particularly useful in plant breeding, but is being used increasingly in the commercial production of meat, eggs and wool. It involves crossing individuals from genetically distinct populations. Outbreeding usually takes place between members of different varieties or strains, and in certain plants between closely related species. The progeny are known as **hybrids**, and have phenotypes showing characteristics which are superior to either of the parental stocks. This phenomenon is known as **hybrid vigour** or **heterosis**. Hybrids produced from crossing homozygous parental stocks from different populations are called F_1 hybrids and show advantages such as increased fruit size and number, increased resistance to disease and earlier maturity. In maize (sweet corn), hybridisation has increased the grain yield of the F_1 hybrids by 250% over the parental stocks (fig 25.5). In the case of double-cross hybridisation, the hybrids produced by crossing two inbred strains are themselves crossed. The resulting hybrid produces ears having the quality and yield which more than covers the costs involved in a two-year breeding program-me (fig 25.6).

Increased vigour results from the increased heterozy-gosity which arises from gene mixing. For example, whilst each homozygous parent may possess some, but not all, of the dominant alleles for vigorous growth, the heterozygote produced will carry all the dominant alleles, as shown in fig 25.7.

Increased vigour in certain varieties may not result simply from the increased prominence of dominant alleles,

Fig 25.6   *The phenotypes produced by double-cross hybridisation in maize. The maize crop on the right was produced by crossing the hybrids of the inbred strain (shown on the left)*

Fig 25.7 *A simple genetic explanation of increased vigour in F₁ hybrids*

Parental genotypes (2n)	**FFgghhIIjj** × **FFGGHHiiJJ**
Meiosis	
Gametes (n)	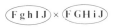
Random fertilisation	
F₁ genotypes (2n)	**FfGgHhIiJj**
F₁ phenotypes	This carries a dominant allele for each gene

but also from some form of interaction between particular combinations of alleles in the heterozygote.

If F₁ phenotypes are continually inbred the vigour will decrease as the proportion of homozygotes increases (fig 25.8).

Selective hybridisation can induce changes in chromosome number (chromosomal mutation), a phenomenon known as **polyploidy**, which can lead to the production of new species. An example of this is described in section 23.9.2.

25.4.3 Artificial selection in Man

Recent advances in Man's knowledge of the structure of the gene, the genetic code, the mechanisms of heredity and the prenatal diagnosis of genetic defects, have opened up the possibilities of selecting or eliminating certain characteristics in Man. The science of **eugenics** is concerned with the possibilities of 'improving' the 'quality' of the human race by the selective mating of certain individuals. This is a very emotive topic and raises all sorts of objections. Aldous Huxley in his book *Brave New World*, published in 1932, fictionalised the day when eugenics would be taken to its extreme possibilities and particular types of individuals would be produced according to the needs of society at that time. Whilst these ideas are repugnant to societies in which the freedom and rights of the individual are paramount, there are strong arguments for the exercise of limited forms of eugenic practice. In medicine, **genetic counselling** is becoming more acceptable as a means of informing couples with family histories of genetic abnormalities about the possible risks involved

Fig 25.8 *Maize stalks of eight generations. The seven stalks on the right demonstrate loss of hybrid vigour as a result of inbreeding from the hybrid shown on the left. The last three generations show reduced loss of vigour as a result of their becoming homozygous. (Photograph by D. F. Jones, Connecticut Agricultural Experiment Station.)*

in having children. By applying the Hardy–Weinberg equation it is possible to calculate the number of carriers of metabolic disorders such as phenylketonuria or abnormalities of the blood, such as thalassaemia, sickle-cell anaemia or haemophilia. Known carriers can be advised as to the likelihood of marrying another carrier and the possibilities of producing offspring affected by the disorder. Such forms of preventive medicine offer advice rather than dictate policy. Any scientific advances which reduce suffering must receive sympathetic appreciation. The dangers of eugenics lie in their possible abuse.

25.5 Natural selection

Natural selection, as postulated by Darwin and Wallace, represented a hypothesis based on historical evidence. For Darwin, the time span involved in the evolutionary change of a population was such that it could not be observed directly. Recent changes accompanying the industrial, technological and medical revolutions have produced such strong directional and disruptive pressures that we can now observe the results of dramatic changes in genotypic and phenotypic characteristics of populations within days. The introduction of antibiotics in the 1940s provided a strong selection pressure for strains of bacteria that have the genetic capability of being resistant to the effects of the antibiotics. Bacteria reproduce very rapidly, producing many generations and millions of individuals each day. Random mutation may produce a resistant organism in the population which will thrive in the absence of competition from other bacteria which have been eliminated by the antibiotic. As a result, new antibiotics have to be developed to eliminate the resistant bacteria, and so the cycle continues. Other examples of the effects of chemicals in producing selection pressure have been seen with DDT on body-lice and mosquitoes and the effect of the anticoagulant warfarin on rats. Following the development of resistant strains they spread very rapidly throughout the population.

Perhaps the classic example of evolutionary change is provided by the response of moth species to the directional selection pressure produced by the atmospheric pollution which accompanied the industrial revolution. Within the last 100 years darkened forms of about 80 species of moths have appeared in varying frequencies throughout the United Kingdom. This is a phenomenon known as **industrial melanism.** Up to 1848 all reported forms of the peppered moth (*Biston betularia*) appeared creamy-white with black dots and darkly shaded areas (fig 25.9). In 1848 a black form of the moth was recorded in Manchester, and by 1895, 98% of the peppered moth population in Manchester was black. This black 'melanic' form arose by a recurring random mutation, but its phenotypic appearance had a strong selective advantage in industrial areas for reasons put forward and tested by Dr H. B. D. Kettlewell.

The moths fly by night and during the day they rest on the

(a)

(b)

Fig 25.9 *Polymorphic forms of peppered moth,* Biston betularia. *(a) The normal form,* Biston betularia typica; *(b) the melanic form,* Biston betularia carbonaria. *(From E. B. Ford (1973)* Evolution studied by observation and experiment, *Oxford Biology Readers,* **55**, *Oxford University Press.)*

trunks of trees. The normal form of the moth is extremely well camouflaged as its colouration merges with that of the lichens growing on the trunks. With the spread of the industrial revolution sulphur dioxide pollution from the burning of coal killed off the lichens growing on trees in industrial areas, exposing the darker bark which was further darkened by soot deposits (fig 25.10).

Kettlewell, in the 1950s released known numbers of marked light and dark forms into two areas, one a polluted area near Birmingham where 90% of the population was the black form, and the other an unpolluted area in Dorset where the dark form was rarely found. On recapturing the moths using a light trap he obtained the following results:

	Birmingham	Dorset
Percentage marked dark form	34.1	6.3
Percentage marked light form	15.9	12.5

Kettlewell demonstrated using cine-film that robins and thrushes feed on the moths. This is a form of natural selection known as **selective predation**, and it acts as a selection pressure on the distribution of the melanic and non-melanic forms.

The results show that the melanic form of the moth, *Biston betularia carbonaria*, has a selective advantage in industrial areas over the lighter form, *Biston betularia typica*, whereas the lighter form has the selective advantage in non-polluted areas.

Subsequent research has demonstrated that the colouration of the dark form is due to the presence of a dominant melanic allele. Fig 25.11 shows a recent distribution of the two forms in the British Isles.

The presence of melanic forms in non-industrial areas of the east of England is explained by the distribution of melanic forms by prevailing westerly winds. Since the introduction of the Clean Air Act in 1956 the proportion of non-melanic forms has increased slightly as the selection pressure on these forms has been reduced in industrial areas.

25.5.1 Polymorphism

Polymorphism plays a significant role in the process of natural selection. It demonstrates many of the principles outlined earlier in the chapter regarding the relationship between genotype frequency within the population and variations in selection pressure. It is defined as the existence of two or more forms of the same species within the same population, and can apply to biochemical, morphological and behavioural characteristics. There are two forms of polymorphism, transient polymorphism and balanced, or stable, polymorphism.

A classic quantitative study of balanced polymorphism was carried out by Cain, Currey and Shepherd on the common land snail *Cepaea nemoralis*. The shells of this species may be yellow (and appear green with the living snail inside), brown, or various shades including pale fawn, pink, orange and red. The lip of the shell may be dark brown, pink or white and the whole shell may have up to five dark brown bands following the contours of the shell (fig 25.12). Both colouration and banding pattern are determined genetically. The colours are determined by multiple alleles with brown being dominant to pink and both being dominant to yellow. Banding is recessive.

Studies have revealed that the snails are predated upon by thrushes which carry the snails to a nearby stone which they use as an 'anvil' to crack open the shell; the snail inside is then eaten. By studying the proportions of types of shell found near an anvil with those in the immediate habitat, Cain, Currey and Shepherd demonstrated that selective forces were at work within the population. In areas where the background was fairly uniform, such as grass and woodland litter, the yellow and brown unbanded shells had a selective advantage as fewer of these shells were found near the anvil (fig 25.13). In areas where the ground cover was tangled and mottled, as in rough pasture or hedgerows, the darker banded shells had a selective advantage. The

(a)

(b)

Fig 25.10 *Melanic and non-melanic forms of* Biston betularia *on tree trunks in (a) an area near Birmingham, and (b) an area in Dorset. (Courtesy of Dr H. B. D. Kettlewell, Department of Zoology, University of Oxford.)*

Biston betularia typica

Biston betularia carbonaria

Fig 25.11 *The distribution of melanic and non-melanic forms of* Biston betularia *in the British Isles in 1958. (After H. B. D. Kettlewell (1978) Heredity,* **12**, *51–72.)*

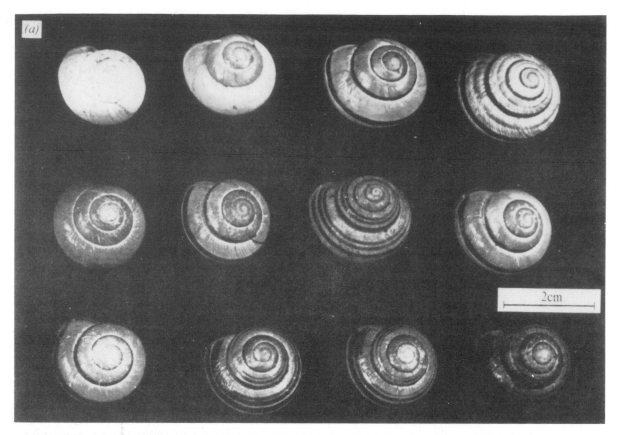

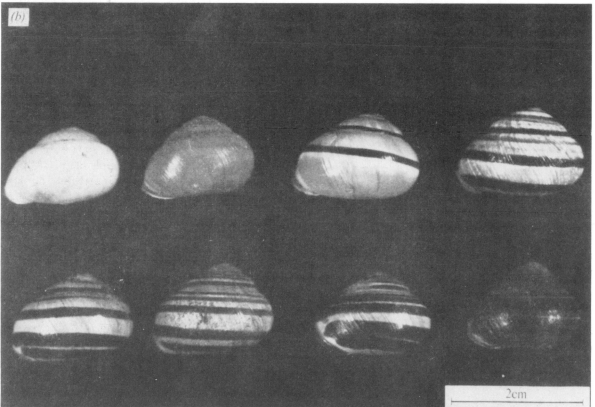

Fig 25.12 *Colour and banding pattern variation in the shells of* Cepaea nemoralis. *The extremes of colour and banding are shown as a progression from yellow unbanded (top left) to brown banded (bottom right). Photographs (a) and (b) show top and side views of the same shells. (After Tribe, Tallan & Erant (1978)* Basic Biology Course, *Book 12, Cambridge University Press.)*

Fig 25.13 *Unbanded shells of Cepaea nemoralis against a background of leaf litter. The shell on the extreme right is yellow, the shell at the top of the photograph is pink and the two shells on the left are brown. (After E. B. Ford (1973) Evolution studied by observation and experiment, Oxford Biology Reader, 55, Oxford University Press.)*

20 mm

forms suffering the greatest predation in any area were those which were visually conspicuous to the thrushes. A large population of polymorphic snails may include several areas with a range of backgrounds. Seasonal effects also produce changes in background colour and pattern. Although predation of conspicuous forms is continuous there is no overall selective advantage for any form, hence the numbers of each form within a population remain fairly constant from year to year.

The balance in numbers of each form may not be determined purely by colour and banding pattern. There is evidence to suggest that physiological effects may help to maintain the polymorphic equilibrium. In some areas where the soil is calcareous and dry and the background cover is light, the dominant forms are not always those with the least conspicuous colour and banding pattern. The genetic basis for the polymorphism shown by Cepaea is thought to rely on the existence of a special form of gene linkage. The genes for colour and banding pattern are linked and form a **super-gene** which acts as a single genetic unit and is inherited as such. These genes determine characteristics which have such a selective advantage that they are maintained within the population. It is the variety of allelic forms of these genes, maintained by the

heterozygotes which forms the basis of the polymorphism. The added linkage of genes controlling certain physiological effects is also thought to contribute to the maintenance of the balanced polymorphism. The existence of a number of distinct inherited varieties coexisting in the same population at frequencies too great to be explained by recurrent mutations, as in the case of Cepaea, is called **genetic polymorphism.**

Transient polymorphism

This arises when different forms, or **morphs**, exist in a population undergoing a strong selection pressure. The frequency of the phenotypic appearance of each form is determined by the intensity of the selection pressure, such as the melanic and non-melanic forms of the peppered moth. Transient polymorphism usually applies in situations where one form is gradually being replaced by another.

Balanced polymorphism

This occurs when different forms coexist in the same population in a stable environment. It is illustrated most clearly by the existence of the two sexes in animals and plants. The genotypic frequencies of the various forms exhibit equilibrium since each form has a selective advantage of equal intensity. In Man, the existence of the A, B, AB and O blood groups are examples of balanced polymorphism. Whilst the genotypic frequencies within different populations may vary, they remain constant from generation to generation within that population. This is because none of them has a selective advantage over the others. Statistics reveal that white men of blood group O have a greater life expectancy than those of other blood groups but, interestingly, they also have an increased risk of developing a duodenal ulcer which may perforate and lead to death. Red–green colour blindness in Man is another example of polymorphism, as is the existence of workers, drones and queens in social insects and pin and thrum-eyed forms in primroses.

25.6 The concept of species

A species represents the lowest taxonomic group which is capable of being defined with any degree of precision. It may be defined in a variety of ways and some of these are summarised in table 25.2.

Organisms belonging to a given species rarely exist naturally as a single large population. It is usual for a species to exist as small interbreeding populations, called **demes**, each with its own gene pool. These populations may occupy adjacent or widely dispersed geographical areas. Spatial separation of populations means that the species may encounter a variety of environmental conditions and degrees of selection pressure. Mutation and selection within the isolated populations may produce the following degrees of phenotypic variation within the species.

25.6.1 Geographical races

Populations which are distributed over a wide geographical range or have occupied well-separated geographical habitats for a long period of time may show considerable phenotypic differences. These are usually based on adaptations to climatic factors. For example, the gypsy moth (*Hymantria dispar*) is distributed throughout the Japanese Islands and eastern Asia. Over this range a variety of climatic conditions are encountered, ranging from subarctic to subtropical. Ten geographical races have been recognised which differ from each other with regard to the timing of hatching of their eggs. The northern races hatch later than the southern races. The phenotypic variations shown by the ten races are thought to be the result of climatic factors producing changes in gene frequencies within their gene pools. The evidence that these variations are genetically controlled is shown by the fact that under identical environmental conditions the different races still hatch at different times.

25.6.2 Ecological races (ecotypes)

Populations adapted to ecologically dissimilar habitats may occupy adjacent geographical areas; for example the plant species *Gilia achilleaefolia* occurs as two

Table 25.2 Alternative ways of defining a species.

Biological aspect	Definition
Breeding	A group of organisms capable of interbreeding and producing fertile offspring
Ecological	A group of organisms sharing the same ecological niche; no two species can share the same ecological niche
Genetic	A group of organisms showing close similarity in genetic karyotype
Evolutionary	A group of organisms sharing a unique collection of structural and functional characteristics

races along the coast of California. One race, the 'sun' race, is found on exposed southerly facing grassy slopes, whilst the 'shade' race is found in shaded oak woodlands and redwood groves. These races differ in the size of their petals, a characteristic which is determined genetically.

25.6.3 Clines

A species exhibiting a gradual change in phenotypic characteristics throughout its geographical range is referred to as a **cline**. More than one cline may be exhibited by a species and they may run in opposite directions as shown by fig 25.14.

Species exhibiting marked phenotypic variation within a population according to their degree of geographical isolation are known as **polytypic species**. One classic form of a polytypic species is illustrated by gulls belonging to the genus *Larus* (section 25.8.4).

All cases of phenotypic variation described above represent varying degrees of genetic dissimilarity which may interfere with the breeding potential of members of the populations if brought together.

25.7 Speciation

This is the process by which one or more species arise from previously existing species. A single species may give rise to new species (**intraspecific speciation**), or, as is common in many flowering plants, two different species may give rise to a new species (**interspecific hybridisation**). If intraspecific speciation occurs whilst the populations are separated it is termed **allopatric speciation**. If the process occurs whilst the populations are occupying the same geographical area it is called **sympatric speciation**.

25.8 Intraspecific speciation

There are several factors involved in intraspecific speciation, but in all cases gene flow within populations must be interrupted. As a result of this each subpopulation becomes genetically isolated. Change in allele and genotype frequencies within the populations, as a result of the effects of natural selection on the range of

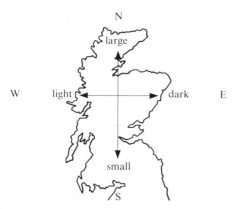

Fig 25.14 *Phenotypic variation in size and fur colour shown by the wood mouse* (Apodemus) *in Scotland*

phenotypes produced by mutation and sexual recombination, lead to the formation of races and subspecies. If the genetic isolation persists over a prolonged period of time and the subspecies then come together to occupy the same area they may or may not interbreed. If the breeding is successful they may still be considered to belong to the same species. If the breeding is unsuccessful, then speciation has occurred and the subspecies may now be considered to be separate species. This is the way in which it is believed evolutionary change can be brought about.

An initial factor in the process of speciation may be the reduction in the intensity of selection pressure within the population. This may lead to increased intraspecific variability. These new phenotypes may enable the population to increase its geographical range if the phenotypes show adaptations to environmental conditions found at the extremes of the range. Providing there is no reduction in gene flow throughout the population, the species, whilst exhibiting the localised phenotypic variation (ecotypes), will still share the same gene pool and continue to exist as a single species. This is the situation found in a cline.

Speciation will only occur as a result of the formation of barriers which lead to reproductive isolation between members of the population. Reproductive isolation is brought about by some form of what the geneticist Theodosius Dobzhansky called **isolating mechanism**.

25.8.1 Isolating mechanisms

An isolating mechanism is a means of producing and maintaining reproductive isolation within a population. This can be brought about by mechanisms acting before or after fertilisation. Dobzhansky suggested a classification of isolating mechanisms which has been modified and is shown in table 25.3.

25.8.2 Allopatric speciation

Allopatric (*allos*, other; *patria*, native land) speciation is characterised by the occurrence, at some stage, of spatial separation. Geographical barriers such as mountain ranges, seas or rivers, or habitat preferences, may produce a barrier to gene flow because of spatial

Table 25.3 Isolating mechanisms (after Dobzhansky).

Prezygotic mechanisms (barriers to the formation of hybrids)

Seasonal isolation	Occurs where two species mate or flower at different times of the year; for example in California *Pinus radiata* flowers in February whereas *Pinus attenuata* flowers in April
Ecological isolation	Occurs where two species inhabit similar regions but have different habitat preferences; for example *Viola arvensis* grows on calcareous soils whereas *Viola tricolor* prefers acid soils
Behavioural isolation	Occurs where animals exhibit courtship patterns, mating only results if the courtship display by one sex results in acceptance by the other sex; for example certain fish, bird and insect species
Mechanical isolation	Occurs in animals where differences in genitalia prevent successful copulation and in plants where related species of flowers are pollinated by different animals

Postzygotic mechanisms (barriers affecting hybrids)

Hybrid inviability	Hybrids are produced but fail to develop to maturity; for example hybrids formed between northern and southern races of the leopard frog (*Rana pipiens*) in North America
Hybrid sterility	Hybrids fail to produce functional gametes; for example the mule ($2n = 63$) results from the cross between the horse (*Equus equus*, $2n = 60$) and the ass (*Equus hemionus*, $2n = 66$)
Hybrid breakdown	F_1 hybrids are fertile but the F_2 generation and backcrosses between F_1 hybrids and parental stocks fail to develop or are infertile, for example hybrids formed between species of cotton (genus *Gossypium*)

separation. This inability of organisms or their gametes to meet leads to reproductive isolation. Adaptations to new conditions or random genetic drift in small populations lead to changes in allele and genotype frequencies. Prolonged separation of populations may result in them becoming genetically isolated even if brought together. In this way new species may arise. For example, the variety and distribution of the finch species belonging to the family Geospizidae on the islands of the Galapagos archipelago are thought to be the result of allopatric speciation. David Lack suggested that an original stock of finches reached the Galapagos Islands from the mainland of South America and, in the absence of competition from endemic species (representing relaxed selection pressure), adaptive radiation occurred to produce a variety of species adapted to particular ecological niches. The various species are believed to have evolved in geographical isolation to the point that when dispersal brought them together on certain islands they were able to coexist as separate species.

Sympatric speciation

Genetic differences may accumulate allopatri-
...n populations which have been geographically
...ted for a much shorter period of time. If these
...opulations are brought together, hybrids may form where
these overlap. For example, both the carrion crow (*Corvus
corone*) and the hooded crow (*Corvus corone cornix*) are
found in the British Isles. The carrion crow is completely
black and is common in England and southern Scotland.
The hooded crow is black with a grey back and belly and is
found in the north of Scotland. Hybrids formed from the
mating of carrion and hooded crows occupy a narrow
region extending across central Scotland (fig 25.15). These
hybrids have reduced fertility and serve as an efficient
reproductive barrier to gene flow between the populations
of the carrion and hooded crows.

In time, selection against cross-breeding may occur,
leading to speciation. Since such speciation occurs finally in
the same geographical area, this is called **sympatric** (*sym*,
together; *patria*, native land) **speciation**.

Sympatric speciation does not involve geographical
separation of populations at the time at which genetic
isolation occurs. It requires the development of some form
of reproductive isolating mechanism which has arisen by
selection within a geographically confined area. This may
be structural, physiological, behavioural or genetic.

Sympatric speciation is more commonly thought of as
providing an explanatory mechanism of how closely related
species, which probably arose from a common ancestor by
temporary isolation, can coexist as separate species within
the same geographical area. For example, in the Galapagos
archipelago the finch *Camarhyncus pauper* is found only on
Charles Island, where it coexists with a related form *C.
psittacula* which is widely distributed throughout the
central islands (fig 25.16). The finch species appear to
choose their mates on the basis of beak size. The range of
beak sizes of *C. pauper* on Charles Island and *C. psittacula*

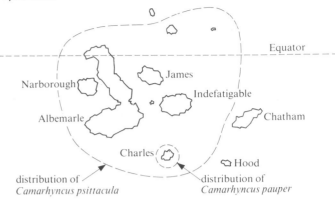

Fig 25.16 *The Galapagos Islands and the distribution of two
species of finch illustrating coexistence following allopatric
speciation*

on Albemarle Island are approximately equal, but on
Charles Island *C. psittacula* has a longer beak. This
difference is significant enough to ensure that the two
species, which feed on different foods, appear unattractive
to each other during the breeding season. In this way the
species remain distinct and are able to coexist.

25.8.4 Ring species

This is a special form of sympatric speciation
which occurs at the point where two populations at the
extremes of a cline meet up and inhabit the same area, thus
'closing' the ring. For example, gulls of the genus *Larus*
form a continuous population between latitudes 50–80 °N,
encircling the North Pole. A ring of ten recognisable races
or subspecies exist which principally differ in size and in the
colour of their legs, back and wings. Gene flow occurs
freely between all races except at the point where the 'ends
of the ring' meet at the British Isles. Here, at the extremes
of the geographical range, the gulls behave as distinct
species, that is the herring gull (*Larus argentatus*) and the
lesser black-backed gull (*L. fuscus*). These have a different
appearance, different tone of call, different migratory
patterns and rarely interbreed. Selection against cross-
breeding is said to occur sympatrically.

Sympatric speciation without geographical isolation in
sexually reproducing species is unlikely. However, in
asexually reproducing organisms, including vegetatively
propagated higher plants, a single mutant so different from
its parent population as to be genetically isolated could give
rise to a new species sympatrically. An example is
polyploidy in *Spartina* (section 23.9.2).

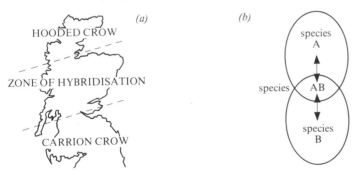

Fig 25.15 *Hybrid barrier as a means of preventing gene flow
between two populations. The maintenance of the two crow
species is shown to be due to the existence of a zone of
hybridisation extending across Scotland as shown in (a). The
existence of hybrid barriers between adjacent populations is
common and functions as follows. Where the geographical
ranges of A and B overlap, mating produces a hybrid with
lowered fertility. A will interbreed freely with AB and AB with B
but the existence of AB prevents free interbreeding of A and
B populations*

> **25.3** Ten subspecies of the *Larus argen-
> tatus–fuscus* population form a continuous ring
> extending from the British Isles through Scandinavia,
> Russia, Siberia, across the Bering Straits, through
> Alaska and Canada and back to the British Isles. If
> the subspecies inhabiting the Bering Straits and
> Alaska was eliminated what predicted effects might
> this have on the population?

25.9   Interspecific hybridisation

This is a form of sympatric speciation which occurs when a new species is produced by the crossing of individuals from two unrelated species. Fertile hybrids usually only appear in cases of interspecific hybridisation as a result of a form of chromosome mutation known as **allopolyploidy** (section 23.9.2). An example of this was demonstrated by Karpechenko in the case of hybrids formed between the cabbage and the radish. The genetic changes involved in this hybridisation are shown in fig 25.17.

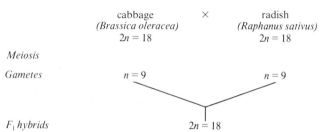

Meiosis

During meiosis in the F_1 hybrids chromosomes from each parent cannot pair together to form homologous chromosomes. The F_1 hybrids are therefore sterile. Occasionally non-disjunction of the F_1 hybrids produces gametes with the diploid set of chromosomes ($2n = 18$).

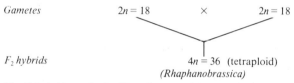

The F_2 hybrids are fertile. Homologous pairing can occur in meiosis as two sets of parental chromosomes are present. Diploid gametes ($2n = 18$), are produced which possess 9 chromosomes from the parental cabbage and 9 chromosomes from the parental radish.

Fig 25.17 *Stages involved in the hybridisation of the cabbage and the radish*

Answers and discussion

Chapter 14

14.1 (a) Solution B (b) Solution A (c) From B to A (d) Solution A (e) (ii) $-1\,000$ kPa. If you find this confusing remember $-1\,000$ is nearer zero than $-2\,000$. Zero is the maximum, or highest, ψ that can occur. (f) Solution B (g) The higher the OP of a solution the lower the ψ (in practice $-\text{OP} = \psi$ for a solution at atmospheric pressure).

14.2 The hypertonic solution. Remember that the cell wall is freely permeable to solutions.

14.3 Zero. The protoplast is not exerting pressure against the cell wall.

14.4 Prokaryotes (the bacteria and blue-green algae) and fungi. Although prokaryotes lack vacuoles, they have the same osmotic properties as plant cells and fungi.

14.5 At the start $\psi^{cell} = \text{TP} - \text{OP}$, $\psi^{solution} = -\text{OP} = -1\,200$ kPa; TP $= 0$ because the cell is at incipient plasmolysis; OP $= 2\,000$ kPa; so $\psi^{cell} = 0$ kPa $-2\,000$ kPa $= -2\,000$ kPa. At the start, ψ of the solution is greater than ψ of the cell. Water therefore moves from the solution into the cell by osmosis. The only term that changes significantly as water enters the cell is TP. As water enters, TP, and hence ψ, increases until it prevents any further net entry of water. At this point ψ of the cell equals ψ of the solution, and the cell is turgid.

Therefore, at equilibrium $\psi^{cell} = -1\,200$ kPa. $\psi = \text{TP} - \text{OP}$ so TP $= \psi + \text{OP} = -1\,200$ kPa $+ 2\,000$ kPa $= 800$ kPa.

14.6 $\text{OP}^{cell} = 1\,100$ kPa; ψ pure water $= 0$; $\psi^{cell} = 0$ at equilibrium. TP $= \psi + \text{OP} = 0$ kPa $+ 1\,100$ kPa $= 1\,100$ kPa.

14.7 (a) ψ^{cell} at transfer $= \psi$ pure water $= 0$, ψ sucrose solution $= -800$ kPa, so the difference in ψ between cell and external solution $= 800$ kPa.
(b) Water would leave the cell (from higher to lower ψ).
(c) TP would decrease.

14.8 (a) Cell B (b) From cell B to cell A
(c) The cells must have the same ψ at equilibrium and this will be the average of the two initial ψs, that is $-1\,000$ kPa.
(d) Cell A at equilibrium: TP $= \psi + \text{OP}$
$\qquad\qquad = -1\,000$ kPa $+ 2\,000$ kPa
$\qquad\qquad = 1\,000$ kPa
Cell B at equilibrium: TP $= \psi + \text{OP}$
$\qquad\qquad = -1\,000$ kPa $+ 1\,400$ kPa
$\qquad\qquad = 400$ kPa.

14.9 $1\,060$ kPa. For intermediate values between those shown in table 14.4, plot a graph of molarity of sucrose solution against osmotic pressure.

14.10 Average OP of beetroot cells is about $1\,400$ kPa.

14.11 ψ beetroot is about -940 kPa.

14.12 A more accurate result can be obtained by taking the mean value of two or more replicates. Some indication of the variation that can be expected between strips is given in table 14.6.

14.13 To prevent evaporation of water, with subsequent increase in concentration of sucrose solutions, and possible drying up of beetroot strips.

14.14 TP $= \psi + \text{OP}$
$\qquad = -950$ kPa $+ 1\,400$ kPa
$\qquad = 450$ kPa.
Note that different beetroots may have different values of OP and ψ.

14.15 (a) The cells of the intact scape are turgid and their walls are therefore tending to expand with turgor pressure. The thick walls of the epidermal cells are less capable of stretching than the thin walls of the cortex cells and therefore exert a restraining influence on expansion of the cortical cells. The latter are under compression. Cutting the epidermis removes the restraint, each cortical cell expands slightly, and there is an overall increase in volume of the cortex which causes the strip to curve outwards.
(b) Distilled water has a higher water potential than the scape cells. Water therefore enters the tissue from the distilled water by osmosis, inflating the cortical cells even further and causing outward curvature.
(c) The concentrated sucrose solution has a lower water potential than the scape cells. Water therefore leaves the tissue by osmosis, causing greater shrinkage of the cortical cells than the epidermal cells and a bending inwards of the tissue.
(d) The dilute sucrose solution must have the same water potential as the scape cells. There is therefore no net gain or loss of water by solution or tissue.
(e) Water potential. An outline of the experiment is as follows.

Prepare a dilution series of sucrose solutions from 1 M to distilled water (such as distilled water, 0.2 M, 0.4 M, 0.6 M, 0.8 M and 1.0 M). The typical curvature of freshly cut dandelion scapes should be recorded by drawing and then two pieces of scape placed in each solution in separate labelled petri dishes (two pieces are preferred so that an average can be obtained). Observe and accurately record curvatures (such as by drawing) after equilibrium has been reached (about 30 min). The solution which induces no change in curvature has the same ψ as the average dandelion scape cell immediately after the cut was made.

14.16 Outlines of two suitable experiments are as follows.
Effect of temperature. Cut cubes of fresh beetroot, wash to remove the red pigment from broken cells, and place in beakers of water at different temperatures over a range, say, from 20–100 °C. The appearance of red pigment in the water would indicate destruction of the differential permeability of the tonoplast (vacuole membrane) and plasma membrane, attended by diffusion of the pigment from the cell sap to the water. The time taken for the appearance of a standard amount of pigment would give an indication of the rapidity of breakdown of membrane structure. The colour could be measured in a colorimeter or simply by using the eye.
Effect of ethanol. Method as above, using a range of ethanol concentrations instead of a range of temperatures.

14.17 (a) Leaves contain a very large number of stomata for gaseous exchange and there is little resistance to movement of water vapour through these pores.

(*b*) Leaves have a large surface area (for trapping sunlight and exchanging gases). The greater the surface area, the greater will be the loss of water by transpiration.

14.18 Light intensity increases as the Sun rises, reaching a maximum at midday when the Sun attains its highest point in the sky. Air temperature rises similarly, but it takes about two hours for the heating effect of the Sun to be reflected in a rise in air temperature (mainly because the soil has to heat up first and then radiate heat to the air). The initial rise in transpiration rate between 3 am and 6 am, before air temperature rises, is due to opening of the stomata in the light. From 6 am onwards transpiration rate is closely correlated with temperature for reasons explained in the text. It is not closely correlated with light intensity, presumably because the stomata are now fully open and any further increase in light intensity has no effect.

During the afternoon, light intensity decreases as the Sun sinks, followed by a drop in temperature with the same lag of about two hours. Transpiration rate decreases both as a result of decreasing temperature and decreasing light intensity, but it is much more closely correlated with a decrease in the latter, probably because this induces stomatal closure. By about 7.30 pm it is dark and the stomata are probably closed. Any remaining transpiration is probably cuticular and still influenced by temperature.

14.19 See table 14.19(ans).

Table 14.19(ans)

Dicots	Monocots
Vascular bundles arranged in a ring	Vascular bundles scattered
Endodermis (starch sheath) present	Endodermis absent
Separate pith and cortex	Ground tissue not split into pith and cortex
Pericycle forms a cap to vascular bundle	Pericycle surrounds vascular bundle
Metaxylem has many vessels	Metaxylem has few vessels (commonly two or three)
Protoxylem present	Most protoxylem breaks down to leave a lysigenous canal
Cambium present and secondary thickening may occur later (some herbaceous plants, such as *Helianthus*, develop secondary vascular bundles; perennials develop wood, rays, annual rings, cork)	No cambium, therefore no secondary thickening (very few exceptions where monocotyledon stems develop a tree-like form)

14.20 (*a*) Hollow cylinder
(*b*) Solid rod/cylinder providing support
(*c*) Solid rod/cylinder providing support
(*d*) Solid cylinder

14.21 (1) Long tubes formed by joining of neighbouring cells, with breakdown of cross-walls between them.
(2) No living contents, so less resistance to flow.
(3) Tubes have high tensile strength so do not collapse.
(4) Fine tubes are necessary to prevent water columns from physically collapsing.

14.22 See table 14.22(ans).

14.23 ψ soil solution > root hair cell > cell C > cell B > cell A > xylem sap

14.24 (*a*) There is a rapid initial uptake of potassium (K^+) at both temperatures (during the first 10–20 min). After 20 min there is a continuous gradual uptake of K^+ at 25 °C but no further uptake at 0 °C. Uptake at 25 °C is inhibited by KCN.

Table 14.22(ans)

Dicots	Monocots
Piliferous layer quickly lost	Piliferous layer remains
Few protoxylem groups (few arms of metaxylem) 2–8, commonly four (tetrarch) or 5 (pentarch)	Many protoxylem groups (polyarch)
Pith not common. Xylem forms a solid cylinder at the centre of the root	Central pith. Xylem forms rods around the pith
Cambium often present, making secondary thickening possible	Cambium rarely present; therefore no secondary thickening

(*b*) There are two distinct phases of uptake. In the initial rapid phase, K^+ diffuses into the free spaces of the root. It enters through the cell walls of the piliferous layer, which are exposed to the solution, and diffuses through the apoplasm, possibly entering the intercellular spaces where these contain solution. The results show that this phase is more or less independent of temperature and therefore not dependent on metabolism (enzyme-controlled reactions would proceed faster at 25 °C than 0 °C). This first phase is a passive process.

The second phase is temperature-dependent, and does not occur at 0 °C when the rate of metabolism is very low. This suggests that the process is dependent on metabolism, and its inhibition by KCN indicates that it is dependent on respiration. The second phase is therefore an active transport across cell membranes into cells.

14.25 Rise in respiratory rate is accompanied by a rise in KCl uptake. Once KCl is available, it is therefore apparently taken up by active transport, the energy being supplied by an increased respiratory rate.

14.26 KCN inhibits respiration and thence active transport of KCl into the carrot discs.

14.27 Much of the phosphate inside the root was in the free space and could therefore diffuse out to the water outside, reversing passive uptake.

14.28 No. The endodermis is a barrier to movement of water and solutes through the apoplast pathway (see section 14.5.2, apoplast pathway).

14.29 Autoradiography reveals the location of the ion in thin sections. Treat one plant with an inhibitor of active transport (such as low temperature or KCN) and have an untreated control plant; allow them both to take up the radioactive ion. In the treated plant ions will move only passively by way of the cell walls. Autoradiography should show that the radioactive ion tends to penetrate the root only as far as the endodermis, whereas the control should show much greater movement of ions to the tissue inside the endodermis.

14.30 (*a*) See table 14.30(ans).

Table 14.30(ans).

Plant part	Percentage distribution when upper leaf treated	Percentage distribution when lower leaf treated
apical region of shoot	4.8	3.6
^{14}C-treated leaf	48.4	53.9
other leaves	1.0	0.8
stem	3.5	5.5
pod	38.7	23.4
roots	3.6	12.8

Similarities in ^{14}C export from upper and lower leaves.
Similar proportions of assimilates are exported by both leaves (compare results for '^{14}C-treated leaf') and similar proportions pass to the other leaves. The major destination of the assimilates in both cases is the pod.

Differences in ^{14}C export from upper and lower leaves.
The pattern of export from a given leaf is affected by its position on the plant. The upper leaf exports a higher proportion of its assimilates to the pod and apical region than the lower leaf, which correspondingly exports a greater proportion to the roots.

(b) Once a pod is formed, it becomes a sink of considerable importance for carbon compounds, particularly from the leaves in its proximity. There are two other important sinks in the mature plant, namely the apical region of the shoot and the roots. The lower leaves export mainly to the roots and the upper leaves mainly to the apex.

14.31 0.72 s. The answer is obtained as follows:
100 cm = 1 000 mm = 1 000 000 μm = 10^6 μm
therefore sucrose moves at 10^6 μm h^{-1},
= 1 μm in $1/10^6$ h,
= 200 μm in $200/10^6$ h = $2/10^4$ h = $(2 \times 3\,600)/10^4$ s = 2×0.36 s
= 0.72 s.

14.32 2 500 sieve plates per metre:
$$1\text{ m} = 10^6\text{ μm},$$
$$400\text{ μm} = 4 \times 10^2\text{ μm},$$
$$10^6/(4 \times 10^2) = 10^4/4 = 2\,500.$$

14.33 Oxygenated blood can be delivered to the tissues rapidly enough to satisfy the increased metabolic demands of the body. Various organs such as the kidney and the capillaries rely on a high blood hydrostatic pressure for effective and efficient functioning.

14.34 This means that oxygenated blood of the systemic circulation reaches the body capillaries at a much higher pressure. This is essential for the efficient function of organs and tissue fluid formation and permits active chemical processes and a high body temperature to be maintained. It is essential that a much lower pressure is developed in the pulmonary artery in order to prevent rupture of the delicate pulmonary capillaries.

14.35 Local vasodilation in the wounded area enables more blood carrying oxygen and nutrients to arrive there and speed up the process of repair and replacement. Increased body blood pressure prepares the body of the animal to respond to any further stress more readily and efficiently.

14.36 Before the race. Adrenaline is secreted in anticipation of the race. This stimulates vasoconstriction throughout the body in all but the most vital organs. Hence blood pressure is raised. Heart rate is also increased. Extra blood is passed to the general circulation from the spleen.

During the race. Increased metabolic activity takes place during the race, especially in the skeletal muscles. Increased carbon dioxide levels in these regions promote local vasodilation. The increased body temperature further enhances vasodilation. However the general increase in carbon dioxide level in blood is noted by the chemoreceptors of the aorta and carotid bodies which in turn stimulate the vasomotor centre to promote vasoconstriction. This increases blood pressure and therefore speeds up blood flow. Heart rate is also increased and a more complete emptying of the ventricles occurs. Towards the end of the race the muscles will be respiring anaerobically and producing lactic acid (section 11.3.8). Strong contractions of the muscles knead the veins and promote faster venous return to the heart.

Recovery. The oxygen debt is paid off and lactic acid removed from the blood system. Tissues subside in activity and the carbon dioxide level decreases. Consequently there is a return to normal of heartbeat and blood pressure.

14.37 In tissues which are respiring actively the partial pressure of carbon dioxide will be high. This leads to a reduced pH and to the displacement of the oxygen dissociation curve to the right. Analysis of fig 14.64 shows that as this occurs it facilitates the delivery of increased quantities of oxygen from the blood to the cells which can be used by respiratory processes for the production of energy. Looked at another way, haemoglobin takes up oxygen less readily initially but when saturated releases it quickly.

Increased metabolic activity increases the temperature in a part of the body. This produces a reduction in the affinity of oxygen for haemoglobin and an increased dissociation of oxygen. Thus the dissociation curve is again shifted to the right. This is physiologically advantageous as more oxygen is delivered to the active regions. The oxygen dissociation curve is not exactly the same for all animals. For example, compared with Man, the curve for small mammals is displaced to the right. Small mammals possess a much higher metabolic rate than Man and therefore it is appropriate that oxygen should be released much more readily.

14.38 The position of the curve of the foetus relative to that of its mother means that its blood has a greater affinity for oxygen than the maternal blood. This has to be so, as the foetus must obtain all of its oxygen from its mother's blood at the placenta. So, at any given partial pressure of oxygen, the foetal blood will take up oxygen from the maternal blood and will always be more saturated with oxygen than the maternal blood.

14.39 This means that the blood has a high affinity for oxygen and that it is able to combine with it at the low oxygen tensions experienced at high altitude. This is another good example of physiological adaptation.

14.40 (1) Carboxyhaemoglobin reaches the lungs and takes up oxygen and forms oxyhaemoglobin,
(2) Oxyhaemoglobin is a weaker base than carboxyhaemoglobin and releases hydrogen ions.
(3) Hydrogen ions combine with hydrogencarbonate ions in the erythrocyte so forming carbonic acid.
(4) Carbonic acid dissociates into carbon dioxide and water.
(5) As a result of the loss of hydrogencarbonate ions from the erythrocyte, further hydrogencarbonate ions diffuse into the erythrocyte from the plasma.
(6) More carbonic acid is formed which dissociates into more carbon dioxide and water.
(7) Carbon dioxide diffuses out of the erythrocyte and is eventually excreted from the body via the lungs.

Chapter 15

15.1 Locomotion is primarily associated with the need to search for food (and is closely associated with the development of a nervous system). Green plants are autotrophic, that is make their own organic requirements, so do not need to search for food.

15.2 See table 15.2(ans) (next page).

15.3 Growth could be inhibited on the contact side, or stimulated on the opposite side, or a combination of these effects might occur. In fact, growth is slowed down (cells become less elongated) on the contact side and growth on the opposite side is stimulated 40–200 fold.

15.4 Various methods are possible. A simple experiment is illustrated in fig 15.4(ans).

15.5 (a) Spirogyra (or any other filamentous green alga).
(b) The bacteria are aerobic and positively aerotactic. Therefore they swim towards oxygen along a gradient from

low oxygen concentration to high oxygen concentration. The highest oxygen concentrations are around the edges of the cover-slip, where oxygen is diffusing into the water from the atmosphere, and adjacent to the algal filament where oxygen is being released as a waste product of photosynthesis.

Table 15.2(ans).

Example	Advantage
Shoots and coleoptiles positively phototropic	Leaves exposed to the light which is the source of energy for photosynthesis
Roots negatively phototropic	Exposed roots more likely to grow towards soil or equivalent suitable substrate
Shoots and coleoptiles negatively geotropic	Shoots of germinating seeds will grow upwards through soil towards light
Roots positively geotropic	Roots penetrate soil
Rhizomes, runners diageotropic	Helps plants colonise new areas of soil
Dicotyledonous leaves diageotropic	Flat surface of leaf will gain maximum exposure to sunlight (at right-angles to incident radiation)
Lateral roots plagiogeotropic	Large volume of soil exploited and the arrangement of roots provides support (similar to guy-ropes supporting a tent)
Branches plagiogeotropic	Larger volume of space occupied for exploitation of light
Hyphae positively chemotropic	Grow towards food
Pollen tubes positively chemotropic	Grow towards ovule, where fertilisation takes place
Roots and pollen tubes positively hydrotropic	Water essential for all living processes
Tendrils positively haptotropic	Essential for their function of support
Sundew tentacles positively haptotropic	Enables plant to imprison insects which walk over the tentacles (section 9.12.2)
Pollen tubes negatively aerotropic	Another mechanism ensuring that initial growth of the pollen tube is towards the tissue of the style (away from air)

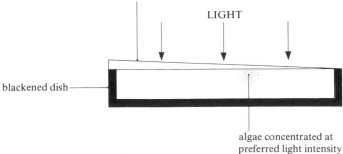

Fig 15.4(ans) *Experiment to demonstrate preferred light intensity of* Euglena *or* Chlamydomonas

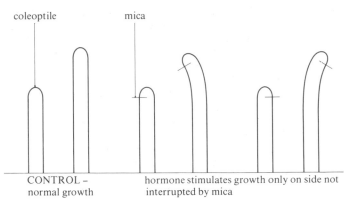

CONTROL – normal growth

hormone stimulates growth only on side not interrupted by mica

Fig 15.8(ans) *Repetition of Boysen-Jensen's experiments in uniform light. Three experiments are shown; treatment left, result right, in each case*

(c) Leave the slide in the dark for about 30 min and re-examine. All the bacteria should now be around the edges of the cover-slip because the alga cannot photosynthesise in the dark.

15.6 (a) The stimulus of light is detected by the coleoptile tip. Some kind of signal is transmitted from the tip (the receptor) to the region behind the tip (the effector).
(b) Experiment c was a check on the result from experiment b which could have been the result of injury to the coleoptile.

15.7 Further evidence of the existence of a signal, presumably a chemical transmitter substance (hormone), has been obtained. It cannot pass through an impermeable barrier. It moves mainly down the shaded side of the coleoptile. In experiment b mica prevented this movement. Light therefore either inhibits production of the hormone, causes its inactivation (stimulates its breakdown) or causes it to be redistributed laterally.

15.8 See fig 15.8(ans).

15.9 The coleoptile tip produces a chemical which diffuses into the agar. It can stimulate growth in the region behind the tip and restores normal growth (experiment a). There is little or no lateral transmission of the chemical (experiment b) under conditions of uniform illumination or darkness.

15.10 The coleoptile would have grown to the left.

15.11 A 100 ppm   B 10 ppm   C 1 ppm   D 0.1 ppm
E 0.01 ppm   F zero

15.12 A relatively high auxin concentration stimulates growth of coleoptiles (or shoots) but inhibits growth of roots. This supports the conclusions drawn from experiment 15.1.

15.13 See section 16.5.6.

15.14 (a) Abscisic acid can be transported away from root tips, undergo lateral transport in root tissues in response to gravity, and inhibit growth.
(b) IAA is probably not involved in the geotropic response of maize since it is apparently not transported away from the root tip.

15.15 (a) starch
(b) maltose
(c) maltase
(d) The main food reserve of cereal seeds is starch, stored in the endosperm.

15.16 Storage proteins are digested (hydrolysed) to provide amino acids, the basic units of proteins. These are reassembled to produce enzymes (which are always proteins), such as α-amylase, which are then used to digest the food stores of the endosperm.

15.17 The amylase activity could be associated with micro-organisms present on the fingers or with saliva which has been transferred from mouth to fingers. Note the importance, therefore, of not handling the seeds after their surface sterilisation in this kind of experiment.

15.18 Incubate seeds with radioactive (^{14}C-labelled) amino acids. This results in production of labelled amylase. Alternatively, incubation of seeds with inhibitors of protein synthesis (such as cycloheximide) prevents synthesis of amylase and no amylase activity is then recorded.

15.19 Dissection of the seeds into aleurone and non-aleurone portions should show that the initial appearance of labelled amylase is in the aleurone layer. Alternatively, separate incubation of endosperm with aleurone layers and endosperm without aleurone layer, with starch–gibberellin agar would result in amylase production only in the former (difficult to do in practice).

15.20 One of the best bioassays for gibberellin (quick, reliable and sensitive) involves incubating embryo halves of barley grains with the substance being assayed. After two days the amount of reducing sugar present is proportional to the amount of gibberellin present.

15.21 (a) The amino acid is retained by the young leaf and does not move very far from the point of application. In the old leaf some of it is exported via the veins and midrib.

(b) The young leaf would use the amino acid to make protein in growth. The old leaf is no longer growing and so is exporting nutrients to other parts of the plant such as roots and young leaves.

(c) Amino acids are retained by, or move towards, tissues treated with kinetin. (The reasons for this are unknown, but presumably connected with the maintenance or stimulation of normal cell activity by kinetin.)

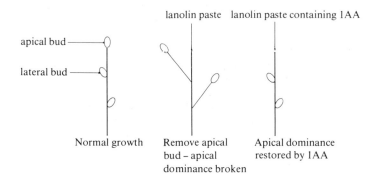

Fig 15.23(ans) *Experiment to show role of IAA in apical dominance*

15.22 One solution would be to take a plant where applied gibberellin is known to affect stem growth and remove its source of auxin by removing the shoot apex. Gibberellin should then prove ineffective. It is important to demonstrate that the response can be restored by addition of auxin (such as IAA in lanolin paste) as injury might be the reason for lack of response to gibberellins, or another chemical might be involved. Such experiments do demonstrate a total dependence on auxin.

15.23 (a) Auxin (IAA)

(b) See fig 15.23(ans).

15.24 Small leaves offer less resistance to passage through the soil (leaves of grasses remain inside the coleoptile). The hooked plumule of dicotyledonous plants protects the delicate apical meristem from soil particles. Elongated internodes ensure the maximum chance of reaching light.

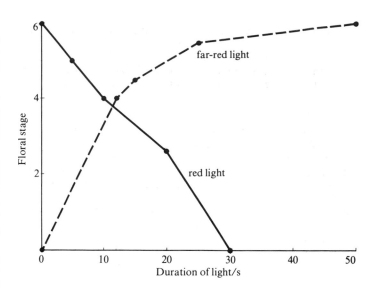

Fig 15.26(ans) *Effects of red light and red/far-red light interruptions of long night on flowering of cocklebur*

15.25 See chapter 9.

15.26 The graph is shown in fig 15.26(ans).

The opposite effects of red and far-red light are demonstrated. Red light exposure of 30 s, at the intensity used in the experiment, completely nullifies the inductive effect of a long night. The effectiveness of red light increases with time of exposure up to 30 s. The red light effect is reversed by far-red light, although a longer exposure (50 s) was needed to completely reverse the effect. These results suggest that phytochrome is the photoreceptor involved.

15.27 There are several possible methods. Fig 15.27(ans) illustrates one simple solution. Boxes represent light-proof covers, used as appropriate to give short days.

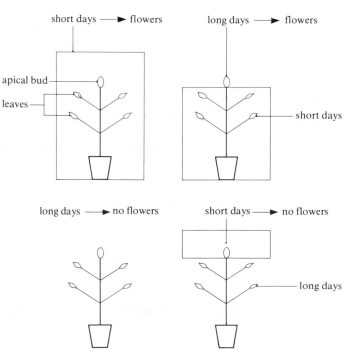

Fig 15.27(ans) *Experiment to determine whether leaves or floral apex are sensitive to the photoperiod that stimulates flowering*

15.28 Lateral bud inhibition or apical dominance is largely controlled by auxins. (See apical dominance, section 15.3.3.)

Chapter 16

16.1 (*a*) A steep concentration gradient of Na^+ ions exists between the outside and inside of the axon and Na^+ ions rapidly diffuse down this gradient.
(*b*) The relatively high negative potential within the axon encourages the inward movement of the positively charged Na^+ ions.

16.2 If the outflow of positive K^+ ions from the axon balanced the inflow of positive Na^+ ions into the axon there would be no change, or perhaps only a slight decrease, in the resting potential. Such a slight change would be insufficient to reach the threshold required to produce an action potential.

16.3 (*a*) Normal sea water
(*b*) One-half sea water
(*c*) One-third sea water
The amplitude of the action potential spike in (*a*) and the depolarised membrane potentials shown in (*b*) and (*c*) is determined by the number of Na^+ ions entering the axon from the extracellular fluid. The solutions in which (*a*), (*b*) and (*c*) were recorded contained progressively fewer Na^+ ions.

16.4 Sodium ions are pumped out of the axon and potassium ions are pumped in. The movements of the ions are linked (coupled) and mediated by the cation pump.

16.5 The longitudinal resistance of axoplasm decreases with increasing diameter of the axon. As the resistance decreases, the length of the membrane influenced by the local circuit increases and this lengthens the distance between adjacent depolarisations and leads to an increase in conduction velocity.

16.6 The frog is a cold-blooded (poikilothermic) organism, active within the temperature range 4–25 °C, whereas the cat, being warm-blooded (homeothermic), maintains a constant temperature of 35 °C. This increase in temperature increases the speed of conduction of the nerve impulses by a factor of three.

16.7 Graph (*a*) indicates that the frequency of impulses in the sensory neurone is directly related to the stimulus applied to the muscle spindle. It is known that the stimulus produces a depolarisation known as the generator potential and, as shown in graph (*b*), the magnitude of this potential is directly related to the frequency of sensory impulses. It may be concluded from these data that increasing stimuli produce increasing generator potentials whose amplitudes are directly related to the frequency of impulses in the sensory neurone.

16.8 The path taken by light as it passes through the eye is as follows: conjunctiva→cornea→aqueous humour→ lens→ vitreous humour→retina.

16.9 Light from an object falling onto several rods which are linked to the brain by separate neurones may not have sufficient energy to produce a propagated action potential in each neurone and therefore the light may not be detected. If, however, the same light falls on three rods which are linked to the same neurone supplying the brain, the separate generator potentials produced by the rods would summate and produce a propagated action potential which would be registered in the brain as light.

16.10 When looking directly at an object, light reflected from it passes along the optical axis of the eye and strikes the retina at the fovea which contains cones only. During daylight this will produce a detailed image in the brain due to the high light intensity activating the cones. At night the light intensity would be too low to activate the cones. By looking slightly to one side of the object the reflected light from it will not strike the fovea but a point on the retina to the side of it where there are rods. At night these will be activated by the low light intensity and an image will be produced in the brain.

16.11 The object will appear yellow. Each retina will distinguish one colour only. In one eye, green cones will be stimulated by light of 530 nm and, in the other, red cones will be stimulated by light of 620 nm. Mixing will occur in the brain due to equal stimulation by these colours and the object will appear to be the colour of the average of the combined wavelengths, that is $\frac{530 + 620}{2}$ nm = 575nm, which corresponds to yellow.

Chapter 17

17.1 The femur is basically a hollow bone. When a compression force is exerted on one side of the bone, the other side is subjected to tension. Along the central axis of the bone the forces diminish and are neutralised. The material in the centre of the bone consequently does not need to contribute to its strength. Reduction in weight of the bone due to the absence of bone along its central axis is advantageous to the animal as it lightens the weight of the femur without reducing its mechanical efficiency. The perimeter of the femur is composed of compact bone which resists the tension and compressional forces. Spongy bone at the head of the femur is a meshwork of interconnecting bony struts. They maintain the rigidity of the bone but with the minimum of weight.
Cartilage acts as a cushion between two articulating bones. Its matrix can be deformed by compression but will return to its original shape because it possesses good powers of extensibility. The cartilage also reduces friction between the smooth, moving articular surfaces.
The tendons consist of inextensible, white fibrous tissue and attach the muscles to the femur. The pull of the muscle is concentrated over a small area. Tendon organs operate to prevent muscle rupture if the muscle is suddenly subjected to a heavy load.
Ligaments are also composed of inextensible, white fibrous tissue and connect the femur to bones articulating with it at joints. They confine the movement of the components of each joint to a specific direction and therefore promote the efficiency of its operation. Ligaments also strengthen the joint.

17.2 (*a*) It allows free movement of the rib cage of the mammal.
(*b*) The flexible suspension enables the animal to withstand the shock sustained by the forelimbs when it lands at the end of a jump.
(*c*) The forelimbs possess a wide range of movement, which is useful for such activities as climbing, cleaning the face, manipulating food and digging.

17.3 A band remains the same length; H band becomes shorter; I band becomes shorter.

17.4 The myosin filaments (constituting the A band) remain the same length whilst actin filaments slide over them towards each other. This effectively shortens the H and I bands.

17.5 (*a*) The central non-contractile portion of the muscle spindle is stretched. Nerve impulses are fired from the annulo-spiral nerve endings and pass to the central nervous system. Impulses are propagated from the central nervous system via efferent neurones to the extrafusal fibres causing them to contract. This is the stretch reflex.
(*b*) The muscle spindle is no longer stretched and the number of impulses fired from the central non-contractile region of the spindle is diminished.

(c) Impulses are fired from the tendon organs which reach inhibitory neurones in the spinal cord. When these are activated this causes a reflex inhibition of contraction of the muscle that is being stretched. Therefore active resistance to stretching is decreased. This mechanism offers a form of protection to the muscles, preventing possible rupture when they are suddenly overloaded.

(d) The central region of the spindle is stretched and fires impulses to the spinal cord. Motor neurones are stimulated to carry impulses to the extrafusal fibres of the muscle causing contraction. When contraction in the intrafusal fibres is matched by an equal contraction of the extrafusal fibres, the central region of the spindle is stretched no further and a state of equilibrium is reached. This mechanism is very important as it sets the tone of muscles. It ensures that the muscle is not completely slack, and by increasing the stretching of the spindle so increases the muscle's response. If the muscle was slack when a heavy load was applied, the muscle could suffer considerable damage.

17.6 It allows greater movement of Ca^{2+} ions needed for muscle contraction.

17.7 Synchronous. This type of muscle has much more sarcoplasmic reticulum because it requires more nervous impulses to operate it, and each nerve impulse depends on the release of Ca^{2+} ions by the sarcoplasmic reticulum.

17.8 (a) Streamlined shape
(b) Smooth surface – scales overlap each other in an appropriate direction
– mucus/oily covering thus reducing friction
(c) Various types of fin to promote forward propulsion and stability during swimming
(d) Highly muscular body
(e) Lateral line (table 4.12)
(f) Swim bladder in bony fishes
(g) Highly coordinated neuromuscular activity

17.9 (a) Large, powerful flight muscles
(b) Streamlined body shape
(c) Sharp narrow wings, designed for low drag
(d) Large wings possess mostly primary feathers (for forward propulsion)
(e) Fast wing beat (10 per second)
(f) Forward thrust achieved by both the downbeat and upbeat of the wings.

17.10 This position increases the effective length of their limbs. Consequently each stride taken is longer and so propels the body forward over a greater distance. Assuming that the speed of movement of the limbs remains the same, the sprinter will therefore move forwards at a faster pace.

Chapter 18

18.1 Hyperventilation increases the tidal movements of air, carbon dioxide is expelled from the lungs and the carbon dioxide tension of the alveolar air decreases. The carbon dioxide level of the blood comes to a new equilibrium with the alveolar air as it passes through the pulmonary capillaries. This reduces the carbon dioxide tension of the blood and increases the blood pH. The abnormal alkalinity of the blood produces symptoms of dizziness and fainting and the inhibitory effect of lack of stimulation of the chemoreceptors supplying the respiratory centres decreases the ventilation rate.

18.2 The rates of transpiration and evaporation are inversely proportional to the level of atmospheric humidity. When humidity is high the rates of transpiration and evaporation

are low and the plant cannot lose latent heat and reduce its temperature.

18.3 19.6%

18.4 During this period the subject was allowed to equilibrate with his surroundings.

18.5 There is a direct relationship between these two variables which suggests that the rate of sweating is controlled by activity of the hypothalamus.

18.6 The direct relationship between skin temperature and evaporation during the first 20 min established that an equilibrium exists between the two. As the evaporation rate falls, due to the action of the hypothalamus in response to the ingestion of iced water, latent heat of evaporation is not being lost from the skin and this accounts for the observed rise in skin temperature.

18.7 'Fever' is due to the resetting of the hypothalamic 'thermostat' at a higher temperature. Until the core temperature rises to that temperature there is a discrepancy between 'normal' body temperature and the cold conditions. In these conditions the body responds by shivering and the body continues to feel cold until the core temperature reaches the temperature of the hypothalamic thermostat.

Chapter 20

20.1 (a) The true statement is (ii), 'Gametes are always haploid'. Even this is not always true since polyploid parent cells would give rise to gamete cells with more than the haploid number of chromosomes; for example the gametes of hexaploid wheat plants would be triploid.
(b) Exceptions to statements (i), (iii), (iv) and (v):
(i) Asexual reproduction in plants with alternation of generations involves meiosis, so the gametophytes produced show variation.
(iii) Gametes are produced by mitosis in life cycles A and D (fig 20.1).
(iv) Meiosis does always produce haploid cells (except in polyploid organisms). Mitosis can produce haploid cells, as in the growth of multicellular haploid organisms (such as *Spirogyra*, life cycle A, and growth of gametophyte, life cycle D, fig 20.1). It can also produce diploid cells as in the growth of multicellular diploid organisms.
(v) Mitosis can occur in haploid cells, as in the examples given in (iv) above.

20.2 (a) If the parent plants that produced the pollen grains can be identified, then certain deductions can be made about the climate that such plants would have grown in.
(b) Any interference by Man with the natural vegetation would be reflected in the pollen record. For example, pollen of weed species and agricultural plants, such as wheat, would indicate clearance of natural vegetation for agriculture. Similarly, absence of pollen from trees in some areas would indicate forest clearance.

20.3 If a plant species is dioecious, half of its individuals do not produce seeds. Also, there is a large wastage of pollen which is a disadvantage in terms of material and energy resources.

20.4 Separate sexes is more economic in animals than in plants because there is less risk in transferring male gametes as a result of locomotion and behaviour patterns.

20.5 $\frac{1}{2}$ (50%). Remembering that the pollen grain is haploid:

Parent plant genotype	Possible pollen genotypes
S_1S_2	$\left.\begin{array}{l} S_1 \\ S_2 \end{array}\right\}$ in equal numbers

S_1 pollen grains would be compatible with S_2S_3 style tissue
S_2 pollen grains would be incompatible with S_1S_3 style tissue

Note that neither S_1 nor S_2 pollen grains would be compatible with the style of the parent plant (S_1S_2), so that self-fertilisation is impossible.

20.6 (*a*) The part of the bee's body receiving most pollen will be that which brushes against the anthers while the bee is taking nectar. Thus pollination will generally occur between anthers and stigmas at the same height within the flower, that is between pin-eyed and thrum-eyed flowers.

(*b*) It encourages outbreeding.

20.7 The functions of the cell organelles suggest that the cells manufacture materials for use within the cell. The raw materials for these processes come from the breakdown of materials entering the cell, using enzymes stored in the lysosomes. The synthesised products are packaged by the Golgi apparatus and stored for subsequent usage.

20.8 (*a*) Adding the numbers of corpora lutea and corpora albicanti together shows the number of ovulations which have occurred, that is 67 in all. Assuming one oocyte was released from each follicle per month this gives the *reproductive* age at 5 years 7 months. Hence the 22-year-old woman began ovulating at approximately the age of $16\frac{1}{2}$ years.

(*b*) Of the 42 000 follicles only 219 were primary oocytes, having a diameter over 100 μm. Again, assuming one oocyte would be released per month, the potential number of years for ovulation would be 18 years, 3 months.

(*c*) Five follicles contained two oocytes each, therefore potentially five pairs of twins might have been produced which would not be identical twins.

(*d*) Non-disjunction occurring during anaphase I of meiosis.

20.9 Blood would flow in the reverse direction along the ductus arteriosus.

Chapter 21

21.1 The following conclusions may be drawn from these curves:

(*a*) relative growth is greatest during embryological development,

(*b*) rate of growth is greatest during infancy and adolescence,

(*c*) maximum growth, in terms of a particular parameter, such as height, is greatest in the adult.

21.2 (*a*) There is loss of mass due to respiration of food reserves in the seed.

(*b*) Green leaves have grown and opened above the ground.

(*c*) Photosynthesis. Its rate must now be greater than respiration.

(*d*) This is due to dispersal of fruits and seeds.

21.3 Body mass averages about 33.5 kg from November to March at a time when the average daily intake is 320 kJ. Throughout this period the mean monthly temperature does not rise above −10 °C. In order to maintain a constant blood temperature of approximately 35 °C, despite a temperature difference of 45 °C, the husky, a homeotherm, must have an extremely high metabolic rate. This places a great demand on an adequate supply of food to provide the energy sources for respiratory activity. Since the data show that the average body mass throughout the winter period is below that of the summer, this provides extra evidence of the metabolic demands imposed on maintaining a constant body temperature.

21.4 Small seeds have relatively small food reserves; it is therefore important that the growing shoot reaches light quickly so that photosynthesis can start before the reserves are exhausted.

21.5 (*a*) Chlorophyll strongly absorbs red and blue light, but not green and far-red light (see chlorophyll absorption spectrum fig 9.9).

(*b*) Red light stimulates lettuce seed germination, but far-red light inhibits it (section 15.4.2). Seeds under a leaf canopy, where the light will be enriched in far-red, might therefore be inhibited from germinating until a break in the canopy ensures that they will not be too shaded for efficient photosynthesis and growth.

21.6 At the onset of germination, food reserves in the barley grain, principally starch, with some protein, are mobilised. Starch is converted to sugars, and proteins to amino acids, and these are translocated to the embryo for use in growth. Therefore, endosperm dry mass decreases while embryo dry mass increases.

At the same time there is an overall loss in dry mass during the first week. This is due to aerobic respiration, which consumes sugar, in both endosperm and embryo (though to a greater extent in the latter). At about day 7 the first leaf emerges and starts to photosynthesise. The resulting increase in dry mass more than compensates for respiration losses so that a net increase in dry mass is observed. At the same time the rate of growth of the embryo, now a seedling, increases.

21.7 (*a*) There is a gain in dry mass of 8.6 g, calculated as follows.
Mass of seeds = 51.2 g
Mass of fatty acid = 51.2/2 = 25.6 g
M_r fatty acid = 256
Therefore 1 mole = 256 g, so 25.6 g = 0.1 mole
From the equation,
0.1 mole fatty acid → 0.1 mole sugar + 0.5 mole water
$\qquad\qquad\qquad\qquad\qquad$ + 0.4 mole carbon dioxide
M_r sugar = 342
Therefore 25.6 g fatty acid → 34.2 g sugar + water
$\qquad\qquad\qquad\qquad\qquad\qquad$ + carbon dioxide
Water is not included in the dry mass and carbon dioxide is lost as a gas, therefore the gain in dry mass = (34.2 − 25.6) g = 8.6 g.

(*b*) Respiration would result in a decrease in dry mass. In reality there would still be an increase in dry mass.

(*c*) Volume of carbon dioxide evolved from the seeds = 8.96 dm³ at STP, calculated as follows:
from the equation, 0.1 mole fatty acid → 0.4 mole carbon dioxide. 0.4 mole carbon dioxide occupies 0.4×22.4 dm³ at STP = 8.96 dm³.

(*d*) By hydrolysis, catalysed by a lipase. The other component of the lipid is glycerol.

(*e*) 51 carbon atoms (the lipid would be tripalmitin; the fatty acid is palmitic acid). Each lipid molecule comprises three fatty acid molecules, each with 16 carbon atoms, plus one glycerol molecule with three carbon atoms.

(*f*) Sucrose or maltose.

(*g*) Oxygen reaches the storage tissue by diffusion through the testa and micropyle.

21.8 (*a*) The dominant food store is lipid, which comprises about 70% of the dry mass of the seeds before germination. By day 4 the mass of lipid is starting to decrease and the mass of sugar to rise. Lipid is therefore being converted to sugar and translocated to the embryo. Note that no sugars can be formed by photosynthesis since germination occurs in darkness. At day 5 the RQ of the embryo = 1, indicating that the embryo is respiring the sugar derived from the lipids. At the same time, the cotyledons (RQ = 0.4−0.5) are gaining energy from the conversion of lipid to sugar, and possibly from oxidation of sugar and fatty acids.

$$C_{18}H_{34}O_3 + 13O_2 \rightarrow C_{12}H_{22}O_{11} + 6CO_2 + 6H_2O + \text{energy}$$
ricinoleic $\qquad\qquad\qquad$ sucrose
acid (fatty
acid derived
from a lipid)

RQ = 6/13 = 0.46

Conversion of lipid to sugar takes place with an increase in dry mass, so total dry mass of the seedlings increases up to 6 or 7 days. Beyond this point, the lipid reserves are running low, so rate of use of sugar starts to exceed the rate of production. Net mass of sugar, and total mass of seedlings, then starts to decrease. Sugar is used in respiration and in anaerobic reactions.

(b) At day 11, the RQ of the whole seedlings would probably be slightly less than 1.0. It is a combination of two reactions: the main one is the oxidation of sugar in respiration, RQ = 1, but there would probably still be a small contribution from the conversion of lipid to sugar, RQ 0.4–0.5.

21.9 Normally insufficient oxygen is able to penetrate the testa to allow exclusively aerobic respiration; the RQ is a combination of the RQ for aerobic respiration (probably about 1.0) and that for anaerobic respiration, which is infinity (∞). Removal of the testa allows more rapid penetration of oxygen by diffusion, with a consequent increase in aerobic respiration and decrease in RQ. Ethanol is a product of anaerobic respiration so less accumulates when the testas are removed.

21.10 During exposure of the pupa to a constant low temperature of 3 °C for 6 weeks thoracicotropin is produced and stored by neurosecretory cells in the brain. Transferring the pupa to a constant temperature of 25 °C causes the release of thoracicotropin into the blood which activates the thoracic glands to produce moulting hormone, diapause is broken and pupal–adult metamorphosis occurs.

Chapter 22

22.1 (a) Meiosis
(b) W – interphase
     X – telophase I
     Y – telophase II
(c) Gamete cells

22.2 See fig 22.2(ans).

22.3

Bases	A	G	T	C
A	AA	AG	AT	AC
G	GA	GG	GT	GC
T	TA	TG	TT	TC
C	CA	CG	CT	CC

22.4 4 bases used once = $4 \times 1 = 4^1 = 4$
4 bases used twice = $4 \times 4 = 4^2 = 16$
4 bases used three times = $4 \times 4 \times 4 = 4^3 = 64$
therefore the mathematical expression is x^y where
x = number of bases and y = number of bases used.

22.5 See fig 22.5(ans).

22.6 UAC AAG CUC AUG GUA CAU UGC

22.7 This suggests that the process of differentiation does not involve the loss of, or damage to, the genetic material (DNA) but the switching off of selected genes. The DNA was still able to function given the new environment of an undifferentiated cell. Further experiments involving transplanting donor nuclei from cells at a later stage of development did not produce viable embryos. This was taken as evidence that certain irreversible changes occur in the genetic material during development which influence differentiation by causing genes to be switched off irreversibly. However, later experiments carried out by Gurdon at Oxford in the 1960s involved transplanting nuclei from endothelial cells of tadpole intestine into enucleate egg cells from a mature frog. In many cases the eggs developed into normal frogs with the characteristics of the nucleus-donor tadpoles. This technique is known as cloning and suggested that whilst the nucleus

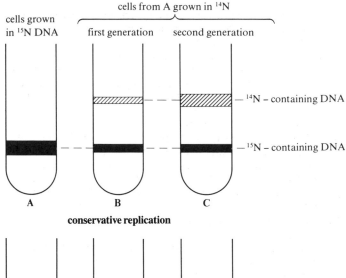
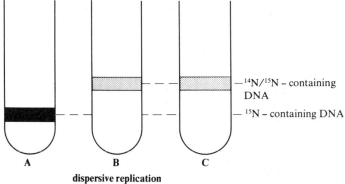

Fig 22.2(ans) *Diagrams explaining two further theories of DNA replication. The appearance of DNA in a caesium chloride density gradient according to the theories presented in Fig 22.14*

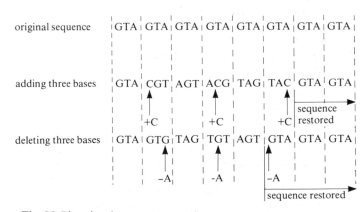

Fig 22.5(ans) *Answer to question expressed diagrammatically. The general principle behind restoring the normal triplet sequence by the addition or deletion of 3 bases is to add or delete three bases at any position along the length of the polynucleotide code*

plays the dominant role in the process of development, the cytoplasm (in this case the egg cytoplasm) plays a major role in determining the extent of the genetic expression of the nuclear material, that is differentiation. In this case it induced the nucleus to fulfil its complete genetic potential and produce a complete organism.

913

Chapter 23

23.1 See fig 23.1(ans) below.

(a) Let:

> **B** represent brown fur (dominant)
> **b** represent grey fur (recessive)

Parental phenotypes	brown fur	×	grey fur
Parental genotypes (2n)	**BB**	×	**bb**
Meiosis			
Gametes (n)	Ⓑ Ⓑ	×	ⓑ ⓑ
Random fertilisation			
F₁ genotypes (2n)	**Bb** **Bb** **Bb** **Bb**		
F₁ phenotypes	all brown fur		

F₁ phenotypes	brown fur	×	brown fur
F₁ genotypes (2n)	**Bb**	×	**Bb**
Meiosis			
Gametes (n)	Ⓑ ⓑ	×	Ⓑ ⓑ
Random fertilisation			
F₂ genotypes (2n)	**BB** **Bb** **Bb** **bb**		
F₂ phenotypes	3 brown fur : 1 grey fur		

(b)

Experimental phenotypes	brown fur	×	grey fur
Experimental genotypes (2n)	**Bb**	×	**bb**
Meiosis			
Gametes (n)	Ⓑ ⓑ	×	ⓑ ⓑ
Random fertilisation			
Offspring genotypes (2n)	**Bb** **Bb** **bb** **bb**		
Offspring phenotypes	1 brown fur : 1 grey fur		

In the case of monohybrid inheritance, the offspring from a heterozygous genotype crossed with a homozygous recessive genotype produce equal numbers of offspring showing each phenotype: in this case 50% brown fur and 50% grey fur.

23.2 If an organism having an unknown genotype is testcrossed with a homozygous dominant organism, all the offspring will show the dominant characteristic in the phenotype, as shown in fig 23.2(ans) below.

Let:

> **T** represent a dominant allele
> **t** represent a recessive allele

Testcross phenotypes	homozygous × homozygous	heterozygous × homozygous
Testcross genotypes (2n)	**TT** × **TT**	**Tt** × **TT**
Meiosis		
Gametes (n)	ⓉⓉ × ⓉⓉ	Ⓣⓣ × ⓉⓉ
Random fertilisation		
Offspring genotypes (2n)	**TT TT TT TT**	**TT TT Tt Tt**
Offspring phenotypes	all tall (homozygous)	all tall (½ homozygous, ½ heterozygous)

23.3 *(a)* If short black hair appeared in the F₁ phenotypes, then short hair must be dominant to long hair and black hair must be dominant to white.
(b) See fig 23.3(ans) below.

Let:

> **B** represent black hair
> **b** represent white hair
> **S** represent short hair
> **s** represent long hair

F₁ phenotypes — short black hair × short black hair
F₁ genotypes (2n) — **SsBb** × **SsBb**

Meiosis

Gametes (n) (as shown by ♂ and ♀)

Random fertilisation (as shown by Punnett square)

F₂ genotypes (2n) (as shown in each square)

♀ \ ♂	Ⓢ Ⓑ	Ⓢ ⓑ	ⓢ Ⓑ	ⓢ ⓑ
ⓈⒷ	SB SB ■	Sb SB ■	sB SB ■	sb SB ■
Ⓢⓑ	SB Sb ■	Sb Sb □	sB Sb ■	sb Sb □
ⓢⒷ	SB sB ■	Sb sB ■	sB sB ▮	sb sB ▮
ⓢⓑ	SB sb ■	Sb sb □	sB sb ▮	sb sb ▯

F₂ phenotypes: 9 short black hair : 3 short white hair : 3 long black hair : 1 long white hair

(Symbols) ■ □ ▮ ▯

23.4 See fig 23.4(ans) below.

Let:

> **R,r** and **S,s** represent two allelomorphic pairs of genes controlling flower colour.

Parental phenotypes	purple	×	purple
Parental genotypes (2n)	**RrSs**	×	**RrSs**
Meiosis			

Gametes (n) (as shown by ♂ and ♀)

Random fertilisation (as shown by Punnett square)

Offspring genotypes (2n) (as shown in each square)

♀ \ ♂	ⓇⓈ	Ⓡⓢ	ⓇⓈ	ⓡⓢ
ⓇⓈ	RS RS ●	Rs RS ●	rS RS ●	rs RS ●
Ⓡⓢ	RS Rs ●	Rs Rs ●	rS Rs ●	rs Rs ○
ⓇⓈ	RS rS ●	Rs rS ●	rS rS ○	rs rS ○
ⓡⓢ	RS rs ●	Rs rs ○	rS rs ○	rs rs ○

Offspring phenotypic ratio: 9 purple : 7 white

(Symbols) ● ○

23.5 The two alleles segregate during metaphase I and anaphase I.

23.6 The number of different combinations of chromosomes in the pollen gamete cells is calculated using the formula 2^n, where n is the haploid number of chromosomes.
In crocus, since $2n = 6$, $n = 3$.
Therefore, combinations $= 2 = 8$.

23.7 The F_1 phenotypes show that purple flower and short stem are dominant and red flower and long stem are recessive. The approximate ratio of 1:1:1:1 in a dihybrid cross suggests that the two genes controlling the characteristics of flower colour and stem length are not linked and the four alleles are situated on different pairs of chromosomes (fig 23.7(ans) below).

Let:

P represent purple flower
p represent red flower
S represent short stem
s represent long stem

Since the parental stocks were both homozygous for both characters the F_1 genotypes must be **PpSs**.

Testcross phenotypes   purple flower, short stem × red flower, long stem
Testcross genotypes (2n)   **PpSs** × **ppss**

Meiosis
Gametes (n)
(as shown by ♂ and ♀)

Random fertilisation
(as shown in Punnett square)

♀ \ ♂	PS	Ps	pS	ps
ps	PS ps	Ps ps	pS ps	ps ps

Offspring genotypes (2n)
(listed in each square)

Offspring phenotypes   1 purple flower, short stem: 1 purple flower, long stem: 1 red flower, short stem: 1 red flower, long stem

23.8 (a) Homologous chromosomes
(b) Body colour and wing length
(c) This cannot be concluded from the data since the position of the antenna shape gene is not shown.

23.9 Out of the 800 seeds produced, only 24 show the results of crossing-over between the genes for seed colour and seed shape. In the other 776, the alleles for seed colour and seed shape have remained linked as shown by their approximate 1:1 ratio.
Hence the crossover value is $(24/800) \times 100 = 3\%$. Therefore the distance between the genes for seed colour and seed shape is 3 units.

23.10 See fig 23.10(ans) below.

(a) Let:

N represent normal wing (dominant)
n represent miniature wing (recessive)
R represent red eye (dominant)
r represent white eye (recessive)
XX represent female fly (♀)
XY represent male fly (♂)

(i) Parental phenotypes miniature wing, red eye ♂ × normal wing, white eye ♀
Parental genotypes (2n) $X^{nR}Y$ × $X^{Nr}X^{Nr}$
Meiosis
Gametes (n) X^{nR} Y × X^{Nr} X^{Nr}
Random fertilisation
F_1 genotypes (2n) $X^{nR}X^{Nr}$ $X^{nR}X^{Nr}$ $X^{Nr}Y$ $X^{Nr}Y$
F_1 phenotypes   normal wing, red eye ♀ normal wing, white eye ♂

(ii) Assuming no crossing-over between the genes for wing length and eye colour in the female, the following results are likely to appear:

F_1 phenotypes   normal wing, white eye ♂ × normal wing, red eye ♀
F_1 genotypes (2n) $X^{Nr}Y$ × $X^{nR}X^{Nr}$
Meiosis
Gametes (n) X^{Nr} Y × X^{nR} X^{Nr}
Random fertilisation
F_2 genotypes (2n) $X^{Nr}X^{nR}$ $X^{Nr}X^{Nr}$ $X^{nR}Y$ $X^{Nr}Y$
F_2 phenotypes normal wing, normal wing, miniature wing, normal wing, red eye ♀ white eye ♀ red eye ♂ white eye ♂

(b) The lack of a 1:1:1:1 ratio of phenotypes resulting from this cross indicates crossing-over between the genes for wing length and eye colour in the female.

Testcross phenotypes normal wing, red eye ♀ × miniature wing, white eye ♂
Testcross genotypes (2n) $X^{nR}X^{Nr}$ × $X^{nr}Y$
Meiosis
Gametes (n)
(as shown by ♀ and ♂)

♂ \ ♀	X^{nR}	X^{Nr}	X^{nr}	X^{NR}
X^{nr} (Random fertilisation, as shown in Punnett square)	$X^{nR}X^{nr}$ ♀	$X^{Nr}X^{nr}$ ♀	$X^{nr}X^{nr}$ ♀	$X^{NR}X^{nr}$ ♀
Y (Offspring genotypes (2n), as listed in squares)	$X^{nR}Y$ ♂	$X^{Nr}Y$ ♂	$X^{nr}Y$ ♂	$X^{NR}Y$ ♂

Offspring phenotypes	wing: eye:	miniature red	normal white	miniature white	normal red
Experimental results		36	35	18	17

The alleles for wing length and eye colour are shown on the two F_1 female (X) chromosomes in the explanation above. Crossing-over between the alleles will give the recombinant genotypes shown above. Out of 106 flies, 35 show recombination of alleles (18 + 17), therefore the crossover value is 35/106 = approximately 30%.

915

23.11 See fig 23.11(ans) below.

Magpie moth

Let:

> **N** represent normal colour (dominant)
> **n** represent pale colour (recessive)

Parental phenotypes   pale colour male × normal colour female

Parental genotypes (2n)

EITHER   OR

Meiosis

Gametes (n)

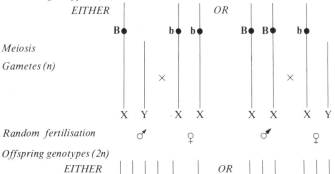

Random fertilisation   ♂   ♀   ♂   ♀

Offspring genotypes (2n)

EITHER   OR

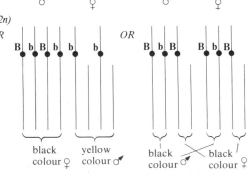

Offspring phenotypes   normal colour ♀   normal colour ♂   normal colour ♂   pale colour ♀

From the results for the offspring phenotypes it is seen that the heterogametic sex in the magpie moth is the female.

Cat

Let:

> **B** represent black colour (dominant)
> **b** represent yellow colour (recessive)

Parental phenotypes   black colour male × yellow colour female

Parental genotypes (2n)

EITHER   OR

Meiosis

Gametes (n)

X Y   X X   X X   X Y

Random fertilisation   ♂   ♀   ♂   ♀

Offspring genotypes (2n)

EITHER   OR

Offspring phenotypes   black colour ♀   yellow colour ♂   black colour ♂   black colour ♀

From the results for the offspring phenotypes it is seen that the heterogametic sex in the cat is the male.

23.12 See fig 23.12(ans) below.

Let:

> **B** represent black coat colour
> **G** represent ginger coat colour
> **XX** represent female cat
> **XY** represent male cat

Parental phenotypes	ginger-coat male	×	black-coat female
Parental genotypes (2n)	X^GY	×	X^BX^B

Meiosis

Gametes (n) X^G Y × X^B X^B

Random fertilisation

F₁ genotypes (2n) X^GX^B X^GX^B X^BY X^BY

F₁ phenotypes   tortoiseshell-coat colour ♀   black-coat colour ♂

(The parental female must be homozygous for black coat colour since this is the only condition to produce a black-coat colour phenotype).

F₁ phenotypes	black-coat male	×	tortoiseshell-coat female
F₁ genotypes (2n)	X^BY	×	X^GX^B

Meiosis

Gametes (n) X^B Y × X^G X^B

Random fertilisation

F₁ genotypes (2n) X^BX^G X^BX^B X^GY X^BY

F₂ phenotypes   tortoiseshell-coat colour ♀   black-coat colour ♀   ginger-coat colour ♂   black-coat colour ♂

23.13 (a) See fig 23.13(ans) below.
(b) There is a probability of $\frac{1}{4}$ (25%) that each child will have blood group A. So the probability that both will have blood group A is $\frac{1}{4} \times \frac{1}{4} = 1/16$ (6.25%).

Let:

> **I** represent the gene for blood group
> **A** represent the allele A
> **B** represent the allele B ⎱ (equally dominant)
> **O** represent the allele O (recessive)

Parental phenotypes	blood group A	×	blood group B
Parental genotypes (2n)	I^AI^O	×	I^BI^O

Meiosis

Gametes (n) I^A I^O × I^B I^O

Random fertilisation

Offspring genotypes (2n) I^AI^B I^AI^O I^OI^B I^OI^O

Offspring phenotypes   blood groups AB   A   B   O

23.14 See fig 23.14(ans) below.

Let:

P represent pea comb
R represent rose comb
a single **P** allele and a single **R** allele occurring together produce walnut comb
a double homozygous recessive genotype produces single comb
W represent white feathers (dominant)
w represent black feathers (recessive)

If eight different phenotypes are produced from the cross, each parent must possess as many heterozygous alleles as possible. Hence the genotypes are as shown below:

Parental phenotypes	black, rose-comb cock ×	white, walnut-comb hen
Parental genotypes (2n)	**wwRrpp** ×	**WwRrPp**

Meiosis

Gametes (n)
(as shown by ♀ and ♂)

♂ \ ♀	WRP	WRp	WrP	Wrp	wRP	wRp	wrP	wrp
wRp	WRP wRp ○	WRp wRp △	WrP wRp ○	Wrp wRp △	wRP wRp ●	wRp wRp ▲	wrP wRp ●	wrp wRp ▲
wrp	WRP wrp ○	WRp wrp △	WrP wrp □	Wrp wrp ◌	wRP wrp ●	wRp wrp ▲	wrP wrp ■	wrp wrp ✹

Random fertilisation
(as shown in Punnet square)

Offspring genotypes (2n)
(as shown in squares)

Offspring phenotypes:
(Symbols)

3 white, walnut-comb: 3 black, walnut-comb: 3 white, rose-comb: 3 black, rose-comb: 1 white, pea-comb:
○   ●   △   ▲   □

1 black, pea-comb: 1 white, single-comb: 1 black, single-comb
■   ◌   ✹

23.15 Since both dominant alleles, **W**, white, and **B**, black, are present in the heterozygous F₁ genotype, and the phenotype is white, it may be concluded that the alleles show an epistatic interaction where the white allele represents the epistatic gene and the black allele represents the hypostatic gene. The F₂ generation is shown in fig 23.15(ans) below.

Using the symbols given in the question,

F₁ phenotypes	white cock × white hen	
F₁ genotypes (2n)	**WwBb** × **WwBb**	

Meiosis
(as shown by ♂ and ♀)

Gametes (n)
(as listed in Punnett square)

Random fertilisation

F₂ genotypes (2n)
(as listed in the squares)

♀ \ ♂	WB	Wb	wB	wb
WB	WB WB ○	Wb WB ○	wB WB ○	wb WB ○
Wb	WB Wb ○	Wb Wb ○	wB Wb ○	wb Wb ○
wB	WB wB ○	Wb wB ○	wB wB ●	wb wB ●
wb	WB wb ○	Wb wb ○	wB wb ●	wb wb ⊘

F₂ phenotypes   12 white colour: 3 black colour: 1 brown colour
(Symbols)   ○   ●   ⊘

Chapter 24

24.1 A control experiment in which each variable was systematically eliminated.

24.2 Redi's basic assumption was that the presence of 'worms' was due to the entry of the flies through the open flasks.

24.3 Sealing the broths would prevent the entry of organisms to the vessels. Lack of air within the vessels may have deprived organisms of oxygen for respiration.

24.4 Pasteur's basic assumptions were that each generation of organisms develops from the previous generation and not spontaneously.

24.5 Micro-organisms develop in the nutrient broth due to contamination of the broth by organisms in the atmosphere.

24.6 Sealed tubes, boiling, autoclaving, direct access to atmosphere, indirect access to the atmosphere.

24.7 Access to atmosphere.

24.8 Pair A are not heated, pair B are boiled for 10 min, pair C are autoclaved at 15 lb pressure for 20 min, pair D have differential access to the atmosphere.

24.9 Spallanzani – tubes 3 and 4
Pasteur   – tubes 7 and 8

24.10 Tubes 1, 3, 5 and 7

24.11 The experimental design takes full account of scientific method. There is a hypothesis and the experimental design includes appropriate controls and systematically eliminated experimental variables. If identical experiments yield consistent results these data may be regarded as valid. The degree of validity attached to conclusions based on these, or any data, depends upon how accurately they interpret the data.

Chapter 25

25.1 The carrier genotype is the heterozygous genotype. The Hardy–Weinberg equation is used to calculate genotype frequencies. The equation may be represented as

$$p^2 + 2pq + q^2 = 1$$

where

p^2 = frequency of homozygous dominant genotype,
$2pq$ = frequency of heterozygous genotype,
q^2 = frequency of homozygous recessive genotype.

The incidence of cystic fibrosis in the population appears in individuals with the homozygous recessive genotype, hence q^2 is 1 in 2 000 or $1/2\,000 = 0.0005$.

Therefore $q = \sqrt{0.0005}$
$= 0.0224$.
Since $p + q = 1$
$p = 1 - q$
$= 1 - 0.0224$
$= 0.9776$.

The frequency of the heterozygous genotype ($2pq$) is therefore

$$2 \times (0.9776) \times (0.0224)$$
$$= 0.044$$
$$= 1 \text{ in } 23$$
$$\simeq 5\%$$

Approximately 5% of the population are carriers of the recessive gene for cystic fibrosis.

25.2 *Fasciola hepatica*, the liver fluke, is a parasite which infests sheep. It has an intermediate host, the snail *Limnaea truncatula*, which lives in fresh water and damp pastures. Draining ponds and wet areas would bring about a change in environmental conditions which would exert a selection pressure tending to eliminate *Limnaea*. As the numbers of the snail fall this would reduce the numbers of available hosts which would lead to a decrease in the numbers of the parasite, *Fasciola*.

25.3 Reduced selection pressure at the extremes of each new population would favour increased variability. New phenotypes may show adaptations to the areas previously occupied by the eliminated subspecies and spread inwards to occupy the vacated ecological niche. The initial geographical separation of the cline may have initiated allopatric speciation. If the ring was reformed, gene flow may be impossible due to genetic isolation and each subpopulation would diverge genetically even further to form distinct species, as is the present case in the British Isles where the species exist sympatrically. If the genetic isolation between the two subpopulations was not too great, hybrids may form when the subpopulations were reunited. This zone of hybridisation may act as a reproductive barrier as is the case with the carrion and hooded crows.

Index